Building Storage Networks, Second Edition

ABOUT THE AUTHOR

Marc Farley is a founder of Teach2Fish, a technology marketing educational company, and an independent consultant in the network storage industry. His career in network storage spans a decade working with a wide variety of technologies and companies. He lives in San Jose, California with Gretchen, his wife of 15 years, and his two children, Laura (12) and Bret (7).

ABOUT THE TECHNICAL EDITOR

Howard Goldstein has over 30 years in the information systems industry specializing in storage, data communications, and telecommunications networking. Howard has a diverse background in technology, management, and education. He has practical experience in all aspects of network technologies including architecture, design, planning, management, implementation, network systems programming and administration, operations and problem determination, and problem resolution. His technical focus has been with various network architectures and products including TCP/IP, SNA, and Storage Area Networking.

Howard holds a Bachelors of Science in Computer Science from the University of Massachusetts at Amherst and a Masters of Science in Telecommunications from Pace University at White Plains, New York.

Building Storage Networks, Second Edition

MARC **FARLEY**

Osborne/**McGraw-Hill**

New York   Chicago   San Francisco
Lisbon   London   Madrid   Mexico City
Milan   New Delhi   San Juan
Seoul   Singapore   Sydney   Toronto

Osborne/**McGraw-Hill**
2600 Tenth Street
Berkeley, California 94710
U.S.A.

To arrange bulk purchase discounts for sales promotions, premiums, or fund-raisers, please contact Osborne/**McGraw-Hill** at the above address. For information on translations or book distributors outside the U.S.A., please see the International Contact Information page immediately following the index of this book.

Building Storage Networks, Second Edition

1235467890 CUS CUS 01987654321

ISBN 0-07-213072-5

Publisher
   Brandon A. Nordin
Vice President and
Associate Publisher
   Scott Rogers
Acquisitions Editor
   Francis Kelly
Project Editors
   Carolyn Welch
   Madhu Prasher
Acquisitions Coordinator
   Jessica Wilson
Technical Editor
   Howard Goldstein
Copy Editor
   Bob Campbell

Proofreader
   Susie Elkind
Indexer
   Valerie Robbins
Computer Designers
   Lauren McCarthy
   Kelly Stanton-Scott
Illustrators
   Beth E. Young
   Michael Mueller
Cover Series Design
   Amparo Del Rio
Series Design
   Peter F. Hancik

This book was composed with Corel VENTURA™ Publisher.

This book, my second,
is dedicated by a second son
with love to my mother
Francis Farley.

AT A GLANCE

CONTENTS

Part II

Fundamental Storing Applications

Part III

The Storage Channel Becomes a Network

Part IV

Wiring Technologies

Part V

Filing, Internet Storage, and Management

FOREWORD

There is an ancient Chinese curse: "…may you live in interesting times." Welcome to the interesting times of data storage.

Data storage is more than doubling every year. This appetite appears to be insatiable with no signs of imminent change. The growth is driven by changes in the types of data being saved, litigation protection, and new regulatory requirements.

The Internet changed everything. This is an overused but appropriate cliché for the growth in data storage. It has spawned new types of data called rich media. Rich media includes MP3, animation, colorful graphics, PDF, PPT, and video streaming. The result is changed user expectations. Rich media data can be up to three orders of magnitude larger (1,000x) than ordinary text data. One other way the Internet has changed user expectations is that all information must be instantly available all the time. This means no data or file can be deleted and everything must be available instantaneously.

The large-scale deployment of e-commerce and managed data in relational database management systems (RDBMS) is also driving data storage growth. IDC and Dataquest both report that more than 70 percent of saved data is managed in a database. RDBMS act as a multiplier of data, increasing it three to eight times its original size.

Litigation is another important driver in the growth of data storage. E-mail continues to play an increasingly important role in lawsuits. Organizations are being told by their attorneys to save ALL of their e-mail.

New regulations, such as the USA's "Health Insurance Portability and Accountability Act of 1996" (HIPAA), require that all patient data be saved for up to seven years. The storage requirements for MRI, PET, and CAT scans alone are enormous.

Managing the exponential growth in data storage is a daunting challenge for most information systems (IS) organizations. Compounding that challenge is the severe shortage of qualified personnel. IDC estimates there will be more than 1.8 million unfilled IS positions by 2003. As the economic expansion slows and IS budgets are cut, even fewer people will be available to manage data storage. One CIO laments: "We have to manage more and more storage with less and less people, until we eventually have to manage Yottabytes (billions of Terabytes) with no one."

So what does all this have to do with storage networks? Everything. This storage explosion and the desire to manage it with increasing productivity have led to the development of storage area networks (SANs) and network-attached storage (NAS).

The concept behind the SAN is to increase IS productivity and efficiency by helping manage the block storage growth with fewer people. It does this by decoupling the storage from the server. The storage can then be shared among multiple servers while both are grown independently. Decoupling and centralizing the storage simplifies management and control, enhancing productivity.

NAS is designed to simplify file-based storage. It does this by using industry standard Network File System (NFS), Common Internet Files System (CIFS), TCP/IP, and Ethernet protocols. NAS is often referred to as "plug-and-play" storage.

Like most simple concepts, vendor delivery adds complexity and confusion that often fails to deliver on the promise. It is very difficult to separate hype from reality until often it is too late.

In the first edition of *Building Storage Networks*, Marc Farley created an incredibly insightful resource for understanding storage and storage networking. It cuts through the chaos of industry propaganda and obfuscation. Mr. Farley clearly articulates in laymen's terms, and illustrates the what, why, wherefores, and hows of storage and storage networking.

Time stands still for no market or technology. Since the introduction of the first edition two years ago, there has been a plethora of emerging storage technologies and storage networking technologies. New technologies bring new jargon, new complexities, new acronyms, new questions, and new confusion.

Many of these new technologies hold great promise while others will be cast on the junk heap of posterity. Separating the winners from the losers will be the market. In the second edition of *Building Storage Networks*, Marc Farley covers these changes and provides a level of clarity not found anywhere else. *Building Storage Networks*, *Second Edition* explores and explains storage management, SAN management, storage virtualization (including host and network based), storage over IP on Gigabit Ethernet (including iSCSI, FCIP, iFCP, and mFCP), and new NAS/SAN files systems (including DAFS and SAFS).

Whether you are an IS professional, a storage engineer, a network engineer, a product manager, an industry analyst, or a corporate executive of a storage, SAN, or NAS company, you should buy this book. It will become an invaluable resource you will use time and again, providing a guide through the interesting times in data storage.

Marc Staimer
President
Dragon Slayer Consulting

ACKNOWLEDGMENTS

Building Storage Networks, *Second Edition* was written with the generous assistance of many friends and business colleagues. I feel a deep debt of gratitude for the hours others spent pitching in to improve this book. Readers have no way of appreciating the impact this has on their experience reading these pages, but I can assure them that it is significant.

Howard Goldstein, the technical editor on this book, provided invaluable help throughout, especially on the new expanded coverage of networking technologies. Other important technical contributors who brought key insights and knowledge include Marc Staimer, Rajeev Shukla, Rich Seifert, Gregory Pfister, Paul Massiglia, Randy Kerns, Dave Hill, Asang Dani, Paul Wang, Brian Berg, Steve Lindsey, Willem van Schaik, Domenic Forgione, Paul Wang, Asang Dani, Tom Curlin, Sandy Frey, Joel Harrison, Larry Boucher, and David Simpson. Apologies to those who slipped my mind.

Big thanks again to the excellent team at Osborne, especially to Jessica Wilson, Carolyn Welch, and Franny Kelly for managing me throughout the process and making it all possible. Thanks again for to Gareth Hancock, the 'G-man', for getting the ball rolling. Also a big debt of gratitude to the production team, especially James Kussow, Michael Mueller, Beth E. Young, Lucie Ericksen, Kelly Stanton-Scott, Tara Davis, and Lauren McCarthy for getting it all put together as the pressure was building towards the finish. What a relief to be done! I get to take a breather, but they all are back on the grindstone.

INTRODUCTION

I understand better today this need of simplifying, of bringing all into one, at the moment of deciding if such a thing should occur or not. Man withdraws reluctantly from his labyrinth. The millenial myths urge him not to go.

—Rene Char, from *Leaves of Hypnos*

Almost as soon as I finished writing *Building Storage Networks* (the first edition), there were things I wanted to do the change the book. I learned things along the way and new perspectives that I came across needed to be written, but they also needed a little time to ripen before expressing them. A tremendous amount of change has taken place in the network storage industry over the last two years and it was imperative for me to get an analysis of this new technology in writing.

This book doesn't so much build on the first edition as much as it uses the first edition as a point of departure. Although a fair amount of the material is the same or similar, significant changes have been made in this second edition. While the book maintains a similar structure to the first edition, there are heavy updates throughout, starting with the first chapter. The only chapters that were not overhauled were Chapters 6 and 7 on RAID and network backup, respectively. Otherwise, there is a lot of new material throughout.

For starters, this book is built around three fundamental storage networking functions: wiring, storing, and filing. Although these topics were covered in some fashion in the first edition, they weren't identified explicitly and were not used as a way to analyze product and technology functions. It's a bit of a risk laying out a new analysis for a new industry, but I feel strongly that the work needs to be done to help people make sense out of this confusion we lump together under the name network storage.

Another goal of this book was to significantly increase the networking content, especially in light of the developments in InfiniBand and Ethernet/TCP/IP storage, such as iSCSI. It is not easy writing about technologies that barely exist and without real products to examine, but such is the nature of on-the-edge timing. A lot of effort went into describing today's vapor in expectation that a fair amount of it will develop as products in the next couple of years. Hopefully, the advance descriptions supplied here will be more revealing than misleading.

As with the first edition, the main emphasis is on explaining things in a way that will help readers understand the technologies and architectures and to be able to gauge the status of the industry as it evolves. To that end, this edition introduces exercises at the end of each chapter to help check the understanding of the major architectural concepts discussed. The exercises are for people with varying skill levels and provide further self-exploration into the topics.

The first edition was very successful and many have commented to me how useful it has been to them. Nothing feels better to me than to hear those comments. It is my sincere hope that this book can also make a significant contribution to people's understanding of this fascinating technology area.

Marc Farley
April 26, 2001, San Jose, California

PART I

Introduction to Network Storage

CHAPTER 1

Getting a Handle on Storage Networking

As with many new technologies, the anticipation accompanying storage networking paints a picture that is more firmly rooted in its potential than in its current capabilities. As a result, IT professionals tasked with evaluating and comparing storage networking products have sometimes had a difficult time making sense of it. This book attempts to fill in the blanks for readers, beginning with this chapter, which lays the groundwork for analyzing and designing storage networks by classifying technologies into three distinct functional elements: wiring, storing, and filing.

THE CHANGING ROLE OF DATA AS A BUSINESS ASSET

A great deal has changed in the computing world over the last 20 years. Inexpensive, powerful computers and networks of computers can do the work that required an expensive mainframe 20 years ago. One thing that has not changed, however, is the importance of the data that computers process and produce. If the data is lost, all the computing power at hand is virtually worthless. So, one of the challenges for the data storage industry has been to provide the type of reliability and protection that is required for 24 × 7 operations on networks of inexpensive systems.

This is easier said than done. Managing storage in a network environment has proved to be generally difficult. A single business location can have several different hardware/software platforms, each with its own systems and storage management utilities. This is an extremely difficult environment for system administrators, who have to deal with all this diversity with little or no margin for error.

There are two approaches to managing storage in network environments. The first is to manage it through a server-provided mechanism, and the second is to manage it through a storage-product direct interface. The latter approach, the most common one taken by companies in the storage industry, leads to a very interesting conclusion: data is an independent asset, separate from the computers that access it and requiring a management system that is independent of host systems management. This distinction between the computer and the data it processes, illustrated here, is germane to the subject of this book.

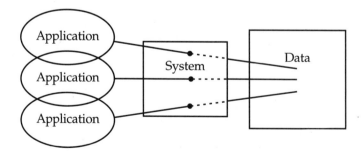

As data is increasingly thought of as its own free-existing entity, not necessarily belonging to any particular system, it is also being viewed as a corporate asset, similar to capital or intellectual property that needs to be preserved and protected. Likewise, storage networking products and architectures, as platforms for data protection and storage management, are also being elevated as a strategic asset worthy of planning and budget meetings formerly reserved for systems and software.

FUNDAMENTAL CONCEPTS OF STORAGE NETWORKING

Given that storage networking is expected to provide the best methods to structure data access in the future, the obvious question is: "What is storage networking anyway?" As with so many things, the answer is more complicated than one might initially think. With several product classes being developed and marketed, and with several variations within each class, storage networking can be a confusing subject, not only for consumers, but also for those within the storage network industry itself.

Requirements for Storage Networking

Before plunging headlong into a technology discussion, we'll first explore the environment storage networks are entering and some of the problems the technology is attempting to solve.

Flexibility

Internet computing is probably the largest and most dynamic environment ever encountered in the relatively short history of computing. The cliché that the only constant is change appears to be true, at least for the next several years. The ability for organizations to regenerate their images and product lines overnight on the World Wide Web establishes a new, fluid way of conducting business.

Storage networking must be able to meet the need for speed in altering systems configurations and supporting constant design and content changes on Web sites. Storage implementations that hinder fast change will be rejected in the Internet data center.

Scalability

One of the most common ways for systems to change is to grow. The amount of growth in the fastest growing environments is limited by the capability to record and process all the information desired. As organizations collect increasing amounts of information in support of all aspects of their operations, they need to maintain access to it. Therefore, storage networking must provide scalable solutions that allow data repositories to expand without service interruptions.

Availability and Access

Stored data could be requested by users at virtually any time. Whether it is a customer service application, research data, sales analysis, or any other type of data, the availability of and access to data will keep organizations running with top efficiency. Storage networks have to be able to provide access to data and withstand threats to local service by rerouting access to secondary locations.

Reliability

Storage networks are fundamentally different than data networks. Failed transmissions in a typical data network using TCP/IP are not catastrophic because the transmission can usually be retried at a later time and the data is still in its original form in its original location.

In contrast, data that is lost in a storage network malfunction may not be able to be recovered. The issue is how storage outages are handled by their primary applications: file systems and database systems. These applications are typically written with the assumption that storage is always available and working. If the storage device or connection fails, these applications often crash, taking the systems they run on along with them. Storage networks have to provide the highest level of reliability, beyond those typically achieved in data networks.

The Pillars of Storage Networking

When a new technology emerges in a highly competitive market, as is the case with storage networking, it is not always clear what the architectural elements of the technology are. There are several reasons for this ambiguity, including the amount of marketing information created in an attempt to justify different approaches and applications. The analysis in this book is independent of existing market opportunities and breaks down the technology of storage networking into three fundamental components:

▼ Wiring

■ Filing

▲ Storing

This analysis offered here differs from the usual approach of separating SAN (storage area network) and NAS (network attached storage) technologies. SAN and NAS technologies are not orthogonal concepts, as they share common characteristics. In fact, they are more complementary than competitive. Using the three pillars of wiring, filing, and storing, most of the confusion about product classification can be avoided. In addition, it is much easier to design a storage network when one has a clear idea of the fundamental components and how they interact.

Wiring

Wiring, simply stated, is the connectivity technology used to connect storage devices to systems and other devices. It includes such diverse technologies as network cabling, host adapters, network switches, and hubs and also includes logical components such as network flow control, virtual networking, link aggregation, and network security. In short, it is everything involved in the transfer of data across a storage network. Figure 1-1 shows both the logical and physical components of wiring.

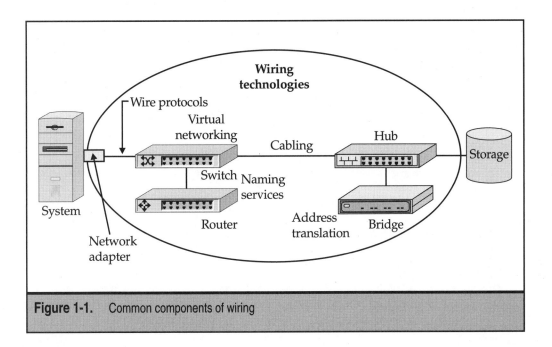

Figure 1-1.   Common components of wiring

Whereas the physical components of wiring are easily identified, the logical ones can be slightly more difficult. Virtual LANs, or VLANs, and the 802.1Q standard defining tagged VLAN switch operations are a wiring technology. The low-level network control logic and device drivers used in storage network adapters are also wiring technology. However, the higher-level storage protocol drivers that manage requests for storage from applications and formulate the storage content of storage network communications are not wiring technology.

Filing

Filing is the intelligent process that organizes stored data. Typically, filing is done by *file* systems and database systems that determine how data is stored and retrieved, what other information is stored with data that describes it (the metadata), and how the stored information is represented to applications and users. The filing function is logical in nature. In other words, it has no dependence on hardware. It is the primary role of NAS technology, although NAS products can incorporate sophisticated wiring and storing technology also. Figure 1-2 shows some of the typical filing implementations in use today.

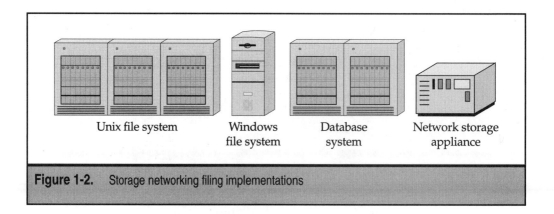

Figure 1-2. Storage networking filing implementations

Storing

Storing technology provides a stable, nonvolatile, reliable place to hold data until it is needed again. Storing technology has both physical and logical components. Physical components include devices such as disk drives and enclosures that provide power, cooling, and connectivity. Logical components include RAID, mirroring, and volume management software that allows multiple disk drives to appear as a single virtual device. The logical component of storing also includes the application-level device drivers of storage network adapters that formulate storage commands and payloads that are sent over the storage network between computer systems and storage devices and subsystems. Storing is distinct from filing in that storing is a device-oriented function and filing is an application-oriented function that makes use of real or virtual storage. Figure 1-3 shows some of the various elements involved with the storing function.

Wiring, Filing, and Storing Combined

Figure 1-4 illustrates the common implementation-locations for wiring, filing, and storing. The filing function traditionally resides in host computer systems, but in NAS environments, it resides within some type of file server. Theoretically, the filing function could reside in several locations in a storage network; it will be discussed in greater detail later in the book as data sharing technology.

The wiring function is represented by the network adapter, cables, and switch/hub—in essence, everything between the computer system and the disk subsystem. Network adapters in SANs are called host bus adapters, or HBAs, and in NAS environments network interface cards, or NICs, are used. HBAs and NICs control network

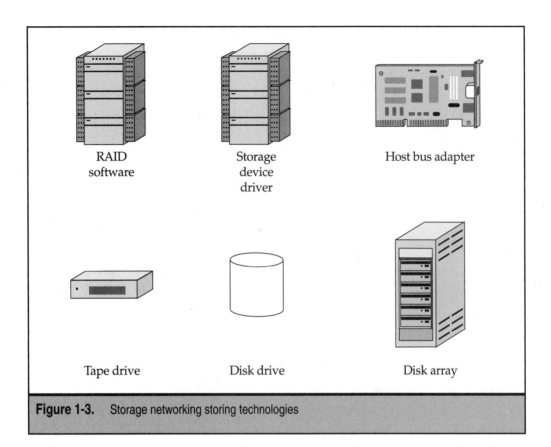

RAID
software

Storage
device
driver

Host bus adapter

Tape drive

Disk drive

Disk array

Figure 1-3.   Storage networking storing technologies

operations for their respective networks and therefore are considered to be part of the
wiring function. The device driver software that controls network communications functions in NICs and HBAs and runs in host systems is also considered to be part of the wiring function.

The storing function is associated mostly with disk devices and subsystems, but in
fact, it is a distributed function with an important piece typically running as device driver
code in host computer systems. This device driver code runs as an application on top of
the wiring function and manages storage commands and data exchanges. It may help
you to think of the storing function as a higher-level network application that uses the
network services provided by wiring to accomplish its tasks.

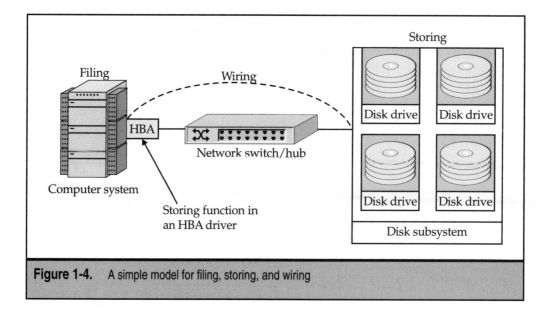

Figure 1-4.   A simple model for filing, storing, and wiring

AN OVERVIEW OF TRADITIONAL OPEN SYSTEMS STORAGE

To understand the new technology of storage networking, it may be helpful to understand the way traditional storage systems have developed. Many of the concepts of storage networking are rooted in mature technology that has existed for several decades.

The term "open systems" is used in this book to refer to the collection of products for Unix and PC systems that support and receive broad industry participation. Considering that open systems computing platforms have been the mainstay of the networking industry, it is probably not too surprising that they will define the primary environment for network storage also.

Within the open systems world, client/server computing has enabled the sharing of data and processing power to fuel an enormous industry. Storage networking shares many of the characteristics of client/server computing by distributing the work of storing and managing data between computer systems and storage devices or subsystems where the data is stored.

The term "subsystem" will be used throughout this book to denote the integration of intelligent controllers, processors, software, and storage devices that provide increased capacity, performance, or ease of use beyond what can be achieved with simple storage devices. The concept of a storage subsystem is shown here:

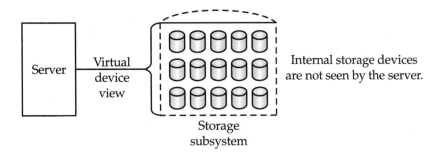

Internal storage devices
are not seen by the server.

Storage
subsystem

Network storage servers and subsystems provide the following capabilities:

▼   Distributing storage responsibilities among multiple machines

■   Storing data in one or more locations easily and reliably

■   Retrieving data from one or more locations easily and reliably

▲   Managing the access to data from multiple systems

Storage on Open Systems Servers

While a fair amount of personal productivity data in open systems networks is stored on client systems, server systems are used to process and store the lion's share of corporate data. This section explores some positive and negative attributes of open systems server storage.

Open Systems Costs

One of the best things about open systems client/server computing is the overall size of the market. Large markets, like open systems computing, invite lots of competition, which drives down the cost of products. While it is certainly possible to spend over $50,000 on a file server these days, it is also possible to spend less than $5,000 for a PC file server system that works very well for a department or a medium-sized business. In fact, there are several small, network attached storage servers on the market that provide excellent, simple storage for less than $1,000.

Among the most interesting developments in the open systems world is the acceptance of open source software, particularly the Linux and FreeBSD operating systems and the Apache Web server. Although there are many interesting aspects to open-source development, one of the most compelling is the potential for rock-bottom-cost software. When one takes all the components of a file server into account, the hardware costs have been decreasing significantly from year to year, while the software costs have stayed fairly level. Open source software drives the software cost down, which certainly promises to significantly reduce the cost of server systems.

The large size of the open systems server market provides a market environment that thrives on a high degree of market segmentation, which translates into a wide variety of products to fit various needs. Customers benefit from this by being able to find products that meet their requirements without having to pay too much for a system that is too powerful or settle for an inadequate, but affordable, system that is too limited.

File servers provide consolidated management for many client systems. When client data is stored on file servers instead of on client systems, system administrators have far fewer storage volumes to manage. This, of course, is a major benefit to system administrators, saving a lot of time and money. As a result, file servers have become a mainstay of open systems computing.

The open systems market also provides a competitive market for network storage management applications such as backup, mirroring, and HSM (Hierarchical Storage Management). Historically, the trend in the open systems storage software industry has been for larger companies like Veritas, Computer Associates, and Legato to purchase smaller competitors. While this consolidation can reduce the number of options customers have, there still appears to be plenty of competition among large competitors to ensure competitive prices.

Open Systems Testing Challenges

Not everything about open systems dynamics is wonderful, however. One problem area is the complexity and cost of testing open systems products that are likely to be integrated together at customer sites. It is disappointing to realize that complete product compatibility testing is prohibitively expensive and very difficult to manage.

The open systems market is based on the notion of industry-standard interfaces that provide mix-and-match flexibility of products from different vendors. Yet these vendors have to be able to differentiate their products in the market to sell more of them than their competitors or to sell them for higher margins. In the absence of proprietary interfaces, price is often the determining factor in building market share because cheaper products tend to be sold in higher volumes. There could be several reasons why one vendor's product is more expensive than another's. Manufacturing expenses, inventory costs, shallower discounts on components, and more time and resources spent on testing can cause products to be more expensive.

Under such heavy competitive pressures, companies feel compelled to reduce their costs. Such reductions in cost have been known to include reducing the engineering staff and operations budget of the systems test organization. The result is sometimes a product that costs less and comes to market faster but lacks the quality desired.

To understand just how difficult open systems product testing is, consider the perspective of an open systems disk subsystem manufacturer. Its products have to connect to many different I/O (input/output) adapter cards and to a wide variety of system processors running a variety of operating systems, possibly under the control of several database systems. Table 1-1 shows a sample compatibility list that would be the basis for a very large test matrix for an open systems disk subsystem.

I/O Adapters	Processor Systems	Operating Systems	Database Systems
Adaptec	HP Netservers	Windows NT	SQL Server
Q Logic	IBM PC servers	Windows NT Server	Oracle
LSI Logic	Dell servers	Novell NetWare	Informix
Interphase	Compaq servers	SCO Unix	Sybase
Troika	Sun servers	Linux	DB/2
Emulex	HP 9000 server	FreeBSD	
JNI	IBM RS/6000 servers	Solaris	
	SGI servers	HP-UX	
	Compaq Alpha servers	AIX	
		Irix	
		Tru64 Unix	

Table 1-1.   A Sample Compatibility Test Matrix for an Open Systems Disk Subsystem

When all of the variations are taken into consideration, the number of test cases grows exponentially. If we wanted to add storage management software to the mix, the number of combinations would grow even larger. The result is thousands of combinations of fairly complicated tests. The expense of establishing, staffing, and maintaining this kind of lab is enormous. So, rather than responding to all the market opportunities, a RAID vendor could choose to limit the scope of its testing and certification programs and sell its products into certain high-volume markets. That effectively limits the platform choices customers have if they want to utilize different server systems while maintaining their investment in their storage subsystems.

Open Systems Support Challenges

The challenges of testing an open systems storage product are also reflected in the challenge of supporting them in the field. Companies building products will try to consider all the various ways a product will be used and test to ensure its correct operation. That said, there is no way a testing group can imagine all of the variations that customers will want to try. Systems professionals occasionally express dismay at feeling like guinea pigs for computer product manufacturers who are trying to work out the bugs of their products. In truth, they are guinea pigs of a sort, although it is slightly unfair to cast the vendor community as technology-mad scientists trying out their cruel experiments on an unwitting public.

So when things do go awry, customers need a place to go for help and vendors need a way to respond. This, of course, is the technical support department. Now, technical support is often the day-to-day hot seat in any computer company where the company's reputation is made or ruined. For storage products, where data is at risk, technical support more closely resembles a crisis intervention hotline than a technical support department. Although one might want to take the cynical view of vendor testing, it is extremely difficult to believe that any vendor would willingly put itself through the excruciating pain of solving a technical problem where data loss is a very real possibility.

SCSI: THE REIGNING TECHNOLOGY FOR OPEN SYSTEMS STORAGE

In the open systems world, the dominant traditional storage I/O technology is SCSI (Small Computer System Interface), pronounced "scuzzy." To be precise, the term *parallel SCSI* refers to the vast majority of traditional SCSI implementations, which were the primary vehicle used to connect storage devices to open systems computers for many years. SCSI transfers data as *blocks*, which are the low-level granular storage units on storage devices. Because it is so difficult for new storage technologies to be integrated into all the various products sold, new storage I/O channel technologies, such as Fibre Channel, are often based on some form of SCSI to facilitate the most rapid development and market acceptance.

Traditional Systems Wiring: the SCSI Bus

Although parallel SCSI storage is not commonly thought of as a storage networking technology, SCSI-based storage utilizes the same fundamental technologies (wiring, filing, and storing) as those introduced previously. The wiring function in parallel SCSI is commonly referred to as the "SCSI bus" but is also sometimes referred to as the "SCSI channel." The wiring components of the SCSI I/O bus are:

▼ **The SCSI controller** Silicon chips and software that control data transfers over the bus. SCSI controllers are commonly implemented in computer systems as host adapters. SCSI controllers are also implemented in intelligent storage subsystems to provide redundancy and performance enhancements.

▲ **The I/O bus** The system of cables and connecting equipment that serves as the medium for transferring parallel SCSI commands and data. This often includes a bus terminating resistor, or circuit, which is used to reduce the effects of signal reflection over the cable.

In addition, the SCSI bus also incorporates storing functionality through the implementation of the logical SCSI protocol: the SCSI protocol is the signaling language between the host SCSI controller and storage devices/subsystems. The SCSI protocol typically cannot be purchased as a separate product or development tool the way IP protocol stacks can be. Even so, the SCSI protocol stack is an essential part of SCSI operations, just as networking protocols are an essential part of networking.

SCSI's Origins

SCSI was developed initially by Shugart Associates and NCR Corporation in 1981 as part of a disk drive interface called SASI. As this specification was submitted and subsequently progressed through the ANSI X3T9 committee, its name was changed to SCSI. This committee continued developing the specification until it became an official ANSI standard in June 1986. Since that time, this committee has continued to evolve the SCSI specification. As the SCSI bus is the intermediary between the host adapter in the computer and the devices, it follows that the speed and flexibility of SCSI I/O operations are determined by the capabilities of the SCSI bus. SCSI has been a very successful technology and will probably continue to flourish for a long time as a high-performance, moderately priced storage interconnect technology. However, the original SCSI specification was never intended to deal with current performance and availability requirements.

Data Availability Through a Single SCSI I/O Controller

SCSI was originally conceived as a way to attach many different types of devices to a common I/O bus, controlled by a single I/O controller. The capability to connect many kinds of devices makes SCSI extremely versatile for customers with a variety of application and storage needs.

However, two SCSI host adapters do not easily share the same SCSI bus. SCSI's evolution as a single-controller architecture allowed it to be very reliable but makes it unpredictable for connecting more than one SCSI host adapter to a single bus. Although the SCSI specification supports this configuration, most implementations of SCSI host controllers do not, which makes it difficult to create an open systems solution with multiple host adapters sharing a single SCSI bus.

Therefore, the typical SCSI implementation has a single server with SCSI adapters providing SCSI channel connections to storage. In other words, the single server becomes a single point of failure and a potential bottleneck between users and their data. Where 24 × 7 high-availability data processing operations are required, allowing any single system to be a source of failure is simply bad business. Figure 1-5 shows a network server as a single point of failure between users and their data. In contrast, the flexible server-to-device connectivity that network storage provides is seen as an important benefit for high-availability computing.

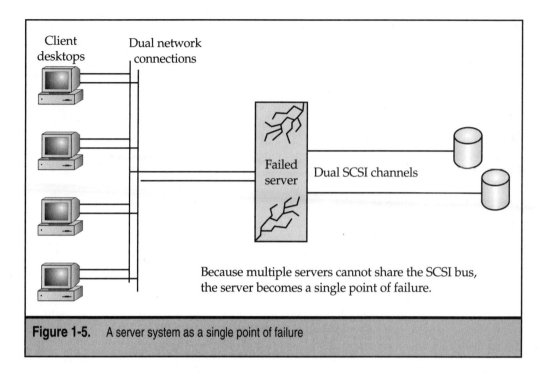

Because multiple servers cannot share the SCSI bus, the server becomes a single point of failure.

Figure 1-5.   A server system as a single point of failure

SCSI Bus Implementation Variables

From its inception, SCSI was developed with the goal of attaching multiple high-speed devices—both inside and outside of the systems that use them. External SCSI cabling was engineered for signal reliability over a reasonable distance, and to withstand normal electromagnetic interference in office environments.

Parallel SCSI Daisy-Chaining

The SCSI bus is a collection of cables that are strung together and connect the various devices and the SCSI host controller on a single logical and electrical I/O transmission system. The term used to describe the way SCSI devices and their controller are connected is called a *daisy chain*. The following example shows several daisy-chained SCSI devices:

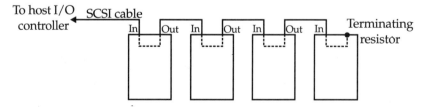

A daisy chain is based on the fact that most SCSI devices and subsystems typically have two SCSI connectors. These connectors are not specifically input and output connectors but provide a way to extend the length of the bus by chaining cables and devices together. Each device has a unique physical address that identifies it on the bus. In that respect, the parallel SCSI bus works like other communication buses or bus networks. For example, parallel SCSI's connectivity can be compared to an ARCnet bus network that consists of multiple segments connected through small nonactive hubs to form a single larger bus.

The length of the SCSI bus is an important variable in the configuration of the I/O subsystem. As is the case for any high-speed transmission, the greater the transmission length, the more the signal spreads and the more difficult it is to receive the signal correctly. It is important to realize that the length of the SCSI bus should include all cable segments, both internal and external.

The configuration of parallel SCSI buses can be changed to accommodate changing requirements. SCSI buses often start with one or two devices and then add several more over time. This flexibility to add devices is a key benefit of SCSI's connectivity. While SCSI might seem slightly archaic compared to network topologies, it was developed before the advent of switched networks at a time when Ethernet networks were lengths of coax cable that supported node connections with viper-like taps that bit into the cable with sharp prongs. SCSI's longevity is a testimony to the quality of its basic design.

That said, when a configuration change is made on a parallel SCSI bus, the system may have to be powered off in order to ensure the safety of data on other devices on the bus. At a minimum, the bus needs to stop its operation and reset its operations to accommodate the new device.

SCSI Initiators and Targets

The SCSI host adapter is typically considered the *initiator* of most SCSI operations, and the device usually takes the role of a *target*. The *initiator* signals an operation to start, and the *target* responds to the initiator's requests for data or status information. Some devices and adapters are capable of functioning as both initiators and targets.

SCSI Addressing, LUNs, and Prioritization

As the SCSI bus is built from discrete segments connected together, it requires a mechanism for identifying each device correctly. The SCSI ID, or *address*, is used to identify each device and controller on the SCSI bus uniquely and to determine bus arbitration priority.

Every host controller and device on the parallel SCSI bus has a configurable address. Unfortunately, the nature of the parallel transmission cables in SCSI limits the number of addresses on a bus. Two data widths are used in parallel SCSI: 8-bit, sometimes called *narrow SCSI*, which has 8 addresses, and 16-bit, also called *wide SCSI*, which has 16 addresses. When one subtracts the address required for the SCSI host adapter, the numbers of addresses left for devices are 7 and 15, respectively.

Narrow SCSI uses a priority scheme where the SCSI ID determines the relative priority of each entity on the bus. For example, the highest address, ID 7, is also the highest-priority address and the lowest address, ID 0, is the lowest-priority address. Things get a little more interesting when the wide SCSI bus is used. To maintain a level of compatibility with the existing narrow SCSI bus, wide SCSI preserves narrow SCSI's priority scheme and places the additional IDs, 8 through 15, at a lower priority. Therefore, the priority of SCSI IDs for wide SCSI is as follows:

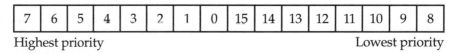

7	6	5	4	3	2	1	0	15	14	13	12	11	10	9	8

Highest priority   Lowest priority

While seven and fifteen addresses are more than enough for most workstation applications, storage networking applications, such as RAID, require more addresses to achieve the capacity desired. For this reason, SCSI also includes a scheme for addressing devices at the sub-ID level, also called a *LUN* (logical unit number). Figure 1-6 shows devices inside subsystems where the subsystem-to-host connector uses SCSI addresses and the devices within the subsystems are addressed as LUNs.

Each SCSI ID can have up to 8 LUN addresses, which means that a single SCSI bus could have up to 56 devices on 8-bit SCSI and 120 devices on 16-bit SCSI. While this many devices would be performance constrained if they were connected to a single SCSI host I/O controller, the potential capacity is greatly improved.

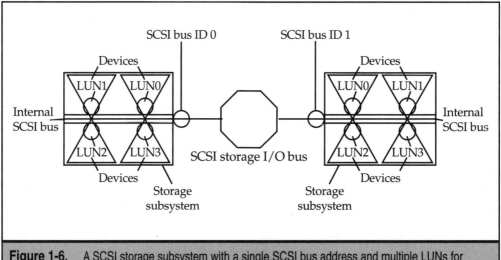

Figure 1-6. A SCSI storage subsystem with a single SCSI bus address and multiple LUNs for internal devices

So, the addressing model used for SCSI bus operations is a *target-LUN* pair. To the operating system, it is an initiator-target-LUN triplet, where the initiator refers to the ID of the SCSI host adapter on the system's internal I/O bus. It is common for server systems to have multiple host adapters.

SCSI devices use several methods to set their addresses. Some use a mechanical method, such as jumpers or switch settings; others use a programmable interface, such as a touch screen panel. SCSI host I/O adapters have their SCSI addresses assigned through software configuration utilities or through jumpers on the board. In general, it is easier to manage products that allow their SCSI addressing to be set by software.

The parallel SCSI bus will not work correctly if two entities are assigned the same SCSI address. SCSI devices with the same address will both respond to requests, a condition that *locks up* the bus and usually requires the system to be powered down if it doesn't cause the system to crash. Whenever parallel SCSI bus problems are encountered, it is always a good idea to verify the uniqueness of all SCSI IDs, including the host adapter.

SCSI Bus Arbitration and Selection

SCSI entities *arbitrate* for control of the SCSI bus. The arbitration process is one of the foundations of parallel SCSI technology and provides an orderly, if not fair, method to determine which adapters and devices can transfer commands and/or data over the bus.

The host adapter and devices needing to access the bus first determine if the bus is available, or free. If the bus is free, the adapter and/or device signals it would like to use the bus by broadcasting its address on the bus. Each adapter and device compares the priority of all the addresses that were broadcast. The highest-priority entity takes control of the bus and begins using it. Lower-priority entities must wait until the bus becomes free again and try to arbitrate again for its control.

Once an entity has control of the bus, it *selects* another entity on the bus that it wants to communicate with. If the controlling entity determines that the other entity is busy, as occurs when it is processing another command, the controlling entity can try to communicate with a different entity or return the bus to a free state.

Parallel SCSI devices can become *starved.* This happens on busy SCSI buses with a high volume of activity. There is so much data being transferred among all addresses that the lowest-priority addresses have difficulty winning an arbitration sequence. The overall effect can significantly slow down system performance, as the data on the starved device is effectively blocked from being available to complete some other process.

TIP: Try to use the highest-priority address, SCSI ID 7, for the SCSI host I/O controller. This is true whether narrow or wide SCSI is being used. Using ID 7 gives the host controller the highest priority for bus arbitration and establishes a consistent assignment, which makes it easier to configure and troubleshoot.

Single-Ended, Differential, and Low-Voltage Differential SCSI

Parallel SCSI technology has evolved over the years to provide performance improvements. Usually these performance upgrades have been accomplished with a trade-off in the length of cables used; particularly for *single-ended* SCSI. "Single-ended" refers to a kind of electrical line driver circuitry used. Another type of line driver technology is called *differential SCSI*. Differential SCSI uses a different type of line driver circuit that enables the longest possible bus lengths for accurate transmissions.

For several years, there was one specification for differential SCSI, but in recent years a second kind of differential SCSI, *low-voltage differential,* or *LVD* SCSI was specified and implemented in products. The original differential SCSI is now referred to as *high-differential* SCSI. It is important to clearly identify low- and high-differential SCSI, as the two are electrically incompatible, and connections between them can result in ruined electronics. High-differential SCSI is also electrically incompatible with single-ended SCSI.

LVD SCSI was designed to interoperate with single-ended SCSI. As a result, it is possible to connect both LVD and single-ended devices on a SCSI bus with an LVD host I/O controller. When this is done, the SCSI bus assumes the length characteristics of a single-ended SCSI bus.

Table 1-2 compares the relative speeds and cable lengths of the various types of SCSI. The table includes multiple entries for Ultra SCSI and Wide Ultra SCSI that indicate the allowed bus lengths for different numbers of devices. The fewer devices, the longer the bus can be. Wide Ultra SCSI does not support single-ended line drivers when the maximum 16 devices are connected.

SCSI Version	MB per Second	Maximum SCSI IDs	Single-ended SCSI Cable Lengths	Differential SCSI Cable Lengths	Low Voltage Differential (LVD) Cable Lengths
SCSI-1	5	8	6 m	25 m	6 m*
Fast SCSI-2	10	8	3 m	25 m	3 m*
Fast Wide SCSI-2	20	16	3 m	25 m	3 m*
Ultra SCSI	20	8	1.5 m	25 m	1.5 m*
Ultra SCSI**	20	4**	3 m**	25 m	3 m*
Wide Ultra SCSI	40	16	Not supported	25 m	Not supported*

Table 1-2.   Relative Speeds and Cable Lengths for Various SCSI Types

SCSI Version	MB per Second	Maximum SCSI IDs	Single-ended SCSI Cable Lengths	Differential SCSI Cable Lengths	Low Voltage Differential (LVD) Cable Lengths
Wide Ultra SCSI	40	8	1.5 m	25 m	1.5 m*
Wide Ultra SCSI**	40	4**	3** m	25 m	3 m*
Ultra2 SCSI	40	8	N/A	25 m	12 m
Wide Ultra2 SCSI	80.	16	N/A	25 m	12 m
Ultra3 SCSI	160	16	N/A	N/A	12 m

*SCSI-1, SCSI-2, and Ultra SCSI devices can be connected to an LVD bus but require cable lengths to be restricted to single-ended cable lengths.

**By reducing the number of attached devices to less than half of the maximum number, the cable length can be doubled for Ultra and Wide Ultra SCSI.

Table 1-2.   Relative Speeds and Cable Lengths for Various SCSI Types (*continued*)

Connectors and Cables

Every SCSI bus should be terminated to ensure reliable data transfers. *Termination* refers to the use of resistors that stabilize the voltage levels across the SCSI bus. SCSI host adapters usually have circuits that provide this termination automatically. Devices can be equipped with internal terminators or without. It is normal to need an external terminator that attaches to the available port. There are several types of terminators available that will do the job, but it is important to make sure that the terminator matches the type of SCSI bus employed: single-ended, HVD or LVD, wide or narrow.

Parallel SCSI connectors come in a wide variety of pin configurations that correspond to various versions of SCSI. Common connector configurations include 25, 50, 68, and 80 pins. While it is best to match the connectors with all entities on a SCSI bus, there may be times when it is not feasible to do so. In that case, cables can be purchased that have different pin configurations on their ends for attaching to different types of connectors. For instance, a cable can have a 68-pin connector on one end to connect to a disk subsystem and a 50-pin connector on the other to connect to a tape drive.

Connector converters are also available that fit between two unlike connectors. That said, it is important to understand that any device on the SCSI bus that is downstream (physically farther away from the host I/O controller) of any narrow SCSI connectors, such as a 50-pin connector, will only be able to receive 8-bit narrow SCSI signals. As illustrated here, a narrow SCSI connector cannot conduct any signals for the additional pins that a wide connector has:

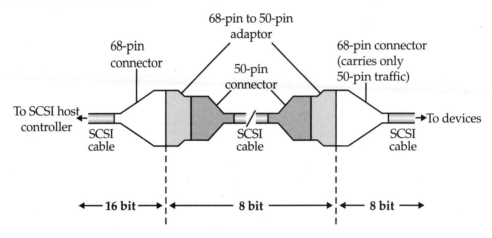

One of the things to watch out for when using connector changers is the termination of the additional wide data lines at the point where the connection conversion occurs. Without proper termination, the wide devices on the SCSI bus may not perform as well as expected and may not even work at all. Such termination problems can be difficult to troubleshoot, because the controller and all narrow devices on the bus will work as they should, not being affected by the missing termination on the additional wide pins.

Wide devices can function in 8-bit mode if it is not possible to exchange wide SCSI signals with the host I/O controller. Therefore, when there is a mix of wide and narrow devices on the same bus, it is recommended that the wide devices be located closest to the host I/O controller. For instance, 68-pin devices should be closer to the host controller than 50-pin devices. Of course, if the host controller has an 8-bit 50-pin connector while some of the devices have 68-pin connectors, it doesn't matter which order is used, as none of the devices will be able to operate in wide 16-bit mode.

While connector pin differences are fairly easy to deal with, changing from single-ended to differential SCSI is significantly more problematic. There are products that do this, although they are not very common and may not work for all applications. Such a device can be used to attach a differential device onto a single-ended SCSI bus.

NEW STORAGE CONNECTIVITY OPTIONS THAT EXTEND THE I/O CHANNEL

Data access requirements for open systems networks are the primary force behind the development of storage networking technologies. As mentioned at the beginning of the chapter, data-driven business processes have become major contributors to business success. It should come as no surprise then that maintaining clear access to data is a priority. If data can't be accessed, then the business will be unable to work normally and it will suffer.

Given this environment, businesses need more flexible options for connecting their servers to storage subsystems. These storage connectivity options are what storage networking is all about. Storage networking makes it much easier to expand capacity, increase performance, and extend distances, but most of all it lays the groundwork for sharing storage subsystems and data among multiple host computers. Figure 1-7 shows the basic relationships between servers and storage in a storage network environment.

The key architectural element that distinguishes storage networks from parallel SCSI is the physical independence of the entities on the storage network. Addressing in a storage network is done as a function of a communications protocol, as opposed to using electrical signaling. In a switched topology storage network, there is no common medium that causes contention, as there is with parallel SCSI, and there is no implied hierarchy, as there is with parallel SCSI. This means the overall performance of the network is more predictable and scales better.

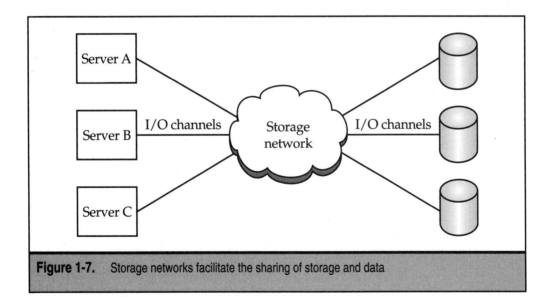

Figure 1-7. Storage networks facilitate the sharing of storage and data

In addition, the configuration of host adapters and devices on a storage network can be changed with minimal impact on production servers. That is not to say that such changes should be made without careful planning, but it is certainly far better than having to power down servers to attach new storage devices.

Network Attached Storage

Network attached storage, sometimes shortened to NAS, is the term used to identify turnkey network file server products. The typical NAS product as pictured here connects to a common network, usually Ethernet, and provides preconfigured disk capacity along with integrated systems and storage management software to create a total storage solution.

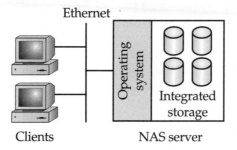

NAS products are also referred to as *storage appliances,* following the lead of Network Appliance, one of the leading companies producing NAS products. NAS systems are characterized as having specialized file systems integrated with thin or stripped-down operating systems that are tuned for the requirements of file serving. This specialization of operating and file systems functions delivers the optimal price/performance ratio for network storage.

NAS products typically communicate with client systems using the NFS (Network File System) or CIFS (Common Internet File System) protocol, or both. These protocols run on top of the IP protocol used on Ethernet networks and the Internet. The purpose of these protocols is to exchange *files* between computers. The relationship between clients and NAS servers is shown here:

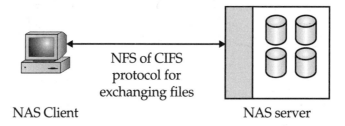

At some point in the future, and possibly very soon, the distinction between an *intelligent* storage device and a turnkey storage server may become more difficult to ascertain. In this book, the term "NAS" will refer to a system, subsystem, or device that has the ability to respond to file requests from a client system. The client that accesses the NAS product can be a server system to the rest of the network, providing typical server functions such as e-mail, Web, or database services.

Fibre Channel

Fibre Channel was the first wiring technology adopted by the broad storage industry as a standard foundation for connecting and managing storage networks. Unlike the terms SAN and NAS, the name *Fibre Channel* defines an actual technology based on the development of a full standard with a great deal of depth and functionality.

Do not be confused by the awkward spelling of "fibre"—after it is typed this way a few times, it doesn't seem so awful. This spelling of "fibre" was not the result of a British influence but was chosen to differentiate Fibre Channel networking technology from fiber optic cabling. In fact, Fibre Channel is designed to run on fiber optic cables and also copper cabling. Perhaps it is too bad that another, less contrived name was not chosen. But the storage industry has not been known for its clever naming conventions; after all, try to remember what flashed through your mind the first time you heard the term SCSI.

Fibre Channel blends gigabit networking technology with I/O channel technology in a single integrated technology family. Whereas SCSI, by default, implies the *parallel* SCSI bus with multiple data lines running in parallel, Fibre Channel implements *serial* SCSI with a single optical or copper cable connecting network nodes, as shown in the illustration that follows. It is the application of a serial SCSI protocol that enables Fibre Channel cables to extend up to 10,000 meters. Compared to the 25 meter maximum of SCSI, this seems almost too good to be true.

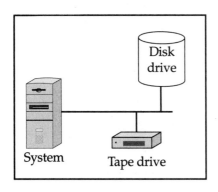

SCSI bus connections
constrained to a single room

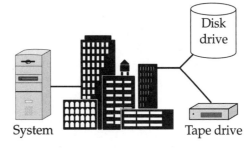

Fibre channel connections
can extend across a campus
or metropolitan area

Two Networks: Loop and Fabric

While generally thought of as a single networking technology, Fibre Channel is more properly thought of as two separate networking technologies. Fibre Channel loop networks use a shared media loop topology similar to FDDI and Token Ring. Fibre Channel fabric networks use a switched networking topology similar to switched Ethernet and ATM. A point-to-point topology can also be configured to connect systems and storage directly without any intervening equipment. Figure 1-8 contrasts the three Fibre Channel topologies.

FCP: Serial SCSI Storing Protocol

Fibre Channel adopted an industry-standard version of serial SCSI and named it FCP, for Fibre Channel Protocol. FCP is a serial SCSI implementation of the SCSI-3 project under development in the SCSI ANSI subcommittee; it has proved itself to be an excellent

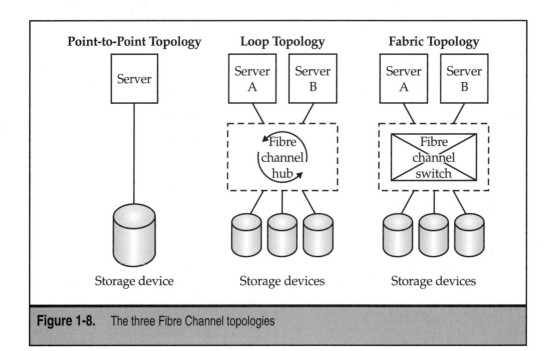

Figure 1-8. The three Fibre Channel topologies

protocol for storage traffic. On the strength of this protocol, Fibre Channel has compatibility with nearly all the file systems and database systems used in popular servers today. The industry's agreement on a single, working storage protocol may prove to be the biggest advantage Fibre Channel has over other wiring technologies.

Interestingly enough, FCP is not a wiring protocol but a storage application protocol layered on top of lower-level wiring technologies built into Fibre Channel. In sharp contrast to parallel SCSI, which has limited support for multiple initiators, FCP on Fibre Channel is designed to easily support multiple host adapters working together on a high-bandwidth, networked environment. Figure 1-9 illustrates Fibre Channel's multi-initiator capabilities.

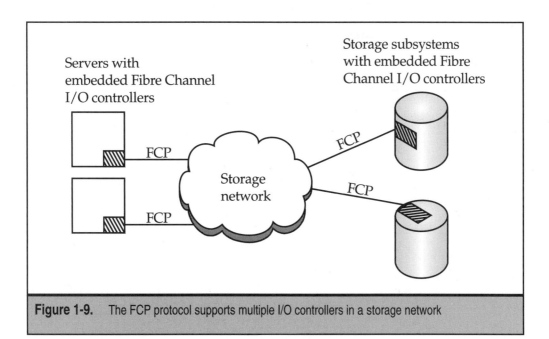

Figure 1-9.   The FCP protocol supports multiple I/O controllers in a storage network

Storage Area Networks

Storage area networks, or SANs, are dedicated networks that connect one or more systems to storage devices and subsystems. One of the ways SANs are often described is as "back-end" networks that carry storage traffic while the "front-end" or data networks carry normal client/server TCP/IP network traffic as shown here:

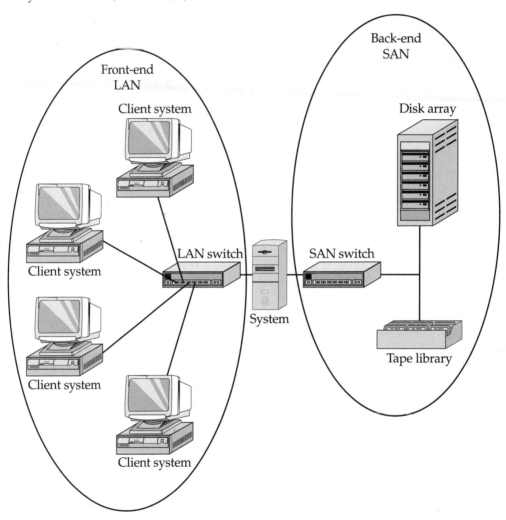

The term SAN has become almost synonymous with Fibre Channel. However, Fibre Channel is not a required component, as other networking and/or serial SCSI technologies could be used to create a SAN. For instance, a SAN could be built with an Ethernet network dedicated to NAS traffic.

A single wiring technology can carry both filing (NFS and CIFS) traffic and serial SCSI storing traffic. Both Fibre Channel and Gigabit Ethernet have the capability to transport NFS and CIFS on top of the TCP/IP protocol stack as well as transporting serial SCSI protocols. In this way, a single network wiring technology can connect all kinds of storage network traffic, including client server NAS as storage devices and subsystems. Figure 1-10 shows both types of traffic working together in a single multiprotocol SAN.

SAN as a System Area Network

Outside the storage industry, people have suggested that SAN stands for "server area network." There is some merit in using the term this way to identify a small low-latency network that connects servers together for the purposes of redundancy and scalability. The term "cluster" or "cluster network" could also be used for this type of network. So, since this is a storage networking book and other words exist for clumps of server connectivity, the term "SAN" in this book means storage area network, unless otherwise stated. The term "storage network" will also be used to describe a network primarily used for connecting servers to storage devices.

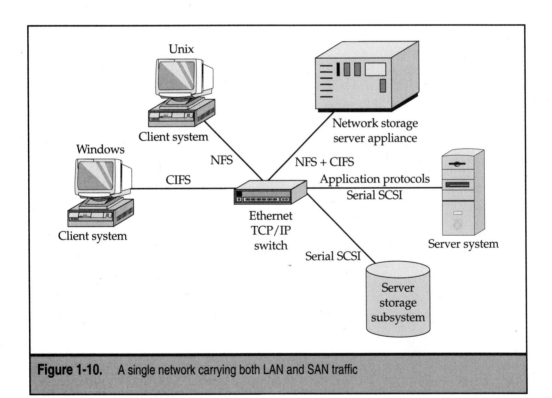

Figure 1-10. A single network carrying both LAN and SAN traffic

Fibre Channel as a SAN Technology

Fibre Channel has been closely associated with the term "SAN" for several years. As discussed previously, while Fibre Channel and SAN may seem like two terms for the same concept, they are not. Fibre Channel is simply the wiring technology that inspired storage industry marketing people to invent the term SAN.

Fibre Channel extends the capabilities of server SCSI channels by employing standard networking technology as the transport for high-bandwidth data transfers. While this idea to integrate storage with networking might be seen as a natural evolution for I/O technology, the fact is, storage connectivity has not always been the primary force behind Fibre Channel. For several years, Fibre Channel was seen by its developers as the next great LAN networking technology. At this point, it seems highly unlikely that Fibre Channel will have much, if any, success as an IP backbone technology.

Ethernet as SAN Wiring

Fibre Channel is certainly not the only technology to build SANs with. For example, a dedicated Gigabit Ethernet network that connects servers to NAS servers is certainly a storage network.

More importantly, there is a great deal of development work going on to develop a Gigabit Ethernet–based storage networking technology to compete with Fibre Channel. This idea is expanded with a fair amount of detail in later chapters, but the basic idea is similar to Fibre Channel's adoption of FCP as an application protocol. A storage protocol will be used that is transported on top of an industry-standard Ethernet protocol layer. For instance, a serial SCSI protocol could either replace IP in the protocol stack or be transported by IP or TCP services.

In general, this type of approach would not work with any nonswitched, sub-100 Mb/s Ethernet network. There are significant differences between storage network requirements and those of TCP/IP data networks, but that does not mean that Ethernet technology could not be developed that meets the needs of storage networks. For instance, it might be necessary to incorporate Gigabit Ethernet with more advanced flow control and a new generation of switches that function more like storage switches than traditional Ethernet switches. Just as Fibre Channel implementers install new wiring to accommodate Fibre Channel, they could also implement new Ethernet storage switches. The result would be a SAN based on Ethernet technology, as opposed to Fibre Channel. The protocol abstraction for this is illustrated here:

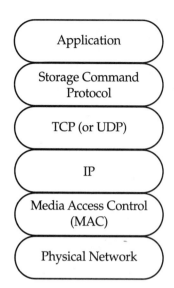

SUMMARY

The growing awareness that data is the ultimate IT asset, along with the need to provide 24 × 7 access to it, is forcing the development of storage technology that can satisfy the requirements for flexibility, scalability, availability, and reliability. Storage networking is a relatively new open systems technology that exceeds the capabilities of bus-connected storage by combining advancements in three fundamental areas: wiring, filing, and storing.

Traditional parallel SCSI technology also incorporated wiring, filing, and storing elements, but it is limited by cabling distances, by the number of addresses and, most importantly, by the physical and electrical nature of its wiring technology. In contrast, storage networks break through the limitations of parallel SCSI by isolating the physical connections from such logical operations as addressing and naming.

The first new technology to be adopted for storage networking is Fibre Channel. Fibre Channel meets the requirements of storage networking and incorporates an ANSI standard serial SCSI protocol called FCP. Fibre Channel is implemented both in shared media loop networks and in switched fabric networks.

Ethernet networks, particularly Gigabit Ethernet networks, may provide the best options for customers if the storage-oriented technology can be developed in time to catch up with Fibre Channel. For starters, NAS servers attached to dedicated Gigabit Ethernet networks are already an alternative approach to building a SAN that provides many of the same benefits of Fibre Channel. A serial SCSI mapping for Gigabit Ethernet would enable it to be used as a high-speed storage network, equal in speed to Fibre Channel and potentially with lower costs achieved through the efficiencies of higher-volume production.

NAS products will also continue to evolve. The spectrum of products in this area spans a price range from two hundred thousand dollars to less than a thousand. As storage device and subsystem companies continue to look for ways to differentiate products in the market, it is likely that new devices and subsystems will be introduced that have higher-level filing capabilities in addition to the storing functions they use today.

In conclusion, we live in a time when the storage and networking worlds are in a state of flux. Established technologies are being adapted to fit a new set of requirements for distributed, high-availability computing. Today's notions of file servers and block storage devices as fundamental storage components are changing rapidly. Customers today are forced to evaluate and purchase products without knowing which direction the industry will turn.

The remaining chapters in this book should help readers understand the many variables at play and help them make choices about storage products that are based on fundamental requirements of flexibility, scalability, availability, and reliability.

EXERCISES

1. Calculate the number of test scenarios needed to uniquely test a storage networking product that works with four operating system platforms, each with three different versions, two file systems for each platform, eight different host I/O controllers, four kinds of switches/hubs, and 15 types of devices/subsystems.

2. Draw a configuration for a wide SCSI bus in which nine devices are wide SCSI devices but the device with SCSI ID 4 is a narrow SCSI device. Assign any device ID you want to the wide SCSI devices and minimize the impact of mixing the narrow device with wide devices on the same bus. Don't forget to terminate the bus correctly.

CHAPTER 2

Piecing Together a Path for Storage I/O

As with any advanced technology, there are a lot of details to consider when implementing storage and I/O systems. When one starts planning a storage network, it becomes immediately obvious that designing, installing, and managing one requires a solid understanding of the total endeavor. A holistic approach enables the design team to define and articulate the requirements and begin the process of testing, recommending, and implementing a real storage network. This chapter takes the reader through an overview of the complete set of hardware and software components that are parts of most storage networks.

IDENTIFYING THE PHYSICAL I/O BUILDING BLOCKS

The exploration of the I/O path begins with the tangible hardware components. Storage networks have six hardware pieces directly involved with I/O transfers:

▼ System memory bus

■ Host I/O bus

■ Host I/O controllers

■ I/O bus and network connections

■ Storage devices and subsystems

▲ Storage media

This section will help the reader understand how, where, and why these technologies are made the way they are, and how to take advantage of their capabilities.

System Memory Bus

Obviously, system CPUs can have an enormous impact on I/O processing—but the CPU is not necessarily part of the I/O path and is not presented that way in the book. In general, there is a desire to relieve the CPU from managing I/O processing in server systems by moving that function to other processors. Therefore, we choose to ignore the CPU as part of the I/O path and assume the presence of intelligent I/O processors that perform this work.

Without considering the CPU, the first leg of the I/O path is the system memory bus:

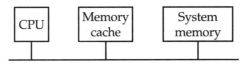

The system memory bus is a physically compact high-speed bus that connects the CPU to its primary memory storage and memory caches. It's not usually possible for a user to add devices to the memory bus, except for memory and cache chips that fit into sockets provided by the system manufacturer. While memory bus architectures are mostly outside the scope of this book, there are a few things that can be said to help form a context for discussing the I/O path.

It is tempting to view memory as some kind of instant grab bag for data, but in the microscopic world of the CPU, that's not the way it works. Memory is an electrical device that responds to service requests like any other device. This signaling takes several CPU cycles to complete. From the perspective of a device like a disk drive, the signaling component of the data transfer to memory is insignificant, but to the CPU, it can be huge. Therefore, slower I/O devices, such as storage devices and network adapters, are usually separated from the system memory by a bridge chip and run on the host I/O bus, as shown here:

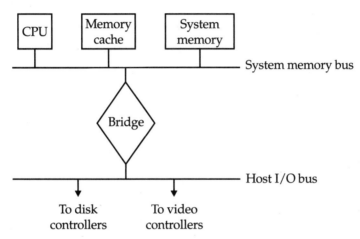

Virtual memory is an important feature of most systems that facilitates multiprogramming and multiprocessing environments. The operating system uses virtual memory to store lower-demand data on disk drives while it keeps higher demand data and instructions in system memory. Two flavors of virtual memory are *demand paging* and *segment swapping*. Most modern operating systems use one or the other to manage their memory resources. When data held in virtual memory is needed by the CPU, it is transferred from virtual memory storage on a disk drive back into system memory. Delays in the transfer from a comparatively slow disk to high-speed memory have a negative impact on overall system performance.

In addition to virtual memory operations, storage-specific applications, such as backup, often depend on moving large amounts of data in and out of the system memory bus. Obviously, delays in moving this storage traffic in and out of the system memory bus will negatively impact these applications. Removing unnecessary processes that contend for memory bus resources can increase their performance.

NOTE: When pondering the amount of memory to configure for new servers, opt for more. There is no substitute for memory when performance is paramount. In a server, additional memory can have a more profound effect than faster processors when it comes to overall system performance.

The Host I/O Bus

Data destined for storage devices leaves the system memory bus and is sent over another system bus: the host I/O bus. The most common host I/O bus implemented in products today is the PCI bus, but there are several others, including the S-bus, the EISA bus, and the VME bus.

The host I/O bus provides several important functions, including:

▼ Connection of system adapters such as network interface cards (NICs) and host bus adapters (HBAs)

■ Transfer of data between external devices and networks and the system memory bus

▲ Transfer of data between system adapters

System architects typically separate the system memory bus from I/O bus actions and interruptions with some sort of bridging device. Figure 2-1 shows a host I/O bus with four add-in I/O cards connecting to the system memory bus through a bridge controller chip.

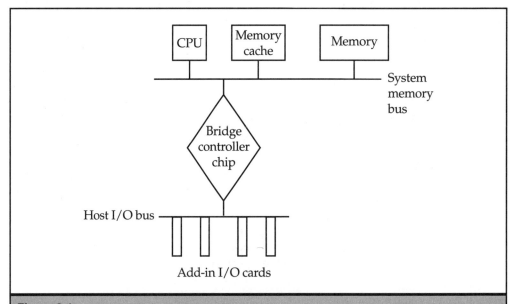

Figure 2-1. Multiple I/O cards connect to the system memory bus through a bridge controller

The host I/O bus is represented in diagrams throughout the book as a hexagon that connects to both storage host bus adapters (HBAs) and network interface cards (NICs), like this:

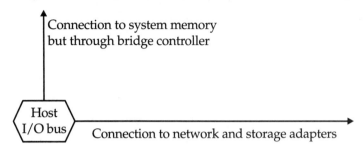

The host I/O bus is the vehicle for moving data from the system memory bus to peripheral devices and networks. If the system CPU is likened to the engine in a race car, then the host I/O bus is analogous to the car's transmission, which transfers the engine's raw power to the wheels that make the car move. Most data processing applications require that lots of data be moved in and out of storage devices. A system that cannot efficiently move its data from the host I/O bus to the memory bus and back again will not provide adequate performance as processing loads increase.

Host I/O bus technology receives a lot of attention from the industry whenever the technology changes, and for good reason. System companies, adapter card manufacturers, CPU companies, software companies, chip manufacturers, and, most importantly, IT organizations are affected. In the PC world, users have had to sort out the advantages and disadvantages of ISA, Microchannel, EISA, and PCI buses, often investing in server I/O bus technologies that have become obsolete.

A new serial I/O bus called InfiniBand is being developed by an industry group led by Intel. The new InfiniBand serial I/O bus is likely to create a fair amount of disruption in the industry because it completely breaks the existing model of using adapter cards that fit into system expansion slots. Instead, InfiniBand provides serial networking interfaces like switches or hubs for adding functionality to systems. Chapter 13 provides a more in-depth examination of this important topic.

Host I/O Controllers and Network Interface Cards

After the host I/O bus, the next stop along the physical I/O path is either a host I/O controller or a network interface card (NIC), depending on the storage technology in use. These host I/O controllers and NICs are end points for the wiring functions of their respective networks and are positioned at the junction of the host I/O bus and the storage bus/network.

They are implemented either as adapter cards that fit into host I/O bus slots or as part of the chip set integrated on the system board. In either case, a physical connector is provided that bus/network cables connect to. In the diagrams throughout this book, host I/O controllers are represented by right triangles and NICs are represented by pentagons between the host I/O bus and the networks they connect to, like this:

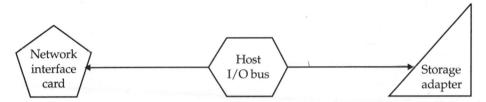

Host I/O controllers and NICs share the host I/O bus with each other as well as with other processors, such as video cards. In general, these other controllers are not relevant to the topics of this book, except for their impact on storage I/O processing.

Software for Host I/O Controllers and NICs

Control software for host I/O controllers and NICs can run in two locations: in the adapter *firmware*, and in the host system as a *device driver*.

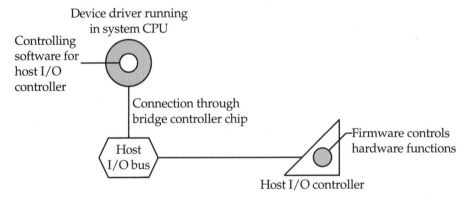

Firmware is controller-specific software that resides and runs on the particular hardware chips implemented on the host I/O controller or NIC. It controls the most basic functions, including such things as power-on testing and error detection.

The device driver resides on system storage and runs as a process on the host computer. Device drivers direct the mode of operations and the transfer of data through the host I/O controller or NIC. They are discussed in more detail later in this chapter as part of the logical I/O path.

A lot of variety is found in the host I/O controllers and NICs on the market. Historically, host I/O controllers have been SCSI and Fibre Channel HBAs, the latter having been central to the development of storage area networks. Alternatively, NICs are associated with network attached storage, although that notion could easily be changed as storage networking technology continues to evolve. It may help readers to associate host I/O controllers with serial SCSI transmissions, as opposed to SANs. A brief overview of some of the various host I/O controller technologies follows.

Parallel SCSI

Parallel SCSI was introduced in Chapter 1 as the traditional storage channel technology for open systems servers. The term "parallel" refers to the structure of multiple connecting wires used for addressing devices and transferring data. The original SCSI specification described these connections in detail—without any discussion of other wiring schemes. So, for many, SCSI simply is equated with parallel data transmission.

Including parallel SCSI in a book about storage *networks* may seem a little strange, because it is not usually thought of as a network. However, open systems server storage has been dominated by parallel SCSI for many years, and it is still the prevailing storage channel for network attached storage appliances. When one considers NAS as a major segment of the network storage market, SCSI obviously has an important place. Perhaps most important, the SCSI command protocol is the established device-level interface for the major storage networking technologies. That makes it virtually impossible to discuss storage networks without discussing SCSI.

The SCSI command protocol provides several significant performance benefits. For example, SCSI allows *overlapped* operations, which means SCSI HBAs can multitask their operations. Overlapped operations take advantage of the speed difference between the relatively fast electrical signaling on the storage bus and the relatively mechanical operations of storage devices. SCSI takes advantage of this timing difference to manage several operations on multiple devices simultaneously. Figure 2-2 shows a single SCSI HBA that has started three operations on three separate devices: a data transfer from device #1, a seek operation on device #2, and a write on device #3 that is emptying its buffer memory to disk.

Fibre Channel

Fibre Channel, the topic of Chapter 11, is one of the leading technologies for storage networks. It is a gigabit technology, similar in transmission speed to Gigabit Ethernet. In storage terms, that equates to 100 MB/s. Like parallel SCSI, Fibre Channel host I/O controllers are usually referred to as host bus adapters, or HBAs. Fibre Channel HBAs are relatively expensive compared to SCSI host adapters, but they can address many more devices than their SCSI counterparts. Fibre Channel host bus adapters are used to provide I/O connectivity to more devices, over longer distances, than SCSI.

Device driver software for Fibre Channel HBAs was developed to allow existing applications and operating systems to use the existing software interfaces that SCSI provided, but through a Fibre Channel HBA. The addressing capability of Fibre Channel is also enhanced over SCSI, allowing for as many as 16 million network IDs, as opposed to SCSI's 16.

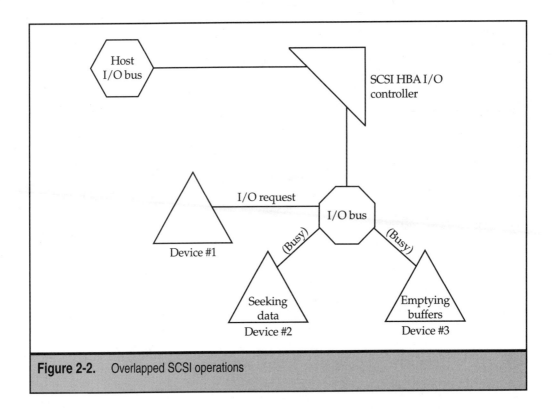

Figure 2-2.   Overlapped SCSI operations

SSA

SSA, or serial storage architecture, was developed by IBM as a storage network technology, primarily for networks of disk drives. While SSA was viewed by others as a competitive proprietary technology, IBM actually tried to make it an open industry standard by publishing the specification and turning it over to the ANSI committee working on SCSI-3. SSA never caught on within the industry and is now mainly an IBM-only technology. Where there once was hot debate over whether Fibre Channel or SSA would prevail, there is now little doubt that SSA's development is drawing to a close. These days there are very few companies making SSA products; in fact, IBM has developed its own Fibre Channel strategy and is also one of the primary companies behind storage over Ethernet and IP networks.

SSA networks are shared-media loops, similar to FDDI, but designed for storage requirements. SSA traffic is bidirectional and uses dual-ported disk drives for optimal availability. SSA has some very attractive attributes such as support for 127 devices per loop, and a transfer rate of 20 MB/s. Devices can be 15 meters apart, without restrictions as to the overall bus length, and the cable connectors are relatively small and only require four pins. SSA was a reasonable candidate to replace parallel SCSI, but it did not succeed in getting widespread industry support.

ATA and IDE

ATA stands for Advanced Technology Attachment, which is closely related to disk drives implemented with IDE (Integrated Drive Electronics). In general, ATA is a controller technology, and IDE is the disk drive technology that matches it. ATA is a low-cost, moderate-performance interface designed primarily for disk drives in desktop computers. Most ATA controllers sold today implement faster versions called ATA-2 and ATA-3, and the matching disk drives use Enhanced IDE, or EIDE. ATA host controller chips are integrated onto almost every PC system board produced, providing the capability to connect four devices. ATA controllers have become so inexpensive and common that it might be impossible to purchase a PC motherboard that does not have an ATA interface built in.

As the primary design goal of ATA technology has been to minimize cost, they have not been marketed for use in high-throughput environments, such as storage networking. ATA was developed primarily as an inside-the-case technology, which means that their cables were not defined for external connections or anything resembling networking. Nor does ATA support overlapped I/Os on multiple drives, so it is slower than SCSI protocols for multitasking server systems. Although its performance on a single device is pretty reasonable—16.6 MB/s—ATA is generally not considered optimal for use as a host I/O controller in storage network applications where overlapped operations are the norm. Some work is being done, however, to develop ATA controllers capable of supporting higher-throughput environments like those found in storage networks.

IEEE 1394, Firewire

One of the serial SCSI implementations in the market is called Firewire, or 1394. The name "Firewire" was coined as the product name for a technology developed by Apple and Texas Instruments based on the IEEE 1394 serial transmission standard. Firewire has not been very successful as a storage interface but has found broad support as an interface for video equipment.

Firewire supports up to 64 devices with a cable length of 72 meters. Data transfers up to 40 MB/s can be achieved. It also supports isochronous communications for video or multimedia streaming applications. 1394 host I/O controllers tend to be more expensive than SCSI, in part because the technology lacks the volumes needed to drive the cost of production down. It is most often implemented as a means for connecting video and audio peripherals to multimedia production systems. After several years in existence, there are not many companies making storage products for 1394 storage networks. Compared to Fibre Channel, and Gigabit Ethernet storage, there is very little investment in Firewire, and it does not appear that 1394 will be considered important to the storage networking industry.

HIPPI

HIPPI stands for high-performance parallel interface, which was developed primarily as a high-speed I/O channel capable of 80 MB/s transmissions. HIPPI is used mostly for scientific/research computing, but it has also been implemented for digital entertainment production. HIPPI was developed as a simplex communication technology, meaning transmissions could only be made one direction at a time. HIPPI cables are big and heavy due to the fact that a single one-way connection with 32 data lines is implemented on a 50-conductor cable with heavy shielding. As HIPPI is a point-to-point technology supporting a single storage subsystem connected to a single computer system, the use of HIPPI for storage networking is not very realistic.

HIPPI host I/O controllers are not plentiful in the market and tend to be expensive. Platform availability (hardware and software) for HIPPI host I/O controllers is poor, with most HIPPI products being produced for Silicon Graphics/Cray systems. While platform coverage could possibly change over time, there are not many companies left investing in the development of HIPPI host I/O controllers and storage devices. Therefore, it is highly unlikely that a HIPPI industry will emerge to become a realistic network storage technology.

However, just as the FCP serial SCSI protocol can be carried over a Fibre Channel network, HIPPI signaling and data transfers are also supported as an application layer protocol in Fibre Channel. If HIPPI is going to evolve as a commercially viable product outside government labs and the film/video industry, it will do so as a technology that finds new life through Fibre Channel.

Ethernet

Ethernet NICs are far and away the most common I/O technology for network attached storage. Historically, Ethernet adapters have not been used as host I/O controllers transporting serial SCSI data. However, this situation has changed as the established Ethernet industry and a number of start-up Ethernet storage companies have developed the capability to transport serial SCSI over Ethernet networks.

One of the interesting details to consider in this development is determining whether or not an Ethernet adapter for serial SCSI is a typical Ethernet NIC or a different type of network controller. It seems a little strange to refer to an Ethernet adapter as an HBA, but there may be significant enough differences between a storage-enabled Ethernet adapter and a traditional Ethernet NIC to call the former something different. The approach used in this book is to use the term "Ethernet SCSI controllers" when it is necessary to identify the host I/O controller as Ethernet technology. Otherwise, the generic term, host I/O controller, will apply to Ethernet as well as Fibre Channel and SCSI varieties.

Storage Networks and Buses

After the host I/O controller, the second wiring component on the I/O path is the storage network, or bus. The topology of the network significantly determines many of the network's characteristics. Just as bus, loop, and switched topologies have been used in data networks, they also have corresponding implementations in storage, as shown in this table:

	Bus Topology	Loop Topology	Switched Topology
Data Networking	Arcnet Thicknet Ethernet Thinnet Ethernet	Token Ring FDDI	10BaseT 100BaseT 1000BaseT ATM
Storage Networking	Parallel SCSI ATA Fibre Channel Pt-to-pt	SSA Firewire Fibre Channel Loop	ESCON Fibre Channel Fabric

The three topologies used in storage networking are illustrated in Figure 2-3.

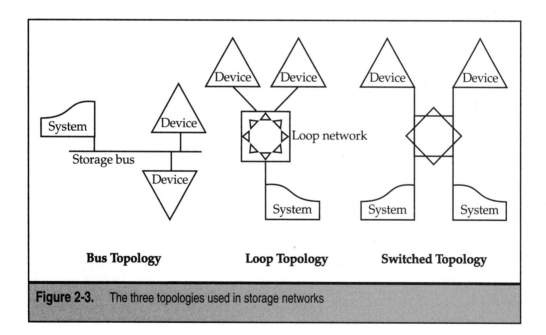

Figure 2-3.   The three topologies used in storage networks

The parallel SCSI bus is based on shared access over a common cable. Each system or device that wishes to communicate over the parallel SCSI bus waits for bus activity to stop and then *arbitrates* for the bus. Arbitration is the combination of algorithms and signals that determine which entity has control of the bus when there are multiple entities wanting to gain control.

Fibre Channel loop networks are similar to the parallel SCSI bus in the way the loop is a shared resource that requires arbitration to determine who controls the loop. Loops are typically connected in a star-wired fashion using a hub that connects each entity via a cable to the hub and then connects these cables together through connections inside the hub. The entire loop of external and internal connections is a shared resource. As Fibre Channel loops use serial transmission instead of parallel, the cables can be made using small connectors and can extend over much longer distances.

Switched topologies also use serial transmission. However, switched networks do not share a common cable; instead, each network node connects to a switch with its own private cable. No arbitration is necessary with a switched topology. Instead, each node wanting to communicate with another initiates the session directly, without regard for other sessions on the network. Aggregate communications on a switched network have much higher throughput than loops or buses because multiple pairs of nodes communicate concurrently. While switches provide the best flexibility and performance, they are also the most expensive alternative.

Depicting Storage Buses as Hubs

Each of the three topologies has an established method for connecting host I/O controllers, devices/subsystems, and networking devices such as hubs and switches. However, this does not mean that there is an implied hierarchy in the way devices are *addressed*. In some cases, the addressing method employed may be better described using the analogy of a simple Ethernet network hub. So, while the physical connection on a SCSI bus could be shown as a daisy chain, the addressing, and access to the devices, may be more accurately shown as a hub. Where storage addressing is concerned, the hub model is more appropriate than the bus. Therefore, SCSI networks are depicted graphically as hubs instead of buses in diagrams in this book.

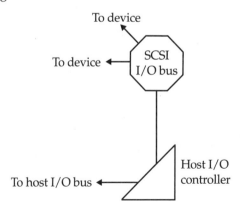

Storage networks will be shown using either hubs or switches depending on whether the network is a loop or a switched network.

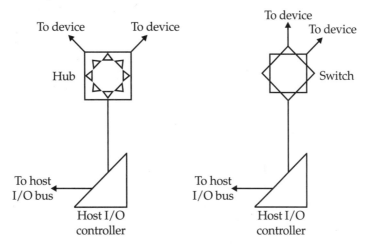

Storage Devices and Subsystems

The next, but not last, stop along the I/O path is the device or subsystem on the opposite end of the network from the host I/O controller.

Storage Subsystems

A *storage subsystem* is a collection of devices that share a common power distribution, packaging, or management system scheme. Examples of storage subsystems include RAID systems, the subject of Chapter 6, and tape libraries, as discussed in Chapter 7. Both of these types of subsystems have multiple devices acting as a single system on the I/O channel.

Storage subsystems range in functionality from simple products, which are basically power and packaging cabinets that consolidate devices in a single "box," to sophisticated computers in their own right that provide storage management functions like mirroring, striping, and backup.

Storage subsystems can have one or more IDs on the storage bus or network, while the devices inside them are addressed as LUNs associated with the higher-level IDs. Another common approach is to use virtualization techniques and present the devices inside the subsystem as a single large device. This is typically accomplished by means of a completely separate and independent I/O bus or network inside the subsystem that connects to all internal devices. The internal bus/network is managed by a subsystem controller that masks the complexity of the subsystem's internal device communications. In other words, the subsystem controller allows the host I/O controller to manage a single virtual device. In that case, the internal devices are not addressable as LUNs.

Disk Drives

The most common electronic storage device is the disk drive. The progress made by the disk drive industry over the past 20 years is practically a miracle. While processor chips tend to get most of the credit for the rapid evolution in computing, this evolution would not have been possible were it not for the incredible achievements in disk drive technology.

Besides capacity, disk drives are measured on two important criteria: reliability and performance. We'll now look at these topics and discuss their applicability to storage networks.

Reliability: MTBF and MTTR   Reliability of disk drives is constantly getting better, even though the tolerances of the technology continue to narrow. One of the indications of reliability is a drive's MTBF (mean time between failures) calculation. In general, MTBF numbers do not indicate how long a particular device is likely to last; instead, they give a statistical approximation of how likely a device is to fail.

Obviously, there is no way to test a product's expected life span if it's only been in development for a relatively short time. For example, there is no way to run an empirical life span test for a product expected to last six years when it takes only 18 months to develop and manufacture it. That's why statistical evaluations are necessary. By the time a company actually tested the device for six years, it would likely have been mothballed already for four!

So, customers need a way to determine reliability, and manufacturers need a way to communicate it. Thus, there are MTBF calculations. There are three basic techniques used for determining MTBF:

▼ Run the same test on lots of devices for a few months. Divide the total hours run for all devices during this time and divide by the number of failures.

■ Continue to run tests over an extended period of time (this is called ongoing reliability testing), and make the same calculations as in the preceding technique.

▲ Multiply the number of devices sold in some time period by the number of hours during that time period. Take this product and divide by the drives that failed and were returned.

MTTR, or mean time to repair, is another measurement companies use to indicate the repair frequency of modules in their products. For some devices, a MTTR number no longer makes sense—it's cheaper to replace the device than repair it. Also, where redundant drives are used in a subsystem, such as a RAID subsystem, the loss of a single drive does not impact the ability to access data and MTTR numbers are less meaningful.

Rotation Speed   The rotation speed on a disk drive gives an indication of the rotational latency of the drive, as well as its performance capabilities for streaming data.

Rotational latency is an important issue in high-throughput network storage applications such as file serving and backup. The faster the rotation speed of the disk drive, the shorter period of time the disk drive head must wait to start reading or writing data and the faster the data transfer can be. While this amount of time may be short, in the range of 2 to 10 milliseconds, when every disk operation is affected, the resulting performance impact can be large. Other processes are delayed while waiting for the data to be read from disk. So, where there is a steady demand to access data on a device, every millisecond counts. To put things in perspective, a single request for a file on a server could result in 5, 10, 25 or more individual read requests from a disk drive. Multiplying those numbers by the number of concurrent requests (100, 200, 500) on a server would indicate the need to reduce rotational latency as much as possible. For example, a 5-millisecond average rotational latency multiplied by ten reads per file with a queue of 200 concurrent users results in a 10-second delay as a result of rotational latency alone. It's no wonder that heavily loaded Web sites can seem so slow.

Rotational latency can also be important in cases where relatively few files are being accessed at a time—if the files are large. Storage networks have been implemented successfully in the computer graphics and image processing industries for their ability to offer high-speed I/O operations on large files. This is an environment where the rotational speed of a disk drive contributes directly to system performance. For example, the Silicon Graphics' XFS file system is optimized for graphics processing by structuring its disk layout in large contiguous blocks of data in order to facilitate long, nonstop disk reads. In this case, faster disk rotation means the data moves faster past the drive heads—in essence, it is read faster.

NOTE: Storage networking requires relatively fast disk rotation speeds. New drives purchased for storage networking applications should exceed 10,000 RPM.

Seek Time After rotational latency, the next most important performance measurement for disk drives is seek time—commonly measured as average access time. This is the amount of time it takes for the drive head to move from one track to another when reading or writing data. Sometimes rotational latency averages are added in the calculation of average access time. Disk actuators, also called disk arms, are complex, high-precision mechanisms that have the read/write heads attached to them. Even though disk arms move at incredible speed over the surface of the disk media, this speed is slow compared to the speed of electrons moving through silicon or copper. So, the time it takes to seek is a system bottleneck.

Memory Buffers Rotational speed is not the only indication of disk drive performance. All disk drives have some amount of *buffer* memory to temporarily store data that they are reading and writing. Buffers provide a way for the host I/O controller to work with a drive to transfer data in and out of the drive while the drive is seeking or performing some other function. All drive reads and writes are done through the drive's buffer. As it turns out, larger buffer sizes reduce the number of transfer operations, thus creating a more efficient I/O channel. As drives have become more intelligent through the use of microprocessors, the memory on the disk is also used for caching in addition to buffering. Caching is the topic of Chapter 5.

Buffer memory capacities in the range of 2MB to 4MB are recommended for storage networking environments.

Transfer Rates   There are two transfer rates used to measure disk drive performance: the burst transfer rate and the sustained transfer rate. Burst rates indicate the speed of data transfers within a track on the disk, and sustained transfer rates reflect the speed of data transfers where there are track changes and gaps in the data on disk. Both are illustrated here:

Disk surface

Data in → Track

Data in →

Burst Transfer   **Sustained Transfer**

Real disk performance is highly dependent on the structure of the file system on the disk and how fully populated, or fragmented, the disk is. For that reason, do not expect to receive performance in the range of the specifications listed for sustained transfer.

In general, for most storage network environments, the most significant specifications are the amount of buffer memory, the rotational speed, and seek times of the disk. Other specifications, such as burst transfer rate and sustained transfer rate, depend heavily on these specs.

Dual Porting   As RAID and storage networking technology have advanced, the requirement to provide alternative access paths to individual disk drives has increased. Disk drive manufacturers have responded with *dual ported* disk drives. Simply stated, dual porting provides an additional I/O channel connector on a disk drive. Dual porting provides a redundant or secondary I/O path in case a failure occurs anywhere in the primary I/O path. Fibre Channel dual ported disk drives are commonly implemented in disk subsystems built with internal Fibre Channel networks.

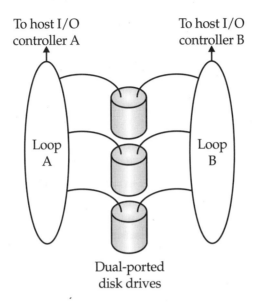

To host I/O
controller A

To host I/O
controller B

Loop
A

Loop
B

Dual-ported
disk drives

Tape Drives

Tape drives are primarily used for backup and recovery; the topic of Chapter 7. They are relatively slow compared to disk drives, and any amount of seeking can take seconds, or even minutes, as opposed to milliseconds. For this reason, tape drives are not practical for random access applications.

Tape drives work best when *streaming* data—that is, when they can maintain a constant, sustainable workload. Streaming depends on having a steady supply of data being transferred to the drive. If the incoming data cannot keep up with the streaming speed of the tape drive, the tape transport mechanism has to stop and rewind slightly in order to *reposition* the tape for when data arrives again. This stopping, rewinding, and restarting obviously can have an adverse effect on performance. The problem can be relieved somewhat by the creation of fairly large memory buffers in the drives, although the average amount of data flowing into the drive from the application using it should be equal to the drive's streaming data rate. Tape drives with 2MB to 4MB buffers are recommended for storage networking environments.

Optical Storage Technology

In general, optical storage technology has not been very useful in storage networking environments. Optical drive technology such as MO (magneto-optical) has been used, especially for HSM (hierarchical storage management) systems, but the MO media have suffered from having limited capacity. Also, storage management of optical jukeboxes turns out to be a difficult problem. Today, with the advent of recordable DVD, MO technology is almost dead. CD-ROM technology has had limited success by providing sharable servers for towers of CD stackers (robotics). CDs are acceptable for reading, but recordable CD technology is far too slow for writing. Perhaps DVD technology will enable optical storage to be used more broadly in storage networks, but given early indications, this does not appear likely.

Media

The final destination along the I/O path from system to storage is the media in the device. This is the disk platter, tape, CD, or whatever media is used in the drive. There's not a lot one can do about selecting the media for disk drives, but it is possible to buy some variety of removable media, such as tapes and CDs. The subject of tapes is treated in Chapter 7 as part of backup.

That said, there are a few things worth knowing about media:

▼ Media is error prone, and most devices have ways to compensate.

■ Media corrodes, even optical media.

■ Dust and humidity are the mortal enemies of media.

▲ All media expires, even under optimal conditions.

Therefore, if you can maintain the environment surrounding your storage devices and media, they will all work a lot better than if they are exposed to hostile conditions. Beware of such elements in your environment as humidity; dust (especially dust raised during construction projects); tobacco smoke; gases such as freon; and electrical fields caused by radar, welding equipment, or elevator power cables.

THE LOGICAL COMPONENTS OF THE I/O CHANNEL

With the physical components of the I/O path identified, we'll move into the logical side of storage I/O. The logical components discussed in this section are:

▼ Application software

■ Operating systems

■ File systems and database systems

■ Volume managers

▲ Device drivers

Application Software

Most I/O processes begin with an application. This can be an interactive end user–driven application, a database operation, a batch processing application, or a systems management application. Applications usually have no visibility to the details of storage implementations, which are provided as an abstracted programmatic interface by the operating system.

An exception to this are specialized applications that utilize storage devices, such as backup/recovery, document management/archiving, and graphics/video processing. Such applications provide their own device and media services that help system administrators manage some part of their computing environments.

Operating System

The operating system provides file system and storage service interfaces that applications and users use to access files and devices. When requests are made for file and storage services, the operating system assumes full responsibility for fulfilling the request to completion. An example of a file service is starting an application and having the operating system open and load the executable files and libraries needed for the application. An example of a storage service is formatting a floppy disk from a command line interface.

On a detailed level, the operating system does not fulfill these requests itself but works through other processes. Acting like a general contractor, the operating system uses specialized subcontractors with higher levels of expertise. For example, file services are handled by the file system, and device operations are often performed by specialized device drivers. Both of these are discussed in the sections to follow.

Not all I/O requests begin with an application or user. Operating systems themselves utilize storage services according to their own requirements, such as virtual memory and system caching. Many operating system components use disk storage for such things as configuration files and system logs.

File Systems and Database Systems

As mentioned, the operating system works closely with a file system to manage data access in the system. In addition to file systems, database systems are another system facility that manages access to data. Both file systems and database systems provide complete and reliable record keeping about what data is stored where on storage devices. The term *metadata* refers to the file system or database management data that describes the data held in the file or database system and provides access information for it. These are very intricate software systems that not only have to ensure reliability and integrity but also must be fast enough to provide excellent performance under heavy loads.

The File System's Role

File systems are usually tightly integrated with operating systems to form an inseparable duo. While the operating system manages the scheduling and resources for the system, the file system manages the storage space for the data that the system creates and uses. The file system distributes data on the logical drive as best it can to ensure reliability and consistent performance.

However, in storage networks, it is possible—and may even be desirable—to separate the operating system from the file system, or divide the file system into smaller parts and distribute them to multiple processors. As the amount of data stored continues to expand, it may become necessary to move some of the file system's functions into storage subsystems in order to achieve the performance levels and scalability required for responsible storage management. Chapter 15 examines this truly fascinating area in much more detail.

Database Storage I/O Operations

A database system can access and store data by making I/O requests of an underlying file system, or it can choose to manage its own block I/O operations by reading and writing directly to a *raw partition*. A raw partition is disk storage that is manipulated directly by the database system, as opposed to being managed by a file system. In other words, the database system figures out how to allocate the storage for its table spaces without requiring this from a file system.

The result can be a faster-performing database system. When one considers that database I/Os are the primary function of the database and that each I/O may involve as many as 20,000 processor instructions, it's not difficult to see why database I/O performance is an important topic. A file system in a computer has to be built to provide services for many applications and types of data. Therefore, file systems are not inherently optimized for database operations. By contrast, raw partitions can be completely optimized for a particular database technology and are tuned for its unique requirements.

Volume Managers

Many systems do not have a component explicitly identified as a *volume manager*. However, just because the name for the function doesn't exist, it doesn't mean the function doesn't. Volume managers are a part of nearly all systems, providing fundamental tools for managing disk drives and partitions. A volume manager can be integrated as part of the operating system, or it can be a separate software module.

In describing the function of the volume manager, it can be useful to clarify its role in relation to what the file systems and database systems do. File systems and database systems perform filing functions, while volume managers provide storing functions, consistent with the descriptions of filing and storing from Chapter 1. File systems and database systems work with either virtual storage or real storage that has been defined by a volume manager.

Volume managers create and arrange disk drive partitions into logical drives where the file system places its data. A simple volume manager function is the capability to create disk partitions and logical drives on those partitions. Volume managers are often used to manage disk subsystems, either by managing the individual disks in a cabinet or by managing the aggregate capacity as a single large virtual disk drive. It is even possible that the volume management concept can be extended to envelope several storage subsystems in a storage network.

Volume Manager Functions

Volume managers can form many kinds of disk configurations from component disk drives and drive partitions. Several examples follow that illustrate some of the capabilities of volume management software.

Mirroring   The volume manager can mirror I/O requests to specific partitions and disk partitions to create redundant data and to improve performance. The mirroring process is shown here and discussed in greater detail in Chapter 4.

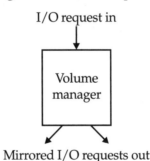

Striping   Volume managers can stripe data across multiple disk drives to attain higher performance. The basic idea here is to set up a round-robin process where I/O operations are distributed to each device in sequential order. When the host I/O controller has reached the last device, the buffer on the first drive may be ready for the next operation. If so, then the operation can continue; if not, it can continue when the device is ready to receive data again.

Striping effectively creates a buffer pool across the devices, that is, N times the drive's buffer capacity, where N is the number of devices in the *stripe set*. This larger buffer pool enables larger overall data transfers that reduce the overhead and latency of working with individual devices in a start-stop fashion. An example of striped I/O is shown here:

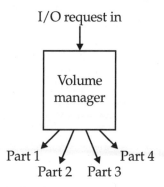

RAID   Volume managers can implement RAID algorithms that turn discrete disks into RAID subsystems. In general, a RAID cabinet has some collection of disks with an intelligent controller to provide a wide range of storage management functions, including mirroring, striping, and more advanced performance and availability techniques. A high-function volume manager can take the place of the intelligent RAID controller. RAID is discussed in detail in Chapter 6.

Concatenation   *Concatenation* is the capability to merge two or more device partitions and create a single virtual device with the combined capacity of all of them. The following example shows concatenation being performed over three separate disk partitions on two different disks:

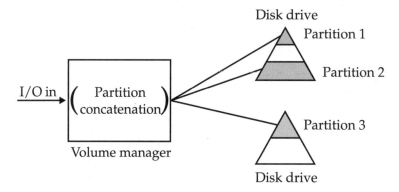

Disk Caching   *Disk caching* is the primary topic of Chapter 5. A disk cache is a collection of memory that holds data temporarily in anticipation that it will soon be requested by an application. The volume manager can allocate system memory to use as a disk cache.

Device Drivers

Device drivers for host I/O controllers and storage devices in storage networks are extremely important pieces of the overall puzzle. A device driver is the last piece of software in the server to see data going out to the hardware, and it is the first to see it coming back in. The volume manager communicates with the device driver directly through an internal function or through a mechanism in the operating system. In either case, the device driver receives the I/O request and generates the proper format and signaling for the targeted device.

Device drivers are often the source of great wonder and frustration. They can be difficult to develop and troubleshoot because they have to be small, fast, and accurate. They tend to run at a system level where errors can result in the crashing of the system and loss of data. They have to accommodate interruptions and delays from the physical world as they occur, not according to some optimized, logical process. It's hard work developing device drivers for storage networks.

Device drivers are sometimes designed in modular layers to achieve independence of host (software) and device (hardware) functions. That way, minor changes can be made to one layer without affecting the other, reducing the chances of creating additional problems. This concept is similar to networking protocol stacks, which have defined interfaces between layers.

Higher-layer device drivers present a programmatic interface that simplifies development work for storage management and other application vendors. An example of such an interface is Adaptec's ASPI (Advanced SCSI Programming Interface). Interfaces like ASPI facilitate innovation in either software or hardware by reducing the overall development and system test effort.

This modular approach in device driver layers has been an important consideration for technologies based on serial SCSI. The storing function of serial SCSI is managed in the upper layers of the device driver, while the wiring function is managed within the lower layers of the driver. By maintaining the storage application layer from parallel SCSI while creating totally new device and network technology drivers, the Fibre Channel industry has proved it is possible to install completely new storage networks that require no adjustments to the application-level software that uses it.

An example of multiple device driver layers supporting independent changes to network hardware and software is shown here:

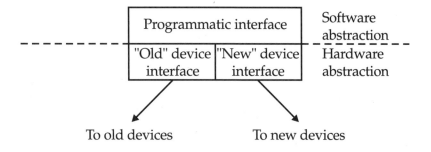

While this approach enabled many of the basic benefits of Fibre Channel to be realized immediately, it also limited the complete potential of the underlying wiring function. For example, Fibre Channel is a full-duplex technology that is sometimes hailed as providing 200 MB/s full-duplex transfer rates. However, serial SCSI is based on parallel SCSI operations, which are simplex (one-way) communications by necessity of parallel SCSI electrical bus design. That means that Fibre Channel FCP storage communications do not use full-duplex transmissions.

COMBINING HARDWARE AND LOGICAL COMPONENTS INTO AN I/O STACK

Systems, especially network systems, are often analyzed as "stacks" of functions. Most readers are probably familiar with protocol stacks that represent functional layers in network communications. This book uses the stack shown in Figure 2-4 to try to clarify some of the various abstract functions that either are, or could be, implemented as independent components of a storage network. This stack model does not represent any industry standard but is offered here as a model for analyzing technology implementations and for gaining a complete end-to-end view of storage I/O transfers.

I/O Stack Functions

One of the important elements of this stack is that it is asymmetrical. In other words, the two end nodes communicating in a storage network do not necessarily implement the same stack. Unlike most TCP/IP data networks where systems communicate as peers on the network, storage networks can use either a peer-to-peer or a master/slave relationship between systems and their storage, depending on whether the storage service is oriented toward filing or storing.

A brief discussion of each of these layers follows.

Application

Applications were briefly discussed earlier in this chapter as the origin of most storage I/O operations. The application layer runs in host systems and is not included as a part of the storing, wiring, or filing function in a storage network. Instead, it is the end point that uses these services.

Application	Business and desktop applications
Presentation (filing)	Logical view of data presented to users and applications: files, directories, folders.
Data structure (filing)	Structure and logic of storing and retrieving data on devices and subsystems
Block (storing)	Storage commands, data transfers, storage location translation, device virtualization
Bus/Network (wiring)	Addressing and naming services, routing, bridging, virtual networking, security and zoning
Media access (wiring)	Arbitration, session negotiation, flow control
Physical (wiring)	Cabling, connectors, network ports, line drivers

Figure 2-4.   The I/O function stack

Presentation

The presentation layer is a filing function and refers to those functions provided by an operating system that allows applications and users to locate and use data. In other words, it is the external view of the file system or database system. For some systems, this may be a collection of folders; for others, it may be a specific syntax used on a command line; and for yet others, it may be a database query generated by an application. There are many possible ways to represent data, and different operating systems take different approaches and support different programming interfaces.

Data Structure

The data structure layer is also a filing function that controls the placement of data within a device, subsystem, or network. It translates logical names used by the presentation layer into *logical block addresses* where the data is stored. The data structure used by a file system or database can be tuned for certain data characteristics to provide optimal performance. For example, a file system can use large contiguous storage locations, which facilitate long reads and writes such as those encountered in data mining or multimedia applications. Alternatively, a database system may use very small block-transfers that facilitate small fast I/O operations such as those found in transaction systems.

The data structure function tracks available free space in storage and is constantly working to calculate how to segment data to fit into the logical blocks that are available. It typically does not have direct control over physical block addresses, even on individual disk drives, which export logical block addresses while maintaining their own internal block translation tables.

Block

Block layer functions perform storing operations, which include the translation of logical block addresses as well as the commands for storing and retrieving data. *Block translation* is commonly used in products such as volume managers and RAID controllers; providing a way to map one block address space into another. As a function that can be implemented in multiple products along the I/O path, block translation can be performed several times before the final block location is defined.

The block layer is built around the SCSI command protocol, which was developed for parallel SCSI and then adopted as a serial protocol by storage network vendors. Device virtualization is specific to the application or process that implements it and depends on a number of variables, including the number and capacity of disk drives being used and the configuration options selected. The block layer is not used for NAS storage appliance traffic.

Network

The network layer is a wiring function that includes network addressing and transmissions. In general, the network layer provides software functions for connecting and managing sessions over the storage network, including routing information.

MAC (Media Access Control)

The media access layer of the storage network is the same as the MAC layer in data networks, such as Ethernet. As in the case of data networking, there are several types of MAC technologies in storage networks, from arbitration-based access schemes in Fibre Channel loops to switched communications in Fibre Channel fabrics and Gigabit Ethernet LANs.

Physical

The physical layer of the storage I/O stack is the same as for any data network. This could represent fiber optic or shielded copper cabling used by either Gigabit Ethernet or Fibre Channel, twisted pair copper for 100BaseT Ethernet, or 68-conductor cables used for parallel SCSI.

I/O Stack Applications

This I/O stack model provides a way to analyze storage networking functionality as a process that encompasses both hardware and software elements. The stack in this book breaks down filing functionality into two layers: presentation and mount point. The storing function is contained within the block layer. Wiring functions are contained in the bottom three layers of the stack and implemented in products using industry standards in Ethernet and Fibre Channel.

Not all components of the I/O stack are present in *all* entities on a storage network. Figure 2-5 shows the differences in the stack implementations associated with host systems, storage devices, and NAS storage appliances.

The Storage Networking Industry Association (SNIA) was formed to help address the need to define interfaces and terminology for storage networking. SNIA is not a standards organization itself but works to make recommendations to existing standards groups. Considering the depth and breadth of functions involving all the various software and hardware product types, it seems unlikely that any one standards organization would be able to span the technology of an I/O stack. SNIA may be able to provide coordination between these different groups.

Application	Business and desktop applications
Presentation (filing)	File systems, databases, network attached storage client software
Data structure (filing)	File systems, databases, network attached storage client software, replication
Block (storing)	Host adapters, RAID, mirroring, device sybsystem controllers, volume managers
Bus/Network (wiring)	Host adapters, NICs, switches, hubs, bridges, routers, virtual network software, devices/subsystems
Media access (wiring)	Host adapters, NICs, switches, hubs, bridges, routers, virtual network software, devices/subsystems
Physical (wiring)	Cables, connectors, lasers, repeaters, host adapters, NICs, devices/subsystems, switches hubs, routers, bridges

Figure 2-5.   Mapping the I/O stack across different types of storage networking products

SUMMARY

This chapter surveyed the complete set of hardware and software components involved in the transfer of data between applications and storage devices. The first half of the chapter examined the hardware components involved, and the second half of the chapter described the software components.

As new storage networking technology is deployed in the coming years, the analysis of I/O dynamics is bound to change. The product classes and functions described in this chapter should be useful as a way to analyze the technology and its implementations for several years to come. We often talk about how rapidly things change in the computer industry, but there are also fundamental processes that change little over time. Many of the concepts in this chapter are likely to be relevant for some time.

EXERCISES

1. If a component's reliability is calculated at 98 percent, what is the reliability of five of these components working together in a subsystem? What is the reliability if there are ten such components?

2. File systems manage free space on storage. Model a storage device with a 5×5 matrix, where each cell represents a single storage address and where cells are accessed by rows, not columns.

Place data in the matrix according to the list of file writes, updates, and delete operations that follow. You cannot use more than three consecutive cells in a row for a single write operation. In other words, writes larger than three cells have to be split up inside the matrix. Try to maintain some consistency in the way cells are distributed in the matrix for a single file. You may want to try using a few different methods to get the most even distribution of data.

Write File A — four cells

Write File B — two cells

Write File C — seven cells

Write File D — three cells

Update File A with another two cells

Write File E — five cells

Update File B with another cell

Delete File D

Update File A with another cell

Delete File C

Update File E with another two cells

Write File F — four cells

Delete File B

Write File G — six cells

CHAPTER 3

Charting the I/O Path

C reating and managing storage networks requires detailed information about all the components along the I/O path. With a solid understanding of the physical and logical components in the I/O path and their respective roles, it is possible to build reasonable models for high availability and performance scenarios.

This chapter examines the fundamental I/O path components in open systems storage, detailing the sequence of components data travels through between an end user system and its final storage destination on a storage network. The diagrams presented here will serve as a basis for understanding the I/O path combinations and variations used throughout the remainder of the book.

The last section of this chapter explores the concept of virtual storage, one of the foundations of advanced storage implementations. Storage virtualization is practically a requirement for all storage subsystems and is one of the most prevalent techniques used in storage software and I/O processing.

THE I/O PATH FOR LOCAL STORAGE

The I/O path commonly starts with a request for file or database services by an application running on a workstation or desktop system. To simplify the analysis, we'll first look at I/O operations in local storage devices. For the purposes of this discussion, local storage defines storage devices in stand-alone systems—in other words, systems that are not on a network.

Local I/O

Almost all systems have the need to store and retrieve files on locally attached devices. While thin diskless clients have been sold for several years, systems with local storage are far more popular and likely to remain so as the cost of disk drives stays so low.

Typical devices used for local storage include IDE and SCSI disk drives, tape drives, CD-ROM drives, floppy disk drives, and high-capacity removable disk drives such as Iomega ZIP and JAZ drives. Users of these systems store all kinds of data, including applications software, e-mail, and work files, on these devices.

Many of the network diagrams in this book use the terminology and icons introduced in Chapter 2. They are grouped together for easy reference in Figure 3-1.

A Detailed Examination of the Local I/O Path

We'll open the analysis of the local I/O path by following the I/O path for a word processing application. Data is originally created by a user who enters it by typing on a keyboard, copying from another application, or using other mechanisms such as speech recognition. The user's word processing software then formats the data by applying the appropriate document tags and descriptive codes; the result is stored as an electronic file.

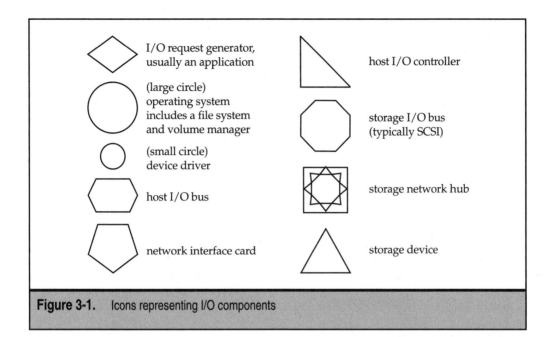

Figure 3-1.   Icons representing I/O components

As the user works, newly created data is saved to disk, manually by the user, or automatically as a background task by the application. The word processor uses a default directory for storing documents so that the end user doesn't have to be actively involved in the detailed instructions for every save operation. More importantly, the end user and application developer do not need to know any details about the storage devices their application saves data to. For instance, it is not necessary to know anything about device addresses or the physical structure on any of the machines their application runs on.

The file system provides an easy way to select a device and a logical location on that device, in other words, its directory and name. This is done through a file service interface that is presented to and used by the word processing application. Using this interface, the word processing application generates an I/O request.

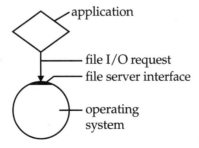

Operating System Components of the I/O Path

The operating system, or OS, is responsible for routing the I/O request from the application to the file system, through volume management functions and then the device driver that ultimately controls how the devices operate. In doing this, several intricate operations are performed. It is not the intent of this book to try to analyze all the possible OS processes that can affect or influence I/O operations. However, a definite model will be used and followed through this chapter and the rest of the book. The three primary OS components are:

▼ The operating system kernel

■ The file system

▲ The volume manager

In addition, the file services interface and the device services interface are also considered to be part of the OS function. They are programming interfaces for exchanging I/O requests with application software and device drivers, respectively.

When the I/O request enters the operating system, it is placed in a queue in the system kernel. The system kernel is composed of all the primary operating system functions, including scheduling system processes and allocating resources for all system functions, including such things as applications processing, communications, and I/O scheduling. The number of processes competing for resources and the capabilities of those resources determine the overall performance of the system, including the servicing of I/O requests.

After the kernel schedules an I/O request, the file system takes over. The file system determines whether or not a file can be accessed, retrieved, created, or updated. While it may seem trivial to write a file, in fact many steps and checks need to be performed. Is there a file with this name already? Is there enough room on the disk for this file? Is the media read-only, meaning it cannot be written to? Does the directory exist to which the user is trying to write this file? Are there security or access restrictions for this directory, media, or device? Is the filename valid? All of these things and more must be checked before the operating system can successfully write the file to a device.

Once this is done, the file system determines where it will place the file on the targeted storage volume. Note that this target volume could be a real or virtual device—from the file system's perspective, it does not matter. While the file system does not work directly with the device, it *does* maintain a complete mapping of all the data on its disk drives, including virtual drives. It uses this mapping to find available space to store the file and then converts the application's original file I/O request to some number of block-level I/O operations. While the application saves fresh data to the file, the file system converts that into specific blocks within the file.

Before the I/O request leaves the file system, the file system creates appropriate metadata that describes the file and determining access rights as well as providing information that can be used for systems and storage management purposes. The following illustration shows a file request being made to the file system, which processes the application's file request into block I/O operations and adds location information and metadata to the request.

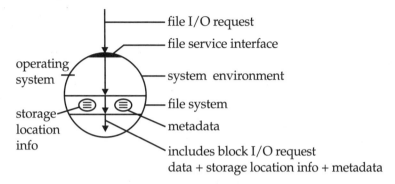

file I/O request

file service interface

operating system

system environment

file system

storage location info

metadata

includes block I/O request
data + storage location info + metadata

NOTE: Metadata is an interesting topic of great interest to the storage industry. As the amount of data continues to increase, it becomes more difficult to manage. Metadata that accurately describes the contents of files can be used by storage and data management systems that help administrators manage their systems. Backup is an example of an application that uses metadata extensively to help administrators manage their systems.

After the file system has determined where it will store the file, the operating system sends its transformed I/O request to the volume manager. The volume manager receives the file system's I/O request and processes it according to the device configuration it manages. This could be as simple as passing the request to a device, or it could involve the generation of multiple requests for multiple device subsystems. The illustration shown here shows the volume manager creating two requests from a single file system I/O request.

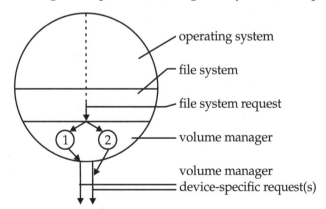

operating system

file system

file system request

volume manager

volume manager
device-specific request(s)

Role of the Device Driver

The device driver is the final component of system software in the I/O path. After the device driver receives the block I/O request(s) from the volume manager, it manages the transfer of the requested blocks to the targeted host I/O controller on the host I/O bus. The device driver and host I/O controller pair manipulates the device across the storage network or bus. The next illustration shows the device driver's role in conveying the request from the system software stack to the host I/O bus.

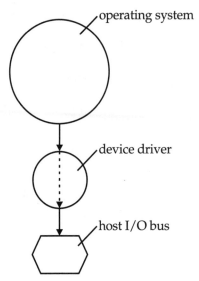

The following diagram summarizes the system software components of the I/O path. At one end is the application software that makes the file I/O request, and at the other end is the device driver that manages and controls I/O controllers.

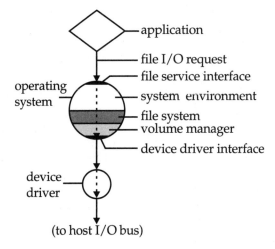

The Host I/O Bus

The device driver assembles the I/O request and sends it to the host I/O controller across the system's host I/O bus. The host I/O bus may appear to be a passive component in this process, but it actually has an intelligent controller for maintaining clock cycles and activities. It can be thought of as a high-speed networking switch that establishes connections between device drivers on the computer's side and the various external equipment interfaces on the other side. In the case of the InfiniBand serial I/O bus, the switch analogy may be more real than analogous. The host I/O bus obviously plays a key role in the I/O path and can have an enormous impact on performance.

The Host I/O Controller

As described in Chapter 2, the bridge between computers and their storage devices is the host I/O controller. The host I/O controller can be integrated on the system board or installed in a slot on the system, in which case it is called an HBA. Most host I/O controllers today use bus mastering technology to keep the system's CPU from being heavily loaded by the details of I/O processing.

The device driver and the host I/O controller can be thought of as two parts of the same process, separated by the system host I/O bus. The illustration that follows shows these three components together forming the complete link between the system and its storage devices. This system/storage link is a critical part of all I/O traffic, whether it is local storage or network storage.

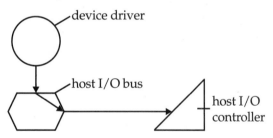

The host I/O controller receives the I/O request from the device driver and conveys it to the specified device. The host I/O controller has the responsibility for correctly addressing each device and transferring the I/O request commands and data completely and without error.

The host I/O controller can be used to create virtual devices, just as the volume manager can. In that case, it receives the I/O request from the device driver and reassembles it for the various real devices it interacts with. In that sense, the host I/O controller provides an additional layer of volume management. This ability to *recurse* the volume management function is an important concept in network storage I/O. There can be many different virtualization levels for a single storage subsystem. The illustration that follows shows a host I/O controller receiving a single I/O request and creating two I/O requests to send to devices, such as it might do when creating a disk mirror.

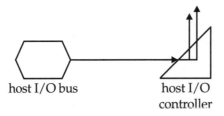

host I/O bus   host I/O
controller

The Storage I/O Network/Bus

The storage I/O network, or bus, is on the other side of the host I/O controller from the system I/O bus. In general, it is a little easier to understand this function by limiting the discussion initially to bus technology; it can then be generalized to include networks.

The Role of the Storage Bus   Storage networking implements a great deal of technology from the parallel SCSI. As mentioned in Chapter 1, serial SCSI protocols such as Fibre Channel's FCP are the basis for transferring commands and data over storage network wiring. In addition, parallel SCSI is widely used as the storage device interconnect for the majority of NAS products sold.

Physical connections on the storage I/O bus are accomplished using daisy chaining. While physical daisy chains of parallel SCSI imply a hierarchy of connections, the addresses assigned to devices on the SCSI bus are established by a system administration. Any device on the bus can be assigned a unique ID and granted the corresponding priority for bus operations—independent of its location on the daisy chain. I/O requests are addressed directly to each device on the bus without the need for other devices to "peek" at the transmitted data as it travels across the bus.

SCSI bus transmissions differ from Ethernet bus transmissions in the following ways:

▼   Ethernet collision-sensing protocols are not used.

■   In Ethernet, all systems have equal access and control. The Parallel SCSI bus has structured priorities that determine control of the bus. Often, a single controller initiates and controls all activities.

▲   Traffic on storage I/O buses typically supports longer data payloads, allowing faster bulk transfers of data. With the elimination of contention for bus access and the use of longer data transfers, extremely high utilization can be achieved, in the range of 80 to 95 percent of available bus bandwidth.

Upgrading the Storage I/O Bus to a Storage Network   One of the simplest models for storage networks is a replacement for the storage I/O bus. This model certainly works for point-to-point storage networks. In fact, a point-to-point storage network over a single cable is much more simple than a bus. The following illustration shows a cable replacing the storage I/O bus in a point-to-point storage network.

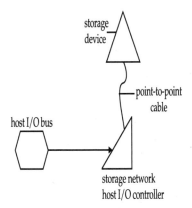

Storage networking makes it possible to connect many devices and systems on the same network. In that case, a switch or hub replaces the bus in the previous illustrations, providing connections to multiple devices and host systems as shown here.

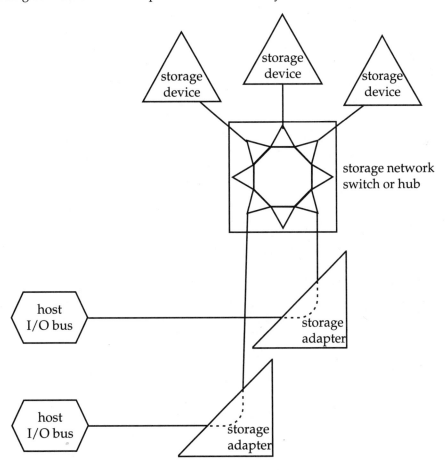

The Final I/O Destination: The Device

The storage device interprets the I/O request and acts on the request. To paraphrase President Harry Truman, the buck stops there. Data is read and written or some other operation is performed and the device creates a response. This response can be a simple acknowledgment that the request was received, or it can be more involved, including status information about the device as well as the device's storage media.

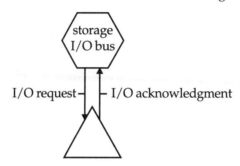

If the device is a storage subsystem, such as a RAID cabinet with an intelligent controller, the I/O request is passed to each internal device for processing. Responses from devices are collected and sent from the RAID cabinet as a single response. The most common I/O request is a read request. In response to the read request, the device reads the data blocks specified and transfers them to the host I/O controller, which packages them for transfer across the host I/O bus to the device driver and up through the system software components to the application.

Command Acknowledgments   Devices typically acknowledge each command sent from the host I/O controller. Storage subsystems presenting virtual devices can acknowledge I/O requests immediately before forwarding the requests to attached devices. While this can accelerate performance, it also creates the risk that the operation requested might never actually be performed on a real device. An example of this is write-back caching, one of the topics discussed in Chapter 5.

Upon receiving an acknowledgment from the device, the host I/O controller interprets it and, if required, sends a corresponding acknowledgment back up the I/O path. Acknowledgments can be required by any of the system software components in the path.

Hardware Components of the I/O Path

The drawing that follows shows the hardware components of the I/O path, beginning with the host I/O bus and connecting through the host I/O controller and the storage I/O bus to the devices.

storage devices

storage I/O bus

host I/O bus

host I/O controller

Diagramming the Complete Local I/O Path

The entire local I/O path described in the preceding sections is shown in Figure 3-2. An application on the upper left of this drawing is able to make I/O requests that result in operations being performed on three storage devices, shown on the upper right.

Notice that the entire path supports two-way communications and that I/O requests and responses can flow in either direction. Local storage is a closed system where the I/O process follows a specified path and retraces its steps back to the application.

Considerations for I/O on Network Servers

The local I/O path for network server systems is basically the same as for other systems, but with additional requirements to support many users and much more traffic. In client/server networks, the real storage and I/O action is on the server.

There are three broad classes of servers considered here:

▼ File servers

■ Database servers

▲ Web servers

Server I/O requirements begin with the types of applications that run on them. Server applications are optimized to respond to client requests. In other words, the work is generated from external sources instead of being initiated by internal processes and schedules. Clients use network communications protocols and wiring to access the server, usually TCP/IP and Ethernet technologies. One of the important enablers is the presence

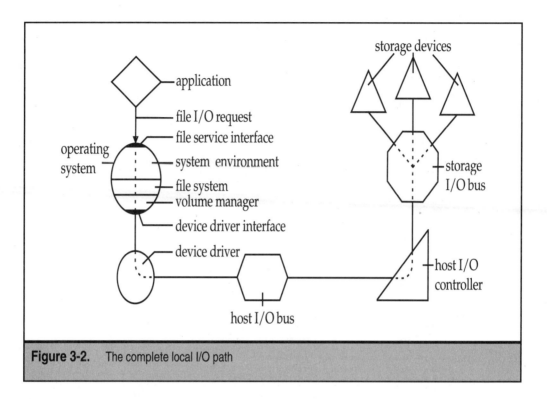

Figure 3-2. The complete local I/O path

of some sort of client-connection handling process running on the server to manage all client interactions.

Figure 3-3 illustrates a simple model for client I/O access to server systems. The figure shows an incoming client I/O request that is read by the NIC (network interface card) and sent over the host I/O bus to its corresponding device driver. The device driver then sends it to the server operating system, where it is processed by the client I/O handler.

File Server Industrial-Strength I/O Processing

A file server's client I/O handler routes network client requests to internal processes, including the server's local storage. While this does not necessarily seem like such an interesting application, from a file server's perspective it is the most thrilling application of all. File servers are required to support large numbers of users simultaneously. A desktop system might manage a handful of requests at a time, whereas a server may receive hundreds of requests simultaneously. Each of these requests must be managed accurately and correctly.

As an example, a file server may have 200 users working on it, each accessing his or her own private storage. That means there can be 100 or more simultaneous requests to access files on the storage disks or subsystem. Each of these requests must be processed

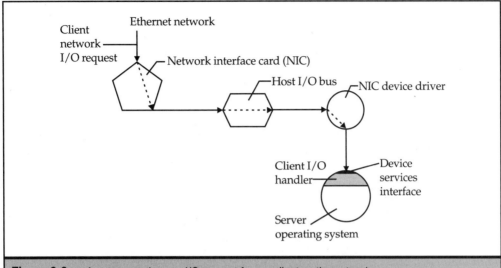

Figure 3-3.   A server receives an I/O request from a client on the network

by the client I/O handling process, placed in a queue, and serviced by the storage I/O subsystem of the file server. The process of moving these requests through the file server's complete I/O path certainly takes time and is an obvious bottleneck point.

Security is another responsibility of the file server, which must ensure that data does not get routed to the wrong user. When a user logs in to a server, that user typically enters a password that verifies who he or she is. From then on, it is unnecessary to log in for each I/O request that is made. This is because the file server client handling process is responsible for keeping track of who is who, according to users' network IDs, addresses, or other identifiers.

While network IDs and addresses work well as a means of identifying users and systems on a network, they do not necessarily work well as file server internal names and references linking users to their data. This means the file server must have a way of converting network identifiers into internal user references that can be easily tracked through the server I/O path. Unfortunately, not all components in the I/O path use the same data structures. For instance, the way a host I/O controller tracks its I/O requests to disk devices is different than the way the file system tracks its I/O requests. Sufficient memory resources are needed to ensure that the various internal references required along the I/O path can be maintained without failing.

TIP: Servers need lots of fast memory for storing internal resources about I/O processes. If possible, install 50 percent to 100 percent more than the minimum recommended system RAM as a preventive measure against erratic performance and reliability.

Database Server Requirements

Database servers can have very definite storage and I/O requirements that are a function of the types of business application they support. For instance, a transaction database typically has small, bursty I/O, while data mining database systems typically have long streaming I/Os. Considering the importance of database systems in supporting various business functions, database systems are often dedicated to one specific application in order to provide the highest service levels possible. This means that the I/O components, configuration, and data structures can be tuned to that application.

The concept of a raw partition for database storage was introduced in Chapter 2 as a way for the database system to implement its own volume management function that manages database I/O operations directly, as opposed to working through the system's file system. This approach makes a certain amount of sense in that databases are not file-oriented structures per se; instead, they are record-oriented. Therefore, the raw partition assumes the role of the file system in the database I/O scheme.

So, when the database application generates an I/O request, it works out the details of storing the data internally instead of passing it on to the file system as a file server does. In other words, the database provides its own complete system mechanism for creating the I/O request. When the higher-level database function determines an I/O operation is needed, it directs that request to a process that maintains a file-system-like lookup table that knows the location of records on devices. This record-level I/O request is passed through the raw partition manager to a device driver. The rest of the I/O path looks the same as it does for a standard file server. The illustration that follows highlights the basic differences between the storage software components in a file server and those in a database server running on a raw partition.

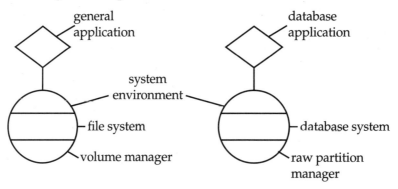

general application

database application

system environment

file system

database system

volume manager

raw partition manager

File Server   Database Server

There are also many database implementations that use the system's file system facilities instead of implementing a raw partition. In this case, the database typically opens a file for updating and leaves it open while it periodically makes I/O requests to update specific block ranges within the file. In fact, this type of operation is quite similar to an operation on a raw partition, but the file used in this instance exists in the server's file system along with many other files.

Web Server Requirements

Web servers have a wide variety of requirements for storage I/O processing. These requirements are relatively simple for HTML Web page serving, but they can become extremely challenging for large search-engine sites, portals, and e-commerce Web sites. As a Web site grows in popularity and the traffic increases, the performance requirements for storage on Web servers can be very difficult to meet. The client I/O handling programs in large Web servers have to be able to accommodate thousands of requests per minute. While some of this processing can be distributed, the sheer number of client requests is staggering. Internet storage requirements and the applications of storage networking technology for Web sites are discussed in Chapter 16.

Theme and Variations on the Local I/O Path

Server systems often need to expand their I/O capabilities beyond the simple models previously explored. The discussion that follows expands the analysis of the local I/O path to include multiple host I/O controllers for handling higher client traffic volumes.

Multiple Host I/O Controllers

Multiple host I/O controller configurations are common. For example, server systems can have two or more SCSI controllers providing high-capacity and/or fault-tolerant storage.

Figure 3-4 shows a system with three host I/O controllers, each managing a single device on a dedicated I/O bus. If placing a single device on a bus seems like a waste of bus

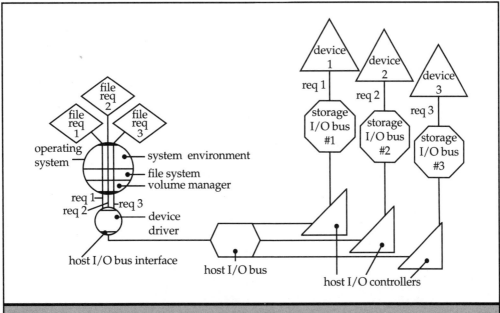

Figure 3-4.   The I/O paths for three I/O requests using three host I/O controllers

bandwidth, just consider that the device might actually be a large RAID disk subsystem with 20 internal disks.

One of the details of this configuration is that the three host I/O controllers shown are all working with a single device driver. This assumes that the host I/O controllers are made by the same manufacturer.

Another variation on the preceding example is where multiple I/O controllers are used to support different kinds of devices. For instance, there could be three host I/O controllers in a server—one for a floppy disk drive and CD-ROM, one for disk storage, and one for tape storage. Depending on the mix of controllers and their characteristics, it may be necessary to have separate device drivers for each host I/O controller. While disk and tape can be combined on the same I/O bus, it is usually better to keep them separate, as discussed in Chapter 4 on mirroring. If the same model of host I/O controller is used for both disk and tape, one device driver can work with both I/O buses. The drawing that follows shows an I/O path where three distinct host I/O controllers are managed by three device drivers in the host system.

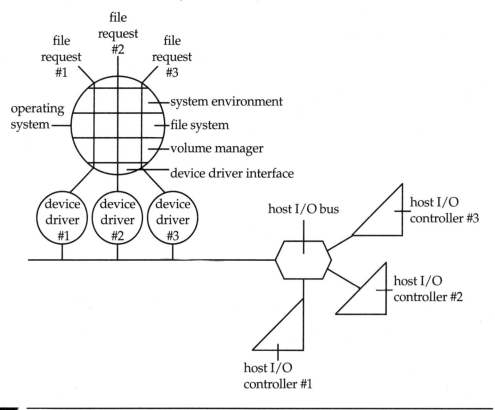

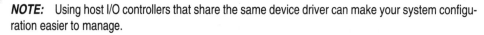

NOTE: Using host I/O controllers that share the same device driver can make your system configuration easier to manage.

THE CLIENT/SERVER I/O PATH

A topic that often confuses newcomers to storage networking is the difference between local storage I/O and network storage I/O. One of the keys to understanding this is knowing that data in the I/O path can be *redirected* to alternate storage destinations. In other words, something appearing to users and applications as local storage is actually being managed by a server somewhere on the network. To say it another way, client-storage redirection software provides *transparent* access to remote storage.

Client I/O Redirection

Applications typically depend on file systems, volume managers, and device drivers to convey all the necessary information about I/O operations through the I/O path to storage devices. From the application's perspective, it does not matter if the storage function is local or is remotely handled over a network as long as its internal operations are not affected. This is an application of *storage virtualization,* and in the context of client I/O redirection, it is usually done on a file level. In other words, the application requests a file from the system and a special virtualization function retrieves the file from an alternative location as pictured.

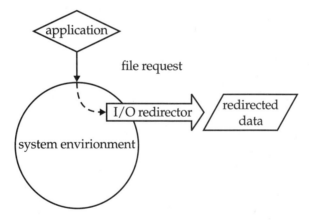

This type of file redirection is called *remote mounting* a file system and is also referred to as *mapping to a network drive* or attaching to a network drive. The general idea is that a file server makes all or some of its stored files available over the network to clients that have the appropriate redirection technology installed and the authorization to access those files. Readers familiar with Microsoft Windows products may be familiar with the capability of these systems to make data available to other systems as well as attach to virtual drives on other Windows systems. It may help some readers to understand that even though this may be called mapping a drive, the actual process being used is accessing a remote file system. The actual disk drive is being managed by the file server, not the client. This is a fairly rich technology area and will be discussed in much more depth in Chapters 12 and 13.

One of the important points in any storage redirection scheme is the amount of time the operation takes. Normally this means that everything works just fine if the requesting application does not fail due to any time delays, or *time-outs*. A time-out in storage I/O processing is some defined length of time that the system will wait before assuming the I/O failed. Time-outs are usually implemented as a system safeguards, not as parts of an application.

The client redirector runs in a client system, providing transparent access to remote storage over the network. It is located in the I/O path immediately prior to the file system. Positioned at a layer above the file system, it merges the view of the remote server's file system resources with the client system's local file system resources.

The client redirector typically does not keep metadata about stored data on a network file server, but it does have to be able to provide access to the data and its associated metadata on the remote server. In general, I/O redirection creates an additional storage resource to the client system; however, the remote storage resource might not behave exactly like a local resource. For example, the remote server might require case-sensitive commands, while the client does not.

Client redirection sends storage requests over a common network, such as Ethernet. This means that the redirected I/O command must be routed internally to the network interface card and its associated protocol and device drivers. The protocol used is typically some type of a network file protocol. The network file protocol specifies the types of operations and exchanges that can be exchanged over the network with affiliated file servers. Depending on the network environments used, there are usually multiple protocol layers implemented, as a sequence of device drivers, as part of normal network operations.

Figure 3-5 shows the client path components for redirecting local file I/O to a remote network file server. The I/O redirector presents a virtual file interface to the application and/or end users. Looking "down" in the I/O path, redirected I/O operations are transmitted through the network file protocol driver and through the system's underlying protocols and eventually onto the network through a network interface card. In general, the network file protocol is layered on top of existing lower-layer communication protocols, such as TCP and IP. When NFS (Network File System) is the network file protocol in a LAN environment, UDP (User Datagram Protocol) is often used instead of TCP for faster performance.

I/O redirection can be analyzed by means of protocol stacks, the same way that network communications can. Built on top of the TCP/IP protocol stack, a network file protocol can be placed in any of several places. Some file protocols, such as NFS, can be implemented directly on top of the TCP/IP stack or, alternatively, use a UDP/IP stack. Some of the common protocols used for transporting network file I/O include:

▼ CIFS (Common Internet File System), used in Microsoft Windows products

■ NFS (Network File System), used in nearly all systems, especially Unix systems

▲ FTP (File Transfer Protocol), used in nearly all systems for accessing files over the Internet

CIFS uses a TCP/IP stack but can also require an additional Netbios layer for identifying systems in networks that do not use domain name services. NFS was originally developed

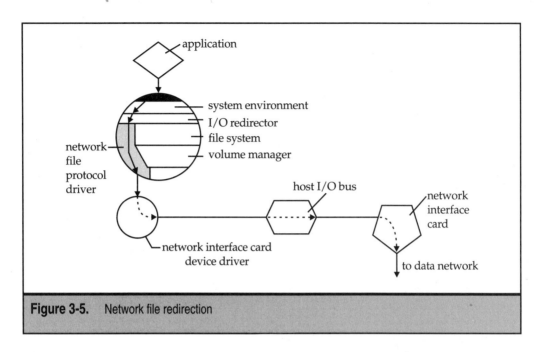

Figure 3-5. Network file redirection

to use the stateless UDP (User Datagram Protocol) and has evolved to also run over TCP. Although TCP is a stateful protocol, NFS is not. FTP has been the primary protocol for Internet transfers and runs on top of TCP in wide area environments. The MAC (media access control) layer most commonly used today follows the standard 802.3 specification for Ethernet networks. Figure 3-6 summarizes these common network protocol stacks.

Network File Protocols		
CIFS	NFS + FTP	NFS
Netbios		
Stateful Transport Protocols TCP		Stateless Transport Protocols UDP
Network Layer - - - IP		
Media Access Control (MAC) - 802.3		
Physical Layer - - Cabling + Connections		

Figure 3-6. Network file protocol stacks

Figure 3-7 shows a picture of both local and redirected I/O. There are two I/O requests made by applications: one for local storage and the other for network storage. The local I/O request follows the path outlined previously in this chapter: through a volume manager, the I/O controller device driver, the host I/O bus, the host I/O controller, the storage bus, and into the device.

The redirected network I/O request is alternatively routed through the I/O redirector down through its network file protocol driver, into the TCP/IP stack over the host I/O bus to a network interface card. From there it will be transmitted out over the network to a network server.

The Server Side of Client/Server Storage I/O

On the other end of the network, redirected I/O requests from clients are received by a NIC in the server. As client requests enter the server, they are "unwrapped" by the server's communication protocol drivers and conveyed to the server's network file protocol handling program.

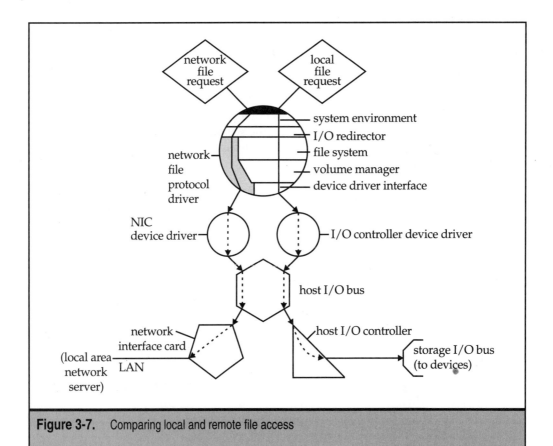

Figure 3-7.   Comparing local and remote file access

From there, redirected I/O requests are sent to the server's file system for processing. At this point, the redirected I/O request is handled more or less as a local I/O request to be fulfilled by a device or subsystem connected to the server. The server software components and the I/O path that client requests take through the server are shown in the following diagram.

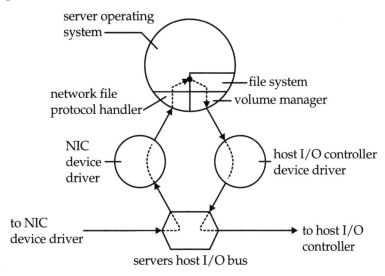

There are five general software processes encountered as data moves from the NIC to the server's host I/O controller. They are:

1. The request arrives in the NIC and is disassembled by the systems communications protocol drivers (typically TCP/IP) and conveyed to the network file protocol handler program.

2. The network file protocol handling program creates all the connection tracking information necessary to exchange data with the remote client. It submits the request to the server's operating system.

3. When the client I/O request is transferred to the server operating system, several types of process and client management operations can be performed, including process scheduling, security control, logging, and process routing.

4. The request is passed to the server's file system, which identifies the file and directory in its own local storage and creates a block-level I/O operation.

5. The request is given to a volume manager that maps the file system's request to downstream block-level devices. From there, the I/O request is passed to the host I/O controller device driver(s) and the hardware I/O path implemented in the server.

Figure 3-8 shows a detailed view of the network I/O process inside a typical network file server and indicates each of the preceding steps.

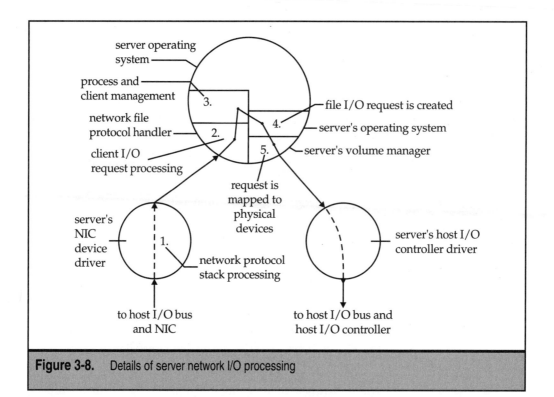

Figure 3-8. Details of server network I/O processing

The complete picture of the server side of client-redirected I/O is shown in Figure 3-9. This drawing illustrates the importance of a robust and fast host I/O bus. Client I/O requests enter the server through the NIC and are transferred over the host I/O bus to its corresponding protocol device drivers. After the request is routed through the server operating system, it may generate one or more I/O operations from the server's volume manager, which are also routed through the host I/O bus on their way to the host I/O controller(s). Finally, the requests are routed to the server's devices over the storage bus or network.

The responses to these requests go back over the same path that was used on their way in. This means that the host I/O bus has to be able to support I/Os between:

▼ Incoming path NIC to NIC device drivers

■ Incoming path host I/O controller device drivers to host I/O controller

■ Outgoing path host I/O controller to host I/O controller device drivers

▲ Outgoing path NIC device drivers to NIC

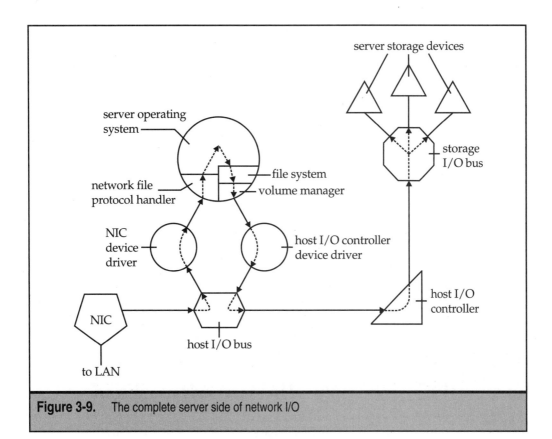

Figure 3-9.   The complete server side of network I/O

Now, if we take these four path components and divide the bandwidth of the host I/O bus evenly, it is easy to see how the host I/O bus could become a bottleneck. Assuming a PCI bus, as is common for most PC-based server systems today, it is a 33 MHz bus with a 32-bit data path—which results in a maximum throughput of 132MB/s. Divided equally and throwing in a small amount of overhead, each process just identified has approximately 30MB of host I/O bus bandwidth.

When one considers that servers often have multiple NICs and multiple host I/O controllers, it is evident that the host I/O bus can easily become overloaded.

Adding a Storage Network and Completing the Big Picture

Now, to make things a bit more interesting and fill out the picture of storage networking better, the storage I/O bus on the server can be replaced with a storage network. Figure 3-10 shows a client system using I/O redirection accessing files on a network server that stores its data on a storage network.

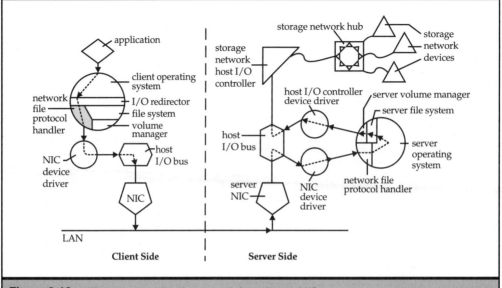

Figure 3-10. The complete client/server path for redirected I/O

IMPLEMENTING DEVICE VIRTUALIZATION IN THE I/O PATH

As new storage technologies are introduced in the market, it is necessary that they be compatible with existing storage. The basic idea is simple: if the interface and management of the I/O channel change too radically, the technology will be too difficult to adjust to implement and it will fail in the market. This has been true for almost all kinds of computer products, not just storage products, and is also true for both file server NAS-style storage networks as well as newer Fibre Channel SAN-style storage networks.

One of the most common techniques to provide compatibility in storage and I/O products and processes is *virtualization*. Just as virtualization is used in client redirection to mask network complexity, storage virtualization, in general, substitutes a virtual file system or device for one or more others. The goal is to create an environment that behaves and responds to commands as if it were real. Stated simply, virtualization "fakes out" an interfacing technology into believing something else is present. Another interpretation is that virtualization makes something new and fabulous look like something old and boring—only better.

Client redirection is an example of file system virtualization. There is another class of virtualization known as *device virtualization*. Device virtualization can be implemented many different ways, but where storage is concerned it has basically three forms:

▼ Virtualization that aggregates multiple resources as one addressable entity

■ Virtualization that subdivides a resource into multiple addressable entities

▲ Virtualization that emulates another product or function

The first kind of device virtualization allows many individual components to be combined to create a single large addressable entity, such as a disk subsystem that creates a single large virtual disk from multiple smaller disks. The second does the opposite; it allows a large entity to appear as if it were many smaller addressable entities, such as when a single disk drive is partitioned into multiple smaller drive images. As it turns out, sometimes both these types of device virtualization are used at the same time, such as when a number of disk drives are combined together in a disk subsystem to form a single virtual disk, which is then parceled out as smaller virtual drives.

The last type of device virtualization is commonly referred to as *emulation* and is typically used to provide compatibility for new products. This is needed when a new device has new capabilities that cannot be exercised by existing system components and software. In that case, the new device may be able to *emulate* an older device. In general, when device virtualization is discussed in this book, it refers to either of the first two types that provide address mappings between some number of real entities and some other number of virtual entities. Figure 3-11 shows the three virtualization techniques.

Locations in the I/O Path for Device Virtualization

Device virtualization can be implemented in many ways all along the I/O path. The most common locations in the I/O path where it is implemented are:

▼ A volume manager in the host

■ Host I/O controllers and device driver software

▲ A storage subsystem

Device Virtualization in a Volume Manager

The primary task of the volume manager is to provide device virtualization services of downstream storage resources. Volume managers partition, concatenate, stripe, and mirror disk drives.

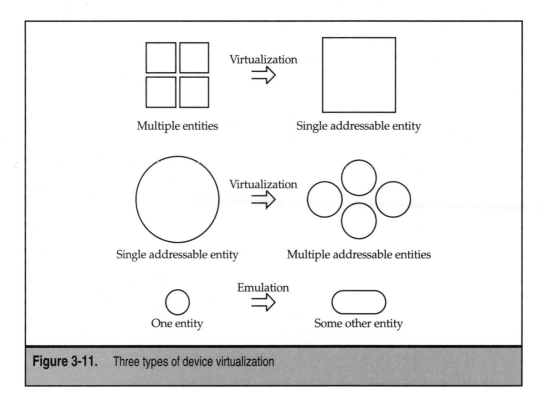

Figure 3-11. Three types of device virtualization

Device Virtualization in a Host I/O Controller and Device Driver

Host I/O controllers and their associated device drivers can also provide device virtualization techniques such as RAID, striping, mirroring, and error correction. An example of device virtualization in a host I/O controller is the formation of two I/O requests for mirrored disks from a single I/O request.

Device Virtualization in a Storage Subsystem

Device virtualization is commonly used in storage subsystems. RAID subsystems, the topic of Chapter 6, are an excellent example of device virtualization at the last stop on the I/O path. Disk subsystems can provide address translation both to form larger virtual drives and to subdivide resources disks into smaller virtual drives. The illustration that follows shows three storage devices forming a single large virtual disk, which is then divided and addressed as four virtual drives.

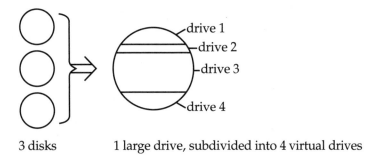

3 disks   1 large drive, subdivided into 4 virtual drives

Figure 3-12 highlights the various places and functions along the I/O path where device virtualization is commonly performed.

Channel Virtualization

Host I/O controllers used in storage networks support SCSI protocols to maintain compatibility with existing applications, file systems, and databases. Parallel SCSI was designed for much smaller architectures than storage networking technology, so the compatibility offered by storage networks also significantly extends the capabilities of the storage channel.

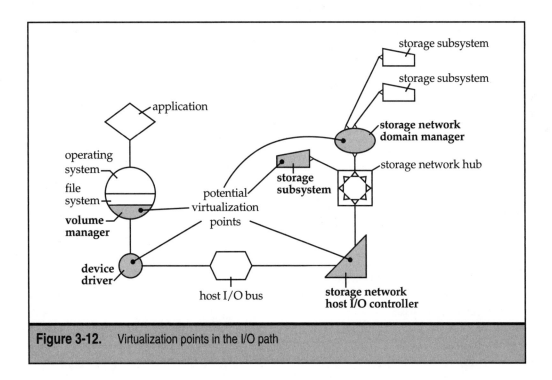

Figure 3-12. Virtualization points in the I/O path

While some might argue that serial SCSI storage over a storage network is not *device virtualization*, it can also be argued that a storage network and a system's storage network device driver constitute a form of channel virtualization.

As storage networking technology continues to evolve and include different types of wiring technologies, the concept of channel virtualization is likely to become an important concept that enables new technologies to dovetail with existing implementations.

SUMMARY

The complete client-to-server I/O path is not too difficult to understand when you have a solid understanding of the basic components and their respective roles. While the hardware components are fairly evident, the software components are often anything but evident and can be confusing. When it comes time to start planning, testing, purchasing, and deploying storage networks, costly mistakes and delays can be avoided if the IT team clearly understands the details of the software implementation.

Operating systems and file systems tend to be proprietary products. Therefore, there is not a standard protocol stack for I/O as there is for networking. Readers that use the I/O paths diagrammed here should be able to discuss their systems clearly and identify potential problems or bottlenecks. Unfortunately, the terminology used for storage and I/O products is not universally defined or agreed upon. For instance, throughout this chapter the term "host I/O controller" was used. To many people, this is called a host bus adapter, or HBA. To other people, it is called a SCSI card, and to still others, it may be referred to as an integrated SCSI chip on the host I/O bus.

As there is no shortage of opinions in the computer industry, when you have a discussion with another person about a system, a fair amount of time is often spent agreeing on terms and understanding each other's language. This is certainly true for I/O technology. It is hoped that the diagrams and the language in this chapter can be used as a jumping-off point for your own discussions.

EXERCISES

1. Diagram the complete process and I/O path used in retrieving data from virtual memory on disk. Include the system memory bus and bridge controller chips. Compare this with a memory access that uses real, not virtual, memory.

2. Consider two disk drives with logical block addresses (LBAs) that can be described by 6 × 6 matrices. For the following virtual devices, create a virtual address matrix and map the addresses of the disk drives' LBAs into the address cell of the virtual device.

    Mirrored virtual device (data copied to both disks)

    Striped virtual storage

    Concatenated virtual storage

PART II

Fundamental Storing Applications

CHAPTER 4

Disk Mirroring and Replication for Data Redundancy

Storage management applications will change dramatically as storage network technology continues to overcome the restrictions imposed by bus-attached storage and pregigabit speed networks. To understand, appreciate, and evaluate these new capabilities, the reader may first want to acquire a fundamental knowledge of their inner workings. The next four chapters explore mirroring, caching, RAID, and backup.

When it comes to storage management applications, there is a great deal to be said for simple concepts and brute force configurations. One of the most basic ideas in storage management is *data redundancy.* Data redundancy is based on the notion that data is maintained in multiple copies or can be re-created by other means. Redundancy roughly equates with disaster tolerance, although it can also provide increased *data availability* when the redundant data can be accessed in real time.

Disk mirroring is an example of a simple *storing* function that has become the most popular method for providing data availability. Disk mirroring is implemented at the block layer of the I/O stack, as illustrated in Figure 2-5 from Chapter 2. There are a wide variety of disk mirroring solutions available in the market with an enormous range of costs and capabilities, but most of them share a common design goal—to be reliable and fast.

Replication is closely related to disk mirroring and provides similar functionality but works at the data structure layer of the I/O stack. Data replication typically uses data networks for transferring data from one system to another and is not as fast as disk mirroring, but it offers some management advantages. This chapter explores the fundamentals of disk mirroring and data replication and also discusses disk drive and I/O channel technologies that will be used through the rest of the book.

SAFEGUARDING YOUR DATA WITH DISK MIRRORING

Disk mirroring has been the foundation of storage management for several decades. This simple technique saves businesses millions of dollars each year. Disk mirroring is to storage management what the hammer is to carpentry—a fundamental tool that is not likely to outgrow its usefulness anytime soon. *RAID 1* is another term for disk mirroring often used by manufacturers and vendors of RAID disk subsystems. The developers of RAID technology started their hierarchy of redundant storage functions with disk mirroring.

Disk mirroring is a block-layer function that applies a basic form of device virtualization that makes two disks appear as one disk by writing identical data to both of them. While disk mirroring is a simple concept to understand, it can have a rather surprising and unexpected impact on system performance. As the term implies, disk mirroring makes an extra, or mirrored, copy of all the data that is written and stores it in two, or more, locations. In effect, a disk drive is transformed into a pair of identical twins, so your data is far less vulnerable than it would be if you relied on a single disk.

The whole reason for implementing mirrored disks is to maintain the ability to access data when a disk drive fails. Most system administrators with more than a few years of experience can tell horror stories about disk drive crashes, of drives that died with the company's accounting data, e-mail, engineering drawings, the CEO's presentation to the board of directors...and the list goes on. The unfortunate truth is that disk drives fail—and when they do, systems administrators need to have technology implemented that circumvents the problem.

Luckily, the track record for disk drive reliability has been fairly amazing. Disk drives are extremely complicated electromechanical devices that integrate a very wide range of technologies. The only reasons that disk drives cost as little as they do are the enormous manufacturing volumes and intense competition in the disk drive industry. A great deal has been written and reported about the steady decline in the cost per megabyte of disk storage, but the improvements in the reliability of storage devices have also been dramatic. In the last 20 years, the reliability measurements for disk drives have improved over a hundredfold.

Given the excellent reliability statistics for disk drives, two drives are not likely to fail at exactly the same time. This means that when something goes wrong with one of the mirrored disk drives, the situation can be put back to normal without having an adverse effect on end users or normal operations. In a 24 × 7 operation, it doesn't get much better than that, and that's the main reason disk mirroring should be applied as the minimum-allowed data redundancy solution.

The Mechanics of Disk Mirroring

On a detailed level, mirrored disks are implemented in many ways, according to the design criteria used. The analysis of mirroring here begins with the relative priority of the disk drives in a mirrored pair.

Primary/Secondary Mirrored Pairs

One common method of disk mirroring is implemented where operations are started on one drive before the other. In this type of mirroring, the system manages the details of their operation in a sequential fashion where one disk is referred to as the *primary,* and the other disk is called the *secondary.* Data that is written is sent first to the primary, and then to the secondary. Designating which drive is which usually takes place when the disk mirror is initially configured. Although doing things twice on a computer can be considered a waste of processor cycles, the additional overhead involved in disk mirroring is relatively small, and the resulting protection is worth the effort. In addition, there are mirroring solutions that operate the mirror as a process in an adapter card or in a subsystem controller and do not add overhead to the system processor.

Whatever the details, the intent is to write the data to the secondary in real time so that any failure on the primary will not impact data integrity. While the write on the secondary occurs after the write on the primary, the delay can be reduced by overlapping the two operations. In other words, the write to the secondary is done before the first drive acknowledges a successful completion of its operation.

A simple disk mirror with a primary/secondary configuration is shown here:

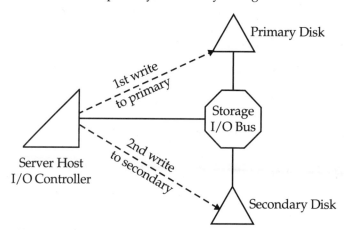

Peer-Mirrored Pairs

As an alternative to the primary/secondary mirroring method, mirroring can also be done by using both disk drives as true peers, without establishing an access sequence. In this case, the drive accessed first depends on the status of the drives or some other criteria such as alternating their use. This peer-mirror approach could improve I/O performance by beginning drive operations as soon as either drive in the pair is available instead of always waiting for the primary drive to be available before starting. On a busy I/O channel, with several disk drives configured in mirrored pairs, the prioritization of the drives, the distribution of the data across the drives, and the arbitration process could create an environment where the peer-mirror approach gives better performance. Otherwise, the operations of the peer-mirror or the primary/secondary mirror appear identical to end users and applications.

The Mirroring Operator

Disk mirroring is more than the attachment of extra disks to the I/O channel. In order for mirroring to work, some software or hardware component in the path I/O channel must process and manage the mirror function. There are several ways to do this that will be explored later in the chapter, but for now we'll simply assume the mirror function is performed in the I/O path between the file system and the storage bus/network. Figure 4-1 shows such an I/O request being processed by a *mirroring operator*. This mirroring operator copies the original I/O request and creates two separate *mirrored I/Os*, which are transferred over the storage bus/network to a pair of mirrored disks.

Synchronous, Asynchronous, and Semisynchronous Disk Mirroring

Disk mirroring can consist of synchronous, asynchronous, or semisynchronous operations, depending on the way I/O write operations are correlated, or not, with responses from the disk drives in the mirrored pair. Synchronous mirrors, the most common type,

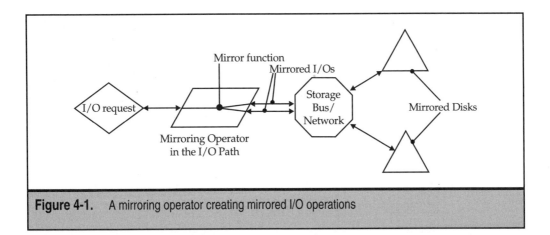

Figure 4-1.   A mirroring operator creating mirrored I/O operations

are typically implemented as pairs of disk drives mounted within the same system or storage subsystem. A high-speed storage bus or network is assumed. Asynchronous or semisynchronous mirroring is usually implemented for remote mirroring purposes, which implies that there are expected transmission delays for one of the disk drives in the mirror pair.

Synchronous Mirrors   In a *synchronous* mirror, the mirroring operator waits for both disk drives to complete writing data before it returns an acknowledgment to the I/O requester initiating the operation. Figure 4-2 shows the process, not to be confused with the physical path, of a synchronous I/O operation. The mirroring operator creates mirrored I/Os,

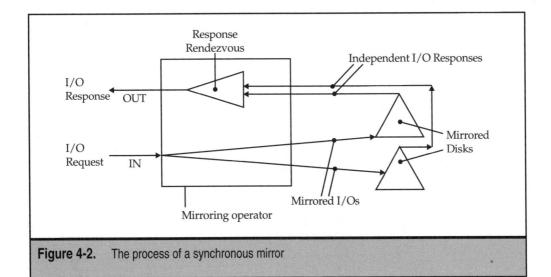

Figure 4-2.   The process of a synchronous mirror

which are sent to the pair of mirrored disks. Each disk responds individually to the request after it completes. A process generically labeled "the response rendezvous" in the mirroring operator waits for the responses from both disk drives before forwarding a response back up the I/O path for the I/O request.

There is a single I/O request being processed at any time by a synchronous mirror. Obviously, if there are lots of I/O requests to process, delays in acknowledging I/O requests from the disk drives could result in a performance bottleneck. This is why synchronous mirrors are usually used with local, high-speed storage buses and networks. On the plus side, synchronous mirroring allows a system to have precise status information of each I/O, and can maintain data integrity should unexpected I/O path errors occur.

Asynchronous Mirrors   While synchronous mirroring is optimized for local high-speed connections with minimal risk to data integrity, *asynchronous* mirrors are designed for remote, low-speed connections, but at the risk of compromising data integrity. Asynchronous mirroring sends I/O requests to the mirrored pair as they are received, without first waiting for acknowledgments from disk drives for the previous I/O operation. This approach can process more I/O operations than synchronous mirroring, especially when the I/O path implementation to one of the mirror pairs is extended over a slow network.

An asynchronous mirror process can be represented graphically like this:

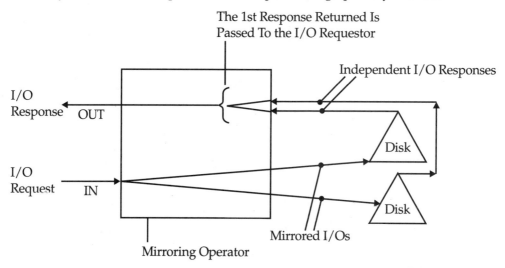

Semisynchronous Mirrors   *Semisynchronous* mirroring represents a compromise between synchronous and asynchronous mirroring. Semisynchronous mirrors put a limit on the number of unacknowledged I/O operations that can be forwarded by the mirroring operator before it stops forwarding I/Os to the drives in the mirror pair. The number of pending operations can be configured at any reasonable amount, including one, as long as the mirroring operator has the means to ensure data integrity in case a failure occurs.

Error Recovery in Disk Mirrors

If one of the mirrored I/O requests fails to complete on one of the disk drives, the mirroring operator has the responsibility of trying to recover and maintaining ongoing I/O operations. For example, if there is a disk drive failure, the mirroring operator might not receive an acknowledgment from the failed drive. In this case, the mirroring operator must determine an error has occurred and initiate its error processing function to inform the administrator about the error. Administrator notification is the responsibility of one or more software packages that alert the system administrator that a problem has occurred in the mirror. For example, the mirroring software could simply post a message on the system log, or it could also be integrated with SNMP network management.

After the failure has been identified, the mirroring operator stops writing to the failed disk drive and continues operations on the remaining drive. Figure 4-3 shows a mirroring operator detecting an error, reporting it to its defined error handler, and suspending operations on the failed disk drive.

Logical Block Addressing in Disk Drives

It is much simpler to mirror drives that are the same model with the same physical characteristics than it is to mirror drives that are different. The I/O requests that are sent to the mirroring operator are typically formulated for a single disk drive before they are copied and transmitted to both drives in the pair. It is much easier and arguably more reliable to use the exact same model in both drives in the pair. Considering the low cost of disk drives today, there are no compelling economic arguments for implementing dissimilar disk drives in a mirror.

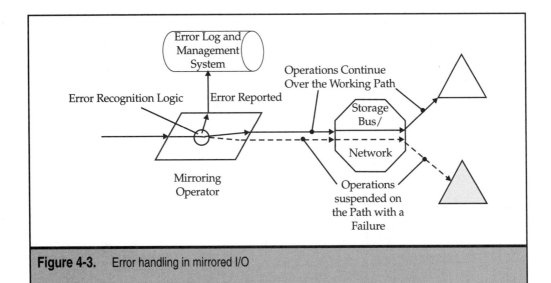

Figure 4-3.   Error handling in mirrored I/O

However, although two drives may come off the manufacturing line next to each other, be formatted identically, be part of the same mirrored pair, and have the exact same data written to them, they are not likely to have the exact same on-disk structure. Why? For starters, modern disk drives use *logical block addressing,* which masks the media-level details of storing data. The disk drive contains its own internal mappings of which logical blocks are associated with which physical blocks. Identical disk drives in a mirror will have the same logical block addresses but have independent and different physical block mappings.

Over time, media errors occur on the drive platters, which create bad sectors that cannot be used. Writes to these bad sectors are redirected to other sectors by the drive's firmware or by the disk device driver. Logical-to-physical block remapping occurs in real time and is not apparent to the user.

Media errors are the result of microscopic damage, shock, and corrosion of the magnetic surface. The major contributors to corrosion are temperature and humidity extremes. As the causes of media damage have random effects across the media, it is virtually impossible that two drives would develop identical media errors and redirected block mappings.

Disk drives all have a number of spare blocks that are used for redirection when they are needed. If media failures occur enough times, the drive can run out of spare blocks. When this happens, the drive fails, which is one of the reasons for using disk mirroring. Considering that the same environmental influences that contributed to the first drive's failing are present for the second drive, one shouldn't feel too secure about the second drive either, which is exposed to the same environmental conditions.

Garbage in ...

Disk mirroring works on the concept of two disk drives containing the same image of the data stored on them. The contents are the same. If one drive has a boot record on it, the other one has one, too. If one drive has database data stored on it, so does the other. If one drive has a bunch of files in the Windows Recycle Bin, so does the other. If the data on one is encrypted, so is the data on the other. If one disk has corrupted files, the other has the same corrupt files. If the data on one is infected with a virus, so is the other. To paraphrase a familiar phrase, garbage into a disk mirror produces twice as much garbage. In other words, disk mirroring offers protection from physical threats to data but does not offer protection from logical threats.

Replacing a Failed Disk in a Mirror

When one of the drives in a mirrored pair fails, it needs to be replaced. The forces that caused the first failure may very well be working on the other drive, which means the failed drive should be replaced soon to prevent data loss if the other drive fails. The system can probably operate without failing for several hours, or even several days, without a replacement drive, but the sooner this is taken care of, the better. Once the new drive is installed, it needs to have the data copied from the other drive in the mirror pair. This might be an automatic process, but could also be a manual one depending on the mirroring technology implemented.

Some disk subsystems support *hot swapping,* which is the ability to remove a disk drive and plug in a new one, without first turning off the power to the system or the drive bus/network. If hot swapping is supported, the administrator can remove the failed drive, replace it with a new one, and start the process of copying data from the active, working drive. This might sound trivial, but it's not: make sure the failed drive is clearly identified before removing it. Removing the good, working drive can have disastrous effects.

If hot swapping is not supported for the mirrored disks, it is necessary to power down either the system or the disk subsystem to remove and replace the failed disk drive. Do not attempt to try hot swapping with a system or subsystem that doesn't support it. Removing or inserting a disk drive into an unsuspecting I/O channel can result in system crashes and loss of data.

NOTE: You will save yourself time and anguish by ensuring the replacement drive is configured correctly with jumpers and address settings.

Mirrored Partitions

Disks are often partitioned to create several logical volumes. For example, a system with a 9GB drive might have three partitions of 3GB each. It is possible on some systems, such as Windows NT, to mirror a subset of these partitions while leaving the rest unmirrored. While this might seem like a clever way to optimize the amount of space on your disk resources, you might want to think twice before doing it. The following example illustrates the potential problems.

Assume you purchase two 30GB disk drives for a Windows NT system that you intend to use as a primary and secondary mirrored pair. The primary drive is partitioned into three logical volumes, identified by the system as the C:, D:, and E: drives. If desired, you could mirror only the partition with the C: drive onto the secondary disk drive. This allows you to create two additional partitions on the secondary drive, say drives F: and G:. That way, you could assign the data for certain applications to different partitions.

Now, let's examine the sense in doing this. For starters, the cost of disk capacity is low and getting lower almost on a daily basis. For this reason, optimizing storage for cost in most cases is not warranted. If you (or your boss) decide later that the data on a nonmirrored partition needs to be mirrored, you will first have to move one of the others. Keep in mind that anytime you move a disk partition, you must take extra time and care to do the job correctly or run the risk of losing data.

CAUTION: Do not mirror a partition onto the same disk—it provides no protection from disk failures and negatively impacts performance.

When establishing mirrors, keep in mind that data growth is unpredictable and that your application's storage requirements may grow and fill the capacity of the partition. In that case, you will have to move the application's data to a larger partition with sufficient free space and redirect the application to access it in its new location. Another unsavory option is to reorganize your disk subsystem. This involves either copying all the data to other systems that might have the capacity or relying on a backup copy to restore all the data. Either way, the work can be problematic and occasionally nerve-wracking. If you are not careful, data can be lost. Unfortunately, there are many stories of serious data losses that occurred while reorganizing disk partitions.

As a rule, any amount of complexity in your disk partitions and mirrors, no matter how simple they seem, can become problematic later. Last, consider the other people who might be called in to recover the server in an emergency. How difficult would it be for them to perform a complete server recovery if some drives are mirrored and others are not? *Disk capacity is cheap; time spent managing disk problems is not.*

Implementing Disk Mirroring in the I/O Path

Disk mirroring is an implementation of device virtualization that can be located in any of the places along the I/O path where device virtualization can be applied.

▼ Volume manager in the host

■ Host I/O controller device driver software

■ Host I/O controller hardware or firmware

■ Storage network domain manager

▲ Storage subsystem

Mirroring with Host Volume Manager Software

Disk mirroring is one of the most frequently used functions in host-based volume management. As it runs as a host process, volume manager disk mirrors can encompass both internal disk drives (drives located within the server cabinet) or external disk drives (drives located in a subsystem cabinet).

JBOD (just a bunch of disks) is a class of storage subsystem that provides power and I/O connectivity for multiple disk drives in an external cabinet but does not create virtual drives from the members. In other words, disk drives in a JBOD cabinet are accessed individually by the host system and can be configured as a mirror by a host-resident mirroring process.

Most major server operating systems and file systems provide basic disk mirroring utilities. For simple installations where optimal performance, remote management, and configuration flexibility are not required, operating system mirroring utilities provide an inexpensive option that works well. Otherwise, volume management software may be available to provide additional capabilities and more control than is typically provided as part of the operating system.

Figure 4-4 shows two different I/O paths for mirrored operations in a volume manager. Two I/O requests, r1 and r2, are created from a single request from a file system. In the top example, a single host I/O controller is used, and in the second example, dual host I/O controllers are used.

Host volume manager mirroring runs on the host system and uses processor and memory resources to do its job. Therefore, this approach exerts a load on the host com-

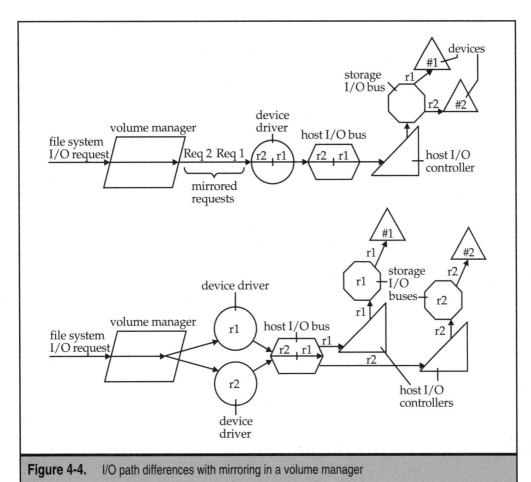

Figure 4-4.   I/O path differences with mirroring in a volume manager

puter's resources. In most cases, that is not much of a problem, but on servers that are already overloaded, host volume manager mirroring will have an impact on performance. Also, the mirror operator must wait its turn to execute on the host computer and therefore may encounter more delays in the mirroring process than some other types of mirroring solutions. Again, this is not much of an issue, except on servers already running at maximum CPU capacity.

However, as a software application that resides within the host, software mirroring can be easily integrated into server management functions. In addition, any updates or bug fixes that need to be made to the host volume manager mirroring software can be done with relative ease compared to mirroring solutions that are implemented in hardware or firmware further down the I/O path.

Host I/O Controller Device Driver Mirroring

The next stop along the I/O path to implement disk mirroring is the host I/O controller device driver. Similar to volume manager mirroring, mirroring in the I/O controller device driver can initiate independent requests on two separate I/O paths through a single or dual host I/O controllers, on through to internal or external disk drives. A single mirroring device driver can be used across two identical host I/O controllers.

The device driver mirror shares many of the characteristics of the volume manager mirror. However, as virtualization is performed at the driver level, the host volume manager sees a single virtual drive and does not have the capability to address both drives individually. Figure 4-5 shows an abstracted "stack" view of the I/O path for a disk mirror implemented in a host I/O controller device driver.

Like volume manager mirrors, device driver mirrors also run as a process in the host system and take system resources. Heavily loaded servers could experience slight performance degradation due to the additional burden of the mirroring function. As host-based software, device driver mirroring integrates well with server management functions and can be updated with software patches or by reloading updated drivers.

Host I/O Controller Hardware Mirroring

In addition to the device driver, it is also possible for firmware and hardware in the host I/O controller to provide the mirroring operator. Unlike the device driver mirror, a disk mirror in a controller only applies to that controller and is therefore limited to using the storage I/O buses or networks they control, as shown in Figure 4-6. While a single host

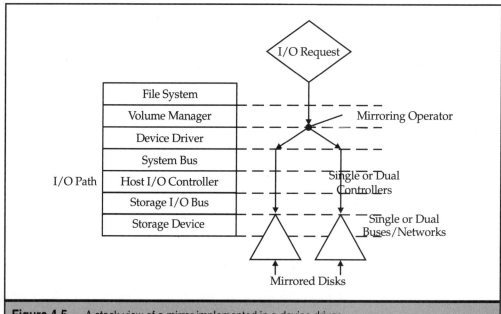

Figure 4-5.   A stack view of a mirror implemented in a device driver

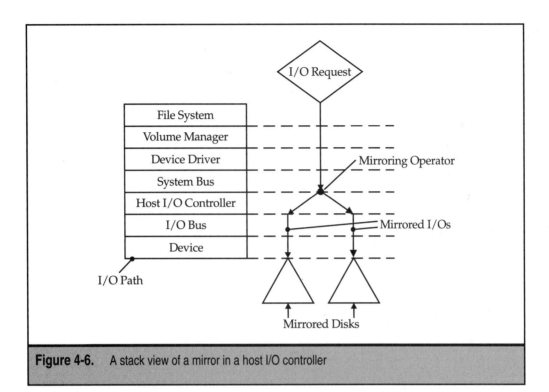

Figure 4-6.   A stack view of a mirror in a host I/O controller

I/O controller can control multiple buses/networks to provide additional capacity, performance, and redundancy, one should question the sanity of using a single controller where high availability is the goal. In such cases, dual controllers are preferable.

In general, host I/O controller hardware (and firmware) is the first point in the I/O path where hardware-based mirroring can be implemented. The primary advantage of hardware mirroring is the excellent performance that can be delivered without loading the host processor. Conversely, hardware solutions tend to be less flexible in terms of upgradability and management integration. As a host server component, I/O controller mirrors have device drivers that run on the server and can provide a direct connection to server-based management systems. Host I/O controller mirroring can provide the optimal balance between performance and manageability.

Mirroring in a Storage Network Domain Manager

A relatively new product class to emerge from the storage networking industry is a storage network domain manager. As a network entity that provides device virtualization, such a product is obviously capable of providing mirroring. Its place on the I/O path can be seen in Figure 4-7. All upstream path participants, such as host I/O controllers and host volume managers, are presented with a single image of a virtual device. The mirroring operator in the domain manager can use one or two network ports for transmitting the mirrored I/O requests.

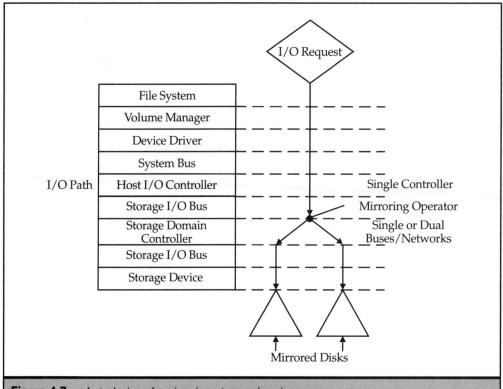

Figure 4-7. A stack view of a mirror in a storage domain manager

Mirroring in an External Disk Subsystem

The final stop in the I/O path where disk mirroring can be implemented is in an external disk subsystem, typically a RAID subsystem. RAID implies the presence of an intelligent processor that can provide advanced disk operations and management. Disks in a RAID cabinet are usually not addressed directly by the server's I/O controller but by an embedded I/O controller. Disk mirroring, or RAID 1, is provided as an option by most RAID subsystems.

With the mirroring operator running in a RAID controller, both the host operating system and the host I/O controller simply "see" a single virtual disk instead of two mirrored disks as shown in Figure 4-8. This approach has minimal impact on the host CPU.

Given sufficient processing power, the performance of a mirror in an external disk subsystem can be very fast. Not only is its processor dedicated to the task of storage management, the subsystem is often designed and tuned for a specific set of components.

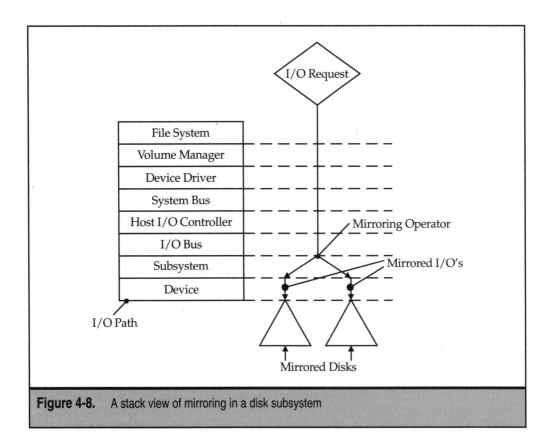

Figure 4-8.   A stack view of mirroring in a disk subsystem

Matched with other high-speed I/O components, including system processor and bus, the external disk mirror can provide optimal performance.

Along with performance, the support for hot swapping, as discussed earlier in this chapter, is an area where external disk subsystems can really shine. Hot swapping in an external disk subsystem is implemented by incorporating a specially engineered I/O bus that provides power and signal buffering for all other devices on the bus.

Increasing Data Protection with Dual I/O Controllers

Dual host I/O controllers are frequently used with mirrored disks to provide protection from I/O controller failures and increase performance. This is sometimes referred to as *disk duplexing*. In general, dual controllers are a requirement of high-availability operations. The mirroring operator for dual-controller mirrors is located either in the volume manager, as shown in Figure 4-4, or in the device driver, as shown in Figure 4-5.

Dual controllers take extra card slots in your servers, which can create configuration problems. For example, it is fairly common for administrators to make a choice between using an additional I/O controller for redundancy or using it to increase a server's capacity.

PERFORMANCE CHARACTERISTICS OF MIRRORING

While disk mirroring is the subject of this chapter, the mirroring concept is certainly not limited to disks, as evidenced by the preceding discussion regarding dual host I/O controllers. The sections that follow discuss the performance potential of mirroring, including ways to balance mirrored I/O traffic across multiple I/O buses/networks.

Increasing I/O Performance with Disk Mirroring

So far, our discussion of disk mirroring has involved how mirrors work when they are written to. But write I/O operations only represent approximately 10 to 20 percent of a disk's normal activities. With reads representing the lion's share of the operations, obviously any performance enhancements that can be applied to reading are significant.

I/O performance has been an important topic for many years and is becoming increasingly important as the amount of data we have online increases. In a basic computer system, the slowest-performing component typically is the disk drive. While memory responses are conservatively measured in nanoseconds, disk access times are measured in milliseconds. Considering how much data resides on disk, anything that improves disk performance is a welcome addition.

As it turns out, disk mirroring can be used to improve performance at the same time it provides redundancy and availability benefits. The key to understanding how this works is analyzing the physical processes that occur when a disk drive reads and writes data. Disk arms and their attached read/write heads are constantly moving across the surface of the drive reading and writing data. The time it takes the arm to position over the proper track is called *seek time*.

Once the heads are in place over the tracks, they must wait for the information on the medium to rotate underneath the head in order to read it. This delay is called *rotational latency*. Once the mechanical processes are accomplished, the actual data transfer is fairly fast, limited by the rotational speed of the drive.

When the drive needs to change tracks to continue reading the data or to service another request, the process starts all over again. This constant delay in positioning the disk arms and waiting for data to rotate under the heads is the fundamental reason why disks are relatively slow. If there was something that could be done to reduce the delays incurred, a significant amount of time could be saved.

For mirrored writes, the disk arms of both drives are positioned over their respective tracks and then transfer the data to disk. By contrast, read operations do not really need to position both disk arms over the same tracks on both drives. A single disk arm on either drive can find the track correctly and read the data correctly, which means that redundancy on read operations is unnecessary. Therefore, when there are multiple read operations in the queue, the work load can be distributed so that one disk will satisfy one set of requests while the other disk satisfies the other set. In this way, the disks can balance the load. Figure 4-9 illustrates load-balanced, or asynchronous, reads from a pair of mirrored disks.

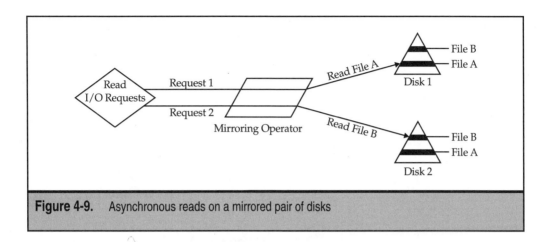

Figure 4-9.   Asynchronous reads on a mirrored pair of disks

Increasing Performance by Increasing the Number of Disk Spindles

Parallel processing is one of the primary techniques for improving system performance. The idea is simple: if one processor can finish a job in ten seconds, it should be possible to make ten processors finish the job in one second. Overlapping reads with mirrored disks are an example of this concept applied to disk drives.

The essence of overlapped reads is to increase the number of disk drives, and therefore of disk arms used to retrieve data. This is sometimes referred to as "increasing the number of spindles." The fact is that with one disk arm per drive, increasing the number of drives for accessing data, as mirroring does, can result in faster read performance.

Disk drives are truly amazing technology devices we tend to take for granted. The disk drive industry is highly competitive and continues to propel its technology in the direction of ever-increasing areal density, delivering greater capacity and faster rotational speeds, resulting in faster performance. There is little doubt that the disk drive industry has continued to amaze the market with its technological advancements over the years.

However, there is a drawback to higher capacity disk drives: a single disk arm reads more and more data. In other words, even though the amount of data has increased dramatically, the number of disk arms has stayed the same. While the average access times of disk drives are getting better and better, they are not progressing at the same rate as capacity. Increased capacity does not correlate with increased platter size.

This is not necessarily a huge problem for single-user systems, but for multiuser server systems with high levels of concurrent access, the disk arms have to seek much more often. For example, consider the scenario depicted in Figure 4-10, where two servers with 36GB of mirrored disk are both managing 20 concurrent disk reads.

In Figure 4-10, Server A uses two mirrored pairs of 18GB drives to total 36GB of online storage. Server B uses nine mirrored pairs of 4GB drives to achieve the same capacity. Server A has four disk arms available to service the 20 requests, while Server B has 18 disk

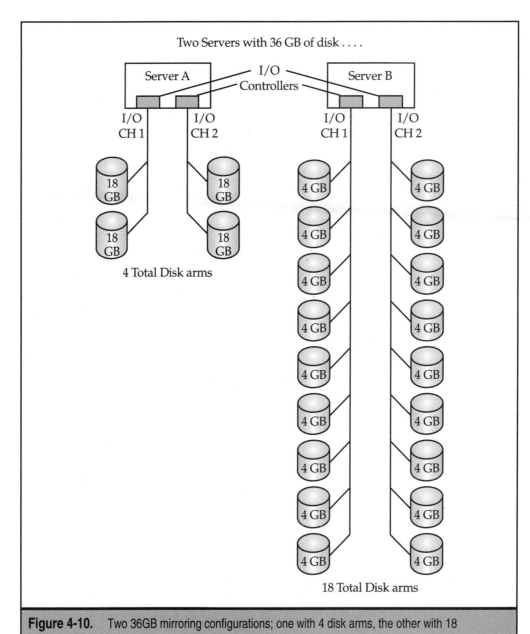

Figure 4-10.   Two 36GB mirroring configurations; one with 4 disk arms, the other with 18

arms. There is no guarantee that the distribution of data would allow all 18 disk arms to be used, but it is almost certain that Server B would use more than 4 disk arms to service the same requests. Over time, the increased number of disk arms would result in clear performance advantages for Server B.

Size Matters

The size of the blocks written to disk is an important element of I/O performance. Many file systems have configurable block sizes, which can be tuned for a particular application or to solve a particular problem.

One such problem is disk fragmentation, which is the phenomenon of having the contents of a file spread all over the disk, forcing the disk arm to move many times in order to read the file. Disk fragmentation occurs as disk capacity fills up and files are updated and expand. To accommodate the larger size, additional blocks are written to open space on the disk. As the disk fills, the amount of data that needs to be placed in "fragments" increases. Fragmentation can cause enormous increases in seek time and rotational latency to read the complete file.

Larger block sizes result in less fragmentation, but more wasted space on the disk. Some of the performance problems with disk fragmentation are reduced by reducing the seek time and rotational latency needed to read a file. File updates are more likely to fit into the remaining space in the file's last block, which, in turn, results in less fragmentation.

In general, the following guidelines will help you select the best block size for your systems.

System Activity	Optimum Block Size
Transaction data	4K to 8K
Office automation	16K to 32K
Data warehousing	64K to 256K
CAD/design	64K to 128K
Multimedia	512K to 4MB

NOTE: It is a good idea to get a recommendation from your application software vendor as to the best block size configuration for its application.

Supporting Disk Mirroring with Additional I/O Channels

When disk mirroring is used to improve performance, it may be a good idea to use additional host I/O controllers also. The logic here is fairly simple: if more disk arms are added, the I/O channel can become a bottleneck. Adding I/O channels can alleviate such problems.

As a rule, try not to configure an I/O channel where the aggregate performance of the disk drives connected to an I/O controller is more than four times the performance capabilities of the controller. Also be careful of using a high percentage of the addresses available on a given I/O channel. The arbitration processes of both SCSI and Fibre Channel arbitrated loops can "starve" the lowest-priority devices on a fully configured channel and hinder overall performance.

As an example, consider a Wide Ultra SCSI bus with a maximum throughput of 40 MB/s and 16 SCSI IDs. Now, let's assume that the disk drives under consideration have a peak transfer rate in the 15 MB/s range. Using the preceding rule of thumb for performance matching, the maximum aggregate speed of the drives would be 160 MB/s, which is equivalent to ten or eleven disk drives. Given that the host I/O controller will use a SCSI ID, that means that eleven or twelve SCSI IDs would be used, with four or five free, reducing the likelihood that device starvation will be a serious problem.

As is true for all complex systems functions, there may be many times when the rules of thumb given do not fit very well.

Avoiding Performance Problems when Mixing Tape Drives with Disk Mirrors

Devices of different speeds can be attached to the same bus/network. However, when different types of devices are used, the resulting performance can be disappointing. One such scenario involves mixing tape drives and disk drives on the same I/O channel. Most host I/O controllers will change their transfer speed to match the speed of individual device, but while slower devices are "hogging the bus," every other device is delayed. Some host I/O controllers support multiple buses at different speeds, especially newer Ultra3 SCSI host adapters.

One of the keys to understanding the performance of a disk mirror with an attached tape drive is following the path of the backup data. It moves from one of the disk drives into the host, through an application or driver buffer, and back out on the host I/O controller to the tape drive. An example of this flow is shown in Figure 4-11, which shows a SCSI tape drive with a maximum transfer rate of 5MB/s attached to an Ultra SCSI bus with two mirrored disk drives.

One would think that adding a single tape drive might not have much impact, especially because the tape drive only runs at night during backups. However, while backups

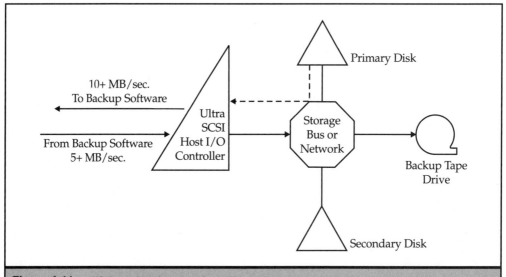

Figure 4-11. I/O flow of backup data from disk to tape over a single storage bus or network

are running, the overall system I/O performance could be far less than expected. If this system has a lot of data to back up, this could become a serious problem for the administrator as backups extend into production hours. Chapter 7 on backup looks at the challenges of backup in much greater detail.

Tape drives tend to respond more slowly to I/O commands than disk drives do. Tape drives running on the same channel as disk drives can add a small amount of latency in the I/O channel that negatively impacts disk performance. Finally, troubleshooting becomes much more difficult when the number of devices increases and the devices are not the same type of device.

TIP: Whenever possible, put tape drives on their own I/O channel, separate from your disk devices.

Planning a Disk Mirroring Configuration

Different storage bus and network technologies support different numbers of devices or addresses. For instance, there can be 8 addressable devices on narrow, or 8-bit, SCSI and 16 addressable on wide, or 16-bit, SCSI. When you count the controller as an addressable device—and you have to—the actual number of devices supported is 7 on a narrow SCSI bus and 15 on a wide SCSI bus. If the goal is to mirror every drive, there will be one drive that cannot be mirrored.

If you are using dual mirrored controllers with software mirroring or host I/O controller mirroring, the total number of devices available doubles, but the number of devices per channel is still restricted to 7 and 15 drives, respectively. By mirroring across the controllers, however, you gain an additional drive pair that is shared across the two controllers. In other words, you can have 7 mirrored pairs on two 8-bit SCSI controllers and 15 mirrored pairs on two 16-bit SCSI controllers.

Rules of Thumb for Mirroring a Server Disk

The following guidelines might be helpful in determining the most appropriate mirroring solution to use:

▼   At a minimum, use disk mirroring to protect server data.

■   If possible, choose at least Ultra 2 SCSI, Fibre Channel, or some other storage networking technology that has the combination of available addresses and channel bandwidth.

■   Use software mirroring on moderately loaded servers where cost is the main factor.

■   Use host I/O controller mirroring for optimal performance, scalability, and administration.

▲   Use external subsystem mirroring with hot-swappable drives when fault-tolerance is required.

MIRRORING EXTERNAL DISK SUBSYSTEMS

Just as disk drives can be mirrored, it is also possible to mirror external disk subsystems. This approach can alleviate a lot of the ugly details of configuring individual disk drives on host I/O controllers as evidenced in the previous section.

Figure 4-12 shows how disk subsystems can replace individual disk drives in a mirroring configuration. The disk subsystems in this example are required to provide device virtualization for their internal drives to allow the entire subsystem cabinet to be treated as a single virtual disk drive. A mirroring operator can be implemented anywhere along the I/O path ahead of the device level. As such disk subsystems typically provide their own additional redundancy protection, this type of configuration provides a great deal of data protection.

Beyond the basic idea of big virtual disks, subsystem mirroring offers other interesting possibilities that are discussed in the following sections.

Mirror-Based Data Snapshots

Not all applications of mirroring are concerned with disaster recovery and availability of data. There are many reasons why an extra set of data could be useful for a company. As an example, consider the difficulties in testing new applications. How can a valid test be run without having real data to work? A test that doesn't include actual data samples is probably not a complete test.

Simply saying that real data is needed is simple, but actually getting real data to work with is not so simple, and it is essential that real, working data never be put at risk. One of the most popular techniques for doing this is called a *snapshot mirror*. The basic idea of a

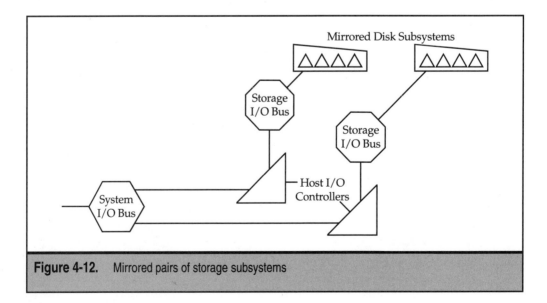

Figure 4-12.   Mirrored pairs of storage subsystems

snapshot mirror is to establish a separate addressable storage entity that has a "snapshot" of some amount of real data—and then run tests against it. Snapshot mirrors can be used for a variety of functions, including backup, application testing, time/date simulation, data conversion, and other batch processes.

A snapshot mirror works by creating a subsystem mirror, which can be disconnected from the I/O path being used. Other subsystems on the I/O path continue to operate normally. On the surface this is fairly simple, but on a detailed level it requires precise synchronization between the snapshot mirror and the host system, which must flush any pending writes that may be stored in the host system's internal caches.

Figure 4-13 shows a snapshot mirror that is created on a separate disk subsystem. In this diagram, the primary subsystem is still connected to the host server and is providing uninterrupted storage to it. The secondary snapshot mirror subsystem has been detached and is connected to another system and is running tests. Although it is not required, the secondary subsystem is shown to be *dual ported*, which means it can be connected to both the host server and the test system without having to switch cables. Obviously, care must be taken to prevent the test system from interfering with the secondary subsystem when it is working with the host server.

One of the most difficult aspects of running a snapshot mirror is the challenge of resynchronizing the snapshot with the primary data when the secondary application is finished. Resynchronization implies that data written to the primary while the snapshot was disconnected is logged or cached in order to accurately synchronize the data. The resources needed to support this logging or caching need to be accounted for in the primary system or subsystem. It is a fair amount of detailed data to track with no room for error.

Conversely, if resynchronization is not done, it is necessary to make a complete copy of all data from one subsystem to the other to re-create the mirror. Depending on the amount of data stored on the primary subsystem, this could be an enormous task, which

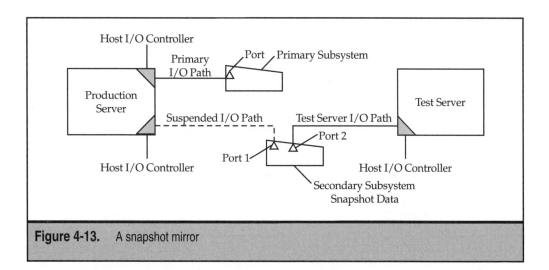

Figure 4-13.   A snapshot mirror

can be a long, slow process impacting server performance. It may seem obvious, but it needs to be pointed out that subsystem resynchronization takes significantly longer and has a larger, negative impact on performance when there are large amounts of data to resynchronize.

EMC Timefinder

One of the most successful snapshot mirroring products has been EMC Corporation's Timefinder. Timefinder is a software product designed to run on EMC's Symmetrix storage subsystems. It is based on a design where the mirroring intelligence is in the subsystem, as opposed to the server. In order to ensure data is never left without a mirror, Timefinder establishes a three-way mirror. The third, or tertiary, mirror detaches from the other two.

Timefinder works with both mainframe and open systems storage. Figure 4-14 shows an installation of Timefinder where the tertiary subsystem is detached for the purposes of running backup. This enables the host system to continue operating without the impact of backup operations dragging on its performance.

Subsystem Mirroring Beyond the Local Area

Business continuity or disaster recovery plans typically involve the ability to resume normal computing operations in some other location if the business's normal data processing facility experiences a disaster. Storage networking facilitates the establishment of remote systems and storage subsystems that can be used to mirror data beyond the radius of certain anticipated disasters. In some locations, the disaster could be an earthquake; in others, it could be a flood or fire; and in others, some sort of storm.

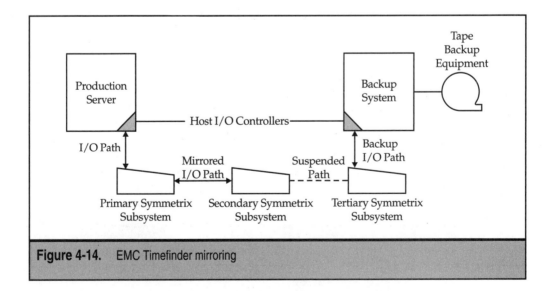

Figure 4-14.   EMC Timefinder mirroring

Mirroring Cross-Campus

In order to protect data from a localized disaster, organizations will establish disk mirrors across a campus environment. That way, if a building should burn, flood, or meet with some other disaster, the data stored there could be available to a machine in another building.

Cross-Campus Mirroring Using Channel Extension

Channel extension is a technology that has been used for several years. The concept of channel extension is to provide some way to transmit distance-constrained storage I/O operations over extended distances. Usually this means converting parallel storage I/O transmissions to a serial signal for transfer over some other type of cable—and back again to its original, parallel format on the receiving end, as diagrammed here:

Cross-Campus Disk Subsystem Mirror

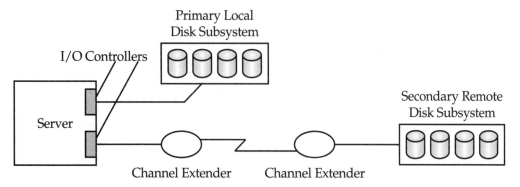

Channel extension solutions tend to be proprietary and not very flexible, using point-to-point links. While they may be compatible with a wide variety of existing storage devices, subsystems, and host I/O controllers, they are usually not compatible with other channel extender products. For that reason, channel extension has typically been sold as a matched pair of extenders. As storage networks become popular, the use of channel extenders is declining rapidly in the market.

Cross-Campus Mirroring with Storage Networks

Storage networking is based on serial SCSI protocols as discussed in Chapter 1. Both Fibre Channel and Ethernet/IP storage networking use serial SCSI application-layer protocols that are transferred over open systems standard networks having their own physical, MAC (media access control), network, and transmission layers. Fibre Channel and Gigabit Ethernet have cable length limitations of 10,000 meters, which is plenty for establishing disk mirroring over a typical campus or MAN (metropolitan area network).

The primary differences between storage networking and channel extension is the fact that storage networks do not require any conversion of a native storage protocol. Traffic that stays in a storage network does not have to have its frames subdivided and reassembled at the remote end. In addition, storage networks are typically not limited to functioning as dedicated point-to-point networks the way channel extenders are. In other words, a storage network might start out as a point-to-point network between a particular server and its storage subsystem, but unlike a channel extension product, the storage network can expand and accommodate traffic from many servers to many storage subsystems simultaneously.

Disk Mirroring over a Wide Area Network

Many organizations may not have a campus to work with or may not feel cross-campus mirroring meets their requirements for disaster tolerance. Many organizations, particularly financial services companies, have decided to mirror data across a WAN (wide area network) to get the data protection they seek.

Comparing Storage and Network Transmission Speeds

People unfamiliar with storage I/O technologies sometimes tend to think of new networking technologies as the fastest way to move data. This is easy to understand, considering the complexity involved in planning for, installing, running, and managing large networks and the amount of marketing this technology and its products receive. Storage I/O, on the other hand, has historically been ignored by the networking industry and market—and with good reason. Prior to storage networking, storage I/O was not a networking technology and storage products were not built to be attached to networks.

So, sometimes it surprises people when they find out how well storage I/O performance has compared to networking technology. Table 4-1 compares the evolution of both common networking and storage technologies. Considering the many possible variations in transmission media and speeds, it would be possible to make many different comparisons in addition to the ones shown. The last column on the right approximates storage transfer speeds in units of bits—as opposed to bytes, the way storage is normally specified.

One of the most interesting aspects of Table 4-1 is how the relative performance difference between networking and storage technologies has been narrowing through the years. The last row shows that OC-48 networking transmissions have higher transfer rates than 2 Gigabit Fibre Channel. Table 4-1 does not indicate the effective throughput of the various technologies. For example, if switched Ethernet transmissions peak at a 50 percent utilization under normal conditions, the effective throughput of a 100 Mbit/s network is 50 Mb/s. This is one of the primary differences between traditional data network transmissions and storage I/O transmissions—storage transmissions can be performed at 80 to 90 percent of

Network Technology	Transfer Rate, in Mbit/s	Storage I/O Technology	Transfer Rate in Mbytes/s	Equivalent Transfer in Mbits/s
T1	1.54 Mb/s	SCSI	5 MB/s	40 Mb/s
Ethernet	10 Mb/s	Fast SCSI	10 MB/s	80 Mb/s
Fast Ethernet	100 Mb/s	Fast/Wide SCSI	20 MB/s	160 Mb/s
ATM over OC-3	155 Mb/s	Ultra SCSI	40 MB/s	320 Mb/s
ATM over OC-12	622 Mb/s	Ultra-2 SCSI	80 MB/s	640 Mb/s
Gigabit Ethernet	1,000 Mb/s	Ultra-3 SCSI	160 MB/s	1,280 Mb/s
OC-48	2,500 Mb/s	2Gbit Fibre Channel	200 MB/s	1,600 Mb/s

Table 4-1. A Comparison of Networking and Storage Data Transfer Rates

the theoretical maximum speed. For instance, it is possible to achieve transmission rates of 18 MB/s over a 20 MB/s channel. Even on a dedicated, point-to-point TCP/IP Ethernet segment where CSMA-CD collisions are avoided, the effective throughput is constrained to between 70 percent and 80 percent of its line speed due to protocol overhead.

The "Big Pipe/Little Pipe" Problem

So, when storage traffic is expected to be transferred over a data networking, one of the major challenges is solving the discrepancy between the speeds of the local storage bus/networks and the data networks linking them. It is a case where the bandwidth available, or the "pipe" used for storage, can be much larger than the bandwidth available for the data network, especially if the data network is a wide area network. In other words, it is a "big pipe/little pipe" problem as illustrated here:

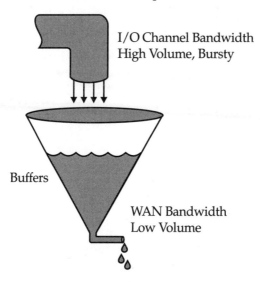

Discrepancy Between I/O & WAN
Transmission Speeds

I/O Channel Bandwidth
High Volume, Bursty

Buffers

WAN Bandwidth
Low Volume

There are a couple of techniques that can be used to work around this problem. The first is to use multiple WAN links in a transmission group. Another term for this approach is "inverse multiplexing"—a concept that has existed for years in the telecommunications industry and can be represented like this:

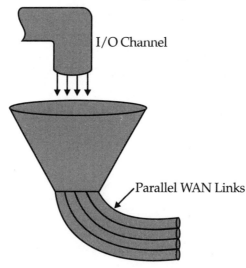

Transmission Group
Inverse Multiplexing

I/O Channel

Parallel WAN Links

The other technique that can be used to deal with the bandwidth discrepancy between storage buses and WANs is filtering. This is based on the idea that a filter selects only the data that needs to be mirrored and everything else is ignored. Data replication products already can do this by operating at the file system level and selecting only certain files or directories to be replicated.

Most organizations are able to prioritize their data and identify what the most important data to be mirrored is. Perhaps over time it will be easier to accomplish, but until WAN bandwidth ceases to be a scarce resource where storage is concerned, selective replication will be a desirable option.

Comparing Synchronous, Asynchronous, and Semisynchronous Mirroring in WANs

Synchronous, asynchronous, and semisynchronous mirroring were introduced early in this chapter as different disk mirroring techniques offering differing degrees of performance and data integrity. In a local storage network, it is possible to achieve excellent performance with synchronous mirroring because the pipe used to connect to the secondary is the same speed as that for the primary. In mirroring across a WAN, however, the WAN pipe will likely be much smaller than the storage network. In these cases, either asynchronous or semisynchronous mirroring may be a better choice.

The best way to understand this is to examine the detailed data flow from the primary local storage bus/network, over a WAN, to the secondary storage bus/network, as shown here:

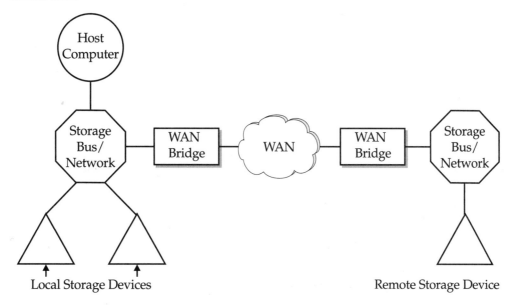

Synchronous mirroring can be thought of as a connection-oriented process that acknowledges every operation before continuing with the next. If local write operations occur at a rate that exceeds the bandwidth of the WAN pipe, it is fairly obvious that the

WAN is a bottleneck with a detrimental effect on system performance because local operations also wait for acknowledgments. Applications with high write I/O rates suffer under synchronous mirroring over a WAN.

Asynchronous mirroring, on the other hand, allows all write I/Os to be sent over the WAN as they are received by the mirroring operator. For the most part, it is able to accommodate speed discrepancies without impacting system performance by waiting for acknowledgments. However, there are serious potential problems due to the fact that many writes sent to the remote secondary storage subsystem could fail without notification. In that case, the mirroring operator must keep track of all outstanding (unacknowledged) writes and have some way of providing a solution for data integrity. If the local storage subsystem has already committed many writes and the remote storage subsystem has unknown results for those writes, it is a difficult, yet essential puzzle to solve to ensure that the data images can be restored to an identical state later.

This points to the core difficulty in any remote data mirroring or replication scheme, which is how to perform error recovery when detailed information about the error is not available and the state of the remote location is unknown. Unfortunately, this is a fairly difficult scenario to test for due to the diversity of system, storage, and application environments.

The performance impact of synchronous mirroring and the data integrity potential of asynchronous mirroring has given rise to semisynchronous mirroring. The idea of semisynchronous mirroring is that the number of outstanding writes is limited to some manageable number. For instance, there could be a maximum of three writes unacknowledged before allowing any more local writes, as illustrated here:

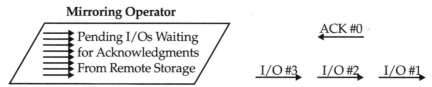

The concept of semisynchronous mirroring is based on the fact that I/O rates are typically not constant but vary over time. Semisynchronous mirroring allows the rate to be averaged out relative to the performance of the WAN pipe. For instance, a semisynchronous mirror could accept two writes in rapid succession and forward them to the remote secondary. The third write I/O might not occur until after the first of the previous writes is acknowledged, in which case it will be processed immediately. If the first write is not acknowledged yet, the third write I/O will be delayed until the first is acknowledged, which hopefully should already be on its way back from the remote site.

Obviously, additional error recovery mechanisms are required beyond those needed for synchronous mirroring. They might not be as difficult to solve as this in asynchronous mirroring, but they still need to be solved in a foolproof fashion and require memory and processor resources to ensure data integrity.

Using Channel Extenders for Remote Mirroring

Channel extenders were introduced previously as a possible solution for cross-campus mirrors. They can also be used across WANs to provide long-distance mirroring. Channel extenders are a "black box" technology and only work when they are implemented as matched pairs—one on each end of the WAN. In other words, don't expect to purchase channel extenders from two different companies, or expect them to work together as a pair. As protocol converters, they certainly comply with the I/O transmission standards such as SCSI on each end of the link, but in the WAN channel, extenders use whatever proprietary protocols necessary to accomplish their task.

Channel extenders are far from being plug-and-play products. They need to be carefully tuned to the specific characteristics of the WAN link used and the sending and receiving storage subsystems. This drawing shows two channel extenders used for remote mirroring over a WAN:

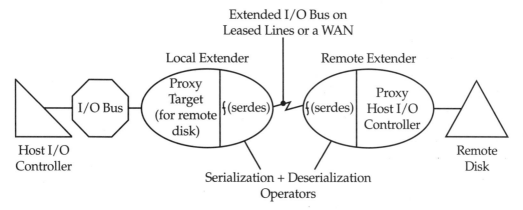

Notice that the extender closest to the host system does work on behalf of the remote target storage subsystems. In other words, it is a *proxy* target device. This function can include "spoofing" the host by prematurely acknowledging a write I/O in an asynchronous or semisynchronous mirror before it actually receives the acknowledgment from the remote storage subsystem. That means the extender needs to keep a cache of data for retransmission until the remote extender acknowledges its completion.

The remote extender does not merely act as a proxy initiator—it *is* the initiator for the remote storage subsystems. It must correctly model the initiator on the host system and perform the types of functions that the host initiator does. While this might seem straightforward, it is actually quite complex, as there is no device driver that is tightly coupled with the initiator in the remote extender. The remote extender instead must be a very effective and autonomous operator that knows how to respond to all the possible variations in timing and status information from its attached storage subsystems. For that reason, channel extenders should be used only with storage subsystems that are certified and supported by the channel extender vendor.

Channel extension is a challenging technology. If you implement channel extenders, try to keep the following recommendations in mind:

▼   Use a dedicated wide area link. Leased lines work best. Although virtual circuits in public networks may "look just like" a dedicated link, they also can introduce transmission variations that are difficult to tune for.

■   Use an isolated I/O channel on the host end. Don't put the channel extender on a storage bus or network with other storage subsystems. It makes it much more difficult to tune and troubleshoot when there are problems. Channel extension solutions are relatively expensive to own and operate, so there must be a good business reason for having them in the first place. Don't try to cut costs by connecting them to a bus with other storage subsystems—it makes it much more difficult to tune and troubleshoot.

▲   Remember that channel extenders are highly sensitive to changes. Changes in devices and I/O controllers could require adjustments to the channel extender and other networking equipment.

File Replication

Standard TCP/IP data networks can also be used to copy data from one storage subsystem to another using a technology called *replication*. Replication is a *filing* process that copies data from one system to another after the data has already been written to disk as a completed I/O. In other words, where mirroring is more or less a real-time storing process using logical block information, replication works with data objects at the file level using file system. It follows that the remote process that receives replicated data is also a filing function that works with a file system of some sort.

The basic idea of replication is fairly simple: identify data that has changed and copy it to another system. This involves running a watchdog or daemon program on the server that periodically looks for such updates. In order to identify a change to data, the replication system may maintain its own information about the data and make comparisons with the state of the data on disk.

One of the key features of replication is the ability to specify the files and directories you want to copy. While a disk mirror copies everything from one device onto another, replication can be configured to copy only the most important files needed to recover from a disaster. By limiting the amount of data that is transferred, the network load and its corresponding performance problems and costs can be significantly reduced.

As mentioned, replication typically uses a data network as the conduit for the copied data, unlike mirroring, which uses a storage bus or network for transferring data. In that sense, replication is much more flexible than mirroring because it can use virtually any TCP/IP network to copy data to any location on the network. However, data networks tend to be slower than storage, and so replication is also more commonly found on machines where the I/O rates are not as high and the requirements for bandwidth are less.

Figure 4-15 illustrates a file replication system that selects certain files from the primary server's file system and transports them over a TCP/IP network to the secondary server, where they are copied to its file system.

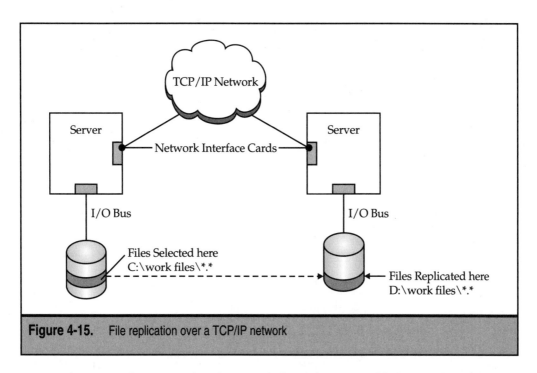

Figure 4-15. File replication over a TCP/IP network

Another nice advantage of replication is the ability to establish a many-to-one relationship between application systems and a specific replication server where the replicated data is stored. This way, a single server can be optimized for replication purposes and can provide a single management point for all replicated data. This illustration shows two servers replicating their data to a single replication server:

Many to One Replication over a LAN

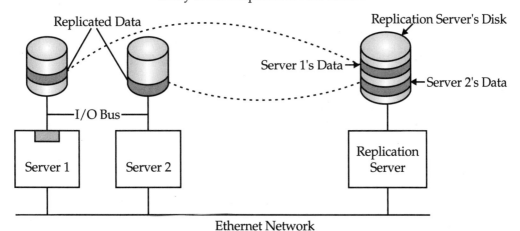

One of the interesting variables in replication is the granularity of the data objects that can be replicated. In many replicating systems, the smallest unit that can be replicated is a file, which means that a 24-byte change to a 150MB file can result in the entire file being replicated, not just the 24 bytes that changed. There are also replication systems that are able to track changes within files and can make copies of just the changed data. Veritas Software makes a volume manager replication product that captures block information instead of file information and copies it to another system with another copy of the software.

One of the problems with replication is the delay in time from when the data was first written to disk to when it gets replicated. Consider the scenario when replication is scheduled to run every hour on the hour. Should a disaster happen 15 minutes after the last replication operation, any new data will be lost. So in that sense, replication does not protect against all data loss, but it can be set up to minimize the amount of data that is lost. Some replication products work constantly, significantly reducing the window for data loss after the last copy operation.

TIP: Replication traffic can be heavy. Use dedicated high-speed LAN links or subnetworks between replicating servers.

Replicating Files over a WAN

File replication is an excellent technology for WANs because it allows the administrator to effectively control which data is transferred. By selecting only the most critical data for transmission over the WAN, it is not necessary to pay the transmission charges for data that might not be needed immediately.

With replication over a WAN, the remote system that receives the replicated data is responsible for storing it on its own managed disks. Therefore, replication is an asynchronous process because it does not impact local I/O performance by waiting for acknowledgments of every write operation on the remote system.

SUMMARY

Disk mirroring is one of the most fundamental of all storage management applications. It is an excellent, time-tested technology that provides data redundancy but can also deliver excellent performance benefits when configured optimally. It is a very simple and powerful concept that can be implemented many different and sometimes sophisticated ways.

In the years to come, mirroring will be expanded to include much more use over metropolitan and wide area networks as high-speed network services become available that can handle much greater amounts of data. In addition, replication technology will also continue to evolve and become much faster and more "real-time" in nature. Many of the later chapters in this book address mirroring again, but as a storage network application that has grown beyond its implementation on storage buses.

EXERCISES

1. Design a mirroring solution using four host I/O controllers.

2. Design a mirroring solution using two 36GB drives and one 80GB drive. Using the same drives, create two mirrors. Why would you want to do this? Why wouldn't you?

3. Design a ten-port disk mirroring subsystem with five 100GB disk drives and an embedded volume manager that exports virtual disk drives with a maximum of 50GB each.

4. Design a 300GB disk mirroring solution for a high-traffic Web site. Assume you have disk drives available in 9GB, 36GB, and 72GB capacities. Pick where you want the mirroring operator to be and how many host I/O controllers you want to use.

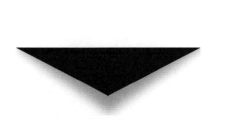

CHAPTER 5

Boosting Performance Through Caching

Increasing system performance is an ongoing goal of most IT organizations. As the amount of data to process increases and becomes more diverse, the available time to run specific tasks tends to get shorter. Either better processing algorithms need to be developed or faster systems need to be deployed. As the development of new algorithms may not be attainable, particularly for off-the-shelf software, the only realistic solution for improved performance is to deploy faster systems and components.

One of the standard techniques for improving I/O component performance is to improve the performance of storage I/O operations through the use of caching. This chapter looks at caching technology, particularly *disk caching*. While disk caching is often associated with RAID disk subsystems, it is independent of RAID and has very little to do with the striping and redundancy technology that are the hallmarks of RAID. Disk caching can also have important implications for data integrity that need to be understood.

Also in this chapter, we'll explore other performance-boosting technologies and techniques such as solid state disks and tagged command queuing.

CACHING BASICS

Caching is a fundamental technique used in most computer systems. The idea of caching is simple: copy data from a location where access is slow to an alternative location where it is faster. In most systems of any complexity, there are usually devices or components that have significantly different performance capabilities. Caching improves performance by shifting data from a slow device to a faster one, as illustrated here:

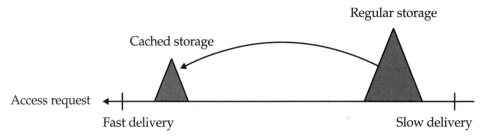

Disk caching stores data in relatively fast memory that would otherwise be accessed on relatively slow disk drives. Disk caching is either a *storing* technology working on blocks of data or a *filing* technology working with files, depending on the implementation, but in both cases it is independent of the *wiring* technology deployed.

The memory used for disk caching is usually *volatile* memory, which means it loses the contents of the data if power is removed. In this sense, the cache memory is temporary storage and the disk devices and subsystems being served by the cache are *nonvolatile*, or permanent, storage. The relationship between volatile (memory) and nonvolatile storage are illustrated here:

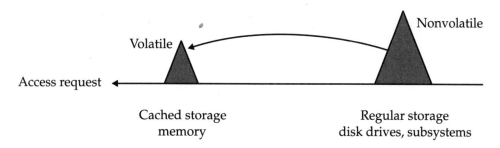

Disk caches can be thought of as distinct devices or memory locations that store data temporarily. Usually some small amount of data from a disk drive or subsystem is kept in the cache. In addition, the data in the cache changes over time. Therefore, caches need to be searched in order to determine if the data being requested or written can use the cache. Searching a cache adds additional overhead to the I/O process, so it is important that the cache be significantly faster than the nonvolatile storage where data is permanently stored in order for the cache to provide improved performance.

Cache Hits and Cache Misses

When the cache is searched and the data requested is found, a *cache hit* occurs. Besides providing fast response from memory components, cache hits can also shorten the I/O path, like this:

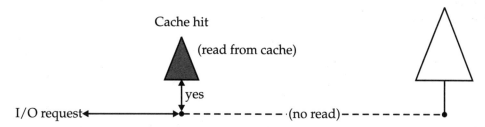

It follows that a *cache miss* is an operation where the cache is searched but does not contain the data requested. In that case, it must be read from nonvolatile storage. Cache misses add time to the I/O operation due to the time it takes to search the cache. A cache miss can be depicted like this:

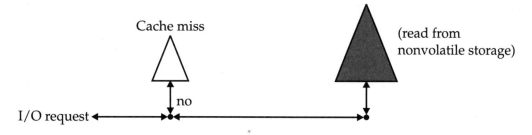

A poorly implemented cache with a high percentage of cache misses will actually degrade performance due to the additional overhead required to search the cache for each I/O operation.

The term used to describe the relative accuracy of the cache is called the *cache hit ratio*. The cache hit ratio is determined by dividing the number of cache hits by the total number of I/O reads. Cache hit ratios depend on many variables, including the data access characteristics of the application and the relative size of the cache compared to the non-volatile storage it works with. In general, open systems servers, such as Unix, NT, and NetWare systems, are usually not able to achieve hit ratios in excess of 50 percent. Mainframe systems can achieve much higher hit ratios (90 percent) due to the differences in the methods used for accessing data in mainframes. The cache hit ratio is calculated as:

$$\frac{\text{I/O Requests fulfilled by Cache}}{\text{Total number of I/O Requests}} = \text{Cache hit ratio}$$

Caching Theme and Variation

As is the case for many I/O operations, caching can be implemented in many different ways at many different points along the I/O path. This section looks at the general operations of disk caches in terms of their locations along the I/O path.

The Difference Between Caches and Buffers

Sometimes the words "cache," "memory," and "buffer" are used interchangeably. However, memory in a disk drive is usually not a cache, but a buffer. While the physical memory components may be the same, buffer memory temporarily stores data that is being transferred from one location or device to another. Buffer memory is under the control of a short-lived process that releases the memory location when the data is done being transferred. Another difference between cache memory and buffer memory is that buffer memory cannot be shared by multiple applications. In contrast, a disk cache can support many different applications at the same time.

A common type of buffer is called a FIFO buffer, for first in, first out, as shown in the diagram that follows:

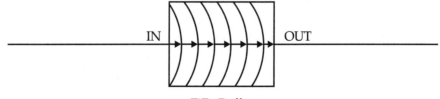

FiFo Buffer

Cache memory is controlled by one or more algorithms that maintain and manage the contents of the cache. Whereas buffer memory typically fills and empties rapidly, data can remain in a cache for an extended period of time, depending on the algorithms used and the access characteristics of the applications being used.

Buffers are useful for matching the data transfer speeds of controllers and devices with dissimilar performance capabilities. In this way, buffers can be thought of as transformers of sorts. The chips in a host I/O controller are capable of transferring data very quickly over the I/O channel. Their performance can be measured in terms of nanoseconds. Electromechanical storage devices, such as disks and tape drives, transfer data in the range of milliseconds. Therefore, device manufacturers place buffer memory in their devices to eliminate access latency and match the performance of the host I/O controller. This is the enabling technology for overlapped I/O operations, as shown in the drawing that follows:

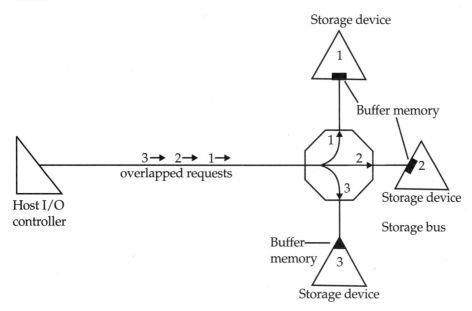

Caching in System Memory

Caching is typically implemented in host systems as part of the operating system. In these cases, the cache is *filing*-based because it operates on files or database objects. This type of cache can be extremely effective because the file system has the intelligence to effectively predict what data might be requested in future operations and load it into cache memory. The cache hit ratio of filing-based caching can be 90 percent or higher, depending on the data access characteristics of the application. This is truly an optimal range for cache hit ratios, especially when compared to storing-based caching.

The amount of memory available for disk caching in the host depends on the application mix and the memory required to run other processes. For the most part, systems allocate whatever memory is not being used to disk caching. The memory used for disk caching is often referred to as "cache buffers"; as discussed previously, however, this memory is used as a cache, not a buffer. Host system caches are extremely fast, as I/O requests can be satisfied over the system memory bus within nanoseconds.

NOTE: Configuring servers with lots of memory is usually a good idea because whatever memory is not being used for application processing will be used to accelerate system performance through disk caching.

The amount of host system cache available can change as the workload changes in a server. As new applications are started, it may be necessary to deallocate some of the memory used for caching to make room for the new applications. When this happens, the data in cache is first flushed to nonvolatile slow disk storage before the memory is assigned by the kernel for use by the applications. The sudden loss of cache memory can have an immediate performance impact on other applications that have been working with cached data and now must access their data from slow disk drives. Conversely, as applications complete, their memory can be allocated again to the cache memory pool. However, this does not result in an immediate performance boost, as the cache memory has to be filled with data before it can speed up I/O processing.

The host software that provides the cache is a low-level filing component that runs as one of the file system/kernel services and above the volume manager level in the I/O path. Using the I/O stack as a yardstick, host caching operates at the data structure level, where it has detailed knowledge of the logical block addresses where data is stored. The presence or lack of host software caching does not effect the representation of data to the end user or application.

The approximate location of host system disk caching on the I/O path is shown next:

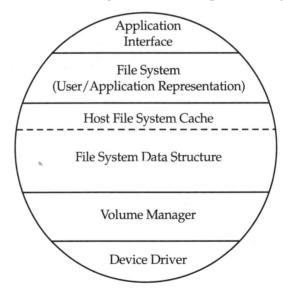

Host system caching is typically implemented as a tightly integrated component of the operating system kernel and the file system. There are usually no external programming interfaces available for applications to manipulate host system disk caching, and the management tools for managing the cache are vendor/system specific. Host system caching is a software "black box" that works as an internal part of the system with somewhat mysterious and unpredictable behavior. This is not to imply that host system caching is bad by any means, but it may not be possible to sustain performance levels over time as the processing load changes on the system.

Caching in a Solid State Disk

A specialized technology for disk caching is *solid state disk*, or SSD, technology. SSDs also use relatively fast memory for storing data, but instead of using system memory, the memory is installed in an external subsystem, which, through the art of device virtualization, is substituted for a slow, electromechanical disk drive.

SSDs address the unpredictability of host system caching by providing a consistent "memory environment." As a virtual device, the operating system kernel cannot allocate, deallocate, and reallocate SSD memory as it sees fit. Instead, SSD memory is managed as a distinct storage resource that can be predictably controlled by system administrators.

SSDs operate as target devices on the I/O path. They are *storing* devices that do not have any inherent filing capabilities. In other words, they operate like a disk drive that receives storage I/O commands from a file system or database, including the placement of data in logical block addresses. Therefore, SSD caching is at the opposite end of the I/O path from host system caching, as shown in Figure 5-1.

Looking at Figure 5-1, I/O operations with an SSD are transmitted over the system memory bus, through the system I/O bus, and out over a storage bus or channel. This is a much longer path with much more latency than caching with memory in the system memory bus. There are several orders of magnitude difference in the response time of system memory and SSDs.

Caching Without Cache Logic   SSDs work under the control of a host file system. Just as the file system allocates and manages free space and the layout of logical blocks on disk drives, it does the same for an SSD. Therefore, there is no inherent logic in the SSD that analyzes I/O traffic to determine what to place in a cache and what to remove from the cache. All the data in an SSD is considered as cached, and all I/O operations to an SSD are fulfilled in the same time frame, irrespective of the logical block address being accessed.

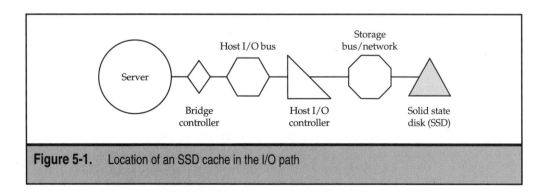

Figure 5-1.   Location of an SSD cache in the I/O path

To use an SSD cache, the data for an application is placed on the SSD through the services of the file system that controls it. This is typically done by copying the data from some other storage device to the SSD with a common copy command. The I/O path for this operation is shown next to illustrate the role of two file systems in this process: one for the disk storage and the other for the SSD.

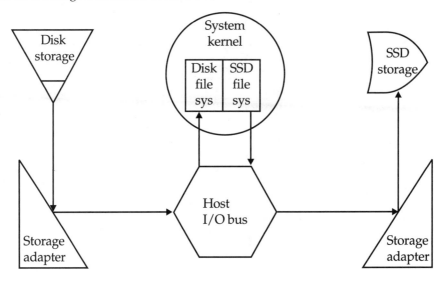

No action is taken by the SSD to accelerate I/O performance; it simply operates as an extremely fast disk drive. Furthermore, all I/O requests to use the SSD's memory are directed by the host file system or database. No block-based caching intelligence is at work with an SSD. For that reason, the SSD's *cache,* which does not use any caching logic whatsoever, operates at a filing level, even though the SSD itself is a storing-level device. It's a little strange, to be sure, but that's the way it is.

After the data has been copied to the SSD, applications that use it need to have device identifiers changed to reflect the new storage location on the SSD. It is important that all such identifiers be changed so that the application does not operate on two different sets of data, which would result in bad and/or corrupt data files, not to mention extremely vexing troubleshooting experiences.

Caching in Host Adapters and Storage Subsystems

Caching is sometimes implemented as a *caching controller* in a host I/O adapter or in a disk subsystem. Caching controllers use memory modules that are built to fit the unique layout, power, and capacity requirements of the storage subsystem or I/O adapter. Like SSDs, this memory is not part of the kernel's resources, but dedicated to providing cache performance benefits. As this memory is outside the system's host I/O bus as well as the system memory bus, its performance is necessarily slower than system memory, even if the memory-component response time is faster or equivalent to the memory used by the system.

This type of disk caching is a *storing* technology that supplies its own intelligence for operating on and analyzing block-level I/O activity. The cache operates by predicting the future blocks that may be requested by the applications that use the adapter or subsystem for storage I/O. As such, caching controllers examine each and every I/O request, adding overhead to the I/O process. As a storing application, the cache is independent of filing intelligence in a file system or database, which means the cache cannot be assigned to specific applications. If the cache hit ratio is too low, the cache can actually degrade performance instead of improving it.

Figure 5-2 shows the relative positions of caching controllers and memory located in a host I/O adapter and disk subsystem. Notice how in both cases the cache controller is in the I/O path, but the cache memory is not. Instead, the cache is accessed through a separate and independent memory bus.

Caching controllers are commonly used for database applications where the file sizes far exceed the maximum memory configuration of a system and where performance stability is required.

Performance Expectations of External Disk Caching   The performance benefits attained from adapter and subsystem caching vary a great deal depending on several variables. Vendors selling caching products may reference customers who experienced performance acceleration of 50 percent or more. Remember to heed the standard disclaimer language about "actual results may vary…" when trying to determine the benefits of a caching controller.

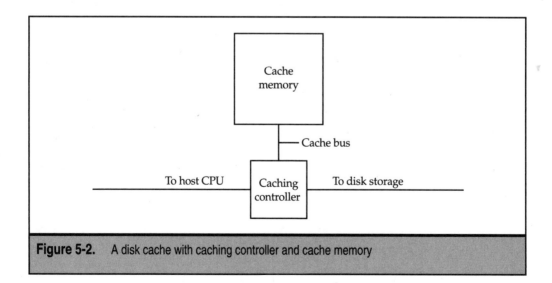

Figure 5-2.   A disk cache with caching controller and cache memory

READING AND WRITING AND (ALGO) 'RITHMETIC'

Disk caching includes both read *and* write I/O operations. All cache implementations should consider both aspects and strike a balance between the two to ensure optimal performance and data integrity.

Implementing a cache is not like pouring a bottle of octane booster in the gas tank to get additional power from an engine. Disk caching uses four basic algorithms, two for reading and two for writing. To receive the most benefit from a cache, the algorithms used should match the data access patterns of the application. The better the match, the greater the performance gain can be.

The following sections describe the fundamental caching algorithms. The descriptions offered here are not based on any specific product's cache design, but are included to help the reader understand caching algorithms and functions.

Cache Reading Algorithms

As discussed, the basic idea of a cache is to intelligently predict what data may be needed next by the system and to place this data in a faster device or location on the I/O path. There are two basic algorithms used when reading data, depending on the type of application:

▼ Recently used

▲ Read ahead

Recently Used Cache

The algorithm for recently used caching is sometimes referred to as a *least recently used*, or *LRU*, algorithm. However, the LRU algorithm was developed for virtual memory technology, not caching, and is used to transfer less active data out of memory to virtual storage on disk. An LRU algorithm selects data to discard, rather than keep or place in higher-speed locations. In that sense, the "L" part is contrary to the concept of a cache.

Where caching is concerned, the inverse of an LRU process is used. Therefore, referring to caching algorithms as *recently used* is more appropriate. The recently used cache algorithm is based on the notion that recently read data tends to be read again shortly thereafter. Applications often develop data access patterns where certain block ranges of data are used much more frequently than others. These high-traffic block ranges are called *hot spots*. When hot spot data is placed in a cache, the access to it can be much faster than if it is on a disk drive. The illustration that follows shows two hot spots that have been copied into a caching controller's memory:

Hot spots copied into fast cache memory

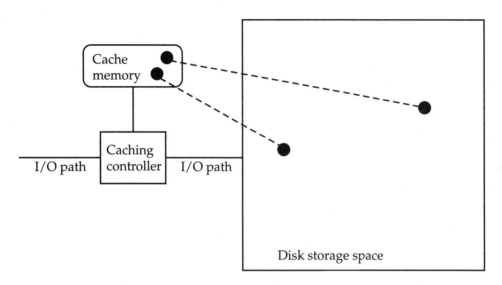

The recently used cache copies data into cache memory as it is requested during normal I/O operations. To do this, the cache controller needs to be able to interpret all I/O requests, extract the data for the cache, put the data in cache, and complete the I/O operation as if the cache never existed.

The process for loading data in a recently used cache is shown in this diagram:

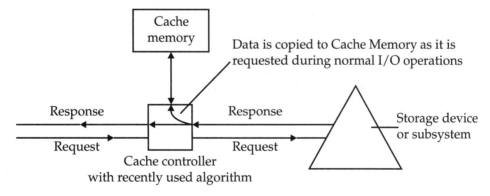

The cache is filled in this manner until it is full. Data that is placed in the cache remains there until it is replaced by some other, more recently used data. Eventually the cache's appetite exceeds its capacity and there is more data to put in the cache than it can hold. At that point the fickle cache employs a less recently used algorithm to determine what data to remove in order to accommodate the new data. In other words, the recently used cache keeps access records for the data it stores to determine what data gets in and what gets thrown out.

Applications for Recently Used Caching   Recently used caches provide the greatest benefit to applications where hot zone data is apparent and heavily accessed in rapid succession. Database applications, particularly the indices used for finding and linking data, often develop hot zones. Transaction processing applications usually perform a series of I/O operations on certain records in quick succession and can attain higher performance if the record's data is loaded in cache. Figure 5-3 shows the data flows for accessing and storing data in a recently used cache.

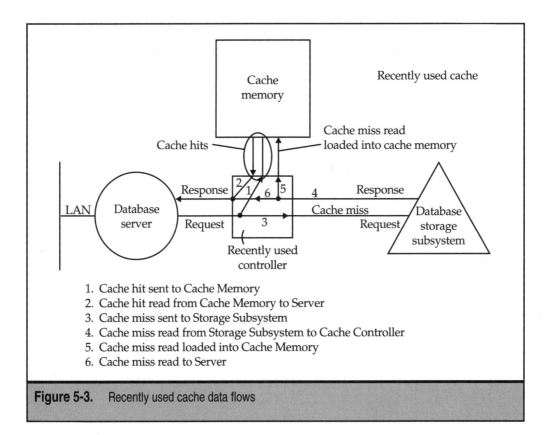

1. Cache hit sent to Cache Memory
2. Cache hit read from Cache Memory to Server
3. Cache miss sent to Storage Subsystem
4. Cache miss read from Storage Subsystem to Cache Controller
5. Cache miss read loaded into Cache Memory
6. Cache miss read to Server

Figure 5-3.   Recently used cache data flows

Here is a short list of application types that could benefit from recently used caching:

▼ Transaction systems

■ ERP and MRP systems

■ Internet e-commerce servers

■ Customer service and support

▲ Other multiuser database applications

Read-Ahead Cache

Applications that access data sequentially are poor targets for recently used caching. Instead, *read-ahead* caching is used to accelerate the performance of these applications.

A read-ahead cache is based on the notion that data is accessed sequentially and that data recently accessed will not be needed again. So, the read-ahead cache attempts to calculate the next several "chunks" of data that will be needed in the sequence. In other words, the read-ahead cache guesses what will be needed next from what was just retrieved from disk.

Central to the concept of read-ahead caching is prefetching. *Prefetching* is copying data from slow, nonvolatile storage and placing it in fast cache memory before it is requested. This differs significantly from recently used caching, which only caches data that was already requested or written. The prefetching process can be pictured like this:

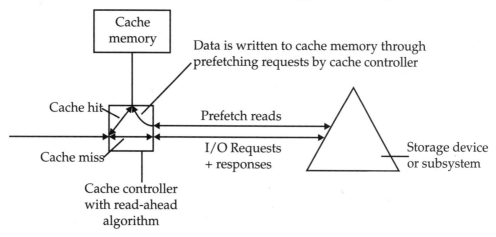

Data is quickly discarded from a read-ahead cache under the assumption that it will not be updated in the near future. The purpose of the read-ahead cache is to move mass quantities of data closer to the CPU for processing. In these types of applications, the total amount of the data is often read, but the majority of the data is unchanged by the process. Hence, there is little need to retain aged data in the cache.

Read-ahead caching is most effective when implemented as a filing technique in host file system software working at the data structure level (see Chapter 2 for a discussion of the data structure level in the I/O stack). As most file systems today control the layout of logical blocks in storage, they have the ability to request logical blocks in advance of their access. This can result in a greater than 99 percent cache hit ratio if the application processes all data in sequence and if that data can be retrieved faster than the application requests it.

Conversely, read-ahead caching is very difficult to implement in caching controllers as a storing technology working at the block level. Caching controllers typically have no visibility to the file system's layout on disk. Considering that data tends to be spread all over the disk surface and that sustained I/O read operations will move the disk arms many times, a read-ahead cache that reads contiguous blocks of data from disk tracks often winds up reading ahead into data that is not needed. More important, these caches have no good way to determine what logical blocks will be requested next. It's somewhat analogous to going to a supermarket to buy hot dogs and yogurt by filling your cart with all the meat and dairy products in the aisle and then discarding them at the checkout counter in order to pay for only the wieners and yogurt that you crave.

Read-ahead caching in caching controllers can benefit a great deal from operations like disk defragmentation that try to store data in fewer and larger contiguous block ranges. Specialized file systems, such as SGI's XFS, that use larger logical storage blocks can make a big difference. Conversely, the more fragmented a volume is, the more difficult it is to succeed with a caching controller using a read-ahead algorithm.

Applications for Read-Ahead Caching   In general, wherever large files are sequentially accessed, there is a need for read-ahead caching. Applications in certain industries, such as the film, video, medical imaging, and graphics production industries, can benefit a great deal from read-ahead caching. A short listing of applications that could benefit from read-ahead caching follows:

▼   File serving

■   Multimedia: audio and video

■   Graphics

▲   Data warehousing

Cache Writing Algorithms

The caching technology for writing data is considerably different than that for reading. Write I/O operations can be written to fast cache memory instead of being written all the way through the I/O path to storage. This can save a great deal of time in a busy system that would otherwise have to wait for storage to acknowledge the completion of the operation before processing more I/O operations.

While the goal of caching is to boost performance, it is not an acceptable solution if the risk of losing data is too great. Therefore, it is essential to get the data written to cache memory into safe, nonvolatile storage. Depending on the write caching algorithm used, the performance-boosting characteristics of disk caching can create a risk for the safe storage of new data that is created or updated.

Write Caching and Data Integrity

The core of the write cache data integrity issue is determining where newly written or updated data is stored—in cache or on disk—and how multiple versions of data can exist in the cache and on disk. At some point, all new or updated data in cache needs to be committed to nonvolatile storage on disk. It is essential to realize that data written to cache is not always written to disk immediately, depending on the write cache algorithm used. Data that is assumed to be on disk but that never actually gets written there will cause data files to become corrupt, or worse, inaccurate. A corrupt file can typically be found out by the application, but an inaccurate file may continue to be used, including all the old, stale data, until another process (or irate person) discovers the error.

Like human memory, memory used for disk caching is volatile (it is also selective, but that's another matter entirely). When power is removed, the cache memory loses its data. Special-purpose power and memory subsystems for disk caching are sometimes used that supply battery backup power to memory for some specified period of time. But power is not the only threat to data integrity in a cache. Other system failures and disasters that can cause a system to crash or otherwise prevent the cache from writing to disk can also result in corrupt or inaccurate data.

Stale Data   Closely related to data integrity concerns is the topic of *stale data*. Stale data is data that is older than some recently updated version of the data. For most of the discussions in this chapter, stale data is data on nonvolatile disk storage that is older than new updated data written into the cache.

Consider a scenario where an application is reading and writing its data to an SSD cache. Assume new updates are placed on the SSD and will not be transferred to a nonvolatile disk subsystem for a few hours when the application completes. Also assume that another application runs asynchronously at a later time and uses some of the data created by the first application, but that instead of using the SSD, it accesses the data from the nonvolatile storage subsystem.

Now, imagine that something goes wrong that prevents the data on the SSD from being transferred to the disk subsystem. When the second application accesses the data from the disk subsystem, it will be accessing stale data that does not reflect the most recent update of the data. Therefore, the results of the second application, and of all other dependent processes, will be incorrect. This problem could go unnoticed and become a major headache for the IT staff. Figure 5-4 illustrates this scenario.

Write Cache Redux

The case just described where fresh data on an SSD does not get transferred to a disk subsystem can be avoided in a number of ways by configuring the application access differently, but it serves to illustrate how stale data needs to be considered by a caching implementation.

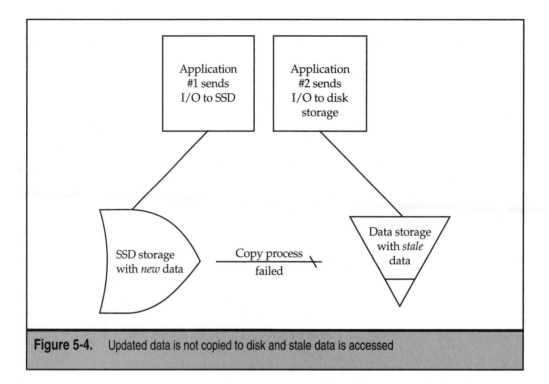

Figure 5-4. Updated data is not copied to disk and stale data is accessed

When data is created or updated by a system using a cache, the data is transferred along the I/O path toward storage. If a host-based software cache or a caching controller is in use, a decision has to be made whether or not to place this new data in the cache or not and whether or not the data should be written immediately to nonvolatile disk storage. Writing data to nonvolatile storage is relatively slow and could degrade the system's performance as it waits for writes to be acknowledged. On the other hand, if data is written to the cache and the eventual write to nonvolatile storage is postponed, it is possible that the data could be lost in a system disaster.

Basically, two approaches are used to manage write I/O operations with disk caches:

▼ Write-through cache

▲ Write-back cache

Write-Through Cache   The write-through cache writes through, or past, the cache directly to nonvolatile storage. It is the most conservative implementation of a write cache, as it basically does not trust the cache to complete the write later. Should the system stop functioning for any reason, the file system or database system that requested the write will have all its data on disk where it can access it and resume normal operations. The write-through cache can mirror its data to the cache or not. However, if the write is a newer version of data that was loaded from cache, the write-through cache must either update the information in cache or delete it from the cache.

This raises an important point about write caches: they must be able to update all instances of the data, including any stale copies of the data. In some cases, it may be simpler to discard stale data than to update it. Figure 5-5 shows a write-through cache that writes or updates new data on nonvolatile disk storage.

Write-Back Cache   The write-back cache, also called a write-behind cache, is optimized for performance. The basic idea of the write-back cache is to provide faster response to the application and to aggregate several I/O operations and write them to nonvolatile storage all at once, as opposed to writing each one as it occurs. Grouping write operations together provides performance benefits on both sides of the cache. The host that generates the write operation receives an acknowledgment faster than it would from a write-through cache, and the aggregated write operations to devices take less total time than they would if they were executed asynchronously. Tagged command queuing, discussed later in this chapter, can be used to combine several writes as a single chain of write I/O operations. Figure 5-6 illustrates a write-back cache grouping several I/Os together before transferring the data to nonvolatile storage.

For database environments where the I/O rate is in the thousands of I/Os per second, the write-back cache can provide significant performance improvements. Not only are the acknowledgments for each I/O operation received faster, but writes that update hot spots can do so without having to write to nonvolatile storage every time. That way, multiple updates to the same block can be reduced to a single physical disk write I/O operation. This process of emptying the cache is called *flushing* the cache.

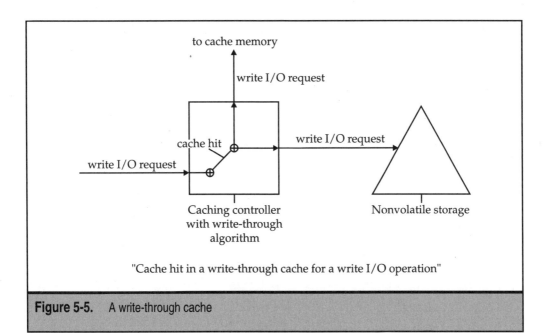

"Cache hit in a write-through cache for a write I/O operation"

Figure 5-5.   A write-through cache

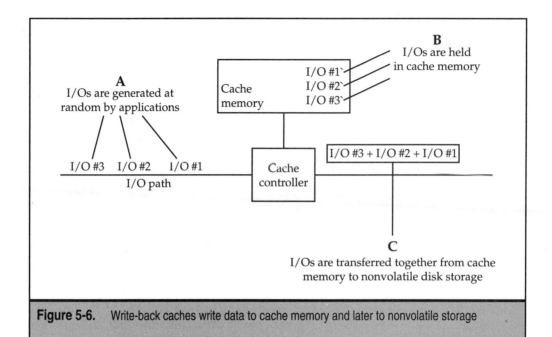

A
I/Os are generated at random by applications

Cache memory

I/O #1`
I/O #2`
I/O #3`

B
I/Os are held in cache memory

I/O #3   I/O #2   I/O #1
I/O path

Cache controller

I/O #3 + I/O #2 + I/O #1

C
I/Os are transferred together from cache memory to nonvolatile disk storage

Figure 5-6.   Write-back caches write data to cache memory and later to nonvolatile storage

As mentioned, the serious problem with write-back caching is the potential for losing data should some disaster strike while data is in cache memory before it has been flushed to disk. There is nothing inherent in the general write-back algorithm to compensate for such an occurrence. Therefore write-back cache implementations incorporate their own technology solutions and configuration options to provide data integrity safeguards. Usually this includes some type of auxiliary battery-based power that will keep the cache and subsystem active long enough to flush the cache to nonvolatile storage.

Of course, if a write-back cache receives an update for data that is stored in cache memory, it must either update the data in cache or discard it to prevent it from becoming stale and accessed again incorrectly.

CAUTION: Write-back caches should never be used without an integrated UPS (uninterruptible power supply) that is rated for the power requirements of the system or subsystem containing the cache and that can force the cache controller to flush the cache and stop accepting new write requests.

Disk Cache Mechanics

Disk caches use a fundamental set of processes that can be implemented in a large variety of ways. As "black box" technology, disk caches are largely determined by the designers and provide varying amounts of end user configuration and control. The following is a list of the basic functions most disk caches use:

▼ Cache storage device(s), usually memory

■ Index for locating cached data

- ■ Data loader
- ■ Activity indicator/discard processor
- ■ "Dirty" block indicator (for write-back caches)
- ▲ Write-back processor

We'll now look at each of them briefly.

Cache Devices

Disk caches store data in fast memory devices. This is true whether the cache is host soft-ware–based, an SSD, or a caching controller. The choice of memory technology imple-mented is normally a design decision of the device, subsystem, or system manufacturer. In general, disk cache memory is expensive compared to disk storage.

Index for Locating Cached Data

Data stored in a disk cache has to be retrieved quickly. With the exception of SSD caches, the cache memory storage needs to be searched to determine if data is in the cache. Although memory access is relatively fast, long searches through cache memory take real time and can have a negative impact on system performance if they do not yield positive results.

Therefore, the cache uses an index of some sort to determine what data is stored in the cache. Basically, two kinds of indexing are used: *direct mapping* and *associative indexing*. Direct mapping creates a bitmap of logical block addresses in fast cache memory that rep-resents every nonvolatile disk storage block address. When the cache receives an I/O op-eration, it quickly searches this index to see if the data is stored in it. The drawing that follows illustrates a cache bitmap that directly maps the storage locations on a disk sub-system to bits in the cache index:

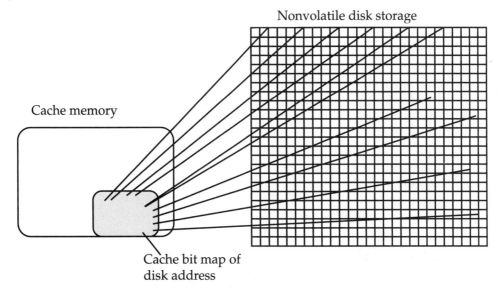

Nonvolatile disk storage

Cache memory

Cache bit map of
disk address

Associative caches are slightly more complicated; they work by representing aggregated storage addresses together by a single bit in the index. A search of the index may indicate the possibility that a particular data location is stored in cache memory. The associative cache then makes a second memory search through the actual cached data to determine if the data requested is there. Of the two, direct-mapped caches are faster but require a bit to represent each storage address on nonvolatile storage. At some point, the amount of data required for this one-to-one bit mapping becomes a problem. Associative caches are slower but require fewer resources to create the index.

Data Loader

Cache memory has to be filled somehow; otherwise, the cache can't do its job. This happens either during the course of normal I/O operations with a recently used cache or as a separate process with a read-ahead cache. The data loader for the cache may also be invoked when copying data to cache as part of a write operation.

Activity Indicator/Discard Processor

An activity indicator is needed to help determine what to discard as the cache fills. In essence, the data loader is constantly trying to load new data into the cache. This means there must be some way to get rid of data that is already there. For this to happen, there needs to be some metric or way to prioritize the data to discard. In conjunction with the activity indicator, a discard processor is needed to ensure that aged data is removed properly.

"Dirty" Block Indicator (for Write-Back Caches)

Write-back caches containing data not yet written to nonvolatile storage need to indicate data that is "dirty" and must be copied to nonvolatile disk storage. This is typically done by marking a dirty bit, which can be part of the cache's index and is similar to a backup bit in a file system that signifies new data that needs to be preserved.

Write-Back Processor

The write-back processor runs periodically as a process of a write-back cache to ensure successful commitment of all dirty data to nonvolatile storage, including writes made after loss of power when the system or subsystem is being powered by emergency UPS batteries.

Caching Comparisons

A disk cache can reside in a few different locations along the I/O path. In the sections that follow, we'll analyze some of the relative strengths and weaknesses of different disk caching alternatives. The options we will consider are:

▼   Host system software and memory

■   Device or subsystem caching controller

▲   Host I/O caching controller

Host System Caches   As mentioned previously, installing excess memory capacity in a system allows memory to be allocated for disk caching. From a physical/device perspective, the system memory used for the cache is located on the system memory bus and managed by a CPU-based cache process as shown:

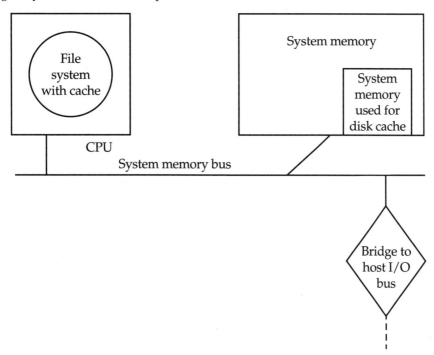

Placing data in a cache in system memory allows it to be accessed extremely fast over the system memory bus. There is virtually no faster access on the system except for the memory cache and the CPU.

However, the system CPU *is* the cache controller and requires system resources to do its work. This adds some level of overhead to the system, including the necessary resources for implementing it, such as the cache index. As the system starts running more applications, some of the memory used for disk caching may need to be returned to the kernel for use by an application. If so, obviously the cache process must remove any related information in the cache's index to prevent "unexpected system behavior," otherwise known as system crashes.

Therefore, host software caching is not recommended for systems that are processor bound. The definition of "processor bound" is somewhat relative, depending on several variables. The general idea is that if the system is already thrashing under too many applications, it is possible that the cache might not have enough memory or available processor cycles to operate as expected.

Host-based write-through caches can be very effective. The performance benefits are not as great as with a write-back cache, but the data integrity risks of write-back caches (as will be discussed) are avoided.

Host-based write-back caches can be incredibly fast because writes to the cache and the subsequent acknowledgment of the I/O request are practically instantaneous. For high-throughput I/O environments such as transaction processing systems, a write-back cache in system memory should provide the fastest overall performance. Care must be taken to ensure that adequate UPS protection is being used with all components in the I/O path so that dirty data in the cache can be written to nonvolatile storage following a loss of power.

> **NOTE:** Random access and transaction applications can benefit most from disk cache implementations in host systems. The optimal performance combination for these applications is likely to be a recently used cache combined with a write-back cache.

Caching in Disk Subsystems

Another common location to implement a disk cache is in a disk subsystem. Just as with host systems, it is possible to install additional memory in storage subsystems. Caching in the storage device or subsystem means the host system's CPU is relatively unaffected by cache operations. Caching logic in a disk subsystem is executed in a caching controller and executes quickly without interruptions from other system tasks, such as application and systems software, that compete for CPU cycles on host processors.

However, placing the disk cache in a device/subsystem means all I/O operations to the cache are likely to be slower than in the case of host-based caching, as each I/O request travels over the complete I/O path from the CPU to the device/subsystem, as shown here:

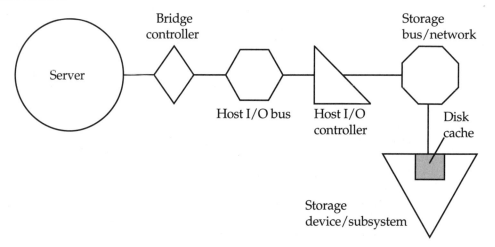

Caching at the storage subsystem may require twice as much cache memory if mirrored subsystems are used. For example, consider an implementation of mirrored storage subsystems where each subsystem has its own cache memory installed. If each subsystem has the same amount of cache memory, then twice as much cache memory must be purchased.

Write-through caches in storage subsystems make a certain amount of sense; after the data has traveled all the way across the I/O path, why not just write it to disk? The reason "why not" is to try to achieve higher I/O rates for a database or transaction system. But if you do not need the I/O productivity and are caching data for a file server or another kind of sequentially accessed application where write operations are minimized, a write-through cache will work well.

Among the most demanding applications in terms of CPU utilization are database and transaction processing applications. As these applications take a great deal of CPU power, which may heavily load the system, it is certainly not a mistake to implement the cache in the storage subsystem. For starters, database and transaction caching might require more memory than the system can accommodate.

NOTE: When using a write-back cache in a storage subsystem to achieve high-performance transaction processing (over 7,500 I/Os per second), try to remove all unnecessary hardware and software components that vie for resources on the I/O path.

Disk Caching with a Host I/O Caching Controllers

Historically, there has probably been more research and development on implementing caching in host I/O controllers than on all other types of implementations combined. This comes from the work of major system and subsystems companies such as DEC, IBM, HP, and STK, who over the years developed tightly coupled host I/O controllers that were linked to both the host OS and the subsystem's implementations.

The caching algorithms for host I/O controllers can be implemented in one of two ways: in a device driver that runs in the host, or with firmware and hardware residing on the circuit board of the I/O controller. Host I/O caching controllers locate the cache function on the host system I/O bus, as opposed to the storage I/O channel. This effectively shortens the I/O path and can provide better I/O response than a caching controller in a disk subsystem.

However, caches on host I/O controllers are somewhat limited in the amount of memory they can accommodate. If several gigabytes of memory are needed for the cache, it is unlikely that a host I/O controller will be able to do the job. Like disk subsystem–based caches, mirrored configurations that use dual-host I/O controllers require twice the amount of cache memory.

Host I/O caching controllers can also implement write-back caching. Like a host memory write-back cache, it needs to be protected by a system UPS that can keep the cache data "alive" while the accumulated data in cache is flushed to nonvolatile disk storage.

Configuring Cache Memory

There are no good, simple ways of determining how much cache memory is needed for a given system and its applications. While one would be tempted to base the figure on the total amount of storage in a subsystem, there are too many variables, such as the amount of inactive data stored. But you need someplace to start when first planning a cache implementation. After the initial installation of the disk cache, you may want to make adjustments in the amount of memory and the algorithm being used.

One reasonable estimate is to plan to have cache memory equal to 0.1 percent of the total storage capacity of the disk subsystems being cached. In other words, if there is 50GB of storage, plan on 50MB of cache memory. For 1TB of storage, use 1GB of cache. While this amount is likely to change (upward), you should be able to tell if the cache algorithm employed is working.

A more sophisticated approach to determine the amount of cache memory needed is to measure the amount of data being used by the applications that you intend to use the cache for. Calculate the required cache memory as 0.5 percent to 1 percent of this total. For instance, if you have a database application with 200GB of storage, you may want to start out by implementing 1GB to 2GB of cache memory.

Multilevel Caches

It is possible to use cache in multiple locations along the path, such as in the host and in a caching controller. Figure 5-7 shows such a configuration.

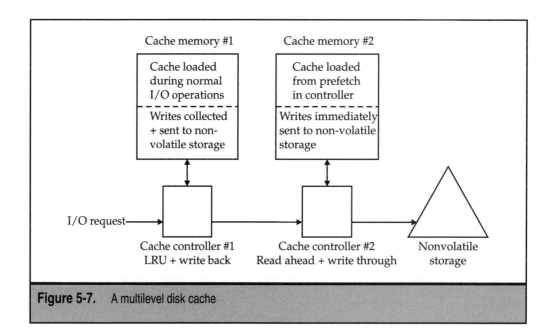

Figure 5-7.   A multilevel disk cache

Multilevel caching may provide benefits by using different types of configurations for different applications. The key to a successful multilevel cache implementation is to understand how writes work and how they are transferred back to nonvolatile storage. The assumption made here is that the multilevel cache runs along the I/O path for a single system that does not allow any applications to bypass any of the caches in accessing data. If a cache in the path could be bypassed by an application, the risk of accessing stale data would be fairly high and a real data disaster could occur that might not be able to be solved.

With that in mind, as usual, it is important to always use UPS or power protection for all caching components in the path. Using only write-through caches reduces the confusion about where the most recent version of data is, but if high transaction processing performance is needed, the caching component closest to the CPU can use a write-back scheme with all other caching components using write-through caching.

TAGGED COMMAND QUEUING

Another performance-enhancing technique is called *tagged command queuing.* In a nutshell, tagged command queuing allows a device to accept multiple commands from a host I/O controller and organize them for the most efficient operations on the disk drive. The host I/O controller and the device keep track of the I/O requests through the use of numbered tags. The overall process of sending a sequence of commands is depicted in this image:

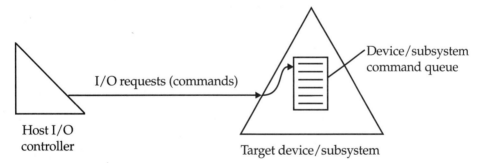

Using Intelligent Processors in Disk Drives

At the core of tagged command queuing is the notion that disk drives can have intelligent microprocessors that can significantly improve the performance of a device. This will be explored more in the next chapter, when XOR disks are discussed. Tagged command queuing is implemented in both host I/O controllers and devices as a way to keep track of commands needed for servicing from the device. The device uses onboard memory and intelligence to manage a queue of commands that the host I/O controller sends it. While the host I/O controller sets the relative priority for each command, a processor in the device optimizes the execution of those commands according to several variables regarding local conditions on the disk drive.

A simple example of tagged command queuing is a sequence of disk reads. By using tagged command queuing, the host I/O controller can send a number of read requests while the disk drive responds to a previous I/O request. The disk drive's command processor sorts these new requests in order to minimize the amount of movement that the disk arm needs to make. Figure 5-8 shows a queue of inbound requests that have been sorted to minimize the amount of jumping around the disk arm must do to satisfy the requests. While certain individual requests may be delayed, the overall throughput of the disk drive can be much improved.

Effectiveness of Tagged Command Queuing

Tagged command queuing can be expected to contribute performance gains as high as 100 percent. In general, tagged command queuing is more effective working with randomly generated I/O traffic, similar to traffic generated by database applications and loaded into LRU disk caches. A queue depth of eight pending commands has been shown to be optimal.

Tagged command queuing can also work with sequentially accessed data, similar to read-ahead caching, but the number of commands in the queue should be less than half of the number for random I/Os. By virtue of sequential access, an implied sorting of commands is already taking place. Therefore, random reads would benefit the most from sorting performed by the disk drive's processor.

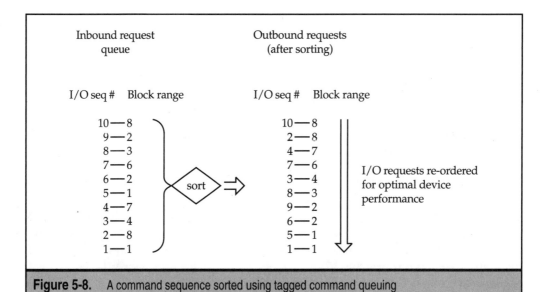

Figure 5-8. A command sequence sorted using tagged command queuing

IMPORTANCE OF THE I/O PATH IN SYSTEM PERFORMANCE

System performance analysis is an extremely complex topic that encompasses all components in a system. Among the most important components are those belonging to the category of storage I/O technology. The discussion that follows takes a "big picture" view of the impact of storage I/O on system performance.

Balancing Processor and I/O Performance

Experts in the field of system architecture and performance analysis agree that balancing the performance of various system components is the key to achieving maximum performance. Intuitively, this makes sense: if the suspension on an automobile does not allow the car to be driven more than 30 MPH on a winding mountain road, a 400 horsepower engine doesn't help much. In a similar fashion, a fast CPU that is constantly waiting for storage I/O processes to complete will not be able to run efficiently. The opposite is also true; putting a very fast storage channel on a system that is processor bound will not result in significant performance enhancements.

System and CPU upgrades are fairly commonplace and occur for the following reasons:

▼ User response time has become unacceptable.

■ The workload has increased and cannot be completed in the time allowed.

▲ The time allowed to do some amount of work has decreased and system performance is no longer adequate.

The expected benefit of a processor upgrade is improved performance to maintain response time or meet new requirements (more work and less time to do it). Unfortunately, simply upgrading the system processor probably won't deliver the expected results if the storage and I/O components can't keep up with the new processor.

Analyzing the Impact of CPU and I/O Performance Gains

For example, let's assume that a process running on the current system takes 10 seconds to complete, including all processor and I/O operations. Detailed analysis of the process indicates that 5 seconds of that time is spent on processor work and 5 seconds is spent on I/O operations. In other words, there is no overlap occurring between processor and I/O work.

A new processor that runs four times as fast as its predecessor is installed in the system. What should the expectation be for the performance gain? The new processor completes the job in a quarter of the time, or 1.25 seconds. That means the time savings from the upgrade for the processor part of the workload is 3.75 seconds. For now, we'll assume that the processor efficiency is not constrained by memory speed or any other variables and an improvement of four times can be realized.

Now, when we consider the I/O side of the upgrade, we realize that there is no guarantee that the processor will provide any benefit whatsoever to I/O processing. In fact, from the previous analysis made, the processor was idle while I/O operations were being run. This indicates that there is not likely to be any improvement in the I/O performance of the system. Assume that the time savings for the I/O portion of the work is zero. In other words, the I/O part takes 5.0 seconds.

Combining the processing and I/O times we see:

New_process_time = improved_processor_perf + I/O_perfor, or 1.25 + 5 = 6.25

So when the relative performance improvement is made for the total process, we see that the improvement is:

old_process_time / new_process_time = 10 / 6.25 = 1.6 times improvement

While a 1.6 boost in performance might be worthwhile, it's pretty far from the fourfold improvement expected.

Now let's assume new I/O technology is used, such as a subsystem disk cache, that doubles I/O performance so the I/O portion completes in 2.5 seconds, the total time for the process is now 3.75 seconds, and the overall performance increase for the process is:

old_process_time / new_process_time = 10 / 3.75 = 2.7 times improvement

This is probably a little closer to the hoped-for results.

Now, we'll start the analysis again from scratch, but this time assuming the processor upgrade under consideration contributes to an I/O performance improvement of 25 percent, so that the I/O component of the entire process completes in 3.75 seconds. Assuming no other I/O performance boost from caching, the time it takes to run the process now is 1.25 seconds plus 3.75 seconds, or 5.0 seconds. Then the overall performance improvement would be:

old_process_time / new_process_time = 10 / 5.0 = 2 times improvement

Our final analysis of this scenario assumes that a disk cache is added to the earlier scenario, cutting the I/O processing time in half again to 1.88 seconds. Now the process takes 1.25 plus 1.88, or 3.13 seconds to complete. The overall performance gain for this scenario is:

old_process_time / new_process_time = 10 / 3.13 = 3.2 times improvement

By looking at the examples just given, it's clear that boosting I/O performance makes a large impact on the overall performance of the system. This is not exactly rocket science, but it is often overlooked by busy network administrators.

SUMMARY

This chapter reviewed disk caching as the primary technology for boosting performance for storage I/O. In general, system software–based caching can provide optimal results because the access to cache memory occurs over the nanosecond-range system memory bus. In addition, host system software caching can be done at the data structure level, which contains complete information about the logical block addresses of the data being accessed.

However, host system caches are not always the best choice, depending on such variables as the workload on the system, processor utilization, the relative size of the data being cached, and the amount of cache memory available to the system. Alternatives to host system caching are using solid state disks, or SSDs, and caching controllers in host I/O adapters and disk subsystems.

One of the most important aspects of any cache is the way write I/Os are handled. The fastest performance is attained by using a write-back cache that stores new data or updates in cache memory and periodically sends it back to nonvolatile disk storage. However, write-back caches add an element of risk to the process due to the time delays that can occur between the time the CPU updates data and the time the data is flushed to disk. Emergency power for systems and cache memory can help prevent permanent data loss.

The topic of cache will be introduced again later in the book in discussions on clustering and distributed file systems. In general, the problems of managing cache in a multihost environment are among the most difficult to solve in the computer industry.

EXERCISES

1. Assume you run an application that routinely accesses a database file that is 40GB in size. The system has a maximum memory capacity of 4GB, the storage subsystem has a maximum cache memory capacity of 12GB, and an SSD disk available to you has a capacity of 36GB. Using these resources, design a caching solution for this application including the selection of read and write caching algorithms.

2. Design an automated data loader process for an SSD that is used to process four different applications during a 24-hour period.

CHAPTER 6

Increasing Availability
with RAID

S torage subsystems that provide data protection and performance benefits are readily available from a large number of vendors. These subsystems combine micro-processors, power distribution, cooling, storage and network management, and plug-and-play packaging in a wide variety of combinations.

Disk subsystems that use device virtualization to represent internal disk drives as larger, virtual drives are typically referred to as RAID (redundant array of independent disks) systems. Subsystems that lack this ability are normally referred to as JBOD (just a bunch of disks). JBOD subsystems can have many of the same physical features of RAID subsystems but work with host-based device virtualization such as volume manager software or RAID host I/O controllers to implement RAID array algorithms. The difference between RAID subsystems and JBOD subsystems is depicted here:

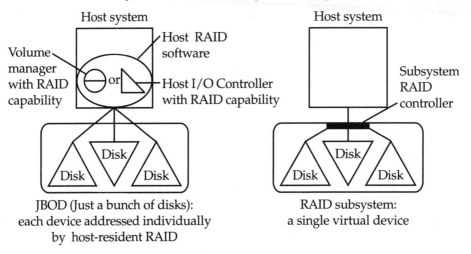

JBOD (Just a bunch of disks):
each device addressed individually
by host-resident RAID

RAID subsystem:
a single virtual device

This chapter examines RAID, primarily as a storing function that enhances the data redundancy, capacity, and performance of storage. Many of the data protection benefits that are inherent in the physical design of the disk subsystem apply equally to JBOD and RAID. As RAID algorithms can be implemented as an integrated part of a disk subsystem or through a separate mechanism, this chapter lumps both JBOD and RAID together for the sake of brevity. However, there are places where the two are distinguished in order to clarify a feature or benefit of one or the other.

THREE REASONS FOR RAID

RAID began in the 1980s as a research project at the University of California, Berkeley and has since been the subject of a great deal of R&D work within the storage industry, with many successful implementations. These days, most disk drives are inexpensive, so the acronym has been adjusted to use the word "independent" in place of the word "inexpensive." Regardless, there are three fundamental reasons RAID has become so popular:

▼ RAID delivers capacity and management benefits.

■ RAID delivers performance benefits.

▲ RAID delivers reliability and availability benefits.

RAID CAPACITY AND MANAGEABILITY

As mentioned, RAID provides device virtualization where several individual disk drives or partitions can form a single composite virtual disk drive, as shown in Figure 6-1.

Scaling Up with Capacity

RAID facilitates building large data processing systems with large amounts of data. For instance, a RAID subsystem with the combined capacity of ten individual disk drives can appear as a single address or LUN on a storage bus or network. As organizations struggle to manage fast-growing data collections, device virtualization in RAID can provide large amounts of storage capacity. Without ample storage capacity, applications have to be spread over multiple servers, which is a real nuisance to manage and increases the chances of failures and errors.

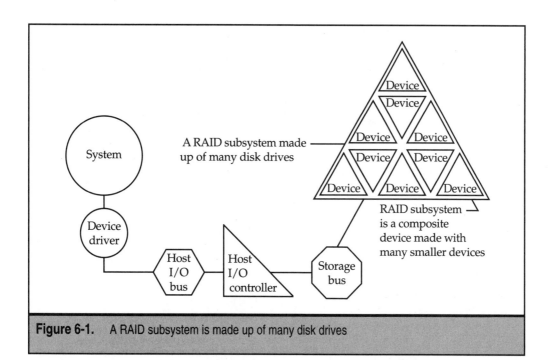

Figure 6-1. A RAID subsystem is made up of many disk drives

Raw Capacity Versus Usable Capacity

Although total capacity in a RAID array is an important advantage, the usable capacity is less than the aggregate capacity of the member disks. (*Member disks* are the individual disks making up the RAID array.) The amount of usable capacity in a RAID array can be calculated from the RAID algorithm and the number of disk drives in the array. In general, the capacity of the RAID array will be between 50 percent and 90 percent of the capacity of the array's member disks. An example of RAID capacity and overhead is shown here:

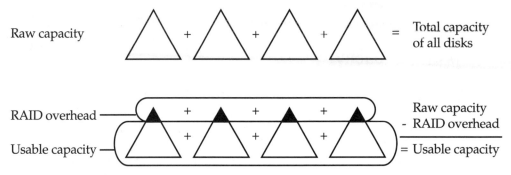

Server Slot Capacity

Device virtualization helps relieve host I/O bus capacity problems also. There are only so many slots available in any system and fully configured systems might not be able to accommodate additional host I/O controllers. The ability to use a single slot to use multiple disk drives inside a RAID subsystem is an advantage over JBOD subsystems.

Consider two disk subsystems with 40 disks each. The JBOD version of such a subsystem would likely require two or more adapters, taking up as many host slots. Depending on the application, such a configuration could realistically require four host I/O controllers to achieve reasonable performance. By comparison, a RAID subsystem that provides a single address could conceivably utilize a single host I/O controller to support all 40 disks.

Management Advantages of RAID

By combining several smaller drives into a large virtual drive, a single file system can be used to store and organize all the information required of an application. This can be a huge advantage compared to manually spreading the data over ten individual file systems on ten devices. It can be a great deal of work continually balancing the capacity and workload of the application over multiple disk drives. The next diagram compares the virtual approach with a single logical drive and file system, as opposed to having ten drives and ten file systems:

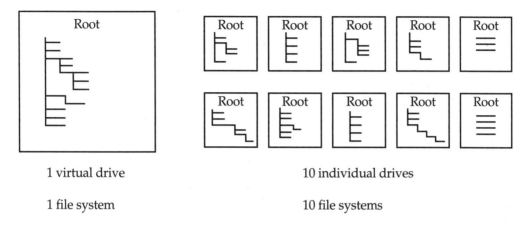

1 virtual drive

1 file system

10 individual drives

10 file systems

So, instead of managing many smaller drives, RAID allows system managers to manage large virtual drives. There are still individual drives to manage when drives fail and need to be replaced, but the work of balancing data over many smaller drives can be avoided.

Reducing the Number of Storage Bus/Network Addresses

Related to slot capacity limitations is the number of addresses available for a given host I/O controller. Eight-bit SCSI is limited to seven addresses in addition to the host I/O controller address. While it is true that each of these addresses can support eight LUNs each, assigning multiple drives to multiple LUN addresses adds complexity and requires management attention that may better be used on other tasks. Instead of configuring many addresses for many individual disk drives, RAID subsystems make it possible to use a single address. Most systems professionals find it desirable to consolidate administrative tasks and minimize the risk of errors. With the explosive growth in storage, reducing the administrative effort is becoming a necessity to keep up with the workload.

JBOD subsystems, on the other hand, do not provide device virtualization and therefore require more addresses and LUNs on the storage bus or network.

RAID FOR PERFORMANCE

Disk mirroring technology provides excellent reliability for relatively moderate costs. Therefore, if reliability were the only benefit of RAID, most RAID users would probably purchase mirroring instead. Therefore, RAID obviously must have some performance benefits over individual and mirrored disk drives if it is going to be useful. In general, the main performance problems that need addressing are those stemming from the electromechanical nature of disk drives: rotational latency and seek times.

Performance Through Striping

One of the concepts most closely associated with RAID is *disk striping.* The basic concept of disk striping is to spread operations on multiple disk drives to allow the host I/O controller to process more operations than if it were working with a single disk drive.

There are basically two kinds of striping arrays used in RAID cabinets:

▼   Interlocked access arrays

▲   Independent access arrays

The original research work on RAID at the University of California defined multiple "levels" of RAID, prescribing the relationship between the member drives and the types of striping algorithms used. Using those definitions as a guide, interlocked access arrays have been implemented using the RAID 3 model and independent access arrays have implemented RAID 4 and RAID 5. RAID levels are discussed in more detail later in the chapter, but for now we'll compare the differences of interlocked and independent access arrays.

Interlocked Access Arrays

Interlocked access arrays synchronize rotating media on member disk drives by taking a single I/O request, dividing it into short I/O operations, and writing them in sequential order to the member disks using data striping techniques. This way, each I/O request is spread immediately across multiple member disk platters.

In order for interlocked striping to work, each drive must perform within fairly close tolerances of the other drives in the array. Disk actuators need to move at the same speed, the rotation speed needs to be the same as the other drives in the array, and the drive's electronics must be able to process commands and move data in and out of its buffers at the same speed. In general, this is relatively expensive and difficult to engineer and maintain.

Figure 6-2 illustrates how interlocked access stripes are written on member drives. The diagram shows four member drives in the array, drive 1 through drive 4. They are shown at five different times, t = 0 through t = 4. They are all spinning at the same rotational frequency.

1. At time t = 0, the first piece of the transferred data is written to drive 1's buffer. All other drive buffers are ready.

2. At time t = 1, the second piece of the transferred data is written to drive 2's buffer. Drive 1's buffer starts writing to disk. All other buffers are ready.

3. At time t = 2, the third piece of the transferred data is written to drive 3's buffer. Drive 1's buffer finishes writing to disk. Drive 2's buffer starts writing to disk. Drive 4's buffer is ready.

4. At time t = 3, the fourth piece of the transferred data is written to drive 4's buffer. Drive 1's buffer goes to ready. Drive 2's buffer finishes writing. Drive 3's buffer starts writing.

5. At time t = 4, drive 1's buffer is filled again. Drive 2's buffer is ready. Drive 3's buffer finishes writing. Drive 4's buffer starts writing to disk.

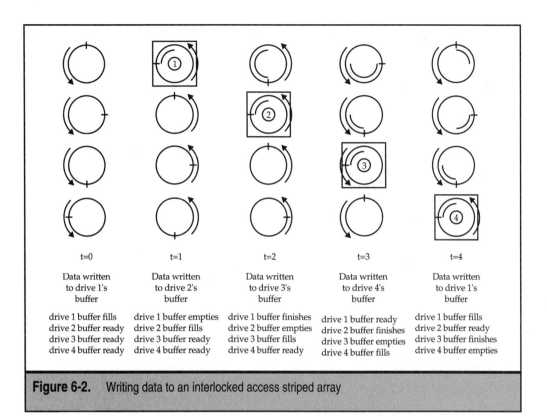

t=0	t=1	t=2	t=3	t=4
Data written to drive 1's buffer	Data written to drive 2's buffer	Data written to drive 3's buffer	Data written to drive 4's buffer	Data written to drive 1's buffer
drive 1 buffer fills	drive 1 buffer empties	drive 1 buffer finishes	drive 1 buffer ready	drive 1 buffer fills
drive 2 buffer ready	drive 2 buffer fills	drive 2 buffer empties	drive 2 buffer finishes	drive 2 buffer ready
drive 3 buffer ready	drive 3 buffer ready	drive 3 buffer fills	drive 3 buffer empties	drive 3 buffer finishes
drive 4 buffer ready	drive 4 buffer ready	drive 4 buffer ready	drive 4 buffer fills	drive 4 buffer empties

Figure 6-2.   Writing data to an interlocked access striped array

The data transfer operation proceeds in this round-robin fashion until there is no more to transfer.

Applications for Interlocked Access Arrays

Interlocked access arrays are very good for applications characterized by long, sequential access to data, such as:

▼ File serving for large sequentially accessed files

■ Multimedia: audio and video

■ Film and graphics processing, animation

■ CAD

▲ Data warehousing

Interlocked access arrays are not effective in environments where I/O transaction rates are high, because they are limited to processing a single I/O operation at a time. While it is possible that each individual transaction may be operated on faster with an interlocked access array, there is no overlapping of operations. Interlocked access arrays reduce some rotational latency by synchronizing the rotation of the member disks. However, rotational latency is still a performance problem: when an operation starts, it has to wait for the first disk in the array to be positioned correctly. More importantly, interlocked access arrays do nothing to alleviate the latency of seek times. In fact, seek times for interlocked access arrays can be longer than for a single disk because of the requirement for all member disks to settle their disk arms before the operation can begin.

Independent Access Striped Arrays

The other type of striped array uses independently accessed disks. In other words, the drives are not synchronized and individual write operations tends to be written in longer segments on individual drives, as opposed to striping data in short segments across all the drives in the array.

The strength of *independent access* arrays is the number of overlapped I/O operations that they can support. For example, an array could have twelve disk drives, each being operated by a single host I/O controller. The I/O operations would be distributed among the various drives according to the RAID levels employed.

While the array does not control which virtual device addresses the host system accesses, the fact that there can be multiple disk drives results in the probability that data requests will generate activity on multiple drives independently. This helps to reduce the likelihood that a single disk drive or disk arm would become a bottleneck for I/O operations. Using tagged command queuing, as described in the preceding chapter, multiple commands can be transmitted to the array, ordered for efficient operations, and passed on to the individual drives.

RAID Controllers

Figure 6-3 shows a *RAID controller* between the storage bus and the member drives in an array. This RAID controller presents one or more virtual devices to the host system and distributes I/O commands to the member disks in an array. In general, RAID controllers receive and interpret I/O commands from host systems and then create a new set of operations for the member disks. The RAID controller is also responsible for maintaining the block translation tables that map storage locations on the *exported* virtual device to the individual disk drives in the array.

Applications of Independent Access Striped Arrays

Independent access arrays excel at transaction processing workloads. The capability to overlap many I/O operations on multiple member drives means that the total throughput of the array can be far better than that of an individual disk drive or a parallel access array.

Independent access arrays work well for most applications, including:

- ▼ Transaction systems
- ■ ERP and MRP systems
- ■ Internet e-commerce servers
- ■ Customer service and support
- ■ Other multiuser database applications
- ▲ File servers with many small files

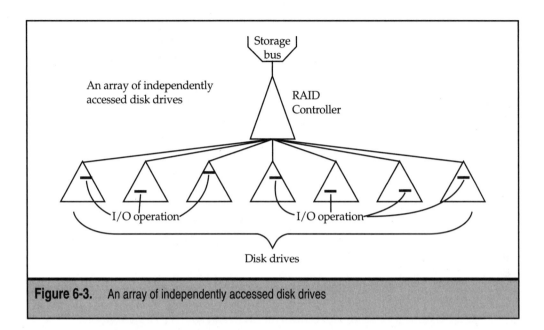

Figure 6-3.   An array of independently accessed disk drives

RAID RELIABILITY AND AVAILABILITY ADVANTAGES

Internet computing practically demands 24 × 7 computing capability. To provide this level of service, the storage devices and subsystems that hold data must be available at all times.

When multiple disk drives are used in combination, the potential for failure increases linearly with the addition of each disk drive. For example, an array with three drives is three times as likely to have a failure as a single drive. Similarly, an array with ten disk drives is ten times more likely to experience a drive failure than a single drive. Therefore, it is essential for RAID arrays to provide reliability features beyond those of individual drives.

Data Reliability Through Redundancy

RAID applies *redundancy* algorithms that allow individual devices to fail while maintaining the ability to maintain data integrity. In general, there are two classes of redundancy:

▼   Mirrored redundancy

▲   Parity redundancy

Mirrored redundancy was discussed in Chapter 4 as a technique that makes an image copy of data on another device or subsystem. Disk mirroring works very well for redundancy purposes but doubles the cost of storage by requiring two disks to form a mirror pair.

Parity Redundancy

Parity redundancy is implemented by calculating a parity value, or *checksum data*, based on the data stored on member disks in the array. Parity redundancy requires additional disk capacity, but less than mirroring requires, for holding the parity information. This additional capacity does not have to be a dedicated disk, as parity data can be inter-mixed on the member drives along with data.

Parity is calculated by performing an exclusive or (XOR) operation on aligned groups of data across multiple member drives. The XOR operation is used to regenerate missing data for a drive that fails by forming the XOR value from the parity data and the actual remaining data on the other disks. This relationship is shown in Figure 6-4.

One of the advantages of parity redundancy is it takes fewer disk drives than mirroring. Generally, an array with any number of member disks can be protected using the additional capacity of a single disk drive. For instance, a five-disk array with parity redundancy would use the equivalent capacity of one of the disks to hold the parity data. This does not necessarily mean that an entire disk will be used as a parity disk, but the capacity value of a disk will be. Therefore a five-disk array will have one-fifth, or 20 percent, overhead for redundancy. As the number of member disks in the array increases, the percentage of overhead diminishes.

Parity Rebuild

When a member disk fails in a RAID array, the data on it can be recovered by using the XOR function on the data from the remaining disks. As data is requested by the host, the existing data and parity data are read from all disks and the XOR function is used to calculate the missing data. This calculated data is the same as the missing data on the failed disk, and this is sent to the host to fulfill the I/O request.

At some point, a new disk will replace the failed disk in the array. At this time, a process called a *parity rebuild* will be run. The parity rebuild process reads all the data on other disks, including the parity data, and begins the process of re-creating all the data on

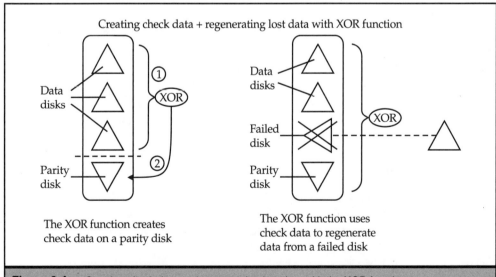

Figure 6-4. Creating check data and regenerating lost data with the XOR function

the replacement drive using the XOR function. Figure 6-5 shows the process for a parity rebuild of a failed member drive in an array.

Power Protection

Redundancy protection through mirroring and parity provides a way to recover data when a device fails. Larger-scale threats exist that affect the entire storage subsystem, not just individual disks. One of the most common and dangerous threats to data is the loss of power. When power is lost, pending I/O operations can be lost or incomplete, resulting in corrupt data.

There are basically two techniques used to protect data from power loss in RAID subsystems:

▼   Redundant power supplies

▲   Battery backup UPS systems

It's a good idea to use both of these to ensure against power-related data loss.

Protecting Against Component Failures with Redundant Power Supplies

RAID subsystems have their own power supplies to control and maintain voltage and current levels for the subsystem's internal circuitry. Just like any other component, these power supplies occasionally fail. There are three requirements to ensure that a failed power supply won't cause a loss of access:

▼   Redundant power supplies are required.

■   Each power supply needs to have the required connections and wattage to supply power to the entire subsystem.

▲   Power supplies need to have power-level sensing and failover capabilities to provide an immediate and smooth transition when failures occur.

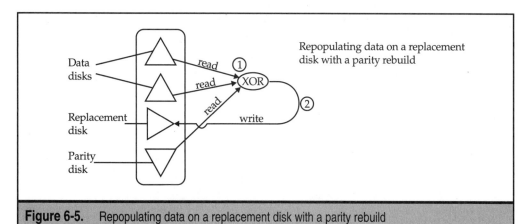

Figure 6-5.   Repopulating data on a replacement disk with a parity rebuild

As an additional measure, different power circuits can be used to provide power the different power supplies. This protects against isolated power problems in a building's circuits that supply power to the subsystem. When a circuit is blown for some reason, it's a good idea if another circuit can deliver power as pictured here:

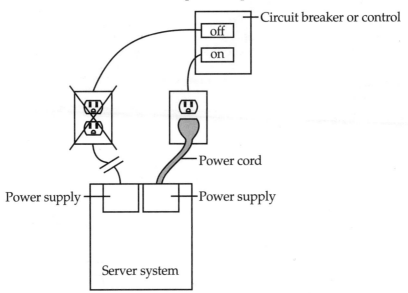

It may even be possible to use different power grids inside a building that protect against a blackout. Power grids are regions, or zones, established by the electrical utility companies for segmenting power distributions in the geographies and neighborhoods they serve. Sometimes it is possible to establish connections to multiple power grids within a building or campus environment. If so, it is possible to keep computer systems and their storage subsystems running, even during a blackout in one of the grids. Of course, it is necessary to know which power circuits belong to which grid and to understand the power-carrying capabilities of those power circuits. The next diagram shows a building in relation to two external power grids:

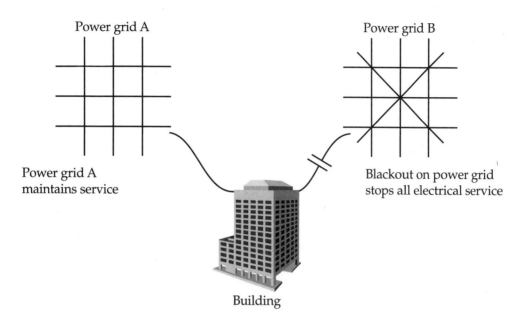

Redundant power supplies can be either load balancing or set up for a primary supply with a hot spare. "Load balancing" refers to a way of distributing the power to the subsystem through both power supplies simultaneously in more or less equal amounts. This technique reduces the load on each power supply, which may help preserve the longevity of the power supplies.

If load-balancing power supplies are being used, it is a good idea to carefully review the wattage ratings for each supply against the requirements for the subsystem. Make sure that each power supply has the capability to deliver the required power to all components in the subsystem following a failure of the other power supply.

The other configuration for redundant power is to use a standby power supply that is ready should the other supply fail. This other power supply is not actively providing power to the system but begins operations when the other supply starts to fail.

Battery Backup for Power Loss

Just as servers use UPS (uninterruptible power supply) systems with emergency backup support, RAID subsystems can also be equipped with battery support. This battery support can be either internal to the RAID system or implemented as an external product.

One of the main issues with RAID subsystems is maintaining power to volatile write-back cache memory. Any loss of power to this memory will result in data being lost by the cache when the system is restarted later. If any of the data blocks in cache are dirty blocks (written to the cache, but not yet written to disk), then data will be lost and possibly corrupted.

For that reason, some disk subsystems integrate backup battery support for internal cache memory that allows the cache to be flushed to disk after a loss of power. An orderly shutdown of the subsystem is always preferable to a sudden halt. Battery support provides a little extra time so that the subsystem can continue running while the host system completes its pending work. Battery backup can also protect data in cache when power is suddenly lost. Even if the subsystem stops functioning immediately, it is still possible for the battery to supply power to cache memory, until line power can be restored and the cached data can be written to disk.

Controller and Cache Redundancy

RAID subsystems can be equipped with redundant RAID controllers and mirrored cache to provide high availability to data. There are three fundamental approaches: the hot spare approach, where one controller does all the work with a spare in reserve; the load-balancing approach, where both controllers work on different operations; and the load-sharing approach, where two controllers can actually work together and share the workload. Load-balanced and load-sharing RAID controllers work in tandem with dual host I/O controllers in the host system. Dual host I/O controllers allow multiple paths to be established between the host system and the RAID subsystem, as shown in Figure 6-6.

Load-Sharing RAID Controllers   Load-sharing controllers use configured I/O paths from each host I/O controller to the RAID subsystem's controller. Each RAID subsystem controller can have its own cache memory to manage and does not have to worry about updating or locking cache memory from other controllers.

Alternative I/O paths are available to be used if the primary paths fail. When a failure occurs, the cache information for the failed link must be made available to the other link, or it must be discarded completely and new I/O paths need to be established for the host I/O controllers and the RAID controllers.

Load-Balancing RAID Controllers   Load-balancing controllers have the capability to distribute I/O operations from either host I/O controller to any of the internal member disks in the array. While this is relatively easy to describe, the implementation of load-balanced RAID controllers is an extremely difficult problem. At the core of the matter is cache. An I/O operation that is written to a RAID controller will be reflected in the controller's

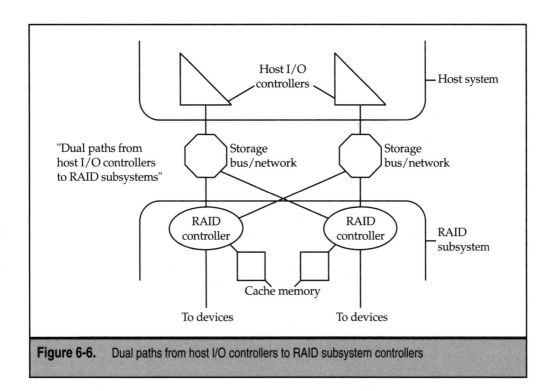

Figure 6-6.   Dual paths from host I/O controllers to RAID subsystem controllers

cache occasionally. If the same application and controller can use another path and RAID controller, it is necessary that the exact same cache information be available to both operations. The timing of the updating on the cache is difficult and requires a shared cache memory implementation and locking mechanism.

Dual Cooling and Fans

Cooling fans can also fail. While the loss of a cooling fan might not be immediately catastrophic, it can cause severe problems, leading to overheating and failure of other components. Additional cooling fans that can provide the required airflow inside if another fan fails are commonly implemented in RAID cabinets today.

Hot Spares and Hot Swapping

When 24 × 7 operations are required, redundancy by itself is insufficient to maintain availability. There must also be a way for redundant components to immediately take over for the failed components without loss of power or connections. In addition, there also needs to be a way for failed parts to be removed and replaced without interrupting operations.

Immediate Failover to a Hot Spare

Redundant components are not useful if they cannot step in and shoulder the burden when another part fails. The concept of a *hot spare* is a part that is capable of substituting for another part when that part fails. Some RAID subsystems contain hot spare disk drives that provide this capability when a disk drive drive fails in the storage subsystem.

A hot spare drive can be used to provide services to more than one array. For instance, a large RAID subsystem may export more than one logical array. A single hot spare can be used to offset a failure with any of the member drives in any of the arrays. Figure 6-7 shows a RAID subsystem with three arrays of five disks each. There are two hot spares that can be used by any of the arrays to replace a failed disk drive.

The main advantage of a hot spare disk drive is that no time is lost waiting to remove the old drive and inserting a replacement. The hot spare disk drive can be logically inserted into the array, where a parity rebuild can be immediately started. This provides the fastest protection against another drive failing and losing data.

Removing and Replacing Parts by Hot Swapping

Whether or not hot spares are used, there needs to be a way to remove a failed component and replace it with a working one. When this is done without interruption to the opera-

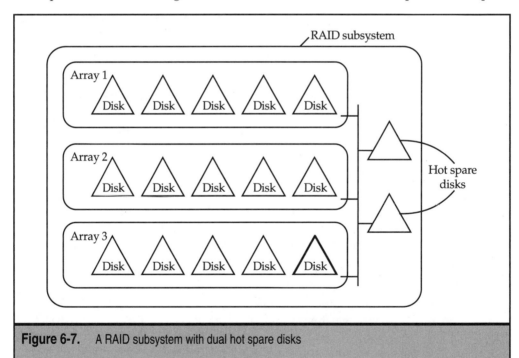

Figure 6-7.   A RAID subsystem with dual hot spare disks

tions of the subsystem, it is called *hot swapping*. Hot swapping might apply to some components and not others in a RAID or JBOD subsystem. Components that are commonly designed for hot swapping are disk drives, power supplies, and fans.

Hot Swapping Disk Drives

Hot swappable disk drives are a valuable feature. They allow failed disk drives to be replaced as quickly as possible without interrupting operations. Once the replacement disk is in place, it can be scheduled to have its data rebuilt.

Hot swapping is easy enough to understand, but it is a fairly complicated process. Because the storage bus/network inside a disk subsystem can have many disk drives connected sharing the same power, signaling, and data circuits, it is risky to remove a component while electrical current is on and data transfers are occurring. Therefore, disk subsystems usually contain special protection mechanisms that allow disk drives to be removed and replaced.

The procedure for doing this depends on engineering decisions made by the subsystem manufacturer. Some subsystems allow disks to be pulled at will, whereas others require software and/or hardware locks to be released before removing a drive. These procedures should be well understood before attempting to hot swap a disk drive.

It may sound a little silly, but it is quite important to correctly identify the disk drive that needs replacing. Hot swapping certainly makes things easier, but it should not be done as an experiment—it can have disastrous consequences. A drive that is removed from a subsystem cannot necessarily be put back in again and expected to work without loss of data. Removing the wrong drive when another drive has already failed can result in a catastrophic loss of data.

Warm and Cold Swapping   A failed component must be removed whether or not the subsystem supports hot swapping. Two other options for swapping components are warm swapping and cold swapping. A warm swap mean that the power to the subsystem is still on, although the subsystem is no longer operating—its operations are suspended while the device exchange is done. A cold swap, on the other hand, means that the subsystem is shut down completely, including turning off power before the component replacement is made.

The Internal I/O Paths in a RAID Subsystem

Chapters 2 and 3 analyzed the I/O path from the system CPU to devices on the bus/network. However, where storage subsystems are concerned, the I/O path is extended within the subsystem from the controller to the destination devices. For the most part, these discussions apply to RAID subsystems, not JBOD. The path to devices in a JBOD cabinet is determined by volume management software in the host or host I/O controller.

The internal I/O path in a RAID subsystem depends on the configuration of the RAID controllers and the interfaces of the member disk drives. The illustration that follows shows a simple RAID controller with a single controller and a single disk cache, addressing the member drives of a single array through a single port, or connector, on each member disk:

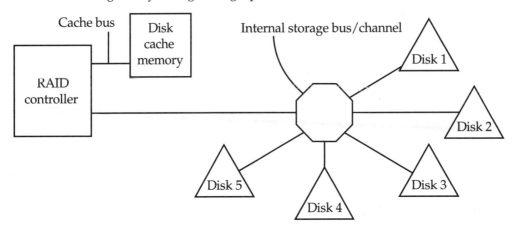

A simple internal I/O path in a RAID subsystem

The RAID controller distributes the I/O operations to the member disks according to the device virtualization scheme employed. A single internal bus (or network) conveys the I/O operations and data between the RAID controller and the member drives. A separate, high-speed memory bus is used to connect the RAID controller to its disk cache.

A variation on the preceding example adds another I/O channel to the RAID controller. Figure 6-8 illustrates this new configuration with two channels connected to two separate disk arrays.

Now, we'll expand the communications capabilities of the member drives by adding an additional port to each drive. In other words, these disk drives are *dual ported,* which means they can communicate to both I/O channels using both of their ports, as shown in Figure 6-9.

The last variation on this theme is shown in Figure 6-10. This RAID subsystem has two dual-channel RAID controllers, and two arrays, with each member disk drive being dual ported. Each disk can communicate with both controllers, providing complete path redundancy within the subsystem to protect against component failures.

Looking at Figure 6-10, there are a few interesting things to discuss. I/O buses A1 and B1 are the primary paths used by RAID controllers A and B, respectively. I/O buses A2 and B2 are secondary paths that are needed only if a channel failure occurs. Both controllers can send I/O operations to any member drive in the subsystem. In the event of a failure, data in either of the RAID controllers or internal I/O channels can be rerouted over the other controller or a secondary path. If controller A fails, controller B performs the duties of both controllers and communicates to the member drives of array 1 through I/O channel B2. Likewise, if controller B fails, controller A communicates to the member drives of array 2 through I/O channel A2.

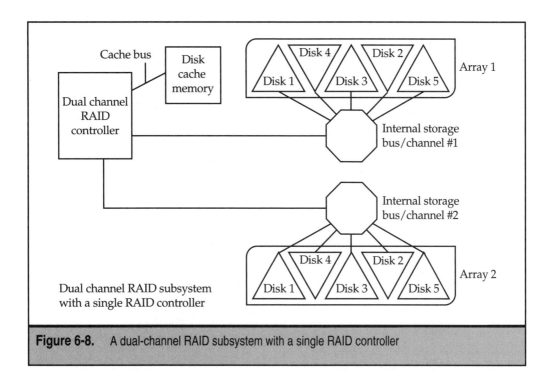

Figure 6-8.   A dual-channel RAID subsystem with a single RAID controller

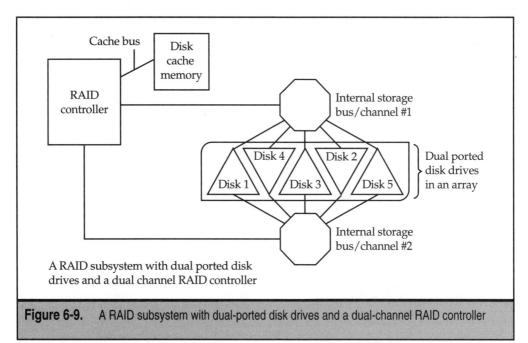

Figure 6-9.   A RAID subsystem with dual-ported disk drives and a dual-channel RAID controller

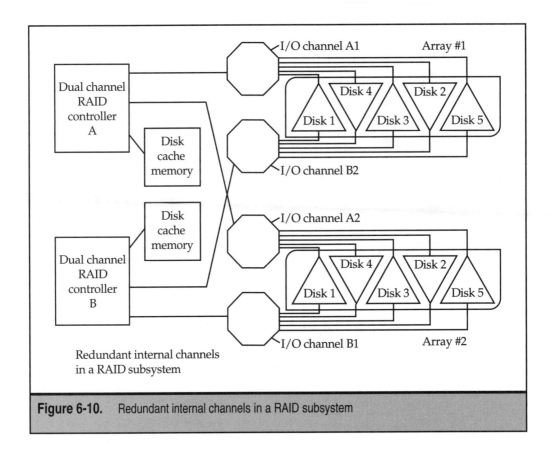

Figure 6-10. Redundant internal channels in a RAID subsystem

Also notice that channel failures can be rerouted through alternate RAID controllers. In fact, two channels can fail as long as they are not combinations of A1+B2 or B1+A2.

ORGANIZING DATA IN RAID ARRAYS: EXTENTS, STRIPS, AND STRIPES

Disk drives are often subdivided into large groupings of blocks, such as disk partitions. RAID arrays can also subdivide member disks many different ways to support a wide variety of storage requirements. These disk subdivisions can also form RAID arrays. In fact, to be technically accurate, disks do not form arrays, but their subdivisions, called *extents*, do.

Array Management Software

Array management software is the implementation of RAID algorithms, or volume management software, in a disk storage subsystem. Both array management software and volume management software can provide the same redundancy functions by subdividing member disks, organizing them into arrays and presenting them as virtual devices to host systems.

Array Management Software Roles

Array management software has three basic functions:

▼ Manage and control disk aggregations.

■ Convey I/O operations in and out of subdivided disks.

▲ Calculate parity values for data redundancy and reassemble lost data using parity.

These functions are discussed in the sections that follow.

Subdividing Disks with Extents

Disk subdivisions in RAID subsystems are called extents. The RAID Advisory Board, or RAB, defines an extent as follows:

A set of contiguously addressed blocks of member disk storage. A single member disk can have one or more extents. If a disk has multiple extents defined, these may be of different sizes. Multiple, possibly non-adjacent extents may be part of the same virtual-disk to member-disk mapping. Extents are sometimes called logical disks, although they are not normally made directly visible to operating environments.

In other words, extents establish boundaries between consecutively addressed groups of storage blocks on RAID member disks. Extents, then, become the individual puzzle pieces that are arranged to form arrays and mirrors and virtual drives of RAID subsystems. Figure 6-11 shows an array of four disks, each of them with multiple extents defined.

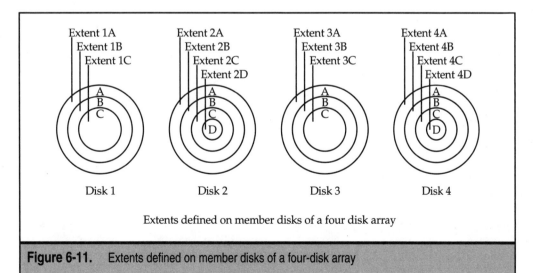

Extents defined on member disks of a four disk array

Figure 6-11.   Extents defined on member disks of a four-disk array

In Figure 6-11, disk 1 and disk 3 both have three extents (A, B, and C) defined, while disk 3 and disk 4 have four extents (A, B, C, and D). There are several ways these could be combined to form arrays. One obvious combination would be to form arrays across all disks using their respective A and B extents. In other words, extents 1A–4A and 1B–4B could be combined to form two separate arrays. The remaining extents could be used as individual drives or combined in mirrored pairs constructed from extents 1C+3C, 2C+4C, and 2D+4D.

Consolidating Addresses with Virtual Drives

Array management software forms a consolidated image of the extents in an array and *exports*, or presents, them to host systems. Figure 6-12 shows an exported virtual drive formed by four member drives. Array management software is responsible for *mapping* data block addresses from the member disk extents into contiguous storage addresses on the virtual drive and making the virtual addresses available for host storage applications such as file systems or databases.

Conveying I/O Operations from the Virtual Drive to Member Drives

As I/O operations are transmitted to the RAID controller, array management software parcels it for the member disks and creates internal I/O operations addressed to the cor-

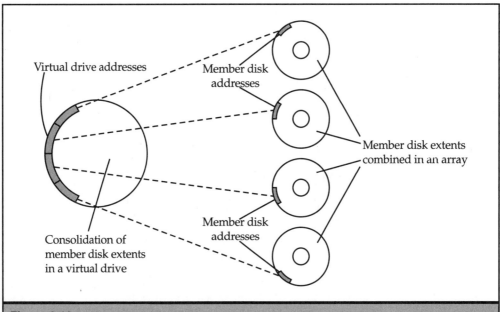

Figure 6-12.   Mapping member disk addresses into virtual drive addresses

responding storage locations on member disks. Array management software is responsible for managing I/O operations in and out of the RAID subsystem. It does this by:

▼ Providing a consistent and reliable way to translate logical block addresses

■ Converting I/O requests intended for the virtual disk to array member disks

▲ Responding to host system I/O requests, including the management and error correction arising from failures or errors from a single member drive

Subdividing the Subdivisions: Extents into Strips

Extents on member disks are subdivided into smaller sections that are used for individual I/O operations. These smaller subdivisions are called *strips.* If the strip belongs to an extent that belongs to an array, the length of the strip is called the *stripe depth.* All the strips in an array have the same length to simplify the mapping of virtual disk block addresses to member disk block addresses. The next drawing shows the relationship between stripes, strips, and extents:

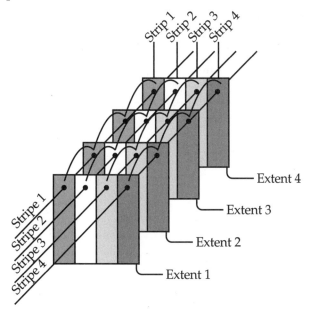

Extents in an array should be the same size. Nonuniform extents create problems for storing parity and in establishing array address mappings. In order to manage arrays efficiently, array management software can adjust the size of larger extents in arrays by not using all the available storage and setting a least-common extent size.

Strips are roughly equivalent to sectors on a disk drive but do not correlate to sectors in terms of determining their size. Strips can hold the contents of several I/O operations. The RAB defines strips as:

> The result of dividing an extent into one or more groups of identically sized, consecutively addressed blocks in a single extent. In some environments, strips are known as stripe elements.

Combining Strips into Stripes

Extents and strips are defined on individual drives, not arrays. Just as extents can be combined to form arrays, strips can be combined to form *stripes*. The RAB defines a stripe as:

> A set of positionally corresponding strips in two or more extents of a disk array. Positionally corresponding means that the first strip in each extent is part of the first stripe, the second strip in each extent is part of the second stripe, and so on.

Another way to describe stripes is to say that stripes are the set of aligned strips that cross extent boundaries in a way that is similar to how cylinders align tracks on disk drives. Figure 6-13 shows four extents with two strips (strip 1 and strip 2) indicated in each extent. The four strip-1s are aligned to form a stripe, as are the four strip-2s.

While the cylinder analogy is intuitive, there is no reason why the extents used in an array need to physically line up the way they are shown in Figure 6-13. For instance, a pair of disk drives subdivided into three extents could form three arrays, none of which are aligned physically but which are aligned by the relative strip location in each extent.

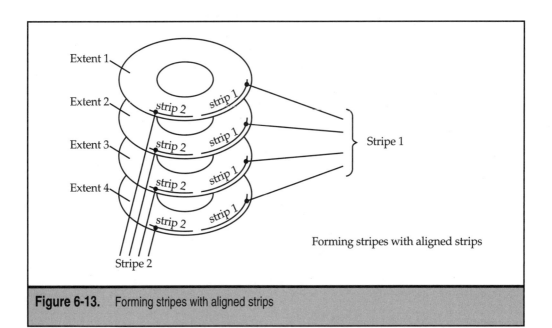

Figure 6-13. Forming stripes with aligned strips

The illustration that follows shows two disk drives, A and B, subdivided into three equal extents. Arrays are formed by combining extents A1+B2, A2+B3, and A3+B1. The strips in these extents do not line up physically from disk to disk, but the relative position within their extents does.

Logically aligned, physically unaligned stripes

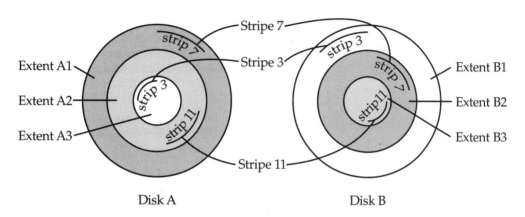

Ordered Filling of Strips and Stripes
--

Stripes in arrays are mapped to contiguous blocks in the virtual drive. As data is written to the virtual drive by the host, the first strip in the first extent is written first, followed by the first strip in the second extent, the first strip in the third, and so on. In this sense, the filling of stripes proceeds in sequence. This drawing illustrates this process:

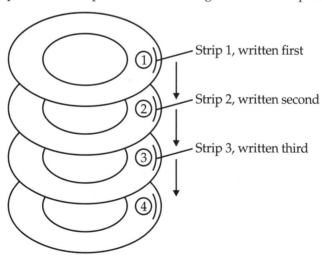

APPLYING PARITY TO STRIPED DATA

Parity was introduced previously as a means of providing data redundancy. We'll now take a more detailed look at parity implementations.

Creating Check Data with the XOR Function

Check data is the redundant data created by the RAID subsystem when it calculates parity. As mentioned previously, the exclusive or, or *XOR*, function is run against the real data on a bit-by-bit basis to create the check data. The sections to follow examine how the XOR function is applied to create parity and regenerate data when a disk fails.

Calculating Parity

The check data for RAID uses the Boolean XOR function. The logic of the XOR function is fairly simple; it behaves like the simple OR function, except that a true + true function gives a false result. The logic of the exclusive or is shown in Table 6-1.

The XOR function can be used on larger combinations of bits. As it turns out, it doesn't matter if the bits are grouped together in pairs and operated on or if each additional bit is XOR'd with the result from the previous XOR operation, as if in an XOR "chain." In fact, it does not matter what order the bits are operated on.

Following standard binary data conventions, a zero bit represents a false value and a one bit represents a true value. Applied to RAID, data bits written to array extents are XOR'd with corresponding bits on other extents and a parity check bit is calculated and written to a parity extent location.

Table 6-2 shows hypothetical strings of bits spanning four extents. The fifth column is the resulting parity bit calculated by the XOR function.

Looking at Table 6-2, one can apply the XOR function to the bits in any four columns to arrive at the value in the other one. For instance, if XOR is applied to columns two through five, the result will be the same as the values shown in column one. This demonstrates the power of the XOR function to regenerate data when a disk fails. If a disk fails and data in an array extent is unavailable, its values can be regenerated using the XOR function from the corresponding bits from the other extents in the array.

Operand 1	Operand 2	XOR Result
False	False	False
False	True	True
True	False	True
True	True	False

Table 6-1.   Exclusive Or (XOR) Operations

Extent 1	Extent 2	Extent 3	Extent 4	Parity
0	0	0	0	0
1	0	0	0	1
0	1	0	0	1
1	1	0	0	0
0	0	1	0	1
1	0	1	0	0
0	1	1	0	0
1	1	1	0	1
0	0	0	1	1
1	0	0	1	0
0	1	0	1	0
1	1	0	1	1
0	0	1	1	0
1	0	1	1	1
0	1	1	1	1
1	1	1	1	0

Table 6-2.   XOR Parity Calculations for Combinations of Four Bits in Four Extents

The Inverse Operation of XOR Is XOR

Part of the power of the XOR function is the fact that it is the inverse of itself. In other words, when you calculate parity with an XOR, you can reverse the calculation by using XOR again. This is a little counterintuitive, as common mathematical functions like addition and multiplication have subtraction and division as their inverse functions. Here are a few examples:

0 XOR 0 = 0; the inverse operation is: 0 XOR 0 = 0

0 XOR 1 = 1; the inverse operation is: 1 XOR 1 = 0

1 XOR 0 = 1; the inverse operation is: 1 XOR 0 = 1

1 XOR 1 = 0; the inverse operation is: 0 XOR 1 = 1

This listing on the previous page is the complete combination matrix for the XOR function. Even though the number of combinations increases, the value of each individual calculation can be derived from the preceding matrix.

Reduced Mode Operations for Interlocked Access Arrays

The term "reduced" in the context of RAID refers to a RAID subsystem where one of the disks fails and the subsystem continues to run without it. When this happens, the RAID array adjusts its functioning to ensure data integrity.

Member disks in an array can function as data disks, parity disks, or both, if RAID 5 is used. If a failed disk is a data disk, the array regenerates data for the failed disk as needed to satisfy read I/O requests. Write I/O requests are handled in exactly the same way they would normally be, except that the data is not written to the failed disk, but the updated check data is written to the parity disk. This way, data on the lost disk can be regenerated, even if it was never actually written to the failed disk. When a replacement disk is installed, a parity rebuild operation repopulates the new disk, as shown in Figure 6-5 previously.

When a parity disk fails, subsystem performance can actually increase. The RAID subsystem works as it normally would—but without any overhead for reading, modifying, or writing parity check data as shown here:

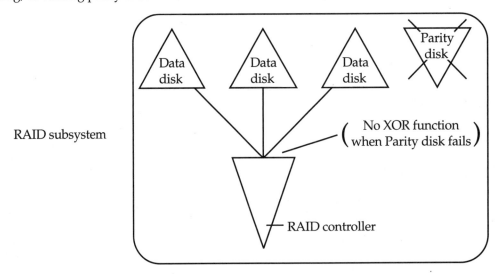

RAID 5 distributes check data across all the disks in an array. In that case, the reduced-mode behavior of the array depends on the stripes accessed. If the stripe loses one of its data disks, then it must be regenerated and written correctly during reduced operations. If the stripe loses its parity disk, then the operation is performed without any parity calculations or overhead.

MTDL

Mean time to data loss, or MTDL, is the probable time to failure for any component that makes data inaccessible. For RAID, it includes the likelihood that a second disk will fail when an array is operating in reduced mode. MTDL is based on the combination of MTBF (mean time between failure) data for individual disk drives and the number of drives in an array. In general, higher numbers of disks in an array equate to lower MTDL numbers.

MTDL should not be taken lightly, as a second disk failure can result in complete data loss. It is recommended that failed disks be replaced as quickly as possible and that the parity rebuild process be started as soon as possible following the replacement of the failed drive.

The array overhead incurred during a parity rebuild can severely impact the performance of the array. Therefore, it may be preferable to wait for a regularly scheduled I/O-intensive application to finish before starting the parity rebuild.

CAUTION: It may be an advantage to adjust the system backup schedule when an array is running in reduced mode. For instance, file systems residing on the array can be placed at the beginning of the backup software schedule to ensure the backup process completes. Keep in mind that backup processing will be slower when data needs to be regenerated. In addition, you may want to verify the backup tapes to ensure all the data was copied to tape from the reduced array.

Parity in Interlocked Access RAID

Calculating check data for interlocked-access RAID is straightforward. As stripes are written across the member disks, the check data is calculated and written to an additional synchronized parity disk. The parity disk has the same extent size and stripe size as the data disks in the array.

Similarly, if the information ever needs to be recovered due to a failed data disk, the XOR function is applied to the data as it is read from the synchronized disks. The stripe components are read from the other disks, including the parity disk, and the values for the missing disks are regenerated.

Parity in Independent Access RAID

The situation for independent access RAID is slightly more complicated. Data is not striped across several synchronized disks rotating at the same speed. Instead, data is written to strips in a single extent and then written to the corresponding extent in the next disk. In other words, the writes do not have to span all the disks in the array.

Write Penalty in Independent Access Arrays

As each strip is written, the check data is calculated to protect the data. The XOR function, as described before, is used to generate the check data. But some of the data used for calculating the check data is on disk already and is not being written by the host I/O controller. Therefore, calculating the check data for the new data requires that some of the existing data be read from disks in the array. This process of reading data and calculating check data in order to write new data and calculate parity is known as the *read, modify, write penalty*.

Calculating the parity for the new data is an interesting process, and not what one would immediately expect. Recall that the check data calculation is independent of the order of the calculation. The contributing bits can be mixed in any order and the same check data value will be arrived at. As it turns out, the XOR function has the ability to retrace its steps to calculate an interim value. For example, applying the XOR function to the check data value and any of the contributing values results in removing the contribution of that value. In other words, it rolls back the check data value by one contributor. The diagram that follows shows the result of the XOR calculation for four disks when the contribution from the second disk is removed:

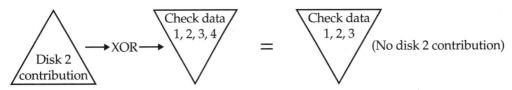

So, when new data is written to an independent access array, the following process is used to update the check data and write the new data:

1. Receive I/O request and new data from the host I/O controller.
2. Read the old data for the strip that is being replaced.
3. Read the check data for the strip.
4. Roll back the check data by XORing it with the old data.
5. Calculate new check data by XORing the rolled-back value with the new data.
6. Write the new check data to disk.
7. Write the new data to disk.

This process is called the *read, modify, write cycle*. Figure 6-14 shows the read, modify, write cycle for an array with four member disks, one of which contains parity for the stripe.

Performance of Read and Write Operations in Independent Access Arrays

The read, modify, write cycle requires four times the data transfers of a write to an individual disk drive. The old data is read, the parity is read, new parity is written, and finally new data is written. This is a significant amount of overhead to a single I/O request.

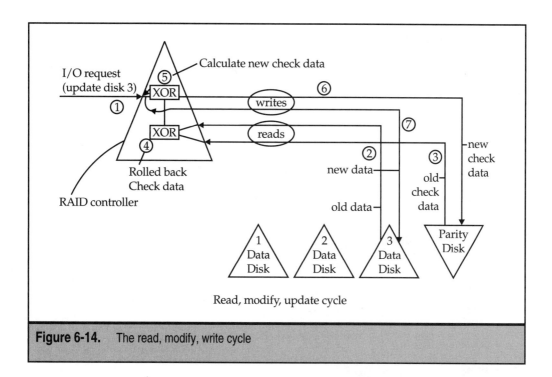

Figure 6-14.   The read, modify, write cycle

Because of the overhead of the read, modify, write cycle, read operations in independent access arrays are much faster than write operations. In fact, the performance of writing in an independent access array is slower than writing to an individual disk or a interlocked access array. For that reason, independent access arrays should be configured with write-back caches when used with applications with a larger percentage of reads to writes.

Using Disk Caching to Reduce the Write Penalty

The write penalty in independent access arrays results from writes that update a minority of strips in a stripe. However, if a write operation can fill more than half the strips in a stripe, the write penalty is somewhat reduced. The general idea is that the existing data on other strips not being updated can be read and XOR'd with the new data being written to the other strips. Then the new data and new check data can be written to their respective locations in the stripe. Notice that it is not necessary to read the old check data first or roll back any existing check data values. This sequence is outlined as follows:

1. Hold new writes for strips being written to.

2. Read existing values from strips not being written to.

3. Calculate new check data.

4. Write new strips and new check data.

A disk cache implemented with a write-back algorithm can hold disk writes until more strips can be written in a single operation. If enough strips can be suspended in the cache, it may be possible to use this second method and avoid having to read and modify data from member disks. Considering that a write-back cache can be employed to suspend write I/Os to disk, it is possible to collect multiple writes until enough strips can be written at once and avoid having to roll back the parity values. Instead, new parity can be calculated from the old and new data without requiring the old parity to be rolled back. If this is done consistently, the performance for writes in an array with a write-back cache can approach the write performance of an individual disk drive. Figure 6-15 shows a write-back disk cache that holds array writes until there is enough data to fill the majority of strips in the stripe.

XOR disks

At the request of certain RAID subsystem vendors, Seagate pioneered the integration of XOR functionality into the disk drive controller. The basic idea of XOR integration is to combine I/O operations and XOR functions in a single request to the disk drive.

As described previously, the order in which the XOR function is computed is not important, which means groups of strips can be combined in any order to achieve the same result. Using the read, modify, write cycle with independent access arrays, the check data is rolled back by XORing it with the old data from the target disk. Then this rolled-back result is XOR'd again with the new data being written to create the new check data value. An algebraic expression of this is:

[(*Old-check-data*) XOR (*Old-strip-data*)] XOR (*New-strip-data*) = *New-check-data*

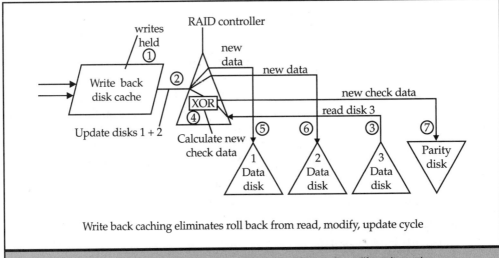

Write back caching eliminates roll back from read, modify, update cycle

Figure 6-15.   Write-back caching eliminates rollback from the read, modify, write cycle

This expression can be slightly rearranged as:

[(*Old-strip-data*) XOR (*New-strip-data*)] XOR (*Old-check-data*) = *New-check-data*

Notice that the first two terms in this second equation are the old data and the new data in the strip. A disk drive with integrated XOR functionality can follow this procedure:

1. Receive new data from the host I/O controller.
2. Read old data from the disk media.
3. Calculate the XOR value of the new and old data.
4. Transfer the resulting XOR value to the disk drive where the check data resides.
5. Calculate a new XOR value for the stripe by combining the transferred XOR data with the old XOR data on disk.

In this list, the first four functions involve the data disk in the array where the new data strip is being written. The fifth function involves the disk where the check data resides. If the disk drive performs the XOR function, the RAID controller does not have to, enabling it to respond faster to I/O requests from the host I/O controller. Figure 6-16 shows a five-disk array using XOR drives to calculate check data values.

When XOR calculations are performed by the disk drives in an array, a high percentage of traffic can be eliminated from the storage bus/channel. Using XOR drives can reduce bus traffic 33 percent to 50 percent, depending on the capabilities of individual drives to act as initiators, bypassing the RAID controller to send parity data directly to other drives.

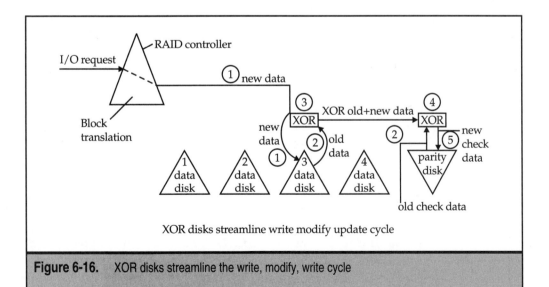

XOR disks streamline write modify update cycle

Figure 6-16. XOR disks streamline the write, modify, write cycle

COMPARING RAID LEVELS

The original RAID work at done at the University of California in the eighties specified five different RAID levels with different characteristics and algorithms. After this original work was done, a sixth RAID level was added. Over time, another RAID level was accepted and recognized by the broad industry—RAID level 0. We will discuss RAID levels 0 through 6 in the following sections.

The RAID Advisory Board

The RAID Advisory Board, or RAB, is an industry association of RAID technology developers and users who work together to develop and promote RAID technology. RAB has four primary purposes:

▼ Promote RAID technology to the market.

■ Establish standardized terminology, classifications, and metrics.

■ Share resources within the RAID community.

▲ Foster the development of related technology to further the development of RAID.

RAB maintains a set of requirements for each RAID level. This book does not list each of those requirements in discussing RAID levels in the following sections, but interested readers are encouraged to visit the RAB Web site at **www.raid-advisory.com**.

RAID Level 0: Striping

RAID level 0 is simply disk striping without parity. It is not really RAID, per se, because it does not provide any redundancy. If a disk fails with RAID 0, data is lost. RAID 0 typically employs an independent access method for striping data to member disks, as opposed to using an interlocked access method. This allows multiple I/O operations to be processed in parallel simultaneously. Without the overhead of calculating parity, these arrays provide the fastest throughput of any type of array.

Applications where performance is paramount and data protection needs are minimal are well suited for RAID 0 arrays. Multimedia production applications such as film and video production can use RAID 0 for storing data as it is being processed. Other applications include high-speed data acquisition where the data is worthless if it cannot be captured completely at high speed. In this case, it is better to ensure performance to capture all the data and then make copies onto other storage media and devices to protect the data.

Data Mapping for RAID Level 0

Figure 6-17 shows how the virtual device for a RAID 0 array is mapped onto the individual member disks of the array. In general, the capacity of the virtual drive is the sum of the member drive's capacities.

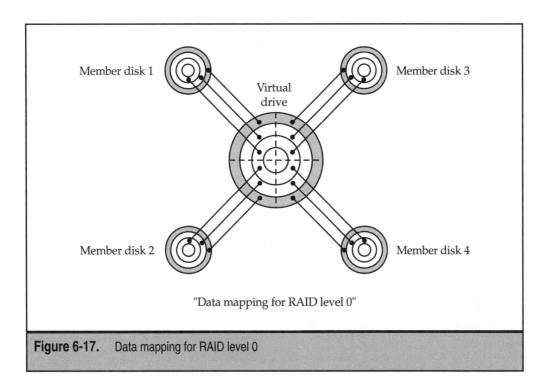

Figure 6-17. Data mapping for RAID level 0

RAID Level 1: Mirroring

For the most part, RAID level 1, or disk mirroring, was covered in Chapter 4. RAID 1 does not calculate parity. Its data protection is excellent and its performance is also very good, as it is not necessary to perform XOR operations while reading and writing data.

Data Mapping for RAID Level 1

The data mapping for RAID 1 is fairly simple. What happens to one disk happens to the other. The virtual drive is directly mapped to the blocks on the mirrored pair. Figure 6-18 shows the data mapping used for RAID 1.

RAID Level 2: Interlocked Access with Specialized Disks

RAID 2 was conceived when disk drives were more expensive and in general did not have as much sophisticated circuitry as they do today. The definition of RAID 2 involves error correction circuitry to be performed by the RAID controller. This role has been assumed by disk drives today. Therefore, RAID 2 is practically nonexistent.

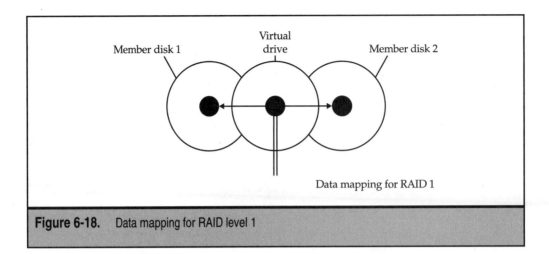

Figure 6-18.　Data mapping for RAID level 1

RAID Level 3: Synchronous Access with a Dedicated Parity Disk

For the most part, interlocked access RAID as discussed previously in this chapter is defined by RAID 3. RAID 3 subsystems "spray" data stripes across all the drives in the array and write check data to an additional parity disk in the array.

Because of the need to synchronize disk rotations for RAID 3, it is seldom implemented in host volume management software due to the difficulty of maintaining close control of the disk operations. For that reason, RAID 3 implementations are usually RAID subsystems with integrated RAID controllers. Even so, RAID 3 is a technology that seems to be dying out in the market. Many of the performance advantages of RAID 3 can be accomplished through caching or through advances in the rotational speed of disks.

Although RAID level 3 is almost always implemented with a dedicated parity disk, it is not required for RAID 3. For instance, the parity location can be spread across different disks for different stripes.

One of the distinguishing features of RAID level 3 is that it always completes stripes of data across all the disks. There are no partial writes that update one out of many strips in a stripe. This eliminates the read, modify, update write penalty that exists in higher RAID levels. For that reason RAID 3 is often employed for applications where write performance is a priority. Other common applications for RAID 3 include large sequential access applications such as data mining and multimedia/film production. Graphics and CAD also tend to have long sequentially accessed files. Data acquisition systems for scientific research can also benefit from the performance of writes using RAID 3.

Data Mapping for RAID Level 3

The data mapping for RAID 3 was shown in Figure 6-2. Notice that only complete stripes are allowed to be written. RAID 3 arrays can be subdivided into many virtual drives, if desired.

RAID 4: Independent Access with a Dedicated Parity Disk

RAID 4 is an implementation of independent access RAID where a single disk is dedicated as a parity disk. Unlike RAID 3, RAID 4 has much larger strips that allow multiple I/O requests to be processed simultaneously. While this provides significant performance benefits for read requests, RAID 4 has a particularly difficult write penalty, as the parity disk is accessed twice in each read, modify, write cycle.

Data Mapping for RAID Level 4

The data mapping for RAID 4 is shown in Figure 6-19. As with other RAID levels, RAID 4 arrays can be subdivided into many virtual drives.

RAID Level 4 Write Bottleneck

By virtue of using a dedicated disk for parity, RAID 4 has an inherent bottleneck for processing write requests. This is a performance "double whammy," considering the performance impact already incurred with the RAID write penalty. As RAID 4 supports independent access to all disks, multiple write operations in the array require the check data to be read and rewritten to a single disk. This dependence on the dedicated parity disk to support all pending writes can be a system bottleneck.

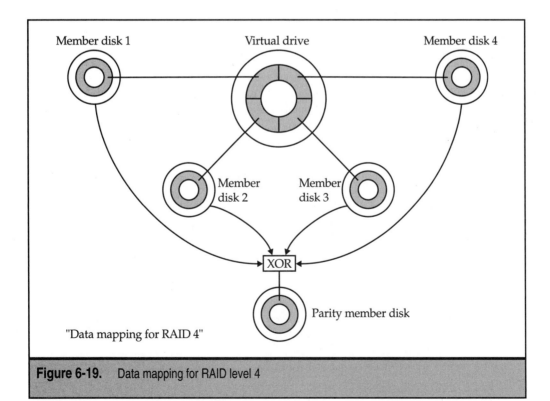

Figure 6-19.   Data mapping for RAID level 4

Limitations to the Number of Disks in RAID 4

Notice that as the number of disks in a RAID 4 array increases, the effects of the RAID 4 write bottleneck increase. To some degree, the number of disks in an array determines the number of overlapped operations at any time. For example, a three-disk array can operate on at most two I/O requests at a time. While there may be additional processing occurring to streamline operations using techniques such as tagged command queuing, the disk arm can work on only one request at a time. Therefore, a five-disk array can support more I/O operations than a four-disk array, a six-disk array can support more than a five-disk array, and so on.

While it may seem plausible that adding more disks will distribute the load and create additional parallelism in the RAID subsystem, it is not necessarily true. It is highly unlikely that the data mapping of the RAID array and access characteristics of the application would be so well matched as to maintain a highly parallel distribution of the workload on all member disks. Still, arrays with more disks have more disk arms to do the work and can potentially deliver performance benefits.

However, in RAID 4, the congestion over access to the parity disk becomes worse as the number of disks and overlapped operations increases. For that reason, RAID 4 disk subsystems are somewhat limited in the number of disks and disk arms they can realistically support. Therefore, the flexibility in configurations and expansion of RAID 4 arrays is constrained. For that reason, RAID 4 is not commonly implemented.

Using Write-Back Caching and Solid State Disks to Reduce RAID 4 Write Congestion

One way to alleviate this problem is to use write-back caching that attempts to update complete strips, or at least the majority of the data in a stripe for each write. This removes the necessity of reading the dedicated parity disk when rolling back the check data during a read, modify, write cycle. Systems that control their write-back cache successfully in this manner can get excellent performance from their disk subsystems. The "Filer" products from Network Appliance are examples of products successfully using write-back caching along with RAID 4 in their disk subsystems.

Another solution to this problem is to use a solid state disk for the parity disk in RAID 4. Using a solid state disk device for the parity drive would likely provide adequate performance to eliminate the bottleneck of the read, modify, update cycle in RAID 4. One potential problem with using solid state disks for parity is matching the capacity and stripe depth configuration of the solid state disk with the capacity and stripe depth of the disks in the array. While this might seem trivial, there are no inherent reasons why a solid state disk's memory-based capacity would match the capacity of magnetic media disk drives. The point here is that there would likely be large or small differences in capacity that would need to be addressed. Of course, to be precise, the *extent* size on the solid state disk would need to match any extents in RAID 4 arrays.

RAID 5: Independent Access with Distributed Parity

RAID 5 is an independent access RAID array that distributes the check data over all the disks in the array. In other words, there is no dedicated parity disk. This means that there is no write bottleneck as there is with RAID 4. The delay still arises from the read, modify, write cycle that occurs for write operations, but no single drive bottleneck is designed into the array as there is with RAID 4.

Increasing Parallelism in RAID 5

As the number of member disks in a RAID level 5 array increases, the potential for increasing the number of overlapped operations also increases. This is in stark contrast to RAID 4 with its write bottleneck on the parity disk. Therefore, RAID 5 arrays can realistically support more disks than RAID 4, allowing RAID 5 to achieve higher capacity and higher numbers of disk arms for better performance. However, some caution is in order: as the number of disks in an array increases, the mean time to data loss (MTDL) is shorter due to the higher probability that a second disk will fail before the failed disk is repaired.

Also, the performance benefits depend heavily on the distribution of data across member disks and the access patterns of the applications. Research at Digital Equipment Corporation on RAID subsystems used across several common applications showed that 55 percent of all I/O operations were directed at 20 percent of the disks in an array.

XOR Disks in RAID 5

The distribution of check data in RAID 5 is an excellent match for XOR technology integration in disk drives. With check data residing on different disks in the array, one can see that simultaneous write operations may use completely different disks for writing data as well as the corresponding check data.

The previous discussion of XOR disks in this chapter shows how old and new data can be XOR'd in a disk and then sent to the parity disk by the controller to calculate the new check data value. Assuming an eight-member array with RAID 5, each strip update involves reading, writing, and calculating check data on two of the eight disks. It is easy to think of many combinations of simultaneous operations that could involve separate disks and avoid contention for a single disk. Of course, there are no guarantees that contention couldn't arise, but in general, the distribution of work through overlapped operations could generate significant performance improvements to certain applications, such as transaction processing. In addition, the bus bandwidth required for disk XOR parity calculations is 33 percent to 50 percent, which results in better throughput of the RAID array.

Data Mapping for RAID Level 5

The mapping of data for RAID 5, including the location of check data, is shown in Figure 6-20. There is no standard or specification for how check data is distributed, so RAID 5 implementations of the distribution of check data vary from vendor to vendor. In

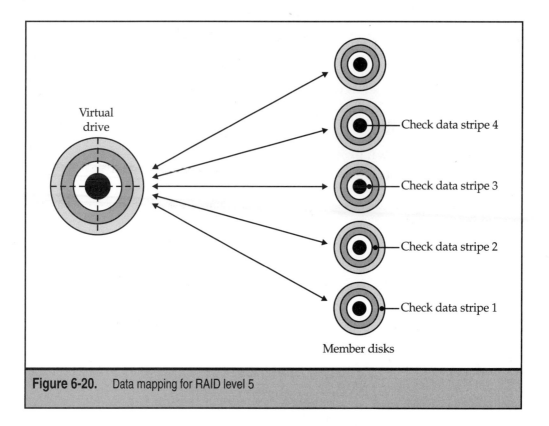

Figure 6-20. Data mapping for RAID level 5

Figure 6-20, the check data for the first stripe is on the first disk, the second stripe's check data is on the second disk, and so on. With five disks in the array, the sixth stripe's check data would "wrap around" and be written to the first drive.

RAID 5 is one of the more common implementations of RAID in the market. Although the distribution of check data on multiple disks appears somewhat complicated, it is fairly simple to compute its location by the stripe number. In other words, the data mapping for the virtual device dictates the stripe and the strip dictates the check data location.

Applications for RAID Level 5

In general, the optimal application loads for RAID level 5 arrays are transaction loads where multiple I/O requests can be overlapped in the RAID subsystem. However, applications with a high percentage of write operations are not recommended for RAID 5. Write-back caching can alleviate many of the problems with heavier write traffic.

RAID Level 6: Independent Access with Double Parity

In all the preceding discussions of RAID levels, the goal is to protect data from the loss of a single disk drive in an array. While MTDL numbers should help bolster one's confidence in the subsystem, it might not give the protection required for extremely sensitive data requiring the highest availability.

RAID level 6 provides two levels of redundancy, meaning two drives can be lost from an array and the array can still continue functioning. To date, RAID 6 implementations are relatively uncommon in the market, the most popular having been the Iceberg RAID subsystem manufactured by Storage Technology Corporation and sold by IBM. In general, implementations of RAID 6 have considerably higher cost than other RAID levels due to the fact that RAID 6 requires more complex and expensive controllers than other RAID levels.

Check Data for RAID 6

RAID level 6 supports the loss of two disks by making two independent parity calculations on each stripe written. This can be done by using multiple algorithms or by creating and using two separate stripe alignments.

RAID Level 6 One-Dimensional Redundancy

The first approach for RAID 6 is to use two different calculations for generating check data. One of the easiest ways to think about this is to have two parity disks available to support the data disks. The first parity disk supports one parity algorithm, while the second disk supports another. The use of two algorithms is referred to as P+Q parity. *One-dimensional redundancy* refers to the use of the additional parity disk covering the exact same striped data.

For example, the P parity value might be generated by the XOR function. In that case, the Q parity function needs to be something else. A strong candidate is to use a variation of Reed Solomon error correction coding used for disk and tape drives. If two disks fail, the regeneration of the data on both disks is accomplished by solving two equations with two variables, an algebraic technique that can be accelerated by hardware assist processors.

Data Mapping for One-Dimension Parity RAID Level 6

Figure 6-21 shows a data mapping for a one-dimension RAID 6 implementation. This diagram shows two different parity values, one labeled Check Data A function and the other Check Data B. Both kinds of check data would be spread throughout the array the way RAID 5 does to avoid the kind of write penalty associated with RAID 4.

RAID Level 6 Two-Dimensional Redundancy

Two-dimensional redundancy is based on an algebraic concept that arrays can be logically arranged in matrices of rows and columns. Data alignments are established across rows and down columns, and parity check data is calculated as orthogonal vectors in the *array space*.

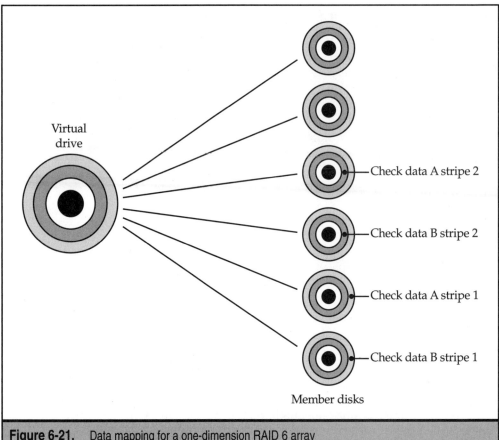

Figure 6-21.   Data mapping for a one-dimension RAID 6 array

Each strip of data belongs to two orthogonal (separate and discrete) stripes, without the possibility that any other stripes in the array can be written to the same parity location.

This approach is fairly simple to visualize as an $M \times N$ matrix, where M parity disks are needed for the N parity calculations and N parity disks are needed for the M parity calculations. The total number of parity disks needed for this arrangement is equal to $M+N$. The parity overhead for this type of array is reduced when the number of rows and columns are equal and the size of the array increases. For example, a 3×3 nine-disk array has six parity disks for an overhead of 66 percent. However, when the array contains 100 disks in a 10×10 configuration, 20 parity disks are needed and the overhead falls to 20 percent.

One of the advantages of the two-dimensional approach is that the same algorithm can be used to calculate check data. This greatly simplifies the mathematical routines used for reduced-function operations such as data regeneration and parity rebuilds. A single program in array management software or the same hardware assist implementation can be used.

Data Mapping for a Two-Dimension RAID 6 Array

Figure 6-22 shows the data mapping for a two-dimension RAID level 6 subsystem. The arrangement of the matrix shown indicates disk alignment. In reality the matrix would be built with extents, not disks.

Combining RAID Levels

Considering how array management software could reside within a RAID subsystem and also in host volume management software or a host I/O controller, it seems logical to consider the effect of layering multiple layers of RAID functionality on top of each other. As it turns out, combining mirroring and striping provides both performance and redundancy benefits. It is not necessary to implement RAID in separate products to implement multiple RAID levels. Many RAID products provide RAID 0+1 within a single subsystem.

Objectives of Multilayered RAID Arrays

RAID levels 0 to 6 all make some sort of trade-off between price, performance, and redundancy. Combining multiple RAID levels makes it possible to use the relative strength of one RAID level to compensate for or overcome the weakness of another RAID level. In this way, it might be possible to create a hybrid RAID array with superior characteristics.

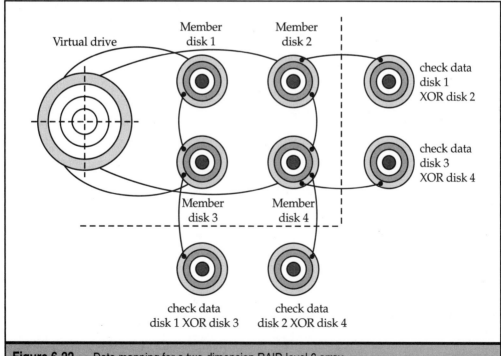

Figure 6-22. Data mapping for a two-dimension RAID level 6 array

RAID Level	Comparative Strength	Comparative Weakness
RAID 0	Performance	No redundancy
RAID 1	Redundancy without write penalty	Cost
RAID 3	Minimal write penalty	No overlapping I/Os
RAID 4	Overlapped small I/Os	Parity disk bottleneck
RAID 5	Overlapped small I/Os	Write penalty

Table 6-3.   Strengths and Weaknesses of Various RAID Levels

The strengths and weaknesses of some of the various RAID levels are listed in Table 6-3.

Multilayered arrays impose multiple block translation mappings for each layer and can cause confusion. For the purpose of the discussions to follow, we will refer to the RAID level that manipulates member disk drives directly as the *lowest position* array and the RAID level closest to the computer's CPU as the *highest position* array. The highest position array is purely virtual and does not directly manipulate hardware.

Another point here is that the highest position array is represented as a single virtual device. The lowest position is actually made up of several physical arrays: one for each of the virtual member drives in the higher position array. Figure 6-23 demonstrates.

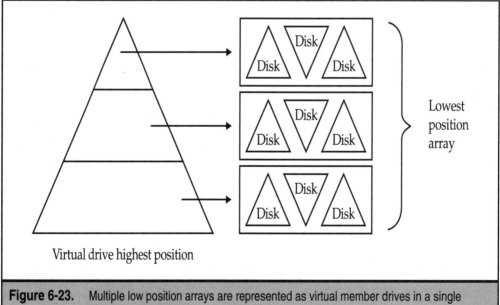

Figure 6-23.   Multiple low position arrays are represented as virtual member drives in a single higher-position array

While it is interesting to think about all kinds of potentially interesting combinations for layered RAID, the only one with widespread product implementation is the combination of RAID 0 striping with RAID 1 mirroring, as discussed in the following section.

Striping and Mirroring Combined—RAID 0+1/RAID 10

The combination of RAID levels 0 and 1 is referred to as RAID 0+1. As we will see, it has some interesting advantages. Combining the speed of RAID 0 striping with the mirrored redundancy of RAID 1, the result is a RAID subsystem that is fast, without write penalties and having excellent redundancy. Figure 6-24 shows a RAID 0+1/RAID 10 configuration, where the RAID 0 component is in the highest position and RAID 1 arrays in the lowest positions.

Notice how this array can lose several disks as long as they do not belong to the same low-position mirrored pair. However, because the array could be wiped out by the loss of one mirrored pair, it does not *guarantee* protection against a two-disk failure as RAID 6 does. Also, the cost of this array is slightly higher than that of parity RAID due to the 100 percent redundancy overhead of the disks.

That said, there are reasons why RAID 0+1/RAID 10 arrays are becoming popular:

▼ Reduced operations do not have reduced performance.

■ There is no write penalty compared to parity RAID.

■ An array with *x* number of virtual member drives can survive up to *x* failed drives.

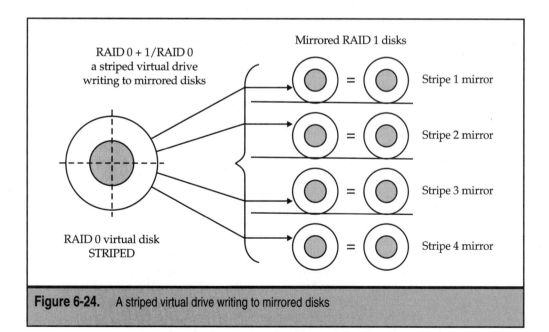

Figure 6-24.   A striped virtual drive writing to mirrored disks

- ■ Array capacity scales without decreasing MTDL.
- ■ MTDL depends on a single drive, not multiples.
- ▲ It is easy to implement with multiple products.

Data Mapping of RAID 0+1/RAID 10

Figure 6-24 showed the preferred data mapping for a RAID 0+1/RAID 10 array, with the RAID 0 striped array in the highest position and the RAID 1 mirrored pair arrays in the lowest positions.

LOCATING RAID FUNCTIONALITY IN THE I/O PATH

Array management and volume management software can reside in several places in the I/O path. Not surprisingly, these are the same locations where one finds mirroring and caching: in the host system, in a host I/O controller, and in a disk subsystem.

RAID in Host-Based Volume Management Software

Volume management software RAID runs in the host system. In this scenario, the host CPU(s) provide the processor muscle for the RAID algorithms. Host-based RAID has proved itself to be fairly effective, but it is more commonly found in Unix environments than in PC server environments.

Operating system and systems vendors sometimes have their own proprietary volume management software that incorporates RAID functionality. Even if higher levels of RAID are not supported, most server operating systems at least support RAID level 1 mirroring. As the market becomes more knowledgeable about RAID and disk subsystems, it is likely that more system vendor and add-on products will be introduced.

Analysis of Host-Based RAID

Host-based RAID requires available processing cycles on the host system CPU(s) as well as taking up bandwidth on the system memory and host I/O bus. Depending on the RAID level implemented, this could cause several I/O operations to traverse the system bus that would otherwise be executed as one request with external array management software. In addition, parity RAID can be CPU intensive when performing XOR operations in high throughput transaction processing environments.

For instance, RAID 1 mirroring is fairly simple to implement and does not involve a great deal of CPU processing. Likewise, RAID level 0 requires the mapping of a virtual drive to member disks. Again, this is not particularly resource consuming. RAID 4, 5, and 6, however, require multiple XOR parity operations and reads from disk drives.

As an example, RAID level 5 running in a host system with a JBOD disk subsystem has to move a fair amount of data over the host I/O bus when updating a strip on disk. In this case, the old data and old parity are read from disk and then new values are written out to disk. Between the reading and writing is the XOR computation. With all this activity going on, it is possible that the host I/O bus could become congested.

Problems with RAID Level 3 in Host-Based Array Management Software

RAID 3 performance depends on writing data to member drives with fairly close tolerances for disk rotation synchronization. However, host-based array management software has to supply its data through the entire I/O path. Delivering RAID 3 stripes to disk drives across the entire I/O path and achieving the desired performance is a difficult problem. The speed of RAID 3 depends on taking advantage of synchronized disks. If delays occur during data transmissions between the host and disks causing member disks to make additional revolutions, the performance of the array will be poor.

NOTE: Many of the redundancy attributes commonly assigned to RAID subsystems are actually part of the disk subsystem and can be provided by JBOD cabinets. These include redundant power supplies and fans and even hot-pluggable disk drives. While host-based RAID can support hot-swapping disk drives, one cannot depend on host software for this support—it must be incorporated in the disk subsystem.

Host I/O Controller–Based RAID

Host I/O controllers have long been a favorite target for applying advanced storage management functionality. This has historically been true for mainframes as well as for mid-range, Unix, and PC systems. RAID-enabled host I/O controllers are available from systems companies and companies specializing in host I/O controllers, such as Adaptec, AMI, Compaq, CMD, and IBM.

Analysis of Host I/O Controller–Based RAID

Located between the host I/O bus and the storage bus, host I/O controllers are an excellent location to implement array management software. The performance of the RAID function can be optimized for the type of storage bus or network being used. Both internal and external storage can be combined into a single high-speed array. It is not unusual for a host I/O controller to support multiple buses and have the capability to combine members to form an array across these buses as shown here:

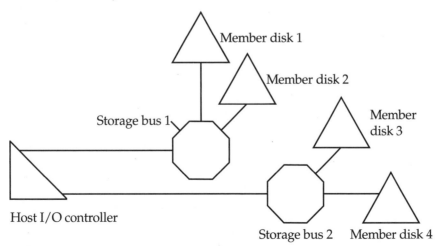

RAID 3 is easier to consider implementing in a host I/O controller than with host-based array management software, as the I/O path components between the host I/O controller and member disks are shorter and faster. RAID levels 4, 5, and 6 all have the read, modify, write cycle to process that would impact the storage bus or network, but this would not have a direct impact on host I/O bus and system memory bus traffic.

Disk Subsystem–Based RAID

RAID subsystems are fairly common in the market and provide a wide variety of functions and RAID levels.

Analysis of Disk Subsystem–Based RAID

The integration of array management software with disk channel technology and disk subsystem redundancy allows RAID subsystems to offer the broadest range of RAID features and functions. By placing the array management software at the "far end" of the I/O path, adjacent to the disk drives, the least amount of "metatraffic" is generated over the host I/O and storage buses.

SETTING FAULT-TOLERANT STANDARDS: THE RAID ADVISORY BOARD (RAB)

Besides helping to standardize RAID terminology and RAID level interpretation guidelines, the RAID Advisory Board also has created several disk subsystem classifications for fault resistance and tolerance.

The following classifications are defined by RAB:

▼ Failure resistant disk system (FRDS)

■ Failure resistant disk system, plus (FRDS+)

■ Failure tolerant resistant disk system (FTDS)

■ Failure tolerant resistant disk system, plus (FTDS+)

■ Failure tolerant resistant disk system, plus plus (FTDS++)

■ Disaster tolerant disk system, (DTDS)

▲ Disaster tolerant disk system, plus (DTDS+)

Interested readers are encouraged to visit the RAB's Web site at **www.raid-advisory.com**. Table 6-4 briefly compares the differences between these classifications.

Class	Protection Offered
FRDS	Disk failures, rebuild, host and bus failures, monitor failures, and warnings
FRDS+	All of the preceding plus hot swapping, cache failure, external power loss
FTDS	All of the preceding plus channel failure, controller failure, power supply failure
FTDS+	All of the preceding plus hot spare disks
FTDS++	All of the preceding plus multiple disk failures
DTDS	All of the preceding plus zone failure protection
DTDS+	All of the preceding plus long distance access protection

Table 6-4. RAB Disk System Classification

SUMMARY

Disk subsystems and RAID are the primary vehicles for creating server-class storage. As storage capacities continue to increase with continued pressure to improve performance and availability, it is likely that RAID subsystems will be the mainstays of the storage industry for many years to come.

Today's RAID implementations are based on striping, mirroring, and XOR-based parity. As the cost of disk drives continues to decrease, it is possible that the cost arguments for using parity RAID will become less interesting and that mirroring-based solutions will dominate. While the discussions of XOR computations in this chapter may be interesting, there is little doubt that they add a fair amount of complexity to the picture, especially for error recovery.

It is hoped that the characteristics of the various RAID levels presented will provide insight for readers looking to match storage system performance and protection with the requirements of their applications. The subject of tuning RAID subsystems by adjusting stripe depth was not included in this book, as it is a topic that is fairly implementation- and application-specific. But the reader should be aware that beyond matching the best fitting RAID level to an application, the adjustments in stripe depth may be the next most important parameter to optimizing performance.

EXERCISES

1. Design a RAID array with an exportable storage capacity that is 90 percent or greater of the aggregate "raw" storage of the member disk drives.

2. Now assume the array designed in exercise 1 implements RAID 5. Assume a stripe depth of 64KB, how much data needs to be held in a write-back cache so that check data does not have to be rolled back when writing to any particular stripe in the array.

3. Design two 500GB 0+1 RAID subsystems using 36GB and 75GB drives. What is the maximum number of disk drive failures that can occur in both arrays without losing data?

4. There are six disk drives in a multiported RAID subsystem, each with 50GB of raw capacity. The array management software allows you to create up to three extents on each drive, none less than 10GB. Configure the following arrays to meet the storage requirements for four exported virtual drives.

   Array #1: RAID 5 with 40GB usable capacity

   Array #2: RAID 5 with 90GB usable capacity

   Array #3: RAID 5 with 20GB usable capacity

   Array #4: RAID 1 with 40GB usable capacity

   What is the maximum number of drives that can fail in the subsystem you designed in Exercise #4 before data is lost?

CHAPTER 7

Network Backup: The Foundation of Storage Management

With so much data on open systems servers, it is important to understand how this data is protected from disasters. Unfortunately, many threats to data that cannot be easily prevented will destroy data and the systems that access it. If that happens, the only viable solution is to restore the systems and data. Several techniques for preserving data availability have already been discussed in previous chapters. Disk mirroring enables data to be recovered from another disk or subsystem. RAID enables data to be accessed when a single disk drive fails.

These techniques protect against equipment failures, but they do not protect against defective human beings. In fact, users constitute the single biggest threat to data by deleting and altering data, including virus activities. In many cases, it is easier to restore a previous version of a file than it is to work with a file that has been tampered with. Backup is a well-known safeguard against all kinds of unexpected data loss, and it is generally considered irresponsible systems management not to perform regular backups.

The realization that data might need to be restored someday is not necessarily a very profound thought. A lot of backup hardware, software, and tapes have been sold over the years. Unfortunately, the challenges of backup and recovery in network environments are great, and many customers experience chronic difficulties in managing backup for their open systems servers. This is somewhat remarkable, considering that network backup is probably the second most prevalent network storage application behind file serving.

This chapter examines the technologies used in network backup today and some of the reasons why backup is a problem for many organizations. Wiring, storing, and filing functions are all used in network backup, and the applications of these functions in network backup are described briefly. The discussions in this chapter set the stage for Chapter 10, which examines storage networking applications, particularly how this new technology can be applied to solving the difficult problems of network server backup and recovery.

NETWORK BACKUP AND RECOVERY

Network backup is typically implemented in three different types of products:

▼ Backup hardware, including systems, adapters, tape storage technologies, and networking

■ Media, usually magnetic tape

▲ Software

We'll look at each of these three product classes in the sections that follow.

Hardware Used in Network Backup Systems

The primary hardware used in network backup is shown in Figure 7-1.

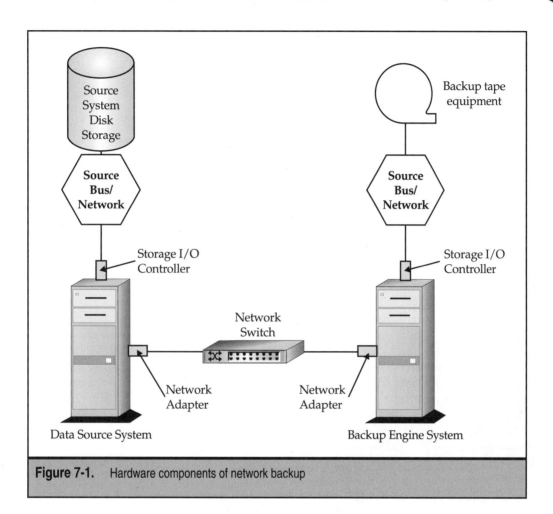

Figure 7-1.   Hardware components of network backup

When most people think of network backup hardware, they typically think of some sort of tape drive. But to get a complete understanding of network backup, it is essential to attain a broader picture of backup hardware that also includes systems, networks, and I/O channels.

System Roles in Network Backup

There are two different types of computer systems in network backup: the *backup engine* system and the *data source* system.

Backup Engine System

In general, backup data is transferred over a network from the data source system to the backup engine system. After the backup engine system receives the data, it writes it to a tape storage device. The backup engine system is the computer where the primary controlling software runs for backup operations. In addition, it is typically where all of the management functions reside, including device operations, backup scheduling, media management, database/catalog processing, and error handling.

Data Source System

The *data source system* is the computer having data that needs to be backed up. Sometimes this is also referred to as the *client system*. However, using client/server terminology for backup can be confusing, as backup clients are often network servers. Therefore, this chapter attempts to avoid using the word "client" when discussing network backup. The term "target system" is also used sometimes to identify the data source system. However, the word "target" is part of the SCSI syntax that identifies a device or subsystem on the bus, including the backup devices or subsystems to which backup data is being written. Therefore, to avoid confusion, we'll use "data source system" to refer to the systems being backed up.

Backup Device and Subsystem Technology

The foundation of most backup and recovery systems is a tape device of some kind that performs the primary *storing* function of backup. As mentioned previously, in SCSI-speak these devices are referred to as *target* devices. This can be confusing when talking about restore operations because the term "target system" is used to identify a system on the network to which data is being restored. In that case, there can be both a *target device* from which the restored data is being read as well as a *target system* to which data is being restored. In general, the term "target" has not been used much in this book to avoid confusion. However, the reader should be aware that the terms are sometimes used in practice.

Tape devices have a mode of data transfers referred to as *streaming*, which means the tape drive is running at full speed without waiting for data to be transferred to it. Streaming speed for tape drives is much faster than nonstreaming speeds, in which the tape mechanism must be continually stopped and restarted, slowing down the overall process and causing extra wear on the tape and drive. Therefore, it is desirable to design a network backup system that can stream a backup drive to attain optimal performance.

Among the most important components of tape devices are the tape heads. Tape heads recognize fluctuations in the magnetic signals that occur as the head and tape move in relationship with each other. Tape head technology is often derived from disk head technology, but tape drives implement completely different methods for positioning the heads over data on tape. This topic is discussed further in the section called "Media Components for Network Backup."

Backup Subsystems

Just as disk drives can be placed in JBOD and RAID subsystems, tape drives can also be combined with other technologies to create subsystems that provide a variety of functions geared to simplifying backup management.

Tape Autoloaders   Tape autoloaders combine an individual tape drive with a tape robot mechanism that can automatically select, grab, remove, and insert tapes under either programmatic or manual control. Typically, autoloaders can hold between four and twenty tapes that are put in the slots of *tape magazines* inserted and removed from the autoloader. The diagram that follows shows the basic components of a tape autoloader:

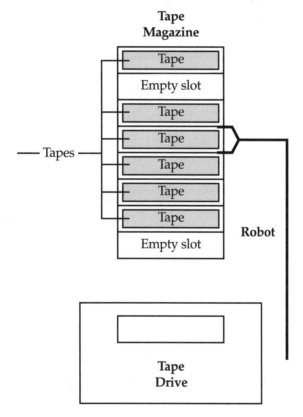

Autoloaders are a good solution for situations where backup commonly extends beyond one or two tapes. In networks where the storage capacity is not large, autoloaders can be used to hold a week's worth of tapes without needing to add or remove any. Because they hold a relatively small number of tapes, they have limited value for managing large amounts of media.

Tape Libraries   Tape libraries refer to any tape automation products that are physically larger than and hold more tapes than an autoloader. They often have more than one tape drive, but that is not a requirement. Tape libraries can be quite large and hold thousands of tapes, although libraries of this size are rare for open systems network backup. Common library configurations have two to four tape drives and can hold 20 to 400 tapes. Removable tape magazines are common in these products, and there are many possible configurations and geometries used in library systems. The next diagram shows the basic components in a typical tape library:

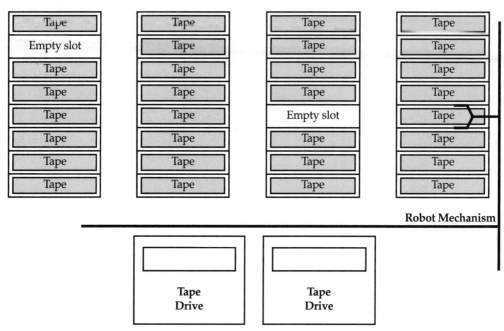

Libraries can use bar code readers to identify tapes as they are inserted. When a large number of tapes are inserted, the ability to use bar code recognition can save a great deal of time. Normally, the bar code information is a sequence of numbers that is applied to the spine of the tape cartridge as a sticker. The bar code number is independent of the name used by the backup software application; however, most library-enabled backup software packages provide a way to correlate bar code information with a more intuitive name.

Wiring Components in Network Backup

The networks that data source systems and backup engine systems communicate over and the storage I/O channels both types of systems use constitute the wiring component of network backup.

Data source and backup engine systems communicate with each other over a data network including such hardware as network interface cards (NICs), switches, hubs, and cabling. Traditionally, open systems network backup has been run over Ethernet. Network backup can quickly saturate a production Ethernet network with its heavy traffic loads: 10 Mb/s networks are inadequate for most server backup operations; 100 Mb/s Fast Ethernet or FDDI and Gigabit Ethernet links obviously deliver much better results. Network backup performance depends on several variables, particularly the amount of network traffic generated by other systems and applications sharing the network. It is important to remember that other network applications can be adversely affected while backups are running. For that reason, dedicated segments can be employed to provide optimal bandwidth for backup with the least impact on normal production network traffic.

Both data source and backup engine systems transfer data to and from storage devices using storage I/O controllers and a storage bus or network. The storage bus or network used on the backup engine system could be used to attach disk drives, but tape drives are often isolated on their own dedicated bus to allow optimal disk performance. Most backup devices in use today implement parallel SCSI controllers.

Media Components for Network Backup

For backup and recovery, the buck stops at media. Neither hardware nor software, media provide the most fundamental storing function and is typically the least expensive and most critical part of the backup system. The entire subject of media and media management is one of the least understood aspects of network backup. Media management becomes increasingly confusing as the capacity of online and stored data increases and the number of media parts needed to store new and historical data increases along with it.

Physical Tape Format

Tape drives and the cartridges that work with them are typically developed together as inseparable technologies. New tape drives usually have larger capacities and faster performance than previous tape drive designs and require new cartridges to take advantage of them. Part of the design of the drive/cartridge combination is its media format, or the specification of the physical and electrical characteristics of how data is written to the media.

The physical format of the tape drive specifies the size of standard unit of data, its orientation on the tape, the location of tracking information, error correction data, and the position and frequency of location markings for locating data on the tape. Design changes to heads in tape drive products often alter the geometry and configuration of the heads as well as making incremental changes to the format. While it is possible for new designs to take existing formats into account, it is virtually impossible for the improved design and its associated format to be achievable with previously existing drives. That's why new tape drives can usually read existing tapes made on older drives while older drives cannot read the tapes written by newer drives. Although the same phenomenon occurs with disk drive technology, it's not a problem because the media in disk drives is not exchanged with other disk drives.

In general, there is an astounding lack of compatibility among various physical and logical tape formats in the market. This situation has frustrated IT professionals for many years, who have had to discard existing tape equipment because it was no longer compatible with newer technology products. Unfortunately, this situation is a by-product of the evolution of tape technology in a competitive market. Tape manufacturers have to be able to produce higher-capacity, higher-performance tape drives in order to stay in business.

The very real problem with this situation is how to read data from tapes that have been stored for many years when the drive technology has long been obsolete and is no longer available to read it. Backward compatibility should not be assumed in future generations of products. For that reason, IT organizations need to plan for the availability of equipment needed to read tapes into the future. This is a much easier issue to discuss than to follow through on, as convenient services or facilities may not exist to adequately store old tape drive equipment.

Helical Scan Technology

Helical scan tape drives use the basic mechanism that has been developed for video tape recorders. The quality of this technology varies from relatively expensive and high-accuracy 19mm professional studio gear to the relatively inexpensive and reasonably accurate high-volume 8mm and 4mm tape technologies used in camcorders and DAT (Digital Audio Tape) recorders, respectively.

The general concept of helical scan tape is that the heads are embedded in a rotating drum that spins at high speed, at an angle relative to the tape's edges. As the tape is passed in front of this moving drum, the heads read and write data in a pattern of diagonal stripes. Typically, helical scan drives have two read and two write heads, which can be positioned in a variety of geometries. The transmission channel for helical drives uses radio frequency transmissions to transfer between the spinning drum and the I/O circuitry of the drive. Figure 7-2 shows the relationship between the head, drum tape, and stripes of helical scan recording.

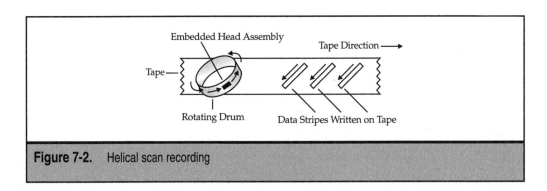

Figure 7-2.   Helical scan recording

One of the advantages of helical scan tape technology is the fact that it is used widely in the film, video, broadcast, music, and home electronics industries. As a result, the cost of parts for a helical scan tape drive can be lower than comparable linear recording technology due to the high-volume manufacturing efficiencies achieved with camcorder production.

Linear Recording Technology

Linear recording technology is similar in nature to common audio tape recording. The head is held stationary while the tape is passed over it. Often several tape heads are stacked next to each other to read and write data on adjacent tracks. (The word "track" in this context refers to a defined strip on the surface of the tape that is parallel to the edge of the tape and maintains its distance from the edge.) Stacking allows linear tape drives to support many tracks at once—from 9 to 128.

The head stacks are connected to servomotor mechanisms and actuators that change the relative position of the heads to enable a track to be read or written. Like audio tapes, with their A and B sides, linear tape drives reverse their direction at the end of the tape and start working in the opposite direction. Some linear tape drives use a *serpentine* tracking system with several such reversals. With the capability to use both directions of the tape, searches for data on tape can be accomplished much faster. Figure 7-3 shows the relationship between the heads, the actuators, and the tape in linear track recording.

The Media Cartridge

Network backup media is almost always packaged in a cartridge mechanism, commonly called a "media cartridge" or "tape cartridge." It's a subtle distinction, perhaps, but the media is the actual magnetic material that receives and retains the signal, and the cartridge is the integrated case with reels, guides, bearings, and all the other small parts that physically support the media.

A media cartridge can be identified by holes and other indicators molded into its shell. These indicators communicate to devices the technology generation of the media and the device used to read and write data to the cartridge. For instance, holes in the

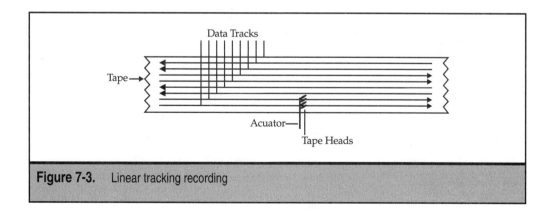

Figure 7-3. Linear tracking recording

cartridge can be detected by a tape drive, which can adjust its operations to provide backward compatibility.

Tape Media

Tape is practically synonymous with backup in network backup for several reasons:

▼   Tapes provide good performance for reading and writing long streams of data typically encountered during backup and restore operations.

■   Tapes provide excellent capacity compared with rotating magnetic and optical media.

■   Tapes are relatively small and can be easily stored and transported.

▲   Tape is cheaper per megabyte than other media, such as rotating magnetic and the various forms of optical media.

Using Sequential Media   Tapes are accessed sequentially. In other words, data is written to tape as sequential blocks starting at the front of the tape and continuing on until the end of the tape is reached.

Sequentially accessed media differ considerably from random access media, such as a rotating disk drive platter. To begin with, tapes are off-line media and do not depend on having a single copy of a file that every user or application accesses. For example, disk file systems typically do not allow different files in the same directory to have the same name. Tape storage, on the other hand, can store many copies and versions of a file with the same identical name in multiple locations on the tape. As files are updated on disk and copied onto tape, the complete new version from the same directory location is written to a new tape location. Existing versions of the file stored on the same tape are not updated with new information—the previously written file version is left intact. This drawing shows how multiple complete versions of files are stored on tape:

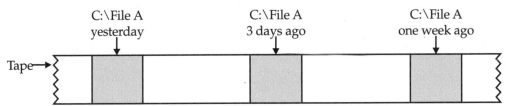

Tapes work well for storing large files. As sequentially accessed storage, tape does not spread data evenly across its surface in small chunks as disk storage typically does; instead, it simply writes it in large contiguous blocks on tape. Therefore, it is well suited for copying extremely large files that would be scattered all over rotating disk platters. While the access time to any random block on a tape is extremely long, tape can achieve streaming speeds in the range of 5 to 15 MB/s depending on the technology used.

The demise of tape has been predicted for decades as other removable storage technologies have been developed and seemingly destined to take its place. However, tape technology continues to prove itself as an excellent combination of performance, capacity, and price. So far, optical media has not been fast enough nor has it supported the required capacity that allows it to compete with tape.

Disk drives have also been used for backup, but they have historically been too expensive and too difficult to remove or transport as dictated by disaster recovery requirements. Both these limitations are becoming less of an issue over time, as disk drive pricing declines to less than $.01/MB and network storage provides the capability to make remote electronic copies of data, circumventing the need to physically move tapes.

Media Sets

Although tapes offer an excellent combination of capacity and performance, sometimes their capabilities are not adequate for the job at hand. In these cases, multiple tapes can be used together as linked sets commonly referred to as *media sets*, or sometimes *media pools*. Media sets enable concurrent and/or sequential backup operations to run on multiple tape drives to achieve the performance and/or capacity required. As these tapes represent a single repository of backup data that may need to be restored together at some time in the future, it's important to be able to schedule sets together as part of the same backup or restore operation. Just as you would not typically cut and splice pieces of tape together from different data tapes to create a merged backup tape, you should also avoid mixing tapes together from different media sets.

Media Magazines

Tape autoloaders and libraries store tapes in slots that are referred to as *elements*. Usually tapes are removed and inserted one at a time; however, many tape automation products use magazines, which are multislot tape containers that can be removed and inserted as single modules.

Tape Formulas   Data tapes are made by combining several different materials to form a single composite ribbon. A great deal of specialized chemical technology is involved in creating data tapes. For example, the largest American producer of data tapes is the 3M Corporation, which is primarily a chemical manufacturing and technology company. For that reason, the tape *formula* is an important technology for backup and recovery systems.

Most tape is made up of the following layers:

▼   A backing layer, which blocks magnetic signals

■   A base layer made out of mylar for strength and flexibility

■   A binding layer for holding magnetic materials in place

■   A magnetic layer, which provides the actual storage function

▲   A tape coating, which protects the magnetic layer and provides lubrication

The backing, base, and binding layers are important for the longevity of the tape. A failure in any of these components can result in the tape literally falling apart. However, problems with tapes can be unknown for many years until the tape has aged and been exposed to environmental influences.

The magnetic layer gives the tape its signal strength characteristics, or *output*. The greater the output level, the stronger the signal. The output measurement of tapes tends to be proportional to the frequency of the signal; as frequency increases, so does the signal strength, until a point is reached where higher frequencies can no longer be supported. In general, a higher-output tape is easier to read and restore data from than a lower-output tape.

Finally, the coating on the tape determines how well the tape will wear over many uses. The coating protects the magnetic layer from small dirt particles that can remove or eclipse the magnetic layer. The coating also helps maintain a constant speed by reducing friction. This is extremely important, especially in helical scan tape drives.

Caring for and Storing Tapes

Manufacturer's specs for tape commonly claim the ability to read data for 30 years. Such claims are based on accelerated tests under optimal conditions and should not be the basis of a realistic tape storage policy. It is much more realistic to think about tapes as lasting for five years, possibly ten if they are carefully stored and maintained. As an advanced chemical and materials technology, tapes require consistent care to maintain their composition and the integrity of the data written to them. Tapes degrade over time due to oxidation of the metal particles within them and aging of the various layers, resulting in cracking and gaps in the magnetic layer. Here are a few maintenance tips to remember about tape:

▼   Maintain low humidity.

■   Maintain cool temperatures.

■   Periodically retension tapes.

■   Limit the number of passes.

▲   Keep tape heads clean.

Humidity is tape's worst enemy because it causes tapes to oxidize. Oxidation adversely affects the magnetic and physical properties of the magnetic layer in the tape. Therefore, one should avoid storing tapes in a humid environment. Also, the backing and binder of tapes stretch and change shape as the temperature increases. This causes the data signal on tape to stretch, which makes it more difficult to read correctly. If possible, tapes should be maintained at consistent, cool temperatures in the range of 40 to 60 degrees Fahrenheit or 5 to 15 degrees Celsius.

Tape stiffens with age if it is not used. Stiffness causes cracks and leads to the breaking apart of the various layers in the tape. Therefore, tapes should be periodically *tensioned*, preferably every six months, if they are not being actively used at least once a year. Tape tensioning is a common operation found in most backup applications that basically un-winds and rewinds the tape. Archived tapes are at the most risk for loss due to tape stiff-ness because they are typically stored out of sight and forgotten.

Tape heads read and write data when the tape comes in contact with the tape head. This causes wear and tear on both the tape and the tape head. A *tape pass* occurs each time a head reads from or writes to a given section of tape. While the data might be dif-ferent, the physical section of tape is the same. Tapes sometimes specify the number of passes allowed before degradation occurs (usually in the range of 2,000), and some backup software packages count the number of tape passes that occur. A tape pass should not be confused with a backup operation. For instance, a section on a tape could have several tape passes occur on it in the course of a single backup operation. This makes counting tape passes extremely difficult, because it is virtually impossible to track each section of tape uniquely. Still, software that counts tape-passes provides backup administrators with the information they need to manage tape-life expectancies and determine when tapes should be "retired."

Tapes shed materials that can coat the tape heads. The more residue there is on the tape head, the less strong the signal will be that is recorded on tape. It doesn't take a rocket scien-tist to figure out that a poorly recorded signal may be harder to read than a strong signal. For that reason, tape heads on tape drives should be regularly cleaned to reduce the effect of dirty heads. Most manufacturers specify cleaning approximately every 30 hours of opera-tion. A weekly cleaning schedule is a good idea.

TIP: Tapes last longest if they are kept in cool, dry conditions, are used in drives that have regular head cleanings, are not overused, and are tensioned twice a year.

Software Components

The software components of network backup and recovery are discussed in the following sections. While hardware determines the maximum transfer rates and seeking perfor-mance of the backup system, software determines how efficiently the hardware is used. Backup software provides wiring, storing, and filing functions in varying amounts de-pending on the implementation and design choices made. Terms and concepts presented here are general and are not intended to represent specific products.

Several generic components are included in most network backup systems, as shown in Figure 7-4.

Job Scheduler

All backup software products have some type of *job scheduler*. This component deter-mines what information to back up, and when backup should start. It also determines what device and media to use. Job scheduling can be done interactively through an inter-face where the administrator selects all the variables, and it can also be automated. In general, backups tend to be automated and restores tend to be done manually.

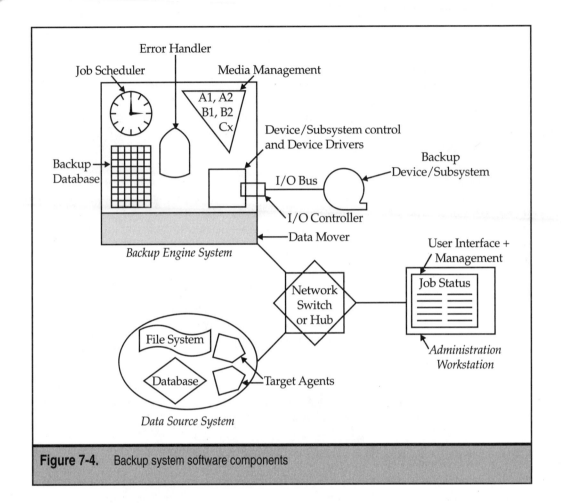

Figure 7-4. Backup system software components

Media Manager

Backup data is written to tapes or some other recording medium. As backup media contain corporate assets, it makes sense to manage their use. In fact, *media management* is one of the most important aspects in any network backup product. There are often many tapes to manage in support of several different backup goals. Tapes that are not used in their correct sequence can result in the inability to restore a complete server. With many tapes within the grasp of hurried administrators, it is easy for mistakes to be made selecting media for backup operations. Automated media management can help reduce these mistakes.

One function of a media manager is to ensure that usable tapes are available for upcoming backup operations. Another important feature is maintaining an inventory of media loaded in an automated autochanger or library. Other functions include determining which tapes to move off site for disaster recovery protection, which tapes to move back on site for backup operations, and which tapes to discard due to error counts or overuse.

Data Source System Agent

The software component running on the data source system is usually called a backup *agent*. Agents are filing functions that are developed for particular file systems or databases and take advantage of special programming interfaces for reading data and their associated metadata.

Backup agents are developed to work closely with a particular backup engine. The interactions between backup engines and data source agents are highly specialized to fit the particular processing sequence of the engine. While standardized backup agents are desired, they are not likely to be developed for existing network backup architectures because that would require backup software developers to make considerable changes to their products.

Network Data Mover

The *data mover* is the higher-level *wiring* function that oversees the copying of data from the data source system to the engine and eventually to tape. The data mover can reside on the engine system and "pull" data from the data source or reside on the data source and "push" data to the engine. The data mover can also run on another server and move data on behalf of the engine to a connected tape drive.

Device/Subsystem Controller

The *device controller* is the software component that manages the detailed operations of the physical storage device or subsystem that writes to media. Usually this *storing* function is part of the backup engine, but it can also reside on a data source system or other system in the network and have its operations controlled remotely by the backup engine. This is called *remote device support.*

Logical Tape Format

In addition to the physical tape format that is determined by the drive design, there is also a logical format that is imposed over it by backup software. The logical format is the higher-level organization used to locate files on tape. Logical formats determine the size and location of:

▼ Header information, including the electronic tape name or label

■ Index information and location markers to quickly locate backup data sets

▲ Backup data sets, including data that may be interleaved

The primary requirement for a logical tape format is locating data correctly on tapes. One of the most common methods used is to keep an index at the beginning of the tape that identifies where *data sets* are on tape. A data set is a file or group of files copied together as part of a single backup job. For example, files copied from a specific disk volume on a server could form a data set; in contrast, an individual file that is manually backed up would be written as a single data set. Individual files are accessed for restores by first reading the index, then locating the data set, and finally locating the file within that data set. There are many ways to structure the information and access to data on tape. One possible structure is shown here:

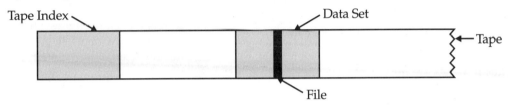

The *index* is usually a fixed-length section of tape that can hold many data set records. When new data sets are written to tape, the index is updated to reflect the presence and location of each new data set. When data is overwritten as tapes are reused in later backup operations, the index is also overwritten to indicate the new data sets. As a result, the index is constantly being used by both backup and restore operations. This is typically the section of tape that has the highest number of tape passes and wears out the fastest.

Several tape formats are in widespread use. The Unix TAR (Tape Archive and Retrieval) format is used by several vendors. The MTF (Microsoft Tape Format) is commonly implemented on products that back up and restore Windows systems. NetWare backup systems tend to use SIDF (Systems Independent Data Format). Legato Systems has a tape format called OpenTape, which is available for other companies to use but has been basically ignored by the other backup vendors. The use of multiple tape formats on different platforms means that it can be difficult if not impossible to read a tape on one platform that was created on another one. Readers are advised to inquire about cross-platform tape format compatibility.

Backup System Database or Catalog

Despite common perceptions, the real heart and soul of any network backup system is its internal database, sometimes called its *catalog*. The backup database provides a filing function for backup that helps administrators locate data stored on backup media that might need to be restored. For the most part, the word "catalog" implies a collection of records of specific backup operations such as what was backed up by those operations and what tapes were used.

A *backup system database,* on the other hand, implies some type of relational database technology that allows views of backup information based on multiple indices, including such things as filenames, file date and timestamps, tape names, pool names, date of backup, and file ownership information. The database is central to the backup process for its capability to support restores. By providing several search views, administrators can quickly find particular files or database tables to restore without having to manually scan backup records. This can save hours and even days, depending on circumstances.

However, this capability has a cost. In order to have a database, the data must first be collected and then entered into the database. Where backup is concerned, these databases tend to be very large, as the number of objects being backed up tends to be large. For instance, if there are 500,000 files on a server, there have to be at least 500,000 records in the backup system database to store records for each file. As backup information is added to those records, it's easy to see where backups of 500,000 files create a large database. The transaction processing alone to update backup records can take hours to complete. Multiplying the number of servers by ten or more, it becomes obvious how large a task the database processing is for backup.

The situation becomes even more interesting when each entity being backed up has a record for each of the copies available on media. Let's say there were 15 records for each file on the system. The size of the database now starts becoming an issue. Most backup systems have a facility for removing backup records from their databases when the size of the database becomes a problem—usually this is apparent in sluggish backup performance and extended database processing cycles. The deletion of a database record does not mean the data on a tape cannot be restored, but it does mean it will take much longer to manually find and restore it.

The key issue in all this is the number of files being backed up and tracked individually. A large database that backs up relatively large (50MB) tables as a single entity can be much easier to manage than a small file server with lots of small (10KB) files.

User Interface

Most network backup software uses a graphical user interface, or GUI, that controls most of the other functions in the software, including the configuration of the data source agent.

Error Handling System

All backup software has some way of communicating errors—and some ways are better than others. There needs to be some way of knowing when backup fails and what caused the failure. The challenge is understanding which errors need to be treated as important and which are less critical. For example, a file that is backed up but does not have its access date backed up could be considered an error. The question is, what kind of alert or report should be generated to draw attention to this? In reality, there are bound to be several such errors every night the backup runs.

Backup error logs should be reviewed regularly to identify undetected problems. Too often, serious backup problems are not uncovered until a restore is needed and it is too late.

Typical Network Backup

The most common network backup system used today is a client/server backup model where the backup engine establishes network connections directly with agents on data source systems and copies data through those connections.

When the engine begins backing up the data source system, it communicates with its agent and begins accessing the file system or database using the programming interface provided. The results of the file system scan determine which files need to be backed up. This information is transmitted back to the engine for the data mover to start working on. The data mover copies files over the network and hands them off to the backup device control system, which eventually writes them to a tape in a tape drive. When the file is completely written to tape, the database can be updated to reflect its successful backup. Figure 7-5 shows the data transfer through the backup engine system starting at the network interface card all the way to the backup device(s).

When one sees the whole picture laid out like this, it's not hard to see why backup over a network is slower than backup over an I/O bus. For starters, a 100 Mb/s network is roughly equivalent to a fairly slow and outdated 10 MB/s storage channel. The inability

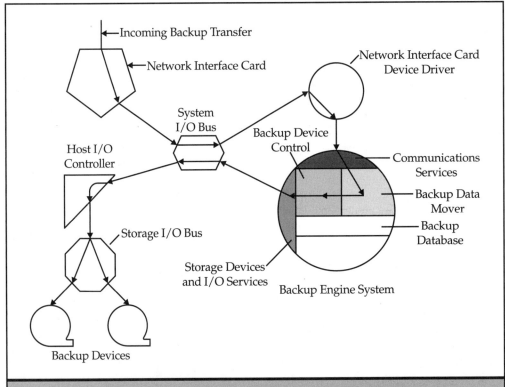

Figure 7-5.   The detailed data flow path through a backup engine system

for the network to deliver data comparable to the speed of the backup channel is one of the typical problems with many network backup systems. Some techniques for circumventing these performance problems are discussed next.

Local Backup to an Attached Tape Drive

The simplest network backup is not really network backup at all—it's local server backup of network servers. This method installs all components on the server: engine, data source, data mover, and everything else. The main reason for running local backup is to get faster performance from a locally attached tape drive. The next diagram shows three servers, each with its own local backup:

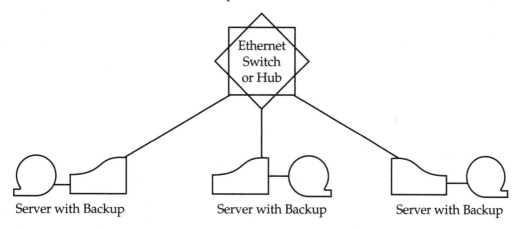

The primary problem with this type of single-server backup is the amount of management support needed. Local backup equates to at least one tape drive per server, one backup software package per server, and multiple tapes for each server. This is considerably more to manage than a single large network backup system. In addition, the workload of the backup engine will compete with other resources on the data source system and impact its performance.

Backup with Remote Devices on Data Source Systems

To achieve the performance of locally attached devices with the manageability of a network system, one can attach tape drives to large data source systems. But instead of operating the tape drive with a backup engine running on the system, the backup operations are managed remotely by a backup engine somewhere else on the network. Figure 7-6 shows a network backup system using this kind of remote device support on data source systems.

Remote device support provides excellent performance for large data source systems that have too much data to be backed up over the network. Media management, however, is almost as difficult as it is for multiple single-server backup systems.

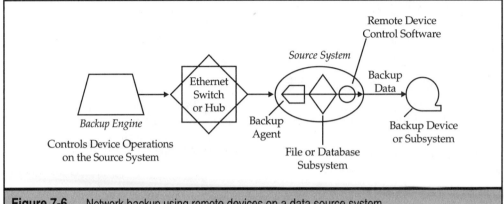

Figure 7-6.   Network backup using remote devices on a data source system

Network Backup with Parallel Data Transfers

Device parallelism is a performance enhancing technique that routes data from one data source to a dedicated device. This way, a backup engine can back up multiple data sources simultaneously to an equal number of devices. Device parallelism provides a way to get more "bulk" backup done, but it does not help stream the tape drives or speed up the backup of any data source system. The primary advantage is the ability to finish the entire backup faster than by processing one session at a time.

Another type of parallelism is called *data interleaving*. Data interleaving combines the data from multiple sessions with multiple data sources onto a single tape. The result is the capability to achieve streaming speeds to a tape drive by combining data from several sessions. Interleaving data cannot speed up the performance of backup on any one data source, but it does make the overall backup process finish faster. The combination of device parallelism and interleaving allows backups to finish faster yet—if the networking capabilities of the backup engine can support the additional traffic. Figure 7-7 shows two data sources being backed up simultaneously by a backup engine that is interleaving their data on a single tape drive.

WORKING WITH BACKUP

Several variations in backup operations can be implemented. This section explores some of these variations and explains how and why they are used.

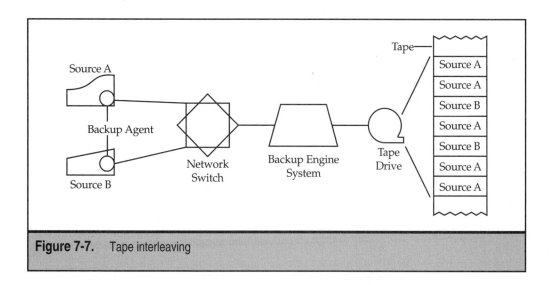

Figure 7-7.   Tape interleaving

Types of Backup Operations

There are a few basic backup operations. Usually, the selection of the backup operation depends on the importance of the data, the amount of time available to run backups, and the day of the week or month. In general, there are four basic backup operations to consider:

▼   Full backups

■   Incremental backups

■   Differential backups

▲   Selective, or on-demand, backups

Full Backup

Full backups copy the complete contents of a disk volume. In other words, a full backup would be used to back up the C: drive, the D: drive, and so on of a system. The term "full backup" can be applied to the server and include all its assigned logical volumes, or it can be applied on a volume-by-volume basis. The best reason for performing full backups is to provide the easiest full restore. With the entire contents of the volume on a single tape, or group of tapes, the restore process is straightforward and easy to follow. Full backups are typically performed on weekends when there is adequate time to finish the job without interrupting the work of end users.

Incremental Backup

Incremental backups copy newly changed data that has been created or updated since the last backup operation. The main advantage of incremental backups is to perform the shortest possible backup operation. When incremental backups are used, the restore process requires data to be restored from the full backup and all incremental backups run since the last full backup. This does not mean that a different tape needs to be used for full and incremental backups. The same tape can be used, or a different tape could be used every day if desired, depending on capacity and off-site storage requirements.

Differential Backup

Differential backup copies all new data that has been created or updated since the last full backup. For instance, if a full backup were performed over the weekend, at the end of the business day on Monday the differential backup would be the same as an incremental backup. However, on Tuesday the differential backup would contain all the data that would have been copied on the incremental backups on both Monday and Tuesday. By Thursday, the differential backup would contain the incremental data from Monday through Thursday. The main purpose of differential backup is to limit the number of tapes needed for a full restore. The data written to tape in a differential backup operation is depicted here:

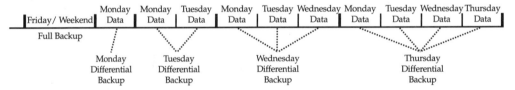

On-Demand Backup

The backup operations listed in the preceding sections normally run as automatic operations that follow a defined schedule established by the job scheduler component of the backup application. However, administrators also need to be able to back up data on demand as situations dictate.

Backing Up Live Systems

Backup is a technology where there is little substitute for brute-force performance and capacity advantages. No matter how clever the algorithms may be for managing backup operations, the capability to move data and finish faster is always a significant benefit. It is hard to go wrong by purchasing the fastest and highest-capacity tape equipment.

One of the trickiest parts of backup is ensuring that the data being backed up has integrity. At the root of the problem is the nature of multiuser, high-availability server systems where many users may be accessing data while the backup system is attempting to make a copy of it. If updates are made to files or databases at the same time backup is copying them, it's likely that the backup copy will have parts that were copied before the data was updated, and parts that were copied after the data was updated. In other words, the data copied for backup represents two different versions in unequal halves. When that happens, the data copied to tape is inconsistent and unusable.

There are two basic ways to deal with this problem:

▼ Cold backups

▲ Hot backups

We will discuss these two types of backup in the following sections.

Cold Backup

Cold backup is a backup operation that makes backup copies of data to tape while the server is not accepting new updates from end users or applications. This completely alleviates the problems of a concurrent update while a backup copy is going on. Cold backups work very well and are often used for backing up parts of databases. Of course, the problem with cold backups is that they make the server unavailable for updates while the backup process is running. If the cold backup runs for six or eight hours, this could be a serious problem for a server with 24 × 7 availability requirements.

Hot Backup

The availability issue with cold backups initiated the development of *hot backups.* The idea of hot backups is that the system can be backed up while users and applications are updating data. There are two integrity issues that crop up in hot backups:

▼ Each file or database entity needs to be backed up as a complete, consistent version.

▲ Related groups of files or database entities that have correlated data versions must be backed up as a consistent linked group.

The simplest solution is to ignore the problem altogether and hope the backup data won't be needed for a restore later. This approach is not recommended for fairly obvious reasons: if you don't want to restore data later, then why bother doing it at all? Another solution is to not back up any files that are being used by other applications while backup is running. This way, there is no risk of backing up a file while an application is updating it. However, it is also possible that some important data files that are always opened by an application will never be backed up.

Copy-on-Write   One of the most promising technologies for hot backup is called *copy-on-write*. The idea of copy-on-write is to copy old data blocks on disk to a temporary disk location when updates are made to a file or database object that is being backed up. The old block locations and their corresponding locations in temporary storage are held in a special bitmap index, similar to a cache index, that the backup system uses to determine if the blocks to be read next need to be read from the temporary location. If so, the backup process is redirected to access the old data blocks from the temporary disk location. When the file or database object is done being backed up, the bitmap index is cleared and the blocks in temporary storage are released to be used again. Figure 7-8 shows the basic components of a copy-on-write process.

Copy-on-write functionality has been implemented most often for database backup. Many database companies have copy-on-write functionality built into their products to enable 24 × 7 operations on their databases. This capability must be matched with a backup software product that takes advantage of this facility. The major database companies have worked with the backup industry for several years to integrate their copy-on-write functions with database backup agents for the major systems platforms.

Software Snapshot Technology   A technology similar to copy-on-write is referred to as a *snapshot*. There are two kinds of snapshots in the market today. One way is to make a copy of data on disk drive, as discussed in Chapter 4 as a *snapshot mirror*. The other way is to implement software that provides a point-in-time image of the data on a system's disk storage, which can be used to obtain a complete copy of data for backup purposes.

Software snapshots work by maintaining historical copies of the file system's data structures on disk storage. At any point in time, the version of a file or database is determined from the block addresses where it is stored. So, to keep snapshots of a file at any point in time, it is necessary to write updates to the file to a different data structure (set of blocks) and provide a way to access the complete set of blocks that define the previous version.

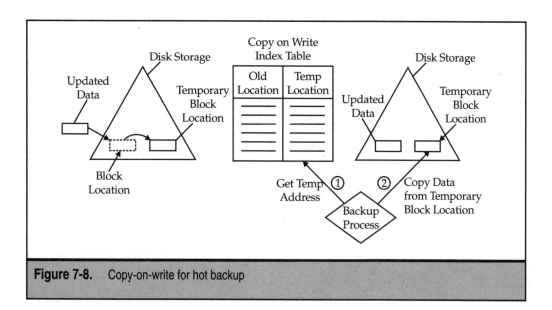

Figure 7-8.   Copy-on-write for hot backup

Software snapshots retain historical point-in-time block assignments for a file system. Backup systems can use a snapshot to read blocks during backup.

Software snapshots require free blocks in storage that are not being used by the file system for another purpose. It follows that software snapshots require sufficient free space on disk to hold all the new data as well as the old data. The amount of free space necessary depends on the activity in the file or database system and how much new data is being generated in relation to the existing old data.

An example of a system with built-in software snapshots is the WAFL (write anywhere file layout) file system used by Network Appliance in their Filer products. One of the primary principles of the WAFL file system is that data can be written anywhere there are free blocks in the system. "Free blocks" in this sense refers to blocks that are not used by the system to store both current as well as historical versions of files. Software snapshots are discussed in more detail in Chapter 15.

The Special Case of Image Backup

Most backup is done as a *filing* process. In other words, backup operations usually incorporate file system or database information that identifies files and database entities by name so that they can be restored individually. However, it is also possible for backup to be done as a *storing* process where the backup process copies bulk data on a block-by-block basis. This approach is called *image backup* because it makes an image copy of the block contents of a storage device or subsystem. The diagram that follows shows the process of an image backup where a data mover transfers block data from a disk drive to a tape drive:

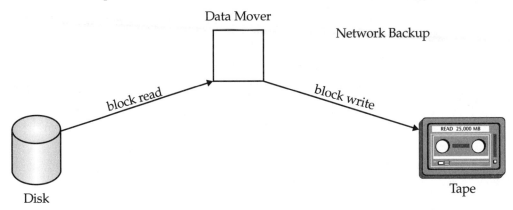

Image restore operations are used to repopulate individual devices or subsystems. Image backup has the advantage of having brute-force performance for both backup and restore operations. When the data is copied from the backup device(s) to the recovery device(s), the recovery device(s) can be disconnected and reconnected to any system with compatible software. This theoretically allows a system that had multiple storage devices to have its devices restored as images in parallel and then connect each of them to a new replacement system.

The primary difficulty in image backup is the problem of restoring individual files and database tables. As the image copy is a block-by-block copy without any information from the file or database system, there is no easy way to identify the blocks holding a particular file or database table. Even with the knowledge of which blocks correspond to a certain file, these blocks are practically guaranteed not to be located in contiguous sections of tape, which renders the individual file restore impractical. Another weakness of image backup and restore is that empty blocks are copied, which is not efficient. An image backup takes the same amount of time whether the storage is 10 percent full or 95 percent full.

It is possible to combine the concept of image backup with file system backup. To accomplish this, each file is copied by first retrieving the block locations for the file from the file system and then moving those blocks to backup media. Notice that the file copy is not performed through the file system interface, but through a device-level block copy operation.

RESTORING DATA

Backup and restore are obviously closely linked processes. Data cannot be restored that has not first been backed up. While backup is a prerequisite for restore, one should not expect restores to be a simple inverse process of backups. Restores are much more complicated than backups and tend to give administrators more problems.

Integrating Restore with File Systems and Databases

Backup operations write data to devices and media that are controlled by the backup engine and not accessed by user applications. While the reading of backup data is usually done using the data source system's file or database system, the actual writing of backup data onto backup media is independent of the file or database system it was copied from.

Restores, on the other hand, create data in the file or database system. The term *restore target* is used here to differentiate a system that has data restored to it from a system that had its data backed up. They are often the same system, but they can also be completely different systems. Just as the data source system has an agent for handling the details of system security as well as file systems and databases, the target system also typically uses an agent to ensure data is transferred correctly into its file systems, databases, and storage devices (Figure 7-9).

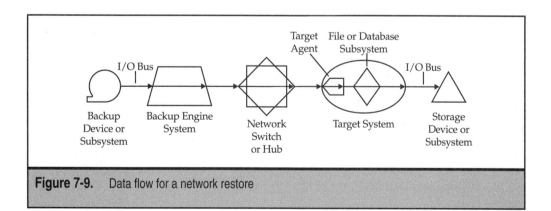

Figure 7-9.   Data flow for a network restore

Types of Restore Operations

Just as there are common backup operations, there are also common restore operations that are called for most often by system administrators. Whereas most backup operations are performed automatically and unattended, most restore operations are manual, where an administrator selects the data to restore. The common types of restore operations are:

▼ Full restores

■ File or table restores

▲ Redirected restores

We'll discuss each of these briefly in the following sections.

The Full Restore Process

The only true single-pass, full-restore operation is an image restore. The idea of an image restore is that a small, specialized operating system is loaded on the target system (system being restored from backup data) that has the required device drivers to perform all necessary disk, tape, and network operations. These can include disk partitioning, block copy, and network transfer operations. Notice that image restores can only work if the disk partitions being restored to are the same size as they were previously. Image restores can be accomplished by a tape drive attached directly to the target system, or by a backup engine connected to the network that manages tape drive operations.

Otherwise, there is a sequence of events that needs to be followed to provide accurate full restore operations over the network. Typically, the server's disk partitions and logical volume assignments must be made first before reloading the target system's operating system. When the operating system is running, the appropriate backup agent can be loaded to provide restore services for the backup engine. Then the file system directory structure, files, user security information, and other system resources, such as the Windows Registry or the NetWare NDS (NetWare Directory Services) tree, are also restored.

The situation for databases is usually considerably more complicated and may require the expertise of the database administrator to ensure the database can be brought back to a functioning system. Databases typically have more interdependent data components that depend on the organization of the database. In general, databases can be restored completely without a lot of difficulty if the database was shut down in an orderly fashion when backup ran. However, if the restore is being done to recover from an unexpected shutdown or failure, the various components probably need to be restored in the proper sequence. Careful attention needs to be paid to the database log files to identify any partially completed write operations and determine if they should be rolled back to ensure a consistent whole database image. Readers interested in more detailed explanations of database recoveries may find the discussion on database replication in Chapter 15 helpful. The drawing that follows shows some of the basic software components involved in database backup and recovery:

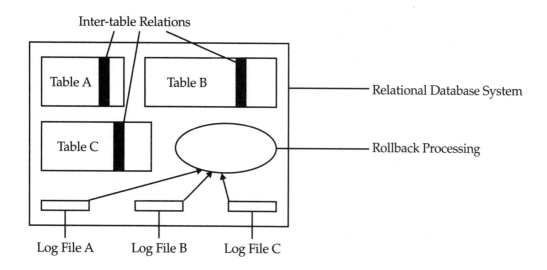

Restoring Files, Tables, and Other Objects

Another common restore operation is for an individual file, table, or other data object. In this case, the administrator uses the backup system interface to select the item to be restored. If a tape autoloader or library is used, the restore process may be able to continue without the administrator's attention; otherwise, the correct tape will need to be manually located.

Restoring Data to Another Location

Another restore operation puts data in a system or file system location that is different than the one it was copied from. Sometimes this is referred to as a *redirected restore*. A redirected restore is commonly done when tape is being used to exchange data between systems as pictured here.

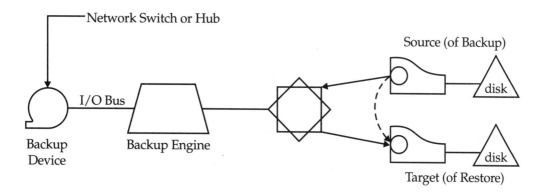

Importance of Media Management to Restores

Backups will write data to almost any tape that is available, even if it's not the best tape for the operation. The goal of backup is typically to copy as much of the data that needs to be backed up as possible. Restores, on the other hand, cannot allow this kind of ambiguity. A tape either has the data that is required or does not. Correct identification of tapes is essential for network restore operations. When there are 50 to 150 tapes to choose from, as is the case for an average network backup system, a trial-and-error method of locating tapes is not very efficient.

Tapes need external labels if they are going to be quickly located for restores. Hopefully the external labels of the tapes accurately and adequately reflect the contents of the tape. This might seem obvious, but incorrect labels are a common mistake that can cause a great deal of frustration. Many times, the problem is not that the tape was mislabeled but that the tape was used incorrectly for backup. For example, a tape with a label of Wednesday that is used on Sunday will not contain the expected data. This simple example underscores the importance of monitoring the use of backup tapes to ensure they are being used in their proper sequence.

If tape labels are suspect or cannot be read, the tape can be inserted in a tape drive and read with a backup utility program to view the tape header and directory information written on it. Although it is time consuming, sometimes this is the only way to determine which tapes are needed for restoring by carefully comparing the header and directory information on the tapes.

The use of tape automation in autoloaders and libraries can help alleviate these kinds of problems. Many backup software products have the capability to force autoloaders and libraries to learn the contents of tapes stored in them. These tape inventory operations read the electronic labels on tape and correctly identify them, regardless of the external labels. Many tape libraries implement bar code readers to speed the tape inventory process. Instead of loading each tape, the bar code reader simply reads the bar code and links it to the name used by the backup system. Bar code readers can save a great deal of time, especially with libraries that contain many tapes. However, it is somewhat dangerous to rely completely on bar code labels, as they usually don't mean much to human beings. Therefore, it is a good idea to use human-readable labels, too.

Restoring Outdated Data

Whatever the reason for using the wrong tapes, the results can be problematic. The potential exists to restore data that no longer exists on the server or should exist in some other location. For instance, a large application's data files may have been on one volume a month ago but been moved to another volume two weeks ago. If a tape is used that contains backup data that is over a month old, it is possible that large amounts of data will be restored to both volumes, overfilling them, as shown here:

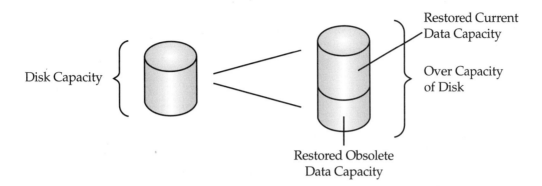

BACKING UP AND RESTORING SECURITY DATA

System security is an extremely vital concern to most organizations. With many other sources of information and expertise available, the discussion here is confined to considering the relationship between backup/recovery and security.

User access management is a common feature of all server systems. Access control enables administrators to establish access privileges and exclusions for specific users and groups of users regarding specific data objects. User access is an important component in the overall system security implementation on any system. Most access control schemes can be broken down into two components: the user trying to gain access and the thing that can be accessed—usually files and directories.

Data Access Components

Users access files when they run applications. System security typically establishes access permissions for files at the directory (or folder) level and also at the file level. Directory-level security is applied to all the files within a directory and allows a user with access to the directory to access all the files it contains. File-level security is applied to an individual file. A user with access at the directory level may not be able to access an individual file in that directory if it has file-level security specifying more restricted access.

Caller ID As an Analogy for User IDs

It is important to understand that security is established using both user and file system entities. Security operations are analogous to using Caller ID, where a user calls for a file and the system checks the user's ID to see if it recognizes the caller. If there is a match between the file system's authorized users and the user requesting access, then the user is allowed to access the file. If there is no match, the user is not granted access as is illustrated in this diagram:

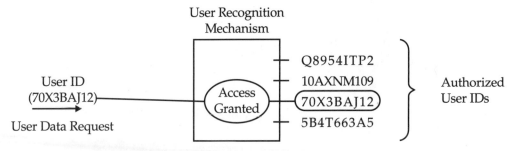

System user IDs are created to represent users as numerical objects. Numerical representations are much easier to manage than alphanumeric names. Unlike a person's phone number, system user IDs are typically not known to their owners—they are probably not even known to system administrators. However, they are known to the file or database system. It's as if you had an unlisted telephone number and the person you called could recognize your number but you didn't know it yourself. Security systems generate user IDs randomly. For that reason, a user that is created once, then is removed from the system, and is created again will have a different user ID number assigned the second time.

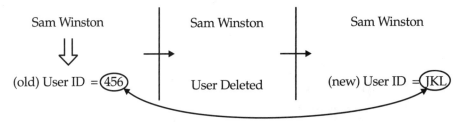

This means that users will not be recognized by the file system if they are deleted and re-created. In other words, administrators have to re-create access permissions if they re-create the user.

File System Metadata

The login process authenticates users by name and password and assigns a system internal user ID to a user's communication session. From this point on, the user's communication sessions are identified by this internal user ID.

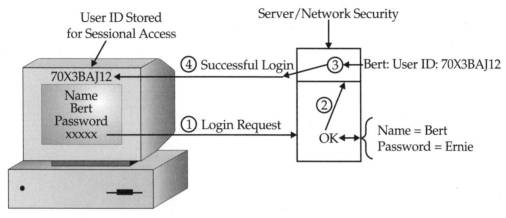

The access permissions for file system objects must be stored where they can be accessed by backup and restore processes. Typically this is done within the metadata of the file system, although it can also be done with an external data file. In Windows systems these data structures are called access control lists, or *ACLs*.

The combination of internal user IDs and file system access permissions determines which user IDs can access which objects in the file system. These two data structures are obviously very closely linked, forming two halves of the file system access system. Figure 7-10 shows these two data structures.

Maintaining Data Access During Disaster Recovery

An important consideration is what happens in disaster recovery situations. The two parts of the security/access system may be able to be backed up and restored independently, but they must be backed up and restored as a single, linked system if they are to

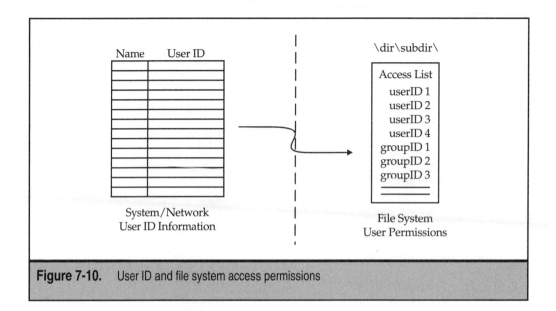

Figure 7-10.   User ID and file system access permissions

work correctly. For instance, restoring files and user ID data—but not access permissions—means new metadata will need to be created for users to access system objects. Similarly, a restore process that restores files and access permissions, but not user ID data, requires that administrators manually re-create users and new permissions for those new users. This security disconnect is illustrated here:

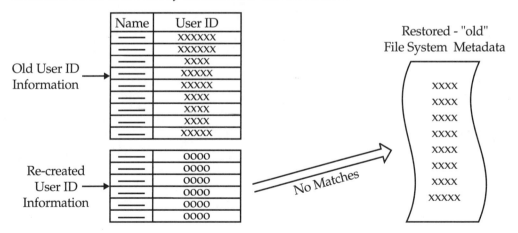

While most network backup software products provide the ability to back up and restore both user ID data and access permissions, it is the responsibility of the backup administrators to know how to back up and restore them correctly.

TAPE ROTATION

Organizations often want to keep several different versions of backup copies to satisfy business requirements. For example, a business may want to keep copies of data from the end of each month for business, legal, or audit purposes. The sequence of tape operations, the naming conventions used, and the frequency of use are known as *tape rotation*.

The Necessity of Tape Rotation

The core benefit of tape rotation is ensuring restore integrity. Tape rotation is needed, in part, because backup operations are not really concerned with the integrity of the restores—just the integrity of the backup.

Restoring data is the inverse of backup in that one knows exactly where the data needs to go but may have difficulty figuring out where it's coming from. For that reason, a structured approach is needed to identify which tapes have the data that is needed. In contrast, a poorly implemented scheme practically guarantees difficult restores and possibly lost data.

Reusing or Recycling Tapes

Tape rotation schedules tapes for periodic use. While tapes are relatively inexpensive for the capacity they provide, they cost enough that most people don't want to use them only once and then place them on the shelf forever.

From a wear and tear perspective, most tapes today are made to last over 2,000 passes. This number is not as high as it might appear, as several tape device operations will cause a tape pass to occur even though it is not apparent to the administrator. But the fact remains that tapes can be used many times in many operations.

Matching Business Cycles with Rotation Schedules

Many tape rotation schemes match business cycles to enable the creation of historically relevant copies of backup data. This way backup data reflects regular accounting and measurement cycles such as sales and inventory data as well as financial statements. These types of business processes are commonly done on a weekly, monthly, and quarterly basis. Some industries are required by law to maintain periodic backups for historical and audit purposes.

Enabling Efficient Backup Operations

Another reason for tape rotation is to implement efficient daily backup operations. Certain media schedules allow more efficient backup operations than others. For example, a simple two-tape rotation schedule could use each tape on alternate days. This method would likely require a full backup every other day to ensure complete restores. Other rotation schedules, as discussed in following sections, provide more efficient backup operations.

Commonly Used Tape Rotation Models

Several types of rotation models are used. The most common ones are discussed in the following paragraphs.

Weekly Rotation

Weekly tape rotation is one of the simplest schemes available. Essentially one tape (or group of tapes) is used for an entire week. The rotation cycle begins with a full backup and adds incremental backup data on the remaining days. Restores are relatively simple, as the number of tapes containing backup data is relatively small. Weekly rotation works best when rotation changes occur on days with the longest backup window. This is typically a Friday night, which allows extra time to run all weekend, if necessary. Two sets of tapes can be alternated, or several sets of tapes could be created for each week of the month.

In many respects, the weekly rotation scheme is an excellent choice. It is easy to adjust for special circumstances such as holiday weekends and business cycle deadlines. In addition, it is fairly easy to understand and work with. A weakness is the potential to lose up to six days of data in a site disaster. For example, a disaster that occurs on the sixth day after rotation could destroy all the data on tape that had been created in the previous six days.

Daily Rotation

To reduce the exposure of catastrophic data loss, the daily rotation model uses different tapes every day. This requires the ability to complete full backups every night, something that cannot be done in many networks. However, if nightly full backups can be done without disrupting normal operations, the protection of data is excellent. This scheme is fairly easy to understand, but it does require more management time than weekly rotation.

Monthly Rotation

Although it is not often used, monthly rotation can be successfully implemented with systems that do not generate a great deal of new data. The general idea of monthly rotation is to make a full backup at the end or beginning of the month and incremental or differential backups on the rest of the days of the month.

Before thinking that a monthly rotation will work in your environment, there are some important considerations to take into account. If the daily operations during the month are incremental backups, restores could require the use of many tapes. If daily incremental backup data is appended to the end of the previously used tape(s), a tape failure could result in the loss of a whole month's worth of data. On the other hand, if different tapes are used every day for incremental backups, the restore process could use 20 or more tapes, which can certainly be problematic—just in assembling the tapes for the restore.

For those reasons, daily differential backups are recommended with monthly rotations. This way, only two tapes are needed for restores—the monthly full and the last daily differential. The implication here is that the amount of new data created during the month is somewhat limited, so that the differential backup does not run too long. In either case, whether incremental or differential backups are used, it is a good idea to make copies of the daily backups to maintain both local and remote copies. Systems that create a great deal of new data should not use a monthly rotation.

Grandfather, Father, Son

The grandfather, father, son rotation model, also called GFS for short, is a combination of the preceding three rotation models. The basic idea is that there are tapes assigned to days of the week, weeks in the month, and months in the year.

In the GFS model, full backups are typically performed every weekend and incremental or differential backups are performed on the other days of the week. On either the first or last weekend of the month, the full backup is written to a monthly tape; on every other weekend, the full backup is written to a weekly tape. Daily tapes are used on nonrotation days of the week. Table 7-1 shows the tapes one could expect to use with a GFS rotation model.

The GFS rotation scheme is popular for good reasons. For starters, it is easy to understand and manage. More important, it has built-in retention of data that keeps weekly

Monthly	Weekly	Daily
January tape	Week 1 tape	Monday tape
February tape	Week 2 tape	Tuesday tape
March tape	Week 3 tape	Wednesday tape
April tape	Week 4 tape	Thursday tape

Table 7-1.   Tapes Used in a GFS Rotation

full backups available for a month, and monthly full backups can be kept available for as long as desired. Table 7-1 shows four monthly tapes, but there is no reason why more monthly tapes could not be used, making it very easy to match a wide variety of data retention requirements.

An important point to consider when keeping monthly tapes for extended periods is the impact it can have on the backup system database. The size of the backup system database can become quite large and have a significant impact on the performance of the backup system. It may be necessary to periodically delete the backup database records for older monthly backups.

Using Rotation Models to Balance Backup Performance and Restore Performance

As it turns out, the amount of time spent on full restores is inversely proportional to the time it takes to run backups. In other words, rotations that enable more efficient backup operations result in longer restore operations. Efficient backup copies only changed data, ignoring data that has already been written to tape(s). Such backup operations proceed very quickly but can result in many more tapes being needed for restores.

As an example, consider a perpetual incremental backup system that runs over nine weeks. Say, on the first day, the full backup operation uses five tapes. Each day after that, a new tape is used for an incremental backup. By the end of nine weeks, 67 tapes have been made. If this system ever needed to be restored, it might be necessary to use all 67 tapes.

While the fastest backups are done with incremental operations, the fastest restores occur as a result of running full backups. Full backups that fit on a single tape work best, but whether it is one tape or several, the key is that the backup has a complete, consistent set of data that is restored in a single operation. Restore operations that require the administrator to pick through tapes looking for the best combination are time consuming and lead to mistakes.

Another reason for limiting the number of tapes for restore is to reduce the likelihood of tape failures. In the example given with perpetual incremental backups, the failure of any one tape could prevent the server from being completely restored.

So, one of the goals of tape rotation should be to balance the performance and efficiency of backup with the ease and reliability desired for restores. That was the motivation for the invention of differential backup operations. Some backup products allow data sets on various tapes to be merged to create a set of tapes containing a complete virtual system image. For instance, they would use the data set from the last full backup and merge it with incremental data sets from other tapes and days of the week. This way, a composite tape or tape set can be generated that provides all the data needed for a complete restore image. The reader should be aware that this is a fairly sophisticated feature not supported by all backup software products.

Marking Deleted Files

Files that were backed up and later deleted should not be restored. It is very difficult to search for deleted files after a restore operation has already put them back on disk. This can be a difficult problem if deleted files are restored, causing the disk to overfill and potentially keeping other files from being restored.

In general, this is a problem for any tape rotation schedule, but some are more problematic than others. The number of deleted files that are restored is typically the number of files deleted since the last full backup operation was run. Full backups are typically used by backup software to determine the "baseline" state of the system. Restore operations will restore all the data from the last full backup and then add newer files created since that time. Files deleted after that full backup operation will likely be restored improperly.

Off-Site Tape Rotation

Backup tapes should be kept off-site for some period of time, enabling a complete restore if a disaster wipes out the organization's systems. When a disaster strikes, the supply of off-site tapes may be the only means of restoring critical business data. Obviously, if an organization depends heavily on its data resources, the ability to restore data is extremely important.

There are services in most metropolitan areas that can be used to deliver and store tapes in off-site storage vaults. These services were developed years ago primarily for the data on mainframe systems, but they can also be used for data tapes from open systems backup. The selection of a service and the verification of their practices could be an important part of a disaster recovery plan.

Duplicating and Mirroring Tapes for On- and Off-Site Protection

An increasing number of businesses have requirements to have copies of backup data available on site and off site at all times. This is a problem for system administrators who need to be able to restore all their data from off-site tapes and who also need to be able to restore individual files for their end users. Obviously a tape that is off-site for a week does not help the end user very much who needs a file now.

A common solution to this problem is to use mirrored tape drives, make duplicates of backup tapes, or run two separate backup operations covering the same data. Similar to disk mirrors, tape mirrors make two tape drives appear as one virtual drive. Duplicating tapes is a simple concept that copies the data from one tape onto another. Most backup software products provide tools for doing this.

The third alternative, running two backups, has some surprising complications because of the way archive bits are used and manipulated by backup software. Archive bits are set by file systems to indicate a file has been modified and needs backup. After the file is copied to tape, its archive bit is reset by the backup engine. With two backup operations running, it is possible that a file needing backup would have its archive bit reset by the first backup system that copies it. The second backup operation might then skip the file when it checks the file system for archive bits.

Maintaining Rotation Order

When tapes are in tape drives and backups are running, there is an excellent chance data that is on them will be overwritten with new data. For the most part, this is the way it should work. However, if the wrong tapes are put in the drive, it is possible that data that is needed for some other purpose could be overwritten and lost. For instance, a tape that was supposed to have been sent to an off-site storage facility may instead have been left behind in a tape drive. When backup runs again, it is likely that the tape will be over-written with new data, making it impossible to restore the overwritten data. Therefore, it is extremely important to maintain the order of rotation.

Simplifying Rotation Management with Automation

Tape rotation can be simplified with the use of tape automation equipment. For starters, automation makes it much less likely to have human error screw up operations (someone using the wrong tape, for instance). In addition, multitape restorations can be much eas-ier if administrators no longer have to search for each tape; the tape subsystem can do it for them. Finally, tape automation provides a good place to store tapes. They are safer in an autoloader or library than they are stacked in a cube or in a desk drawer.

Problem Areas for Backup and Recovery

Problems with network backup and recovery are common. Some of them are opera-tional, some are environmental, and others have to do with the technology of network-ing. In this section, we'll review some of the typical problems affecting the success of backups and restores.

Inadequate Oomph!

One of the most common problems with backup systems is trying to do too much with too little. Often the requirements for backup are overlooked and not given adequate analysis. Backup is a big job that involves heavier network and I/O traffic than any other application. If it is not analyzed as such, the backup system is likely to be inadequate.

One way to prevent this from happening is to analyze the network backup system as the primary application in the network. In other words, try to understand the complete network as existing for the purpose of performing backing.

Insufficient Management Resources

Without sufficient oversight of the backup process, there is an excellent chance that backup problems will go unnoticed. In addition, overworked administrators are also more likely to make mistakes with some aspect of backup.

Insufficient Capacity and Time

If the media and devices do not have adequate capacity to complete the backup job, there will obviously be some amount of data that does not get backed up. Automated tape changers and libraries can overcome most capacity problems. It is necessary to monitor tapes in autoloaders and libraries to make sure tapes are available for the next expected operation, including the rotation schedule.

Ample capacity can't help, however, if there is not enough time to finish backups before they have to be stopped. Some organizations require backup operations to be completed by a certain time, such as the start of the next business day. Obviously, data that doesn't get backed up can never be restored.

Hardware Failures

It's important to realize that tape drives are highly sophisticated electromechanical devices that are exposed to dust, dirt, and airborne contaminants. As a result, tape mechanisms and heads require cleaning. The more dust and dirt there is inside a tape drive, the more likely it is to have errors. Weekly cleaning with nonabrasive head cleaners is recommended.

Improper termination of the SCSI bus causes data transfer errors. Although the problem is the bus, termination problems appear to the backup software as either hardware failures or media failures. Terminating resistors are needed on both ends of the bus. Host I/O controllers have electronic terminators, and most devices use external terminators. The terminator must match the characteristics of the bus, 8-bit or 16-bit and single-ended or differential.

Media Failures

Tapes exist in a hostile environment. They are wound and unwound many times, stretched over transport mechanisms, and exposed to external elements in the air and on the surface of rollers and capstans inside the tape drive. It's no surprise they fail from time to time.

Network Problems

Network backup creates huge data transfers that can flood a network, causing a variety of congestion-related problems, such as slow performance and transfer failures. It's not unusual for network routers, hubs, and switches to become congested and drop packets. For most data processing applications, dropped packets cause the data to be transferred again, which degrades performance but maintains the connection. When the level of network traffic is heavy enough, as can occur during backup operations, it is possible that retransmitted packets can also be dropped. When this happens, network performance can degrade to unacceptable levels and cause backup and other applications to fail.

Lack of Practice, Planning, and Testing

Restores often fail because administrators are unfamiliar with the necessary procedures. Therefore, the first rule of disaster readiness is to practice recovering data. Keep in mind that there are many types of restore operations and that they don't all work the same way. Here are a few exercises to help you prepare for an unexpected restore scenario:

▼　Restore an entire server.

■　Restore a disk volume, or a logical disk drive.

■　Restore a directory to a different location in the directory tree.

- Restore a directory to a different server and file system.
- Restore an empty directory.
- ▲ Restore a file to a new location in the directory tree.

Tapes Have No Data on Them or Cannot Be Read

Data can't be restored if it doesn't exist on tape. This happens when:

- ▼ Backups fail or are stopped prematurely
- Tapes are used out of order and their data is overwritten
- Tapes wear out
- ▲ Tapes are destroyed by heat, humidity, dust, and other threats

If a tape failure occurs during a restore, stop the operation and clean the heads on the tape drive. It is possible that dirt deposits on the tape head have temporarily reduced the ability of the tape drive to read the data. Sometimes it is necessary to clean the heads twice.

Tapes with extremely important data on them that need to be read but cannot, due to the effects of contaminants and humidity, can be taken to facilities that have special techniques for baking tapes and making them readable again. The services are costly without any guarantees that data can be recovered.

NOTE: Retensioning tapes (unwinding and rewinding them again) periodically extends their shelf life. If possible, try to do this every six months, but at least once a year.

Data on Tape Is Corrupt or Incomplete

Another related problem occurs when the data on tape can be read just fine, but the data itself is corrupt and worthless. This can happen because of some flaw in the backup system, but it is more likely to be caused by data being updated as the backup is running. This is particularly problematic for database systems, due to the amount of data they have and the requirements for high availability. An adequate live or hot backup product is needed to ensure data integrity.

File System and System Configuration Changes

Most network backup systems default to restoring data to its original location in the network, server, and file system. If the directory structure in a server has been reorganized, the name of a server changes, or other network-location information changes on a server, it is possible that data will be much more difficult to restore.

Sometimes people will use a system crash as an opportunity to upgrade their server—especially if they have been limping along with an underpowered server for some time. So, they build a whole new server with new disks, a new operating system, new disk volumes, and new users and passwords. New operating systems often have new backup system requirements and may not work with an older backup software package.

Software and Equipment Is Unavailable or Not Working

Physical and logical tape formats could be incompatible with the equipment available for restoring data. It is important to plan to have compatible systems, host I/O controllers, cables, terminating resistors, drives, and software to be able to read off-site tapes.

Capacity Overflow

In the earlier section on tape rotation, the problem of restoring more data than expected was discussed. More is definitely not better when it comes to restore operations. If too much data is restored, disk volumes will fill and the restore will halt or even crash the server.

Measurable Variables in Backup

There are several key items that must be considered when putting a backup plan in place:

- ▼   Backup window
- ■   Largest backup data source
- ■   Amount of total data
- ■   Amount of updated data
- ■   Network transfer rate
- ■   Speed of backup devices
- ▲   Backup engine performance

We'll look at each of these briefly in the following sections.

Backup Window

The *backup window* is the amount of time available to run backups. The backup window is often thought to be useful for cold backups, but it also applies to hot backups. Just because a server can be backed up without downing the server does not mean that it ought to be. The performance impact of backup can still limit the hours that backups can run.

There are basically two backup windows to consider. One is the nightly backup, which is performed overnight between normal business days. This is typically a backup window of three to eight hours and is used primarily for incremental or differential backup operations. The other backup window is the window to complete weekly or periodic full backups. It's not unusual for this backup window to extend over 24 hours, sometimes lasting from Friday evening until late in the day on Sunday. The backup system needs to have the capability to work within the constraints of both backup windows.

Largest Backup Data Source

It is not unusual for one particular file to be significantly larger than the others and contain important data that must be protected by backup. Unfortunately, such files are often too large to be backed up in the normal nightly backup window by the network backup system. In such cases, sometimes the best solution is to use a dedicated backup system installed directly on the system. Snapshot technology could also work well.

Total Amount of Data

The total amount of data stored on the network is significant for determining the dynamics of full backups. It is also significant when trying to plan for recovery requirements. Notice that this is not the total capacity of storage, but the amount of data residing in storage.

Amount of Updated Data

It is much more difficult to determine the volume of data that is updated on a daily basis that needs to be backed up. Backup records probably give a good idea of day-to-day backup loads. The amount of updated data is used to determine the capabilities of the backup system to complete incremental or differential backup operations on weekdays.

Network Transfer Rate

As mentioned previously, network backups can drive network utilization to saturation and cause severe performance degradation. There are many variables to consider when projecting the impact of backup on a network. However, with careful thought and planning it is possible to make some realistic estimates. For the most part, daily backups are the main problem, because weekdays have short backup windows that restrict how long backups can run. Weekend backups usually have much more time to finish and do not put the same amount of pressure on administrators.

Speed of Tape Devices

Even though the network is the most likely bottleneck for backup transfers, it is not necessarily the only one. Most network backup transfers are much slower than an average tape drive's capabilities, but interleaving data, dedicated local backup, and remote device operations can generate data transfers to tape that exceed their performance capabilities.

Tape drives are capable of maintaining streaming speeds if data can be supplied fast enough. It is normal for tape device manufacturers to publish the sustained throughput specification of their tape drives assuming that a 2:1 data compression ratio can be achieved. For instance, 8mm helical scan drives that list their transfer rates as 6 MB/s have a noncompressed transfer rate of 3 MB/s. The transfer rate attained has more to do with how compressible the data is than any I/O technology.

Backup Engine Performance

The ability for the backup engine to make the transfer from network I/O to storage I/O is significant for network backup. This dictates a system with an efficient host I/O bus, such as the PCI bus, as well as using high-speed adapters. In order to conserve the number of slots in the backup engine, a multiple-port NIC could be considered. As discussed previously, the database processing requirements for backup can be challenging. For that reason, the more processing power and system memory in the backup engine, the better.

SUMMARY

This chapter examined the technologies and processes of network backup. As one of the stalwart applications of systems management, backup is a part of most data processing installations. The chapter introduced the basic hardware, media, and software components of backup before discussing the types of backup operations commonly used. The topic of backing up live data was discussed, and the concept of copy-on-write was introduced. Restore operations, media management, and tape rotation were also discussed, including the relationship between them. Finally, some of the most common trouble spots for network backup were discussed.

EXERCISE

Develop the specification and administrative operations for a network backup system to replace existing stand-alone backups for five servers using the following data:

1. There is an average of 200GB of data stored on each server.

2. On average, 5 percent of the data changes every day.

3. Assume there is an existing Fast Ethernet network in operation and a switch with two ports available.

4. All backup data should be available on site and off site to facilitate restores.

5. The IT standard for backup approves 40GB tapes and tape drives capable of transferring data at 6MB/s, including autoloaders with either six- or nine-cartridge magazines.

6. The backup window is six hours.

PART III

The Storage Channel
Becomes a Network

CHAPTER 8

SAN and NAS as Storing and Filing Applications

The first part of this book was spent describing the fundamental technologies of server storage that have been used for many years. From this chapter on, we'll turn our attention to the specifics of storage *networks,* including the integration and application of the traditional storage technologies in a networked world.

To date, storage network products have been identified as either NAS (network attached storage) or SAN (storage area network). NAS products have a heritage rooted in Ethernet-accessed data and are modeled after the concept of a network file server. SAN products are rooted in SCSI storage technologies and include several types of products designed to provide familiar functions all along the I/O path, including host I/O controllers and storage devices and subsystems. Some of the most noticeable SAN products are those that have replaced the parallel SCSI bus with switches and hubs.

NAS products were in the market for several years before SAN products. When SANs arrived, a great deal of confusion followed surrounding the relationship between the two. The situation turned into a minor industry power struggle where both camps tried to gain the upper hand. This led to a number of interesting analyses, including some attempts at distinguishing the two as different architectures. While the two are structurally different, they are much more alike than they are different, and they have the potential to be integrated together in a number of ways. In fact, there is an excellent chance that NAS and SAN will be integrated and eventually viewed as feature sets of future storage networking products.

This chapter sets the stage for the second half of the book by analyzing both NAS and SAN as filing and storing applications. By distinguishing NAS and SAN in this way, it is possible to find some solid ground for developing storage network designs and evaluating the potential of new products and technologies. But in order to understand SAN and NAS in these terms, it is important to understand the wiring component also. This chapter looks at some of the wiring characteristics that are optimal for storage network applications.

RECAPITULATING WIRING, STORING, AND FILING

As discussed in the first chapter, storage networking is built on top of three fundamental components: wiring, storing, and filing. All storage products can be broken down into some combination of functions from these three areas. The way these components are combined in products can be a little bit surprising because storage products have not been developed along these lines and so a great deal of functional overlap occurs.

Storage Networking Is an Application

Many people have spent many hours trying to determine what the killer applications for storage networking might be and how to make the technology easier to understand by virtue of its successful application. While there are many opinions on this point, the view taken in this book is that storage is itself an application. Just as client/server applications and distributed applications of many kinds run on a variety of networks, storage is a unique and special type of application that runs on multiple networking technologies.

As storage processes are tightly integrated with systems, it may be more appropriate to say that storage networks are systems applications. Higher-level business and user applications can use the services provided by storage networking applications. As is true with all technologies, some types of systems match the requirements of various higher-level applications better than others.

Wiring

The term "wiring" in this book applies to all the software, hardware, and services that make storage transport possible and manageable in a storage network. This includes such diverse things as cabling, host I/O controllers, switches, hubs, address schemes, data link control, transport protocols, security, and resource reservations. So, if this is a book on *network* storage, why use the term "wiring"? The answer is simple: bus technologies like SCSI and ATA are still heavily used in storage networks and will probably continue to be used for many years to come. In fact, SCSI and ATA bus products are by far the most common storage technologies used by the NAS side of the storage network industry today.

Optimal Characteristics for Storage Network Wiring

Storage networks differ from data networks in two very important ways:

▼   They transfer data that has never existed before between systems and storage. In other words, data can be lost if the network loses packets.

▲   Systems expect 100 percent reliability from storage operations and can crash when failures occur.

Storage networks demand a high degree of precision from all components to implement a reliable and predictable environment. Parallel SCSI, despite its distance and multi-initiator limitations, is an extremely reliable and predictable environment. New wiring technologies such as Fibre Channel, Ethernet-Storage and InfiniBand have to be able to provide the same, or better, levels of reliability and predictability if they are to succeed as replacements for SCSI. Another perspective views wiring as a storage *channel.* The term "channel," which originated in mainframe computing environments, connotes a high degree of reliability and availability.

The following sections look at some potential characteristics of wiring that would allow it to operate as a channel. This is not to say that available wiring technologies incorporate all these characteristics, because they don't, but it is important to understand how the various technologies compare relative to these ideals.

Minimal Error Rates   Storage networking involves massive data transfers where it is essential for all data to be transferred correctly. Therefore, storage networks demand the lowest possible error rates. Not only is there less risk for data corruption or failures, but lower error rates also reduce the amount of retransmitted data and the accompanying network congestion that can occur.

Success in Moderation: Flow Control   *Flow control* is the capability to limit the amount of data transmitted over the network. This involves some method where the receiving entity sends a message to the sending entity telling it to stop transmissions so that it can complete processing the data it has already received. Alternatively, flow control can be implemented where a sending entity has the capability to send a certain amount of data but must wait for a signal from the receiving entity before sending more.

The goal of flow control is to prevent network entities from having *buffer overflow* conditions that force them to discard data transmissions when the amount of incoming data exceeds its capacity to temporarily store and process transmissions. With the assumption that a high percentage of wiring technologies have gigabit/second transfer rates, the flow control mechanism should be implemented in hardware at the data link layer to be quick enough to be effective.

There are two types of flow control to consider. The first is flow control over an individual network link between adjacent entities, such as a system and a switch. The other is end-to-end flow control between the sending entity and the receiving entity in the storage network. The two types of flow control are independent of each other, as there is no way to guarantee that implementing one type of flow control will prevent buffer overflows from occurring elsewhere in the network.

Full-Duplex Transmissions   Full-duplex communications provide separate send and receive circuits between communicating entities. This is an important function for supplying the most immediate and accurate flow control. While data is being transferred from the sender to the receiver on one circuit, the receiver can *throttle back* the sender immediately on a separate circuit without having to wait for data transmissions to stop first.

In addition to flow control benefits, full-duplex communications provide a fast means for acknowledging completed transmissions between receiver and sender. For high-throughput transaction processing environments that also require high reliability, the capability to quickly process transmission acknowledgments is paramount.

Low Latency   *Latency* is the amount of time required for a network entity to queue, transfer, and process transmitted data. Most data networks have fairly relaxed latency characteristics. For storage I/O, however, latency can be a major issue. Transaction systems that process a high number of interdependent I/Os per second cannot afford to be slowed by latency in the channel.

For example, a hypothetical storage network with a latency of 10 milliseconds would have a minimum transaction rate of 20 milliseconds/second to account for the initial I/O request and its returned data or acknowledgment. Without including the time required by the subsystem, this translates into a maximum I/O rate of 500 I/Os per second, far below the I/O rates desired for most transaction systems. To ensure minimal impact, the wiring in a storage network should operate with a latency of 20 *microseconds* or less.

In-Order Delivery   When data transmissions are received out of sequence relative to the order they were sent, the receiving entity has to sort them and detect missing or corrupt frames. This reordering is not necessarily common, but it can happen and therefore must be protected against. Traditionally, this is not an issue with storage channel technologies, including parallel SCSI. The speed that storage runs at demands the most efficiency from the channel. Out-of-order delivery in wiring can add unnecessary overhead to systems and storage subsystems.

A good question to ask is what component of the wiring should be responsible for ordering data in the network. There are two approaches: the first approach places the burden on network switches and routers to ensure that transmission frames are transported in sequence, and the other is to place the burden on the receiving storage I/O controller to reorder frames as needed.

Independence of Wiring from Storing and Filing

The wiring used in storage networks is independent of the storing and filing functions that may be used. This allows any networking technology with the characteristics listed previously to be used for storage networking. In other words, both NAS and SAN can use any available, qualified network. It's the word "qualified" that makes things interesting.

The subtle point to make about the independence of wiring is that both NAS and SAN products can use the exact same wiring—or type of wiring. Again, this requires the implementation details to be worked out sufficiently, which takes a tremendous amount of effort on the part of many companies and engineers. However, there are no architectural blocks preventing NAS and SAN products to work together on a single storage network.

Multiplexed Communications and Multiple Protocols

Storage networking requires new methods for starting, establishing, and managing communications, which are considerably different than those used in bus technologies such as parallel SCSI or ATA. For example, storage networks, by their nature, provide the capability for a storage subsystem to carry on multiplexed communications with multiple hosts simultaneously. Multiplexing in this context refers to the capability to transfer and receive individual data frames with different network entities. This is considerably different from bus technologies such as parallel SCSI and ATA where there is only one entity controlling the bus at any time.

In addition, many more types of transmissions and protocols are typically used in storage networks than on storage buses. There are protocols used to coordinate the activities of switches and protocols, for addressing, for link state changes, and for all sorts of services provided by the network. There can also be different storing, filing, and communications protocols. Storage devices and subsystems on storage networks have to be able to screen all of them and accept or reject them with 100 percent accuracy. This is a major shift from bus technologies, where the number of protocols and services is much less.

Storing Recap

A great deal appears about storing technologies in the first seven chapters. The independence of wiring from storing allows all those concepts, including device virtualization, mirroring, and RAID, to be implemented over a variety of networks.

Storing is mostly concerned with operations covering a logical block address space, including device virtualization, where logical block storage addresses are mapped from one address space to another.

In general, the storing function is mostly unchanged by storage networks, with two noticeable exceptions. The first is the possibility of locating device virtualization technologies such as volume management within storage networking equipment. This type of function is sometimes referred to as a storage domain controller or a LUN virtualization.

The other major shift in storing is scalability. Storing products such as storage subsystems tend to have more controller/interfaces than the previous generations of bus-based storage and also have much more storage capacity.

Filing

The filing function has two roles: representing abstract objects to end users and applications and organizing the layout of data on real or virtual storage devices. These two roles were identified in Chapter 2 in the discussion of the I/O stack as the representation layer and the data structure layer, as depicted here:

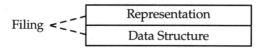

File systems and databases provide the lion's share of the filing functionality in storage networks, with storage management applications such as backup also functioning as filing applications.

The topic of file systems (filing) is treated in more depth later in the book. While the filing function has been mostly unchanged to date by storage networking, an obvious exception has been the development of NAS file systems, such as the WAFL file system from Network Appliance.

A Simple SAN/NAS Paradox

SANs have been touted as a solution for high availability. The basic idea is that host systems no longer have to be single points of failure or network bottlenecks. The concept of SAN *enterprise storage* places the responsibility for data longevity on the storage subsystem. In other words, storage subsystems assume the responsibility to manage themselves and the data that resides on them. Implied in this notion is the possibility that host systems will come and go and change their processing mission, but the data these systems process will be safe and secure on the enterprise storage platform.

Enterprise storage makes a certain amount of intuitive sense. It's a nice idea, with a gigantic problem: how is the self-managing storage subsystem going to become intelligent enough to provide the management services and control of the data it stores? The capability of storage subsystems to support storing-level functions allows them to function as "super virtual devices," but it does not provide any power to act on data objects such as files the way IT managers would like.

Typical Implementations of Filing, Storing, and Wiring in Host Systems and Storage Subsystems

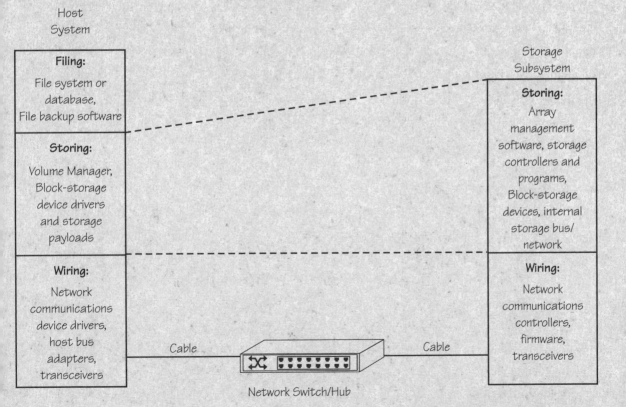

Host System

Filing:
File system or database,
File backup software

Storing:
Volume Manager,
Block-storage device drivers and storage payloads

Wiring:
Network communications device drivers, host bus adapters, transceivers

Storage Subsystem

Storing:
Array management software, storage controllers and programs, Block-storage devices, internal storage bus/ network

Wiring:
Network communications controllers, firmware, transceivers

Cable

Cable

Network Switch/Hub

Segregating Traffic in FC SANs

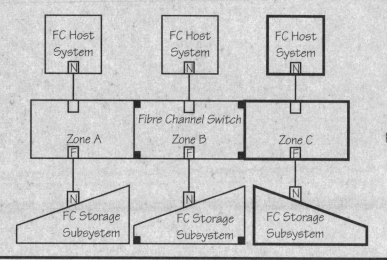

FC Host System
FC Host System
FC Host System

Fibre Channel Switch

Zone A   Zone B   Zone C

FC Storage Subsystem
FC Storage Subsystem
FC Storage Subsystem

Fabric Zoning

Fabric attached N-ports can communicate only with other N-ports belonging to the same zone.

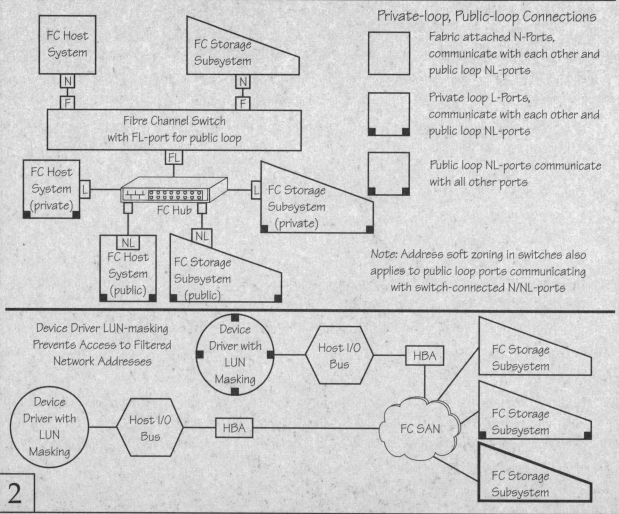

FC Host System
FC Storage Subsystem

Fibre Channel Switch with FL-port for public loop

FC Host System (private)
FC Hub
FC Storage Subsystem (private)

FC Host System (public)
FC Storage Subsystem (public)

Private-loop, Public-loop Connections

Fabric attached N-Ports, communicate with each other and public loop NL-ports

Private loop L-Ports, communicate with each other and public loop NL-ports

Public loop NL-ports communicate with all other ports

Note: Address soft zoning in switches also applies to public loop ports communicating with switch-connected N/NL-ports

Device Driver LUN-masking Prevents Access to Filtered Network Addresses

Device Driver with LUN Masking
Host I/O Bus
HBA
FC Storage Subsystem

Device Driver with LUN Masking
Host I/O Bus
HBA
FC SAN
FC Storage Subsystem
FC Storage Subsystem

2

Two Models for Transporting SAN Traffic over Ethernet/TCP/IP Networks

1. Bi-directional E-port to E-port SAN Tunneling

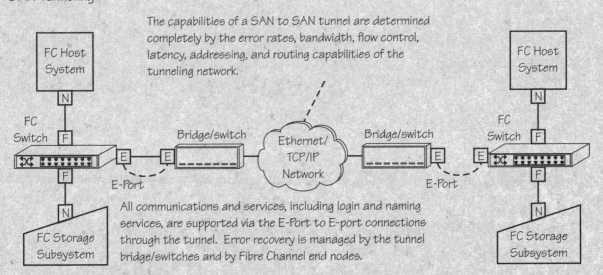

The capabilities of a SAN to SAN tunnel are determined completely by the error rates, bandwidth, flow control, latency, addressing, and routing capabilities of the tunneling network.

All communications and services, including login and naming services, are supported via the E-Port to E-port connections through the tunnel. Error recovery is managed by the tunnel bridge/switches and by Fibre Channel end nodes.

2. Uni-directional SAN Extension with Remote Device Spoofing

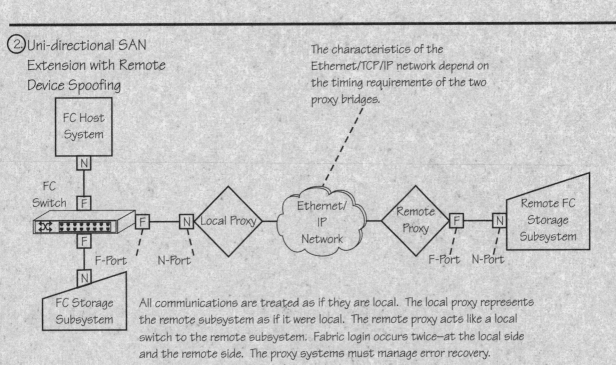

The characteristics of the Ethernet/TCP/IP network depend on the timing requirements of the two proxy bridges.

All communications are treated as if they are local. The local proxy represents the remote subsystem as if it were local. The remote proxy acts like a local switch to the remote subsystem. Fabric login occurs twice—at the local side and the remote side. The proxy systems must manage error recovery.

SAN Core Mesh Networks

Larger SANs can be built by connecting multiple switches together in a mesh network where each switch has a single direct connection to every other switch in the mesh. The number of interswitch links required is x(x-1), where x is the number of switches in the mesh. The number of user node ports is x (p-x+1), where x is the number of switches and p is the number of ports per switch.

In the following examples, 16 port switches are assumed. As the number of switches in a mesh increases, the percentage of ports used for interswitch links increases. The maximum number of user ports in such a mesh is attained when the number of switches is equal to half the number of ports in any given switch.

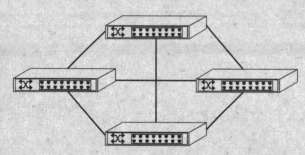

A 4 switch mesh SAN core network with 64 total ports. There are 12 interswitch links and 52 user ports.

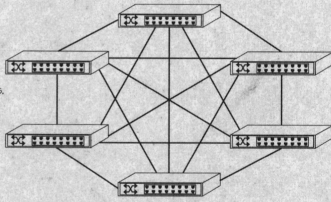

A 6 switch mesh SAN core network with 96 total ports. There are 30 interswitch links and 66 user ports.

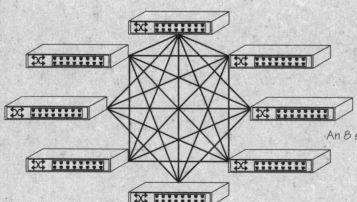

An 8 switch mesh SAN core network with 128 total ports. There are 56 interswitch links and 72 user ports.

InfiniBand Storage Subsystem Connections

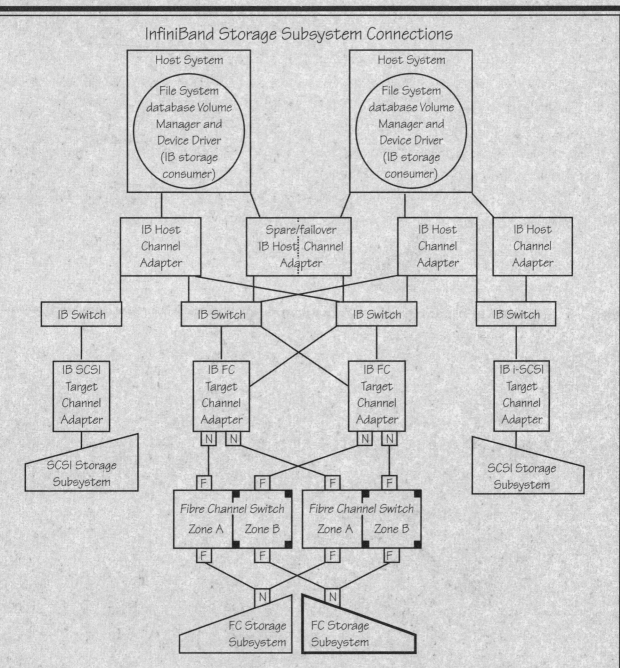

Any kind of wiring can connect to the IB network, including parallel SCSI, i-SCSI (Ethernet), and Fibre Channel. A host system communicates over an InfiniBand (IB) network through a host channel adapter. Connectivity to storage subsystems requires a target channel adapter that bridges the IB network and the storage network. Storage network connections can be made over isolated IB subnets as shown for SCSI and i-SCSI as well as over interconnected subnets as shown for Fibre Channel. This example shows path redundancy through both the IB and FC networks, with an N+1 configuration featuring a spare redundant host channel adapter that can be used by either host if their primary host channel adapter fails.

InfiniBand NAS Shared-Nothing Cluster

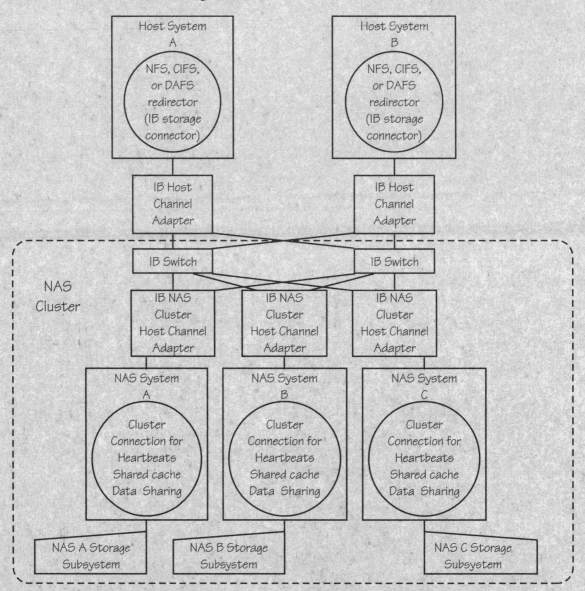

The NAS cluster maintains a single data representation image on all three NAS systems. In other words, the data representation image is replicated across the NAS cluster members. In this shared nothing cluster, pictured here, each NAS system maintains the data structure and control of its own storage subsystem and all access to it, including locking. Host system clients access the cluster through any cluster member. Cluster members access their own storage subsystems directly and access storage on other members' subsystems through the cluster network and a lightweight messaging and data transfer protocol.

Storage subsystems can be connected to cluster members by any suitable wiring technology, including parallel SCSI, FC, or i-SCSI. Path segregation may be needed to protect the control and management of each subsystem.

Multi-level RAID (Plaid)

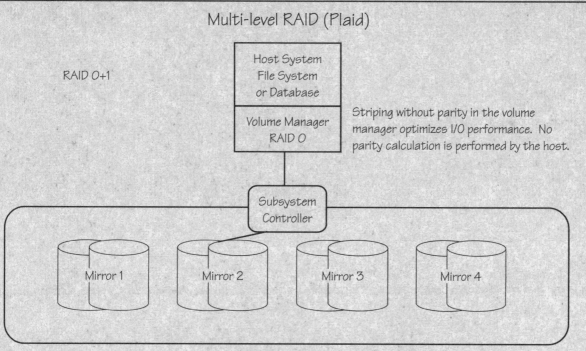

RAID 0+1

Striping without parity in the volume manager optimizes I/O performance. No parity calculation is performed by the host.

A disk subsystem exporting four virtual drives, each composed of two drives forming a mirror. Multiple disk drives can fail without impacting performance as long as two drives from the same mirror pair do not fail. Rebuilds only copy the contents of a single disk drive to the new drive.

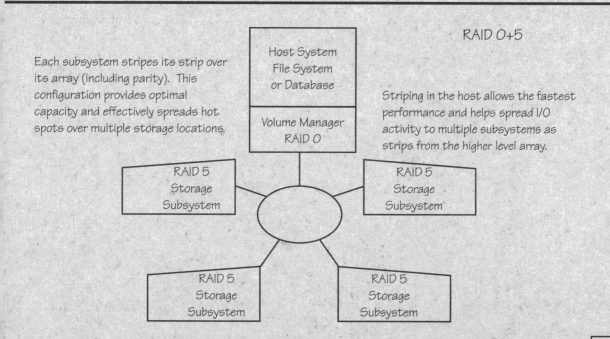

RAID 0+5

Each subsystem stripes its strip over its array (including parity). This configuration provides optimal capacity and effectively spreads hot spots over multiple storage locations.

Striping in the host allows the fastest performance and helps spread I/O activity to multiple subsystems as strips from the higher level array.

Storage Pooling
With a Large Multi-Port Subsystem

A large multi-port storage subsystem provides centralized storage for eight different servers in this drawing.

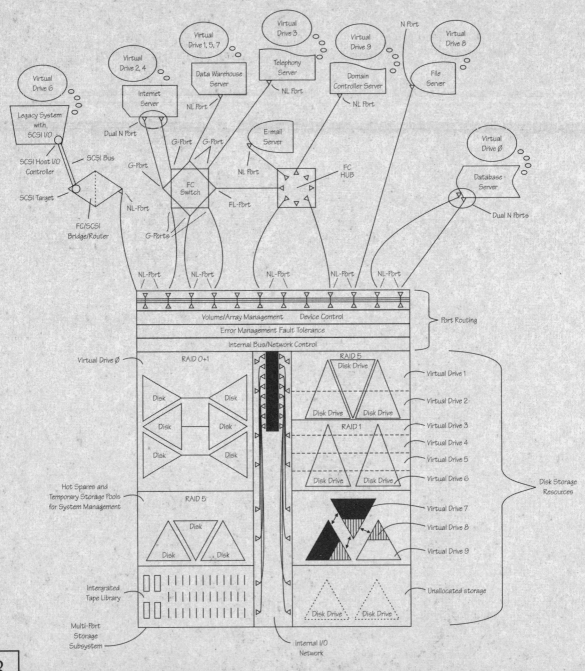

The solution is much more difficult than simply placing microprocessors in the storage subsystems. Self-managing storage subsystems must have the capability to determine what blocks correspond to specific data objects (files, database tables, metadata) if they are going to manage them. The missing link appears to be some amount of embedded filing functionality that provides the capability to associate data objects with their storage locations. This is squarely in the realm of the data structure layer of the I/O stack, as introduced in Chapter 2. The data structure layer can be thought of as the "bottom half" of the file system that controls the placement of data objects on real or virtual storage.

So here is the architectural problem for NAS and SAN: storage subsystems with embedded filing technology are generally thought of as NAS products. So, what would you call a storage subsystem with half a file system? It's neither fish nor fowl. That's why analyzing storage network products as either SAN or NAS does not work. NAS and SAN are not orthogonal, independent entities. Wiring, storing, and filing are.

THE INTEGRATION OF WIRING, STORING, AND FILING IN STORAGE NETWORKS

Storage networking provides storage applications on any number of suitable wiring technologies. In general, storage networking products have been associated with specific network technologies. SANs have been associated with Fibre Channel technology, and NAS is thought of as an Ethernet technology. Unfortunately, identifying storage network technologies with specific data networks has not helped people understand the abstract architectural components of storage networking.

Storing and Filing as Network Applications

Filing is familiar as a client/server application where both client and server perform similar communications functions. For example, a server for one group of clients may itself be a client of some other server. It is slightly strange to think about it as such, but on a communications level, not an application level, clients and servers are peers.

Storing, however, is built on a different type of relationship. Storing-level communications are based on a master/slave model where host system initiators are master entities issuing commands and storage devices/subsystems are slave entities responding to those commands. In general, the slave entities have much less flexibility than the masters that direct their operations. Notable exceptions to this arrangement include devices and subsystems with implemented embedded initiator functionality such as disk drives with integrated XOR processing (Chapter 6) and backup equipment with third-party-copy capabilities (Chapter 10). Even in these cases, however, the embedded initiator in the device is used for specific applications and not used for general-purpose storage communications.

The Hierarchical Relationship Between Storing and Filing

There is an implied hierarchy between storing and filing, where users and applications access data on the filing level and where filing entities such as file systems and databases access the data on a storing level. This hierarchy exists as an internal relationship within nearly all systems used today. This hierarchy is depicted in Figure 8-1 along with the corresponding I/O stack functions.

Wiring's Independence of the Storing/Filing Hierarchy

Although a hierarchy exists between storing and filing, it is not always necessary for it to be implemented as depicted in Figure 8-1. Filing can access the wiring function independently without first passing through a storing function, as shown here:

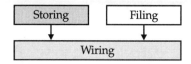

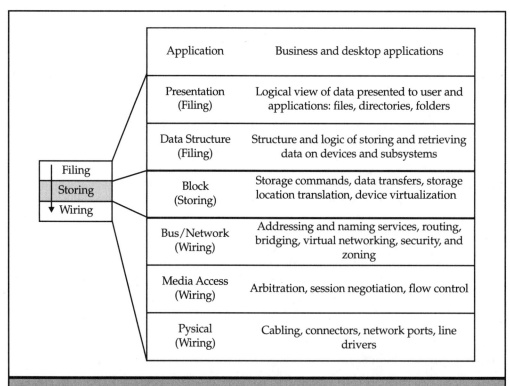

Figure 8-1. The hierarchy of storing and filing in a single system

NAS as a Filing Application

The preceding drawing is the scenario usually used to depict how NAS systems work. Analyzing the I/O path in more detail, however, one realizes the necessity for the client/server filing operation to be converted to a master/slave storing function and transmitted by the server over some sort of wiring to the destination storage devices. This conversion is done by a data structure function within the server's file system that determines where data is stored in the logical block address space of its devices or subsystems.

For most NAS products today, the wiring function used for storing operations is a storage bus. When all the pieces of the I/O path are put together for NAS, we see that the NAS system provides filing services to network clients and incorporates some type of storing function, typically on independent sets of wiring, as shown next:

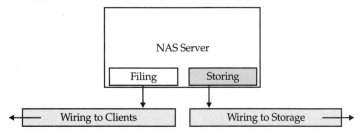

While individual NAS vendors and their particular products may have specific storing and wiring implementations, no architectural requirements for storing or wiring are implied by the NAS concept. Therefore, NAS is considered to be mostly a filing application that uses the services provided by storing and wiring. Although a particular NAS product may implement specific wiring and storage technology, the primary external function provided to customers is its filing capabilities.

SAN as a Storing Application

Storing functionality can be generalized as the master/slave interaction between initiators and devices. Storing is deterministic by design to ensure a high degree of accuracy and reliability. To some degree this is a function of the underlying wiring, but it is also a function of the command sequences and exchanges used in storing. Several storing technologies are available, the most common being the various flavors of SCSI commands.

It can be very hard to separate the storing function from the wiring function when one looks for product examples. For instance, a Fibre Channel HBA is certainly a part of the wiring in a storage network, but it also provides functionality for processing SCSI-3 serial data frames. It is important to realize that the SCSI-3 protocol was developed independently of Fibre Channel technology and that nothing inherent in SCSI-3 ties it to Fibre Channel. It is independent of the wiring function and could be implemented on Ethernet or many other types of network.

Similarly, there is no reason another serial SCSI implementation could not be developed and used with Fibre Channel or any other networking technology. In fact, there is no reason that SCSI has to be part of the equation at all. It is one of the easiest storing technologies to adopt because it has been defined for serial transmission, but there certainly are other ways to control devices and subsystems.

So what is a SAN? It is the application of storing functionality over a network. SANs by definition exclude bus types of wiring. SANs provide deterministic control of storage transmissions, according to the implementation details of the storing protocol used and the capabilities of the underlying network.

ALIGNING THE BUILDING BLOCKS OF STORAGE NETWORKING

Storage networking is certainly not "child's play," but that doesn't mean we can't approach it that way. Certainly the SAN industry has made a number of ridiculous puns and word games surrounding SAN and sand, so with that as an excuse, we'll close this chapter with exercises in building blocks.

The three building blocks we are interested in, of course, are these:

As discussed previously, the implied and traditional hierarchy of these building blocks within a single system is to place wiring on the bottom and filing on top, such that storing gets to be the monkey in the middle, like this:

Of course, in the worlds of NAS and SAN, these blocks have been assembled like this:

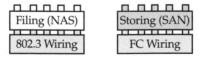

But if we want to take a detailed view of NAS, we know that NAS actually has a storing component as well, which is often parallel SCSI, and we place the building blocks within client and server respectively, like this:

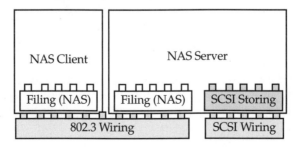

But as we've been saying all along in this chapter, wiring is independent from both storing and filing and, in fact, can be the same for both. So we've structured the building blocks of filing (NAS) and storing (SAN) on top of a common wiring, like this:

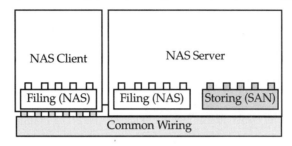

Now the preceding drawing is probably only interesting in theory, as something to illustrate the concept. In actual implementations, it is probably a very good idea to segregate client/server traffic from storage traffic. This provides the capability to optimize the characteristics of each network for particular types of traffic, costs, growth, and management.

That said, it might be a very good idea to base the two different networks on the same fundamental wiring technology. This allows organizations to work with a single set of vendors and technologies. As long as a common wiring technology can actually work for both types of networks, there is the potential to save a great deal of money in the cost of equipment, implementation, training, and management. This type of environment, shown in Figure 8-2, includes a storage device as the final destination on the I/O path.

Start Your Engines, the Race for Wiring Supremacy Has Begun!

Three networking technologies have the potential to provide a common wiring infrastructure for storage networks. The first is Fibre Channel, the next is Ethernet, particularly Gigabit Ethernet, and the third is InfiniBand. Each of these will be discussed in detail in its own chapter. For now, we'll make a brief comparison of their potential as a common wiring for storage networks.

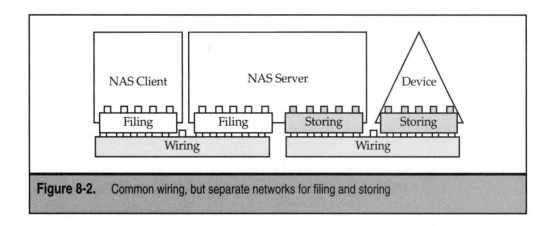

Figure 8-2.   Common wiring, but separate networks for filing and storing

Fibre Channel Strength in Storing

Fibre Channel's primary strengths are precisely where Ethernet has weaknesses. It is a high-speed, low-latency network with advanced flow control technology to handle bursty traffic such as storage I/O. However, its weaknesses are the major strengths of Ethernet. The Fibre Channel industry is still small compared to Ethernet, with limited technology choices and a relatively tiny talent pool for implementing and managing installations. The talent pool in Fibre Channel is heavily concentrated in storage development companies that have a vested interest in protecting their investment in Fibre Channel technology. This does not mean that these companies will not develop alternative wiring products, but it does mean that they will not be likely to abandon their Fibre Channel products.

Of the three technologies discussed here, Fibre Channel was the first to develop legitimate technology for common wiring. But technology alone does not always succeed, as has been proved many times throughout our history. The Fibre Channel industry has never appeared interested in its potential as a common wiring. Although it has a technology lead, having begun as the de facto standard for SANs, it is extremely unlikely that Fibre Channel will cross over to address the NAS, client/server market.

Ethernet's Move into Storing

Ethernet has the obvious advantage of being the most widely deployed networking technology in the world. There is an enormous amount of talent and technology available to aid the implementation and management of Ethernet networks. While the 10Mb and 100Mb Ethernet varieties are sufficient for NAS, they are probably not realistic choices to support SANs because of their overall limitations and lack of flow control implementations. Therefore, Gigabit Ethernet would likely be the ground floor for storing applications such as SANs. However, even though Gigabit Ethernet has the raw bandwidth and flow control needed for storage I/O, most Gigabit Ethernet switches do not have low enough latency to support high-volume transaction processing.

There is little question that Ethernet will be available to use as a common wiring for both filing and storing applications, but its relevance as an industrial-strength network for storing applications has to be proved before it will be deployed broadly as an enterprise common wiring infrastructure.

InfiniBand Incubates and Waits in the Wings

The latest entrant in the field is InfiniBand, the serial bus replacement for the PCI host I/O bus. InfiniBand's development has been spearheaded by Intel with additional contributions and compromises from Compaq, HP, IBM, Sun, and others. As a major systems component expected to be implemented in both PC and Unix platforms, InfiniBand is likely to become rapidly deployed on a large scale. In addition, a fairly large industry is developing the equivalent of host bus adapters and network interface cards for InfiniBand. Therefore, InfiniBand is likely to grow a sizable talent pool rapidly.

In relation to storage networks, the question is: will storing and/or filing applications run directly across InfiniBand wiring, as opposed to requiring some sort of InfiniBand adapter? Immediately, soon, years away, or never? The technology probably needs to gain an installed base as a host I/O bus before it can effectively pursue new markets such as storage networking. However, InfiniBand certainly has the potential to become a legitimate storage wiring option at some point in the future. As the apparent method of choice for connecting systems together in clusters, along with their associated storage subsystems, this could happen sooner than expected. As with any other networking technology, it is not so much a question of whether the technology can be applied, but rather when attempts will be made and by whom with what resources.

The Significance of Common Wiring

There aren't any crystal balls to predict the future of storage networking. However, any time functions can be integrated together in a way that reduces cost and complexity, the only question is whether it can be marketed successfully. Common wiring is more than a theoretical abstraction for storage networks, but it represents a large opportunity to integrate data networks and storage channels under a single technology umbrella.

As Fibre Channel, Ethernet, and InfiniBand technologies evolve in response to this integration gravity, it is almost inevitable that NAS and SAN developers will look for ways to combine functionality and their products will look more and more alike. The terms "NAS" and "SAN" will seem completely arbitrary or obsolete, and it will be necessary to distinguish storage products by the storing and filing applications they provide, as opposed to the limitations of their initial implementations. At that point, a whole new level of storing/filing integration will become visible and true self-managing storage networks may be possible. But first, the wiring slugfest!

Table 8-1 briefly summarizes the competing technologies that could be used to form a common wiring and their current status.

	Filing (NAS)	Storing (SAN)	Comments
Ethernet	The incumbent, with the dominant installed base	Several initiatives, but few products	Requires further refinement for legitimacy in storing
Fibre Channel	Supported, but rarely deployed	First to market, with an established lead	Insufficient critical mass to penetrate Ethernet's realm
InfiniBand	Nothing yet, initially through an adapter	Nothing yet, initially through an adapter	Will develop native wiring capability VIA clusters*

*Pun intended

Table 8-1.   Comparison of Storage Network Wiring Technologies

SUMMARY

This chapter discussed the fundamental components of storage networks—wiring, storing, and filing—in relation to the most common applications of storage networks today: NAS and SAN. More than just the similarity of the acronyms used, NAS and SAN have confused the industry and the market because of their similarities and the lack of an architectural framework to view them in.

NAS, the application of filing over a network, has two important roles. First, it provides a service that allows applications and users to locate data as objects over a network. Second, it provides the data structure to store that data on storage devices or subsystems that it manages.

SAN, on the other hand, is the application of storing functions over a network. In general, this applies to operations regarding logical block addresses, but it could potentially involve other ways of identifying and addressing stored data.

Wiring for storage networks has to be extremely fast and reliable. Fibre Channel is the incumbent to date, but Gigabit Ethernet and InfiniBand are expected to make runs at the storage network market in the years to come. The development of a common wiring infrastructure for both filing (NAS) and storing (SAN) applications appears to be inevitable, and it will deliver technology and products that can be highly leveraged throughout an organization.

EXERCISES

1. Design a storage network for carrying both filing and storing applications using common wiring.

2. Detail the I/O path for client systems that request filing services from a server over the network you just designed. Include the file I/O redirection in the client system.

CHAPTER 9

SAN Structures and Topologies

Storage area networks, or SANs, are among the most interesting topics in the networking world today. While the future of wiring technology for SANs may be up for grabs between Fibre Channel, Ethernet, and InfiniBand, the reasons for deploying SANs and the primary applications they support are the same across all three technologies. This chapter outlines the primary benefits of SANs, discusses the basic topology possibilities, and explores some of the techniques involved to make them useful.

TRANSFORMING THE NETWORK STORAGE CHANNEL WITH SANS

SANs break the traditional binding between storage and computers by allowing storage to communicate with multiple servers. In other words, SANs reintegrate storage as part of a networked storage channel, instead of belonging to a single-controller bus. The following drawing shows how storage has moved from a host-centric architecture to a network-centric one:

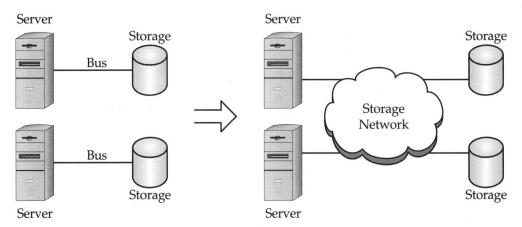

There are some significant benefits in moving storage onto a multiaccess network. One of them is the ability to scale storage far beyond the constraints of bus architectures. Another primary benefit is vastly improved data availability through more flexible, logical host connections.

Running storage I/O over multiple-access networks significantly disrupts the tight control systems have exerted over storage for many years. It is not immediately clear what this will mean over time, but the results are likely to be important. Tightly integrated system software, such as file and database systems, have been developed with the assumption that the storage devices and subsystems would be closely controlled by the host system. However, this assumption is not necessarily valid in a network storage environment. When these system-level applications are forced to adapt to network storage architectures, many other aspects of computing are likely to change also.

Structures for Scaling

Bus storage technologies, by their electrical nature, usually have some small, finite limitation on the number of devices they support. In contrast, SANs can significantly improve the number of devices attached to each host I/O controller. The number of devices that can be attached to a SAN depends on the technology used. For example, a Fibre Channel loop networks supports up to 127 devices, while switched Fibre Channel networks can address millions of devices.

In contrast to parallel SCSI, with its limitation of 15 addressable devices, switched SANs are virtually unlimited. Some might scoff at the idea of connecting a thousand devices to a single host I/O controller, but the evolution of computing is full of examples where innovations and advancements have broken barriers previously thought to be impenetrable. The scalability differences are summarized in the following illustration:

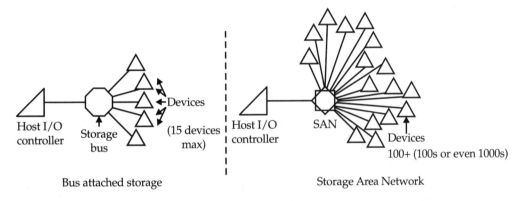

Bus attached storage   Storage Area Network

Scalability Through Cascading Switches

The number of addresses available in a SAN can be increased by *cascading* SAN switches. Cascading connects one or more ports on a switch to downstream switches, forming a hierarchy of switches, as shown in Figure 9-1.

Two levels of 16-port SAN switches can support up to 225 directly attached devices. An additional level of switches (225 switches is a lot of switches and would be expensive) would increase the number of attachable addresses to 3,375. Using 50GB drives, and mirroring them for redundancy, this translates into over 84 terabytes of storage on 1,687 mirrored pairs, all of which could be accessed relatively quickly.

Scalability Through Storage Routers

Storage bridges, sometimes also called storage *routers,* are used to transport block I/O traffic between SANs and other types of networks or buses. These kinds of products provide a variety of boundary services including address translation, protocol and signaling conversion, data buffering, and the capability to interact correctly with all other entities in the SAN and the other bus or network.

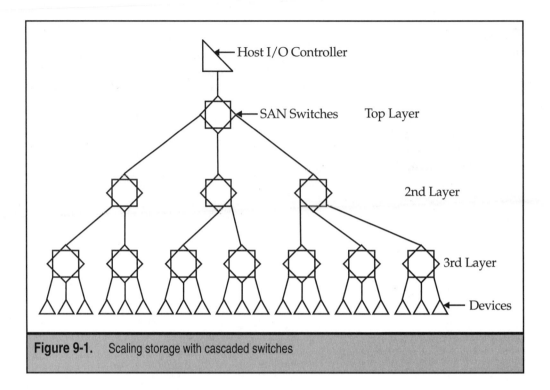

Figure 9-1. Scaling storage with cascaded switches

Figure 9-2 shows a storage router being used to connect seven bus-attached SCSI devices to a Fibre Channel SAN. Notice that the number of devices on the SCSI side of the router is the maximum number addressable for narrow SCSI and how this number is relatively small compared to the number of devices supported by SANs.

Performance Scaling Advantages of Switched SANs

In general, the bandwidth capabilities of SAN technology increase the throughput of the storage channel relative to some existing implementation of bus storage technology. However, that should not be taken to mean that SANs are always faster than buses, because they aren't in all cases. At least in the short term, parallel SCSI technology has continued to increase its performance capabilities and has maintained a performance advantage over SANs.

By taking advantage of switching technology, SANs have an important architectural advantage over bus technology. Switching was introduced years ago in wide area networks and later in local networks as a way to isolate traffic at the data link layer. Instead of many nodes competing for the same shared wiring resource, switching limits the traffic over an individual network link to two nodes. This significantly reduces the congestion on

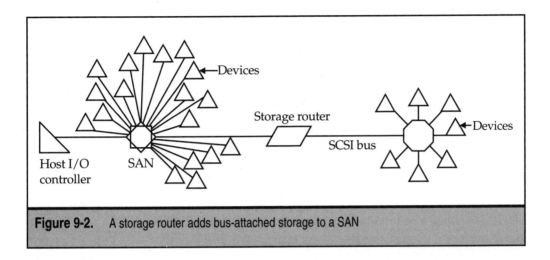

Figure 9-2. A storage router adds bus-attached storage to a SAN

any individual link in the network, which practically eliminates extended arbitration cycles and the starving of devices that cannot win arbitration. By eliminating link congestion, it is possible to significantly increase the number of devices connected to a storage channel without degrading performance.

The difference in link level characteristics between bus and switched technologies is pictured in Figure 9-3.

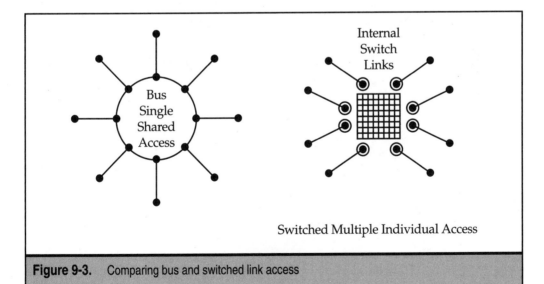

Figure 9-3. Comparing bus and switched link access

Distance Scaling Advantages of SANs

SANs can be run over considerably longer distances at high speed than bus technologies. Serial transmission technologies used in SANs can transmit information over longer distances than parallel bus transmission technologies. Not only are the cable lengths much longer, but it is also much easier to bridge over wide area links. For example, specialized lasers support distances up to 100 kilometers without repeaters on single-mode cable. Less expensive multimode cabling supports transmission distances up to 500 meters. Even copper-cabled Fibre Channel, with its distance limitation of 30 meters, supports distances that are more than twice as long as parallel Ultra SCSI technology operating at 80 MB/s or greater.

With the longer cable lengths supported by SANs, many more options are available for locating storage devices and subsystems. Network cables, particularly fiber optic cables, are smaller and more flexible than bus-attached cables. Combined with the distance supported, the physical locations of subsystems and devices can be arranged where they are easiest to manage. For example, a server room could be planned where servers are located on one side of the room and storage on the other, as shown here:

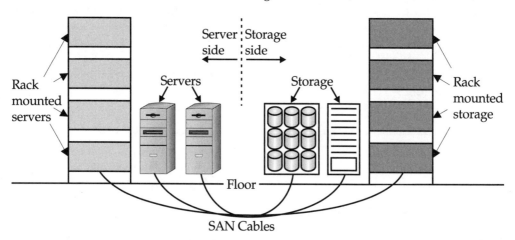

More important, longer cable lengths in SANs allow physically dispersed storage subsystem configurations that provide better data protection and availability. An example is a remote-mirrored disk subsystem that takes advantage of the extended distance capabilities of a SAN instead of relying on expensive and touchy channel extenders. Figure 9-4 shows a remote mirrored disk subsystem located in a different building from the server, that is part of the same SAN I/O channel, providing data protection from a catastrophic local site disaster.

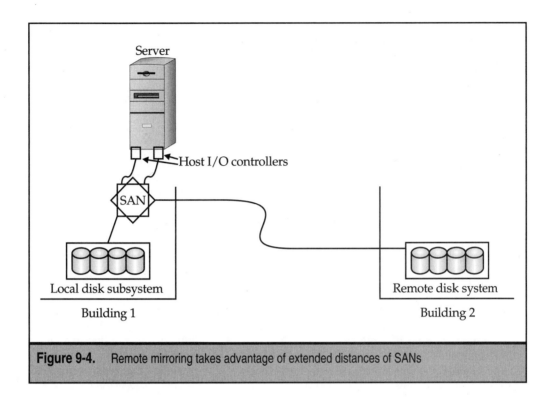

Figure 9-4.   Remote mirroring takes advantage of extended distances of SANs

Structures for Availability

The other key architectural benefit of multiaccess SAN connectivity for storage is the relative ease and speed in establishing connections between storage and servers that are connected to the same SAN. This is not to imply that connecting anything to a SAN is necessarily easy, but it refers more to the ability to add and remove servers and storage independent of each other without having to first shut both down to prevent a catastrophe.

The electrical nature of bus technology does not accommodate "hot" changes to the bus without a fair amount of expensive specialized equipment, and then only under very limited conditions. SAN technology relies on network access protocols to make connections between servers and storage and therefore has no inherent electrical circuit shared between them. Therefore, when changes are required, they can be made relatively quickly.

Advantages of SAN Storage for Storage Upgrades

SANs allow storage to be connected and disconnected to the I/O channel without interrupting server operations. Furthermore, devices and subsystems can exist on the SAN without "belonging" exclusively to any particular server system, which means new storage equipment that is intended to replace existing, operating equipment can be added to the network without interrupting storage operations between the server and the existing storage.

Not only that, but replacement storage subsystem can be tested in parallel with the continued operation of the device or subsystem being upgraded. In theory, most of the data can potentially be transferred from the existing subsystem to the replacement one using a specialized data copy/synchronization operation. This way, the new subsystem can be prepared for operation with minimal impact on the production server, with minimal, or even no, downtime during the upgrade process. Figure 9-5 shows how a new storage subsystem can be added to a SAN without upsetting server operations.

Upgrading and Redeploying Servers on SANs

Just as storage can be upgraded without interrupting normal processing, servers can also be replaced following a similar process. The one major difference in replacing an existing server with a new one is that the two servers may not be able to access the same storage subsystem for the purposes of testing. In general, only one server's file system can control the block structure on a storage device. Even so, some Unix operating systems allow a certain amount of device-sharing by restricting one of the servers' operations to read-only so that two independent software systems are not allocating block storage space on the subsystem.

Specialized distributed file systems and clustered file systems have been developed to allow multiple servers to share access to a single device or subsystem. This topic is discussed in Chapter 15 later in the book.

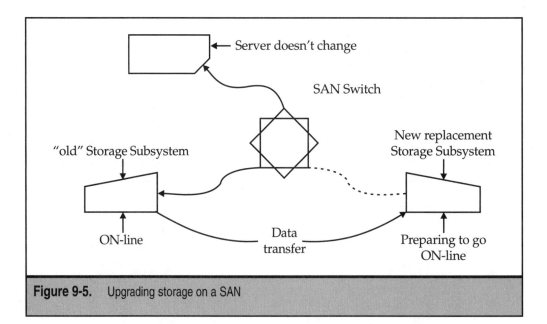

Figure 9-5. Upgrading storage on a SAN

As data does not reside on servers per se, but on storage, it is possible to think of SANs as a medium for matching servers to storage. As applications change their processing requirements over time, the SAN provides the flexibility to upgrade and reassign server hardware as most appropriate for the given workload. Servers that run out of gas for high-demand applications may be able to be redeployed to improve the performance of other less-demanding ones, just by changing the file system mount points for the server. Obviously this is not the sort of thing one would want to do without careful planning, but it would certainly be much easier than changing bus configurations.

High Availability Clustered Configurations

One of the main shortcomings of bus technology is the exposure to server failures. If the server that owns the storage bus fails, access to data can become blocked. High-availability, or HA, technology has been developed to circumvent such problems by allowing the processing load to be shared by multiple servers or making it possible to allocate a spare server as a standby system that can take over the workload should the primary server fail. The goal of HA systems is to never have unexpected loss of data access.

Typically, the combination of servers is called a *server cluster*. There are several types of cluster architectures, classified according to the method used to control and access data on the varying systems that belong to the cluster. The most basic cluster involves a pair of systems, where one is designated as the primary to run all applications until it fails, at which point the other secondary system takes over all operations. SAN technology enables a pair of servers to access the same pair of mirrored storage subsystems using a crisscrossed connection scheme that provides duplicate paths designed to sustain a failure anywhere in the I/O path, as shown in Figure 9-6.

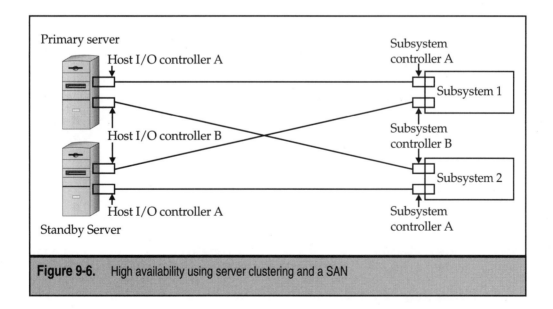

Figure 9-6.   High availability using server clustering and a SAN

NETWORK TOPOLOGIES IN SANS

SANs acquire many of their characteristics from the topology of the underlying wiring function. In the section that follows, we look at the characteristics of two major networking topologies—switched and ring—and discuss how well they match the requirements for a storage channel.

The topology illustrated in Figure 9-6 shows point-to-point links between servers and storage. While point-to-point is a legitimate topology, it is hardly much of a network, as it is severely restricted in functionality and only connects two entities. It is worth mentioning that the one advantage of point-to-point wiring is the extended distances that can be attained using it.

Transmission Frame Structure

Systems and storage communicate with each other using highly structured mechanisms that define all the various parameters of communication. In this chapter, we are mostly concerned with the exchange of *transmission frames* between systems and storage. A transmission frame can be thought of as a string of bits that is delivered and received over the network as a single, granular amount of work. Frames are the most basic intelligible unit for communicating.

Frames are similar to words in a verbal dialogue. The sounds that make up words are unintelligible and not so useful until they form words. The words then are typically pieced together to form a thought or sentence that conveys much more meaning than just the words alone.

So it is with frames. Frames are processed by the receiving entity on a network and often are pieced together to create more meaningful communication. To understand how frames are generated, transferred, and received through a network, it is useful to know a little bit about how they are made.

There is a great deal of detail to the structure of frames, and there are many books available that discuss this topic. For the purposes of the discussions to follow, frames basically have seven parts:

▼   **Start delimiter** Signals the beginning of a frame

■   **Destination address** Identifies what entity should receive the frame

■   **Source address** Identifies the entity that originated the frame

■   **Protocol metadata** Information used to process frames

■   **Data payload** The data being transferred

■   **Error check value** An integrity check to ensure accurate delivery of the frame

▲   **End delimiter** Signals the end of a frame

These pieces are laid out horizontally from right to left in the figure below, indicating the order this information is processed as the frame travels through the network:

End Delimiter	Parity Checksum	Data Payload	Protocol Metadata	Source Address	Destination Address	Start Delimiter

This basic frame structure is used for most types of storage networking technology. In general, the storage I/O controller-initiator receives the data payload and any protocol metadata from higher-layer functions, assembles the frame using the frame elements listed above, and sends it out over the network. The frame is transferred through the network unchanged until it arrives at the destination; it is then received by a storage I/O controller-target and checked for integrity using the error check value. The protocol metadata is interpreted by the appropriate storage network function, and the data is loaded into its proper location. If a response or acknowledgment is required, the target generates another frame using the source address as the destination address for the acknowledgment frame.

Switched Networks

At this stage in storage networking's development, it appears that switched-topology SANs will become the wiring of choice. This is not really too surprising, as switched networking has been widely deployed in Ethernet LANs and has been one of the most successful technologies in a large and dynamic industry.

Congestion at the link level in the storage channel has been one of the most difficult hurdles for bus-based storage. In essence, sharing the wiring of a storage network establishes a system with both capacity and performance limitations. Switching solves this problem by eliminating link congestion and moving the traffic management into the switch itself.

A *switch* is a network device that has multiple ports that connect to other entities such as network interface cards, host I/O controllers, storage subsystem controllers, bridges, routers, and other switches, as depicted here:

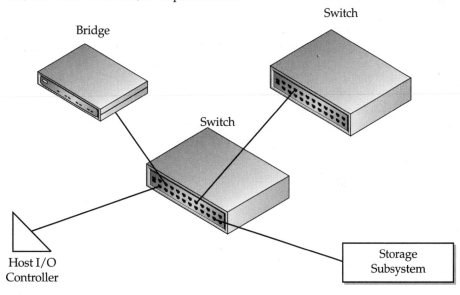

Bridge

Switch

Switch

Host I/O Controller

Storage Subsystem

Inside the Switch

There is a great deal of sophisticated technology inside network switches that has been the subject of many books already and is beyond the scope of this book. However, the basic concepts of switching are presented here to build an understanding of how switched networks for storage can be constructed.

In the parlance of storage, the entity that begins an I/O operation is the *initiator* and the entity that the I/O operation is directed toward is the *target*. The switch transfers incoming traffic from a link with an initiator to a link with a target, as shown next. To be accurate, the switch routes the traffic from an incoming port to an outgoing port.

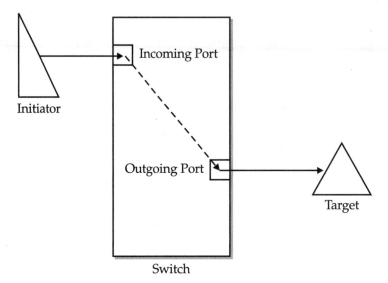

In general, any port in a switch can communicate with any other port in the switch. Switch ports commonly have buffer memory to temporarily store data as it passes through the switch. The switch component that transfers data between ports is called the *backplane*. Several types of backplane architectures are implemented with varying characteristics for such things as throughput, latency, and scalability. The basic components of a switch are shown in Figure 9-7.

In essence, switching moves the storage channel congestion problem from the bus to the inside of the switch. Instead of initiators and targets competing to access the bus, ports in a switch compete to access the backplane. The major difference is that the switch backplane is typically capable of transfer rates much, much faster than are possible in a storage bus.

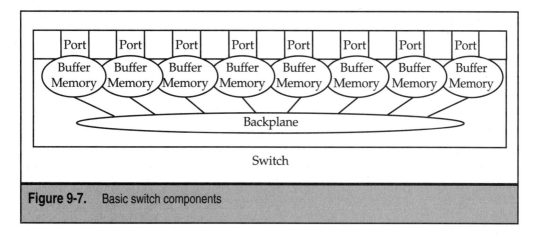

Figure 9-7. Basic switch components

Blocking

Even though the switch backplane can be quite fast, there are still plenty of situations where congestion occurs inside the switch. This can happen when an initiator attempts to send data to a target that is already communicating with another initiator, as depicted here:

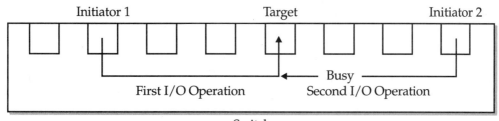

When this happens, some of the data must be held in buffer memory until the target is freed from its previous communication session. This conflict for port access, called *blocking*, occurs in virtually all switches under excessive loads. While most switch vendors promote their switches as nonblocking, it is impossible to design a switch that compensates for a poor network design.

Address Mapping

The switch has to know how to direct incoming traffic arriving on one port to the proper outgoing port. It first reads the destination address in the transmission frame and then tries to match that address with information it keeps about the various network addresses that can be accessed through its ports and connecting links. Therefore, the switch has to have some mechanism or data structure for knowing which addresses are available on which ports. In other words, the switch "maps" its ports to certain addresses and uses this mapping for connecting initiators and targets through an internal port-to-port connection.

Switches can *filter* frames by choosing to discard frames instead of making port-to-port connections for a number of reasons, including address restrictions, invalid addresses, and parity calculations that do not match.

Store and Forward Versus Cut-Through Switching

The logical mapping of ports only determines which ports to send data through; it does not determine how this is physically done. Two basic implementations are used to forward data through a switch. The first is called *store and forward.* As the name implies, the transmission frame that comes into the switch is read completely into the incoming port's buffer memory before it is transferred across the backplane to the outgoing port. Store and forward switches commonly employ various filters to help manage network traffic.

The other approach to switching is called *cut-through* switching. In cut-through switching, the frame's destination address is read at the incoming port and the data is immediately routed to the proper outgoing port. With cut-through switching, it is possible that a frame may already be on its way over the outgoing port's link before the entire frame is received on the incoming link. In other words, the whole frame may never actually be in buffer memory at the same time.

Trunking

Switches can be connected together on switch-to-switch links called "trunks." These links can have different characteristics trunk links that are used to connect targets and initiators to the network. Special protocols can be used on trunk links that allow switches to exchange information that pertains to network operations, but not to any initiators and targets. Furthermore, trunks may use different types of line-driver technology to allow them to run over longer distances or carry more traffic. Virtual networks can also be established over trunk links that provide prioritization and security capabilities that do not exist otherwise in a network.

Priority is an especially interesting topic. Most switched network links do not have to be concerned much with priority because there are only two entities communicating on a link with a limited amount of traffic. However, in a trunk link between switches, many initiator/target pairs may be communicating with each other through the trunk link, and this situation could result in an unexpected bottleneck requiring higher performance levels from the trunk or a way to prioritize data flowing through the trunk.

Ring Networks

Another high-speed network topology used in SANs is a ring, or loop, network. Loops have been used in several networking technologies, including Token Ring, FDDI, and Fibre Channel Arbitrated Loop networks.

Ring networks are shared media networks, which means that all entities on them compete with each other to access the network. Typically there is only data exchange going on in the ring at any given time. In contrast, switched topologies can have many simultaneous transmissions occurring and have much higher aggregate bandwidth capabilities than loops. For this reason, rings, or loops, are viewed as appropriate for departmental SAN solutions, but they are considered too limited to be used in an enterprise-level SAN.

The Hub's Role

Ring topologies are typically built using what is called a physical star, logical ring topology. This means the physical cables are connected to a common network junction point, sometimes referred to as a *hub*. Like a switch, a hub may have several ports connecting multiple initiators and targets on the ring. However, unlike a switch, the hub does not read the frame's address information but sends it out the next active port. The frame is passed through the ring in this fashion until it reaches its destination.

The physical path in a ring network is used to transfer data out to a storage I/O controller and back again through the same port. While the physical path forms a star or a wheel with spokes, the logical path is best described as a ring or loop. In essence, the hub acts as coupling mechanism for the cables in the network. Viewed this way, the logical path forms a ring topology that gives the technology its name. This kind of physical star, logical ring network created by a collection of storage I/O controllers and a hub is pictured here:

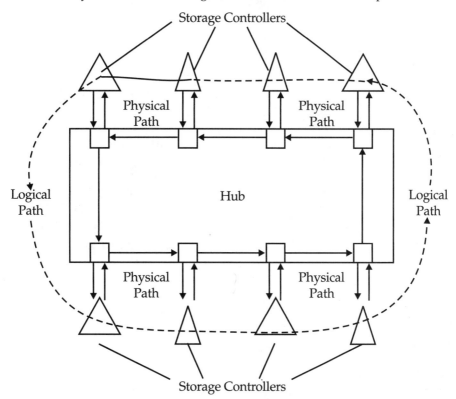

The Team Approach to Networking

A ring network does not depend on the presence of an intelligent switch to transfer data. Hubs are essentially transparent entities that do nothing to read or otherwise process the frame. In fact, hubs are not needed to make the ring work, but they do make it easier to install and can provide some management functions. So instead of a network device making decisions based on frame contents, the individual storage I/O controllers in the ring have to do this. Furthermore, every I/O controller in the ring handles every frame in one way or another, even if it is not acting as the initiator or target in the data exchange. At a minimum, each controller acts as a *repeater* on the ring by regenerating the frame's signal and sending it along to the next controller in sequence.

This creates a kind of network "community" where all the controllers in the ring must be functioning correctly to ensure the integrity of the network. If any controller fails to work properly, the entire network fails.

Addressing in a Ring Network

There is no centralized location to store address information in a ring network. This means that the individual network nodes in the ring must generate their own addresses and maintain their own address and routing information. The situation is more difficult than it first appears, especially when one considers the consequences of a complete network failure resulting from something like a power loss. As the network comes back on line, the nodes need to work as individuals and as members of a group to determine their addresses and remap these addresses to the applications that use them.

Expanding the Ring

Ring networks can expand the number of ports by adding additional hubs and connecting them through port-to-port links. Unlike in switched networks, this is not a trunk link that may carry many storage I/O operations simultaneously; instead, it is a fairly simple network expansion that participates in the single storage I/O operation that the ring supports. As the frame travels around the logical ring, it is passed from one hub's physical network to the next hub's physical network in virtually the same way it is passed from one hub port to the next. Ring expansion is illustrated in the following diagram:

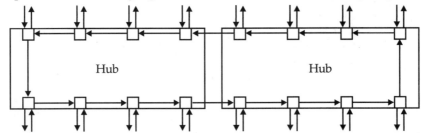

Accessing the Ring

Targets and initiators must have a way of accessing the storage network to transfer data. As shared-media networks, ring networks establish an environment where all targets and initiators compete with each other for control of the ring. Obviously, this could be a horrendous problem with many entities on a single large ring. Fortunately, the ring topology lends itself to a fast and orderly process for determining which storage I/O controller gets to access the network.

At any time, every storage controller on the ring knows the status of the ring. This is a by-product of the ring's standard operation of forwarding frames from node to node in the network. As each frame passes through each controller, the controller checks the frame's protocol metadata to determine if the transmission is starting in mid-stream or is about to end. If a controller sees that the current I/O operation on the ring is about to end, it can prepare to compete to win control of the ring.

When an I/O operation ends on the ring, the ring transfers a special frame indicating that the ring is available for another. This frame is read by each controller in the ring, and the first controller with data to send creates a frame that contains its own ring address. This frame is passed through the ring in sequence, and controllers with higher priority that have data to send can alter the frame, indicating their desire to send data by inserting their ring address. Eventually, the frame is updated by the highest-priority controller with data to send. As no other controllers have higher priority, this frame is passed unaltered around the ring until it arrives back at the controller that last changed the frame. When that controller recognizes its own address, it assumes control of the ring.

Managing Rogues in a Ring

Because each controller in a ring network handles the current frame each time it passes by, a single misbehaving controller in a ring network can destroy the ring's operation. Therefore it is highly desirable to be able to quickly identify rogue controllers and remove them from ring operations. Most ring technologies have some way for any controller in a ring to determine if it is malfunctioning and to remove itself from normal operations.

However, a rogue controller might not be able to recognize it is causing the problem and must be removed some other way, such as by a network administrator who disconnects the cables. Some hubs provide the capability to identify rogue controllers and to virtually remove them from the ring by bypassing their ports in operations. Bypassing a rogue controller is a logical operation. The link to the rogue stays connected to the hub, but instead of the hub forwarding the frame to the controller, it forwards it instead to the next port in the hub like this:

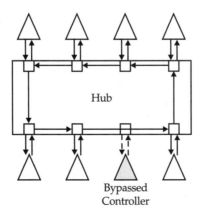

Bypassed
Controller

Switching and Rings Combined

It is possible to combine ring and switched networks to form a hybrid network that is compatible with both kinds of network. In essence, the switch provides a virtual ring port that can be used to establish connections between controllers in the ring network and those in the switched network. In other words, switched networks are extended into ring networks by bridging through specialized ports. Another approach uses specialized switch ports for ring expansion by logically linking individual rings into a single ring.

From the ring's perspective, these specialized ring ports function like normal ring ports in a hub; in other words, they are transparent. From the switch's perspective, however, such a port is an oddball, functioning completely differently than the way normal switch ports do. This port must wait for current ring operations to end before vying for control of the ring—which it might not get for several arbitration cycles of the ring. While waiting, the switch may have to buffer more data than it typically does for normal switching operations. These effects can be minimized by ensuring that rings connected through virtual ring ports in switches are fairly small with relatively few controllers.

A mixed switch-ring network is shown in this drawing:

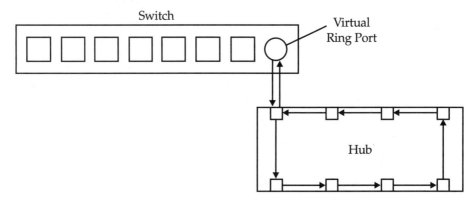

VARIATIONS AND EXTENSIONS TO SAN STRUCTURES

While switched and ring topologies provide the major structure of any SAN, there are additional network software technologies and other techniques that determine the architecture of SAN implementations. In this section, we'll look at some additional structural components that can be used in SANs.

Segregating Access to Storage in SANs

Open systems storage was developed over many years prior to storage networks to work with bus technology storage. Therefore, it's not too surprising to find out that the software components of the I/O path, the file system, the volume manager, and device drivers were also developed to work with bus-attached storage. Unfortunately, some of the assumptions made for software that work for bus-attached storage are no longer valid for SANs and can even threaten data integrity.

Bus storage technology assumes that a single host system controls each storage device or subsystem. Not surprisingly, most operating and file systems weren't developed to support shared access to storage from more than one host system. Coordinating the data structure of data in storage is a very difficult problem to solve with 100 percent accuracy—and 100 percent accuracy is required.

But sharing access to storage is more than just having to worry about which file system manages the data structure on storage. The file system's VTOC (volume table of contents) is a private data structure the file system uses for its internal configuration. Some operating systems and file systems, particularly Microsoft Windows operating systems, will overwrite an existing VTOC with one of their own when accessing storage, making the existing data on the subsystem inaccessible.

SAN vendors have developed a few different methods to overcome these shortcomings of operating and file systems. In general, these methods attempt to partition, or segregate, the access to storage with functions *in the I/O path*. The idea is that segregation will prevent the wrong systems from accessing another system's storage, causing mayhem in the storage channel.

There are three ways to segregate storage access in the I/O path:

▼ Zoning in SAN switches

■ Port zoning in multiport storage subsystems

▲ LUN masking

Each of these methods of segregating storage traffic is discussed in the sections that follows.

Zoning in SAN switches

Just as there are virtual storage devices, there are also virtual networks. In general, virtual networks are subsets of physical networks that provide special connectivity and security functions. Where storage networking is concerned, virtual networks provide a way to segregate I/O traffic among the various controllers in a SAN and create *access zones*, or more simply stated, zones.

Zones in SANs allow controllers to form virtual private access groups that block I/O traffic from controllers outside the group. Zone membership uses the mathematical concept of sets. Controllers can belong to any number of zones and are not required to belong to any. The zoning function prevents I/O operations that originated from nonmembers to enter the zone. Zoning does not necessarily reserve storage subsystems for a particular server, but it can be used this way by creating zones that only contain a single server and the storage it uses.

Table 9-1 indicates the zone assignments of a switched SAN with three servers and four storage subsystems segregated in various ways with three zones. Servers 1 and 2 and subsystems 1 and 2 all belong to Zone A. This zone configuration supports high-availability (HA) connections between a pair of servers and storage subsystems. Server 2 also belongs to Zone B, which is a private connection between server 2 and subsystem 3. This zone could be

	Zone A	Zone B	Zone C
Server 1	X		
Server 2	X	X	
Server 3			X
Subsystem 1	X		
Subsystem 2	X		
Subsystem 3		X	
Subsystem 4			X

Table 9-1. Zoning Assignments

used to provide a snapshot mirror for data stored by the cluster in zone A. Finally, server 3 and subsystem 4 communicate in their own zone. This represents a completely different server and its application that share the wiring infrastructure of the SAN but otherwise share nothing.

A visual picture of this SAN with its zone configuration looks something like this:

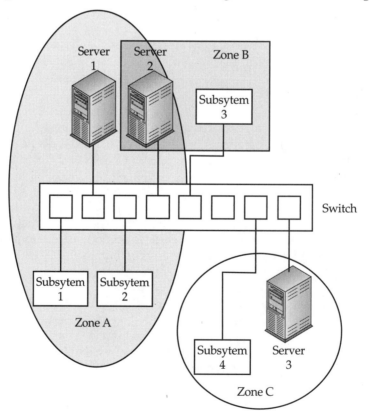

Implementation Options for Switched Zoning

The abstract concept of zoning can be implemented in either switch hardware or software. This has given rise to the terms "hard zoning" and "soft zoning" to identify the main different approaches to zoning. Both types are briefly examined in the following sections.

Soft Zoning by Network Address   *Soft zoning* is accomplished in switches by reading transmission frames as they enter the switch and determining whether or not the destination and source addresses in the frame belong to the same zone. If both addresses are not in the same zone, the frame is discarded with or without an error message, depending on the specific implementation.

Soft zoning requires the switch to support an additional internal data structure that lists all the zones defined to the switch and all the addresses belonging to each zone. This could be done by adding additional information to the switch's internal port mapping information or by creating a completely different data structure. In both cases, the switch has to perform an additional process to test for the presence of zoning and comply with its intended directions. This adds a certain amount of additional latency to the switch's process and has some performance impact on the switch. For instance, a cut-through switch might not be able to forward frames to the output port as quickly as it otherwise would due to the necessity to process zoning information on all its ports. Take, for example, a 64-port switch that queues all zoning operations in a single queue; it would likely introduce more latency to I/O operations than a similarly designed 8-port switch.

There are many ways zoning can be implemented in a switch. A generic soft zoning process is shown in Figure 9-8.

Soft zoning quickly adapts when SAN servers and storage subsystems change the switch ports they are connected to. This is a real benefit in environments where changes are expected to controller-port configurations in the SAN. Network administrators working

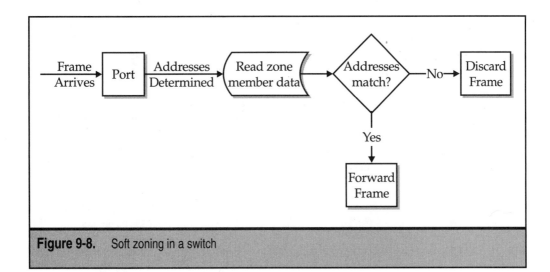

Figure 9-8.   Soft zoning in a switch

with the SAN should be able to unplug cables from switch ports and plug them into other ports without affecting the zoning function.

> **TIP:** As a word to the wise, the capability to remove and reinsert cables in different switch ports should be verified before assuming it works as expected.

Another advantage of soft zoning is that it can support zones that span multiple switches connected by trunk links. Just as a single switch uses both destination and source addresses in soft zoning, multiple switches connected together in a SAN could share and use the same address information and zoning algorithms. However, zoning is not yet standardized within the industry, and it is highly unlikely that soft zoning will work in heterogeneous switched environments.

A potential liability with soft zoning lies in the security risks that accompany internal algorithms in a switch. For example, attacks that spoof frame addresses may be able to infiltrate switch zones by trying various combinations until successful. In addition, denial-of-service attacks that bombard a switch port with excessive requests could result in algorithm processing errors that allow unauthorized entry into zones.

Hard Zoning   *Hard zoning* works by creating an exclusive set of internal circuit links between ports in a zone. Hard zoning is intended to be implemented in hardware and is designed to be impervious to security attacks. In essence, the destination address of a transmission frame is not used to enforce hard zoning, but it is necessary for the switch to read this address to understand what the intended output port is. If the output port is not a member of the zone, the switch will discard the frame with or without an error message being returned to the originating node.

There is a very subtle difference between hard and soft zoning. Both types of zoning read the destination address of the frame, but hard zoning does not process this information explicitly in the zoning function. Instead, some other hardware-based process in the switch prevents the ports from exchanging data.

Hard zoning has advantages and weaknesses opposite of those associated with soft zoning. The main advantage of hard zoning is its security protection. If the hardware does not allow certain port-to-port connections, it is extremely unlikely that network-born security attacks can succeed.

However, link and port changes are not automatically recognized and adjusted for by hard zoning switches, because the zoning is not dependent on destination and source addresses. In fact, an entity that changes ports with hard zoning could cause considerable damage if it is connected to a port with access to the wrong subsystems. This means SAN administrators who remove cables from switch ports and reinsert them into other switch ports could instantaneously cause other systems to crash and storage to lose data.

> **CAUTION:** Never remove and reinsert cables in a hard zoning switch unless you understand all the consequences of doing so.

Also, it is very difficult to assign hard zones across multiple switches through trunk links. By definition, hard zoning ignores address and protocol metadata information and establishes port-configuration connections and exclusions. This makes multiplexed traffic over switch trunks incompatible with hard zoning. Therefore, hard zoning across multiple switches requires a dedicated switch-to-switch link for each zone spanning multiple switches.

A hard zoning process is illustrated next. In this diagram, the incoming frame is mapped to an output port, but the internal switch connection is blocked by a hardware mechanism:

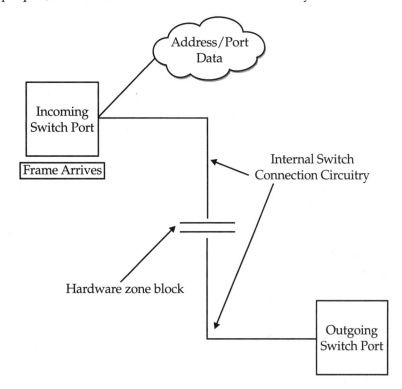

Differences Between Hard Zoning and Port Zoning

Sometimes hard zoning is referred to erroneously as *port zoning*. It should not be assumed that they are the same. The operations and implementation of hard zoning in switches can also be accomplished through software that zones by port, as opposed to by destination and source addresses. Doing this will result in a switch that behaves like a hard zoning switch, except that it does not have the same protection from network-born security attacks as a hardware-based solution.

Why Hubs Don't Provide Zoning

Zoning is a technology that depends on the address and port mapping that is the hallmark of switching technology. Rings and their associated hubs, on the other hand, do not have a natural mechanism to process frames in a similar fashion. Hard zoning in hubs is simply out of the picture. There is no way to physically restrict any of the hub ports from working in a ring network that works by forwarding frames in order through each node in the network. The situation for soft zoning in hubs is not much better. It is conceivable that hubs could be designed with soft zoning that reads destination and source addresses, or protocol metadata, and that, based on the zoning configuration, bypass ring links that do not belong to the zone.

However, such a bypass scheme would require the hub to perform its zoning process every time a frame entered a hub port. Considering that this happens once for every entity on a ringed SAN, this approach would add a significant amount of latency to the network as the number of controllers in the SAN increases. Part of the attraction in ring networks is the relative low cost of hubs. By adding zoning to the hub, the hub takes on more of the attributes and cost of a switch.

Port Zoning in Multiport Storage Subsystems

Controllers in disk subsystems can slice and dice storage many different ways. They can make an entire physical disk drive available, as is, or they can create virtual devices that are smaller or larger than physical devices by partitioning, concatenating, striping, mirroring, and applying RAID algorithms to them. In essence, a range of logical block addresses are made available as a single, manageable storage space. The terms *exported drive* and *exported volume* refer to this range of logical block addresses that servers and databases create data structures for and place data in.

Multiported storage subsystems have more than one SAN connection port (network interface) to support the needs of multiple servers. This is in line with the philosophy of enterprise storage, which asserts that data storage should be the most important platform in the IT world. Obviously for this to work, all these servers must have some way of accessing their data in such a subsystem. This capability is commonly referred to as *port zoning*. The basic idea of port zoning is that internal logic and hardware in a multiport disk subsystem segregates I/O traffic from attached servers to their exported drives.

Figure 9-9 illustrates port zoning in a disk subsystem. The configuration of servers and exported volumes is borrowed from Table 9-1. Servers 1 and 2 form a small HA cluster that works with identical exported volumes A and B. In addition, server 2 has a private connection with exported volume C and server 3 has a private connection with subsystem D.

Implementations of Port Zoning in Disk Subsystems   Port zoning provides guarded connections between the SAN ports in the subsystem and exported volumes. There are many ways to do this, which the vendors of disk subsystems use to differentiate their products. But basically the operations of port zoning follow a sequence something like this:

Frames arrive at the subsystem port, where hardware or software logic validates the frame for transmission errors, formatting, and address correctness. Validated frames are then interpreted for the type of operation they are. If a frame is an I/O request (as opposed to a simple port query), the data payload is extracted and an internal I/O request is generated and transferred over an internal bus or network that connects to storage. The port ID of the internal I/O request can be encoded several different ways depending on the port zoning algorithms employed and the architecture of the subsystem. Some of the possible ways this could be done are as follows:

▼ The port could address the request internally using a unique bus or network ID, which is processed by another internal virtual device controller.

■ A new internal logical block address could be assigned that maps directly to exported volumes and is processed by an internal volume manager.

▲ A special port identifier and protocol could be used to treat the internal request like a message, as opposed to a storage operation.

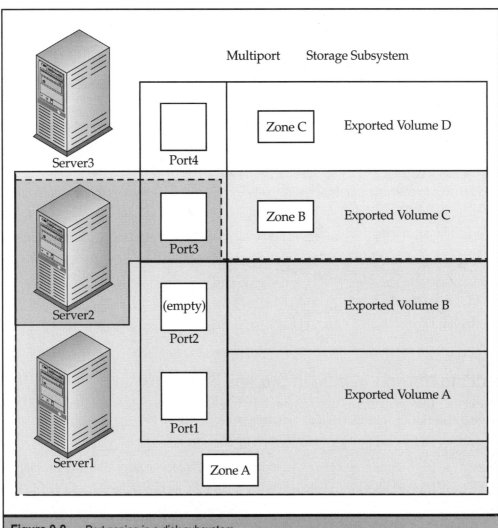

Figure 9-9. Port zoning in a disk subsystem

Whatever mechanism is used to uniquely identify the port, the I/O request is passed to an underlying storage system that manages the configuration and operation of physical disks. Multiported storage subsystems are intricate systems with a great deal of architectural complexity. The process of configuring such a subsystem can be very complex, requiring vendor-specific training and skills.

It should also be pointed out that some manufacturers have developed multiported disk subsystems with port zoning that works with parallel SCSI bus connections. Such a subsystem forms its own subsystem-centric SAN that can operate without any switched or ring network wiring.

LUN Masking

LUN masking, or *address masking*, is a feature of some host I/O controllers that filters access to certain storage resources on the SAN. To be precise, address masking is usually a function of the device driver, not the hardware of the host I/O controller.

Address masking puts the responsibility of segregating I/O paths on the individual servers in the SAN, and requires full coordination of all servers in the SAN to be effective. Each server must be configured correctly to avoid access collisions while accessing storage. If any single server is not configured correctly, the access segregation scheme will fail. Unfortunately, there are no centralized management systems for address masking, which makes it difficult to use in larger environments with many types of servers to manage. In other words, managing paths by address masking is a reasonable solution for small SANs but is not recommended for larger SANs. The following graphic depicts address masking in a host I/O controller:

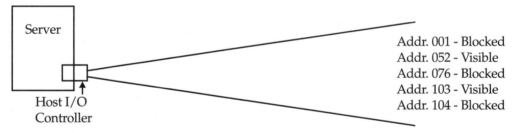

Embedding Network Wiring in Storage Subsystems

One of the more intriguing ideas in storage networking is removing the network between servers and storage by embedding switches and/or hubs within storage subsystems. In other words, the storage network would be practically invisible without discrete, external networking equipment. The only visible item is cabling. Embedding network functions in storage connects servers and subsystems together in exactly the same way as if external network equipment is used. It is simply a matter that the switch or hub provides the boundary of the storage subsystem.

Integrating the wiring components of a storage network together with the storing components potentially makes the SAN easier to manage. It is even possible that all internal or external storage network functions and components could be located behind the boundary of the initial subsystem that acts as the boundary to storing functions. There is no reason why an integrated SAN subsystem management console could not be used to manage all other connected subsystems and SAN devices.

One intriguing aspect of embedded networking in subsystems is that the functionality and value of the network technology are subsumed by the storage subsystem. IT administrators can get the benefits of SANs without having to integrate one themselves from open systems parts. Of course, the downside of this is that subsystem manufacturers may choose to limit support for other products in the market, resulting in a proprietary system that has higher costs and limited functionality compared to open-system SAN solutions.

Figure 9-10 shows embedded networking technology in a storage subsystem. The boundary subsystem in Figure 9-10 may use an additional subsystem to expand the capacity of its exported volumes and use another additional subsystem for remotely mirroring its data over an extended link.

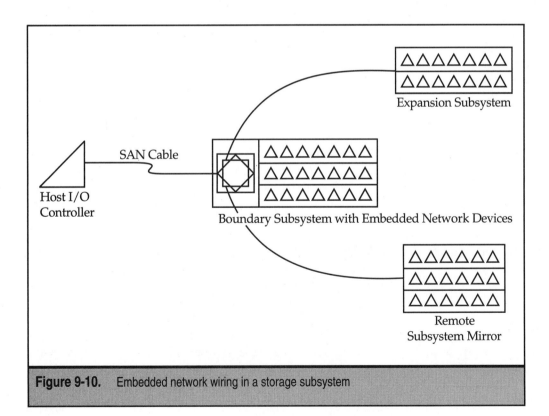

Figure 9-10.   Embedded network wiring in a storage subsystem

Storage Domain Controllers

Another interesting SAN technology is the *storage domain controller*. The basic idea of the storage domain controller is to provide a specialized system in the SAN, sometimes referred to as a *SAN appliance*, that provides storing functions, including device virtualization, volume management, caching, RAID, and even block-based backup. However, the storage domain controller does not necessarily have much in the way of its own integrated nonvolatile storage. They typically are designed to "front" other storage devices and subsystems for this purpose. The illustration that follows shows the location of a storage domain controller in a SAN.

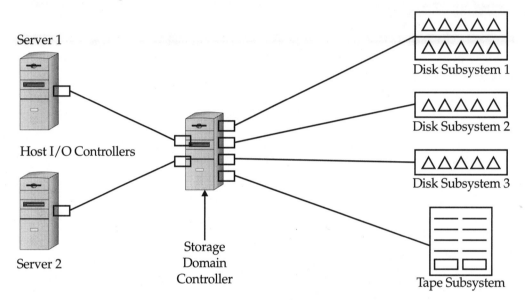

In essence, storage domain controllers are the inverse of embedded networking in storage subsystems: instead of putting the wiring inside storage, they put storing functions in the network. Frames arriving in the storage domain controller are validated and interpreted, and subsequent I/O requests are generated. If it provides caching, the storage domain controller may be able to fill the I/O request from local cache memory. If the I/O is a cache miss, the storage domain controller generates a transmission frame and sends it to the appropriate downstream storage device or subsystem.

Options for Storage Domain Controllers

Storage domain controllers could be constructed any number of ways, including packaged appliance-style products or using specialized storage domain controller software with off-the-shelf parts such as computers, host bus adapters, and memory. The performance, reliability, and scalability of such a "Heathkit" solution would depend on the usual system variables—the various buses, the memory technology, the processor technology, and the network interfaces selected.

One of the interesting items to ponder with this approach is how much storage can be "fronted" by what size and configuration storage domain controller? Another way to think about it is to ask whether or not the storage domain controller is an expensive and large enterprise type of product, or is it a smaller component in a larger overall SAN system?

The answer to these questions will be determined by the requirements of the applications using the SAN. High-performance transaction processing requires large amounts of cache relative to the amount of data stored. In that case, there could be many storage domain controllers with a maximum memory configuration fronting some number of individual disk drives. The optimal ratio of storage domain controllers to disk drives would have to be determined by experimentation and analysis of I/O activity. Alternatively, a storage domain controller could be used to build a large virtual storage devices out of re-purposed older and slower storage subsystems for historical archiving or seldom-accessed data.

Strengths and Weaknesses of Storage Domain Controllers

By turning disk subsystems inside-out, so to speak, storage domain controllers allow caching and volume management functions to be allocated on an application-by-application basis. The pay-as-you-go open systems model of storage domain controllers may be easier to swallow than the seemingly outrageous prices of expensive storage subsystems and their proprietary memory.

Storage domain controllers could be very attractive in environments with many different storage requirements. They allow storing resources to be deployed in a fairly precise manner without much waste. In a similar vein, storage domain controllers can be installed as needed in a growing and changing environment. If the caching for an application becomes inadequate, it is possible that the caching function of a single storage domain controller can be upgraded by replacing it with a pair of them. Finally, storage domain controllers allow a certain amount of mix-and-match hardware to be applied directly to specific applications. For instance, a solid state disk (SSD) device could be used to mirror data for maximum performance for read-intensive applications.

On the negative side, storage domain controllers introduce additional points of failure in the SAN. If the SAN is only as strong as its weakest link, the storage domain controller probably has to be more reliable than standard off-the-shelf system parts. If not implemented correctly or not matched well with applications, the storage domain controller will add latency to the I/O channel. In order to interpret the I/O request, the storage domain controller has to read the entire frame and process it. Depending on the structure of the storage domain controller, this could take several milliseconds. Compared to the microsecond range speed of some SAN switches, this is an awful lot of time. If the cache hit ratio is not very good, there will be performance degradation instead of acceleration.

SUMMARY

SANs have significant architectural strengths compared to bus-based storage channels. The scalability and availability capabilities of SANs are far beyond those of bus technologies. Some functions and configurations, particularly high-availability configurations that were nearly impossible with bus storage, can now be delivered with relative ease on SANs.

Several types of architectures and structures are used in SANs. The most obvious ones are those imposed by the underlying wiring technology. While there are several wiring options to choose from for SANs, switched networking appears to be on the way to becoming the network architecture of choice for connecting systems to storage. Ring topology networks can also work but do not have as rich a set of features and lack the scalability and bandwidth of switched topologies. For that reason, ring networks should probably be restricted to smaller departmental installations.

Among the most liberating advancements of SANs is the capability to share access to storage using network addresses as opposed to electrical signaling. Unfortunately, some of the host system software is not ready to make that leap yet and special precautions have to be made to ensure data integrity. In response to that need, zoning technology was developed to provided access segregation to prevent unexpected data loss. SAN implementers need to pay close attention to the zoning technologies in their products to avoid creating the kinds of problems zoning is intended to avoid.

EXERCISES

1. Assume you have a SAN with three servers and three subsystems in three different zones. One of the subsystems is running out of capacity and needs to be replaced with a new subsystem of larger capacity. List the steps you would use to replace the old storage subsystem with the new one—with as little interruption as possible to the operation of the SAN.

2. Write an algorithm to implement software port zoning in a switch. What data structures are needed?

3. Design a two-server, HA cluster in a switched SAN with complete path redundancy to mirrored storage. Include private storage for each server that cannot be accessed by the other server. Use whatever storage subsystem(s) you believe can do the job.

CHAPTER 10

SAN Solutions

Among the most challenging problems facing IT organizations is the burden of managing their storage infrastructure. Large environments with hundreds, or even thousands, of server systems under management are particularly troublesome. These types of environments may have to adopt a management-by-crisis mode in response to their ever-increasing capacity requirements. But large businesses are not the only ones seeking more effective management solutions for storage. While smaller companies typically have far less storage to manage, they also have far fewer administrators to do the work.

IT managers have been telling storage vendors for several years that they want to reduce their overall storage management efforts by centralizing storage and storage management. Centralization brings multiples of efficiency that make a significant difference in the cost and quality of management. SANs allow both storage and storage management facilities to be centrally located and deliver significant advances in meeting the storage management needs of IT organizations. In addition, SANs also extend the capabilities of data protection applications and technologies by allowing data transfers to occur over longer distances at very fast speeds. This chapter examines some of the primary solutions enabled by SAN technologies and examines the applications that will likely have the most impact as storage moves from buses to networks.

SOLVING STORAGE PROBLEMS WITH SANS

The flexibility and scalability characteristics of SANs provide the underpinnings for several significant storage solutions. Among the most interesting SAN solutions examined in this chapter are:

▼ Storage pooling

■ Pathing

■ Data moving

▲ Backup

Storage Pooling

Configuring storage in a busy and complex environment is similar to solving a puzzle where many pieces have to fit together into a single coherent scheme. Before SANs, one of the more frustrating problems with managing bus technology storage was caused by the lack of multi-initiator access. For example, the only server that could access vacant storage space on a disk subsystem was the server connected to it over the SCSI bus. So, if a server had excess storage space, the other servers in the environment could not access it. This resulted in long, involved processes for adjusting storage configurations in response to changing capacity and performance requirements.

SANs can alleviate these difficulties by allowing all servers to easily access all the storage in a SAN. With the potential for a many-to-one relationship between servers and storage in SANs, any unused storage can be made available to the servers that need it. Such storage could be used for several different purposes, including temporary space that could be accessed by any server, on demand. Figure 10-1 shows a virtual disk volume in a designated "emergency overflow" disk subsystem that is allocated to a server that has run out of available storage on the volumes it has been assigned.

The architectural shift from single-initiator bus storage to multi-initiator storage networks allows all the storage components in a SAN to be treated as part of a large, consolidated set of resources. This ability to aggregate storage resources into *storage pools* that can be managed as a single versatile collection may be the single most important application of SANs.

Device Virtualization in Storage Pools

SANs are the application of storing functions on networks. Storage pooling is a storing function that transforms aggregated storage into more manageable virtual storage. Its primary role is to translate logical block addresses from contributing devices and subsystems into exported volumes that are used by servers. The next illustration shows how the

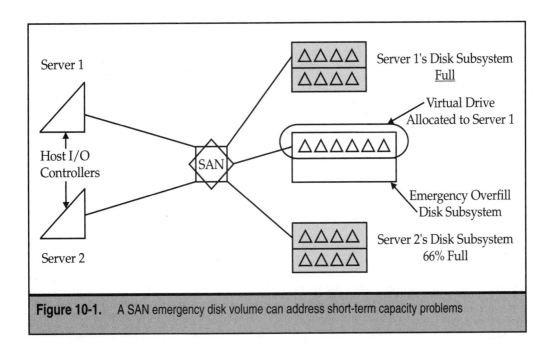

Figure 10-1. A SAN emergency disk volume can address short-term capacity problems

logical block addresses from two disk arrays in a storage pool are first aggregated and then subdivided into multiple exported volumes:

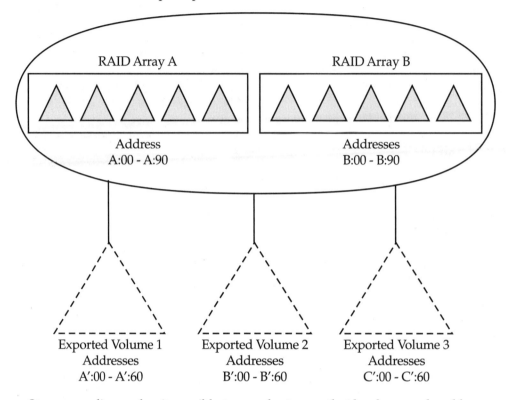

Storage pooling makes it possible to recycle storage that has been replaced by new, larger and faster, storage. Recycling storage in storage pools can extend the useful life of storage by making it available for other servers and applications with less stringent performance requirements.

From another point of view, storage pooling enables vendors to build extremely versatile storage subsystems that allow their customers to buy storage in bulk and allocate it as it is needed over time. For instance, consider a scenario like the one in Figure 10-2, where a one-terabyte storage pooling subsystem has 20 ports that can be accessed by all the servers in a SAN. If the data was allocated in uniform amounts, each port could export a 50GB virtual volume to its connected servers in the SAN.

As shown in Figure 10-2, the 50GB exported volumes can be allocated sequentially. This makes it very easy to assess the amount of storage capacity remaining in the storage pool. This method of allocating storage allows storage administrators to create and follow proactive policies about when to purchase and install additional storage.

Storage pooling provides significant benefits for planning the acquisition and implementation of storage, including the notion that some amount of storage can be implemented as "standby storage" that is ready and available for circumstances when storage

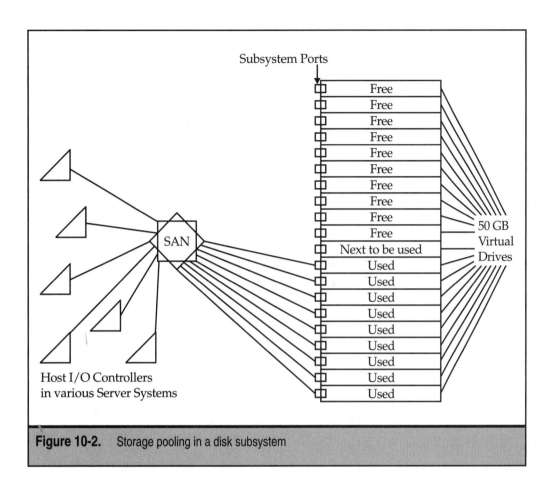

Figure 10-2.   Storage pooling in a disk subsystem

capacity is unexpectedly needed. This can happen for a variety of reasons, depending on application and system management issues that arise. This notion of having ready-reserve storage could be an extremely important benefit for IT professionals who want to systematically deploy storage, as opposed to doing it one crisis at a time.

Independence of Storage Pooling   Storage pooling is a storing-level function that is independent of both wiring and filing implementations. That means storage pooling can be used over any available network to support either file system or database data structures. Implied in this independence is the notion that storage pooling is also platform independent, which means the exported volumes from a storage pool can be used by heterogeneous platforms connected to a SAN for a variety of needs. For instance, a storage pool that was last used for a Solaris system can be recycled to support a Windows 2000 server.

NAS Integration with Storage Pooling   There is no implied filing function with storage pooling, but vendors may choose to integrate NAS functionality into their storage pooling products. In that case, the filing function would be internal to the storage pool and would control one or more of the virtual storage volumes. The network, or wiring, ports for the storage pool function and the NAS function could be different. For instance, a storage pooling product that exports storage volumes through SAN ports could also export a NAS file system through an Ethernet port. The structure of such a storage pooling product with integrated NAS is shown here:

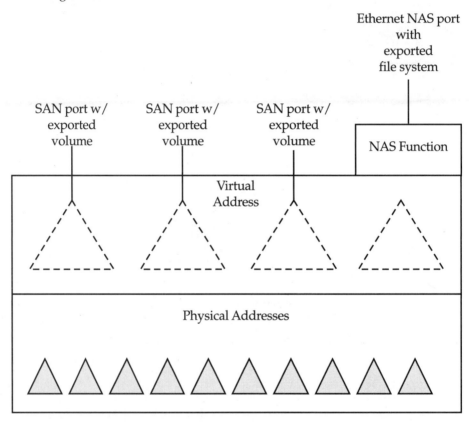

I/O Path Considerations for Storage Pooling

When thinking about any storage networking technology, it is valuable to understand how the I/O path is established between the server and storage.

Three network-resident locations along the I/O path need to be understood in any storage pooling environment. First, the host I/O controllers in the SAN need to be configured correctly to be able to access the exported volumes from the pool. Although the storage might be centralized in bulk, each of the multiple ports in a storage pooling product has its own unique identity, address, or name in the SAN. Those identities need to be included in any list of SAN entities kept by the server or its associated host I/O controllers. In general, this should not be expected to be too difficult as long as all other links in the path are configured correctly. A more likely scenario is that the host I/O controller would use some form of LUN masking as an additional safety measure to prevent servers from accessing storage resources they should not.

Next stop along the I/O path in a SAN is a switch or hub. If a switch is used with zoning, the zones need to be defined that include both host storage I/O controllers and storage pool exported volumes. Again, this does not add any unusual amount of difficulty as long as the identities of the exported volumes in the pool are clearly delineated.

That brings us to the last location, the storage pool itself. It only makes sense that a multiported storage subsystem segregate its internal connections in a way that does not allow data integrity to be compromised by internal "crosstalk." This requires the presence of some type of port zoning in the subsystem along with an associated management interface for it. There are likely to be as many management interfaces for doing this as there are vendors of storage pooling products. However it is done, it is a very good idea for the administrator to always keep up-to-date documentation showing all ports assigned to all exported volumes.

The three I/O path locations involved in creating and completing the I/O path for two servers using a storage pool are shown here:

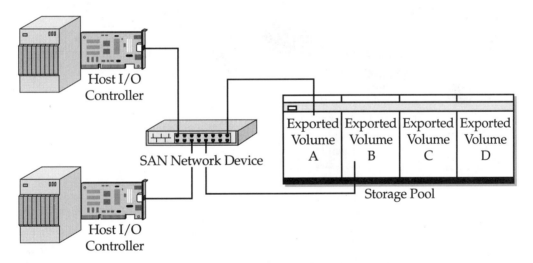

Volume Management in Storage Pooling Products

The storage devices and subsystems that contribute to the storage pool can theoretically be combined in any number of ways by the internal volume management software in the pool subsystem. For instance, storage devices can be mirrored, concatenated, striped, and given parity (RAID) in a number of ways, depending on the design of the pool system.

For example, it might be possible to mirror disk drives in a pool if both drives are the same capacity. Alternatively, it could be possible to mirror a physical disk drive with an equal-sized partition from another drive. As the concept of a storage pool works with logical block addresses, which can be theoretically combined and used in virtually any configuration and order, there are many ways to slice and dice physical storage as exported volumes. There are also many ways to do it poorly.

In general, one should always try to keep in mind the underlying physical structure of the devices and subsystems used. For instance, assume the disk drives in the multiported, pooling subsystem are all 50GB in capacity. The usable capacities of these drives and their combinations in mirrors and arrays will be 50GB, 100GB, 150GB, 200GB, etc. Therefore, it may be a good idea to think about using exported volumes with the same capacities.

The question then is: "Should I use mirrored drives, concatenated mirror drives, small arrays, or huge arrays to form the internal virtual devices that would be segregated into exported volumes?" The answer is that it depends a lot on the design of the pooling subsystem and the possible configurations it supports. But beyond the limitations imposed by a specific product, there are some things to keep in mind.

First, disk arms can easily become I/O bottlenecks if they support too many servers. How many is too many? It depends on the application load. A hypothetical disk drive with five partitions and five ports could easily support five servers and applications as long as none of them are doing very much. To play it safe, try not to have two different filing entities (file systems or databases) driving a single disk arm. This means that individual drives, mirror pairs, and arrays will be dedicated to a specific server. In that case, the capacity of the exported drives should equal the capacity of virtual device.

Second, try to avoid "stacking" virtual devices on top of each other inside the pool. For instance, do not build a three-member RAID 5 array where the members of the array are themselves RAID arrays. This adds unnecessary complexity to the overall scheme and may make it very hard to recover following a disaster. One of the reasons why you might consider stacking RAID on RAID is to increase the capacity of an array to match the storage requirements of a large application. In this case, it may be much better to concatenate RAID arrays to increase capacity.

Third, try to match the capacity of the exported volume with the capacity of the internal storage resources. For instance, it is possible to create a 12-disk RAID array with 75GB disk drives that has a capacity of 825GB and to export volumes of 25GB each on all 32 ports of a 32-port subsystem. This establishes an I/O system within the storage pool that would be prone to bottlenecks and would be nearly impossible to identify. At any time, any number of the 32 connected servers might all be trying to access data from one of the 12 disk drives. Statistically, if all servers were processing I/O simultaneously, and those operations were evenly distributed across all exported volumes, each disk drive would be processing I/O operations for three different servers. This would result in excessive seek times and rotational latency overhead for most I/Os. Not only that, but it would also wipe out the effectiveness of most caching as the access patterns across an average of three servers, and often more, could not be correlated.

Granted, the preceding example is extreme, but it illustrates the point that storage pooling and large-scale device virtualization should not be employed without understanding the low-level devices that support it. The thing to keep in mind is that disk drives are not like memory, where access times are relatively independent of the access patterns and characteristics. Disk drive performance is very sensitive to access patterns, and the more random they become, the less efficient the disk drive becomes. It follows that increasing the number of file systems and databases accessing data on a single disk drive, the more random the I/O activity will appear to it.

It is possible that a storage pool could combine devices and subsystems of many different sizes and capabilities. In that case, it makes sense to try to combine storage resources with similar capacity and performance characteristics as best as possible. If the goal you are trying to achieve for the exported volume cannot be attained from the combination of resources in the pool, you should add different resources to the pool or choose not to use the pool for that particular exported volume. There will be plenty of other opportunities to use the available storage in the pool.

Implementations of Storage Pooling   There are basically two different types of implementations of storage pooling in the market. The first is a large multiported disk subsystem. The available capacities of these subsystems can be very large, and they can support many external connecting ports. For the most part, these subsystems are not intended to be used with any old recycled storage looking for a home. Instead, they are engineered to fairly close tolerances and interfaces and use particular disk drives and components.

The other type of product supporting the pooling concept is the storage domain controller. These products are SAN appliances that provide logical block translation for other devices and subsystems in the SAN. As they typically come with minimal storage capacities of their own, they depend on other storage to be attached to them to form a complete solution.

High Availability Through Pathing

Pathing is a function that manages redundant connections between servers and storage in order to maintain access to data. Typically, pathing is applied across two paths working as a pair to support instantaneous rerouting of I/O operations from one to the other in case a path failure is encountered. SANs promote the use of pathing by virtue of supplying logical network connections between servers and storage, as opposed to the electrical nature of storage buses. Gigabit speed network access to storage in SANs significantly improves the time and accuracy involved in managing storage connections while simultaneously reducing the risk of something going wrong.

Pathing can be done with bus I/O technology also, but the electrical, codependent nature of bus connections and the challenges of implementing multiple initiators on buses make it much more challenging. For that reason, pathing is expected to be much more widely implemented as a SAN function than as a bus storage function.

Sometimes people are confused between pathing and clustering. Pathing is not the same as clustering. Pathing is designed to provide high-availability services for storing functions. Clustering is designed to provide high-availability services to applications. Clusters usually implement some sort of pathing technology as part of the overall effort to maintain application availability. Pathing can easily be implemented without clustering, and clustering can be implemented without pathing, although clustering is expected to provide some form of pathing to manage redundant server/storage connections.

The Pathing System

Pathing is a process that involves several components, including host software, device drivers, host I/O controllers, cabling, switches/hubs, and multiport storage subsystems. For that reason, we refer to the *pathing system* in this discussion to include all of these components working together.

Pathing implies the presence of a constant monitoring process that detects failures in one of the I/O paths and switches its I/O operations to the alternative path. The two paths used in a pathing system are normally implemented as duplicates of each other; path duplication is not necessarily required. For instance, it may be possible for a pathing system to have one path going through a switch and the other implemented as a point-to-point link. The structure of a simple pathing system using duplicated paths is shown in Figure 10-3. Using language similar to that of disk mirroring, this model labels one of the paths as the primary path and the other as the alternative path.

The control of the pathing system typically runs as a host process that manages multiple initiators. However, this process needs to be transparent to volume managers. There-

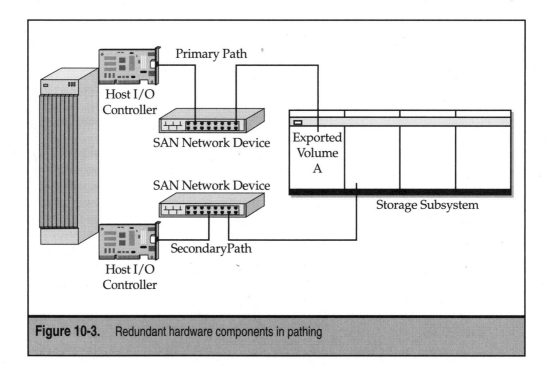

Figure 10-3. Redundant hardware components in pathing

fore, pathing is most likely to be implemented as a process that runs below volume managers and either above or below device drivers in our I/O path model. A pathing process running as a type of super device driver is pictured here:

Volume Manager
(Manages Logical Block Addresses)

Pathing Process
(Manages Redundant Paths to Storage)

Device Driver
(Manages Communications with Devices)

Implementations of pathing use exacting tolerances requiring strict compliance with the specifications. In plainer English, this means it is vendor-specific and proprietary.

Pathing Is an In-Band Process   By definition, pathing needs to have very fast response times to perform its function. That dictates a constant monitoring of the path to detect a failure, and when one is detected, the pathing system must immediately react. The only way to do this is for pathing to work "in-band" and manage the path by monitoring the path operations directly. Viewed another way, the idea of using an independent path monitor based on agents reporting to a management console will not be fast enough to provide the path switch from a failed path to a good one. At some future point, that might be possible, but it is generally not achievable with current network monitoring and management systems.

The Role of Initiators in Pathing

Initiators and targets in storage connections form a tightly coupled pair where activities in the target are driven by the initiator and where the target sends acknowledgments to the initiator for most commands it receives. In most products, pathing depends on the implementation of timers in the initiator that determine when a particular I/O path has failed. The idea here is that the initiator waits some prescribed amount of time after issuing a command for an acknowledgment before it tries to take some corrective action such as reissuing the command.

After some prescribed number of error correction attempts, the initiator will signal to the pathing control process that a particular path has failed. At this point, there may be several alternative paths to choose from including connecting to another target with the same initiator or choosing another initiator/target pair, as shown here:

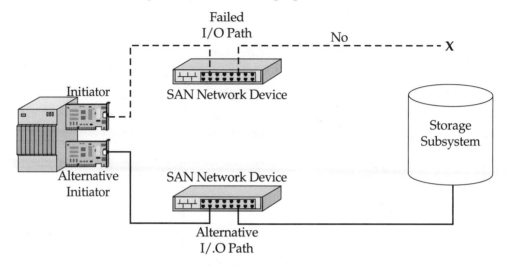

It is also possible to use heartbeat signaling, similar to heartbeats used in clustering to determine if a path has failed. But as pathing uses in-band monitoring, the heartbeats should also travel the same I/O path as storage operations. Therefore, multiplexing storage I/O and heartbeats would be required. While heartbeats could be transmitted as a special type of serial I/O command, it is more likely that the heartbeat would use a different protocol. Multiprotocol host I/O controllers are already in the market, but their subsystem counterparts are not necessarily readily available yet. Not only that, but the distributed design of a server-to-storage heartbeat monitor is not at all trivial. So don't hold your breath, but someday more advanced monitoring of paths through heartbeats will be a reality.

Redundant Path Components

Three usual components of the physical I/O path need to be considered:

▼ Host I/O controllers

■ Network devices

▲ Devices and subsystems, their ports and internal connections

We'll examine each of these in the context of pathing in the following sections.

Host I/O Controllers Used in Pathing Systems   Where pathing is concerned, the host I/O controller implements the initiator and therefore is the place where failures in the I/O path are detected. To be more precise, the device driver for the host I/O controller is the element that determines whether or not the path has failed. When failures occur, the device driver needs to inform the pathing control process so that it can switch paths.

It is possible that another path may be available through the same controller by using an alternative target address, like this:

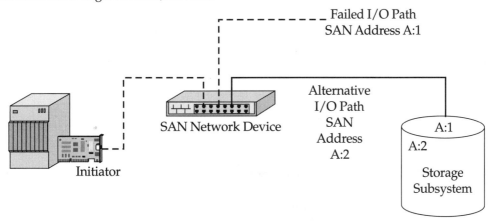

If another path is not available through the controller or if the design of the pathing system requires switching controllers, the operation is switched to the alternative controller. More than simply waking up and starting transmissions with the alternative controller, the pathing system needs to be able to correctly retransmit data that may have been lost in operations that were not acknowledged. On the surface this might not seem so difficult, but the speed at which I/O processing occurs and the amount of data waiting to be transmitted pose some significant design challenges. Everything must work perfectly; otherwise, data will be corrupted. Therefore, the host I/O controllers and their associated device drivers used in pathing systems may have specialized designs and capabilities that ensure the highest degree of accuracy during the failover process.

Switches and Hubs Used in Pathing Systems   For the most part, the switches and/or hubs in a SAN are transparent to the pathing process and have no active role. However, that does not mean that they do not deserve careful thought.

In general, using redundant switches or hubs provides availability protection against a complete failure in the network device. A single port-in, port-out design, as shown in a pair of switches/hubs, does the trick and is fairly simple to understand:

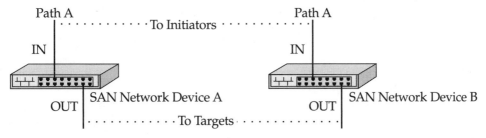

One can also connect both paths through a single switch/hub. However, this obviously makes the network device a single point of failure and is not advised. However, fault-tolerant switches are available with the capability to withstand internal component failures and reroute traffic internally through redundant components. These require redundant power and backplane connections to ensure constant availability. These types of high-end switches, sometimes referred to as *storage directors*, typically are designed for higher port configurations, such as 32-, 64-, or 128-port products. Check product specifications and capabilities carefully. The internal configuration of a hypothetical fault-tolerant ten-port storage switch looks something like this:

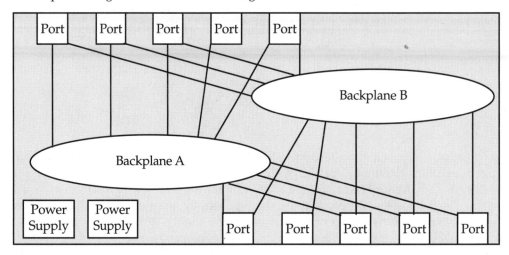

Try to avoid cascading switches used for high-availability pathing. Cascading adds complexity, cost, and failure points. If cascading must be used, there should be complete redundancy in all parts of the I/O path and the total amount of traffic transmitted over switch-to-switch links should be kept at moderate levels. It would not be prudent to have a pathing failover operation threatened by overloaded cascaded switch ports that have to regularly discard frames.

Also, make sure that zoning configurations do not interfere with pathing. Zoning to protect path connections from potential interruptions is a good idea. Special care should be taken to ensure that zoning for alternative paths will work as planned. Depending on the design of the pathing system, the alternative path might be standing by during normal operations and not actively transmitting data, which could make it difficult to notice any zoning problems until it is too late.

Finally, pathing does not require switches or hubs. Point-to-point links between host and subsystem controllers provide a simple solution to pathing that works. As mentioned, it may be possible to use a point-to-point link for an alternative path for the sake of simplicity and to reduce cost. If a point-to-point link is used, make sure to understand how other SAN-internal operations such as backup may be affected.

Subsystems Used in Pathing Systems   Pathing and mirroring both provide redundancy but are mostly different functions. In mirroring, two different I/O operations are generated to create redundant copies of data on separate devices or subsystems. In pathing, a single I/O operation is created that is transmitted over one of two different I/O paths to a single, common subsystem. The differences between mirroring and pathing are illustrated here:

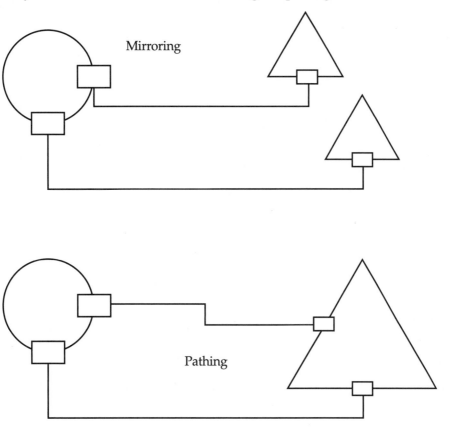

One of the keys to pathing is the capability for the storage subsystem to connect two of its external ports to a single exported volume. At any time, only one of the ports is involved in transferring data to a particular exported volume. Similar to the situation with switch zoning as previously discussed, the storage subsystem in a pathing system should implement port zoning or some other path segregation to guard against unexpected and unauthorized access.

Of course, pathing is not capable of protecting against device failures. For that reason, pathing implies the presence of a storage subsystem that provides its own data redundancy through mirroring or RAID. Storage subsystem designs can implement redundant data paths internally to prevent against internal component failures, as described in Chapter 6 and recapped in Figure 10-4.

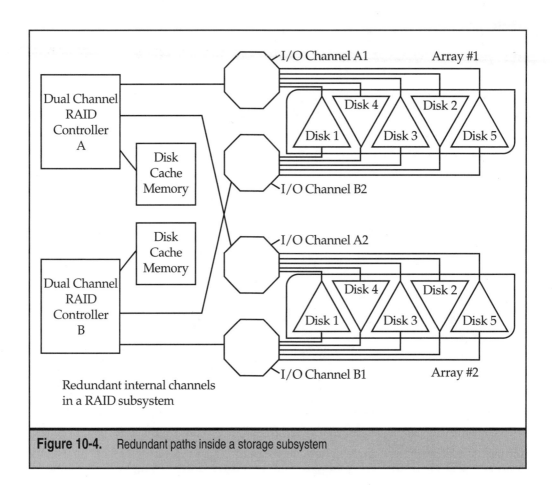

Figure 10-4.   Redundant paths inside a storage subsystem

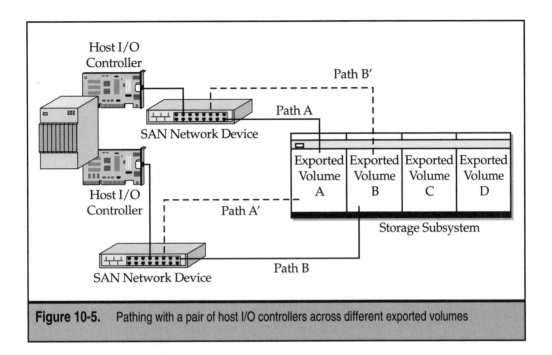

Figure 10-5. Pathing with a pair of host I/O controllers across different exported volumes

The exported volumes in a pathing subsystem can use either target or target/LUN addresses. If target/LUN addressing is used, it is possible for a single physical subsystem port to export multiple virtual volumes on different LUN addresses. In that case, a single host I/O controller could connect to a single subsystem port and act as initiator for each of the LUNs.

Consider a design where a pair of subsystem ports export the same two virtual volumes. That way, a corresponding pair of host I/O controllers could be configured so that each of them would access a different exported volume during normal operations. Should a failure occur on either path, the other path's host I/O controller would assume the work of both controllers with both exported volumes. This fairly intricate scenario is shown in Figure 10-5.

Data Moving

Although it's not an application, per se, another interesting potential SAN technique is *data moving*. The idea of data moving is fairly simple: an initiator in the SAN transfers data from a device or subsystem directly to another device or subsystem by reading from the first and writing to the second, as shown here:

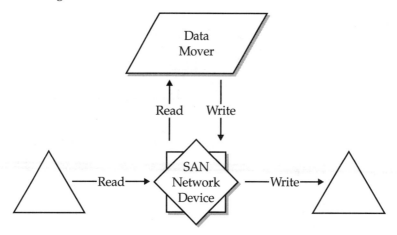

   While data moving is a simple concept to understand, the details of data moving implementations can be extremely challenging. It has terrific potential for use in systems management, especially SAN-based backup, which is discussed at length later in this chapter. Many other storage management applications, such as file transfers, software distribution, and data replication, could also use data moving technology.

   The primary advantage of data moving is performance. By making direct device-to-device transfers, data movers have the potential to bypass many parts of the I/O path that introduce latency and congestion. More important, data moving frees host servers from managing data transfer tasks directly, freeing cycles for application processing.

   Data moving could be implemented in nearly all components of the I/O path, where they can start their operations as initiators in the SAN. Possible implementation points include SAN bridges and routers, disk and tape subsystems, SAN switches and hubs, host I/O controllers, and host-based storage applications.

Problems to Solve in Data Moving

Before jumping too far ahead in planning all the wonderful ways data moving could be used, we'll examine some of the truly difficult issues involved in making it work. It may be that data moving is an unattainable holy grail, but the discussions that follow are still worthwhile for illuminating some interesting details of SAN operations.

Synchronizing Data Between Data Movers and Caches   One of the many details needed to make data moving work reliably is ensuring caches in the I/O path are flushed before trying to read data from a device. For example, consider a system that writes data with an assumption that it is being written to permanent storage. However, the data might not actually be written to the physical storage device yet, because it is being held in a cache somewhere in the I/O path. In that case, the file or database system's data structure will have information about the logical block address of the moved data—even if there is still old, stale data stored in those addresses. The situation is pictured here:

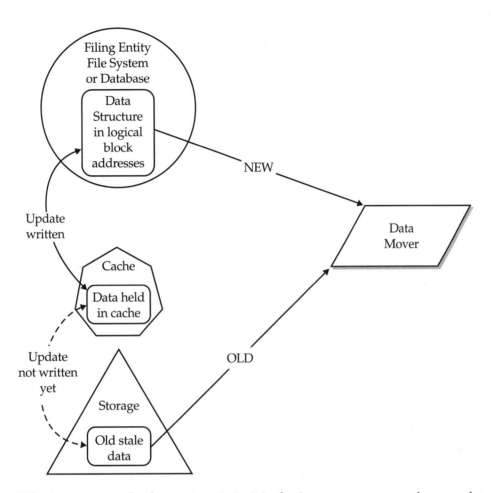

What's more, once the data mover starts, it is also important to suspend new updates to logical blocks being read until after the data mover finishes its work. A copy-on-write function, as described in Chapter 7, could be used.

So, a data moving function must be coupled with any caches that exist in the I/O path, except for those residing in the subsystem the data mover is accessing. In general, this means that the data mover needs to synchronize activities with applicable host system and host I/O controller caches.

Flushing host-resident caches can be accomplished through the use of agent programs that run in the host system and take their direction from the data mover or some other storage management application, such as serverless backup, discussed at the end of this chapter. Outside of backup, the programming interfaces for synchronizing data mover and caching activities do not exist. Therefore, most data moving solutions are likely to have platform dependencies and will be proprietary in nature for several years.

Data Moving and Data Structures   One of the main difficulties in data moving is determining how to correctly locate the data to move from device to device. The data structure that determines the logical block address locations of data is managed by a filing function such as a file system or database in the server. The data mover, however, is not a filing entity and has no direct knowledge of the logical block address data structures in storage.

This poses difficult challenges for both reading and writing data. In order for data to be read correctly from the system where it is stored, the data mover must know the data's logical block addresses. As data could be anywhere—and scattered all over storage—there is no way to calculate the logical block addresses. This means the data mover needs a way to communicate with the filing entity about the data. In general, the interfaces used to support these communications do not exist.

File system and database system developers have an understandable aversion to making this information known to third-party developers, including those making data movers. In essence, this type of interface cannot help the file system or database work better; in fact, it could only have a negative impact on performance or reliability. Therefore, file system and database developers must first understand their role in a larger network storage environment before they are likely to open up the data structures to published programmatic interfaces.

Device Virtualization Address Scrambling   Another hurdle to data moving is the very real possibility that device virtualization functions in the I/O path will invalidate the logical block address information of the filing entity. In a nutshell, the logical block address translation that is the hallmark of device virtualization can occur in practically any component of the I/O path, changing its values. For the data mover to access the data correctly, it needs to use the same address translations as those encountered by I/O operations in the system. This is not at all a trivial matter, depending on the amount of device virtualization encountered in the I/O path.

Now That I Have It, Where Do I Put It?   While reading data with a data mover is difficult, writing data with a data mover is even more challenging. The main issue is that data written by the data mover has to be accessible by a filing entity afterward, or the whole process is a big waste of time. The data structure information on the source storage (where the data was read from) cannot be used on the target storage (where data is being written).

This means the data structure of the filing entity has to be invoked to make decisions about where the "moved" data is placed. If the data structure of filing is not used, it is very likely that existing data in the volume will be overwritten, causing loss of data. Even if the data mover were to write data to an empty storage volume controlled by a file system or database, if the data structure process is not used, the file system or database would have no information about where the data was and would therefore be unreadable.

Kernel Integration   Another even stickier problem is the way most file and database systems are integrated with the system kernels on the platforms they run on. The relationships between the file system and the kernel are very close, involving many nonpublished and difficult-to-understand processes. So it is not really a matter of working with the filing component necessarily. A data mover may also have to integrate with kernel-level functions in order to write data safely and accurately that can be read later. Such kernel-level functions are extremely challenging and may not even be possible, depending on the development support made available by the operating system vendor.

BACKUP OVER THE SAN

The rest of this chapter explores SAN technology as a new approach to the problems that have plagued network backup for years.

Centrally controlled network backups provide significant savings in the time spent managing backups. Organizations that have implemented dedicated backup backbone networks have appreciated this already. But with SAN technology, the dedicated backup can be implemented exclusively on the storage I/O side, without having to transfer data back and forth over the data network.

Three Stages of SAN Backup Development

This section identifies the three different ways to apply SAN technology to backup and explores their effectiveness in solving some of the chronic problems in network backup.

First Stage: LAN-Free, Virtual Private Backup Networks

The first big application of SANs for backup is to move backup traffic off the data network and put it on a SAN. This concept, called LAN-free backup, is shown in Figure 10-6. The idea is the same as a dedicated backup network, but this time it's a SAN instead of an IP data network.

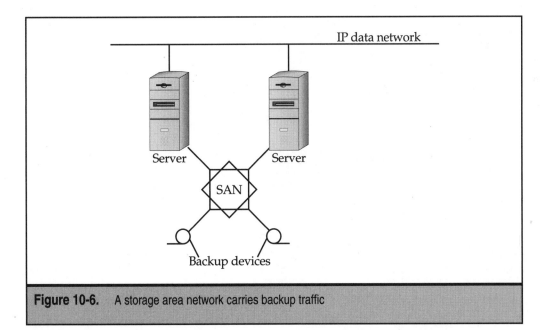

Figure 10-6.   A storage area network carries backup traffic

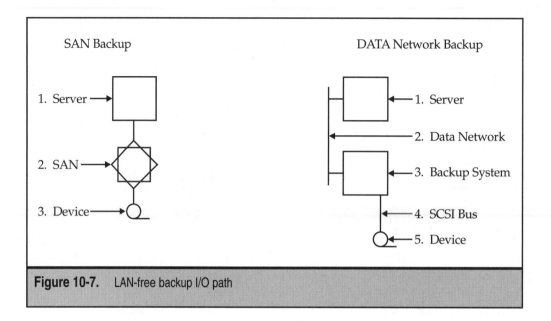

Figure 10-7.   LAN-free backup I/O path

A high-level view of the I/O path for LAN-free backup is shown in Figure 10-7, which illustrates the efficiency of using a SAN as opposed to routing backup over a data network. The SAN approach requires the data to pass through only one system, whereas moving backup traffic over the data network means it must pass through two systems.

Mixing Platforms with LAN Free Backup

SAN technology is platform-independent with broad connectivity support across all open systems server platforms. Unlike bus-attached storage, SANs were designed for use in multiple-initiator, shared-access environments, which means several computers can connect and work on a SAN simultaneously. It follows that multiple independent backup systems can share a single SAN, carrying backup data concurrently for multiple servers to their corresponding backup devices.

The servers, backup applications, and backup devices can be any combination. In other words, different backup systems can be deployed to match the requirements of individual servers. Figure 10-8 shows a SAN backup network with three independent backup systems on three different types of servers, sharing the network, each reading or writing to its own tape device.

Segregating Devices for SAN Backup

The SAN network device in Figure 10-8 connects all three servers, their storage, and backup subsystems on the same network together. While this looks great, there are potentially serious problems to work out in the way devices are accessed and shared in the SAN. Just as operating systems are not consistent in their level of sophistication for shar-

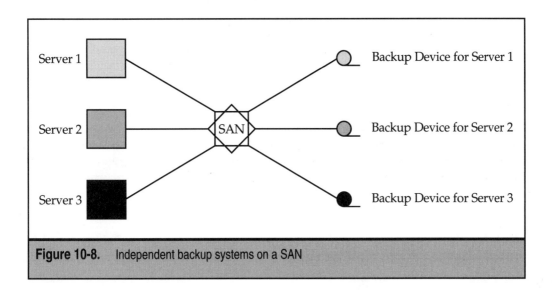

Figure 10-8.   Independent backup systems on a SAN

ing access to SAN-resident disk volumes, there is no standard method yet for making sure that tape drives are accessed correctly without errors by different backup systems. Backup vendors do not yet have a standard mechanism for interoperating on the SAN, although there have been solutions proposed for many years. More on that will come later in the discussion of the second stage of SAN backup.

Zoning with Backup

Zoning can be used to segregate backup components and platforms in the SAN. While zoning is not necessarily required, it may be helpful by creating virtual private backup networks for the various platforms, as shown here:

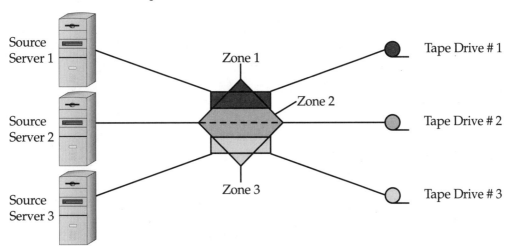

Reserve/Release

Another way to circumvent the problems of concurrent access to backup devices over the SAN is to use a bridge, router, or other SAN device that provides support for SCSI *reserve/release* functions. Reserve/release was originally developed for parallel SCSI operations and is also supported by mappings of serial SCSI in storage networks. The concept of reserve/release works pretty much the way it sounds. An application can *reserve* a particular backup device and save it for its own use until it no longer needs it, at which time it *releases* it for other applications. Compared to more sophisticated device and sharing management systems, reserve/release is pretty basic, but at least it provides a way to keep two initiators from fouling up by sending backup data to the same device concurrently.

Figure 10-9 illustrates a reserve/release function implemented in a SAN device where the SAN device has reserved the access to the backup device for one server and replies to other servers that the device is busy and unavailable.

Robot, Robot, Who's Got the Robot?

Automation of media handling for removable media devices, such as tape libraries, is a fairly mature technology that has been implemented for server systems since the early 1990s. The capacity and automation benefits of such equipment are clear—they reduce errors and allow unattended tape changes whenever they are needed. This last point has not been lost on network administrators who no longer have to visit their computer rooms on weekends to change backup tapes. However, with every silver lining comes a cloud: one of the drawbacks of automated tape products has been the difficulty in sharing this resource between applications, not to mention servers.

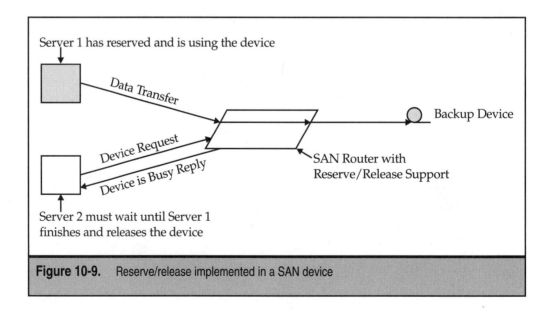

Figure 10-9. Reserve/release implemented in a SAN device

As SANs increase in popularity, it is highly likely that tape libraries and other media automation devices will also become more popular as SAN technology enables them to be shared by multiple servers. In a multiple-drive tape library, it's easy to see how the various drives in the library could be allocated to different servers in the SAN.

Multi-drive Library

Source
Server 1

Source
Server 2

Sharing a Library with Reserve/Release and Application Conflicts   The robot component of a library automates media changes and movements. While there may be multiple tape drives within a tape library being used by multiple servers, there is usually only one robotic mechanism. So, the question then is, how is the robot controlled?

Zoning does not provide a solution to this problem. The tape library and its robot are a single entity that cannot be split or shared across zones. Reserve/release provides the basic capability to share a robot. While one server is using the robot and has it reserved, another server cannot use it. When the first server is done, it releases the robot and another server can access it.

Role of the SAN to SCSI Bridge/Router   The majority of tape drives and libraries have parallel SCSI bus interfaces and not native SAN interfaces. Therefore, one should expect that a SAN bridge or router will be required to connect tape drives, autoloaders, and libraries to the SAN. Even if a library has an external SAN connection port, it probably has an integrated bridge or router within. An advantage of using a bridge or router is that it can provide the reserve/release mechanism for all the tape devices and the robot in the library. This allows unintelligent tape libraries lacking reserve/release capabilities to be shared in the SAN.

Protecting Tapes in Shared Libraries   While reserve/release allows the robot to be shared, it does not do anything to protect the media inside it. Using reserve/release, any application on any server is free to use the robot and access any of its tapes, including tapes that it does not control. If the application does not recognize the tape as one of its own, it may decide to format it and overwrite it with its own data.

This scenario can be prevented by configuring backup software applications to access only certain slots in the library. For instance, assume a 60-slot library is being shared by three different servers. To divide the capacity of the library equally among the three servers, you would configure the library control software in each server to access 20 slots;

server 1 would access slots 1 to 20, server 2 would access slots 21 to 40, and server 3 would access slots 41 to 60. This way, tapes used by different backup applications can be kept apart. This approach works pretty well but does not guarantee against improper tape use. Changes to backup software configurations need to be carefully controlled and managed to prevent slot assignments from overlapping.

When multiple copies of the same backup application are installed on multiple servers sharing a library, it is likely that each server will recognize the tapes from the other servers because they will all have a familiar tape format. In this case, it is less likely that tapes will be overwritten when accessed by a different server, and it may not be necessary to segregate slots as discussed previously. However, it is very important in this case to ensure that a unique naming scheme is used for each server sharing the library, to prevent the server's library control software from selecting the wrong tape. Using unique naming for each backup installation is a good idea in any case, but it is imperative for library sharing.

CAUTION: When sharing a library using reserve/release, one should ensure that the applications using it can either recognize each other's tapes or not access them. Slot restrictions should be used in the library if necessary.

Zoning and Reserve/Release Working Together

Zoning and reserve/release are two different approaches to the same problem. As it turns out, there may be cases where an organization will implement both techniques at the same time. Zoning can do many things, but one of its most important functions is segregating different platforms on the same SAN. Reserve/release, on the other hand, works very well in homogeneous environments where multiple servers using the same backup application (and on the same platform) can share the backup devices on it. Reserve/release sharing depends on all applications being well-behaved citizens, and violations of good citizenship can cause backup failures.

So it is likely that there will be SANs implemented with zoning to segregate platform traffic and reserve/release to share devices within these zones. For instance, a two-platform SAN with a pair of Unix systems and a pair of NT servers could have two zones in the SAN and two different backup systems, backing up data to a pair of tape libraries through two storage routers or bridges. Figure 10-10 illustrates this example.

Comparing SAN Backup to Other Methods

LAN-free backups over virtual private SANs is quite similar to the idea of dedicated stand-alone backup. The primary difference is the use of a high-speed, shared I/O channel to route all the backup traffic to a centralized location. Because all the backup equipment is centrally located, backup administrators don't have to visit backup systems in different locations to verify that the correct media are loaded and the devices are ready. Backup administrators can save hours every day by having all the media and devices in the same location.

Even more important, the performance of SAN backup is excellent. With transfer rates of 100 MB/s (whereas most tape drives for servers support less than 10 MB/s), there

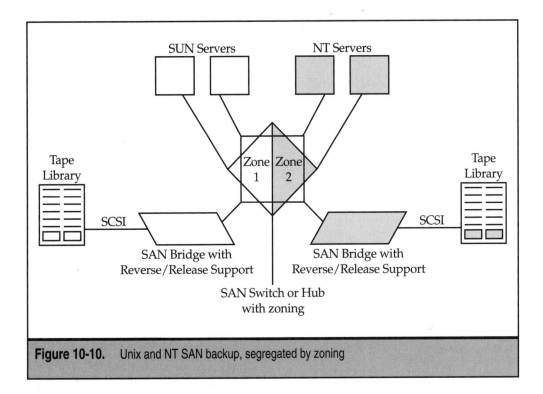

Figure 10-10.   Unix and NT SAN backup, segregated by zoning

is no lack of bandwidth to support backup. So, not only can it cost less to manage backup, but there is no performance penalty to pay for achieving these savings. It's not always possible to scale performance and achieve management efficiencies at the same time, but LAN-free backup does just that.

While LAN-free backup has some significant advantages, it still has its shortcomings. Reserve/release provides device sharing, but it does not provide centralized control and management of how devices are accessed. One can imagine a backup system where the backups of certain business applications are given higher priorities and device assignments than less important applications. Also, segregating media access by server is certainly not the best solution either, as distinct media collections have to be managed separately. A single integrated media management solution could simplify things a great deal. This topic is discussed in the section following on the second stage of SAN backup.

Likewise, improvements are needed for other logical backup components such as operation schedules, device managers, media managers, and metadata access. It should also be pointed out that just because backup data transfers move across the SAN, that does not mean they relieve servers from the problems associated with running CPU-intensive backup applications alongside other business applications.

Overall, LAN-free virtual private backup networks are a vast improvement over LAN-based backup solutions, including backup backbones. In addition, the installation of a LAN-free backup system builds the infrastructure for later developments in backup and data management over SANs.

Stage 2: Integrating Media and Devices

The second stage of SAN-enabled backup integrates the device and media management components that were intentionally segregated in the previous stage. As discussed previously, the selection of devices for specific backup tasks and the segregation of media into discrete collections are two shortcomings of the LAN-free backup approach.

In contrast, if any machine could access any device in response within the limits set by system-wide policies, it would also be advantageous if similar policies could enable the selected device to use any media available. In fact, it might be more proper to select the device according to some combination of media availability, capacity, and performance needed for backup operation. In addition, a consistent logical and physical format across all tapes and a structured naming system can simplify matters considerably.

A single integrated SAN backup system can encompass all logical components of a backup system, including operations management, data transfers, error reporting, and metadata processing. Not only can an organization realize cost savings through less administration effort, it also contributes to better disaster preparedness if common backup software and hardware are deployed throughout the organization on all platforms.

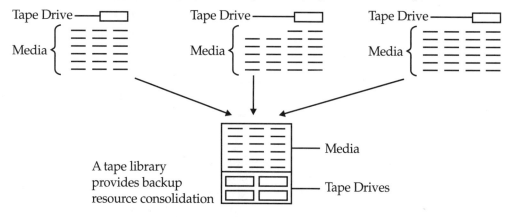

Media and Device Standardization

An open systems integrated backup system depends on backup vendors working together and agreeing on standards for identifying and accessing devices and media. Unfortunately, this hasn't been the norm for the backup industry. Instead, backup systems are likely to be somewhat proprietary, with some partnerships occurring between vendors until standards can be adopted.

The fact is, standards for implementing some of these functions already exist today but have not been widely implemented. In the early to mid-1990s, some of the large government laboratories began working on a storage management standardization effort. Known as the 1244 Mass Storage Reference Model, this standardization work covered a broad range of storage management functions. By and large, the work done by this group was intended to apply to its particular large-scale data processing needs. However, as the amount of data continues to increase in the commercial data centers, this technology has become more relevant. Commercialized versions of various pieces of this specification are starting to make their way into leading network backup products. Legato sells an implementation of parts of this work in a product called Smart Media, and Veritas's Virtual Media Librarian has also borrowed from the concepts in this work. Time will tell how these products evolve and whether or not real open systems interoperability can be achieved. Backup vendors will need to find a way to jointly define interface specifications and test procedures to ensure interoperability in the market.

Integrated SAN Backup Design

Whether this type of implementation is proprietary or open, there is still a common design ideal at work. Figure 10-11 shows one example of an integrated backup system where multiple servers have their data backed up to a single tape library.

While it is possible to build an integrated backup system with individual tape devices, it is much more likely to deliver management efficiencies by using multiple drive tape libraries. Tape libraries provide the means for the backup system to automatically react to problems as they occur. This can include the requirement for loading blank tapes as well as previously used tapes belonging to the same media set, or pool.

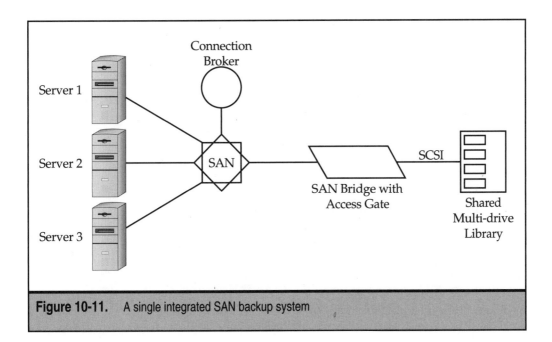

Figure 10-11. A single integrated SAN backup system

Establishing Connections in an Integrated SAN Backup System

Although the tape library pictured in Figure 10-11 has a SAN bridge for SAN connectivity, it is not providing reserve/functionality in this drawing as it did in the previous examples of LAN-free backup. Instead, the bridge/router implements an *access gate* through which each of the servers can establish backup sessions. The access gate provides a function similar to reserve/release but uses a higher-level security mechanism as opposed to a device command.

With a security mechanism in the tape library, each server requests the services of a device in the library as it is needed. The library can then control which device it makes available. This approach makes all devices generally available to all servers and establishes an orderly mechanism supporting path routing and error recovery as well as the prioritization of applications and the policies for managing their activities.

Besides the access gate described, this integrated system adds another global management function: a *connection broker*, which generates the security keys used by servers when communicating with the access gate. The connection broker and the access gate form two halves of a key-based security system in an integrated SAN backup system. The precise roles and scopes of the access gate and the connection broker could differ, depending on the level of intelligence in both components. For example, the connection broker could determine the best device for the server to use and provide that information in the key or directly to the access gate. Similarly, the connection broker could provide the priority level of the server with the key, and the access gate could determine the best drive to use.

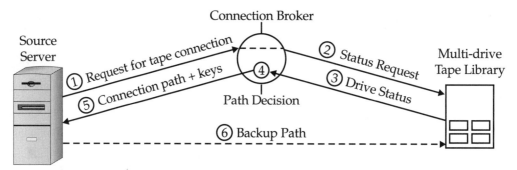

This type of connection mechanism is well suited to large systems with policy management that can enforce priorities during backup operations. For instance, it is theoretically possible to reroute a high-priority operation over a lower-priority connection should the situation require it.

Separation of Control Path and Data Path

The connection broker does not have to be in the path between a server and the device it is working with. It only needs to be able to communicate with both servers and devices. In fact, it is not necessary that the connection broker be connected to the SAN at all; its function could be provided over the data network as long as the access gate is also capable of communicating on the data network. The entire key exchange mechanism could be handled on the data network.

This raises an important architectural point about SAN-oriented backup: the communications that control the operation and the backup data can travel on different paths and networks. This practice is sometimes referred to as separating the *control path* and the *data path*. SANs are the data path used for transmitting backup data, but the control path for backup is typically a data network connection between the backup engine and the various other backup system components, such as backup agents. The difference between the control and data paths can be visually represented like this:

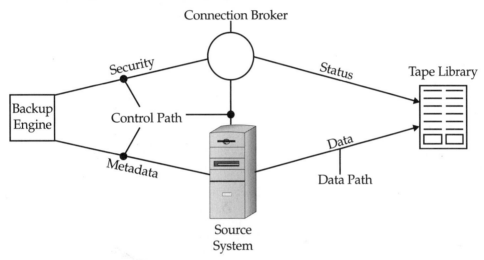

Sharing a Robot with an Integrated Backup System   One of the concepts central to an integrated SAN backup systems is library sharing, including the access to the robot. There are two basic ways this access could be shared:

▼ Brokered access with decentralized robotic control

▲ Programmatic interface to a centralized media changing service

The idea of brokering access is exactly the same as described in the previous sections for creating connections between servers and drives. The problem with this approach is that an individual application could load or change tapes in the library regardless of what other applications or the connection broker are expecting. For instance, a poorly behaved application could unload tapes in the middle of another server's operations.

The other way to share access to a library is to provide a media changing service using a client/server model. For instance, an application could request that a tape be loaded as part of an upcoming job. If there is heavy competition for the library's resources, the media changing service could determine if this request is a high enough priority to interrupt work in progress. In addition, the media changing service could be configured to restrict access from certain applications to specified media locations in the library as an extra means of protecting high-priority data.

Stage 3: Serverless Backup

Another technology area being developed for SAN backup systems is one where independent entities on the SAN provide the device-to-device operations on behalf of servers and data management applications. This is being called *serverless backup* and has also been called *third-party copy*.

Data Movers

As discussed, one of the most important benefits of SANs is the physical independence of devices from systems. That means a function in a server can access an available backup device in the SAN to run operations. In fact, the entities accessing devices in a SAN do not have to be servers or systems at all. They can be any type of SAN component, including hubs, router, switches, even host I/O controllers. The idea is that such an entity that has the intelligence and the hardware necessary can access devices in the SAN and act as a data mover, transferring data from one device to another. A data mover in a SAN could be used to perform data and storage management functions.

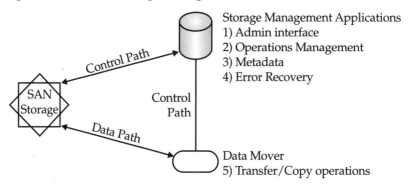

Third-Party Copy Transfers

Given the number of processors and resources available in SAN devices that could function as data movers, it's not difficult to imagine how or where data movers could be created.

SAN-enabled backup application could query the filing information in a server about the data structure and logical block addresses of its data residing in the SAN. Knowing the exact logical block addresses of individual files and database tables allows the data mover to act as an initiator for moving data from its stored location to a backup device in the network. This is known as *third-party copy,* and its process is illustrated here:

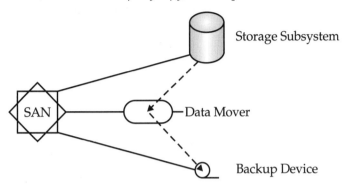

The independence of devices and applications is the impetus for the term *serverless* backup. By removing both hardware control and software resources from a server, the load of backup is reduced enormously.

Serverless Backup Server Agent

In serverless backup systems, the backup application first queries an agent on the server, which identifies the data to back up. But instead of sending a list of files to back up, the agent sends a list of logical block addresses for each of the files to back up. The backup application then transfers the list of logical block addresses to the data mover in the SAN, as shown here:

When the data mover receives the list of logical block addresses, it begins reading data from its stored location and writing it to tape.

The source agent that generates the list of logical block addresses is a key element of serverless backup. An agent for serverless backup must be able to successfully query the file system on the server and receive back the list of logical block addresses where the file or database object resides. It is not even necessary for the data mover to know which file or database table it is performing work on—it just reads and writes data.

Copy-on-Write for Hot Serverless Backup

Serverless backup can be cold or hot. Cold serverless backups are much easier to accomplish than hot serverless backups. The performance and centralized management benefits of running cold backups over the SAN may make cold backup a realistic alternative for some organizations.

However, cold backups are probably not realistic for most networks on a regular basis, and hot backups must be employed. Therefore, a critical component of serverless backup is the copy-on-write function that was discussed in Chapter 7. Copy-on-write for serverless backups provides a way to ensure that new data written by an application during backup operations does not create data integrity problems on SAN-attached storage.

In essence, this is the same problem as bus-attached hot backup, except that it is being done in a multi-initiator SAN environment in a distributed fashion where the serverless backup agent conveys block information to an independent data mover. Serverless hot backup creates a point-in-time backup that manages new writes while it is backing up the data.

Hot backup provides the ability for the source system to copy existing stored data to a temporary storage location when new updates to data overwrite it. As backup progresses, the old data is copied by the backup system from the temporary storage location, then deleted. However, for serverless backups on a SAN, the copy-on-write process runs in a backup source system while the backup block list is transferred to the data mover somewhere in the SAN. This is a distributed process involving remote interprocess communications between the source system and the data mover.

The challenges in implementing this are nontrivial and will require a great deal of work. The copy-on-write process starts in the source system before it sends a block list to the data mover. Instead of the block list's being kept locally in memory, it has to be successfully transferred to the data mover. The data mover has to receive the block list without errors and initialize its process soon thereafter to prevent the copy-on-write process from exhausting the allocated disk space of the source system with too many redirected copy-on-write data blocks.

Serverless Backup and Data Sharing

Serverless backup raises an interesting contradiction in SANs regarding the independence of storage and raises the importance of distinguishing between storage and data. Third-party copy works because data movers are able to read data blocks from SAN storage. The independent nature of SAN storage makes this possible.

However, there is an important difference between *storage* access and *data* access. While SANs allow great connectivity flexibility, the file systems for sharing data among servers are a different story. Theoretically, data movers can communicate with any storage in the SAN. They are platform-independent, block-access functions. The agents they depend on, however, are completely platform-dependent functions that run on single-server systems and are not intended to work across multiple servers or clusters. During serverless backup, an update to data from a server that does not have the serverless backup agent running on it will likely corrupt the backup data. The data mover component would have no way of knowing if something has changed on the storage subsystem.

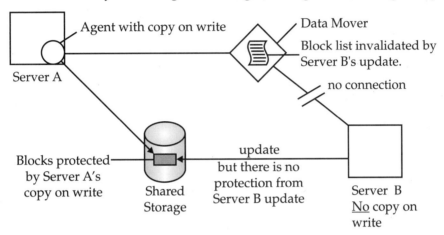

So, as it turns out, the independence of SAN storage that allows data movers to access *data* also allows other servers and systems to interfere with serverless backup processing. Data sharing in a SAN thus opens a subtle exposure to backup integrity. Therefore, data-sharing file systems also require the presence of a distributed copy-on-write function if serverless backup is going to be used.

Designing a SAN for Serverless Backup

Figure 10-12 shows a SAN with two servers and two storage subsystems and two tape libraries segregated into separate zones. A data mover system belongs to both zones and can access all the storage subsystems and tape libraries.

Serverless backup agents in both servers communicate to the data mover and send it logical block address lists for data needing to be backed up. The data mover then reads data from those blocks in their respective subsystems and writes it to the corresponding tape drive in a tape library. Again, as in previous examples, the tape library is "fronted" by a SAN bridge or router that provides connection of the SCSI tape equipment to the SAN. In Figure 10-12, the data mover is located in a separate system instead of in the bridge or router.

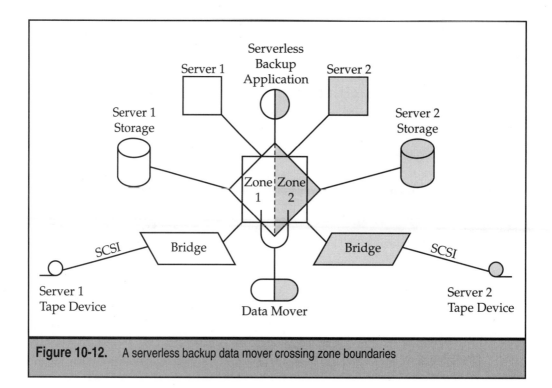

Figure 10-12.   A serverless backup data mover crossing zone boundaries

Combining Serverless with Integrated SAN Backup

Figure 10-12 shows a SAN with two tape libraries serving two different servers. While this is a beautiful picture for tape library manufacturers, it begs the question as to whether or not a single library could be used. The answer is maybe someday, if data mover functionality can be included as part of an integrated SAN backup system.

The challenge in combining serverless backup with the total integrated SAN backup system lies in figuring out how the connection broker, device, robot, and media management of the integrated SAN backup concept can be implemented with serverless backup systems. Serverless backup is being developed with a design goal of minimizing the resource requirements of the data mover so that it can be implemented in various SAN devices. For that reason, it might not be realistic to expect the data mover to also take on the work of the connection broker or access gate.

However, the data mover *does* have the resources to support login functions and access keys for establishing a communication session with a tape library. One possibility is that backup traffic would flow through data movers while the *negotiation* for these sessions and the transfer of communication keys would be managed by the serverless backup application and the connection broker. Figure 10-13 illustrates a hypothetical structure for such a serverless, integrated SAN backup system.

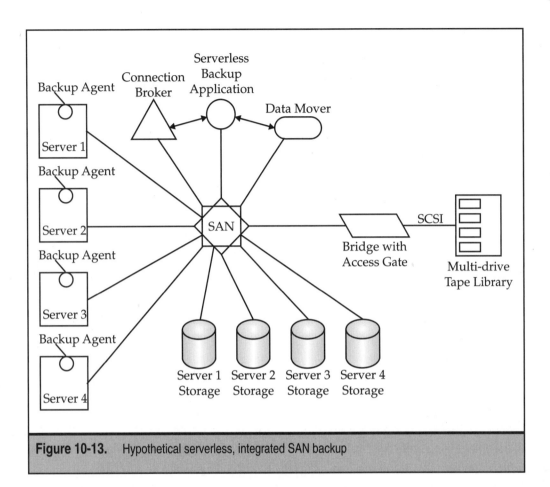

Figure 10-13.   Hypothetical serverless, integrated SAN backup

SUBSYSTEM-BASED BACKUP

In addition to the preceding SAN-based backup approaches, there is another perspective on SAN backup that merits attention, that of an integrated SAN backup system located within a multiported disk subsystem.

A Brief Overview of Subsystem-Based SAN Backup

Figure 10-14 shows the basic physical layout of a storage subsystem with integrated backup capability.

Integrated SAN backup in a subsystem puts the backup functions as close to the physical storage location of data as possible. Transferring SAN backup functions into a disk subsystem's controller circuitry provides direct manipulation of storage devices, as opposed to accessing them over the SAN. The end result is an off-server backup system that is extremely efficient but is likely to be proprietary. As discussed previously in this

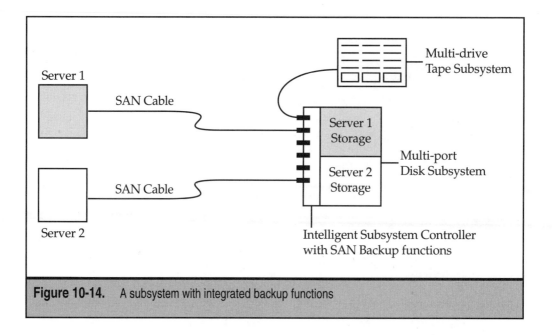

Figure 10-14. A subsystem with integrated backup functions

chapter in the sections on pooling and pathing, the internal capabilities of enterprise storage systems are complex and require sophisticated management. The management of multiple ports, the traffic management in and out of them, and the capability of these ports to access different resources within the system without losing data are not trivial. Needless to say, this type of product is a *system* in the true sense of the word.

Data Movers and Connection Brokers in Subsystem Controllers

Locating data movers in subsystem controllers provides very fast third-party copy operations. Besides the immediate proximity to the subsystem's internal devices, data movers that are internal to the subsystem can circumvent some of the security checks that might be needed for external data movers.

Similarly, connection brokers for setting up paths to tape libraries can also be implemented in disk subsystems. However, this functionality is much more difficult to port to proprietary environments such as disk subsystem controllers because they are far from being standardized platforms capable of supporting third-party application development.

SAN Backup Implemented in Tape Libraries

Another variation on SAN-based backup places the SAN backup functions within a tape subsystem. For the most part, tape subsystems for server systems have been fairly unintelligent devices, but several of the leading tape library companies have integrated intelligent processors and are developing the ability to implement such components as data movers, connections brokers, and, especially, access gates in their products.

As embedded processing capabilities continue to improve, the possibility of locating a small computer within a tape library gets better every day. Such a computer could be general enough to provide the necessary resources to support more heavy-duty, off-the-shelf data management applications. Someday, the entire backup system may be contained within the tape library itself, where it can most directly control all device and media operations.

SUMMARY

Storage applications for SANs promise to greatly simplify the installation and management of storage. The network communication model allows storage resources to be centralized, or at least located together within data center facilities.

Among the most important applications for SANs are storage pooling, pathing, data moving, and backup. While all of these applications could be done with bus technology, they are likely to be easier and less prone to problems when implemented in SANs.

Storage pooling is the ultimate application of device virtualization. Multiport storage subsystems allow storage administrators to flexibly manage the connections between physical SAN ports to the exported storage volumes created in the subsystem. As the amount of storage continues to increase, pooling provides a way to proactively acquire and implement storage, as opposed to managing storage on a crisis-by-crisis basis. Pathing provides connection management between servers and storage subsystems, with the ability to transparently switch from a failed path to an alternative path that is functioning. It is likely to be a key component of many mission-critical, high-availability systems, including clustered servers. Data moving is viewed as a promising area for enhancing systems and storage management in SANs. Unfortunately, the problems with creating general-purpose data moving technology are considerable and depend heavily on the file system and database companies.

SAN backup was the final application analyzed in this chapter. There were three evolutionary stages identified; one characterized by virtual private networks, another based on a brokered security service that manages resource sharing, and the last one built on the data moving concept. The leading network backup vendors have all embraced SAN as their strategic technology platform and have strategic initiatives to develop this technology and deliver it to the market in quick order.

The continued development of standards and the willingness of companies to work together on them will determine how quickly this technology becomes usable and valuable to the market. There is a long way to go, but the beginning is extremely exciting.

EXERCISES

1. Assume you have a storage pool with 30 external SAN ports managing the storage of 28 75GB disk drives and two RAID 5 disk subsystems with 500GB of exportable capacity. Create evenly sized exportable volumes; one for each SAN port. Each exportable volume should be protected by device-level redundancy of some kind.

2. Sketch several designs for a high-availability pathing solution using ring network technology. Do you need a network device to connect host I/O controllers and storage subsystem ports? Does it change your design if the ring has two separate, counter-directional paths? If there are two distinct paths in the ring, what is the minimum number of ring networks needed?

3. Assume you are designing part of a serverless backup application. Your job is to figure out how to write data to tape that has already been read by the data mover. Write a high-level algorithm for writing backup data to tape in a way that allows individual files to be identified on tape so that they can be restored.

PART IV

Wiring Technologies

CHAPTER 11

Wiring SANs with Fibre Channel

F ibre Channel was the first networking technology to be broadly implemented in SANs. Like other networking technologies, such as Ethernet, ATM, and Token Ring, this technology comes in several different flavors.

One of the common variables for most networking technologies is speed, or transmission rate. Fibre Channel also has several speeds defined, including 25 MB/s (megabytes/s), 50 MB/s, 100 MB/s, 200 MB/s, and 400 MB/s. In practice, the 25 MB/s variety, also called quarter speed, is obsolete, 50 MB/s was rarely used, 100 MB/s is the most common, 200 MB/s is starting to be deployed, and 400 MB/s may be used in products some day or may be passed over for faster technology such as 1 GB/s.

Understanding how to put the various pieces together is important. In this chapter, we examine the various implementation details of Fibre Channel, including some analysis of fabrics and loops, the two wiring topologies most often used to build Fibre Channel SANs.

THE STRUCTURE OF FIBRE CHANNEL

In traditional networking technology, the layer above the physical layer composed of cables, connectors, and transceivers is commonly referred to as the *media access control*, or *MAC*, layer. Conceptually, the MAC layer is an implementation of the algorithm used to determine how systems communicate over the network. For example, Ethernet uses the CSMA-CD protocol, and FDDI uses the 802.5 protocol for token passing. Together, the physical layer and the MAC layer form the bottom-most abstract, modular layers in the TCP/IP and OSI protocol stacks.

By contrast, the Fibre Channel standard defines five modular layers that provide the same functionality:

▼ FC-0, the physical layer, including cables, connectors, and transceivers

■ FC-1, the wire transmission protocol, including encoding, timing, and error-detection

■ FC-2, the transport and signaling protocols, including port operations and classes of services

■ FC-3, open for development, expected to provide services between multiple ports

▲ FC-4, which is the mapping layer to upper-layer protocols, such as IP and SCSI

The various layers can be represented graphically like this:

```
┌─────────────────────────────────────────────┐
│                                               │
│      FC-4 Upper Layer Protocol Mappings       │
│                                               │
├─────────────────────────────────────────────┤
│                                               │
│       FC-3 Common, or Group Control           │
│                                               │
├─────────────────────────────────────────────┤
│                                               │
│    FC-2  Network Access and Data Link Control │
│                                               │
├─────────────────────────────────────────────┤
│                                               │
│        FC-1 Transmission Control              │
│                                               │
├─────────────────────────────────────────────┤
│                                               │
│        FC-0  Media and Transceivers           │
│                                               │
└─────────────────────────────────────────────┘
```

Fibre Channel's FC-0 is the *physical layer* foundation for Fibre Channel's gigabit-speed transmissions. It was also used later by the developers of Gigabit Ethernet. It incorporates both copper and fiber optic components.

FC-1 is closely linked to FC-0 in the way it provides the initial checks and conversions of data sent and received over the physical layer. In essence, Fibre Channel was designed for superior reliability and integrity. Its error rates are no greater than 1×10^{-12}. This is roughly equivalent to a single correctable error for every few terabytes of data transferred.

The FC-2 layer contains the bulk of the information pertaining to how data transmissions are structured. As such, it is similar to the MAC (media access control) layer found in other networking technologies. Among the more interesting aspects of Fibre Channel are the port definitions, classes of service, flow control, and communication syntax.

There has not been a lot of work within the industry at the FC-3 level. Most of the investigations and development at this level involve ways to work with multiple links or nodes simultaneously.

The uppermost layer of the Fibre Channel stack, FC-4, provides mappings of the various upper-layer protocols (ULPs) implemented on Fibre Channel. One of these protocols, the Fibre Channel Protocol (FCP), is the implementation of the SCSI-3 standard that translated the commands and operations developed for parallel SCSI into a serial version for use over networks.

THE PHYSICAL ASPECTS OF FIBRE CHANNEL WIRING

The physical layer of any high-speed network is extremely important to the success of the technology. In the sections that follow, we'll examine the physical, or FC-0 layer, parts of a Fibre Channel network. The physical parts of a Fibre Channel network are mainly made up of the cables, connectors, and transceivers that are used to generate and interpret signals on the network.

Cabling

Although the name Fibre Channel would appear to imply a connection with fiber optic cabling, Fibre Channel is a networking technology that supports a wide variety of cabling, including copper cabling. In practice, fiber optic cables are more commonly implemented than copper cables for their superior distance and reliability characteristics. While both copper and fiber optic cables are capable of supporting gigabit transmission speeds, upgrades to higher speeds, such as 200 MB/s, 400 MB/s, or 1 GB/s, will only be supported over fiber optic cabling.

Signal Quality and Cabling

One of the key characteristics of any transmission medium is how the quality of the signal is maintained as it travels through it. All signals *disperse,* that is, become less clear, as the transmission distance increases. In other words, the signal becomes less clear and takes longer for the receiver to interpret. The situation is similar to listening to somebody speaking through a pipe: when the pipe is short, it is easy to understand the speaker; when the pipe is long, there are echoes and other distortions to contend with that make it more difficult to understand.

Different cabling technologies have different characteristics for signal dispersion. In general, electrical signals in copper cables disperse much more quickly than light signals in fiber optic cables. The frequency of the signal also impacts how the signal disperses. In general, high-frequency, shorter-wavelength signals disperse more quickly than low-frequency, longer-wavelength signals. The internal diameter of a fiber optic cable also impacts the quality of the signal. The larger the diameter, the more signal reflections, or harmonic modes, there are, a fact that has a negative impact on signal quality. The phenomenon is analogous to being in a room with a great deal of echo. If the echo is too strong, it can be difficult to discern the details of speech sound. Therefore narrow-diameter optical cables that reduce the amount of reflected signals help maintain signal quality over longer distances.

Finally, signals are susceptible to various types of interference. Electrical signals in copper cables are extremely sensitive to external magnetic fields. The higher the transmission speed used, the more susceptible the signal is to interference. Therefore, copper cables need excellent shielding to diminish the impact interference has on the signal. For the most part, light signals in fiber optic cables are impervious to most common types of interference.

Cable Lengths

The cable lengths supported in Fibre Channel are determined by the capability of the cable to transmit high-quality signals. This does not mean that cable lengths cannot be exceeded, but it does mean that longer cable lengths may not work as well and may not be supported by vendors.

In optical cabling, the internal diameter of the cable and the wavelength of the signal are typically matched. The cables capable of supporting the longest transmissions have internal diameters of 9 microns, and the signals passing through them are in the range of 1,300 nanometers. The lasers used to generate these signals are referred to as *longwave* lasers. As the manufacturing of 9-micrometer cables is something of an expensive process, these cables tend to have the highest cost.

There are two different-sized fiber optic cables used with *shortwave* lasers, which transmit signals in the range of 780 nanometers. One has an internal diameter of 50 microns, and the other is 62.5 microns. The 50-micron variety typically supports distances that are twice those of 62.5-micron cables, but both have far shorter ranges than 9-micron cables.

Basically, two types of copper cabling are used for Fibre Channel implementations. One is the coax cable commonly used for cable television applications, and the other is shielded twisted pair found in many LANs. The primary advantage of copper cabling is its cost; however, copper cabling distances are limited to 25 meters, far shorter than fiber optic cables and roughly the same as differential SCSI. While the distance constraints of copper cabling might limit its use in data center applications, it can be an excellent choice for cabling inside subsystem cabinets.

Speed Versus Distance

The transmission rate deployed has an inverse relationship to the distance that transmissions are supported. The faster the transmission rate is, the shorter the distance will be. A potential problem where SANs are concerned is that existing SANs may not be able to be upgraded to higher-speed equipment if the distance of the links exceeds those supported by the new technology. For instance, a Fibre Channel SAN built with 100 MB/s products, with link distances well below the maximum for 100 MB/s SANs, may not be upgradable to operate at 200 MB/s. Even if 200 MB/s SANs might be supported, it is possible that other implementations at higher speeds will not be supported.

Table 11-1 summarizes the maximum cable lengths for various transmission rates and the type of fiber optic cable used.

One of the most striking aspects of Table 11-1 is the sharp decrease in distance for long wavelength transmissions over 9-micron cables. Over time, this distance will likely increase as the transmission technology improves.

Just because the standard does not support certain transmission rates above certain distances, that does not mean that longer distances can't be achieved. Specialized optical transmission lasers and receivers can provide significantly longer distances than those specified by the standards organization. Some of these products have been implemented in other vendors SAN offerings.

	Maximum Cable Lengths		
Transmission Rate	9 micron	50 micron	62.5 micron
100 MB/s	10,000 meters	500 meters	300 meters
200 MB/s	2,100 meters	300 meters	150 meters
400 MB/s	2,100 meters	175 meters	90 meters

Table 11-1.   Distance as a Function of Transmission Rate for Fiber Optic Cables in SANs

TIP: The error rates expected in Fibre Channel are 1×10^{-12}. Before implementing any long-distance link technology, it is important to understand if its error rates are in the same range as Fibre Channel's. If not, the expectations for performance may not be attainable.

Cable Connectors

Fibre Channel connectors are manufactured in pairs; one for transmitting data and the other for receiving it. The connectors on Fibre Channel cables are engineered to be plugged in only one way to ease installation and troubleshooting by guaranteeing that signals will only move in one direction over a single fiber. The relationship between transmitters and receivers can be pictured like this:

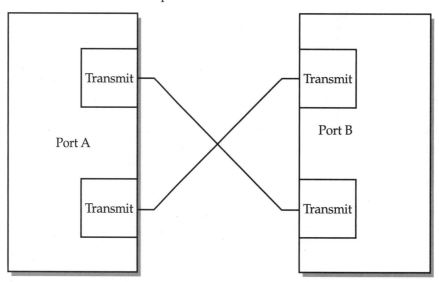

Copper cables used with Fibre Channel provide the lowest-cost option. The most common copper cables for Fibre Channel networks are Type 1 shielded cables with two pairs of twisted pair conductors enclosed in each cable sheath. Each twisted pair consists of a conductor that carries the signal and a ground wire. The connector for this cable is a 9-pin DB-9 connector using 4 pins. Fibre Channel coax cables use BNC connectors similar to those used for cable TV connectors.

Fibre Channel optical cable connectors are called *SC connectors*. These SC connectors are side-by-side connectors, one for transmitting and the other for receiving. The transmitting connector on one end of a cable connects to a receiving connector on the other end.

Figure 11-1 summarizes the types of cables and connectors commonly used in Fibre Channel networks.

Transceivers: The System-to-Network Interface

Cables and connectors are passive components of the I/O path. The active optical/electronic components that transmit and receive signals over cables are called *transceivers*. Fibre Channel has different types of transceivers, depending on the type of cabling used and such other requirements as cost, serviceability, and manufacturing considerations. Transceivers are placed wherever fiber optic cables are inserted into systems, storage, or networking hardware. They are part of all SAN hardware products, including HBAs (host bus adapters), hubs, switches, bridges, devices, and subsystems.

The number of cabling types is certainly a challenge for Fibre Channel vendors who want to provide the most flexibility for their products. GLMs, or gigabit link modules, are modular media connectors that mount on hardware interfaces, like a daughter card that can be removed and replaced as necessary in the field. For instance, equipment with GLMs for shortwave lasers could be modified to work with longwave lasers by removing and replacing the GLM. GLMs can incorporate additional signaling functions and facilities for low-level diagnostics and network management.

Another common type of transceiver used in Fibre Channel is called a GBIC (pronounced "jee-bick"), short for gigabit interface converter. GBICs are integrated more closely with the hardware and typically cannot be exchanged to work with another cable type. GBICs do not have to support field replacement and are less expensive to manufacture and integrate. Like GLMs, GBICs, can integrate low-level diagnostics and management functions.

The last type of transceiver is a 1X9 (one by nine). 1X9s are single-purpose components that provide signaling capabilities. They typically do not provide much in the way of additional functions for management purposes. Another related technology that converts optical signals to copper is a media interface adapter, or MIA. MIAs may seem like a way to extend the life of copper-based Fibre Channel hardware in fiber optic environments, but MIAs might not provide the capabilities and reliability desired, as they can be somewhat problematic.

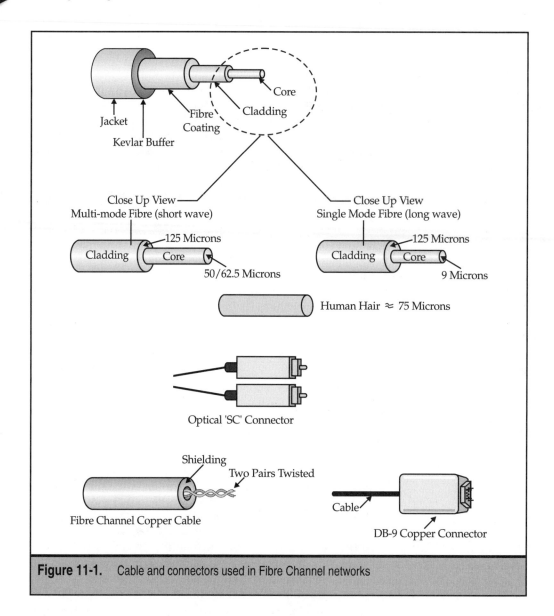

Figure 11-1. Cable and connectors used in Fibre Channel networks

Encoding and Error Detection at FC-1

Fibre Channel transmissions are encoded by an FC-1 layer function as they are sent over the physical network using a scheme known as 8B/10B. The 8B/10B encoding scheme transmits 10 bits of information over the physical plant for every 8 bits of data that is being transferred. In essence, the encoding scheme is a parity mechanism that ensures the integrity of the data transmission.

Gigabaud and Gigabytes

Signaling rates in Fibre Channel can differ, as discussed in the previous section. For the first wave of popular Fibre Channel products, the signaling rate is 1.0625 *gigabaud.* Gigabaud is an expression for the total bandwidth that is available for sending signals.

As a measurement, gigabaud includes all the encoding data as well as the data to be transferred. So, to find the actual, end-result transfer rate, one needs to remove the extra encoded bits. For Fibre Channel, the actual transfer rate is 80 percent of its physical layer bandwidth. That means that Fibre Channel 1.0625 gigabaud transmissions are equivalent to 850 MB/s. However, storage transfers are measured in bytes, not bits. With eight bits per byte, the transfer rate for 1.0625 gigabaud Fibre Channel is approximately 106 MB/s. To make things easier to talk about, this number is rounded down to an even 100 MB/s.

THE LOGICAL SIDE OF FIBRE CHANNEL

A great deal of effort was spent by Fibre Channel's early developers in creating a versatile and orderly high-performance environment. Most of the technology they developed is now part of the FC-2 layer definitions. With an underlying hardware specification that was specified for extremely high reliability, most of the remaining attributes of Fibre Channel networks are drawn from its FC-2 network access and control functions, including its flow control mechanisms and multiple classes of service. In the sections that follow, we'll look at these and other logical structures of Fibre Channel networks.

Fibre Channel Port Types

One of the major differences between Fibre Channel and other networking technologies is the amount of intelligence implemented in the physical hardware that connects all the components to the network. The "tiny little super-guy" of Fibre Channel is called the *port.* Understanding Fibre Channel is much easier if one can understand the relationships of ports in the network. Knowing the interworkings of ports is essential for planning, installing, and troubleshooting a Fibre Channel SAN.

A Brief Word About Nodes

The term *node* applies to any entity that can send or receive transmissions in a Fibre Channel network. A node can be a computer system, a storage device/subsystem, a storage router/bridge that connects SCSI equipment, a printer, a scanner, or any other equipment, such as data capture equipment. In the discussions in this chapter, the term "node" refers to *end node* and does not refer to networking equipment such as switches and hubs that do not initiate and receive data transmissions. However, to be precise, a switch can be considered to be a network node.

A node can have multiple ports into the Fibre Channel network, as shown in the following diagram. This is similar to having multiple I/O controllers in a system or subsystem.

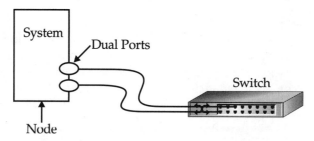

While nodes are interesting from a higher-level storage application perspective, they are not one of the defined logical elements in a Fibre Channel network.

Port Types

Systems, subsystems, devices, switches, and bridges all function as some kind of *port* in a Fibre Channel network. This word "port" refers to a single entrance or connecting point in the network. There is a one-to-one relationship between cables and ports in the network; a cable connects to a single port on each end of the cable.

The type of port that is defined for an entity determines what it can do and how it initiates and responds to network transmissions. There are eight port definitions commonly used in Fibre Channel networks:

▼ **N-ports** Commonly found in systems and subsystems for connecting to fabrics

■ **L-ports** Commonly found in systems and subsystems for connecting to loops

■ **NL-ports** Commonly found in systems and subsystems for connecting to both fabrics and loops, including connecting to fabrics *through* loops

■ **F-ports** Switch ports for connecting to N ports

■ **FL-ports** Switch ports for connecting to NL-ports in a loop

■ **E-ports** Switch ports for connecting to other switch ports

■ **G-ports** Generic switch ports that can be F, FL, or E-ports

▲ **B-ports** A relatively new type of port for bridging transmissions over other networks

N-Ports   The original Fibre Channel concept was based on communications using N-ports and F-ports. N-ports are the logical network function implemented in host bus adapters and storage subsystem controllers that access the Fibre Channel network. Another way to think about them is that N-ports represent storage initiators and targets communicating over a Fibre Channel SAN. They have the responsibility to manage the exchange of frames. Without N-ports there would be no traffic on the network.

N-ports, like all Fibre Channel ports, are strictly a wiring element, as they do not perform any operations based on logical block addresses or filing information. The HBAs or subsystem controllers where the N-port is implemented will provide some storing or filing functions, but the N-port itself is restricted to wiring operations. Addressing operations within N-ports are also restricted to wiring functions. Addressing in Fibre Channel is discussed later in this chapter.

F-Ports   F-ports are implemented in Fibre Channel switches to provide connectivity services to the N-ports that connect to it. Requests from one N-port to access another one are serviced by the switch when it makes a connection between corresponding F-ports in the switch. In other words, the switch completes the I/O path between N-port targets and initiators. Connection services for N-ports are performed for any combination of two different N-ports. The possible N-port to N-port connections inside a four-port switch are shown here:

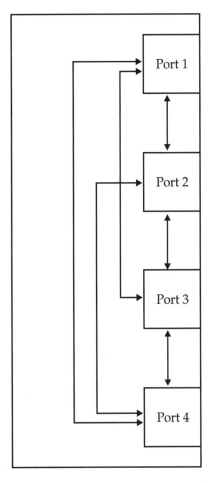

N-ports and F-ports are constantly communicating with each other, whether or not they are transmitting data. During periods of transmission inactivity, N-ports send IDLE words to their corresponding F-port on the switch. These IDLE words establish a "heartbeat" between the N-port and the F-port that allows problems with the link to be identified immediately.

In addition to providing connections between N-ports, Fibre Channel fabrics also provide a variety of network services used for coordinating functions in the SAN. The access to these services is provided to N-ports through special reserved network addresses that are accessed through the switch's F-port.

L-Ports   Entities on loop networks share a common cabling structure and communicate directly with each other as opposed to using a switch to complete the connection. Therefore, a different type of port, called an L-port, is used on loops. Whereas N-ports were designed to initiate and control communications in fabrics, L-ports are designed to initiate and control communications on loops.

Hubs in loops do not have any explicit role in SAN communications. Fibre Channel loops are ring networks that can work without the presence of any hubs. Therefore, hubs do not contribute networking services, with the exception of bypassing malfunctioning links. Without network services provided from a fabric, L-ports contain some additional logic to manage network functions.

FL-Ports   When loops were added to the family of Fibre Channel topologies, it became clear that it would be necessary to allow N-nodes in fabric networks to communicate with L-nodes in loop networks. Two new port definitions were devised to do this: the FL-port and the NL-port.

FL-ports are implemented in switches and enable them to participate as a special node in Fibre Channel loop networks. By definition, the loop network reserves an address for one, and only one, FL-port. In other words, there cannot be two active switches communicating at the same time in the loop. A loop can be constructed with several hubs, but it still functions as a single loop and therefore does not provide a way to attach more than one switch to it. So, while there may be plenty of loop hub ports available to plug switch FL-ports into, there can only be a single active switch connected. It is possible to have other switches connected for redundancy purposes, but they would operate in a standby fashion and not insert themselves in the loop unless the first switch lost the ability to communicate with the loop.

FL-ports are part of the Fibre Channel standard for making what are called *public loops*. In short, public loops allow ports in loops and ports in fabrics to communicate with one another. There are other ways to connect loops to fabrics using proprietary technologies. Proprietary methods for communicating between fabrics and loops create what are called *private loops*. Public and private loops are discussed further in this chapter in the section called "Public loops and Private loops."

NL-Ports   An NL-port is a port that has both N-port and L-port capabilities. Such ports can initiate and manage communications in fabrics and loops, allowing storage initiators and targets to communicate from one to the other. NL-ports in loops can also access the networking services provided by fabrics. Along with switch FL-ports, NL-ports provide the foundation for making public loops.

One of the advantages of NL-ports is that they allow the network topology to change without creating unexpected incompatibilities. An HBA or subsystem controller that has been implemented with an NL-port for public loop operation can be used in either fabrics or loops and can change its mode of operation should the network configuration change.

One should not assume that equipment used in loops will also work in fabrics. A significant number of products installed have controllers that implemented L-ports, and not NL-ports, that have no way of communicating with switches.

E-Ports Switch ports that are used to communicate with other switches are called *E-ports*. In other words, E-ports provide connections for trunk links between switches. E-ports provide the way to build fabrics from multiple switches. An initiator N-port connected to one switch can transfer data to a target N-port connected to another switch through the interswitch E-ports as shown here:

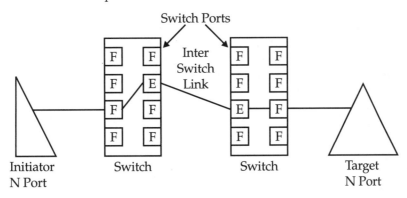

More than just providing an I/O path for data transmissions between switches, E-ports are also used to transfer information about network services between switches.

G-Ports Switch ports are typically made to automatically configure their function by identifying the type of port on the other end of a link. This type of port is called a G-port, for generic port. If the port on the opposite end of the link is an N-port, the G-port configures itself as an F-port; if the opposite port is an E-port, the G-port configures itself as an E-port; and if the opposite port(s) are NL-ports, the G-port configures itself as an FL-port.

B-Ports B-ports were developed in response to requests to be able to use other kinds of networks such as ATM and Ethernet to carry Fibre Channel storage I/O traffic from a local SAN to a remote site. B-ports are part of the FC-BBW specification (for Fibre Channel WAN Backbone), which is discussed in the next chapter along with the integration of Ethernet and IP networking for storage tunneling.

Flow Control in Fibre Channel

One of the most important aspects of any wiring technology for storage networks is its ability to manage network congestion. Most storing traffic can be characterized as "bursty," which means that it is irregular, at times with high levels of traffic, followed by periods of low levels of traffic, and very difficult to predict. This causes some challenging problems for switched communications because it is not possible to know which N-port initiators might want to communicate with which N-port targets. At times there are bound to be conflicts for resources between N-ports wanting to communicate over the same links. If network congestion occurs, system performance can become unpredictable and may not meet expectations for service levels.

Fibre Channel implements two different flow control mechanisms to manage congestion between N-ports and between adjacent ports in the I/O path. An analysis of Fibre Channel's flow control follows.

Buffer Credits

When N, L, or NL-ports begin communicating in a Fibre Channel network, they negotiate about several parameters affecting how they will communicate, including how they will adhere to flow control rules. Fibre Channel ports agree on the number of *buffer credits* that an N, L, or NL-port can use for transmitting data. The buffer credit represents a certain amount of data, similar to blocks used in traditional I/O transmissions. Buffer credits are a little bit like having a debit card or a prepaid calling card. You get a certain amount of money to spend, and you can spend it until you run out. The drawing that follows shows the flow of data and credits between two ports:

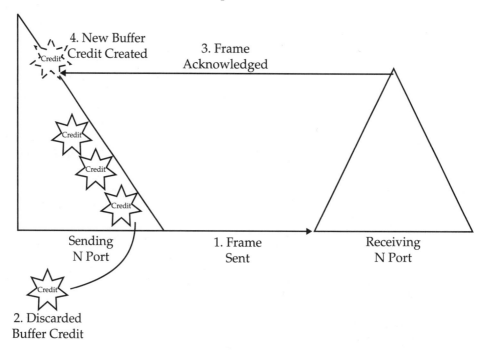

There are two different types of buffer credits used in Fibre Channel, *end to end* and *buffer to buffer.* Both are described in the following sections.

End-to-End Flow Control

As data is sent from the sending port to the destination port, the sender subtracts a credit from its end-to-end credit pool. When the destination N, L, or NL port receives the transmission, it sends an acknowledgment (ACK) control word back to the sender indicating that the frame was received. When this acknowledgment is received back at the sending port, it adds a credit back to its credit pool. In this way, the end-to-end credits used by the sending port are replenished when it receives the acknowledgment from the destination port.

Buffer-to-Buffer Flow Control

The other kind of flow control in Fibre Channel is buffer-to-buffer flow control between adjacent ports in the I/O path. Buffer-to-buffer flow control provides transmission control over individual network links. In other words, buffer-to-buffer flow control is managed between pairs of L or NL-ports in loops and N-ports and F-ports in fabrics.

A separate and independent pool of credits is used to manage buffer-to-buffer flow control. Just as in end-to-end flow control, buffer-to-buffer flow control works by a sending port using its available credits and waiting to have them replenished by the port on the opposite end of the link. The control word R-RDY (receive ready) is sent by the receiving link port to the sender, as opposed to sending a frame acknowledgment.

Class of Service

Fibre Channel defines multiple *classes of service* that define how N, L, NL, and F-ports interact when transmitting data. Class of service definitions were developed to categorize the certainty of data transmissions through the SAN. There were three original classes of services, Class 1, Class 2, and Class 3, defined for Fibre Channel, of which Classes 2 and 3 have been implemented in commercial products. The Fibre Channel standards group spent a considerable amount of time working out the details of Class 1, but it is extremely rare to find implemented in products. Class 1 is discussed in this book more to show what the potential of Fibre Channel technology is than to show its current status or capabilities.

Beyond the first three classes of service, there are three additional classes of service that have not been implemented yet in products. They are not covered in this book.

Class 1

Class 1 service is a shining example of what can happen when a group of engineers gets together in a standards body to design something wonderful without thinking enough about whether anybody would pay for it. When one reads through the standards documents for Fibre Channel, it is obvious that a great deal of time and effort went into the development of Class 1. But when one reads through the product literature of Fibre Channel companies, it is also quite clear that the enormous effort spent was mostly a waste of time, as Class 1 products are extremely rare. It's interesting that the lack of actual Class 1 products has not stopped the Fibre Channel industry from claiming several Class 1 characteristics in its public messages. So even though Class 1 is not being used in products, it is being used for promoting the technology.

Class 1 is a connection-oriented service with guarantees made about the availability of a connection between two N/NL-ports. Class 1 is a virtual point-to-point link that runs through a fabric. No other traffic can interfere in any way with a Class 1 connection. Traffic that is sent over a Class 1 connection arrives in order at the destination port. This saves a great deal of time at the destination node, as it does not have to reorder transmission frames.

Theoretically at least, Class 1 frames cut through the switch and are forwarded immediately to the switch's output port without needing to see if the internal switch connection could be made. In Class 1, the internal switch connection is "always on." Combined with the ordered delivery of Class 1, this virtual point-to-point link results in what would be a very low latency connection. Data passing through the fabric would move as quickly as possible with minimal latency.

Loops do not support Class 1, as it is not possible for a shared media network to provide a dedicated connection.

With a virtual point-to-point connection, there are no acknowledgments between switch F-ports and N/NL-ports. That means that buffer-to-buffer flow control does not apply to Class 1 service. Only end-to-end flow control was defined for Class 1.

The primary disadvantage of Class 1 is the amount of resources required to keep its promises. Switching equipment typically performs its work by multiplexing many things at once, so dedicating a connection between F-ports in the switch cuts against the grain of most switch designs. Perhaps this is the main reason Class 1 has not been more widely implemented. But even if Class 1 were achievable in a single switch, it is doubtful whether or not it could be implemented over trunk links between two switches' E-ports. To adhere to the definition, it could require a dedicated trunk link for each Class 1 connection. Class 1 might be an impossible dream in multielement (multiswitch) fabrics.

A variation of Class 1 is called Intermix. Also theoretical at this point due to the lack of Class 1 products, Intermix provides a way to piggyback Class 2 and 3 transmissions over a Class 1 connection while the Class 1 link is open.

Class 2

Class 2 is a connectionless service that provides multiplexed communications with acknowledgments of transmitted frames. Multiplexed communications implies that there is no dedicated path between a pair of sending and destination ports; this service allows N, L, and NL-ports to communicate with a number of other N, L, and NL-ports in the SAN. Each N, L, or NL-port that wants to communicate has to make its intentions known to the switch or to the other ports in the loop so they can get a connection established.

Although it is unlikely, the possibility exists for frames to arrive out of order at the destination, and therefore Class 2 communications have to assume that reordering of frames may be required. As is possible with any type of network, Fibre Channel frames can be discarded or have errors injected during transmissions. The delivery acknowledgments in Class 2 provide a very fast mechanism for identifying communications problems at both the sending and destination ports.

Both buffer-to-buffer and end-to-end flow control are used in Class 2. Buffer-to-buffer flow control is accomplished when the receiving link port sends an R-RDY control word back to the sender after receiving a frame. End-to-end flow control is accomplished when the destination port sends an ACK control word back to the sending port. Even though a loop does not have a switch port interceding between L or NL-ports, Class 2 transmissions in a loop use both end-to-end and buffer-to-buffer flow control.

The sequence of transmissions and acknowledgments in Class 2 communications is shown in Figure 11-2.

Class 3

Class 3 is the most common class of service used in Fibre Channel networks. It is a multiplexed, connectionless datagram service. Datagram service refers to communications that do not include acknowledgments of delivery. Class 3 can be thought of as a subset of Class 2, but without any way of knowing whether or not data that was sent was received correctly.

Only buffer-to-buffer flow control is used with Class 3, as there are no acknowledgments from destination N/NL-ports. In other words, Class 3 does not monitor transmission problems in port hardware, which means that errors have to be identified using higher-level protocol processes, which adds latency. In general, Class 3 error recovery is

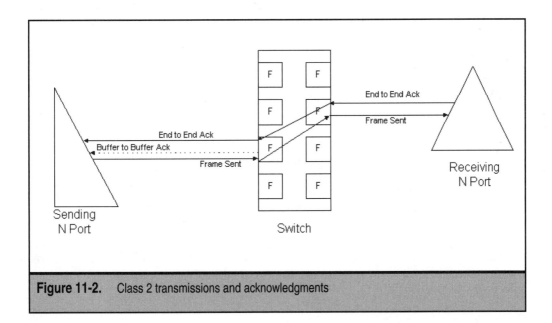

Figure 11-2.   Class 2 transmissions and acknowledgments

based on timeout values being exceeded, as opposed to identifying errors as they occur. Therefore, it takes longer to recognize a transmission error in Class 3 than in Class 2.

The flow control mechanism for Class 3 is done one link at a time. This means a problem at the far end of a connection could go unnoticed while buffer-to-buffer flow control continues to allow new frames to be sent into the network. As there are no end-to-end credits to deplete, sending ports will continue to send frames into the network until they are out of buffer-to-buffer credits. In general, Class 3 is less deterministic about the status of communications in the network and is more likely to have frames discarded in heavily loaded fabrics than Class 2.

The Independence of Flow Control and Error Recovery

Debates over the applicability of Class 2 and Class 3 have been going on for several years within the storage networking industry. There has been a great deal of confusion surrounding this topic, with strong conflicting opinions. This confusion is an indication of how new the field of storage networking is and how much there is yet to learn about the combination of networking and storage. This book hopes to inject some objectivity into these discussions and clarify the issues.

It is important to understand that Fibre Channel is a networking technology and is independent of storing functions. From its inception, Fibre Channel was developed as a networking technology capable of supporting many different types of data transmissions, including the diverse needs of backbone, storage, and real-time traffic. In other words, Fibre Channel as a technology was not developed solely for storage, and it should not be assumed that its architectures were made for storage.

It is also important to realize that error recovery is independent of flow control in Fibre Channel, as it is in most networking technologies. Flow control is managed at the FC-2 layer. Error recovery is managed by upper-layer protocol entities. In the case of SAN storage traffic, error recovery is the responsibility of the FCP protocol's implementation of SCSI-3. The choice of Class 2 or Class 3 flow control is independent of the error recovery mechanism used, although the flow control mechanism can influence how quickly error recovery occurs. Error recovery in Class 2 can begin sooner because the flow control acknowledgments in Class 2 identify problems faster than the SCSI timeout process that Class 3 depends on.

It may help to consider the fact that other types of traffic can exist in a Fibre Channel network, including real-time traffic, such as video transmissions. This type of transmission might not require retransmissions of corrupted or missing frames, but it could still have a requirement for end-to-end acknowledgments to prevent buffer overruns in the destination node. The sending port in this example should certainly not automatically retransmit frames but leave it up to the higher-level protocol to decide whether or not it wants to.

Comparing Class 2 and Class 3

Discussions about which class of service is best for storage have centered around whether Class 2, with its end-to-end acknowledgments, might be required for certain types of storing traffic, such as transaction processing or backup. In essence, there are two conflicting perspectives: those that believe using end-to-end flow control provides a more stable network with fewer errors and faster error recovery and those who believe using end-to-end flow control consumes more network bandwidth than it saves. There appear to be some problems associated with running Class 2 over long distances or networks with higher latencies where the end-to-end buffers are exhausted before acknowledgments are received from the destination port. In this case, the Class 2 flow control would inhibit the performance of the connection by stopping traffic, even when there are no transmission errors or congestion problems.

The resolution to the conflicting opinions about Class 2 versus Class 3 is likely to vary according to the network configuration and the mix of storing applications used. For instance, a network with a single host system and a single storage subsystem could certainly use Class 3 to excellent advantage. If the controller in the subsystem is capable of keeping up with the transmissions from the host, there would be little need for end-to-end flow control. On the other hand, a very busy network with several hosts and subsystems communicating with each other might be able to benefit from having end-to-end flow control limiting some of the traffic among certain communicating pairs of ports.

Flow Control Impact on Error Recovery for Transaction Processing   Although error recovery and flow control are different mechanisms, Class 2 end-to-end flow control can start error recovery earlier by identifying transmission problems faster. Using Class 3, if the SCSI timeout period is long enough, the latency incurred waiting for error recovery could be a problem for high-throughput applications such as transaction processing. The timeout period can change depending on the node technology used. For instance, a Fibre Channel disk drive might have different time-out values than a tape library or an HBA in a host. This makes it difficult to generalize how time-out-generated error recovery will respond.

Flow Control to Maintain Effective Delivery Rates   A discarded frame is not a transmission error; it is a result of network congestion. In effect, a discarded frame is like a transmission error in the way it requires the frame to be retransmitted. Fibre Channel's link error rates are approximately one transmission error for every few terabytes of data transferred, which translates into an error every few hours of operation. If a switch or router in a SAN discards frames due to congestion, the effective delivery rate of frames will be somewhat less than expected and retransmissions will be required more frequently.

In addition, as the number of links in a fabric increases, the frequency of errors in the SAN as a whole will increase. It follows that if a single link has an error every three hours (180 minutes), then ten links, collectively, will have an error every 18 minutes. In addition, if the presence of more links in the SAN also indicates some level of congestion and dropped frames, then the effective delivery rate of the SAN will decrease. It is possible that end-to-end flow control will help larger SANs maintain a consistent effective delivery rate in a storage network.

Most early SAN installations have been designed with limited configurations with relatively small numbers of nodes and ports. For that reason, the effectiveness of Class 2 end-to-end flow control has not been easy to observe in actual SAN implementations. Based on these early SAN implementations, it appears that Class 3 flow control is adequate for most storage networking applications. However, as SANs grow and become more complex, it is possible that the potential benefits of Class 2 will become realistic.

Naming and Addressing in Fibre Channel

The addressing scheme employed by a networking technology is an important architectural consideration because it determines how well the technology can scale to meet future requirements. The methods used to assign and access addresses are also very important because they determine how easy it is to use the technology. Naming is a way to assign aliases to network entities that makes them much easier to recognize and work with than if they are identified only by network addresses. This section discusses Fibre Channel's naming and addressing schemes for ports in both fabric and loop networks.

The basic elements of network names and addresses in Fibre Channel are as follows:

▼ World Wide Name

■ Port address

▲ Arbitrated loop physical address (ALPA)

Each of these is briefly discussed in the following section.

World Wide Name (WWN)

The term *World Wide Name (WWN)* sounds impressive enough, as if there might be some large network plan in which all Fibre Channel ports could be used together in some grand scheme. Instead, it refers to a 64-bit identifier assigned to each product by the manufacturer. The WWN is stored in nonvolatile memory and is typically stamped on the surface of the product and used as a serial number. The format of the WWN is determined by IEEE numbering conventions and is used to provide a means for each product to be uniquely identified in any network it is installed in. This can be very useful when troubleshooting problems with network installations.

The complete WWN for an N-port can be exchanged with a switch when a node initially logs into a switch. If the switch has no information about the N-port, a process called *registration* takes place in which the N-port sends information about itself, including its WWN, to the switch. The switch stores this information so other ports and management applications can access it through a switch service called a *simple name server*.

Port Addresses

A unique *port address* is assigned to each port in a Fibre Channel network. Port addresses in a Fibre Channel are 24 bits long, which means over 16 million addresses are possible in a Fibre Channel network. The port address can be determined by the WWN or by other means. In fabrics, for instance, switches are responsible for assigning unique addresses to all ports. They could choose to use the WWN or some other name/number scheme.

The address space of a network includes all ports in a cascaded network and all loop ports that might be connected through FL-ports. A single node with more than one port uses a unique address for each port.

Arbitrated Loop Physical Address (ALPA)

An 8-bit identifier called the *arbitrated loop physical address,* or *ALPA,* uniquely identifies each port on the loop. Each port in the loop stores the ALPAs of all the other ports in the loop, providing a means for each port to communicate with any other port in the loop.

Public Loops and Private Loops

The ALPA is used in loop arbitration as well as forming the lowest-order 8 bits out of the 24 bits in a loop port's address. If the port is an NL-port and a switch with an FL-port is connecting the loop to a fabric network, the NL-port receives the highest 16 bits for its port address from the switch. If the port is an L-port or there is no connection through an FL-port in a switch, the highest order 16 bits in the port's address are set to zero. A port on a loop where the highest-order 16 bits are zeros is *private* and cannot be accessed by ports in a fabric.

A private loop is a virtual closed system with no access to other networks. Figure 11-3 compares a private loop and a public loop network.

Even though a loop may be public and able to communicate through an FL-port, an individual loop node can still be private by restricting its functions to those of an L-port. In other words, although the loop may be public, any device within it could be private. A private device can communicate with other devices in the same loop, but it cannot communicate with devices outside the loop.

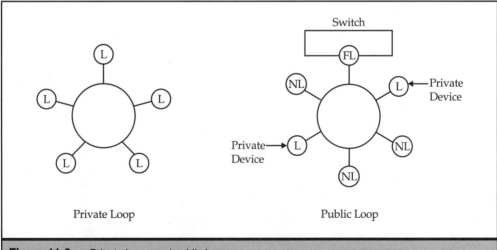

Figure 11-3. Private loops and public loops

Establishing Connections in a Fibre Channel Network

Fibre Channel has a structured method for establishing connections between N, NL, and L-ports. In the sections that follow, we'll first look at how communications are established in fabrics and then we'll look at how it's done in loops.

Fabric Login

Initiating communications in a fabric requires a multistage login process in which communications are first established between an N-port and an F-port in the switch and then with the destination N-port. The process used is as follows:

1. Fabric login
2. Node login
3. Process login (optional)

When an N-port is not transferring data, it sends IDLE control words to its associated F-port on the other end of its link. When an N-port wants to initiate a data transfer, it starts by performing a *fabric login* with a login server process running in the switch. The N-port uses a reserved port address of hex FFFFFE, which the F-port recognizes as a login request and routes to the switch's login server process. Fabric login establishes the class of service to be used within the fabric and other communications parameters including flow control information. While the login is done with a specific F-port on a switch, the login server represents the common capabilities of all the switches in the fabric.

After the fabric login completes, the initiating and recipient N-ports in the network establish communications with each other through a second login process called *node login.* Again, several communication parameters are exchanged and the two nodes can start transmitting.

As Fibre Channel networks can be used to connect nodes with multiple types of internal resources and processes within a node, an additional login called a *process login* is used. Ports use the process login to select the upper-layer protocol they will use. For Fibre Channel, this is the FCP serial SCSI protocol.

Logins are used for all topologies, including point-to-point topologies. The login process for loops and point-to-point networks does not use a switch and therefore does not require a fabric login step.

Loop Arbitration

Fibre Channel loops were developed as a low-cost Fibre Channel disk drive interface with similarities to parallel SCSI semantics. So instead of using switch ports and login servers to establish connections between ports, loops use an arbitration scheme, similar in concept to SCSI bus arbitration. For this reason, the loop technology is called an *arbitrated loop.*

Fibre Channel loops have several nodes sharing the same connected media. This necessitates a method to manage contention. As in SCSI arbitration, the port with the highest priority that participates in any arbitration cycle "wins" the arbitration process. Unlike SCSI arbitration, loop arbitration is achieved through an exchange of control words, whereas SCSI arbitration is done through electrical signals that are asserted on a shared bus.

When one of the L/NL-ports on a loop wants to establish communications with another L/NL-port, it starts generating arbitration control words onto the loop. These arbitration words are passed from port to port on the loop, informing all participants about the intentions of the arbitrating port. As the arbitration words are passed from port to port, each port has the option of forwarding the word or creating its own arbitration word. This process continues around the loop, with each port determining if it can arbitrate for control of the loop.

When the loop becomes available, the arbitrating port assumes control of the network unless another, higher-priority port has assumed control.

An arbitration word is passed from port to port in this manner until it is returned to the port that initially sent it. If the port sees its own arbitration word, it knows it has successfully gained control of the loop and can begin communicating with another port. This process is shown in Figure 11-4.

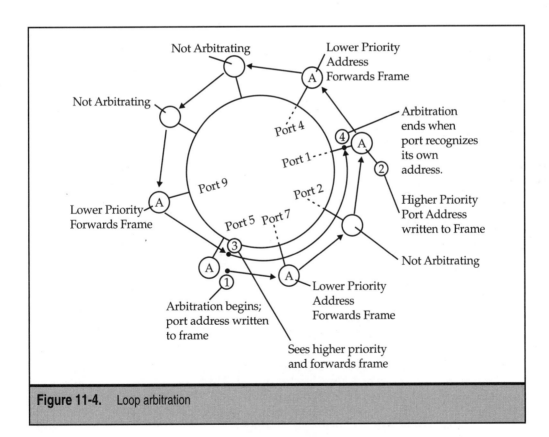

Figure 11-4.   Loop arbitration

After the port has won the arbitration cycle, the next step is opening a loop circuit with the destination port. At this time, the other ports on the loop have stopped generating frames and are forwarding frames for the active loop circuit. This forwarding of frames introduces a small amount of latency, but it does not impact throughput, as the full network bandwidth is still available from port to port.

When the two communicating ports are finished, they close their loop circuit and relinquish control of the loop to another arbitrating port. If another port is arbitrating, it can gain control of the loop almost immediately. No ports need to be told that the network is now available because they all have been monitoring the communications and arbitration words in the loop already.

This capability for ports to monitor communications on the loop makes it possible for any port on the network to shut down another port that is not operating correctly on the network. A quiet port that needs to interrupt the communications of a renegade port that is controlling the network can do so by starting a process called *loop initialization,* which is described later in this chapter and is a required step in removing a port from the loop.

The process for accessing an N-port in a fabric from an NL-port in a loop involves the following five steps:

1. Arbitrate for the loop, and win.
2. Open a loop circuit with the FL-port in the switch.
3. Make a fabric login to the FL-port in the switch.
4. Make a node login with the destination N-port.
5. Make a process login with the destination N-port.

Figure 11-5 shows the process required for establishing public loop communications between a server system in a public loop and a large storage subsystem in a fabric.

Communication Syntax in Fibre Channel

Error recovery in high-speed networks requires fast responses when things go awry. Identifying what went wrong is the most important step in the process. Fibre Channel has a three-level structured syntax of communications that allows the network to quickly identify where errors occurred so that it can respond immediately to resolve them. This syntax is described in the sections that follow.

Exchanges

The highest level in the Fibre Channel syntax is called an *exchange.* Exchanges can be either unidirectional (one way) or bidirectional if two N/L/NL-ports are sending data back and forth. As the top-level structure, exchanges tend to take place over a relatively longer time frame. Exchanges between ports do not prohibit a participating port from also exchanging information with other ports. A single port can manage several exchanges simultaneously.

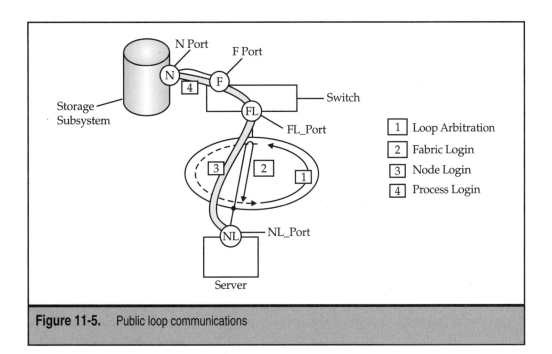

Figure 11-5.   Public loop communications

Sequences

Exchanges consist of *sequences*. An exchange can have as few as one sequence in it. Sequences are unidirectional transmissions between two N/L/NL-ports in a network. A single sequence is a transfer between an initiating node and a destination node. Sequences are processed as a single, discrete transfer entity before subsequent sequences in the exchange can begin. An exception to this is a *streaming sequence* that allows the next sequence in the exchange to begin before the final acknowledgments have been received for the previous transmitted sequence.

With the exception of streaming sequences, sequences are not allowed to be transmitted out of order. (That's why they are called *sequences!*)

Frames

The smallest granule of communication in a Fibre Channel network is a *frame*. The typical frame size in a Fibre Channel SAN is 2KB, although the frame size can theoretically vary according to login negotiations. One or more frames that are part of the same transmission constitute a sequence.

Fibre Channel frames are similar to frames in other network technologies: they have start indicators, header fields, address fields, application data, error detection fields, acknowledgment data, and end-of-frame markers. Fibre Channel frames also have a sequential numerical identifier that is used to identify and correct transmission problems, as described in the following section. Frames belong to sequences and by extension belong to exchanges, as shown in Figure 11-6.

Applying these constructs to storage I/O operations, an exchange correlates to an I/O process that reads or writes some type of data object, such as a file. Sequences are roughly equivalent to commands with several associated processes such as sending a command, reading data, and requesting status. Frames are equated to individual SCSI data block transfers, including all requests, acknowledgments, and error transmissions.

Error Recovery with Class 2

Flow control using sequences and frames can be precise and fast, especially when using Class 2. (Class 1 would be as fast, but it doesn't exist in real-world products.) Destination ports track the order of frames they receive, sending acknowledgment words back to the sender that include the frame's numerical ID. If the sender does not receive an acknowledgment for a certain frame, it can signal the upper-layer protocol to retransmit it to the destination port.

Where SANs are concerned, the SCSI protocol drivers or adapter firmware in the sending and destination nodes communicate by transmitting SCSI-3 commands to each other. These commands could be to resend the entire transmission or just a portion of it, depending on how much of the sequence had been properly received and accounted for.

Error Recovery with Class 3

As Class 3 is a datagram service without acknowledgments, there is no way to notify the sending port that a frame is missing. In that case, the destination port needs to initiate the recovery through an upper layer protocol function on its end.

Frames sent in Class 3 have the same numerical identifiers as used in Class 2. That means the destination port can immediately determine if a frame was not received by

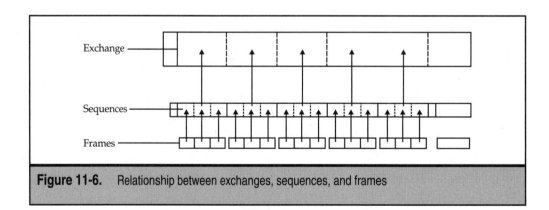

Figure 11-6. Relationship between exchanges, sequences, and frames

looking for out-of-sequence and missing numerical identifiers. At that point, the FC-2 layer at the destination notifies the corresponding FC-4 upper-layer protocol interface (see the section that follows this one) that a problem occurred. Then it is up to the protocol handling logic to determine what recourse it will take.

FC-4 Protocol Mappings in Fibre Channel

One of the strengths of Fibre Channel is its ability to adapt a wide variety of upper-layer protocols (ULPs) at the FC-4 layer that can be transported by the underlying Fibre Channel network. The adaptation of ULPs on top of Fibre Channel transport is referred to as protocol *mapping*. The protocol mapping describes the location and order of message blocks within the Fibre Channel transmission frames.

The FC-4 layer is an *abstraction layer* that allows virtually any type of application or network communication to take advantage of Fibre Channel's underlying structure. This abstraction layer allows networking developers to use the same system-level interfaces that they always have, which greatly simplifies the porting of other functions onto Fibre Channel. The only change that is required is to transfer the physical network operations of those other networks to the logical mapping that the FC-4 layer provides. Then the Fibre Channel network provides its own transport for the ULP. In essence, Fibre Channel is a virtual networking technology that can accommodate any other type of network transmission, as long as it has an FC-4 layer mapping.

An example of how protocol mapping works is error recovery, such as those methods described for Class 2 and Class 3 in the preceding section. All networks have some methods for recovering from network transmission errors, but when these other network types are ported to Fibre Channel, their native physical-level error recovery mechanisms are replaced by Fibre Channel's. They do continue to use the same error recovery logic they always have, but they take their cues from messages provided from the FC-2 layer. The recovery actions of the mapped protocol are handled by device driver software, just as they always were. Where SANs are concerned, a SCSI device driver is responsible for error correction that is passed up from the FC-2 level.

Defined Upper-Layer Protocol Mappings

Among the protocols that have already been mapped to Fibre Channel are the following:

▼   **Small Computer Systems Interface (SCSI)** A mapping of the SCSI-3 protocol, called the *Fibre Channel Protocol (FCP)*, is the primary protocol mapping for Fibre Channel. FCP has the widest implementation of any protocol mapping for Fibre Channel.

■   **Internet Protocol (IP)** Implementations of Fibre Channel IP mappings are now in the market.

■   **Virtual Interface Architecture (VIA)** VIA establishes network communications directly between an application and the network adapter. VIA is targeted at clustered applications.

- **High Performance Parallel Interface (HIPPI)** HIPPI is an aging system and storage connection technology used for high-throughput processing applications. Mapping HIPPI onto Fibre Channel extends HIPPI technology by exploiting Fibre Channel's superior performance and distance capabilities.

- **IEEE 802 logical link control layer (802.2)** The IEEE (Institute of Electrical and Electronics Engineers) has specified several protocols for local area networks, including the IEEE 802.3 media access control protocol for Ethernet and the IEEE 802.5 media access control protocol for token ring networks. The 802.2 protocol provides independence from the media access layer and directs network communications to higher-level protocols such as NetBIOS and IP.

- **Single Byte Command Code Set (SBCCS)** SBCCS is an implementation of the command and control protocol implemented in the ESCON storage I/O channel used by IBM mainframe systems.

- **Asynchronous Transfer Mode Adaptation Layer 5 (AAL5)** While ATM was designed primarily for transporting voice communications, its AAL5 protocol is independent of media access methods and provides scalable system-to-system communications.

- ▲ **Fibre Connectivity (FICON)** FICON is the mapping of IBM S/390 mainframe ESCON traffic as an upper-layer protocol on Fibre Channel networks.

TWO DIFFERENT NETWORKS USING A COMMON NAME

One of the most unusual and confusing aspects of Fibre Channel is the fact that it encompasses both switched and ring topologies. Furthermore, instead of referring to them as switched and ring networks, the Fibre Channel industry adopted the terms "fabric" and "loop" to distinguish the technology from other networking technologies. There is also a third Fibre Channel topology, called point-to-point, that defines connections over a single physical link. Point-to-point connections certainly have a role in SANs, but they are not generally considered to constitute a general-purpose network and are mostly ignored in this chapter.

While the Fibre Channel industry includes both fabrics and loops as parts of a single technology, the analysis in the remainder of this chapter separates the two as being fundamentally different networking technologies sharing common implementations, characteristics, and structures. To be clear, all Fibre Channel topologies use the same physical cabling and transmission technologies. Also, the general frame structure for transmitted data is the same. The payload information is also the same and the communication syntax is the same. Storage I/O operations on fabrics, loops, and point-to-point links can carry the exact same data.

But although there are many similarities, there are also several important differences between fabrics and loops. The fundamental node-port definitions, N and L-ports, which are so important in Fibre Channel's FC-2 layer, are completely different. Their access methods for establishing orderly communications could hardly be more different. Fabric access is based on a login process, and loop access is based on arbitration, similar to parallel SCSI. Flow control and the method of establishing credits are also different between fabrics and loops. Fabric communications are one-to-one connections made between network nodes and switch ports. Loop connections, on the other hand, are a shared media network. Therefore, fabrics have far greater aggregate bandwidth than loops. In addition, fabrics support several services for coordinating network activities. Loops have none of these services and instead must be connected with a fabric in order to take advantage of them. Fabrics provide segmentation of ports in zoning. Loops do not have a way to do this.

The bottom line for Fibre Channel is that the compatibility of fabric and loop products has historically not been very good. The fabric versus loop issues have been addressed by the standards organization, but the implementation history still lingers, creating problems and confusion. For the most part, the fabric/loop problem is gradually disappearing, as fabric products appear to be well on their way to establishing dominance as the Fibre Channel SAN wiring of choice.

A Historical Perspective

On the surface, it is difficult to understand how a standards effort could produce both fabrics and loops. But in fact, there were good reasons for both being developed, and one can argue that Fibre Channel would not have been successful as a SAN wiring technology without both fabrics and loops.

Fibre Channel's Origins as a Backbone Technology

From its inception in 1988, Fibre Channel was developed to be a very flexible, high-speed, scalable networking technology that was originally designed as a backbone network technology. Started as a research project in the R&D labs of such companies as Hewlett-Packard, Sun, and IBM, the early vision of Fibre Channel was to be a high-speed backbone technology for several purposes, including IP data networks. For several years the developers of Fibre Channel believed the technology would someday replace 100BaseT Ethernet and FDDI. In the mid-1990s, in fact, there were published articles on Fibre Channel written by R&D professionals espousing its capabilities for backbone applications and relegating storage as a secondary, less interesting application.

To provide fast performance and accommodate unforeseen changes in technology in the future, Fibre Channel was imbued with the following design elements:

▼   Serial transmission for scalable performance, small cables/connectors, and extended distance

■   Interchangeable, low-error-rate transmission media for high reliability and cost flexibility

■   Switched network interconnections for low latency and aggregate bandwidth

- Connection-oriented and connectionless link-layer functionality implemented in network hardware for highest reliability, lowest latency, and smallest impact on host processors

▲ Modular, layered protocol structure, including upper layer protocol abstraction to allow transport of any data type

As it turns out, these ambitious design goals apply equally as well to storage channels as they do to backbone networks, if not more so.

Turn Left at Scott's Valley; Fibre Channel as a Disk Drive Interface

In the early 1990s, Seagate Technologies entered the standards effort for Fibre Channel and began working on an implementation of Fibre Channel technology for use as an interface for disk drives. Seagate's interest in Fibre Channel was mostly motivated by competition; Seagate wanted to continue to lead as an innovator in the disk drive industry, and wanted to keep their rival IBM from determining the next great storage interconnect technology.

Parallel SCSI was never intended by its inventors to be the last interface for disk drives and serial transmissions, so there had been a long-standing interest in trying to understand how to make serial connections work with disk drives. IBM began working on a disk drive interconnect technology called SSA, or *serial storage architecture,* which was built on a ring network topology. SSA allowed many more disk drives to be connected to a common cabling technology than parallel SCSI and also provided distance benefits far beyond those of parallel SCSI.

Seagate understood the threat that SSA posed to their business and went to work on a parallel effort of their own that could credibly rival IBM's. The choice of Fibre Channel was an astute one for Seagate; Fibre Channel had an existing standards organization behind it with broad support from the major industry participants. If Seagate could successfully get endorsement from the Fibre Channel industry for a new disk drive interface, it could best IBM as a standards-compliant technology. Seagate succeeded in doing this, and by inviting the rest of the disk drive industry to participate, Seagate built the backing it needed to beat SSA in the industry.

Why Loops?   So if Fibre Channel existed as a switched technology, why did loops need to be invented at all? The answer is simple: Seagate and its partners needed to be able to deliver technology to the market as quickly as possible and at a price point that could compete with IBM. That meant shortening the development effort in any way possible while looking to reduce costs.

The first obstacle to Fibre Channel fabrics as a disk drive interface was the associated cost of the switch ports: they were extremely expensive on a port-by-port basis compared to SSA, which did not require any switch or hub but worked by connecting drives together sequentially on a physical ring. Therefore, the disk drive interface needed to work with networking devices or controllers that were much less expensive, or had no cost.

The second obstacle for Fibre Channel was translating the link-level signaling of parallel SCSI to the new Fibre Channel drive interface. There was already an enormous installed base of parallel SCSI equipment and a sizable I/O industry with lots of engi-neers who were experienced with making parallel SCSI solutions. If the new disk drive interface could somehow leverage these external, existing resources, it would gain sup-port much more readily. That effectively ruled out fabrics and forced the development of another topology that more closely resembled the SCSI bus. The ring topology used by SSA was a model for building a shared access network with similarities to parallel SCSI. By implementing an arbitration scheme with a heritage in parallel SCSI and by including the SCSI-3 serial SCSI protocol as an upper-layer protocol, the Fibre Channel disk inter-face made it easy for storage companies to "port" their technologies to the new interface. It was a brilliant business decision that worked extremely well for Seagate.

Fibre Channel Finds Its Killer App   With the advent of storage I/O over Fibre Channel technology, the Fibre Channel industry had an application that could use it. The original design goal of Fibre Channel as the next anointed backbone technology was in serious jeopardy with the emergence of Gigabit Ethernet as a market and technology force. In a not very flattering sense, the Fibre Channel industry had finally found something that the market could get excited about. This didn't mean there was no internal squabbling within the Fibre Channel industry, and many of the participants in the industry under-stood that loop/fabric compatibility would be a major problem to overcome. But the fact was, the largest disk drive company at that time, Seagate, was moving forward with its development plans and had a big stick to swing: a reason for somebody to purchase the technology.

Of course a disk drive interface could also be used as an interface for storage subsys-tems. This fact led to a broadening of the technology to include many subsystem develop-ers who could bring more attention and demand for the technology. To make a long story short, it did not take long for the number of companies working to deliver loop-based products to vastly outnumber the number of companies developing fabric products. Loop was much easier to convert to and was much cheaper overall than fabrics. The mar-keting messages of the loop community fostered the development of the SAN concept as the "killer application" for Fibre Channel. Without the development of loop-based SANs, it is likely that Fibre Channel would never have reached critical mass as a technology.

The Future of Loops   With fabrics dominating the customer site implementations of SANs, there are serious questions about the future of loop technology. If one views the situation as loops versus fabrics, then it is fairly clear that fabrics will dominate as the core technology in SANs. However, loops and fabrics can also complement each other in SAN installations. Loops provide a way to aggregate ports together that connect through a sin-gle switch port. In other words, a SAN constructed with a 16-port switch can add port ca-pacity by attaching loops through an FL-Port.

But even if loops fall out of favor completely as a SAN topology, the technology will still be used to connect devices inside subsystems for a long time. Just as parallel SCSI is used inside storage subsystems, loops are also used with great success to provide fault-tolerant I/O paths to dual-ported disk drives. As Fibre Channel technology matures and improves, disk drive manufacturers are likely to continue supporting loop interfaces for a long time.

Figure 11-7 shows a two-port storage subsystem with two internal Fibre Channel loops connecting to a RAID 0+1 disk array, using dual-porting for fault-tolerant connections inside the cabinet. The loop is a physical star, logical loop, where the loop controller provides the ability to bypass links and drives that fail.

FABRICS

Fibre Channel networks built with switches are referred to as *fabrics*. A fabric can be composed of a single switch or multiple switches. In essence, a fabric is the composite switched environment that connects N-ports. Fabrics have some unique capabilities and requirements that will be examined in the sections that follow.

Latency

Latency is roughly equivalent to the amount of delay in a communications path. In a perfect world, data transmissions would occur as if the network were some sort of large integrated circuit where data arrives immediately after it is sent. In reality, this is far from the

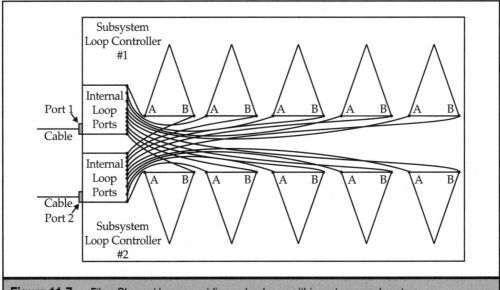

Figure 11-7.   Fibre Channel loops providing redundancy within a storage subsystem

case; every point of control or change in the path introduces some amount of latency to the transmission. This does not mean that it slows down the transmission, but it does delay it.

Latency in fabrics is typically measured as one to four microseconds for switches and as several milliseconds for bridges and subsystem controllers. The difference between the latencies usually has to do with whether or not transmission frames need to be read completely and stored in buffer memory or whether they can be rerouted on the fly to another point or destination in the network without stopping to read the entire frame.

Low Latency for Transaction Processing

Latency is only significant when the communications between systems and storage have to have a quick turnaround or when the number of frames processed is a higher priority than the total amount of data transferred. The systems environment with these characteristics is high-throughput transaction processing.

Transaction processing needs to be able to be very reliable and very quick. I/O processing failures in transaction systems can be disastrous and take many hours to correct. Beyond that, the service-level requirements for transaction systems can be quite demanding. Performance problems caused by latency in the I/O path could severely hamper the output and productivity of a transaction system. That is why there is a focus on the latency in Fibre Channel components. Most Fibre Channel switches have latency measurements in the one- to two-microsecond range.

Switches in Fabrics

Switches in fabrics utilize high-speed integrated circuit and backplane technology with the capability of supporting gigabit transmissions for multiple concurrent sessions. For the most part, Fibre Channel switches provide cut-through switching that forwards transmission frames to outgoing ports before the incoming port has finished receiving the entire frame. This allows the switch to work very quickly.

Almost all Fibre Channel switches are described as *nonblocking* switches. A nonblocking switch can have multiple concurrent connections traveling through its internal infrastructure without requiring data to be delayed by internal congestion in the switch. In other words, it does not *block* or suspend other communications while transferring data internally between two internal ports. The interpretation of what is blocking and what is nonblocking is highly subjective. As it turns out, none of the switch vendors describe their products as having blocking. Still it is worth understanding the concept, as it might be useful in testing and evaluating switches. Figure 11-8 visually contrasts blocking and nonblocking switches.

Notice that a fabric can add many more nodes and switches without significantly increasing the latency of the I/O transmission between nodes. Figure 11-9 shows a before and after picture of a Fibre Channel fabric after new switches were added to the fabric and connected by their E-ports and additional nodes were connected.

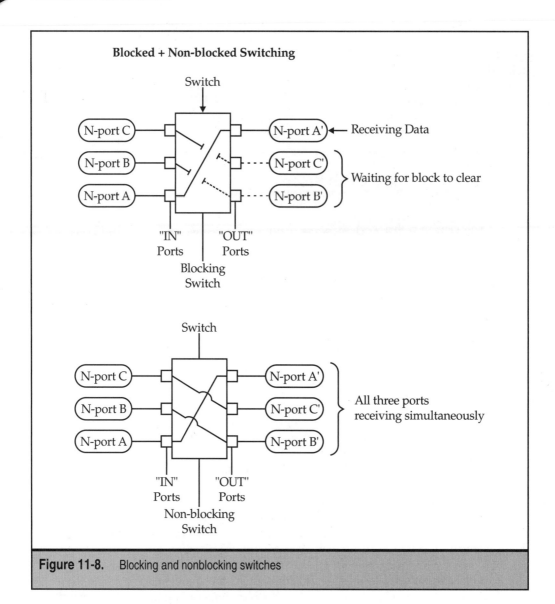

Figure 11-8.   Blocking and nonblocking switches

In Figure 11-9, notice that four new nodes were added to the network, C, C', D, and D', without affecting the latency of the existing paths. The math to calculate path latency is fairly trivial and can be generalized as follows:

```
2 x (node-to-switch latency) + N x (switch internal latency)
```

In general, the latency in Fibre Channel switches is far less than in the nodes. Switches read minimal information in the transmissions and have optimized hardware for very

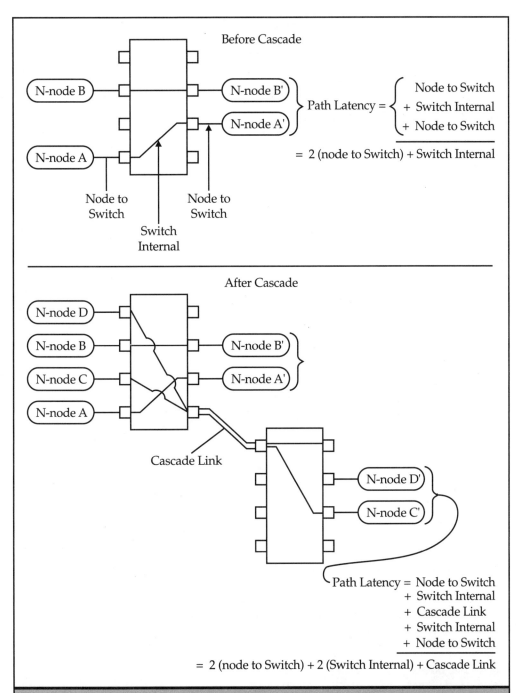

Before Cascade

$$\text{Path Latency} = \begin{cases} \text{Node to Switch} \\ + \text{ Switch Internal} \\ + \text{ Node to Switch} \end{cases}$$

$$= 2\,(\text{node to Switch}) + \text{Switch Internal}$$

Node to Switch

Node to Switch

Switch Internal

After Cascade

Cascade Link

$$\begin{aligned} \text{Path Latency} = \; & \text{Node to Switch} \\ & + \text{ Switch Internal} \\ & + \text{ Cascade Link} \\ & + \text{ Switch Internal} \\ & + \text{ Node to Switch} \end{aligned}$$

$$= 2\,(\text{node to Switch}) + 2\,(\text{Switch Internal}) + \text{Cascade Link}$$

Figure 11-9.   Latency in a multielement fabric

fast data transfers. Nodes, on the other hand, usually have to read or write the complete transmission, including error-checking data, before conveying the contents of their payloads to higher-level system functions. This destination node processing involves a fair amount of work and takes considerably more time than the time it takes to transfer frames through a switch.

Multielement Fabrics and High-Port-Count Switches and Directors

As a SAN expands in size, it may be necessary to increase the number of ports available in a fabric by adding another switch to the SAN. Fabrics constructed of more than one switch are referred to as *multielement* fabrics, and the links between the switch E-ports are called *interswitch links.* The topology of a multielement fabric can be a chain of switches, a hierarchy of switches, or a mesh, as pictured.

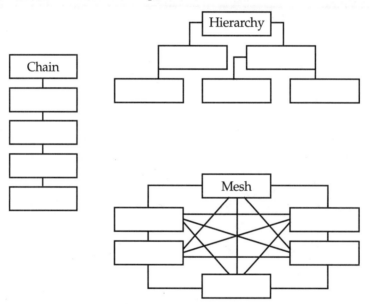

If heavy traffic is flowing over interswitch links, it is possible that blocking could occur. In general, the problem of providing nonblocked communications in multielement SANs is a tough one to solve because it depends a great deal on the specific applications being run and the location of initiators and targets in the fabric.

TIP: To prevent overloading interswitch links, try to connect the cables for target/initiator pairs to the same physical switch, as opposed to connecting them to different switches.

Head-of-Line Blocking As N/NL-ports in Fibre Channel networks can have connections with several other N/NL-ports, it is likely that some of them will have multiple exchanges and sequences in progress between some random combination of N/NL-ports in the fabric. Even though multiple exchanges and sequences can be in the works, the physical connection between the N/NL-port and the fabric is a single link to a single F-port with some amount of buffer memory.

It is possible that a blocking condition for one sequence can keep the data from other sequences from being transferred. This situation, called *head-of-line blocking*, can cause serious performance problems for fabrics.

Consider an N/NL-port that has three active sequences with three other N/NL-ports. Now imagine that one of its sequence-partner N/NL-ports is connected over an interswitch link to a remote N/NL-port.

To make things more interesting, assume there are also other exchanges established between other local N/NL-ports to destinations across the interswitch link.

Let's say the first N/NL-port wants to transfer data over the interswitch link to the remote port and uses all its buffer-to-buffer credit buffers. But let's further assume that another N/NL-port is already transmitting data over the interswitch link and that several other N/NL-ports are already waiting to transfer data across the same interswitch link.

Now, the first N-port attempts to start communicating with a local N/NL-port connected to the same switch. However, it can't, because it does not have any credit buffers available and the F-port does not have enough buffer memory to store any additional data. Put another way, the transmission at the head of the line at the F-port is blocking all other transmissions from the N/NL-port. Head-of-line blocking can undermine an otherwise good SAN design when data transmissions clog interswitch links, preventing higher-priority, low-latency traffic from being transmitted through the switch.

Even though head-of-line blocking can occur, it is a good idea to structure SANs so that transaction-processing systems and their storage do not communicate across interswitch links. That way, adjustments to the structure of multielements SANs won't interfere with the connections between the transaction processing systems and their storage.

High-Port-Count and Director-Class Switches   Another way to increase the number of ports in a fabric is to use switches with more ports. If a SAN installation plan includes many ports in a large SAN, it may be advisable to install switches with 32, 64, 96, or even 128 ports. The primary advantage of this approach is that interswitch links may be able to be avoided completely. That is not to say there won't be blocking within the switch itself, but blocked communications within a single switch are typically resolved much faster than blocked communications over interswitch links.

High-port-count switches are referred to as *storage directors*. The concept of a storage director is based on having lots of ports to connect to as well as having redundant internal components to prevent a disaster if something goes wrong in the switch. With many servers and systems connecting through a director, it is essential that these products be as error free as possible. Therefore, director products typically have sophisticated diagnostics and failure analysis technology so that they can immediately switch to a redundant set of components if something goes awry.

Directors can make the design of a fault-tolerant Fibre Channel SAN much easier by reducing the need for trunk links between switches and by eliminating the need for redundant switch hardware.

Routing in Fibre Channel SANs with FSPF   The I/O path in a multielement SAN is determined by the Fabric Shortest Path First (FSPF) routing protocol. FSPF is a derivative of the common Open Shortest Path First (OSPF) protocol used in Ethernet and I/P networks.

Routes through the SAN are determined by calculating the "costs" of the various paths presented and choosing the path with the least cost. Cost is roughly analogous to physical forces such as friction or impedance, in the way that higher baud rates (faster transmission rates) present less transmission resistance and therefore equate to less expensive costs. Administrators can skew the cost calculation by assigning a numerical value multiplier to the calculation. Once a path is established for two N/NL-ports communicating in a fabric, it is not changed and all communications between those ports follow the same path.

FSPF uses a replicated topology database that is common to all switches in the fabric. As links in the SAN are changed, the FSPF database is updated in all switches throughout the fabric. The process of updating the database in a Fibre Channel fabric is referred to as *flooding the network.* A special class of service, Class F, which is similar to Class 2, is used for exchanging FSPF database information over interswitch links.

Neighboring switches in Fibre Channel fabrics are defined as those that are connected physically through an interswitch link but have not yet exchanged their routing topology databases. *Adjacent switches* are those that are connected through interswitch links and have exchanged topology databases—and that have a common view of possible paths in the fabric.

When an N/NL-port in a Fibre Channel SAN attempts to communicate with another N/NL-port that is located remotely, the switch queries its topology database, matches the communication request to a known path, and forwards the frame through the appropriate E-port and interswitch link.

Fabric Services   Fabrics provide a variety of services to N/NL-ports in a SAN. Among the services provided are a login server for establishing and negotiating communications, a simple name server for locating entities, a time server for synchronizing operations, a fabric controller for operating the switch functions, and an SNMP server for managing and reporting on operating status.

Fibre Channel services are addressable by N/NL-ports using reserved port addresses. When an N/NL-port attempts to use one of the services, it addresses a frame to the reserved address. The fabric controller then routes the request to the appropriate server process running in the switch.

The services provided are coordinated among the switches in the fabric. Information pertaining to these services that needs to be distributed among the switches is done using Class F communications over interswitch links.

Zoning in Fibre Channel Switches   Another special type of service provided by fabrics is zoning, as discussed in Chapter 9, as a way to segregate storage I/O traffic between groups of servers and their affiliated storage subsystems and devices. Most zoning implementations in Fibre Channel SANs use address zoning, or soft zoning.

Loop Communications

The remainder of the chapter looks at some of the unique details of establishing ordered communications in Fibre Channel loops.

Loop Internals

Unlike other ring networks such as token ring, FDDI, and SSA, the Fibre Channel loop is not constructed from two counter-rotating rings, although that could change with some of the work being considered by the standards body. The Fibre Channel loop is unidirectional. That means a failure in any of the connections between loops can take the loop out of commission. This is one of the main benefits of using a hub—a hub can bypass a link or a node that is malfunctioning, as shown in Figure 11-10, where malfunctioning node C was bypassed.

Unlike a fabric network, every time a new node is added to a loop network, the I/O path gets slightly longer. However, the additional length is not as large a problem as it might seem due to the way nodes communicate in the loop. Once two nodes in a Fibre

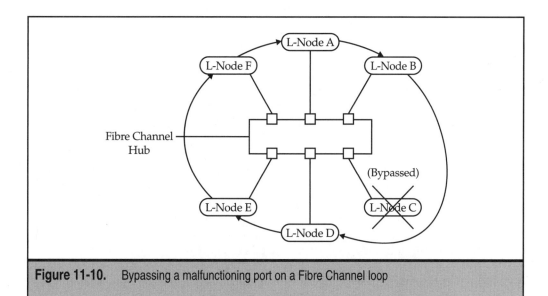

Figure 11-10.   Bypassing a malfunctioning port on a Fibre Channel loop

Channel loop start a communication session, the other nodes in the loop begin acting as repeaters, forwarding each transmission to the next downstream node. In other words, the noncommunicating nodes virtually take themselves "out of the loop" until the session is finished. The following diagram illustrates a four-node loop in which two of the nodes are communicating and the other two are forwarding frames:

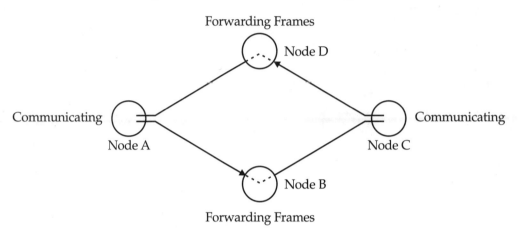

This way, the communication characteristics of loop networks closely resemble those of point-to-point or fabric networks that have the full 100 MB/s bandwidth available to them. This method effectively "flattens out" what would otherwise be a significant performance disadvantage for Fibre Channel loop communications.

Loop Initialization

Ports in loop networks use a process called *loop initialization* to establish their port addresses and establish the pecking order used by all ports on the loop to control communications. Whereas N-ports in fabric networks perform fabric login individually, L-ports and NL-ports in loop networks perform loop initialization as a group, which involves every port in the loop.

Loop initialization occurs whenever there is a break in service in the loop, when a port leaves the loop, or when a new port needs to acquire a port address. Any port in the loop can request loop initialization to proceed. The term *loop initialization primitive (LIP)* refers to a special Fibre Channel sequence that is used to start loop initialization. Any port on a loop can start loop initialization by sending a LIP to its neighbor on the loop. As the saying goes, a chain is only as strong as its weakest link; likewise, a loop is only as stable as its least reliable port. A malfunctioning port on a loop is a very bad thing indeed. That's why port bypass, as illustrated in Figure 11-10, is so important to building reliability in loops.

Loop initialization is not used to recover from transmission errors. The mechanisms described previously for Class 2 and Class 3 error recovery apply in the same way to loops as they do to the fabrics. However, when loop initialization occurs, any ongoing transmissions taking place are interrupted and do not complete. If this happens, the transmission will need to be recovered or retransmitted after loop initialization completes. Loop initialization includes the following seven fundamental steps:

1. Select a temporary loop master.
2. Assign a port address stored in a switch's simple name server.
3. Assign the port address that was previously assigned.
4. Assign a port address based on hardware settings or WWN.
5. Assign a port address through software algorithms.
6. Create a relative position mapping.
7. Circulate the relative position mapping.

Choosing a Temporary Loop Master

Loop initialization specifies that one of the ports in the loop needs to function as a temporary loop master that manages the initialization process. This process is similar to the process of loop arbitration described earlier in the chapter, except that all ports participate in locating the port with the highest priority, which becomes the temporary loop master.

After the loop master is selected, it begins the process of loop initialization by creating a mapping of the loop address space, called the ALPA bitmap. The ALPA bitmap represents all 126 potential L-port addresses in a loop. When the process begins, the ALPA bitmap does not have any ports assigned to, or claimed by, any of the ports represented. The next four steps circulate the ALPA bitmap through the loop four times, giving ports an opportunity to claim an address by manipulating and forwarding the ALPA bitmap.

Claiming Addresses Used with a Fabric

The loop master begins by sending a special frame called the *loop initialization fabric address frame,* or *LIFA.* NL-ports that had previously been logged into switches may claim their previous port address in the ALPA bitmap. The LIFA frame is sent from port to port in the loop, giving each port a chance to register its previous address in the LIFA frame and reclaim the address used by a switch with an FL-port.

Claiming Previously Used Addresses

The next frame circulated by the loop master is the loop initialization previous address frame, or LIPA. The purpose of the LIPA is to allow ports to attempt to reclaim their previously assigned port address. While this step should provide persistent port addresses, it cannot guarantee that this will always happen, especially if two or more previous loops are being combined. Each port that had not previously received an address during the preceding step has the opportunity to claim its address in this step.

Claiming an Address Based on a Hard Address or World Wide Name

When the LIPA frame is returned to the loop master, it generates a loop initialization hard address frame, or LIHA. This step takes advantage of optional hardware settings or the

WWN of the port. Notice that if the WWN had been previously used as this port's address, this step gives the port a second chance to reclaim its previous port address.

Claiming an Address from a Software Process

If the previous three loop initialization frames were unable to establish a port address, the loop initialization soft address frame, LISA, is circulated; and each port employs an algorithm to claim one of the remaining available ports in the ALPA bitmap. When this frame returns to the loop master, all ports participating in the loop have ALPA addresses assigned to them.

Creating a Relative Position Mapping

After the LISA frame has been circulated, the loop master begins the process of mapping the relative locations of all participating ports on the loop. At this point, the ALPA bitmap has been established by ascending ALPA numerical order—not by the actual physical order of ports on the loop. This relative positional order is needed to facilitate communications in the loop.

The loop master sends a loop initialization report position frame, or LIRP, around the loop. Each port that claimed an address during the ALPA address assignment phase enters its address and relative loop-location information into this LIRP frame.

Circulating the Relative Position Mapping

When the LIRP is completed, the information needed to locate addresses in the loop is complete. For the final loop initialization task, the loop master circulates the loop initialization loop position frame, or LILP. Each port in the loop copies the LILP information to internal storage so that it can use it when the loop is up and running again.

SUMMARY

Fibre Channel was initially developed to be a high-speed, high-reliability, and flexible backbone network. Although it does not appear to be destined to be a backbone network, the characteristics of Fibre Channel lend themselves very well to a storage I/O channel.

Although the name Fibre Channel implies fiber optic cabling, copper cabling can be used. The distances attainable with Fibre Channel vary significantly depending on the type of cable used and the transmission speed. The faster the transmission and the larger the cable diameter (for optical cables), the smaller the distance is. Future speed improvements to Fibre Channel will likely be limited in product implementations to fiber optic cabling. Fibre Channel's physical elements are specified for error rates that occur in the range of one error for every terabyte transmitted.

As is the case with most networks, a great deal of functionality is provided in software. Fibre Channel's FC-2 layer shoulders the burden of providing highly structured communications through the implementation of advanced flow control technology that significantly reduces congestion and a communications syntax that quickly identifies transmission errors so that they can be immediately corrected. Together, these facilities make Fibre Channel an extremely reliable wiring option for storage I/O traffic. Fibre Channel's class of service options provide several alternatives, although only two of them have been implemented in products to date. Fibre Channel's Class 2 service uses both end-to-end and buffer-to-buffer flow control as well as incorporating transmission acknowledgments with built-in error detection and recovery.

Fibre Channel has been very effective as a SAN wiring option. Its implementation of its FC-4 protocol mapping of serial SCSI has enabled practically all SCSI storing applications to run over it. Its low latencies, which are in the range of several microseconds, are capable of supporting high-throughput transaction processing.

The two major topologies for SANs, fabrics and loops, have historically created compatibility problems. At the core of these problems is the different access methods that are necessary for switched and shared access networks. In general, the situation appears to be taking care of itself, as fabrics have become more heavily favored for data center installations. Loop technology will continue to exist as an interconnect technology inside storage subsystems.

EXERCISES

1. Using 16-port switches, design a high-availability SAN with redundant path components for four servers, each connecting to two dual-ported storage subsystems. Design the same SAN using a 64-port fault-tolerant storage director.

2. Design a fabric with at least 50 ports using 16-port switch elements where each switch has a minimum of two interswitch links connecting to other switches and where the maximum number of interswitch links needed to connect any two N/NL-ports is 2.

3. Write an algorithm for load balancing across multiple interswitch links that connect any two switches in a SAN. Assume FSPF is the routing protocol.

4. Design a SAN using a single 16-port switch with 8 servers, each communicating with 2 storage subsystems (8 servers + 16 subsystems).

CHAPTER 12

Wiring Storage with Ethernet and TCP/IP Networks

Although the advancements in network storage over the last several years have been enormous, they have not generated as much excitement as the recent initiatives by several companies to create wiring technology for carrying storing traffic over Ethernet and IP networks. Until the advent of SANs, storage was primarily a subset of systems development, and storage networking has only recently been seen as a new and separate technology. With Ethernet and TCP/IP technology being considered for storage network wiring, it seems as if storage networking could become part of the mainstream networking industry.

There is no question that running storage traffic over Ethernet and TCP/IP networks could disrupt the established order in the storage industry as networking vendors begin to see the opportunity to enter the storage marketplace. However, as is true with most technologies, the marriage of Ethernet and TCP/IP networking with storage poses serious technology hurdles for everybody involved, including the established networking vendors.

This chapter takes a look at some of the potential for crossing storage with Ethernet and TCP/IP technology and attempts to analyze the strengths and weaknesses of some of the approaches being developed. This is certainly an exercise in crystal ball gazing, as there are very few products that mix storing with Ethernet and TCP/IP today, so it is still quite early to tell what kinds of functions and features such products would have.

A HISTORICAL PERSPECTIVE ON STORAGE AND ETHERNET/TCP/IP

Ethernet and TCP/IP networks have been used for many years as a wiring layer for a variety of filing-based products. File servers, NAS appliances, network backup and file replication products have all used Ethernet/TCP/IP networks for a long time and will continue to do so. For the most part, these products took advantage of existing network technologies to provide filing functions over a network. Although most of the networking technologies were already in place, it was necessary to invent new network file redirection technologies such as NFS and CIFS to enable filing to work over Ethernet/TCP/IP networks.

The situation today with the development of storing capabilities over Ethernet/TCP/IP networks is similar. There is already a great deal of networking technology that can be used, and the engineers developing it are trying to make the best use of the rich heritage of Ethernet and TCP/IP. To clarify, while network attached storage is mostly file-based today, the new Ethernet/TCP/IP storage networking technology under development today is built around storing technology, specifically serial SCSI.

Clarification in Terminology Used for Ethernet and TCP/IP

Ethernet, TCP, and IP technologies are closely related and are often implemented together in networks. However, they are different technologies that need to be understood individually for their abilities to support storing and filing applications in storage networks. In this chapter, the general network environment that includes all three components is referred to as "Ethernet/TCP/IP" for brevity's sake.

There are many instances where Ethernet, TCP, and IP are discussed separately or as either "Ethernet/IP" or "TCP/IP" networks. When "Ethernet/IP" is used, the implication is that other transport protocols besides TCP are likely to be used, such as UDP. When "TCP/IP" is used, the implication is that Ethernet is not necessarily the underlying physical network—although that will be the case most of the time in situations described in this chapter. It is hoped that the context will make clear which protocols are being considered. The term "Ethernet" in this chapter is often used to refer to both Gigabit Ethernet as well as slower versions of Ethernet. In general, storing traffic is expected to require gigabit-level performance, although there may be instances where 100Base-T technology is adequate.

A Brief Overview of Ethernet and TCP/IP

Some of the important differences between the roles of Ethernet, TCP, and IP are as follows:

- ▼ Ethernet is primarily targeted at operating a physical network. That is not to say that Ethernet does not have logical components and software, but compared to TCP/IP protocols, Ethernet is far more physical in nature. TCP/IP protocols, on the other hand, are mostly logical entities that are used to manage the transmission of data over multiple and/or different physical networks.

- ■ Ethernet was developed as a general-purpose network to work on local networks. It has a network addressing scheme, which was developed to establish unique identities on a network but is not necessarily easy to manage in large networks. Ethernet addresses are commonly referred to as MAC (media access control) addresses. IP, on the other hand, was developed specifically to provide addressing capabilities across multiple numbers and types of networks and has a structure that is relatively easy to manage. The transmission of data over an IP network can span global networks composed of many different technologies. For example, IP addressing forms the foundation for communications on the Internet. TCP does not incorporate network addresses, per se, but it does provide a local port identifier to direct data to the proper application in the receiving system. For instance, HTTP, FTP, SNMP, and telnet communications all have unique, universal port addresses that systems use to communicate with each other. For instance, telnet uses port 23, HTTP uses port 80, and SNMP uses port 25.

- ■ Ethernet transmits data directly over Ethernet networks in discrete entities called *frames*. Ethernet frames have MAC addresses and error correction information to determine if errors may have been introduced while transporting data across Ethernet networks. IP does not transmit data directly over any particular type of network but uses the underlying transmission services provided by the physical network, typically Ethernet. IP transmission entities are called *packets*. They have

IP addresses and independent error correction information that determines if errors may have been introduced during transmissions over whatever network(s) are being used. TCP data transmission units are called *segments.* Segments identify the port number that is being used to communicate between two end nodes. TCP error correction is somewhat different from Ethernet's and IP's in that TCP incorporates the capability to retransmit data. By contrast, Ethernet and IP error detection schemes are used to discard data that might be corrupt.

■ Ethernet frames can be *forwarded* by bridges or switches to other Ethernet network segments that are part of the same addressing scheme. In other words, Ethernet switching takes the entire Ethernet frame from one switch link and retransmits it to another switch link. This is known as layer-2 switching. In contrast, IP packets can be forwarded by IP routers over different physical networks. These can be other types of physical networks or the same type of physical network with an independently managed address scheme. IP routers extract the IP packet from the incoming lower-level transmission unit (Ethernet frame, for example) and place it in the outgoing lower-level transmission unit of the other network. IP routing is also commonly called layer-3 switching.

▲ Ethernet has responsibility for local flow control within the Ethernet network. This is roughly equivalent to Fibre Channel's buffer-to-buffer flow control. IP has no flow control capability. TCP has a flow control mechanism that is responsible for end-to-end flow control between different physical networks; it will be described later in this chapter.

The Ethernet/TCP/IP Protocol Stack

Ethernet and TCP/IP protocol stacks are described in many other books on networking in a great deal of depth. The description here is intended to introduce the stack, not necessarily convey its nuances. In the sections that follow, we briefly outline four layers in the stack that correspond to Fibre Channel's protocol layers. Both the physical and logical components of the Ethernet/TCP/IP stack are included in what this book refers to as the *wiring* function in a storage network.

Ethernet Protocol Contributions   Ethernet has a physical layer, which includes the encoding system used in Gigabit Ethernet, which is the same 8B/10B encoding used by Fibre Channel.

Above the physical layer is the data link layer. In general, the data link layer incorporates all the network adapter firmware and device driver software that is used to manage the physical connections between two adjacent connecting points on the network. In other words, the data link layer manages network links.

The entities communicating can be a network interface card and a switch port, two switch ports, two hub ports, a hub port and a switch port, and so on. The next illustration shows two end systems communicating over a network with four distinct data links.

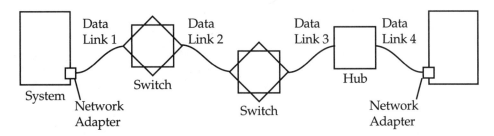

Architecturally, the data link layer is divided into two different components to separate the control of physical operations from an abstraction layer that provides a consistent interface for higher-level network functions. In Ethernet, the physical control layer is called the media access control layer, or simply the MAC layer. In traditional shared-media bus-based Ethernet networks, this included listening to the network to determine if there were other transmissions in progress and waiting until the coast was clear before transmitting data over the network.

From time to time, new functions are added to the existing standard specification for the MAC layer. One of the most important additions was a new access method for switched networks, where each network node had its own private data link to connect to a switch. Other significant additions to the MAC layer have included the capability to aggregate links together so that multiple physical links can operate as one logical connection, as well as the incorporation of full-duplex communications.

The other major component of the data link layer is the logical link control, or LLC. The LLC provides a level of abstraction that allows higher-layer network functions such as IP to use lower-level network transports without having to know about the implementation and technology details.

The TCP/IP Protocol Suite   The TCP/IP protocol suite operates on top of the physical and data link layers provided by Ethernet. The architectural parts of the TCP/IP suite are the Internet layer and the transport layer, both of which are discussed in the text that follows.

IP, the Internet Layer Protocol   The foundation of the TCP/IP protocol suite is IP, or the Internet Protocol. It provides the network layer function in Ethernet/TCP/IP networks that is used to locate resources and route information across different physical networks. While Ethernet has its own local addressing scheme, it is often necessary to build larger integrated networks that use IP as a single addressing scheme.

Over the years, IP has been revised several times, with the current standard being IP version 6, or more simply IPv6, also referred to as IPng, for IP next generation. While IPv6 is the current standard, it is not the most commonly implemented version. IPv4, which has been used for many years, has an enormous installed base that is expected to take several years to migrate to IPv6. Among the improvements in IPv6 is an expanded address space to accommodate the rapid growth of Internet computing.

TCP and UDP Transport Protocols   Above the IP network layer is the transport layer, typically implemented as the Transmission Control Protocol, or TCP. TCP was developed to address two prevailing needs in the early, relatively unreliable, Internet. The first TCP functions were to manage transmission errors and provide an end-to-end flow control to match the transmission rate of a sending system with the capabilities of a receiving system that could be on a completely different network. Over time, TCP/IP networks have become much more reliable through the use of fiber optic media and other advancements in networking technology. Today, therefore, TCP mostly provides end-to-end flow control.

Another commonly used transport layer protocol is the User Datagram Protocol, or UDP. In essence, UDP does not provide user error management or flow control. UDP makes what is called a "best effort" to transmit data but provides no mechanism to ensure data is delivered efficiently or completely. This can be a real advantage for certain types of network communications where the amount of data transferred is small or where it is desired to have higher-level processes manage the error correction and flow control.

WIRING ETHERNET/TCP/IP INTO STORAGE NETWORKS

There are several different approaches and possibilities for integrating Ethernet/TCP/IP networks with storage channels. The primary integration opportunities are:

▼ Server boundary

■ Storage tunneling

■ Native storing transport

▲ Cross-network bridging

The remaining sections of this chapter take an extended look at the integration opportunities in each of these areas.

Server Boundary Integration

The idea of server boundary integration is hardly new and has been discussed already in different parts of the book, so we won't spend much time on it here. Server boundary Ethernet/IP storage integration is modeled after the traditional file server and NAS architecture in which client communications are made over an Ethernet/IP network and storage connections are made over separate wiring, such as parallel SCSI or Fibre Channel. Another way of saying it is that the Ethernet/IP network provides the front-end network and the storage wiring is the back-end network.

On a detailed, system-internal level, the border between the Ethernet/IP network and the storage network is the internal interface between the data representation and data structure functions of the filing system in the server. The data representation function exports a view of data over the Ethernet/IP network. The data structure function directs the storing access to the data over the storage network as shown here:

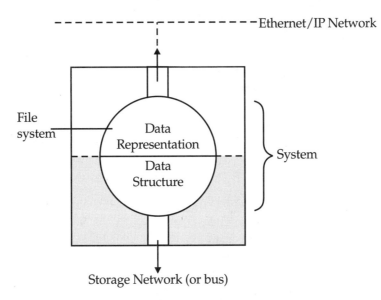

An interesting special case of server boundary integration is where the server network forms a hierarchy of multiple IP network tiers. The most common example of this is a Internet server "farm" where the servers for a large Web site access their data on NAS appliances over an IP network. This architecture is shown in Figure 12-1.

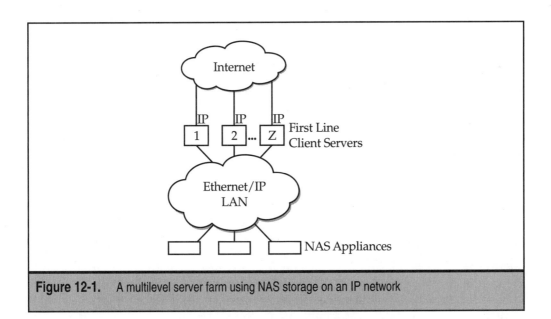

Figure 12-1. A multilevel server farm using NAS storage on an IP network

Storage Tunneling

Storage tunneling is one of the most interesting and multifaceted aspects of Ethernet/TCP/IP storage integration. The basic idea of storage tunneling is to transmit storage traffic from a storage bus or network over a "foreign" Ethernet/TCP/IP network and back to a familiar storage environment. In other words, the Ethernet/TCP/IP network acts like a "wiring splint" that joins together two separate Fibre Channel networks. This process is illustrated here:

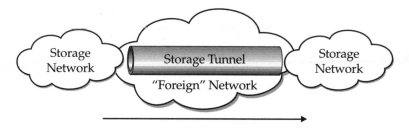

There are many interesting things that need to be thought through in a storage tunneling design. Among the more important items are:

▼   The manner in which data is packaged as it moves across the various networks

■   The way that addressing, naming, and routing are used to direct traffic

▲   The way that error recovery and flow control are implemented and coordinated (or not)

Encapsulation

Different networking technologies have different methods and structures for transmitting data. The differences are analogous to the various ways capital goods are shipped: they are often placed in containers, which can then be transported by boat, airplane, trains, and trucks, with different levels of effectiveness and cost. Data in networks can be thought of as being placed in "protocol containers" that can be transported by different networking vehicles. Just as truck trailers can ride on rail cars and as rail containers can be loaded on cargo ships, network protocol containers can be moved from one network to another.

Networking technologies refer to the transmission units of data they transmit by a variety of names. For instance, Fibre Channel and Ethernet transmissions are called frames and ATM transmissions are called cells. Standards documents refer to these transmission segments generically as protocol data units, or PDUs. For the sake of brevity, we will simply refer to network transmissions generically as frames, unless it is helpful to specify IP-level packets, in which case they will be referred to as IP packets.

One of the main concepts in tunneling is the ability to take an entire network frame and place it inside, or *encapsulate* in it, another frame on the other type of network, like this:

Frame Type #1
Frame Type #2

The concept of protocol encapsulation is fairly simple, but the implementation details can be complex. One of the interesting problems to solve is placing a frame from one network inside the frame of a second network when the second frame is smaller than the first. The technique for breaking larger frames into smaller ones is called *segmentation*. When data transmissions are segmented, the smaller frames are given sequence numbers that allow the receiving station to correctly reassemble the original frames, if necessary. This process is shown in Figure 12-2, where an original frame that is 2K in size is segmented in two tunneling frames that are both 1K in size.

While it would seem that the process of frame segmentation and reassembly would be a real performance problem for the network, it can be done efficiently by implementing the function in network hardware controllers such as network interface cards. For example, ATM networks use 53-byte cells, which of course are quite small compared to most Ethernet frames. But ATM networks today can be used both effectively and efficiently to connect Ethernet/TCP/IP traffic over ATM wide area networks.

Addressing and Naming

Entities in a network that wish to communicate with each other need a rigorous and well-defined method for correctly identifying what systems are communicating. This is typically done through the network addressing scheme, which often also includes some sort of naming service for mapping numerical network addresses to more intuitive and manageable names. Examples of network naming conventions are Fibre Channel world wide names and the domain name services used in the Internet to associate Web site URLs (Uniform Resource Locators) with IP addresses.

Correlating destination and source addresses is an obvious issue for tunneling technologies, which have to correctly identify networking entities from two different networking technologies. For instance, the Fibre Channel address scheme is different from the Ethernet/IP address scheme, and the tunneling solution needs to provide a transparent and accurate I/O path through two different sets of addresses.

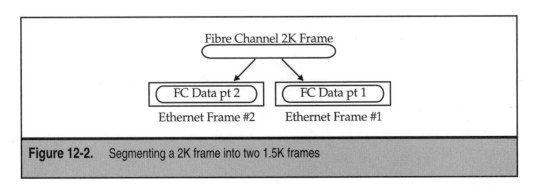

Figure 12-2.   Segmenting a 2K frame into two 1.5K frames

Figure 12-3 shows three different networks. Networks A and C are Fibre Channel networks, and network B is an Ethernet/IP network. Consider what happens when the HBA in network A needs to send data to the storage subsystem in network C. The HBA is not capable of creating any addresses other than Fibre Channel addresses to put in the destination ID of the Fibre Channel frame. Yet, somehow this data must be transmitted using Ethernet/IP addresses because Ethernet/IP network entities cannot use Fibre Channel addresses.

Gateways

The inability of the various network entities to create or use multinetwork addresses means that a network "junction," or *gateway* of some sort, must be in place that can represent the various Fibre Channel and Ethernet/IP addresses correctly. It follows that two such gateways are needed: one between networks A and B and another between networks B and C.

Assuming the HBA in network A needs to transmit to the subsystem in network C, the gateway must be able to recognize those transmissions intended to go over the tunnel. This could be done by configuring and assigning a special port to the gateway function or by reading the destination ID in the Fibre Channel frame and automatically forwarding any incoming traffic across the Ethernet/IP network.

After the gateway has recognized the transmission as one that will be forwarded through the network tunnel, it can segment and encapsulate the Fibre Channel frame within some number of Ethernet frames. The next order of business is determining the

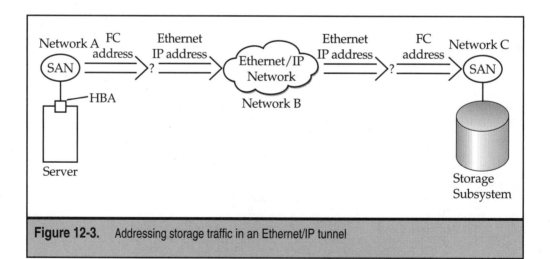

Figure 12-3. Addressing storage traffic in an Ethernet/IP tunnel

Ethernet/IP destination ID that needs to be placed in the Ethernet/IP frame to correctly forward the transmission to the proper remote gateway. There could be several potential gateways, each with its own IP address on network B, as pictured here:

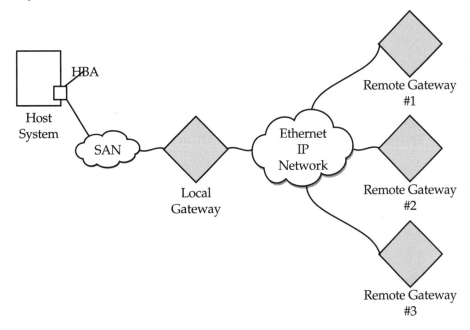

Again, the decision for which Ethernet/IP address is assigned by the gateway is determined according to the incoming port or the destination address in the Fibre Channel frame.

Now we will shift the perspective of the receiving gateway. When the receiving gateway receives the transmission through the tunnel, it sorts the Ethernet/IP frames as necessary and reassembles the Fibre Channel frames. It then transmits Fibre Channel frames over the Fibre Channel network to the storage subsystem. The destination address placed in the Fibre Channel frame by the HBA could be used by the gateway when rebuilding the original Fibre Channel frame, or the gateway could use a different local address.

Using a different Fibre Channel destination address on the reassembled frame allows administrators of both Fibre Channel networks, A and C, to maintain and manage independent address domains. If separate addresses are to be used, then it is necessary to provide some sort of address translation function in the gateway that matches incoming addresses with outgoing addresses in the gateway.

Gateways can be either stand-alone products or integrated into network switches. The gateway function, however, is slightly different than your average run-of-the-mill Fibre Channel port function, as it has to manage multiple network and protocol operations, including the mapping of addresses between two different networks.

Error Recovery and Flow Control in a Tunnel

One of the more difficult aspects of tunneling is managing the communications syntax across three different physical networks. All networks have some method of identifying transmission errors, and all networks implement some form of flow control.

Error Recovery with Tunneling   Error recovery in a tunnel is slightly more complicated due to the fact that three different networks are involved. As the tunnel is transparent to the end nodes, it is possible to have a situation where the error recovery in the tunnel pinpoints a transmission entity that doesn't really exist from the perspective of the applications using the tunnel. As a result, things can be confusing when one tries to understand how transmission errors are corrected.

For example, we'll follow the transmission of a frame using the example network from Figure 12-3. Assume the Fibre Channel HBA transmits a frame through the local gateway, which is segmented and sent over the Ethernet/IP network as two "tunnel" frames. There are now three types of potentially significant network transmission errors:

▼   The tunnel fails to transmit both tunnel frames.

■   The tunnel fails to transmit one tunnel frame.

▲   The transmission fails between the remote gateway and the storage subsystem.

First, we'll discuss the complete failure of the tunnel to transmit either tunnel frame. In this case, the HBA and the local gateway will eventually time out waiting for transmission acknowledgments. If the local gateway times out, it could potentially resend the two tunnel frames if it still has them in buffer memory. If the local gateway does not have the tunnel frames in memory, then the transmission will be regenerated by the HBA.

However, this raises an interesting potential problem. It is possible for the local gateway and the HBA to time out in relatively the same time frame. Both the gateway and the HBA could resend their frames, causing duplicate error recovery frames in the network. In that case, the receiving end node should be able to detect duplicate transmissions and discard them to prevent data from becoming corrupted.

Now let's assume that the remote gateway does not receive the second of these tunnel frames for some reason. It will acknowledge the receipt of the first tunnel frame, but not the second. At some point, the local gateway will realize that the second tunnel frame has not been successfully transmitted and will try to resend it if the frame is still available in its buffers. If the local gateway no longer has a copy of the frame available, it will not be able to respond, leaving it up to the sending end node. The gateway's error recovery process is shown here:

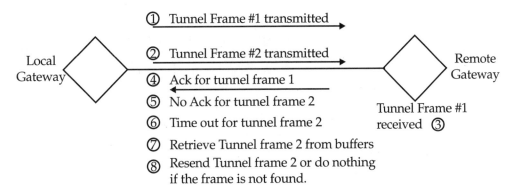

When the sending HBA retransmits the duplicate Fibre Channel frame, the local gateway will transmit both tunnel frames. In this case, the retransmission would be treated as a completely new transmission in the tunnel, although the sending and receiving end nodes would treat them as a retransmission of the original Fibre Channel frame.

A transmission failure can also occur between the remote gateway and the Fibre Channel subsystem. Without receiving an acknowledgment from the destination subsystem, the remote gateway will eventually discern that the transmission error occurred and can attempt to retransmit the frame if it is available in its buffers. If the frame is not in the gateway's buffers, the sending system's HBA will have to retransmit the original Fibre Channel frame, which would be transported through the tunnel and on to the receiving subsystem end node, as shown here:

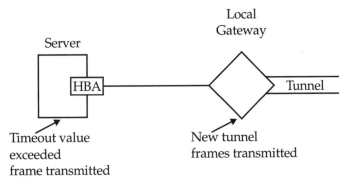

Flow Control in the Tunnel   Flow control is needed to keep transmitters from sending too much traffic into the network, overrunning slower receivers, or causing congestion within the network. Flow control is implemented according to the length of anticipated transmissions as well as the characteristics of the network. There is no reason to believe that flow control for different types of networks would be similar. For the case of storage tunneling, the flow control mechanisms used in Fibre Channel and Ethernet/TCP/IP are considerably different. (The flow control mechanisms used by Gigabit Ethernet and TCP are not similar either, for that matter.)

For the most part, flow control is not as critical a function as error recovery, but poorly implemented flow control can certainly have a negative impact on performance. Considering that low latency is an expected goal of storage networking, flow control that relieves congestion through tunnel paths is certainly desirable.

But just saying that flow control is desired in the tunnel is much easier than providing it. Flow control mechanisms are heavily dependent on the characteristics of the networks they are used in. Whereas Fibre Channel uses buffer credits for both link-level and end-to-end flow control, Ethernet/TCP/IP networks use two different types of flow control. Gigabit Ethernet has a link-level flow control *pause* facility, for stopping transmissions over a link. The TCP protocol uses a "sliding window" flow control that dynamically allocates the buffer size, and therefore the packet size, of network transmissions.

Ethernet/TCP/IP Storage Network Tunnels

In essence, there are two types of open systems storage traffic to consider for tunneling through Ethernet/TCP/IP networks: parallel SCSI and Fibre Channel transmissions. We'll first discuss parallel SCSI briefly and then turn to a more in-depth analysis of Fibre Channel tunneling.

SCSI Tunneling

SCSI tunneling in one form or another has been available for several years already as SCSI bus extender products that were introduced in Chapter 4. In essence, a SCSI extender uses a proxy system where the local SCSI extender assumes the role of representing a remote SCSI HBA or subsystem and takes on the difficulties of synchronizing high-speed SCSI operations over a much slower and typically less reliable network. One of the difficult challenges of SCSI extension is taking the parallel data lines used in SCSI, parsing them into a serial network transmission frame, and then re-creating them properly at the receiving end. SCSI extension is difficult and often requires precision tuning that is based on the host bus adapters, storage controllers, and operating systems used. As a result, it tends to be expensive.

Architecturally, SCSI extension lengthens the parallel SCSI bus to an almost arbitrary length, as long as the parallel data can be reliably reassembled after traveling the length of the tunnel.

Two parallel SCSI buses are required for SCSI extension. The first is a local SCSI bus that typically has a system and a host bus adapter as the initiator. The second is a remote SCSI bus that may have some combination of SCSI target devices on it but probably does not have a host system with an HBA. This design is illustrated here:

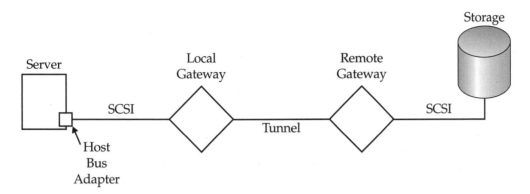

SCSI extension products can use whatever networks the product designers want to. In the past, these have included all types of LANs, particularly Ethernet and FDDI as well as ATM and other kinds of wide area networks. The gory details of the tunneling network must be planned for properly by the tunnel's designers. In essence, there are few standards that specify how parallel SCSI extension works, although it is certainly possible for SCSI extension to make use of standards-based networks.

Fibre Channel Tunneling

Tunneling Fibre Channel data is much easier than parallel SCSI because Fibre Channel is already a serial transmission and can be encapsulated much more easily than parallel SCSI. When tunneling Fibre Channel transmissions over Ethernet/TCP/IP networks, segmentation is almost always a necessity because Fibre Channel frames are typically larger than Ethernet frames. Although it is theoretically possible to negotiate smaller Fibre Channel frame sizes, it may not be achievable in practice due to the way various products implement their session setup and login negotiations. Some of the products in the market today do not negotiate smaller frame sizes, as the assumption has been that the maximum frame size is an advantage.

Ethernet/IP Tunneling: What Level? One of the interesting questions in Fibre Channel tunneling is where the encapsulation should take place in the Ethernet/IP protocol stack. There are four options, with different ramifications:

▼ Ethernet Mac encapsulation

■ IP layer encapsulation

■   UDP encapsulation

▲   TCP encapsulation

Each of these will be discussed briefly in the sections that follow.

Ethernet MAC Encapsulation   There is no overwhelming need to use the IP protocol suite at all for transporting storage traffic over Ethernet local area networks. All of the addressing needed to locate receiving nodes on an Ethernet network can be done using Ethernet MAC addresses.

Encapsulation in Ethernet would be done by creating a storage tunneling protocol that would be implemented within standard Ethernet payloads. In essence, Ethernet-level encapsulation can be viewed graphically like this:

Storage Payload
Ethernet Frame

One of the challenges of Ethernet-level encapsulation is understanding how flow control would be implemented for the tunneled storage traffic. But as motivational speakers like to point out, these are not challenges, they are opportunities. The potential exists to build very fast and highly reliable storage tunnels this way. It would also be possible to build fast storage networks, although it is a good idea to think of tunneling as an independent storage network function.

While Ethernet encapsulation appears to be out of favor within the industry today, it is certainly not a dead issue. For instance, the ability to build a storage tunneling protocol directly on top of 10 Gigabit Ethernet could be very appealing to some.

With Ethernet-level encapsulation, Ethernet's native addressing scheme would be used to enable the tunnel to extend over individual or bridged Ethernet networks. In other words, it would not be possible to route this type of tunnel traffic using standard IP routing equipment.

IP Layer Encapsulation   The next step up the Ethernet/TCP/IP stack is the IP layer. Just as TCP and UDP data is placed in IP packets, there is no reason that tunneling could not be done on the IP layer, as shown here:

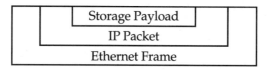

In essence, this approach is similar to Ethernet encapsulation as discussed previously, except that IP addressing would be used, which would allow the IP-encapsulated storage to be routed using industry-standard IP networking equipment. Like Ethernet, IP does not provide its own flow control, and it would probably be necessary for a tunneling protocol to do this.

UDP Encapsulation UDP is sometimes viewed as an inferior protocol to TCP because it does not provide flow control or error recovery. However, UDP has its advantages in that it provides a simple and uncomplicated transmission mechanism. In general, UDP works very well for NFS and SNMP transmissions. Where tunneling is concerned, the lack of flow control and error recovery may not to be such a big problem for UDP. Instead, its lightweight operation may give it a distinct advantage over TCP. If the end nodes are going to perform error recovery anyway, the overhead of error recovery in the tunnel may be unnecessary. UDP encapsulation can be pictured like this:

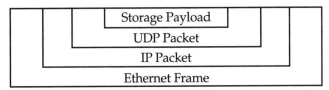

TCP Encapsulation The highest level for storage encapsulation is the TCP protocol. As discussed previously, it is likely that error recovery would be handled by the end node as opposed to the tunnel gateways. On the other hand, flow control in the tunnel could be valuable, especially if the tunnel extends over bridges or routers. Placing the tunnel function on top of TCP can be graphically viewed like this:

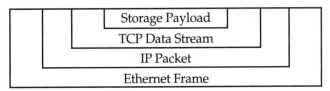

Tunneling Variations for Fibre Channel Components

Now that we have examined the Ethernet/TCP/IP side of the tunnel, we will turn our sights on the Fibre Channel side to examine how Fibre Channel entities could be developed.

N-Port Proxy Gateway Tunneling to Remote Devices A Fibre Channel storage tunnel can be created by implementing a gateway that assumes the role of an N or an NL-port in the Fibre Channel network. In this type of design, the gateway assumes a local address and participates in all local network operations such as port logins and loop initialization. In this respect, the gateway creates a virtual local presence for entities in the remote Fibre Channel network. The term "proxy" refers to the actions that the gateway does on behalf of the remote devices and subsystems it represents.

Because the gateway assumes a particular address, there are some restrictions on the number of remote entities it can represent. But that does not mean the gateway can only represent a single device or subsystem. Just as an N-port for a storage subsystem can represent multiple LUNs, the proxy gateway can provide a level of device virtualization and represent multiple remote devices or logical block address ranges as LUNs in the local Fibre Channel network, like this:

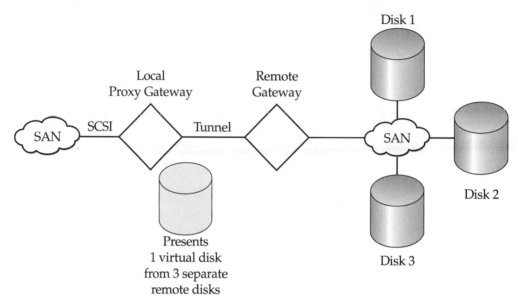

The local and remote gateways form a distributed system that provides local proxy functions for remote Fibre Channel network entities. There are several ways proxies can be designed: As mentioned previously, a gateway can provide some level of device virtualization to aid in the management of remote devices and bulk storage capacity. Sometimes proxy gateways are designed to "spoof" all communication responses in the local network by making all responses expected for network operations locally. In other words, the local gateway would acknowledge all transmissions immediately without waiting for the operation to be completed in the tunnel.

Error recovery is obviously a tricky deal for a gateway that spoofs. Applications and filing systems in host systems in the local Fibre Channel network may have continued processing with the assumption that remote operations succeeded already. Therefore, a gateway that spoofs needs to be able to hold all the information in its buffers in order to recover from unexpected errors. Not only should "spoofed" data be held in buffers, but it should also be kept in nonvolatile memory such as flash memory so that it can survive an unexpected power loss. Depending on the types of application data sent over the tunnel, it may be preferable not to spoof in order to maintain precise control of data transmissions through the tunnel.

Another way to work through a proxy is to use a "pass-through" mechanism, where the proxy forwards frames between the network entities and does not respond until it receives a response from the entity on the other end of the tunnel. With this type of proxy, there is never a premature acknowledgment for undelivered data. On the down side, the performance of a system waiting for acknowledgments from a remote device could be poor. For that reason, it is recommended that Fibre Channel Class 2 not be used with storage tunneling. The time it takes to receive acknowledgments back through the tunnel could bring Class 2 performance to its knees. The process of a pass-through proxy is shown here:

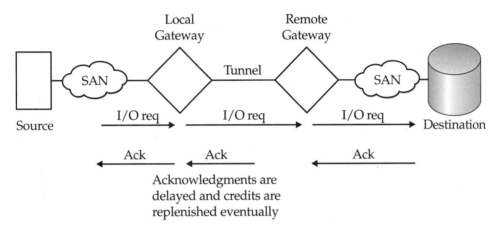

Zoning in a Proxy System   It is possible to implement several zoning variations in a proxy tunnel. First, access zones can be established in the gateway by filtering frames by source ID and rejecting frames from nonmembers of the zone. Essentially, this is a process that is already being done by Fibre Channel to SCSI routers and bridges. LUN masking in an HBA would also effectively limit the access to LUNs presented by the gateway. Finally, it is possible to implement LUN-level zoning in a switch, where the switch would filter frames by "peeking" at the SCSI CDB (command descriptor block) inside the FCP frame. However, this type of LUN-level filtering may have a negative impact on the performance of a switch, as the switch must wait to scan the contents of FCP frames before deciding whether or not to forward them.

A proxy tunnel gateway that provides zoning is shown in Figure 12-4. The gateway in this figure is representing three different disk subsystems as three different LUNs under a single target address. The gateway is implementing zoning for each of these LUNs to segregate access to three different servers in the local SAN. This technique is sometimes referred to as *LUN virtualization*. Although LUN virtualization is performed in the gateway, which is primarily a *wiring* entity in the storage network, the LUN virtualization feature is a *storing* function.

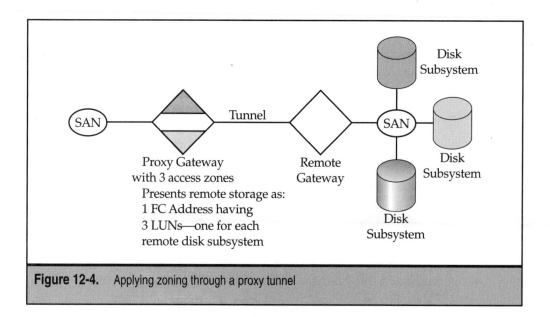

Figure 12-4. Applying zoning through a proxy tunnel

Tunneling Through Private Switch and Hub Ports

The other way to connect Fibre Channel SANs to devices over a tunnel is to use a special "private tunnel port" in a Fibre Channel switch or hub. This is not such a foreign concept, as both Fibre Channel switch and hub vendors have developed specialized functions in their products as optional features. The basic idea is that a port could be configured with special interface capabilities that allow it to connect through tunnel networks to remote devices. In essence, this is analogous to some of the private loop attachments that switch manufacturers developed that allowed them to access certain entities on Fibre Channel loops.

With a specialized switch or hub port, there is no need for a local proxy function and the tunnel port can pass through all commands and addresses as if the remote device or subsystem were local. The latency characteristics of these specialized links would not likely be as good as native Fibre Channel links, but it could be plenty good for many storage applications including remote backup and multimedia data access.

While a private port can be designed to have special functions, it is difficult to understand why switch manufacturers would choose to develop this type of capability when it is possible to construct extended SANs as discussed in the following section.

Building Extended SAN Fabrics with Tunnels

While it is interesting to connect to remote devices using Ethernet/TCP/IP tunneling, it is probably more interesting to understand how to connect SANs together over tunneling networks.

The SAN-to-SAN tunnel also requires a gateway function, but it is somewhat different from using either the proxy or private gateways discussed previously. Instead, the

SAN-to-SAN tunnel gateway connects via an E-port to a corresponding E-port on a Fibre Channel switch. This E-port connection is important in that it allows switches to provide network services, such login functions, routing, and name services, across the tunnel. Architecturally, this independence and interoperability of the two SANs is an important point. The two SANs on either side of the tunnel can be locally administered and can work as part of an extended distance fabric the same as locally connected switches.

Figure 12-5 shows the SAN-to-SAN tunnel with two systems and subsystems in both SANs. The switch in each SAN maintains all the same local information they usually do, but the switches have the additional capability to work together as a multielement fabric. This means it is possible to connect virtually any pair of entities in both SANs, as opposed to configuring particular ports for remote communications.

While Figure 12-5 shows a specific case of an extended fabric with two discrete SANs joined by a tunneling network, there are certainly more interesting configurations. For instance, it is also possible to build multipoint fabrics using multiple tunneling connections. For instance, a distributed SAN could be constructed out of several switches in geographically dispersed regions. Using such a topology would allow extended SANs to have redundant paths between geographically dispersed SANs.

Of course, the range of services in an extended fabric depends on the interoperability of the services implemented on the various switches. As interoperability has been a historical problem with Fibre Channel, it should not be assumed that an extended SAN can be built from switches from different vendors. In addition, there are other SAN functions, such as zoning, that are not well defined yet for multielement fabrics and may not work as well as desired for several years in extended fabrics.

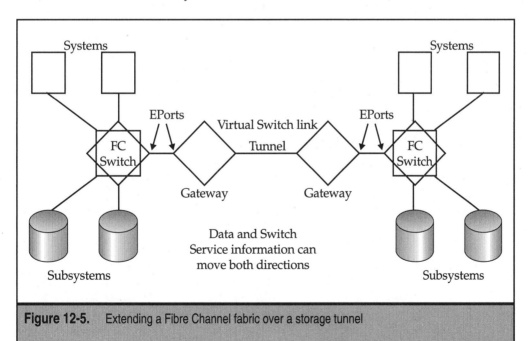

Figure 12-5. Extending a Fibre Channel fabric over a storage tunnel

iFCP as an Extended SAN Tunneling Standard

A proposed standard for an extended SAN-to-SAN tunnel between Fibre Channel networks is called iFCP. The general idea of iFCP is to provide a virtual Fibre Channel fabric to entities in a Fibre Channel network over Ethernet/IP networks.

iFCP uses the extended SAN tunneling model discussed previously, where the gateway function provides an F-port into a Fibre Channel SAN and forwards this information and all other information that commonly flows in a Fibre Channel SAN over the Ethernet/IP network to another gateway.

One of the more interesting aspects of the iFCP proposal is that it is based on an F-port implementation and not an E-port. This is a subtle but important point, as the use of an F-port assumes that SAN entities will connect directly to the iFCP gateway instead of a Fibre Channel switch. In general, Fibre Channel SANs are viewed today as the central entity in a storage infrastructure, and the Ethernet/IP network is perceived as the "external" network that has the potential to connect them together.

However, iFCP assumes that an Ethernet/IP network is the core network and that the iFCP-enabled SAN is a connectivity vehicle for integrating SAN storage into the Ethernet/IP core network, as pictured below:

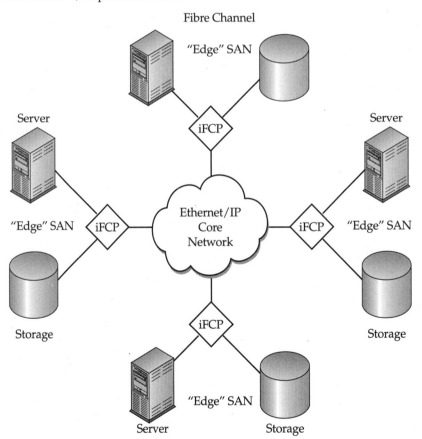

As it is with all the emerging standards involving Ethernet/IP storage, it is not clear what the future holds for iFCP, but there is more potential for iFCP than its use as a SAN-to-SAN gateway. It is certainly possible that end nodes could incorporate iFCP controller technology and participate in a storage network using the iFCP protocol to transmit data to both Ethernet/IP resident storage as well as Fibre Channel storage.

Tunneling Ethernet/TCP/IP Traffic Through a Fibre Channel Network

Although few see this as a highly likely scenario, Fibre Channel networks can be used for transporting Ethernet/TCP/IP traffic. This type of "inverted" storage tunnel involves similar protocol variations to those discussed previously with a few interesting twists that will be explored in the section that follows.

Selecting a Fibre Channel ULP for an Ethernet/TCP/IP Tunnel

One of the first problems with tunneling Ethernet/TCP/IP traffic over a Fibre Channel network is which upper-layer protocol to encapsulate the Ethernet/IP traffic in. The most popular Fibre Channel protocol, FCP, could certainly be used, but it might not be the best choice for a number of reasons. Designed as a backbone technology, Fibre Channel can carry nearly any kind of network traffic through its *link encapsulation* capabilities. For example, link aggregation provides the capabilities to develop a new tunneling protocol for Ethernet/TCP/IP traffic.

Selecting the Frame or Packet

Fibre Channel networks typically use larger frames (2K) than Ethernet/TCP/IP networks (1.5K). Therefore, it is not necessary to segment and reassemble Ethernet/TCP/IP frames that are tunneled through a Fibre Channel network. One way to provide a tunnel is to encapsulate the entire Ethernet frame in the gateway, like this:

Ethernet Frame
Fibre Channel Frame

Another option would be to extract the IP protocol packet from the Ethernet frame and place it in a Fibre Channel IP frame. In essence, this is not encapsulation nearly as much as it is protocol conversion from Ethernet to Fibre Channel. The process for doing this is shown graphically like so:

IP Data Payload
Fibre Channel Frame

It would probably not be very useful to operate above the IP level, such as by tunneling TCP traffic. Selecting TCP payloads from the Ethernet/TCP/IP network for transport across Fibre Channel networks would exclude all non-TCP traffic from passing through the tunnel, such as UDP-based NFS and SNMP. Excluding these other common but non-TCP types of traffic would probably not deliver the full functionality and network transparency required of a tunnel.

Tunneling over ATM with FC-BBW

Although it does not involve Ethernet/TCP/IP networking, we'll spend a little time discussing a Fibre Channel specification called FC-BBW, for Fibre Channel Backbone WAN. The primary idea of FC-BBW is to tunnel storage traffic over an ATM or SONET wide area networks. Although FC-BBW does not involve Ethernet or IP in its current form, the Fibre Channel standards group has been considering an additional specification for Ethernet and IP that will be incorporated in a future revision.

FC-BBW provides a point-to-point facility where Fibre Channel frames are directed through a special kind of Fibre Channel port, called a B-port. Traffic enters the FC-BBW gateway through the B-port and is transported to another SAN transparently. In essence, the B-port provides switch-to-switch connections over ATM and SONET networks. FC-BBW does not support Fibre Channel Loop networks.

Transporting Fibre Channel traffic over an ATM network poses some interesting challenges. The root of the problem stems from the fact that ATM networks have highly structured bandwidth allocation rules that must be followed. End nodes establish service "contracts" with switches within the ATM network for expected amounts of bandwidth. End nodes must not exceed the bandwidth limits they contracted for. The ATM switches in the network can, at their discretion, drop frames in order to keep steady traffic flows for all contracted sessions. To ensure consistent operations over an ATM network, end points often use a mechanism called *shaping* that buffers incoming data and releases it into the ATM network at the contracted transmission rate. While shaping solves many of the issues with "bursty" traffic in ATM networks, the shapers used in ATM equipment may not be large enough to handle the amount of bursty traffic storage can generate.

The ATM frame is 53 bytes long. Fiber Channel frames are 2,000 bytes long. It takes roughly 40 ATM frames to equal one Fibre Channel frame. That means the segmentation and reassembly of frames can be taxing. However, ATM has worked fairly well with other networks besides Fibre Channel, such as Ethernet, and it appears that ATM networks can support most storage applications except transaction processing.

The most difficult aspect of transporting storage traffic over an ATM network lies in managing all the various types of traffic being transported over the network. Storage traffic might not be the only consumer of the ATM network. In fact, ATM network operators like to have many subscribers to their networks to establish a broad income base for their services. Storage, as a heavyweight bandwidth consumer, can easily consume all of the available bandwidth of common ATM network deployments. This obviously creates some economic problems for either the network operators or the storage network operators who want to use the ATM network. ATM network operators probably cannot generate as much revenue from one or two storage customers as they can from hundreds of voice and data customers.

So it is likely that storage traffic will coexist on the ATM network along with other types of traffic that may have varying loads over time. That makes it rather difficult to predict the stability of the ATM network for storage traffic. For instance, if video network loads increase, switches could potentially become overburdened, with the result being more dropped cells. While the video customers might not notice a few dropped cells from time to time, the storage customers might see reduced network bandwidth, as a single dropped 53-byte cell would require Fibre Channel error correction for a 2,000 byte frame. It's not so much a matter of the ATM technology being inadequate, but a case where storage traffic exceeds the expectations of the ATM network managers.

Tunneling over DWDM Networks

Another variation of storage tunneling is to move Fibre Channel traffic over dense wavelength division multiplexing (DWDM) networks. DWDM is a relatively recent networking technology designed primarily to take advantage of the available unused fiber optic cabling that exists in many urban areas. Similar to ATM, DWDM storage tunneling does not use Ethernet/TCP/IP networks, but it needs to be mentioned as a tunneling technology.

In essence, companies have been installing fiber optic cabling for many years with the expectation that it would be needed at some point in the future. Unfortunately, there have not been economical ways that utilize this fiber cabling to its full potential. That's where DWDM comes in. Designed as a tunneling facility, DWDM can transport virtually any kind of network traffic, including high-speed networks such as Fibre Channel and Gigabit Ethernet.

The general idea of storage tunneling over DWDM is to encapsulate the entire Fibre Channel frame within DWDM protocol data units. The DWDM service would provide point-to-point service for two Fibre Channel networks. The DWDM network would be completely transparent to the Fibre Channel entities, which would be responsible for all error correction and flow control. It is not expected that any segmentation and reassembly would be needed for tunneling Fibre Channel traffic over DWDM networks.

Operating as a point-to-point network, a Fibre Channel network that uses DWDM tunneling could be established between any two types of Fibre Channel ports. Several variations are possible:

▼   Point-to-point links between pairs of N/NL-ports in system HBAs and subsystem controllers

■   Fabric links between N/NL-ports and F-ports in switches

■   Interswitch links between E-ports in switches

■   Public loop links between an FL-port in a switch and a hub

▲   Private loop links between a hub and an L-port

At some point in the future, DWDM may allow multipoint connectivity, which would allow Fibre Channel frames to be routed over a virtual *multielement* Fibre Channel mesh fabric.

NATIVE ETHERNET/TCP/IP STORAGE NETWORKS

While storage tunneling is interesting to many, the ability to run storing and protocols natively, or without encapsulation, on Ethernet/TCP/IP networks is garnering a fair amount of attention in the industry. In general, the requirements for storage tunneling and native Ethernet/TCP/IP storage networks are similar; however, there are also some significant differences.

The primary difference between tunneling and native storage over Ethernet/TCP/IP is the fact that Ethernet/TCP/IP protocols do not run in the storage end nodes in a tunneling scenario. On the other hand, Ethernet/TCP/IP protocols must run in the storage end nodes for a native Ethernet/TCP/IP storage network. On the surface, this might not seem like such a significant change, but in fact it is an enormous change that requires a great deal of thought and technology development.

While it may not be necessary to provide error recovery and flow control within a storage tunnel, it definitely is a requirement for native Ethernet/TCP/IP storage. That means that some of the implementation details that are not required of a tunnel must be thought out thoroughly for any native Ethernet/TCP/IP storage network.

Before launching into the protocol story, we'll first try to define the anticipated environment and characteristics of a native Ethernet/TCP/IP storage network. In general it is expected that Ethernet/TCP/IP storage networks will have a high-speed local component and an optional slower-speed wide area component.

The Local Native Storage Network

A local native Ethernet/TCP/IP storage network is composed of Ethernet network interface cards (NICs), Ethernet network cabling, switches, hubs and routers, and all the software necessary to make it all work. Storage I/O is typically very fast and requires low latency. Therefore, if Ethernet/TCP/IP storage networks are going to work well, they need to use high-speed and low-latency Ethernet/TCP/IP technologies. The transmission rate of a 100 megabit Ethernet link is approximately one-tenth the speed of a Fibre Channel network or ultra SCSI bus. For that reason, it is anticipated that local native storage networks will be based on Gigabit Ethernet.

The Optional Wide Area Native Storage Network

The optional wide area native storage network can be constructed from many types of physical network components, including IP network routers as well as interface equipment to ATM and SONET backbone networks. There are no assumed performance minimums for the wide area component, but obviously implementations of storage networks over wide area networks need to take performance into consideration.

While the wide area component is not required to have a native TCP/IP storage network, it is anticipated that this will become commonplace in the future because wide area storage connectivity is seen as one of the driving forces behind Ethernet/TCP/IP storage in the first place.

Although native TCP/IP storage networks are anticipated, there is no expectation for systems and storage subsystems to be connected directly to a wide area network. It is certainly possible for storage products to incorporate their own IP wide area network connection capability, but it is expected that networking equipment will assume the responsibility for providing wide area transport. For instance, it is likely that host bus adapters and subsystem controllers will incorporate Gigabit Ethernet technology and that IP routers will be used to transport storage traffic over the IP wide area network.

Characteristics of Gigabit Ethernet for Storage Wiring

The physical components of Gigabit Ethernet are based on those used for Fibre Channel. Its error rate is the same low bit error rate of 10^{-12}. Gigabit Ethernet incorporates either full- or half-duplex transmissions. The capability to use half-duplex transmissions is for compatibility with the existing Ethernet standard; otherwise, full-duplex transmissions are assumed for native Gigabit Ethernet storage networks. In general, Gigabit Ethernet, like Fibre Channel, will use fiber optic cabling, but it also has the ability to use copper cabling. Gigabit Ethernet and Fibre Channel both use the same encoding method of 8B/10B, which transmits 10 bits of data over the network for every eight bits of information shipped.

Traditional Ethernet does not have much of a flow control mechanism. Gigabit Ethernet added that capability with the *pause* function. Pause lets a receiver on a link signal to the sender that it is running low on buffer memory to store incoming data transmissions. When the sending station receives a pause, it completes its current transmission operation and waits for another pause command from the receiver before it starts sending data again. Using pause, a single data link should not be the cause of dropped frames. In some respects, Gigabit Ethernet's pause is a more straightforward flow control method than Fibre Channel's credit buffers. Whereas credit buffers must always be accounted for in Fibre Channel transmission, pause is only used when it is needed and therefore requires less overhead from the controllers that implement it.

One of the main differences between Gigabit Ethernet and Fibre Channel is the actual transmission rates of the networks. Whereas Fibre Channel transmits at 850 Mb/sec., Gigabit Ethernet transmits at 1 Gb/sec. By virtue of its heritage in Ethernet technology, Gigabit Ethernet inherits a few interesting capabilities, such as link aggregation, which allows multiple physical links to be used as a single link in terms of sending and receiving data over the network. This capability might not be so critical for Gigabit Ethernet, but it could allow 100Base-T equipment to be used for storage transmissions to achieve an aggregate transmission rate of 200 to 400 Mb/sec.

Latency Issues in Ethernet/TCP/IP Networks

One of the weaknesses Ethernet/TCP/IP has for storage networking is longer latency. This added latency comes from two sources: the first is protocol processing latency in end node systems (and subsystems), and the second is switch latency. In the sections that follow, the shortcomings of TCP processing are discussed at length, but for now it is enough to know that TCP/IP processing adds considerable latency to I/O path processing.

Several years ago, several Ethernet switching companies developed cut-through switching and attempted to highlight this in their marketing message. While the technology certainly worked, it was not that big a deal to most customers because there weren't many applications that needed cut-through switches. So cut-through switching dropped out of favor in the Ethernet/TCP/IP industry.

Of course, the situation today is different if Gigabit Ethernet networks are going to be considered for native storage networks. In general, Gigabit Ethernet switches have not been designed with the same low latency specifications as Fibre Channel switches. It's certainly not a case where the Ethernet switch manufacturers can't do it—it's just that they haven't done it yet.

Characteristics of the TCP/IP Protocol Suite

Wiring is made from both physical and logical components. In the case of Ethernet/TCP/IP networks, the TCP/IP protocol suite provides most of the logical management and control of data transmissions for the network. Where native storage networks are concerned, the TCP/IP protocol does not have any particular advantages compared to Fibre Channel protocol functions, although TCP/IP addressing may be an advantage for transmitting storage data over wide area networks.

VLANs

The capability to segregate traffic between storage and servers is an important application for storage networks. Ethernet networks do not have zones, per se, but they do have virtual LANs, otherwise known as VLANs.

VLANs are used to segregate access and traffic between switches in Ethernet networks. The implementation of VLANs involves extending the length of the standard Ethernet frame by four bytes. This means that Ethernet networking equipment built for VLANs has to be "VLAN aware" and able to process extended-length frames. In general that refers to switches, but networking adapters can also be VLAN aware and developed to support application-specific requirements. Therefore, the possibility exists to develop VLAN-aware adapters for storage networking that have the capability to assign tags to certain storage applications.

VLAN Membership

End nodes typically are assigned to VLANs by the switch port they are connected to, by their IP addresses, by the protocols they use, or by just about any other attribute that a switch can determine from the incoming frame. In most implementations, VLAN membership is determined by the switch port used.

VLAN Tags

The additional four bytes in a VLAN frame are used to form a VLAN tag. The VLAN tag identifies the VLAN, or VLANs that an end node belongs to. When end nodes send frames into a switch that supports VLAN tagging, the switch determines which VLANs the end node belongs to and appends the tag to the Ethernet frame before forwarding the frame to the next switch in the network.

When the next switch receives the VLAN frame, it reads the tag and the destination address of the frame. If the destination address is for an end node connected to the switch, it looks to see if that end node is a member of the VLAN. If it is, the switch forwards the frame to the destination node after stripping off the VLAN tag. If the destination address is for an end node connected to another switch, this switch forwards it on to another switch, keeping the VLAN tag in the frame.

If in the rare case when an end node is VLAN aware, the switch does not remove the VLAN tag from the frame when it forwards it to the end node. The end node reads the frame to help determine how it should process it.

A Comparison of VLANs and Zoning in Fibre Channel Networks

VLANs are roughly equivalent to Fibre Channel zoning, but they are different. The section that follows compares the two technologies. Other path segregation techniques such as LUN masking or subsystem zoning are not included in this discussion because they are not impacted by the wiring used, as they are implemented in end node equipment and have little to do with protocols.

The most important difference between VLAN tagging and zoning is the presence of the tag itself, which carries with it the notion that multiple switches in the network will all have the same VLANs identified and configured. This universality of the VLAN function is a by-product of VLAN being a defined industry standard. Fibre Channel zoning is not yet a standard, and therefore there are no common methods for associating zone membership within frames that are transmitted through Fibre Channel fabrics. Notice that the switch's internal data structure to support VLANs is not an issue; as long as a switch can process VLAN tags correctly, it can use whatever internal data structure it wants to.

VLAN tags can also be used to assign priorities to network transmissions. While prioritization schemes cannot solve problems for networks that are chronically overloaded, they can help provide consistent service levels for the highest-priority applications during short-term peak network loads.

In addition to its standard base, a VLAN has the capability to determine membership from information within the frame itself. While parsing frames at gigabit speeds may not be the best way to achieve fantastic performance, the possibility exists to assign frames to VLANs according to the application that generates them. In storage terms, this could effectively be used to restrict access to certain devices by certain applications. For example, a tape library could be placed on its own VLAN and have its access restricted to tape

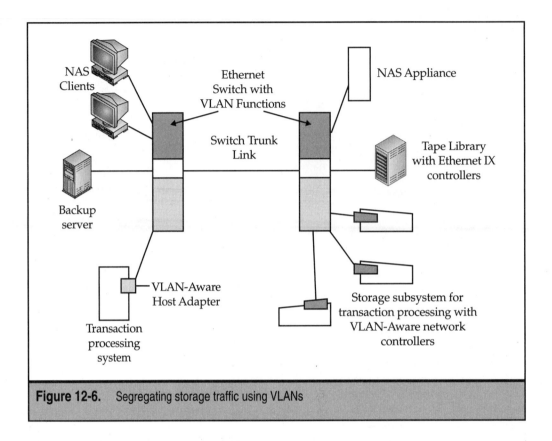

Figure 12-6. Segregating storage traffic using VLANs

backup applications. An application-oriented VLAN, including storage applications, is shown in Figure 12-6. This drawing shows VLANs that are being used for segregating NAS traffic, backup, and a transaction processing system. The transaction processing system in this figure is using a VLAN-aware adapter.

The Performance "Gotcha!" of Processing TCP Algorithms

The main issue with native Ethernet/TCP/IP storage networks is how to handle any TCP processing that may be required. It appears that TCP is becoming the de facto standard by virtue of its selection for the iSCSI protocol. While iSCSI is discussed later, we will now take a look at TCP and its anticipated impact on storage I/O.

TCP was developed to solve problems in unreliable networks many years ago. In general, the processing capabilities of the computers connected to these networks far exceeded the capability of the network to deliver data. In other words, processor cycles were relatively cheap compared to network bandwidth. As a result, much of the error recovery and flow control capabilities of TCP were developed as algorithms that run as software processes in host systems. These TCP algorithms include calculating the proper size of the TCP segments sent and received and calculating the checksum values for data transfers. In addition, TCP processes must also make several memory copies of data as it passes through the protocol stack, which adds latency and impacts performance. Viewed one transmission at a time, these operations may not seem so horrendous, but when one considers the speed of networks today, and the amount of traffic that is moved, the cumulative effect of the TCP overhead becomes extremely problematic.

Even on a microscopic level, TCP processing can have a severe impact on transaction I/O performance. It is not clear what the ramifications would be of trying to transmit transaction data over TCP, but the results are not likely to be favorable. As a rule of thumb, one can approximate that for each bit of data transferred, a processor instruction is needed to process the TCP algorithms that accompany it.

So, if we choose Gigabit Ethernet as a reference point, it means systems and storage subsystems will need to dedicate a gigahertz CPU in their systems for the sole purpose of processing the TCP protocol. When one realizes that an entire processor can be devoted to handling network transmissions in a dual-processor system, it is clear that there is a serious problem brewing.

To get a perspective on the situation, we'll compare anticipated processor and memory performance with network performance. Processors tend to double their capabilities every three years, according to Moore's law. If one assumes that today's processors are capable of delivering 1,000 mips (million instructions per second), in three years they should be able to produce approximately 3,000 mips.

Unfortunately, system memory performance is expected to be mostly flat over the next several years. As TCP stack protocol processing typically makes two or three copies of data as it is passed from the network to the application, the performance improvements of the processors will be compromised by the lack of improved memory response. In other words, the TCP processing capability of the CPUs does not scale linearly but is dragged down by memory performance. Again, two or three memory copies do not seem like much, but the performance effect is amplified by the relatively large amount of traffic that gigabit-speed networks support.

But for now let's be generous and assume that memory performance doesn't impose any performance constraints and that TCP protocol processing can scale linearly with the clock rate of the CPU. That would mean that in two years, a common system CPU would be capable of processing the protocol stacks for three-gigabit network links.

That's not too bad, but in three years time, 10 Gigabit Ethernet will be coming to market and instead of having a scenario where a single CPU can manage a single data link, it will take the processing power of three CPUs to manage the TCP processing for a single data link. In fact, when one factors in the lack of memory performance and the problem of coordinating TCP processing among multiple processors in a system; it could easily take a four-processor system just to handle the communications of a single 10 Gigabit Ethernet link! This situation is pictured in Figure 12-7, which shows the estimated allocation of processor cycles relative to the network bandwidth of data links for Gigabit and 10 Gigabit Ethernet networks.

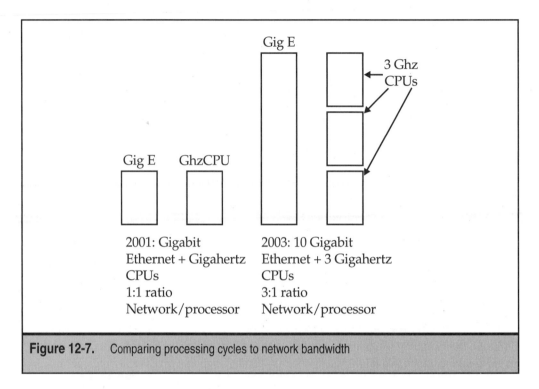

Figure 12-7.   Comparing processing cycles to network bandwidth

The processing concerns with TCP apply to more than host systems in native Ethernet/TCP/IP storage networks. Storage subsystems in these networks must also implement the TCP/IP stack, something they are not equipped to do with their current controller architectures. Therefore, a new type of Ethernet/TCP/IP storage I/O controller needs to be developed that has adequate performance for supporting the broad range of applications expected of storage. This could be done with standard CPU processors, such as the Power PC or the Pentium.

It is probably not necessary to implement native Ethernet/TCP/IP storage interfaces for storage devices like disk drives. Just as many Fibre Channel storage subsystems have external Fibre Channel ports with internal SCSI disk drives, it is most likely that native Ethernet/TCP/IP storage networks will use SCSI and Fibre Channel disk drives as subsystem components.

Network Protocol Processors

So, it looks like we are headed for a major power shortage in the ability to handle Ethernet/TCP/IP network communications in a relatively short period of time. It would appear that there are three possible solutions to this problem:

▼ Don't deploy 10 Gigabit Ethernet.

■ Stop using TCP and replace it with other protocols.

▲ Reduce the overhead of processing TCP.

The first solution—"don't deploy Gigabit Ethernet"—violates the laws of commerce and progress. The second solution—"stop using TCP"—violates the laws of compatibility. That leaves the third option to reduce the overhead of processing TCP as the only viable option for the storage network industry. Not only that, but opportunities like this tend to inspire entrepreneurs to start companies that try to solve them.

Saved by the Network Protocol Processor

In response to the need for more efficient TCP processing, several companies have started development efforts to create specialized Ethernet/TCP/IP protocol processors that would place the burden of TCP processing on network interface cards or storage I/O controllers, as opposed to the system CPU.

The concept of a network protocol processor is hardly new. Special Ethernet network interface cards called TCP/IP offload adapters have had the capability to process IP checksums for several years. These products work by processing the checksum data to determine if the incoming frame is valid. Upon verifying the integrity of the frame, the TCP/IP offload adapters transfer the remaining protocol information to the host system to complete the TCP/IP stack functions and give the payload to the application.

So, in order to meet the TCP processing demands of gigabit-speed networks, specialized network protocol processing chips are being developed that accelerate TCP processing. Used in network interface cards, Ethernet/TCP/IP host bus adapters, and storage subsystem controllers such as TCP accelerators effectively minimize the burden of protocol processing on system CPUs.

In general, most TCP/IP hardware acceleration techniques work by sharing the workload between an adapter and the host processor. As the highest-layer protocol in the IP stack, TCP has to be able to direct data to the proper application port. There is no easy way to do that if the TCP/IP processing functions are performed entirely on a network interface card.

The situation is somewhat different, however, for native Ethernet/TCP/IP storage networks. The complete TCP/IP stack used for storage transfers can be processed in an adapter because the application for storage traffic can be a known, higher-level storage I/O device driver. The data delivered by a native Ethernet/TCP/IP storage network protocol processor is not general-purpose application data, but instead is a very specific type of storage data such as a SCSI command descriptor block (CDB).

This capability to process the complete TCP/IP stack in an adapter can generate a significant performance improvement over processing it on a system CPU. Not only is the processing overhead removed from the system, but the multiple copies of protocol data in system memory can also be avoided. Avoiding the memory copy functions in the host system is known as "zero copy" processing.

There will likely be several different varieties of storage network protocol processor in the market, just as there are several choices for Fibre Channel and SCSI chipsets now. These products are likely to be specialized ASIC designs that are integrated into system and storage I/O controller chipsets.

iSCSI

Today, the storage protocol for native Ethernet/TCP/IP storage networks with the most momentum in the industry is called iSCSI, which is designed to be transported over Ethernet/TCP/IP networks as a payload in TCP. The iSCSI protocol uses the existing serial SCSI standard, just as the Fibre Channel FCP protocol does, but iSCSI and Fibre Channel transmissions are considerably different. For starters, FCP was designed as an upper-layer protocol for Fibre Channel networks and is tightly integrated to work with lower-level network functions.

The iSCSI protocol, on the other hand, is being developed to use the existing, entrenched transfer mechanism provided by TCP. The processes of creating the data transmissions in TCP and Fibre Channel are quite a bit different. So, although the application data may be very closely related, the iSCSI and FCP protocols themselves are not expected to be compatible.

To understand this completely, one needs to understand the nature of TCP transmissions. TCP is a byte stream protocol, which means that it is not so much concerned with transmitting discrete frames of data as it is with properly ordering data that is being transferred to applications. TCP creates 64KB segments for each application that uses its services. It receives data from an upper-level application and prepares it for network transmission over the network.

It helps to think about TCP's heritage as the transfer mechanism for the old Internet. In the old Internet, processing power was relatively cheap, and network bandwidth and reliability were more scarce. TCP managed the entire process for a system that needed to send and receive data on the network. So TCP creates segments for multiple applications and hands them off to IP for transport across the network. On the receiving end, IP transfers the byte stream data back to TCP, which transfers it up to the application by its port identifier. As there can be many different types of applications and networks involved in the transfer of TCP data and as network errors can occur, TCP has the capability to correctly assemble all the data it receives in the proper order before handing it up to its application.

TCP's byte stream approach poses some potential problems for storage traffic because storage typically works with instructions of a specific length, not byte streams. While TCP delivers data in order, it does not deliver data as discrete storage commands. TCP was developed to stop and restart transmissions from the point errors occur. Using byte stream data transfers, there is no correlation of what TCP delivers with the established data formats storage equipment requires. When network traffic levels are low enough, this is not expected to be much of a problem for storage. However, when network traffic levels are high, it could result in inefficient delivery of data, requiring additional buffering in receiving nodes, adding latency to storage transmissions. For instance, TCP could retransmit data that has already been processed correctly as a storage command by the receiving system.

In response to this problem, the iSCSI standards group is working on the incorporation of "markers" to signal the boundaries of iSCSI frames within a TCP byte stream. In theory, the TCP receive process would use these markers to identify discrete SCSI commands that should be buffered individually. The concept of markers is not new to the Ethernet/TCP/IP standards world. Markers have previously been incorporated as a standard MAC-layer function to support link aggregation. It is not yet clear that the larger TCP standards body will agree to accept markers as a change to TCP, as they could potentially affect all TCP processes.

It remains to be seen how this situation will be resolved. It is possible that the theoretical problem stated here will never develop into a pathological problem in practice. It may also be possible that the Internet TCP standards group will decide that markers are a good idea and incorporate them into the standard. It could also develop into a worst-case scenario where an early decision to use TCP-level encapsulation might hinder iSCSI implementations and products for many years; eventually leading to the development of some other Ethernet/IP storage protocol.

SUMMARY

This chapter looked at the various issues surrounding the deployment of Ethernet and TCP/IP networks as the wiring function for storing traffic. The potential of leveraging established skills and business involving Ethernet and TCP/IP is attractive to many.

Two major ideas were discussed. The first was tunneling Fibre Channel storage traffic over Ethernet and TCP/IP networks. The issues of addressing, error recovery, and flow control across multiple networks were discussed. In addition, the protocol options for tunneling at the Ethernet, IP, and TCP layers were analyzed. A new protocol for tunneling called iFCP has been proposed as an industry standard for storage tunneling. In addition to Ethernet and TCP/IP networks, storage tunnels over other networks were discussed, particularly tunneling over ATM using the FC-BBW standard as well as the potential for tunneling Fibre Channel traffic over DWDM metropolitan networks.

The second major topic of this chapter was using Ethernet and TCP/IP networks as the native wiring for storage traffic. While various potential options were looked at, most of this section involved an analysis of using the TCP-based iSCSI. A fair amount of time was spent looking at TCP issues, including its algorithm-heavy design and the technologies that will be needed to enable it to work for storage transmissions.

EXERCISES

1. Plot the addressing scheme for a storage tunnel over an Ethernet/IP network.
2. Does your addressing scheme in question #1 include TCP components? Why or why not?
3. Design a native Ethernet storage network (does not use IP).
4. Now design a tunneling approach for transporting storage traffic from the network you designed in question #3 across multiple networks.

CHAPTER 13

Wiring Storage Networks and Clusters with InfiniBand

This is the third and final chapter that discusses wiring technologies, specifically a new and fascinating wiring technology called *InfiniBand*. InfiniBand is a serial networking technology that is the heir apparent to the PCI bus used in most open systems servers today. As a system-level component designed into systems at low cost, the InfiniBand serial bus/network is expected to be one of the fastest-growing networking technologies ever introduced. The potential uses of InfiniBand go far beyond the realm of system buses as we know them today. InfiniBand is a wiring technology that could be used for all kinds of purposes, including carrying both filing and storing traffic. This chapter looks at InfiniBand technology and its expected capabilities and requirements.

One of the advanced capabilities of InfiniBand is to enable high-speed communications between systems and storage working together in clusters. Clustering is one of the most complex topics in computing technology today. In a nutshell, clustering is a way to aggregate the processing and storage capacity of several systems together as a single entity. Historically, clustering has mostly been concerned with systems operations. Storage, as a slave component of systems, was an important design component of those systems, but not necessarily of the *cluster*. However, the perspective on storage in clusters is changing as new I/O bus, processor, and software technologies are transforming storage into an independent and peer role in the cluster. Where clusters had been thought of strictly as server clusters in the past, they are now being seen as having the potential to incorporate intelligent storage subsystems in the mix.

This chapter begins with a brief overview of InfiniBand as a replacement for the PCI bus and then takes a long detour through the topic of clustering, with a special emphasis placed on storage in clusters. The chapter ends with a return to InfiniBand and discusses some of the more advanced topics related to InfiniBand-based storage I/O.

INFINIBAND AS A PCI REPLACEMENT

All technologies come to an end of their useful life and cease their production. Many reach a point where they can no longer keep up with changing requirements of the leading technology, and so they are maintained for a long time without innovation until they are unprofitable to manufacture and sell. This can take decades or it can take months, depending on the type of technology and how it is used.

In the next several years, we will witness the introduction of a new system I/O bus/network technology called InfiniBand that will start replacing the familiar and low-cost PCI bus used today in most systems. PCI will probably continue to live on in the industry for many years as a viable bus for all kinds of embedded information systems and appliances, but it will likely disappear quickly as part of the I/O path for servers in storage networks.

The InfiniBand System Network

InfiniBand is being developed as a new networking technology that integrates with system functions, allowing it to replace PCI's system bus function. The specifications for

InfiniBand are aggressive and clearly are designed to take advantage of advancements in networking technology. Some of the important characteristics and effects of InfiniBand as a bus replacement are these:

▼ InfiniBand is based on full-duplex, switched serial transmissions.

■ Transmission rates will begin at 2.5 GB/sec for one-way transmissions.

■ System expansion will be external, rather than through system "card cages."

■ System dimensions will shrink as internal expansion requirements disappear.

■ Hot swapping will be supported, in contrast to PCI.

■ Power will be provided independently for each external peripheral, as opposed to being provided through the system.

▲ Host I/O controller functions become network bridge functions.

Each of these characteristics is discussed in the following sections.

Serial Transmissions

Just as mainframe systems switched to serial transmissions over ESCON years ago, InfiniBand uses serial transmission techniques to provide much better distance and addressing capabilities than PCI's parallel bus design.

InfiniBand has an architectural component called the *host channel adapter,* or *HCA,* that will take the place of PCI bridge chips for connecting peripherals to the system bus. However, a single host channel adapter will be capable of supporting many more peripherals than is possible through a PCI controller. The following diagram shows an InfiniBand Host Channel Adapter controller attached to the system's internal CPU and memory bus:

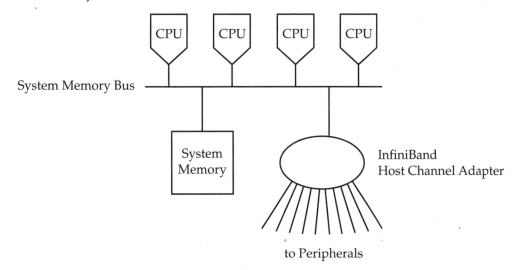

to Peripherals

Transmission Rates

InfiniBand is a full-duplex communication technology capable of link speeds of 2.5 GB/s in one direction. Full-duplex communications for the first version of InfiniBand are then 5 GB/s.

In addition, InfiniBand will support link aggregation to build multilink transmission groups that span 4 and 12 links providing 4× and 12× performance improvements. That means the one-way transmission speeds for InfiniBand could be 2.5 GB/sec, 10 GB/sec, and 30 GB/sec. These transmission rates are considerably faster than the 1 GB/sec maximum transmission rate of PCI.

External System Expansion

Peripherals have been installed inside systems for years as the easiest and most reliable way to add high-speed system-level functions. One of the reasons for this is that parallel bus signals cannot be easily transmitted over external cables. In fact, one of the reasons for replacing PCI with InfiniBand is the fact that system board dimensions were being compressed by the distance limitations of running PCI at faster and faster speeds. In other words, as the PCI bus speed increases, the length of the physical circuits as laid out on system boards decreases, making it much more difficult to design reliable, high-throughput, expandable systems. This fact alone is driving the adoption of InfiniBand—it is a necessity to building larger and faster server systems.

As a serial transmission technology, InfiniBand permits circuits and transmission distances far greater than with PCI, including the transmission of signals over external cables that extend from systems to peripherals. In other words, there is no reason to put expansion adapters inside the cabinet, where they cannot be accessed. This design element facilitates much simpler system configuration management by making all system components easier to access and visible.

System Dimensions Will Shrink

Without the need to support internal controllers that fit into large physical bus slots, InfiniBand-based systems will be smaller. Compact, powerful, six-centimeter-high rack-mounted systems will become common. Big server systems will be physically much smaller than servers built with PCI. A server system the size of a cereal box could be loaded with CPUs and InfiniBand host channel adapters and capable of controlling terabytes of storage in a SAN.

Hot Swapping

InfiniBand uses logical network addressing to establish connections between systems and peripherals instead of using a physical/electrical bus with all its shared data and address lines. This of course means it is easier to isolate connections with entities on the InfiniBand system network without screwing up the entire channel. One of the results of this is the ability to incorporate hot swapping devices. A device on an InfiniBand network is capable of being removed and reinserted without affecting the physical stability of other entities on the channel.

Power Will Be Provided Separately, Not Through the System

If peripherals are external, then they will also be powered by external power lines instead of being powered through the system bus. This could be perceived as an advantage because power capabilities can be added as a system grows and it is no longer necessary to purchase power supplies that are larger than necessary.

Unfortunately, this also means that external power cables for each peripheral attachment will be cumbersome and problematic. Consider having a power connection for all the components in a server today. If this is not solved through the ability to aggregate peripherals into a common power distribution system, it could force the installation of many new power outlets in systems rooms. Consider the situation of managing the physical placement of external controllers that may be able to be 15 meters from the system but are limited to being 2 to 3 meters from a power outlet.

The problem of power distribution may be overcome by using common power services for new, external InfiniBand controllers. This would be a type of external bay that provides power capacity and wiring connections across a backplane to the controllers that are plugged into it.

NOTE: Start planning for additional power receptacles for server rooms to accommodate the additional power line requirements of externally powered peripheral equipment.

Host I/O Controllers Become Network Gateway Functions

With the current system bus architectures, I/O controllers and adapters are located within the system case and provide connectivity to external networks and buses. With InfiniBand, however, I/O controllers can physically be placed anywhere in the network, embedded in systems and storage subsystems, and as independent entities in the network as shown in the following illustration:

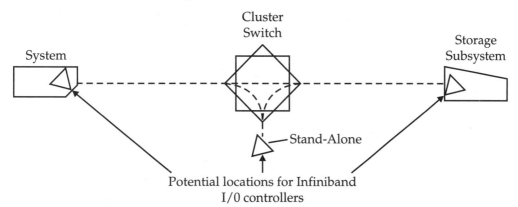

Architecturally, InfiniBand controllers behave more like gateways that span two different networks. In this case, the networks are the InfiniBand network and the external peripheral network such as Ethernet or a Fibre Channel SAN.

AN OVERVIEW OF CLUSTERING

While it is true that InfiniBand is being developed to replace the PCI system bus, the requirements for InfiniBand are much broader than those for a single system I/O bus. InfiniBand is also expected to facilitate the development of high-availability, high-performance, scalable clustering solutions. As a serial system networking technology, it follows that InfiniBand could be used to connect systems together very close to the system memory bus. InfiniBand's capability to link systems at this level is a big advantage over other networking technologies that connect through adapters and bridges, as shown in Figure 13-1.

Clustering has been viewed as a way to bring open systems computing capabilities up to the level of the redundancy, processing power, and storage capacity of mainframe systems. Whether or not those lofty goals can be met, there are plenty of other ways clusters will be used to create new computing solutions.

The main challenge in clustering is finding a way to combine systems together so that the aggregate benefits made by the cluster significantly outweigh the resources needed to make it all work together. It's like riding a bicycle built for two; you don't really get where you are going twice as fast just because two people are pedaling, and steering can be an interesting problem if both riders do not agree on the route. As it turns out, the more systems and storage there are to tie together in a cluster, the greater the management cost is as a percentage of the total aggregate resource.

The Market Context for Clustering

The following sections examine some of the dynamics of clustering technologies in the market.

Multiprocessor Systems

Clustering efficiency is related to the ability to scale multiprocessor stand-alone systems. In essence, clusters have to manage the same types of memory and process sharing problems as multiprocessing systems. As the number of CPUs increases, the system overhead of integrating them as a percentage of total CPU cycles also increases. The efficiency of a multiprocessor system design depends primarily on the operating system kernel responsible for scheduling all the work in the system and directing access to memory resources. The gap between Unix systems and PC systems is narrowing. Unix systems today can effectively use 64 processors in a single system, while the most recent advancements in PC systems software support up to 32 processors.

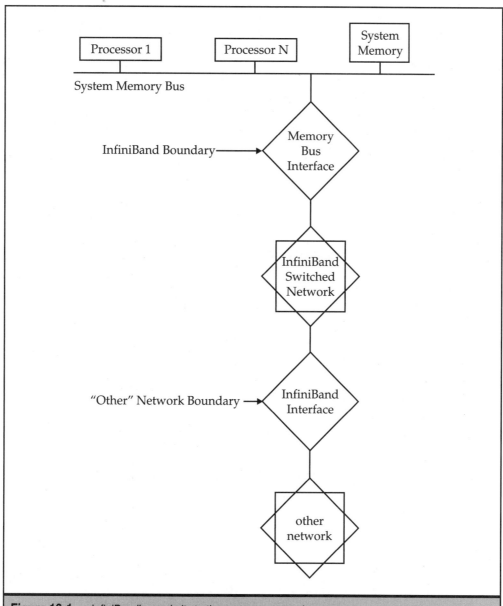

Figure 13-1.   InfiniBand's proximity to the system memory bus

But the operating system is certainly not the only variable. Systems hardware designs also have to be able to support the high-speed communications and chip capacities needed for the operating system to do its work. The integration of software and hardware in multiprocessor systems is a complex effort. Typically, the companies who succeed with multiprocessor systems are those companies with long-standing data center experience, including mainframe and midrange systems.

Similarities Between Clusters and Multiprocessor Systems

Clustering implementations have had similar market dynamics as those in multiprocessor systems, and the most successful clustering products have been those that were developed under one company's "roof." However, this has been changing as software vendors have created strong development partnerships to create viable cluster solutions. The most notable open systems software products include Oracle Parallel Server Database, Novell NetWare Cluster Services, and Microsoft Windows 2000 Datacenter Server.

Some of the most successful clustering products have been built for mainframe computing, including the Digital VAX cluster products and the IBM System 390 product family. This latter example is especially interesting, considering that for many years, IBM sold their huge monolithic mainframe systems arguing that clusters of smaller systems could not compete with single large multiprocessor systems. Eventually, cost and scalability issues forced IBM to change to a different processor technology base (CMOS instead of bipolar) and to broadly adopt a clustered approach to link these new processors.

A SAN Is a SAN Is a SAN. Isn't It?

The term "SAN," when used in the context of clustering technology, normally stands for "system area network." Even though system area networks came first, this is, after all, a storage networking book; and the term "SAN" in this chapter will continue to mean "storage area network," as it has throughout the book. The network that connects systems in a cluster will be referred to simply as the *cluster network*. Things get a little confusing when the network that connects the servers is the same one that connects the storage, but it is hoped that context will make things clear enough.

Why Clusters?

Clustering is a solution for higher availability, improved processing performance, and larger storage capacities. As applications grow, they tend to encounter problems in these areas that cannot be addressed by single systems. Some applications may only need one of these benefits, and others might need all three. The primary availability, performance, and storage benefits of clustering are discussed in the following sections.

Clustering for Availability

One of the advantages of clusters is a higher level of application availability. Applications typically are developed to run on a single system. This means that if something happens to the application's system, the application and its data may be unavailable. With a cluster system, the application can continue running on another system in the cluster, as shown in the following diagram:

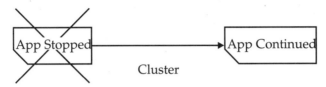

Availability requirements of Internet Web site servers are very challenging. The Internet is a 24 x 7 operating environment that demands an incredible amount of technology and systems administration effort to support it. Clustered computing is common throughout the Internet's infrastructure.

While the ability to realize application availability through clusters is an easy concept, as the saying goes: the devil is in the details. Some very difficult decisions need to be made in designing clusters, including establishing time-out parameters that determine whether or not a system in the cluster is still available. The methods used to determine system availability are grounded in the detailed characteristics of the cluster network.

Clustering for Processing Power

Another advantage commonly attributed to clustering is the capability to process more work in less time as the application and its data continue to grow. The idea is that a cluster of more than one machine ought to be able to finish the work faster than a single machine can. While this depends heavily on the type of application and the characteristics of the clustered systems, including the I/O load requirements, parallel processing in clusters can certainly deliver performance benefits.

This can certainly be seen by looking at transaction processing benchmarks. In general, the systems used in competitive benchmarks do not represent real-world implementations but instead are highly optimized for optimal benchmark results. Regardless, it is clear from reviewing the benchmark results that clustering technology can be very effective for transaction processing work. The Transaction Processing Performance Council TPC-C benchmarks for database performance are reported on the World Wide Web at **http://www.tpc.org**. Several types of transaction processing benchmarks are posted on this site, which lists the results by performance as well as the price-to-performance ratio. One could argue about the relevance of these benchmarks to actual production performance results, but they are interesting to peruse, especially the descriptions of the massive configurations used to achieve the latest results. Some of the cluster-configurations are quite large, including clusters of 24 systems.

Clustering for Storage Capacity and I/O Performance

Clusters also allow the amount of available storage to be expanded, by adding the raw storage capacity of the cluster members together. For instance, a stand-alone system with a maximum disk storage capacity of 10TB could be expected to support 20TB with two equal-sized members in a two-system cluster as shown here:

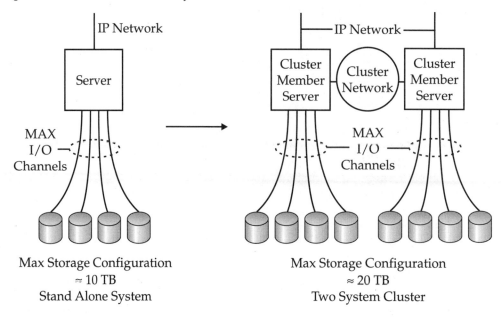

Max Storage Configuration
≈ 10 TB
Stand Alone System

Max Storage Configuration
≈ 20 TB
Two System Cluster

While the storage capacity is an important benefit, a related advantage of clusters is the ability to provide an additional system and its inherent I/O capabilities. For instance, if a large stand-alone server had four I/O channels accessing the data, two of them in a cluster would have eight I/O channels. This might not seem like a big deal, when you consider a transaction processing system that stores data across a large number of I/O channels, subsystems, and disk drives, the ability to aggregate I/O channels through clustering is an important advantage. The method used to access storage in a cluster is an interesting and extremely important design point for the cluster, which will be discussed in more detail in the following sections.

CLUSTER PROCESSES

We'll now start analyzing internal cluster operations in more depth. We'll begin by creating a two-node model for a cluster using NAS and SAN technologies and then expand the analysis into implementation of clustering concepts that would support our two-node cluster.

Creating a Two-Node Cluster with NAS and SAN Elements

NAS servers can be joined by clustering, just like any other pair of systems, and since this is a book about storage networking, we'll use a pair of NAS servers to discuss clustering operations. The I/O channel in our cluster example will be a SAN that connects the two NAS servers to two storage subsystems. For now, we won't worry about how the NAS systems access the storage; we'll discuss that later.

Figure 13-2 shows this cluster configuration with two NAS servers and two storage subsystems. The NAS systems achieve high availability through redundant connecting equipment including dual network interface cards for the Ethernet network and dual HBAs for the SAN. In addition, the storage subsystems are dual ported.

NOTE: Storage for clustered servers should be in external cabinets, not internal to servers. This simplifies connectivity and management of the cluster's storage resources. The multi-initiator support in Fibre Channel provides significant benefits for attaching multiple systems to clustered storage.

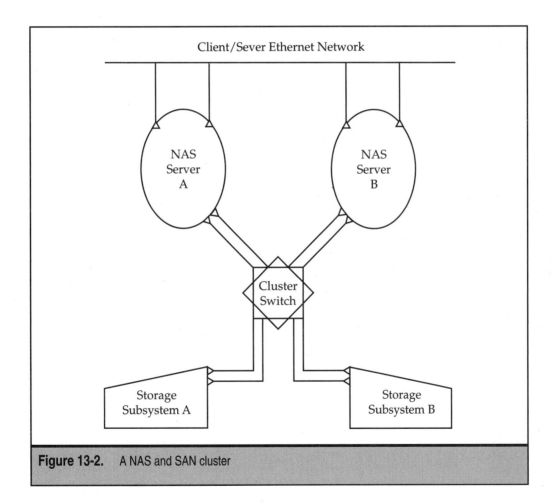

Figure 13-2.   A NAS and SAN cluster

Assumed Goals

The assumption used in this example is that the cluster is being used for optimal avail-ability and that the speed of recovery is of paramount importance. In general, that means that the data replication techniques discussed in Chapter 4 would not meet the requirement following a failover of one of the NAS servers.

Monitoring Cluster Status by Heartbeat

One of the fundamental components of a clustered system is the use of *heartbeat* messages between members of a cluster. The heartbeat message is a constant connection between systems that lets all members know that the other systems in the cluster are functioning normally. Heartbeat signals are typically lightweight (small) messages that take a mini-mum amount of system and network resources. They are the equivalent of the occasional "uh-huh" that people use in conversation with each other on the phone to let the other person know that they are there and (supposedly) listening.

There is a corresponding process in each cluster member that responds to the heart-beats that it receives from other members. More accurately, this process takes action if it does not receive an expected heartbeat from another member. If the expected heartbeat does not arrive, this process begins the process of moving the responsibility and workload of the failed member to other cluster systems.

For our two-member cluster, the heartbeat system is fairly simple. Each member sends a heartbeat to the other at regular, prescribed intervals. If there were more members in the cluster, however, the complexity increases considerably. Consider a cluster with five mem-bers instead of two. It might not be possible for all members to communicate with each other any more, so a new method must be employed. This could be done a number of dif-ferent ways, but it increases the complexity and the likelihood that something could go wrong. For instance, the members could be assigned to subgroups, and the subgroups could occasionally communicate through representatives.

There are many challenges to recognizing failed members. One of the primary problems is getting communications transmitted and received in the time required. In general, the tol-erances for heartbeats are not very big. If the goal is to have transparent failover capabilities, the cluster cannot afford to wait too long before determining that one of its members is down and assuming its work. The problem is that a heavily loaded cluster could have a large amount of work in communications queues waiting to be processed. If the sender and re-ceiver combined inject too much latency into the heartbeat delivery, the wrong decision could be made and a perfectly healthy member could be removed from the cluster.

So, in order to get the most reliable heartbeat transmissions, it may help to use a separate, isolated connection. In the case of our two-system NAS cluster, this could be accomplished with an Ethernet crossover cable that directly connects two intercluster network interface cards, as shown here:

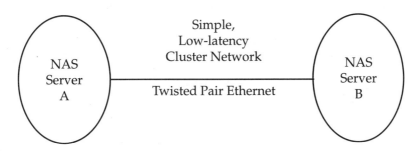

Although heartbeat messages are small, they need to be processed as a high-priority communication. Therefore, a network that can transmit heartbeats quickly over an uncongested link is a real advantage. This is one of the highlights of InfiniBand that will be discussed later.

Another potential problem with heartbeats is that a cluster member may be incapable of doing any work, but could still be sending and receiving heartbeats on the network. In other words, the failing member can still "look good" to the other cluster members, even though cluster clients may not be able to use it.

Failover Process

Once a failure has been identified, there has to be a way for another system to assume the responsibility for running the failed server's halted applications. The system that assumes responsibility for the application is referred to here as the *failover member*. The system that fails is referred to as the *downed member*. Notice that the relationship between downed members and failover members is not necessarily one-to-one. In other words, in a cluster of more than two members, all the other members of the cluster can each assume some of the workload of the downed member. This approach is shown is the following diagram:

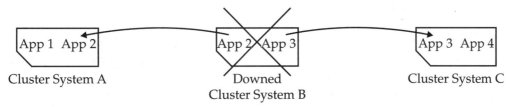

When it is apparent that a member is down, the other members in the cluster need to take action to remove the downed member from the cluster, the LAN, and the SAN. The downed member has to be removed from the cluster heartbeat pattern and any other intercluster processes.

Referring to our two-member NAS cluster, if member A fails, there are no other heartbeat processes to run on member B. The only heartbeat adjustment is to stop processing heartbeats. Member B then needs to prepare to take over the workload for member A.

Shared Storage in Clusters   For a failover member to take over for the downed member, it must be able to access any and all storage and data that the downed member was working with. There are two important points to consider:

▼   The failover member needs to have access to the downed member's data.

▲   Any data partially written when the failure occurred must be found and rolled back.

The first of these objects can be accomplished through the use of I/O pathing technology, but with some modifications for cluster scenarios. In this case, the pathing control in the failover member responds to the failover process instead of to a failure in an HBA. In the case of our two-member NAS cluster, the spare HBA in member B could already have an idle session established to member A's storage and data.

The second consideration regarding partially written data can be resolved with database and file system technology that treats all I/O operations as if they were a transaction. The basic idea is that the file system or database has a way of knowing whether an I/O operation has completed correctly by scanning a log file that keeps records of all I/O activities. These log files can be quickly read to determine what, if any, work needs to be done to fix mangled writes. If problems are found, they can be quickly corrected by changing the data back to the state it was in prior to when the write occurred.

Database Transaction Commitments   Database systems employ transaction commitment mechanisms that determine whether a transaction is completely written to all necessary parts of the database. As fairly complex systems, with many operations and multiple writes required for a single transaction, database developers understand the ugly consequences of having incomplete writes occur when a system unexpectedly tanks. To address this situation, database systems use internal handshaking between different parts of the database that decide jointly if the new transaction data is committed.

Database systems keep logs of every write operation performed during a transaction, so if something goes wrong, the process can be reconstructed or deconstructed, depending on the desires of the DBA (database administrator). One of the main job requirements of a DBA is the ability to understand his or her database's commitment mechanism and how to recover the database to a safe state following an unexpected failure. This process of *rolling back* transactions is one of the cornerstones of relational database technology. This is not something that needed to be invented for clusters necessarily, but it was needed for any database system that experiences a system crash during transaction operations.

Journaled and Log-Structured File Systems   Similarly, *journaled* file systems provide a way to identify and repair incomplete writes to a file system. The basic idea is that the file system maintains a journal file, or files, that track the status of write operations in the file system. For example, the journal could indicate that the data was written, but that pointers to the new data were not. In essence, a journaled file system has the capability to roll back incomplete file system writes.

The journal provides a nearly instantaneous way to check on the integrity of the file system. Without a journal, each directory and file entry needs to be checked against the file system's organizational data, which can take several minutes or even hours on large systems. This time frame is clearly not what people expect from a cluster implementation. Like database transaction commitment control, journaled file systems were not invented for clustering operations, but for individual systems that quickly need to recover from a failure.

Verifying Data Integrity   The point of the preceding discussions was to show that there are software methods for ensuring data integrity that can be implemented in clusters. The failover process in a cluster member can use them to verify that partially written data can be discovered and corrected without causing further problems. For this to happen, the failover member must be able to access the log files for the downed member's data prior to starting operations on it.

Assuming IP Addresses   One of the final tasks in the failover process is for the failover member to assume the IP address of the downed member. Once this is done, the failover member can begin processing service requests from cluster clients intended for the downed member. This process is shown here:

Client/Sever Ethernet Network

Data Access Designs in Clusters

Two fundamental data access methods are used to communicate between servers and storage in clusters:

▼ Shared nothing storage

▲ Shared everything storage

We'll examine each of these in the following sections.

Shared Nothing Storage   The *shared nothing* storage model isn't quite what it sounds like, as the whole idea of a cluster is to combine the resources of several systems into one entity. The term "shared nothing" refers to the fact that individual cluster members control their own resources and that access to them is managed through intercluster communications where requests are made from one cluster member to another.

The important elements in the shared nothing structure are the memory cache in each system and the storage subsystems they control. Figure 13-3 shows the relationships between the servers and storage in a two-system NAS cluster.

In the shared nothing cluster, when one of the cluster members wants to access data on one of the other cluster member's storage subsystems, it has to make a request for it over the cluster network. The member that receives the request does the work and sends it back to the requesting member. The process of servicing data between members in a shared nothing cluster is illustrated here:

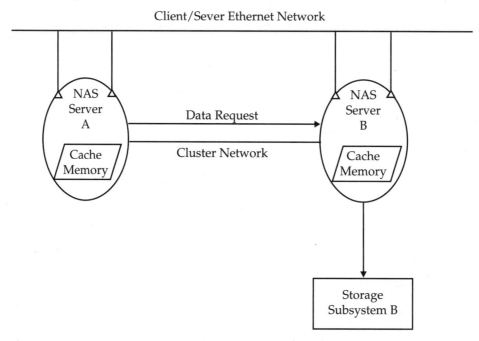

The primary advantage of the shared nothing approach is that data caching and data locking can be managed by individual members, as opposed to trying to work out the details of managing these processes among multiple systems. This makes the cluster operations somewhat simpler to understand and slightly more predictable. Not only that, but in a shared nothing cluster, some of the data access will be made by members onto their own storage resources. In that case, there is no cluster-associated overhead with accessing the data. For instance, using the two-member NAS cluster example, it seems likely that 50 percent of all accesses would have no intercluster access overhead.

Of course, the downside of a shared nothing cluster is that bottlenecks can occur within the cluster between cluster members. For instance, a member with an instantaneous heavy load of requests from other cluster members could become a bottleneck for

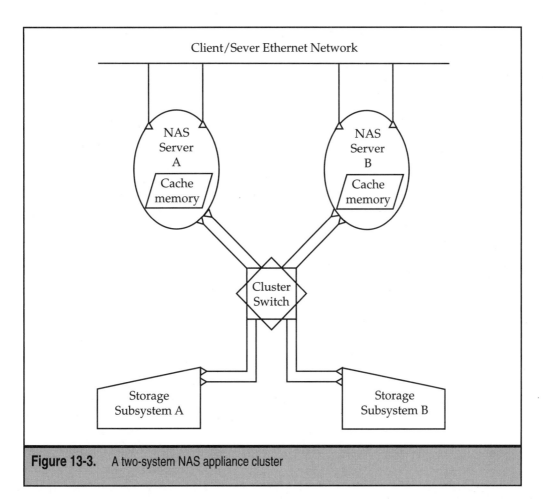

Figure 13-3.   A two-system NAS appliance cluster

all the other cluster members. Another weakness of the shared nothing cluster design is the resulting "private" filing system that each member has on its storage resources. This means that whenever a failover situation occurs, it is necessary for the failover member to access and mount the file system of the downed server.

Shared Everything Storage   The alternative data access method for clusters uses what is referred to as a *shared everything* approach, where all members of the cluster have access to all the storage resources. The most popular implementation of the shared everything approach is the Oracle Parallel Server technology for clustering Oracle databases. Figure 13-4 shows the relationship between systems and storage in a shared everything cluster.

   The primary advantage of the shared everything approach is that failover operations can commence quickly when a downed member has been identified. With immediate access to resources by other members in the cluster, the step for connecting to the downed member's storage is circumvented and data integrity checking can begin immediately.

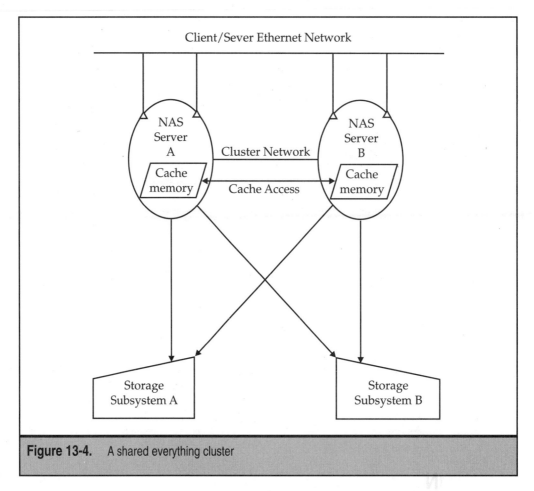

Figure 13-4. A shared everything cluster

However, there is no question that shared everything clusters are much more intricate systems than shared nothing clusters. To begin with, the tricky mechanisms of lock management must be dealt with. As any member can access any data, it is necessary for members to determine if other members have locks protecting data before accessing it. This can be dealt with several ways with various levels of difficulty. For example, the locks could be written to disks in the metadata for the data so that other members would see them before accessing the data, but then those locks would have to be cleared when members of the cluster were downed. This could be a real problem considering that there might not be any way of knowing which locks a downed server had made. Alternatively, there could be a centralized lock manager, which could be checked for all I/O operations. Such a mechanism could work but would require a lightweight intercluster locking protocol that would be an obvious risk as a cluster bottleneck.

Another difficult issue for shared everything clusters is how data written to cache from cluster members is made available to other cluster members and eventually flushed to storage. In essence, there needs to be some mechanism to ensure that data recently written by any of the cluster members is signaled somehow to other cluster members. It is not necessary to write all the data immediately, but it is necessary for other members to know if the blocks they expect to access are invalid.

This raises the concerns about how any members in the cluster can avoid accessing data that was partially written by a downed member. The answer again lies in the method of transaction logging used by cluster members. The difference here is that every member in a shared everything cluster has to perform logging on all the storage in the cluster. This could be done individually by each cluster member, or it could be done collectively into shared log files. If each member has its own individual log files, there is no contention for writing to the log and it is practically impossible for a single downed server to corrupt the log file when it fails. On the other hand, if the log file is shared, then it is very easy to locate it in storage to start the integrity check phase of the failover process.

Data Sharing with Intelligent Storage Subsystems   The management of writes, commitment processing, and rollbacks could potentially be enhanced through the use of an intelligent storage subsystem that functions more as a peer then a slave to cluster servers. Instead of transferring block data, a cluster server would write larger units of data that have a better chance of containing complete file updates or database transaction information in a single operation. In addition, such a "cluster-peer" storage subsystem would be able to maintain its own log files and cluster-aware processes to facilitate orderly failover processing. For example, a cluster-peer storage subsystem could be part of the heartbeat and health monitoring system in the cluster and report any systems that were maintaining their heartbeat signals but may have ceased sending and receiving data from the storage subsystem.

In addition, a cluster-peer storage subsystem could provide lock management for the cluster by identifying and releasing locks that were held by the downed system. This would require the implementation of new distributed locking protocols.

INFINIBAND IN CLUSTER NETWORKS

Figure 13-1 showed the relative proximity of InfiniBand to the system processor and memory core. This is an incredible system architecture advantage for InfiniBand compared with other networking technologies that might be used for clustering. But system architecture is only a part of the story. A successful cluster network technology has to have a successful *network* architecture to achieve the latency, flow control, and communications characteristics required.

Components of InfiniBand Networks

InfiniBand is designed as a switched fabric networking topology similar to Fibre Channel fabric networks and switched Ethernet networks. This is quite a radical departure from the previous bus architecture of PCI. The significance of a switched I/O fabric may not be known for several years, but it is bound to have a major impact on systems designs.

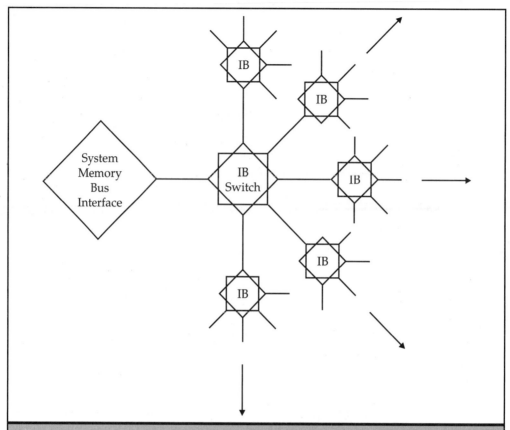

Figure 13-5. InfiniBand expands and extends the system interface.

Figure 13-5 shows how the InfiniBand network quickly expands the size and dimensions of the system interface.

Beyond having a switched topology, InfiniBand is made up of many other networking technologies. In the sections that follow, we'll discuss the various design concepts and specifications of InfiniBand.

Error Rates, Encoding, and Cabling

Similar to Fibre Channel and Gigabit Ethernet, InfiniBand includes both copper and fiber optic cables. Like Gigabit Ethernet, InfiniBand uses cabling and connector technology that is derived from those introduced by the Fibre Channel industry.

The error rates for Infiniband are the same as for Fibre Channel and Gigabit Ethernet: 10^{-12}. In addition, InfiniBand uses the same 8B/10B encoding scheme that Fibre Channel and Gigabit Ethernet do. That is, for every 8 bits of data that are sent, 10 bits are actually transmitted over the physical cabling.

Multiple Physical Lanes   The most interesting aspect of InfiniBand cabling is the support for new cabling technology that aggregates links together in physical *lanes,* of four and twelve cables. There are two variations on this concept; one for four-lane cabling and the other for twelve-lane cabling, called 4X wide and 12X wide respectively. In essence, these are equivalent to grouping four or twelve cables together for faster aggregate throughput speeds. However, 4X and 12X cables are *not* groups of 1X cables working together; instead, they are specially designed cables with connectors called MPO connectors, also known as MTP connectors.

All InfiniBand cabling is full duplex, meaning a 4X cable is made up of 4 transmit lanes and 4 receive lanes. Similarly, a 12X cable is constructed with 12 transmit lanes and 12 receive lanes. The MPO connector is designed with 12 physical link sockets. The 4X cabling uses a single MPO connector and uses sockets 0–3 for transmit lanes and socktes 8–11 for receive lanes. Sockets 4–7 are not used. The 12X cabling uses dual MPOs where one MPO is dedicated to transmit lanes and the other to receive lanes. The 4X and 12X MPO configurations are shown here:

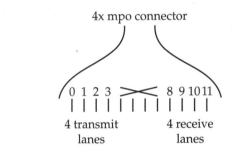

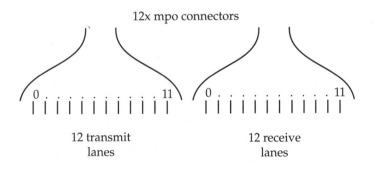

The copper equivalents of MPOs are specially designed connectors being developed for InfiniBand. For 4X copper cabling, the connector is referred to as the 8-pair MicroGigaCN connector, and the 12X copper cables will use a 24-pair MicroGigaCN connector. The connectors for 4X and especially 12X cabling are relatively large compared to their sibling 1X varieties. It is not clear if this will present difficulties in implementing these higher-density connectors, but it is likely that host channel adapters using 12X connectors could cause difficulties for systems and subsystem manufacturers trying to miniaturize the physical dimensions of their products. For that reason, InfiniBand may need to adopt higher line speed technologies, similar to 10 Gigabit Ethernet, in order to fit the changing requirements of data center operations.

The 4X and 12X cabling form a single link from the perspective of higher-level network control and management functions. In other words, the physical lanes in 4X and 12X cables are treated as a single unified entity and are not addressed and managed separately.

The distance capabilities of InfiniBand cabling links are summarized in the following table:

Cable Type	Wavelength	Max Distance
Copper	NA	17 meters
1X 50 micron	850nm	250 meters
1X 62.5 micron	850nm	125 meters
1X 9 micron	1,300nm	10,000 meters
4X copper, 8 pair MicroGigaCN	NA	TBD* ~ 10 meters
4X 50 micron single MPO	850nm	125 meters
4X 62.5 micron single MPO	850nm	75 meters
12X copper, 24 pair MicrogigaCN	NA	TBD* ~10 meters
12X 50 micron single MPO	850nm	125 meters
12X 62.5 micron single MPO	850nm	75 meters

* Copper distances may differ as the technology is introduced.

Another option for InfiniBand that is not typically thought of for Fibre Channel or Ethernet is the capability to connect through a backplane or system board. In fact, because PCI was most often implemented on these types of printed circuits, it is quite likely that one of the most common connecting methods for InfiniBand will be circuit boards. This is not exactly what one thinks of in thinking about a network.

Virtual Lanes   As if the terminology for new technology isn't confusing enough, the developers of InfiniBand incorporated a method of segmenting bandwidth on physical links called *virtual lanes*. Not to be confused with the physical lanes discussed previously, logical lanes can subdivide the bandwidth on any link to be used by one or more consumers. InfiniBand allows configurations consisting of 1, 2, 4, 8, and 15 virtual lanes. Virtual lane 15 (VL15) is reserved for use by InfiniBand subnetwork management. Buffering and flow control mechanisms in InfiniBand are applied at the virtual lane level and are managed independently for each virtual lane. VL 15, however, as a management layer is not subject to flow control.

One of the advantages of virtual lanes is the capability for any link to support multiple communication sessions concurrently. This means that an end node can be communicating at the same time with several different end nodes having completely different transfer characteristics, without having to worry about traffic being blocked in the link. In other words, virtual lanes have the potential to circumvent head of line blocking. This is important for InfiniBand, because it is used as a system channel and may need to support relatively slow legacy devices at the same time it has to support fast, low-latency storage subsystem and cluster heartbeat communications.

Switches and Routers   Switches and routers in InfiniBand networks assume more or less the same roles they do in Ethernet/TCP/IP networks. Switches provide fast packet forwarding within a single physical network, while routers provide packet forwarding across multiple physical networks. Switches are transparent to normal network operations except for when they are accessed for services using reserved, well-known port addresses, similar to Fibre Channel networks.

Switches and routers do not have to support 4X and 12X links, nor do they have to support virtual lanes. It is hard to imagine how a switch would be designed that could accommodate all three speed links—1X, 4X, and 12X—within the same physical form factor. While virtual lanes do appear to have advantages for establishing priorities and circumventing blocking scenarios, they also require more processing and memory resources to manage switch port buffers. It is possible that these advanced capabilities will not be implemented much in actual InfiniBand products, just as Class 1 service in Fibre Channel has been mostly a theoretical exercise for the Fibre Channel standards organization.

Partitioning   Just as Fibre Channel networks can have zones and Ethernet networks can have VLANs, InfiniBand has *partitions*. The mechanism to establish and manage partitions is different than it is for zones and VLANs, but the end result is mostly the same. Partitioning systems and subsystems from each other is a way to avoid potential access conflicts, establish management areas, and facilitate the addition of new equipment into the network in a smooth, structured, and nonintrusive manner.

End Nodes in InfiniBand Networks

Nodes in InfiniBand networks are considered to be systems, I/O devices, or routers. While I/O devices can be simple peripherals such as a scanner or CD-ROM drive, in the descriptions here I/O units are considered to be storage subsystems. While InfiniBand routers might be interesting for many network configurations, they are not likely to be important components of cluster networks.

Sometimes technologies define familiar terms with specific meanings and architectural roles. For example, Fibre Channel "ports" and their varied definitions are an example of using the familiar term "ports" and giving it an architectural meaning. Similarly, InfiniBand uses the term "node" to refer to systems (processor nodes), subsystems (I/O nodes), as well as the adapters and controllers inside them. From the InfiniBand perspective, *end nodes* incorporate a new type of network adapter called a *channel adapter*. A channel adapter in an InfiniBand network can have multiple ports for connecting to the InfiniBand networks. When a system or subsystem has multiple channel adapters, it presents multiple end nodes to the InfiniBand network. The hierarchy of nodes in an InfiniBand system is illustrated here:

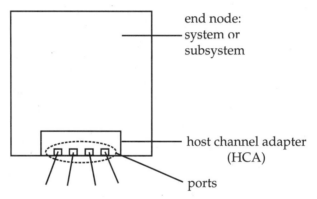

InfiniBand Consumer Processes   Processor and I/O nodes in InfiniBand networks can have many applications and systems functions transmitting data through the cluster network to storage subsystems. In the parlance of InfiniBand, these end node system and storage processes are called *consumers*. Most consumers run in host systems, but they also run in storage devices and subsystems as controller processes.

Consumers in InfiniBand networks take on a slightly different role than applications do in other networking technologies. Applications in traditional networks communicate using high-level system interfaces that pass transmissions through multilevel protocol stacks that provide several standard abstraction layers for communication functions.

InfiniBand consumer processes, on the other hand, are tightly integrated with the communications functions in the network. That is not to say that InfiniBand does not use abstraction, because it does, but it is designed to bypass the multiple layered protocol stacks of traditional networks and all their associated processing overhead.

While most legacy applications in InfiniBand networks will use system services as their interface to the I/O path, InfiniBand-oriented applications in the future will be able to bypass these familiar interfaces and function on a peer level with such low-level system software as network device drivers. While this approach has powerful architectural benefits, they are only architectural and not real until they are developed and implemented in products. Due to the complexity involved, it is most likely that InfiniBand will be developed initially for specific services and functions that can work more or less as a closed system. In other words, InfiniBand software applications are likely to be solutions-oriented cluster appliances. Some examples of these types of cluster appliances are database clusters and network attached storage clusters. The development of DAFS (Direct Access File System) for NAS is an example of work in this area.

Channel Adapters

As mentioned, the equivalent of host I/O adapters in InfiniBand networks are called *channel adapters*. Products that are currently sold as HBAs for storage and NICs for networking will be transformed into channel adapters to work with InfiniBand technology servers. InfiniBand specifies two types of channel adapters: *host channel adapters (HCAs)* and *target channel adapters (TCAs)*.

Host Channel Adapters   Host channel adapters have the responsibility of interfacing with the system processor and memory bus. As such, they are specialized parts of the system and will be core designed-in system components, rather than being add-in components. In general, host channel adapters may have to be designed to accommodate fairly high levels of traffic. InfiniBand networks are unlike other networks in that they are centered around specific systems. In other words, the system in an InfiniBand network is the primary entity in the network. Where clusters are concerned, the systems in the cluster are the primary entities. As the host channel adapters are the main conduit between the system memory bus and I/O subsystems, they have to be able to accommodate the highest traffic levels in the network.

Target Channel Adapters   Target channel adapters provide end node interfaces to non-InfiniBand networks such as Ethernet and Fibre Channel networks. Target channel adapters also provide the interface with non-network peripherals of all sorts, including various bus technologies like the SCSI bus or USB bus.

The relative roles of host channel adapters and target channel adapters are shown here:

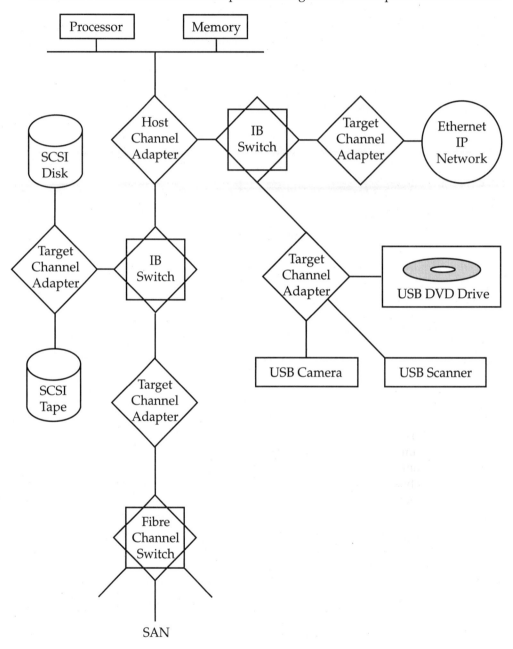

Channel Adapters and Multiple Lane Technologies   Host and target channel adapters can optionally implement the controller technology and physical connectors for 4X and 12X links as well as implementing the logic and hardware resources needed for virtual lanes. Neither of these implementations are likely to be trivial for channel adapter developers who have to understand how other hardware and software companies are going to implement them in their products. For that reason, products that incorporate multiple physical and virtual lanes will probably take longer to come to market than compatibility-oriented products using 1X links and single virtual lanes.

Channel Adapters in Storage Subsystems   Storage subsystems in InfiniBand networks will typically connect to the network through target channel adapters. One of the interesting differences between SAN networks and InfiniBand networks is the location of the host I/O controller. When systems have PCI host I/O buses, there is no choice except to locate the host controller inside the host and connect it to SAN storage using a storing protocol running over some type of SAN wiring.

With InfiniBand, however, there is no need for the host I/O controller to actually be located in the host; in fact, there is no reason to think of it as a *host* I/O controller. Just as Fibre Channel subsystems can have external Fibre Channel ports with parallel SCSI devices, subsystems in InfiniBand networks can have external InfiniBand ports and internal Fibre Channel or parallel SCSI devices. The differences in these two approaches are shown in Figure 13-6.

While it is more likely for storage subsystems to implement TCAs, there is no reason why a subsystem could not have its own HCA. For example, a subsystem with a shared locking or caching manager may need to take a more active role in the network than the usual TCA implementation.

Managing Remote Systems Memory with the VI Protocol

The protocol chosen for InfiniBand is called the *virtual interface architecture* or more simply *VI*. While this name may not spark one's imagination much, the technology of VI is an extremely important part of InfiniBand. The general idea of VI is to allow applications to transmit data between systems and storage by manipulating memory resources remotely over the cluster network. The notion of *remote direct memory access (RDMA)* is the hallmark of VI, and by extension, InfiniBand. The whole point of RDMA transfers is to use systems-like memory operations in lieu of networking functions to transfer and receive data over a network.

VI and RDMA are not feasible without a low-latency, high-reliability network to run on. Although VI is the protocol selected for InfiniBand, there is no reverse requirement, as VI and RDMA can be used on other networks. For example, VI has already been defined as an upper-layer protocol (ULP) at the FC-4 level of Fibre Channel, and RDMA is being discussed within the iSCSI workgroups.

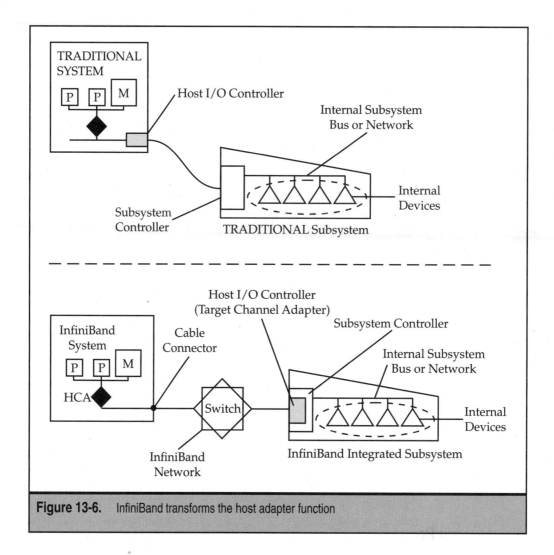

Figure 13-6. InfiniBand transforms the host adapter function

The *virtual* in VI comes from the implementation of virtual memory ports that InfiniBand consumers (applications) use to send and receive data over the network. Similar to virtual memory in systems, VI provides a virtual memory address translation function that enables applications to reserve and access memory resources in other nodes across the cluster network.

Work Queue Pairs

The VI protocol works by establishing *work queue pairs,* or simply *queue pairs,* that serve as the interface mechanism between InfiniBand consumers and the InfiniBand network. Each queue pair has a queue for sending and another for receiving. The queue pair matches well with cabling structures and their dual transmit and receive components. Data that is sent from one node to another on the network is first placed on the send queue of the sending node and then transferred to the receive queue on the receiving node.

Queue pairs are dedicated to specific consumers, and all queue pairs within a channel adapter are isolated and protected from other queue pairs. A single consumer can be using multiple queue pairs.

In summary, channel adapters can have multiple consumers, each of them with its own private queue pair(s) communicating over the InfiniBand network, like this:

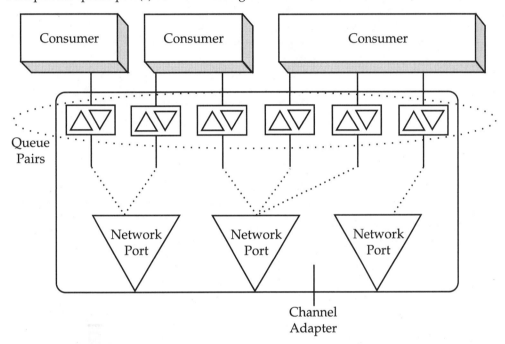

Comparing Protocol Processing on InfiniBand, Fibre Channel, and Ethernet/TCP/IP Networks

The issue of fast protocols can be confusing considering the various approaches taken by the Fibre Channel, IP, and InfiniBand industries. In general, Fibre Channel is a high-reliability, low-latency network. Due to the reliability of the network in Fibre Channel, error recovery by higher-level protocols is expected to be minimal. The protocol suite for Fibre Channel is defined by the FC-0 through FC-4 layers. The FC-2 layer, which is implemented largely in hardware, provides many of the protocol processing functions.

TCP protocol processing in hardware was discussed in Chapter 12 as a way to allow Ethernet/TCP/IP networks to support SAN traffic. As mentioned, opportunistic companies in the storage networking industry are developing network protocol processors that reduce the latency of TCP processing. This is a case where protocol processing methods developed decades earlier are being reengineered to fit the requirements of new networking capabilities and applications.

InfiniBand, as the newest kid on the block, promises to avoid the protocol overhead altogether by using highly reliable networks for making RDMA memory transfers. While the imagery of this is powerful, the fact is that InfiniBand transfers have to take place over some type of network that can inject errors. For that reason, it should not be assumed that transmission overhead can be completely eradicated just because RDMA is being used. Instead, it is probably more correct to think that the overhead of network error and delivery can be moved to other, more efficient components in networking hardware. In essence, this is approximately the same approach taken by the Fibre Channel and Ethernet/TCP/IP industries, the difference is that InfiniBand uses command syntax that originates in systems memory operations.

The table that follows summarizes the protocol processing approaches of the three major storage networking wiring options:

Wiring Option	Operation Semantics	Implementation Point
Fibre Channel	Fibre Channel network	Fibre Channel chipsets
Ethernet/TCP/IP	TCP/IP network	Network processor
InfiniBand	System memory transfers	InfiniBand chipsets

Transport Services

Queue pairs have an associated transport service that determines the overall reliability of the communication between systems and storage. The available transport services in InfiniBand are:

▼   Reliable connection

■   Unreliable connection

■   Reliable datagram

■   Unreliable datagram

▲   Raw datagram

Reliable connection service is a connection-oriented transport service that acknowledges all transmissions. It is called "reliable" because the network provides all error recovery and retransmission at the network level, including network congestion, buffer over- and underruns, and link and fabric failures. Unreliable connections do not acknowledge transmissions and are similar to Fibre Channel's class 2. The reliable datagram service is similar to the reliable connection service except that data frames can multiplex transmissions to and from multiple end nodes. In other words, the network will recover transparently from many types of network errors. Unreliable datagram service is roughly equivalent to Fibre Channel Class 3 communications. Raw datagram service exists primarily to provide compatibility from legacy protocols onto Fibre Channel.

Flow Control

InfiniBand supports both link-level and end-to-end flow control methods that are similar to Fibre Channel's buffer-to-buffer and end-to-end flow control. The flow control mechanism in InfiniBand implements a buffer-refill mechanism that is similar to Fibre Channel's but with subtle differences. However, just as in the case of Fibre Channel, where Class 3 service is much more broadly implemented than Class 2, it is expected that InfiniBand networks will primarily use link-level flow control and ignore the end-to-end flow control. For applications where InfiniBand replaces PCI, it is difficult to imagine why end-to-end flow control would be needed all of a sudden when things have worked well without it for so long.

VI over Fibre Channel

The VI protocol has also been developed as an upper-layer protocol for Fibre Channel. So far, this protocol has not seen much use, but it certainly could be used to form an InfiniBand-like cluster network function with VI running on top of Fibre Channel. Given that a Fibre Channel network has the same error characteristics as InfiniBand technology, it is technically feasible that Fibre Channel–based clusters could develop in the market. This is probably a real long shot, however, as the majority of the research work with VI is targeted to InfiniBand, not Fibre Channel.

IMPLEMENTING INFINIBAND WITH STORAGE NETWORKS

Now that InfiniBand has been described, we'll look at some of the ways it is likely to be implemented with storage as it enters the market.

InfiniBand Clusters

A simple model for an InfiniBand shared nothing cluster is shown in Figure 13-7. This cluster has two systems controlling two SCSI disk drives through two target channel adapters. A separate set of links carries system heartbeats between the two systems. In addition, partitions are used to enforce the shared nothing structure.

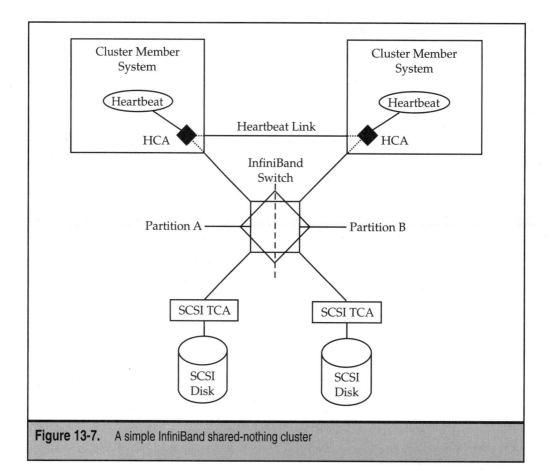

Figure 13-7. A simple InfiniBand shared-nothing cluster

A shared everything cluster is shown in Figure 13-8. The disk drives have been replaced by intelligent storage subsystems that implement a distributed locking manager function in embedded HCAs in both subsystems. All four entities, the two systems and the two storage subsystems, are running a shared caching system "consumer" that coordinates the application.

The idea of a shared caching consumer is an interesting one to ponder. A hypothetical design for such a caching system would use a modified locking mechanism where writes into system cache would also cause a cache-indicator RDMA operation to update a shared memory map of storage contained in the storage subsystems. When a system flushes its cache, it could perform an inverse RDMA operation to remove the cache indicator for the data. Requests for data would also involve a process in the intelligent storage subsystem that checks its cache-indicator mappings. In a two-system cluster, if a subsystem discovers that a data request is held in a system cache, it immediately knows that it is in the cache of the system that did not generate the I/O request.

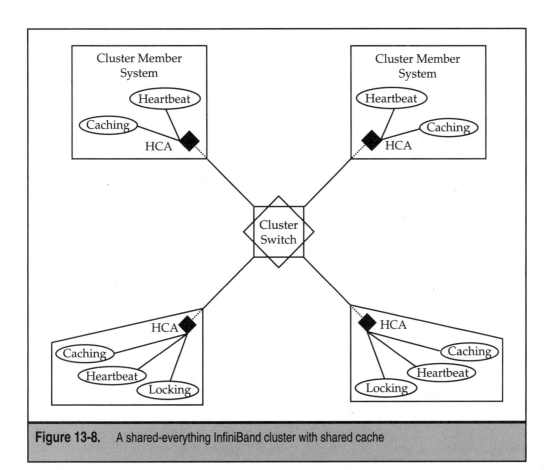

Figure 13-8.   A shared-everything InfiniBand cluster with shared cache

PCI Replacement Structures

The most obvious InfiniBand configuration is a replacement for a PCI bus connecting to a SAN. Figure 13-9 shows such a network where the HCA is located within the host system and where a Fibre Channel TCA is adjacent to the host system.

In Figure 13-9, the Fibre Channel TCA could be replaced by an Ethernet/TCP/IP TCA to connect instead to an iSCSI SAN.

Another interesting extension of this idea is one where an InfiniBand network connects to a local Fibre Channel network, which in turn is tunneled through an IP network to a remote SAN. This scenario is illustrated in Figure 13-10.

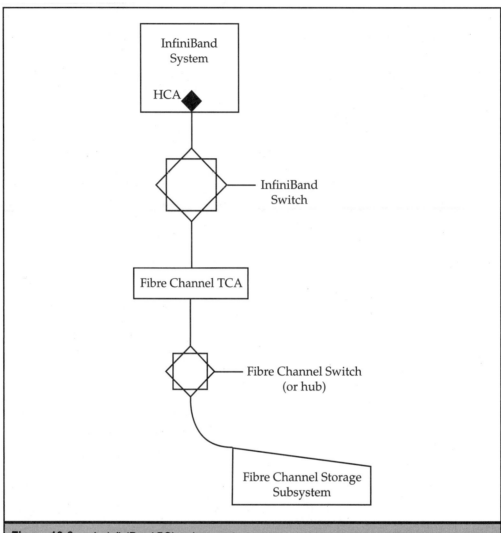

Figure 13-9. An InfiniBand PCI replacement

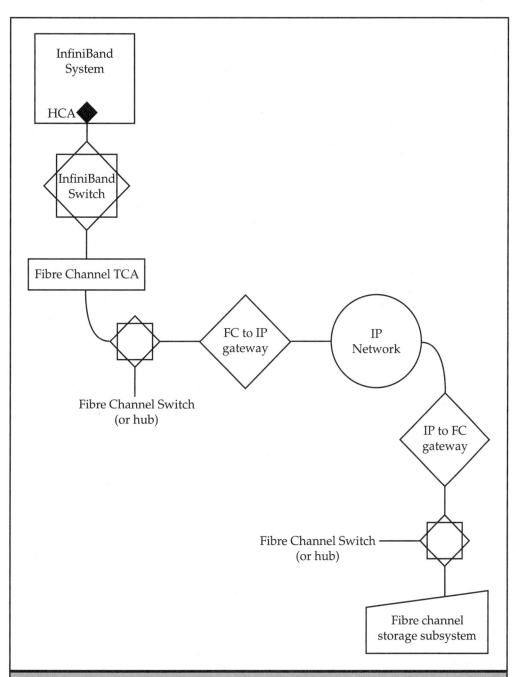

Figure 13-10.   InfiniBand to Fibre Channel, tunneled over an IP network

SUMMARY

This chapter examined the new technology of InfiniBand and its potential impact for storage networking. InfiniBand can impact storage networking in fundamental ways. Its first role will be as a replacement for the PCI I/O bus in systems. Its second role will be as a wiring function for storing and filing applications.

InfiniBand revolutionizes the host I/O bus in much the same way that Fibre Channel revolutionized the storage bus. InfiniBand is based on serial transmissions over a switched topology network that significantly extends the distance and the number of controllers that can be attached.

Using the assumption that modern, high-speed networks have low error rates, InfiniBand is based on the notion that data transfers can be made by manipulating memory resources on remote systems or subsystems. While Fibre Channel and Ethernet/TCP/IP networks can both do similar things, InfiniBand is being developed to support this method of transferring data.

As a result, InfiniBand is well suited to function as a network technology for clusters. It has very low latency characteristics, a feature that is needed for intercluster communications. These latency characteristics also could be adopted for database transaction processing, as will be discussed further in Chapter 14, in the discussion on DAFS.

EXERCISES

1. Design an InfiniBand network for a shared everything cluster made up of three servers and two storage subsystems. Include host channel adapters and target channel adapters in your design.

2. Given the network designed in question #1, write an algorithm for a lock management system for this cluster. Assume the storage subsystems are intelligent and can process any parts of the algorithm you create.

3. Does the design of the lock management system in question #2 change the nature of the channel adapters you designed in question #1? Why or why not?

PART V

Filing, Internet Storage, and Management

CHAPTER 14

Network Attached Storage Appliances

Filing in storage networks is one of the most intriguing areas in storage networking. While it is quickly identified as the primary function of NAS (network attached storage) technology, it will also play a major role in the development of SANs. Filing, like wiring and storing, is a high-level network storage function made up of several lower-level discrete functions. Historically, the internal workings of filing products (file systems and databases) have been among the most complicated aspects of computing and have been difficult to learn about. The next two chapters in this book should help the reader understand the role and technologies of filing. This chapter analyzes the various aspects of filing in NAS appliances, including protocol support, access control, and backup/recovery. The end of the chapter looks at a couple of new and exciting initiatives for network attached storage that have the potential to radically change how network attached storage will work in the future. The first one is called *DAFS*, for *Direct Access File System*, and the other is *NASD*, for *Network Attached Secure Disks*.

NAS SOFTWARE

NAS technology began as an open systems technology in 1985, when it was introduced by Sun Microsystems as NFS, or the Network File System. NFS was an integral element in the growth of network computing, as it allowed Unix systems to share files over a network. After the introduction of NFS, there were many other network operating system (NOS) products introduced from such companies as Novell, Banyan, IBM, Digital, 3Com, and Microsoft. While these products had a variety of features, their primary function was to provide a way to store and share files for groups of users.

Where the network storage industry is concerned, the focus has shifted away from specialized server network operating systems to embedded filing technology in specialized file-server systems called NAS appliances. The appliance concept in storage is borrowed from the ease of use characteristics of kitchen appliances where a user simply plugs in the necessary cables and begins using the appliance with minimal effort or training. While the installation of server appliances is usually more involved than simply connecting power and networking cables, they are typically very simple to install and configure compared with most other storage products. For that reason, NAS appliances have become very popular and are now available in a wide variety of capabilities and price ranges.

Filing in NAS

Storing and wiring are both made up of physical and logical components. Filing, on the other hand, is a logical component that runs as a system application on a wide variety of processors and platforms. That does not mean, however, that filing is a single process; in fact it is made up of many smaller subprocesses that contribute to a complete filing system. In this book, filing has been generalized as having two main roles in the I/O path: its "external" role that presents data to users and applications and its "internal" role that organizes the structure of data on storage in logical block addresses. Using an abbreviated version of the I/O path discussed in Chapter 2, the dual roles of filing can be pictured like this:

Application
External Representation
Internal Structure
Storing
Wiring

In general, NAS appliances are viewed as single-dimension products that provide easy access to data, while hiding the complexities of how the internal data structure and underlying wiring and storing functions work. Considering that the business application resides on some other system in the network, NAS can be thought of as primarily providing storage services through its external representation of data and its internal mechanisms for data structure, storing, and wiring, like this:

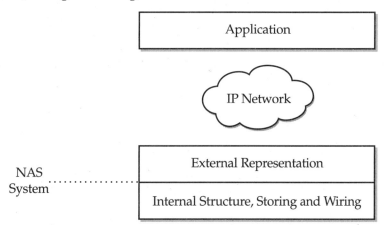

Specialized Operating Systems in NAS Appliances

One of the distinguishing features of most NAS products is the use of the specialized operating system and/or applications system to provide the storage function. Sometimes these specialized operating systems are called microkernel operating systems. A *microkernel* operating system typically has only the communications and storage services necessary to provide its special storage application. In other words, most of the capabilities of a desktop or server operating system are not supported. A NAS product does not necessarily have to be built on top of a microkernel operating system, however. Several NAS products are based on the Linux or FreeBSD operating systems, where some of the functions of the operating system were removed to provide a smaller, faster, specialized version for use as a NAS function.

Microsoft has also entered the business of providing NAS appliance operating systems with its Windows 2000 operating system. It remains to be seen how Microsoft's appliance operating systems products will be customized by NAS vendors, but it seems likely that the core function of their products will integrate well with Windows client software.

As the word *appliance* connotes, a NAS appliance provides a specialized function, such as file serving. Many of the functions associated with typical desktop or server computers are not needed, such as printing, telephony, or Web browsing. Therefore, many, many lines of code can be removed from a general-purpose operating system to make a storage appliance. As they lack many of the usual functions of off-the-shelf operating systems, they typically have problems running off-the-shelf software, as well as compilers and interpreters for "home-made" applications. Instead, an appliance only runs the required components to provide the storage function. The illustration that follows compares a general-purpose operating system with a network storage appliance operating system:

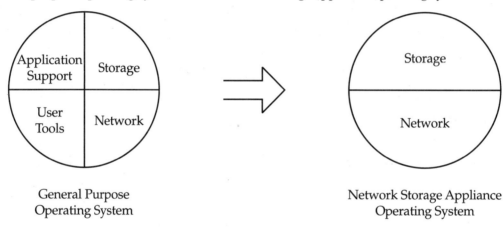

General Purpose
Operating System

Network Storage Appliance
Operating System

The storage appliance operating/application system does not have to be built by removing code from an existing operating system. Instead, it can be constructed as a completely new operating system with a limited and specialized scope. In some respects, a new specialized operating system may have significant advantages over a "parts-missing" operating system for optimizing the performance and capabilities of a storage appliance. For starters, processes that are normally structured as independent functions by a general-purpose operating system can be integrated more tightly in an appliance. Other processes such as protocol processing can be streamlined with specialized hardware and software to provide higher performance levels.

Client Software Compatibility

NAS appliances take advantage of the technologies developed over the history of client/server computing. One of the key concepts in client/server storage is the I/O redirector that was discussed in Chapter 3. Figure 3-10 illustrated the complete client/server I/O path, including the client I/O redirector. In that drawing, a NAS appliance could be substituted for the server on the right side. Through this path, the client system remotely mounts the file system on the appliance.

Transparent access to data through the redirector is essential for the successful implementation of NAS. In general, client redirection software is included as a feature with most general-purpose operating systems. One of the goals of most NAS appliances is the capability to be quickly installed without having to change much, if anything, on client systems. For that reason, NAS appliances are typically designed with networking capabilities that match those of most client systems on the network. For example, a Windows client system that is capable of using the Network Neighborhood function in the Windows operating system should be able to locate and use the appliance just as if it were a local device.

Client redirection software presents NAS storage to users and applications in any of several ways. The most common methods are using a drive letter assignment, such as C: or D:, or using a folder view. In the discussions that follow, the term "drive mapping" will refer to both of these client views of NAS storage.

The capability to use network drive mappings is a large advantage for NAS compared to adding storage devices and/or functionality directly on the desktop system. Typically, adding new devices to a desktop system requires the system to be powered off before the new device software can be installed and configured. This may take more time than it is worth. Not only that, but if the device is to be shared on a network, the work is only halfway done. In contrast, the access to a NAS appliance uses network protocols and existing LAN connections instead of a physical connection. This means NAS appliances can be added or removed from the network without affecting the physical status of any of the clients that use it.

Not only do appliances integrate with client systems for storage purposes, but they can also "plug into" the overall network management structure. For example, a storage server appliance may be able to use the Windows Domain Controller security mechanism and may even be able to function as a primary or secondary Domain Controller in a network of Windows PCs. In addition to integrating with client access and security methods, it is also desirable for storage appliances to be managed with the common server management tools used in typical networks. The management goals of an appliance can be summarized visually like this:

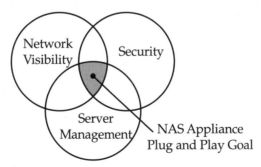

Appliance Scalability Strengths and Weaknesses

As discussed in the preceding section, one of the primary characteristics of a storage appliance is the fact that it can be inserted into network operations with minimal interruption to client systems. A useful by-product of this characteristic is the ease of expandability or scalability of the appliance's function. The ability to add storage capacity that is immediately accessible to clients creates the ability to quickly add new storage to the network. While the various appliances may not be able to merge their storage capacity as a single storage repository or use a single logical view, at least the additional storage can be added without stopping existing operations.

However, scalability within the NAS appliance itself is not necessarily seamless. If a NAS appliance needs to have its storage capacity upgraded, the appliance will likely need to be taken offline while the new storage devices are added. Like any other system, when the appliance is offline, its data cannot be accessed.

For the typical NAS appliance, after the maximum storage capacity is reached, there is no way to expand its capacity and another appliance needs to be added to the network. This might not be much of a problem as long as the new appliance is used for new data and new applications that are not stored on an existing appliance. However, if the new NAS appliance is expected to assume some of the load from the first appliance and data is moved from the old NAS appliance to the new one, it is then necessary to change the client redirector software configurations for any clients that access the relocated data. If the number of affected users is in the hundreds, or even thousands, this can cause a sizable work interruption.

Dynamic File System Expansion

The capacity problem just described can be avoided if the appliance uses a file system that can dynamically expand its usable capacity.

Dynamic file system expansion is not a NAS technology, per se, but originates from general-purpose file systems such as the Veritas file system and Sun's Solaris file system. File system expansion is mostly a data structure process that has the capability to restructure the distribution of data on a new and larger logical block address space, as shown here:

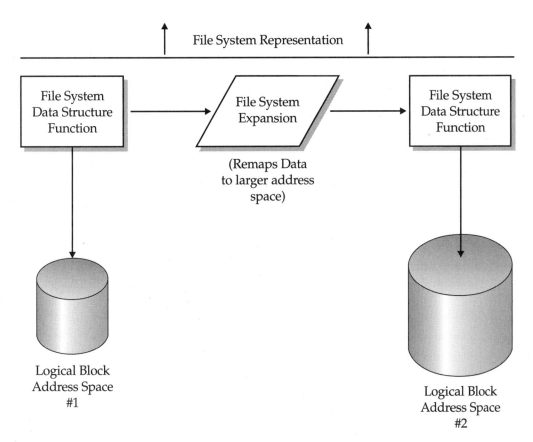

For dynamic file system expansion to work, there needs to be a volume manager that can dynamically integrate additional storage at the logical block level and add it to the available logical block address space of an exported volume. The file system then has to be able to interact with the volume manager to discover the new available space before starting its expansion.

NAS HARDWARE IMPLEMENTATIONS

Server appliances assume the network storage functionality of general-purpose servers and place them in special-purpose packaged systems. Distilling network functionality this way is hardly a new idea. For instance, several years ago network routing was a function that ran in computer systems, as opposed to running on specialized routers, as is the case today. A similar transformation occurred with network printing. Network print serving was commonly implemented in network operating system software, which meant server software needed to be implemented everywhere printers were located. Today, print serving appliances are used that are packaged as small network stations or are embedded as part of the printer for direct attachment to the network.

NAS Appliance Hardware Components

NAS products are available in a wide range of performance levels, degrees of functionality, and prices. The NAS concept is easily translated to a wide variety of processors, chip sets, I/O technology, and storage capacity. This allows an organization to start using relatively small and cost-effective NAS appliances and move into larger ones as its needs expand.

Hardware Requirements for a NAS Appliance

The minimal hardware requirements for a NAS appliance are:

▼ Processor and system board capable of supporting a small system

■ Enough memory to store the OS, client connection data, device drivers, and file system

■ Network interface for Ethernet connectivity

■ Storage I/O channel interface, such as IDE or SCSI

■ Storage device, such as disk drives

■ Power supply

▲ Enclosure

The microprocessors used in NAS appliances can vary greatly, including Strongarm, x86, and PowerPC chips. Likewise, the storage channel and devices used in NAS appliances encompass a broad range of components, including IDE, SCSI, and Fibre Channel devices.

NAS Applications and Configurations

While NAS appliances might have similar components lists, they can be integrated many different ways for a variety of different purposes. In the following sections, we'll examine several types of network storage appliances, including:

▼ Large enterprise appliances

■ Lightweight thin server appliances

■ Database appliances

■ Internet server appliances

- CD and DVD appliances
- ▲ Backup appliances

Large Enterprise, "Heavy Lifter" Appliances

Some NAS appliances simply do not resemble the kitchen toaster or blender that one thinks of with the word "appliance." Companies such as Network Appliance, EMC, and Compaq, for instance, build NAS file servers that can fill large racks with disk drives. Large NAS file servers are built to support hundreds of users in high-volume, high-traffic environments. Such systems typically have specialized hardware and software components that allow them to handle the number of users and traffic volume they have. These "heavy lifting" file serving appliances can support several terabytes of storage capacity using RAID technology, specialized file systems, protocol processors, and fully redundant hardware designs. These large enterprise NAS appliances may also integrate SAN wiring, such as Fibre Channel, as the interconnect for their disks and subsystems. Ethernet connectivity for client connections is provided by one or more network ports typically running at 100Mb Ethernet speeds, but it can also include FDDI, ATM, and Gigabit Ethernet, as shown here:

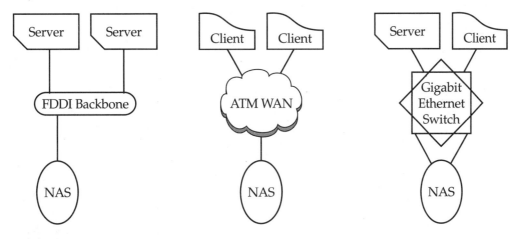

Lightweight Thin Server Appliances

Another trend in NAS appliances addresses the opposite end of the spectrum and fits the mold of the storage "toaster." There are several manufacturers of these small appliances, including some of the disk drive companies who are looking for new ways to package and sell their products. These appliances typically have one to four IDE disk drives inside small form-factor cases with capacities ranging from 20GB to 200GB; they tend to be based on either Linux or FreeBSD microkernel operating systems running on Intel processors. The internal disks in a network storage "toaster" may be able to support basic mirroring and striping. Ethernet connectivity is normally provided by a single 10/100Mb Ethernet port. To keep costs down, these small NAS appliances often have no repairable or replaceable parts. When something fails, the entire appliance is replaced.

NAS Database Appliances

Some attempts have been made to produce specialized NAS servers that operate as single-purpose database servers. So far, these attempts have generally been unsuccessful, but that does not mean that the idea is necessarily bad. NAS database appliance products significantly simplify the installation and integration of database systems in networks. Just as file serving NAS products depend on providing tight network integration with file access protocols, database NAS products will also be required to tightly integrate with database access protocols. Oracle and other database companies have publicly discussed their intention of providing software and even hardware for these kinds of NAS-database appliances.

NAS Internet Server Appliances

NAS servers that provide HTTP (Hypertext Transfer Protocol) Internet services have been actively sold for several years. These servers can provide a variety of Internet server functions including the capability to store and retrieve files using HTTP and FTP (the File Transfer Protocol). Because these Internet server appliances can be used to store files on Web sites, they can be thought of as storage appliances, although their main function is to be a Web server.

CD and DVD Servers

Among the earliest storage appliances were those built to allow workstations on a network to share CD drives and media. Pioneered by Microtest Corporation, the same company that led the early development of print servers, the earliest CD-sharing NAS products shared a single CD drive containing a single CD. Over time, it became obvious that companies that had libraries of CDs for use in their engineering, equipment maintenance, and software development work needed to provide access to entire libraries of CDs to large departments and organizations of workers.

The basic concept of reading a CD has been expanded by some vendors to include disk caching of recently or often used CDs. CD drives are sequential-access devices that are not good at servicing multiple inquiries at the same time. Each user of a shared CD must wait until the previous user has finished with a request and then wait for the CD drive to begin seeking its data from the beginning of data on the CD. This is not very satisfying for multiple users who may be accustomed to much faster performance from CD drives on their workstations. Caching CD information on a disk drive enables multiple users to concurrently access data from a single CD much faster.

Backup Appliances

Another type of NAS device with a limited record of successes is a network backup appliance. Backup appliances are built to back up network servers and clients. However, the use of a backup appliance does not do much to change the performance limitations of network backup. By definition, a backup appliance package would not provide remote device support with external tape drives that attach to the local I/O channels of high-capacity production servers. In other words, a backup appliance is a nice idea, but they do not address the most pressing unmet backup needs in many data centers.

Network Considerations for NAS

While the idea of NAS is to make network integration easy, there are many important network characteristics that need to be considered to create a reasonable set of expectations for how it will work. This is not to imply that NAS doesn't work well, because it often does, but the network that a NAS appliance runs in has a large impact on its performance and reliability. In essence, the network should be viewed as a replacement for a local I/O channel and if the network is weak, the NAS appliance will not work optimally. (Of course, neither will most other network processes.)

In the sections that follow, we'll examine a few network characteristics affecting NAS appliances.

Network Performance for NAS

In general, the networks used to transfer data between clients and NAS appliances do not require the same microsecond-range latency and structured flow control as needed for SAN environments, although that is not necessarily true if the NAS system is storing database transaction data. While SANs have latencies in the order of several microseconds, latencies for Ethernet networks with NAS appliances are expected to be in the millisecond range. Also, where SANs are typically implemented as separate storage networks, NAS appliances are expected to run on existing Ethernet networks with all the other traffic that typically exists on those networks. In other words, there will likely be network congestion and delays that impact the performance of the NAS appliance.

Loss of Packets

The presence of nonstorage traffic over Ethernet/IP networks implies that redirected file storage operations from client systems may be discarded by network devices or be delivered out of order, meaning the NAS appliance has to provide error correction and packet ordering. While this is a normal part of most server operations, it is important to understand this aspect of NAS appliances, especially if high performance is expected. If high performance is required from a NAS appliance, it is a good idea to try to isolate NAS traffic from non-NAS traffic, as discussed in the text that follows, to minimize the effect on the appliance's performance.

Dedicated Ethernet NAS-SAN Networks

To deliver the best network performance with NAS appliances, it is possible to build dedicated physical or virtual NAS networks. A virtual network could be built using VLAN tagging or some other virtual network technology. When the NAS network is "privatized" this way, it functions like a SAN that carries filing traffic as opposed to storing traffic. By limiting the traffic to NAS-only, NAS appliances can support some of the higher performance application requirements of server systems. Figure 14-1 illustrates an Ethernet NAS-SAN network environment where one network is established for common data traffic and the other network is used only as storage traffic.

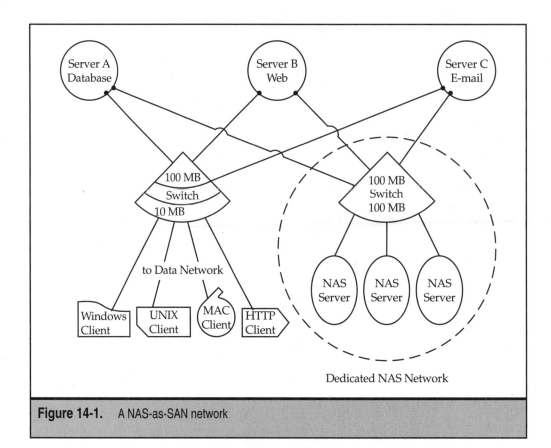

Figure 14-1.   A NAS-as-SAN network

Local Area and Wide Area Considerations

Unix-oriented NAS products typically use NFS as their *network filing* protocol. NFS will be discussed further in following sections of this chapter, but for this discussion we want to examine its suitability for WANs and LANs. Originally designed as a local area file sharing mechanism, NFS was designed to run on top of UDP (User Datagram Protocol), as opposed to the more popular TCP (Transmission Control Protocol). UDP is a connectionless protocol that does not provide transmission acknowledgments and, therefore, can provide faster transfers than TCP. UDP is well suited for LAN environments because it is lightweight and fast—much faster to process than TCP.

However, UDP was not developed for WAN applications where it is often necessary to reassemble data from multiple transmission paths. TCP, on the other hand, was developed specifically to manage the reassembly of data over the Internet. Although TCP is slower on a frame-by-frame basis than UDP, its ability to provide ordered transmissions is a major benefit when transferring large amounts of data in a wide area network. For similar reasons, NFS added support for TCP as a transport protocol to support file access functions over larger LANs where data may pass between multiple subnetworks between client and server.

Storage Applications of NAS Appliances

NAS is a storage product that provides filing services that take the place of other servers in the network. In the sections that follow, we'll first look at NAS as a way to consolidate file storage and simplify file management, then we'll discuss how NAS can be used to support a group of associated load-sharing application servers. Then we'll take a brief look at how NAS can be used to support databases and what some of the challenges of doing this are.

Consolidating Files on NAS Appliances

One of the most common applications for large enterprise NAS appliances is server consolidation. The general idea is to replace several smaller file servers, or move the file serving functions from several servers onto large serving appliances. Consolidating files onto a single large server enables the IT organization to achieve better management efficiencies in managing user accounts and file resources.

Server consolidation affects several aspects of the computing environment. Among the I/O and storage items the IT organization should take into consideration are:

▼ Network I/O channel throughput requirements

■ Cache requirements

■ Disk subsystem structure

▲ Backup requirements

Network I/O Channel Throughput   One way to look at server consolidation is from the perspective of the network I/O elements, such as Ethernet connections and storage I/O buses, being merged in a single NAS system. The aggregated peak I/O transfer requirements of the existing network links need to be accommodated by the new NAS implementation. The network may need to be changed to consolidate server bandwidth through fewer network connections. Similarly, the requirements of the existing server's storage I/O buses or channels need to be accommodated by the new NAS server. In other words, any NAS appliance that replaces existing servers should have the potential to deliver equal or faster file storage services through its network connections and storage I/O channel than the collective servers were providing.

Typically, the measurement to be concerned with is the average transfer rate during peak access periods. A NAS appliance that replaces several general-purpose file servers should be able to process the same and greater peak traffic loads as the file servers can. If an appliance is underpowered for the load it is expected to carry, users will be disappointed with the performance. Peak access periods occur several times during the day, serving as a constant reminder when there are problems.

For large NAS appliances, another consideration is using RAID for the appliance's storage. An integrated RAID subsystem in a NAS system naturally balances the I/O workload over the member disk drives in the appliance's array. This provides disk-level redundancy for all client data as well as establishing a consistent performance level for all clients.

Cache Requirements   Similarly, some amount of memory cache used in existing file servers should be implemented on the NAS appliance. However, if different cache algorithms are used on different servers, it could be difficult replicating their capabilities on a single cache in the appliance. For example, if two file servers are tuned for performance where one uses a read-ahead cache and the other uses LRU caching, it is unlikely that a single cache in an appliance will be able to deliver the same overall results. In this case, it may be a better decision to not consolidate the files from a server effectively utilizing a caching strategy that differs from the other servers being combined.

Another important consideration for caching in server consolidation is planning for concurrent access by multiple users to individual data files. For example, one of the reasons for consolidating servers in the first place may be to enable certain files to be concurrently accessed by many client systems that previously could only have been accessed by one user at a time. While most NAS systems do not incorporate solid state disks (SSDs) in their configurations, the use of SSDs could significantly increase the performance of certain applications running on multiple clients.

Disk and Disk Subsystem Organization   The various servers being consolidated into a single NAS appliance may be using different disk structures. For instance, one server may have mirrored disks, while another has RAID 5. For many workloads, the selection of the disk organization will not make a huge difference in performance; however, it is important to watch out for servers supporting applications with a high percentage of write operations. When writes are relatively heavy (over 25 percent), it is advisable to use disk mirroring (RAID 1). A notable exception to this are Network Appliance Filers that integrate RAID 4 disk arrays with solid state disk storage and their WAFL file system to alleviate the RAID 4 write bottleneck and provide fast disk operations.

For the most part, one should not expect too much flexibility in the disk subsystems of NAS server appliances. The ease of use goal of the appliance concept tends to contradict the complexity of volume management.

Data Sharing for Loosely Coupled Servers

Another excellent application of NAS appliances is to provide file storage for multiple servers that run the same application and need access to a common data pool. Specifically, this works well where the application servers are expected to change often, but where the storage requirements are more stable.

An example of this type of environment is a Web site. Chapter 16, on Internet storage, discusses this application in more detail, but the basic idea is that a "server farm" can access the storage on a large NAS appliance. New application servers can be added, old application servers can be removed, and individual servers can fail without affecting the capability of the site to function and provide all of its data. Similarly, other systems composed of loosely coupled systems working together to provide a single application image can use NAS appliances effectively as the "back-end" storage facility.

NAS Appliances for Storing Database Data

Many database systems can read or write their data either using block storage operations on a raw partition or using file storage operations using a file system. Using file operations, the database system does not have to calculate a logical block address about where to place the data in storage. Instead of sending SCSI commands to a storage controller, the database sends file requests dictating the relative position of the data within the database's file. This is called a *byte-range* file operation and is the way most applications read and write data through a file system. The database request includes an offset number, which indicates the number of bytes from the beginning of the file the transaction is to occur. The receiving file system uses this offset to determine where the data belongs in the database table and can then calculate the location of the data in logical block addresses used on storage. The file system does not necessarily know the database's structure within the file, but using offsets, the database can restore and retrieve all its data.

NAS appliances can be used to support databases by exporting their file system for use by the database system. The database system redirects its database operations using byte-range offsets, over the network to the NAS system, which interprets the request as a file I/O operation, which it then translates internally into a logical block address, as shown in Figure 14-2.

In general, this can work well, but there are some surprising network transmission problems to deal with. Most Ethernet/IP networks are not built for the low latency that is needed in transaction processing. However, a great deal of database I/O is not transaction-oriented, and NAS appliances would work fine for these applications. On the other hand, the transmission characteristics of IP networks present a situation where database requests could be delivered out of order to the NAS system, creating data integrity risks.

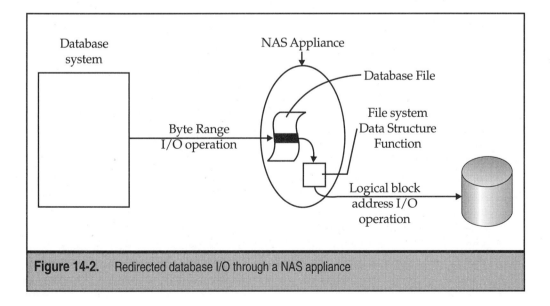

Figure 14-2.   Redirected database I/O through a NAS appliance

To understand the potential of the risk, consider a database system that generates a write and then a read in quick succession to the same piece of information. Many times the read would be satisfied from system cache, but that is not always guaranteed, and for this example we will assume that the data was discarded from cache to make room for new data. As the write request is transferred across the network, assume that it was discarded by a switch or hub due to temporary congestion. The second request to read the data that was supposedly just updated is then sent over the network, and as congestion has cleared, it succeeds. The result is that the database reads stale data that should have been overwritten and the data integrity is lost. Even in dedicated Ethernet networks, this scenario is possible, which has led to the common perception that database systems should not be used with NAS appliances.

This does not mean that NAS will not work for database applications, but it does indicate that NAS, in its current technology state, may not be the best choice for storing transaction data. This topic is being addressed through a new VI-based initiative called DAFS, a topic discussed at the end of this chapter.

Backup and Recovery for NAS Appliances

One of the foundation storage management applications in storage networking is backup. As it turns out, backup and recovery in NAS appliances can be much more complicated than desired. At first glance, backup and recovery of NAS appliances should be easily accomplished by simply reading and writing files using file I/O over the network. Unfortunately, the reality is that backup and recovery for NAS appliances is a fairly difficult and serious challenge. While NAS appliances have been developed to easily integrate with clients and networks, they are rarely developed to integrate with backup systems. The following sections examine NAS backup and recovery in detail.

Netting Out NAS Backup

In general, the performance issues of network backup and recovery are slightly worse for NAS appliances than they are for full-function servers because:

▼ They hold large amounts of data, which takes a long time to back up and saturates the network when it is running.

▲ They use specialized operating systems that cannot run off-the-shelf backup products. This not only includes backup engines, but also the agents that these engines use to back up servers over the network.

As discussed in Chapter 7, backup of any server over the network is only feasible if the amount of data being transferred is relatively small. As a specialized server that may have a lot of data to back up, the NAS appliance may need to exercise alternative backup methods in order to get the job done.

Typically, the backup and restore of metadata and security information is made possible through special programming interfaces provided by the operating system and file system vendors. Backup system agents are developed specifically for each platform to work with these programming interfaces to ensure the correct copying and writing of metadata and security information. However, NAS operating and file systems typically lack these interfaces and/or the system resources to run them and therefore cannot run off-the-shelf backup agents. As a result, it can be very difficult to correctly back up and restore a complete NAS system.

The difficulties in backing up and recovering data stored on NAS appliances create product problems for NAS appliance vendors. There are four basic approaches they can use:

▼ Develop their own proprietary backup scheme.

■ Ignore the problem and tell users to back up their NAS systems as network mapped drives.

■ Develop specialized backup agents and remote device support that works with existing backup products.

▲ Implement a network backup protocol called NDMP.

Backup with a Proprietary Backup Program   System vendors have been designing and implementing proprietary backup systems for years. Some NAS vendors have also taken this approach by developing specialized backup and recovery procedures for the specific requirements of their platform. However, there are NAS vendors that have avoided doing this in order to save development time and cost. While there is little doubt that proprietary backup systems can work for particular NAS appliances, such backup approaches do not integrate with existing backup products in the market. Organizations that have made strategic decisions about backup and recovery systems want better integration with their existing methods than a proprietary backup solution can offer.

That said, the ability to perform high-performance backup that includes a complete backup of all security and metadata information is certainly possible through a proprietary approach—but the NAS vendor has to develop it and maintain it over time for it to be a solution.

Backup Using Mapped Drives   If performance and completeness of data protection are not issues, backing up a NAS appliance as another drive on a workstation or server is a valid approach. The basic idea of backing up data on a mapped drive is the same as backup for any local drive. Just as network attached servers rely on client redirection, this type of backup takes advantage of the same redirection capabilities. Backing up a mapped drive will work with virtually any desktop or server backup product that has the capability to back up local drives.

For instance, NAS appliances implemented in small businesses or branch office locations may be able to be backed up as a mapped drive. Typically, these environments do not have the same backup performance requirements as data center systems and do not need to have direct-attached tape devices.

One of the problems with backing up a mapped drive is that there is usually no way to back up and restore the appliance file system's metadata, including file access permissions. Normal file read and write operations do not copy this information over the network to the client machine. As a result, backing up a mapped drive doesn't copy that information either. This is not necessarily a show-stopper as long as the data on the NAS appliance is shared by all users, in which case the inability to restore security and metadata information may not be an important concern.

However, if users have their own private permissions where information cannot be accessed by all the users, the inability to preserve security after a restore presents a serious problem. As with any file access operation, there is a user defined for backup who gains access to the NAS server and starts reading files. For a complete file backup to work, this user is typically a system administrator with access permissions to all the data stored on the appliance. Using this administrator ID, the backup system reads all the files and then copies them to tape.

Similarly, restores also would use the same administrator ID to write each file to its original location. However, if another user who does not have complete access to the system attempts to restore data, it is possible that the backup system will not be able to access the directories it needs to and subsequently be unable to restore the data.

Also notice that data written by the administrator during restores is not written by the original creator but by the administrator. This could cause access problems for the original user, who may not have the rights to access data that belongs to the administrator. At that point, it may be necessary for the administrator to reassign access privileges to every user who is unable to access the data. Figure 14-3 illustrates this.

The bigger issue for NAS appliances using mapped drive backups is the necessity to re-create every user account following a disaster. Since no security information is maintained by backup, there is no way the backup program can re-create users automatically and reassign their access permissions to shared storage locations (directories, for

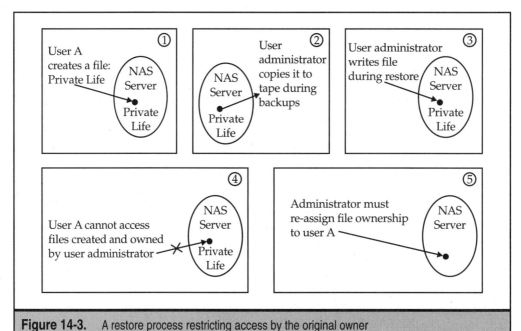

Figure 14-3.   A restore process restricting access by the original owner

instance) on the NAS appliance. For a small NAS appliance covering a relatively small number of users, this is not such an enormous problem, but for a large NAS appliance with many users, the administrative effort of re-creating and reassigning users to directories could take a long time. This scenario is illustrated in Figure 14-4.

There are several potential workarounds for these issues that could be implemented by a NAS appliance. For instance, the file system metadata could be exported to a data file that is copied by backup, and an inverse process could be invoked to reapply metadata from that file. Readers who are interested in understanding the recoverability of NAS appliances using mapped-drive backup should ask the various NAS appliance manufacturers for detailed explanations of their backup and recovery capabilities.

Customized Backup Agents and Remote Device Support for Backup Software Products

Another approach to solving the backup problem for NAS appliance vendors is to develop backup agents and/or remote device support that works with certain backup software products. This approach provides more or less the same capability as developing a proprietary backup system, but with the added benefit of integrating with an existing product in the market. Remote device support allows backup to be done locally at optimal performance. The backup agent provides the ability to back up and recover all required security and metadata information.

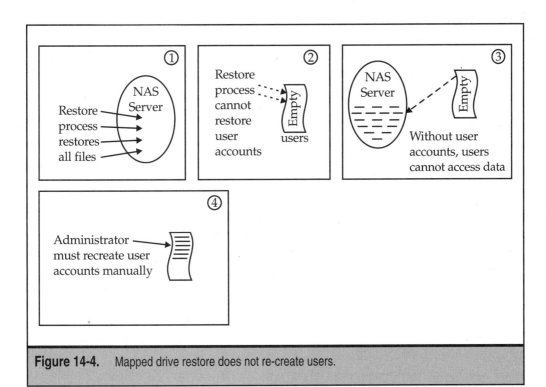

Figure 14-4. Mapped drive restore does not re-create users.

While this might seem like the logical or responsible path to take, there is a tremendous amount of work involved. The process of developing a backup agent for a NAS appliance is not necessarily straightforward and is usually different for each backup software product. The lack of standards for backup agent technology does not allow the appliance vendor to simply implement an available standard. Furthermore, backup software vendors do not all have an open technology policy regarding their backup agent technology and may be reluctant to share the technology.

These difficulties aside, there are significant hurdles to overcome caused by the use of the NAS operating system. Backup agents and remote device support programs can be large and may use programming interfaces and functions that are not provided by the limited resources in the NAS operating system. Even if the functions are provided, there may not be enough resources in the NAS appliance, such as memory, to support the operation of these elements.

NAS Backup Using NDMP   Realizing the problems of implementing backup and recovery on NAS appliances, Network Appliance Corporation and Intelliguard Software, which was acquired by Legato Systems, developed a method to back up and recover NAS-resident data. Their invention, called NDMP, for Network Data Management Protocol, is now one of the first industry standards in storage networking.

The concept of NDMP is to circumvent the need to run backup processes in the NAS appliance by using standardized data mover technology and a proxy service that controls local backup devices. In other words, NDMP provides remote control capability for backing up and restoring data on the NAS appliance. Using NDMP, a NAS appliance is backed up, not by a backup vendor's backup agent, but by an industry standard backup facility. While it would be nice to call this an agent, that is not correct in NDMP-speak. NDMP calls the component that runs on NAS products the NDMP server. The relationships between the backup engine, a NAS server, and an NDMP server are shown here:

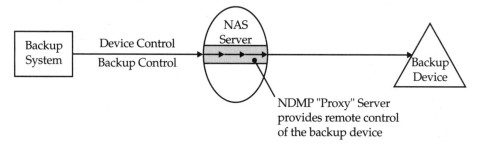

There is an underlying assumption in NDMP that there is a locally attached backup device or subsystem that can be operated by remote control through the NAS appliance from a backup system on the network. This requires an integrated I/O bus or channel interface on the NAS appliance to connect the tape equipment. However, it is also possible for the NDMP server on the NAS appliance to redirect backup traffic to another system on the network.

The NDMP architecture is illustrated in Figure 14-5. The assignment of the terms "client" and "server" follows that used in the X Window System, where the server provides access to a device and is not necessarily driving an operation. For many backup installations, the *NDMP client* would be a system that is designated as the *backup server*.

The NAS appliance in an NDMP relationship is called the *NDMP host*. The NDMP application that runs and provides communications to a single backup device is called the *NDMP server*. There can be many NDMP servers running simultaneously within an NDMP host, providing remote control of multiple drives and automated tape library robots.

NDMP Limitations   For NDMP to work correctly, the NAS appliance vendor must provide NDMP capabilities for its product. In keeping with the terminology used by various backup products, the term "agent" might be used to identify this function, instead of "server." In addition, there must also be an NDMP-compliant backup software package that can send the remote control information to backup devices.

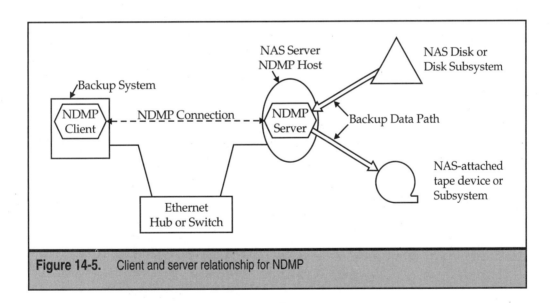

Figure 14-5.   Client and server relationship for NDMP

Another problem with NDMP is that is does not provide a defined method for backing up and restoring security and metadata information. In other words, NDMP can provide fast, system-independent backup functionality, but it cannot provide complete backup functionality. A NAS vendor that wants to provide security and metadata protection will need to provide its own proprietary method for making this information available in files that store the metadata and can be backed up and restored. While the preparation of files containing this information could be automated, the restore process for recovering this information would likely require manual operations that trigger the metadata reconstruction process. This two-step restore process is illustrated here:

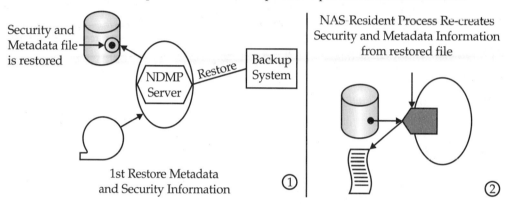

NDMP technology has been open and available to the industry for several years. Interested readers can get current information about NDMP backup software by visiting the NDMP Web site at **http://www.NDMP.org**.

Security and Metadata Implementations in NAS Appliances   There are basically two approaches to storing metadata information in NAS appliances. In most commercial file systems, file system metadata is stored within the file system in data structures on disk. This approach provides fast performance for file operations but can restrict the amount or type of metadata that is used to describe a file. Considering the flexibility of platforms that must be supported by a NAS appliance, restrictions on metadata information can create some usability problems. For example, different client systems' file systems have different types of metadata with different attributes. Not only that, but the file system metadata structure can change with different versions of the operating system. If the metadata is stored in fixed-sized disk locations, it is possible that the NAS appliance's file system will not be able to store all the variations in metadata that the clients have. In that case, certain client systems might not have the same support they expect from the file system.

For that reason, NAS appliances sometimes use an separate "look-aside" file that holds the metadata for the file system. This type of metadata file mirrors the entries in the file system with its own record keeping on every file that exists.

The primary advantage of using a metadata file is that the format of the file can be changed or expanded as necessary to accommodate changes to file metadata that occurs over time. For example, it would be possible for a version of the Linux operating system to incorporate a new kind of object-oriented file description that does not exist in any current file system implementation. Adding this data to the metadata structure within a file system would probably require a complete redesign of the file system. However, by using a metadata file, it is possible to change the information in this file as if it were another application data file.

The primary disadvantage of using a look-aside metadata file is performance. When a file is accessed, its metadata must be viewed from some other location in the file system as opposed to being available in an adjacent location where the file is stored. Considering the load on the system, the time it takes to view this independent metadata file could negatively impact system performance. Therefore, NAS appliances sometimes implement solid state disks or caching to provide optimal performance when accessing metadata information in a metadata file.

Regardless of where the metadata is stored, backup systems need to be able to access it, copy it, and restore it in order to completely protect the data in a NAS file system.

Comparing Different Backup Alternatives for Backing Up NAS Appliances   Table 12-1 summarizes the relative strengths and weaknesses of the various backup approaches for NAS appliances. Unfortunately, there are no clear winners to recommend. In the long haul, NDMP shows the most potential, but it may never come to pass. This will likely be an area where NAS vendors are able to differentiate their products.

	Proprietary System	Mapped Drive	Custom Agent	NDMP
Performance (local or network)	Local	Network	Network	Local
Integrates with existing backup	No	Yes	Yes	Possible
Metadata and security coverage	Yes	No	Yes	No
Relative cost	High	Low	High	Low

Table 14-1.   Comparing NAS Backup Approaches

Snapshots and Backup

Snapshot technology is not necessarily a backup technology, but it often is implemented to work along with backup and recovery. The idea of the snapshot was first introduced in Chapter 4, where hardware-based snapshot technology was discussed. However, snapshot technology can also be implemented in software and is particularly powerful when integrated with a file system. The WAFL file system used in Network Appliance filers is an example of a NAS file system with integrated snapshot functionality. Software snapshots are discussed in more detail in Chapter 15 on file systems.

Once a snapshot has been created, it is possible for backup to access the data in the snapshot without having to worry about managing a copy-on-write process for handling backups for changing files. New data written during backups is ignored and backed up during the next backup operation. Hardware snapshots allow backups to use a "quiet" storage subsystem that has excellent backup performance. In contrast, software snapshots typically use the active storage subsystem of the NAS appliance and contend for storage resources such as disk arms and spindles to read data for backup. However, software snapshots can replicate data to other appliances where the backup can proceed at optimal speed with minimal impact on the original system's performance.

In general, using either hardware or software snapshot technology makes backup and recovery of NAS appliances much easier to manage and improves backup performance significantly. Snapshot technology is not necessarily trivial and has an associated cost that exceeds the pricing of toaster-type NAS appliances. Therefore snapshots are usually only available in high-end NAS appliances.

PROTOCOLS AND FILE SYSTEM OPERATIONS WITH NAS

NAS appliances provide filing services over a network. Not too surprisingly, the foundation of NAS appliances is the file system that can be remotely mounted by client systems. The file system in a NAS appliance typically uses a native file system that is extended through the use of an additional network access protocol and network security technology.

Comparing NAS Communication and Filing Methods

For the most part, the NAS appliance file system is a combination of this network file protocol and the local file system, as shown here:

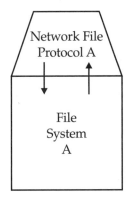 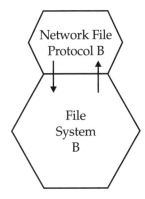

The two primary file system/file protocol pairs:

▼ UFS+NFS: Unix-based, Unix file system, and Network File System, invented by Sun Microsystems

▲ NTFS+CIFS: Windows-based, NT file system, and Common Internet File System, invented by Microsoft

Comparison of NFS and CIFS Access Control

NFS and CIFS have some important differences, especially where data access control is concerned. Among the fundamental differences between the two are:

▼ System login security

■ Stateful and stateless connections

■ File and directory security

▲ File and directory locking

We'll now look at these differences in the following sections.

System-Level Security Differences in NFS and CIFS   System-level and file-level security are separate, but related, issues. System-level security involves the ability to establish a communication session between entities on the network. A network file system obviously needs to provide this to allow a user to search for data and, once it finds it, to begin working with it.

In NFS, users are authenticated at the client by logging into the machine they are working on. After that, their system accesses data from other systems on the network that have *exported* their file systems with NFS. From that point on, the user can access any other file systems on the network by using the NFS protocol. In other words, access using

NFS is a system function, not a user function. The NFS server does not authenticate the user, although it does compare the user ID against security information stored in the Unix file system metadata to determine directory and file access permissions. In general, NFS security is considered adequate for many environments, but it is open to attacks from anyone who can access a Unix system on the network. The diagram here shows the client-location security of NFS:

While NFS systems export their file system to other systems on the network, CIFS systems create *shares* that are accessed by authenticated *users*. CIFS authenticates users at the server, as opposed to the client. In other words, the CIFS security model does not trust that a client was authenticated on another desktop system. CIFS systems use Windows domain controllers for authenticating users. For the most part, CIFS security is stronger than that of NFS, which is both an advantage and a disadvantage. Network reconnections with CIFS are more complicated. The authentication for CIFS access is diagrammed here:

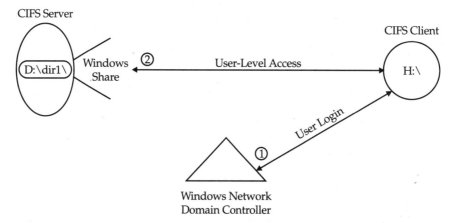

Statelessness and Session Orientation   NFS is referred to as a *stateless* protocol. "Stateless" refers to the fact that NFS has no intrinsic awareness of the historical relationship between client and server. In other words, NFS is like Zen practice, where both client and server deal with each moment as it occurs. This way, if a network problem occurs, it has absolutely no effect on the relationship between client and server. When either the server or the client is available again after an unexpected absence, the two systems can immediately begin working together.

CIFS, on the other hand, has a definite *stateful* session orientation. The client and server share a history and know what has happened during that session. If a session breaks off for some reason, the user will need to authenticate himself or herself again to the NAS appliance or the domain controller. This approach can be somewhat problematic for applications that expect the network storage to always be immediately available, as opposed to being accessed after completion of a login process. One of the reasons CIFS uses a session orientation is to be able to enforce the locking model used of its native file system, as discussed in the text that follows.

User Access and Security

Directory- and file-level security determines whether or not a user, application, or system on the network has the privileges and authorization to access a particular data object. Unix file systems have a three-level security model that defines three different kinds of access permissions: user, group, and other. The *user* of a file is usually the creator of the file; a *group* is a set of users sharing a common ID; and *other* means no associated ID is used. Within these three ID levels three types of access are identified: read, write, or both. Each ID level and access type is represented by a bit set to 0 or 1. A 0 means no authority is granted and a 1 means authority is granted. Unix file-level security is represented as three triples, or nine bits of information.

Each NFS request is accompanied by the user ID and any group IDs assigned to the user. These IDs are checked against the security information in the Unix file system's metadata for the file and/or directory. Even though two systems may be communicating via NFS, that does not mean that the user will be able to access any files if the IDs do not match.

CIFS uses ACLs (access control lists) that are associated with shares, directories, and files. ACLs can be considerably more descriptive than the three-triple system used by Unix and provide for certain condition testing in addition to direct access characteristics. When a CIFS user accesses a share, the user ID is checked against the ACL for the share. CIFS is session-oriented, which means there is an implied connection between clients and servers that maintains the tight control over all communications.

Locking Mechanisms in NFS and CIFS   One of the main differences between NFS and CIFS is how file locking is accomplished in the NAS appliance. This section explores these differences.

PC operating systems, including DOS, have implemented fairly strong file locking for many years. A PC application can open files using system interfaces that specify what I/O operation it expects to perform on the file. Not only that, but within those file open requests is another request that determines whether or not other applications can open the file, and if so, how they will be allowed to use it. These restrictions, or locks, are enforced by the file system. In other words, the first application to access a file in the PC file system determines the behavior of all other applications that come afterward.

This is why CIFS requires a session orientation. The management of the Windows file system lock manager requires historical information about which client has opened which file for what operation in what order.

NFS, on the other hand, doesn't provide mandatory locks; instead, it provides what are called advisory locks, which inform subsequent applications whether or not another application is using the file and what it is using it for. From this information the second and later applications can choose if they want to adhere to the lock request. In other words, any Unix application at any time can go in and do what it wants to with any file. There are no rules, just good citizens.

NAS NFS-based systems can use the facility of an add-on locking manager called the network lock manager, or NLM. Applications that use the NLM will provide more consistent locking behavior in NFS environments. However, the NLM is strictly an optional facility that functions as an application on top of the foundation NFS function. An application that uses the NLM has no guarantees that some other application will use the lock. An application that ignores the lock could access the data and corrupt it through unstructured, uncoordinated updates. This may not be a big concern if data sharing and concurrent access are not common. In fact, it is not an issue at all if the concurrent users are only reading the file and not updating it. However, this situation is one of those systems-level "gotchas" that could be a potential problem well into the future as the application mix changes.

CIFS Emulation for NFS Servers

NFS appliance manufacturers initially built their business around serving Unix files to Unix clients. As the presence of Windows clients is practically a given in most businesses, NFS appliance vendors have had to come to grips with how they will provide services to Windows clients. One way to do this is to add NFS client software to the Windows system. While this works, it requires installation and management on the client Windows system and comes at additional cost.

An alternative is to emulate a CIFS server in an NFS appliance. The emulation functions like a Windows server system, but with a non-Windows file system providing the storage. Figure 14-6 shows the network file protocol stack for a UFS+NFS appliance with a virtual CIFS server providing access to Windows clients with their native CIFS network file protocol.

Locking and CIFS Emulation

With significant differences in the way files are locked between UFS/NFS and NTFS/CIFS, designers of NAS appliances have a difficult task in determining what level of locking to provide in network storage appliances supporting both NFS and CIFS protocols. In general there are two approaches:

▼ Choose one network file system, implement it, and emulate the other.

▲ Develop an independent technology that can encompass both Unix and Windows locking methods and commands.

Linux and Free BSD have virtually no license fees, and NFS is an open standard. This makes them a popular choice for appliance designers who want to develop relatively inexpensive products. Linux- and FreeBSD-based appliance developers that want to provide

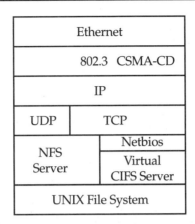

| Ethernet |
| 802.3   CSMA-CD |
| IP |

Figure 14-6.   Combining NFS and CIFS access in a network file access protocol stack

both NFS and CIFS protocol support for Unix and Windows clients can do so by emulating CIFS locking support in a software application that runs as a service on the appliance.

CIFS emulation identifies requests from Windows clients and provides the same type of behavior as an actual Windows server—including locking. When the first Windows user opens a file, the CIFS emulator will service its request as well as deny subsequent service requests from other users or applications that attempt to open the file. From that point forward, the CIFS emulator is responsible for tracking which users have access to which files in what order.

The difficult aspect of CIFS emulation is determining how NFS clients are to be handled when accessing files that have been opened and locked by Windows users. For CIFS emulation to work correctly, all client access attempts, NFS and CIFS alike, should be funneled through the CIFS emulator to ensure that Unix NFS clients do not step on data that Windows clients have already opened and locked. This funneling of NFS client access through an emulation is not standard NFS behavior and requires additional development work.

The other approach to solving *bimodal* Windows and Unix client access to a NAS appliance is to implement an independent network file system on top of a platform-independent operating system. While this approach carries considerably greater cost, it can also accommodate multiple access methods without compromise.

When the operating system and file system used in a NAS appliance are independent of native implementations, all access, regardless of the platform or protocol used, is handled as an application service by specialized access processes, which can include lock resolution across the various access methods used. Figure 14-7 compares the two methods for resolving locks.

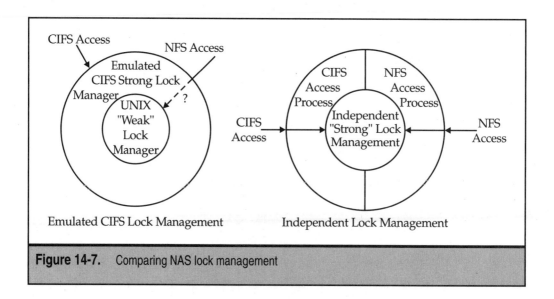

Figure 14-7. Comparing NAS lock management

SAMBA CIFS Emulation   One of the available CIFS emulation technologies developed for Unix systems, or more specifically Linux systems, is Samba. The name "Samba" has its roots in the SMB (Server Message Block) protocol that preceded CIFS in Windows products. Samba is an open-source development project that benefits from the work of many independent software developers and has been implemented as part of commercial products from several NAS vendors. For more information on Samba, visit **www.samba.org** on the World Wide Web.

NEW DEVELOPMENTS IN NETWORK ATTACHED STORAGE: NASD AND DAFS

Like any storage technology, NAS continues to evolve to meet the demands of the market. Sometimes technology is developed to address areas of weakness, and sometimes it is developed to take advantage of market opportunities. In the case of NAS, both types of development are furthering the capabilities of the technology in interesting ways.

NASD

One of the more recent and interesting developments in network storage is a joint research project between Carnegie Mellon University and several companies in the storage industry called NASD, which stands for Network Attached Secure Devices. The main idea behind NASD is that higher levels of intelligence can be incorporated in disk drives to manage network communications as well as storage functions. By allowing disk drives to manage their own network communications, it is believed that the file server can be removed as a potential bottleneck in client/server storage. If there are no servers in the network I/O path, they cannot malfunction or become overloaded and introduce latency or failures.

Professor Garth Gibson of Carnegie Mellon University (CMU) is one of the principal authors of the original RAID papers published in 1987. His work at CMU has continued to examine ways to provide more scalable access to data and circumvent I/O bottlenecks. This work led to the development of the NASD research project. The NASD storage model places NAS-type functionality directly on a disk drive, without the presence of server hardware or a server operating system. In essence, it takes the concept of a NAS appliance to an extreme by placing the appliance-enabling function inside the disk drive.

NASD takes advantage of embedded intelligence in disk drives. The idea is straightforward: as processors become increasingly powerful and small, they can be integrated directly in disk drives and manage their own security, file system, and network communications. NASD researchers have been working on developing and testing these capabilities using a network architecture similar to the SAN integrated network backup scheme discussed in Chapter 10. In this type of design, the security function is managed by a connection broker process running in a network system that distributes access keys to clients who want to access a network attached disk drive. The client then uses the key when establishing a connection with a disk drive, and the key is validated by the embedded intelligence in each disk drive.

The security model is based on the concept of private key/public key authentication technology, in which the connection broker, which NASD refers to as the *file manager*, provides private keys to disk drives and public keys to user client systems. Beyond the role of key distribution, the file manager can perform other roles, such as acting as a domain controller for a network of Windows clients.

When a user logs into the file manager, authenticating himself or herself to the NASD network, the file manager can determine which disks the user has access to and can exchange disk addresses and access "credentials" needed to access NASD resources. With security control placed in a separate file manager, each individual NASD disk drive only has to know whether or not to accept a request by examining the user's public key.

The communications to NASD disk drives use typical client redirector software and protocols with the additional capability to exchange keys when required. Figure 14-8 illustrates the distribution of public and private keys from the file manager to client systems and NASD disk drives.

One of the interesting parts of a NASD network is how often clients communicate with the file manager system in relation to how often they communicate with NASD disk drives. Essentially, the file manager only needs to be accessed to initialize a session between a client system and its disk drive(s). After that, all communications can be handled between the client and the NASD disk drive. Data transfers that are broken off prematurely will need to be re-established, but it may not be necessary to authenticate again with the file manager if the public key received is still available to use. This design removes the file manager as a potential storage I/O bottleneck.

Potential NASD Implementations

NASD is an interesting concept for several reasons. First, it promises to significantly reduce the cost of NAS appliances by adding low-cost parts to low-cost products. Second, the use of networking technology, especially lightweight, small twisted pair wiring, is a very attractive interconnect compared to traditional device cabling. Third, the ability to create specialized ASICs (application-specific integrated circuits) that support different network access protocols could be very useful. For example, the ability to put FTP or HTTP server protocols on a disk drive may make them immediately deployable for certain Web applications.

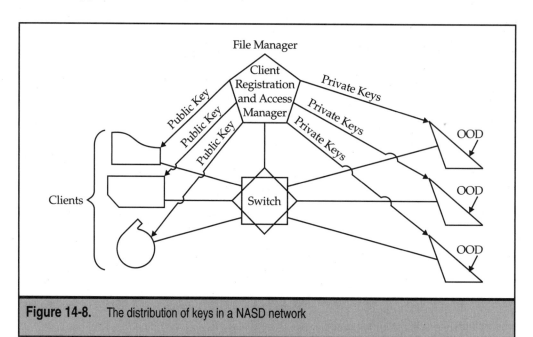

Figure 14-8.   The distribution of keys in a NASD network

Integrating network and file system functionality with a storage product can add a tremendous amount of value to one of the best technology deals going—a big disk drive. Even if a NASD packaged disk drive appliance were to cost three times as much as its unintelligent version, it would probably still be an excellent value. Twisted pair wiring and RJ-45 connectors makes connections very fast, inexpensive, and easy to implement. The ability to connect intelligent disk drives to inexpensive Ethernet hubs may provide the easiest and cheapest way to share and store data in networks.

DAFS

While NASD addresses the opportunity for NAS technology to become less expensive overall than most other types of storage options, DAFS, the *Direct Access File System,* promises to take the technology upstream as a data center storage facility.

DAFS takes advantage of new VI and InfiniBand technologies as discussed in Chapter 13 to provide very fast, very reliable connections between multiple NAS appliances and between clients and NAS appliances. The anticipated result of DAFS is to remove the scalability limitations and management problems associated with individual NAS appliances as well as to allow NAS to provide the performance and reliability required by transaction processing systems.

Scaling Up with DAFS Clusters

One of the design goals of DAFS is to allow a single file system image to continue to expand, even if a single NAS appliance reaches its capacity limitations. Built on the capabilities of VI, and in particular of InfiniBand wiring, DAFS provides a fast, lightweight, and reliable communications mechanism for building clusters of NAS appliances that communicate with each other about I/O processes.

Clustered DAFS appliances share a common, aggregate presentation of the data stored on all participating DAFS appliances. To borrow the overused parlance of the industry, it allows a single system image of the aggregate file system to clients. The major benefit of this aggregation is that clustered DAFS storage can be accessed by client systems as a single mount point. This, in turn, enables client drive mappings to continue to grow beyond the capacity of a single appliance, which means client configurations do not need to be changed regardless of the number of different network connections and DAFS appliances used. Figure 14-9 shows how three DAFS appliances present a unified file system image from the three file systems running on each node in a DAFS cluster.

The DAFS cluster uses a shared nothing approach, as discussed in Chapter 13. Each DAFS appliance presents the same external representation of an aggregated file system, but it only manages the data structure for its own storage. In other words, each DAFS appliance manages its own internal storage space.

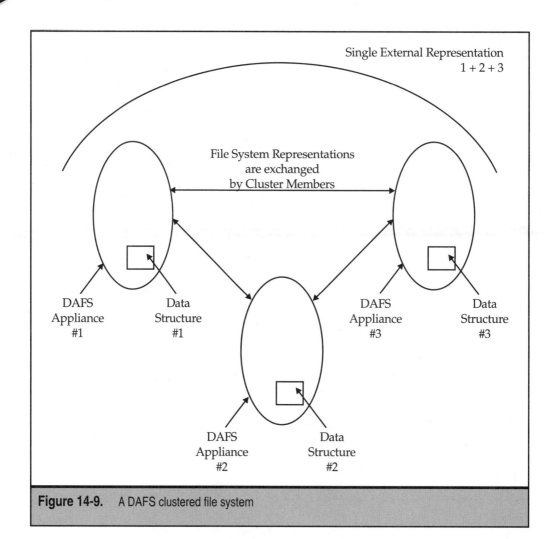

Figure 14-9. A DAFS clustered file system

When a client accesses data from the DAFS cluster, either the DAFS appliance fulfills the request directly if the file resides on storage that it manages, or it requests the data from the DAFS appliance that manages it. After the other appliance forwards the data to the requesting appliance, the requesting appliance can then satisfy the end user's request. This process is shown here:

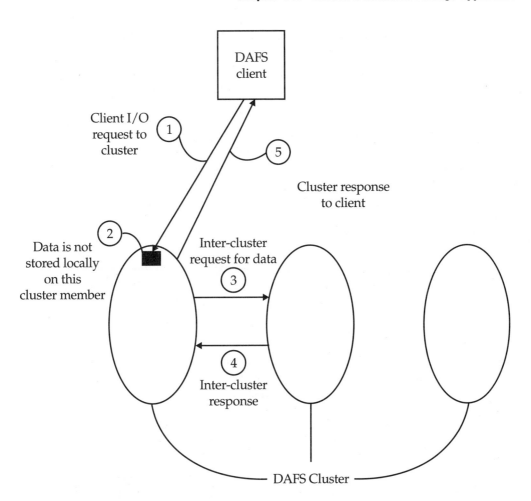

DAFS Transaction Client Connections

DAFS appliance clusters also extend the communications capabilities of VI and InfiniBand to span the connection between NAS and database systems. As discussed previously, there are valid and serious concerns regarding the use of NAS appliances for transaction processing systems. Typical NFS communications over IP networks are neither fast enough nor reliable enough to serve as an interconnect for transaction I/O.

The use of VI and InfiniBand in DAFS changes this situation considerably by providing a highly structured and extremely fast and low-latency connection between database systems and DAFS appliances. In essence, DAFS replaces the ambiguity of Ethernet/IP networks with highly reliable channel-class wiring. Using the structured communications and flow control of VI and InfiniBand, the data integrity issues of NFS-based storage are negated. Transaction data that is lost in transmissions in a DAFS connection is recognized immediately by the communicating nodes, and subsequent transmissions can be delayed until the transmission is recovered.

In addition, the speed of RDMA memory-to-memory transfers for transaction data exchanges could provide optimal performance and database I/O rates. While transmission rates for the InfiniBand links are fast, the biggest performance potential lies in moving the data structure calculations from the database system to the DAFS appliance. It remains to be seen whether or not DAFS technology will include data structure processing accelerators, but the potential exists for a DAFS appliance to be able to provide this function far faster than a general-purpose system that does this work using host processors and memory.

The I/O path for a transaction storage operation over a DAFS connection is shown in Figure 14-10. Notice that the transaction system uses byte-range offsets to access data and that the DAFS appliance provides the data structure translation to logical block addresses on storage.

Figure 14-10 indicates a DAFS file redirector running on the database client. This DAFS file redirector is likely to be considerably different from the file I/O redirectors that have been used for NFS and CIFS. While DAFS is structured to use many of the same functions as NFS, the underlying communications structure is considerably different and is not likely to be incorporated in host operating systems. Therefore, DAFS database support will require the installation and integration of specialized DAFS client software. As always happens with network redirection software, there is likely to be some number of iterations and releases before the DAFS client works as anticipated without bugs.

DAFS Scalability for Database Support

It is not clear if the scalability capabilities of DAFS technology will also apply to its transaction processing functions. The issue is that the data structure elements of the DAFS cluster file system are controlled by individual appliances. So, if a database's storage requirements exceed the capacity of a single appliance, the data would have to be distributed to other appliances in the cluster. The time consumed by coordinating database I/O across cluster links would likely have a significant adverse effect on overall database performance, especially when compared to transaction rates achieved with a single DAFS appliance. This could be circumvented by placing database files on different DAFS appliances, but there would still be an issue if any one file exceeded the capacity of a single appliance.

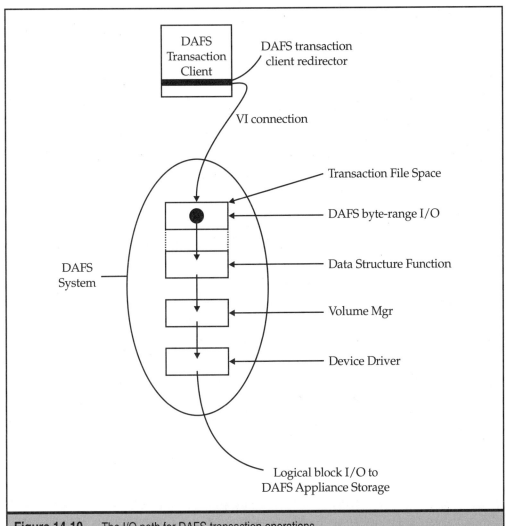

Figure 14-10.   The I/O path for DAFS transaction operations

SUMMARY

Network attached storage integrates system, storage, and networking technologies to reduce the cost of installing and managing storage. NAS is born from the concept of moving functions out of general-purpose servers into special network storage appliances with spartan operating systems that are tuned to provide the best possible storage performance at a given price point. Compared to general-purpose systems, NAS products can be installed much more quickly and provide the flexibility required to quickly adapt to a changing environment. Several types of NAS products are available, including CD-ROM servers and thin file servers. By far the most common of these is a file-serving appliance.

Over time, the technology driving most NAS developments is client redirection software, especially those functions integrated into Windows operating systems. Where NAS products originally were strictly Unix NFS servers, today they accommodate both Unix/NFS and Windows/CIFS client systems.

A lot is being made of open source software in the NAS space. The Linux operating system provides an excellent platform on which to build inexpensive and customized NAS products. The jury is still out as to whether Linux systems will be able to provide the same type of functionality as proprietary operating system NAS products. The Samba server software that allows a Unix system to support Windows clients shows that the open source development community has taken notice of NAS and responded with an important piece of the puzzle.

Finally, the future for NAS is likely to be very rosy. Significant R&D efforts are underway in the NAS industry to develop new capabilities beyond its current role as a file server replacement. NASD promises to take NAS functionality down to the device level, while DAFS has the potential of elevating the role of NAS into an all-encompassing data center solution.

EXERCISES

1. Five departments are using the corporate LAN, each with its own 50GB NAS appliance. Within each department, all users share all their data with each other, but different departments do not share data. Design a backup and recovery plan for these NAS appliances.

2. Twenty-four file servers, nearing the end of their life, are serving files to 1,250 users. Each file server has 120GB of disk storage running at an average of 85 percent full. These file servers are all connected through a pair of 16-port 100BaseT switches. Your job is to plan the consolidation of these servers onto NAS appliances and upgrade the network, if needed. Assume you have the OK to purchase NAS appliances with capacities up to 1TB in capacity and the ability to install up to four network interface cards, including Gigabit Ethernet. As usual, you will be rewarded for keeping the project under budget.

CHAPTER 15

Filing: The Great Frontier of Storage Networking

Filing claims the topmost layer in the hierarchy of storage network functions. While filing is independent of storing and wiring, it determines how these other functions are used. Therefore, filing has a great deal of potential to change the way storage networks are structured and deployed.

The most obvious filing products in the storage networking industry are NAS appliances. (The preceding chapter introduced DAFS as an exciting new technology for clusters of NAS appliances.) But filing is not restricted to NAS; it is used in all systems that store data in storage networks. Some of the most interesting research and development projects in the storage networking industry today are working to distribute filing functionality across network connections. There are many ways this can be done with a wide variety of complexity and sophistication.

The chapter begins with a discussion of three important filing technologies used in storage networking—journaling, snapshots, and dynamic filing system expansion—followed by a discussion of two important database system I/O technologies: direct database file I/O and database log mirroring and replication. After that, the chapter turns to look at the integration of intelligent processors in storage devices and subsystems, particularly for object-based storage, or OBS. From that base, several different models of distributed filing systems are analyzed, and the chapter closes with a brief discussion of file-level virtualization, including hierarchical storage management (HSM) and derivatives of the HSM concept for dynamically moving data for optimal performance.

REQUIREMENTS FOR FILE SYSTEMS IN STORAGE NETWORKS

The dynamic nature of storage networks requires a few additional capabilities from file systems, such as:

▼ Journaling

■ Snapshots

▲ Dynamic file system expansion

Journaling File Systems

File systems are complex and intricate software systems that are responsible for the safe-keeping of all the data stored by a computer. Multiple internal relationships exist in the data structures of the file system that can be used to check for and repair flaws in the file system's structure.

One of the most common file system integrity tests is invoked when a system restarts following an unexpected shutdown. In this situation, the system runs a thorough file system integrity check to ensure that all its internal data structures are correct. For small systems, this test does not usually pose big problems, but for large servers with large file systems, such as those typically found in storage networking environments, these tests can take several hours to run. When end users or applications are waiting for this data to be made available, the inability to get work done can be expensive.

To circumvent this problem, file systems that have different internal data structures, called *journaling*, or *journaled*, file systems, have been created to allow file systems to be quickly checked for errors following an unexpected system crash or loss of power.

Logging File System Activities

The basic idea of a journaled file system is to copy the commands for all write I/O operations occurring in a file system to a separate system journal file. This is the same concept used for databases or any other kind of system that keeps records of its internal status. The process of writing to the journal and writing the data is shown here:

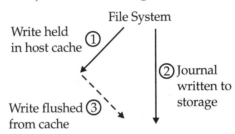

At some unknown point in the future, following a system failure, the system can be restarted and its status checked by comparing the last several actions posted in the journal with the status of the file system's data structure. The process of checking the journal, as shown here, is much faster than running a complete file system data structure analysis:

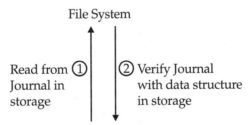

Log-Structured File Systems

A file system technology closely related to the journaled file system is a *log-structured file system*. Where most file systems distribute data across the logical block address space using some fairness algorithm, log-structured file systems write new data to free blocks at the end of the file system's used block addresses. In other words, the log-structured file system is constantly appending data to the end of the used block range. A log-structured file system does not keep a separate journal file to log writes in the system; instead, the actual file system write operations become a log of all write activities. When a log-structured file system restarts after an unexpected shutdown, it first looks for the most recent writes to storage at the end of the file system's data and then immediately begins working again, starting from where it left off, appending any new data following the last complete I/O operation on disk.

One of the key ideas of a log-structured file system is that the data most often requested is the most recently used data. This means it is data that is located at the end of the file system's used logical block addresses. Therefore, the disk arms in disk drives in a log-structured file system do not have to move as far as with a normal file system to read recently written data.

While log-structured file systems are interesting, not very many are implemented in products. They require regular maintenance to recycle free blocks that become available in the middle of file system's used blocks. As these blocks are freed, other data in the file system has to be moved into the available "holes" to ensure that there is enough free space to continue to write new updated data to the end of file system's used addresses. As it turns out, this constant maintenance, which can be compared to disk defragmentation, can require an enormous amount of system overhead to keep the system from reaching the end of its address space while writing. For that reason, the journal approach discussed previously is much more widely deployed.

Software Snapshots

Software snapshots take the concept of hardware snapshots as introduced in Chapter 4 and implement it in filing system metadata to allow data to be virtually "frozen" and accessed as it existed at some point in time. It is one of the hallmarks of the Network Appliance WAFL file system and is likely to become an important ingredient of other filing systems used in storage networks as end users and administrators become familiar with the benefits it delivers.

While hardware-based, block-based snapshots work very well for making extra copies of data for backup and testing purposes, they do not provide an easy way to keep multiple point-in-time images of the file system. This capability to keep and retrieve multiple images, or versions, of files is a valuable capability for many system administrators who are asked by their end users to restore older versions of files. While backup systems can provide the ability to restore individual file versions, the restore process can be difficult and time consuming. Snapshot file versions, on the other hand, are relatively simple to work with.

Also, the difficulties of making backup work were discussed at length in Chapters 7 and 10. One of the difficulties in backup is the requirement to run "hot" backups that need copy-on-write functions to ensure data integrity during the backup operation. While copy-on-write works, it also poses a few risks and adds a significant amount of overhead to I/O processes while backups are running. Software snapshots circumvent copy-on-write altogether by allowing backup data to be read from a virtual snapshot file system within the real file system.

Software snapshot technology will also be very useful for allowing data mover technology to be implemented in SANs for similar reasons. As discussed in Chapter 10, data movers must use a facility such as copy-on-write to make sure the data that is moved has integrity. Again, software snapshots circumvent the need to use copy-on-write to support this important capability in storage networks.

First a Word about Free-Space Allocation

Data structures in filing systems keep information about the location of all used and unused (free) blocks in the system. This includes a large number of temporary files and other files that are short-lived. It also includes information about all new updates to files that overwrite older data but may be placed in different logical block addresses for one reason or another. As files are deleted or as spaces within files are no longer being used, the filing system's data structure function keeps track of these free blocks so that it can place them in the *free space pool* and reallocate them to other files as needed. This free space allocation and management of the free space pool is one of the most important internal workings of all filing systems, as it enables data locations to be recycled over and over again.

Snapshots and Free Space

In essence, the concept of software snapshots delays the freeing of blocks back into the free space pool by continuing to associate deleted or updated data as historical parts of the filing system. In other words, filing systems with software snapshots maintain access to data that normal filing systems discard. It sounds like it could be black magic, but software snapshots follow a very structured and logical process. After some number of snapshots have been processed, the deleted or overwritten data will age sufficiently to be removed from the filing system and its blocks will be returned to the free space pool.

Filing Metadata Used in Software Snapshots

The idea of software snapshots is grounded in the use of filing metadata that identifies historical versions of data. The data structure in a filing system maintains complete knowledge of where all data is stored in logical block addresses. The metadata in a filing system maintains all sorts of information about the data, including its creation date and time, the date and time it was last updated, who owns the data, etc.

In a filing system with software snapshots, the metadata also includes some attributes that indicate the relative age of the data. For instance, historical snapshot metadata can be represented as several bits in a row that represent the history of every block in every file used by the system. The snapshot function in the filing system manipulates these bits, turning them on or off to indicate the time periods when data blocks were current. "Current" in this case refers to the fact that this data block is part of the file or object that would be acted on if the file were to be accessed. The snapshot does not associate a specific date and time with each block but simply identifies whether or not the block was current at the time the snapshot ran.

As the snapshot process runs, it first flushes all system buffers to ensure that all pending writes are committed to disk storage, and then it performs a rotation operation on the bits in the metadata. In other words, it shifts the pattern of bits in the row and adds a new "current" bit to the beginning of the row. The bits can be represented like this row of ten bits shown here:

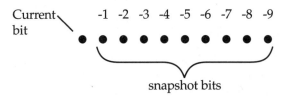

When new data is created, its metadata is also created with a snapshot bit row that has only the current bit turned on, like this:

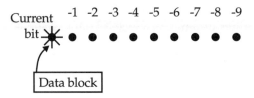

When the snapshot runs the next time, we'll assume that data is still current and the sequence of bits is shifted and the current bit is regenerated, like this:

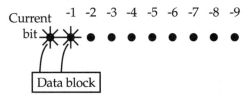

Notice that the data is now associated with a single bit that links it to the specific date and time that the snapshot process ran. The metadata does not know when the process ran, but the snapshot process can make that connection through its own historical information. This process repeats and continues to shift the snapshot bits, and as long as the data is current, the current bit will stay turned on. Eventually, data that has been current for an extended period of time will have all the snapshot metadata bits turned on. There is a lot of data in a file system that will be represented this way. For instance, any file that was created and held by the file system for an extended period of time will be represented this way. The snapshot metadata does not depend on whether or not a file is being accessed. Dormant files that were created months and years ago and are no longer being used will still be current and have their current status maintained by the snapshot process.

When data is deleted or overwritten, its current bit is turned off, like this:

C -1 -2 -3 -4 -5 -6 -7 -8 -9

From this point on, whenever snapshots run, the snapshot bits are shifted and the data can be seen as aging from its metadata bits. For instance, assume a block was deleted four snapshot periods in the past. Its snapshot metadata bits would look like this:

C -1 -2 -3 -4 -5 -6 -7 -8 -9

● ● ● ● ✳ ● ● ● ● ●

Storage Management Applications and Snapshots

Now, when storage management operations are run against a filing system with snapshot capability, the storage management application can read data that is associated with the last snapshot, instead of the active data. This way, the storage management application works with a complete set of data that is guaranteed to have integrity, and there is no need for a copy-on-write process to run.

Filing systems with snapshots are well suited for replication over LANs, MANs, and WANs. The snapshot data is read and transferred across slower and smaller-bandwidth links. As discussed in Chapter 4 regarding replication, the cost to replicate data over relatively expensive WAN links can be minimized compared to block-level mirroring by only transmitting stabilized snapshot data that is known to have good integrity.

It is also possible to work with previous generations of data, not just the last known snapshot. This way, complete sets of older versions of associated files can be recovered or preserved. A hidden benefit (or risk) of software snapshots is that system administrators can identify data that they want to preserve after the data may have already been overwritten or deleted.

It is worthwhile to recognize that some of the data being read during a snapshot data access is data that may be in use by the system. Data that existed at the time of the last snapshot may still be current and in use by the system. For that reason, software snapshots can still theoretically be affected by locking. More importantly, the storage devices and subsystems that are used for snapshot access are the same ones used for production applications. Therefore, software snapshots will almost certainly create some contention for storage resources, such as disk arms, that will have a negative effect on other applications running concurrently.

Dynamic Filing System Expansion

As said many times in this book already, dealing with the constant growth of stored data is a difficult challenge. When the capacity of a storage volume is reached by a filing system, there are few good options with traditional filing systems. Usually it means shutting down the system, attaching new, larger storage devices, turning the system back on, mounting the new storage hardware, and copying the old data from old storage or restoring it from backup tapes.

Unfortunately, many things can go wrong with this process, and many experienced systems administrators have some first-hand knowledge of disastrous data loss that occurred during a capacity expansion process. To address this need, several companies have developed filing technology that allows the data structure of the filing system to expand as new logical block addresses are made available. This allows a single storage volume to scale up in capacity to meet new requirements with minimal interruption and administrative effort. This is not to say that this can be done automatically without planning, but it does greatly simplify the process and reduce the risk of data loss.

Dynamic Filing System Expansion and Volume/Array Management

Before the filing system can expand its capacity, a volume manager, device driver, or array controller needs to be able to associate some new range of logical block addresses with an existing volume. There are several ways this could be accomplished. For starters, a volume manager could use concatenation to add logical block addresses to an exported storage volume. An example of this would be adding a new disk drive to a storage network and then concatenating the available capacity of logical block addresses of this new drive to the capacity of an existing drive. The new blocks from the new drive could be made available as an additional range of logical block addresses, which could become part of the filing system's free space pool. New data could be written by the filing system into this new address space as determined by the filing system's data structure algorithms.

Expanding Capacity in RAID Arrays   Concatenation is certainly not the only way to organize storage, as there are many possible configurations of storage subsystems. For instance, it is possible to add additional disks to RAID arrays and have them integrated into the RAID structure by restriping the data and parity across the new array configuration. In essence, this is somewhat similar to performing a parity rebuild of data, except there is a little extra storage space to work with. This reallocation of data onto array blocks needs to preserve the existing exported logical block address space by establishing new translation tables for the data in the array. When all is said and done, there will be new, additional logical block addresses available to use by the filing system. Figure 15-1 shows this process of expanding the array's capacity.

Integrating Address Space Changes with the Filing System's Data Structure   After the new address space has been created and integrated by the volume manager or array manager, the filing system needs to be able to discover that the additional address space is available so it can integrate it into its functions. In general, there are three issues to take care of: establishing the total size of the new available address space, redistributing data across the new addresses, and incorporating the new space in the filing system's free space pool.

For the filing system to know what its new logical address space is, it needs to be able to communicate with the underlying volume manager that exports it. For the most part, this only happens with tightly coupled filing systems and volume managers developed by the same software developer, such as Veritas or Sun. The file data structure process of the file system has to know the total address space to accomplish its work.

Just as RAID arrays can redistribute data across new drives added to an array, the filing system will probably also need to redistribute data according to its data structure process to ensure fairness in accessing data. Obviously any metadata that relates to the location of the data also has to be altered accordingly. If the data structure function redistributes the data, it is possible that data may be redistributed twice in this process—once by the volume

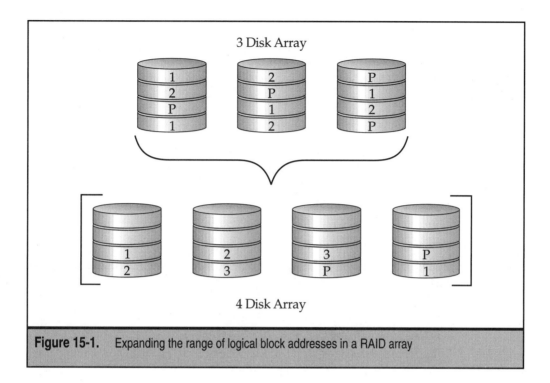

Figure 15-1.   Expanding the range of logical block addresses in a RAID array

or array manager in adding disk drives to the array and once by the filing system's data structure process.

Finally, after all the data has been redistributed, the new available free space created by the previous two processes needs to be integrated into the free space pool. Notice that some of the block addresses that were previously in use may now be free space as determined by the redistribution of data by the data structure function.

DATABASE FILING TECHNOLOGIES

Databases have their own unique filing requirements that stem from their use in high-throughput transaction processing. We'll now look at two of the more interesting filing technologies: direct file I/O and database replication and mirroring.

Direct File I/O

Databases often use *raw partitions* to provide the data structure function and calculate the logical block addresses for database data. This bypasses the process of sending file I/O requests to the file system, which in turn would calculate the block addresses for the database's file I/O operations. While raw partitions work well for performance, they leave a little bit to be desired for systems management. Raw partitions tend to look like black boxes to storage management applications that do not have any way of dealing with the database's storage except as bulk addresses.

So, the idea of direct file I/O is to allow a file system to identify certain files that are accessed directly by the database as a range of logical block addresses, but can also be managed by the file system and any storage management application as a discrete file. To do this, the file system has to be able to accept storing-level logical block operations for the particular range of block addresses that represent the database file, as shown here:

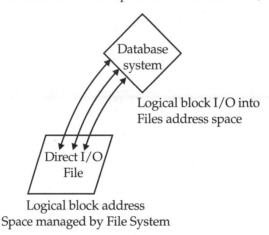

Direct file I/O is an interesting combination of both filing and storing functions and, as such, is not the same as sending byte-range file I/O operations from a database to a NAS appliance, as discussed in the preceding chapter. The database I/O is done at a storing level, while any storage management is managed at a filing level. Direct File I/O has several interesting problems to solve, including how database files are created initially and how the sizes of the files are adjusted as their capacity needs change. The management of this special type of file is not necessarily trivial technology, as filing systems are written to control the entire data structure, as opposed to ignoring certain address ranges that are reserved for the database. It is difficult to assign metadata for file activity that bypasses the filing system's normal operations.

These issues aside, direct file I/O provides an excellent compromise between performance and management goals. When the database is accessing data in the file, performance is roughly equivalent to that for raw partitions. In addition, when the database is not working with a particular file, backups or mirroring can progress without risking data integrity and without having to shut down the entire database.

Database Mirroring and Replication

Another important aspect of database filing related to storage networks is the way database data can be replicated and mirrored over a storage network. As businesses push toward higher availability to data, they want to protect their database and transaction data on a regular basis several times a day, not constantly. In this section, we look at a process for mixing file-level replication with storing-level mirroring to protect databases in an efficient and effective manner.

Netting out the Database I/O Mirroring

Database I/O is an involved process. Databases tend to generate a large amount of I/O traffic, and it is nearly impossible to tell what is going on at any moment. Transactions are multistepped processes that require many individual I/O instructions to complete correctly. While mirroring block I/O is a viable way to prepare for a database system disaster, it is very difficult to tell what the status of mirrored I/Os is if the system should fail suddenly. There are bound to be several incomplete transactions underway that need to be identified and completed or removed. While each I/O operation is essential to process data correctly on the local site, it is not necessary to mirror them all to a remote site if the goal is to synchronize stable data at some point in time. For instance, a record that is updated several times in succession on the local database system only needs to have the final results transmitted to the remote database to synchronize the data. In other words, it is possible to mirror all database activities over a MAN/WAN link, but that is not a very efficient way to work.

Replicating Transaction Logs

Database systems use transaction logging processes to monitor the activities of the database. In essence, the logs contain lists of commands and transactions that were performed by the database. Database administrators are familiar with using these log files to put the database back in functioning order following a system failure. Any transaction posted to the log file can be "replayed" (rolled forward) to run the transaction process again, and transactions can also be "played in reverse" (rolled backward) to remove the results of the transaction process from the database. The decision to roll transactions forward or backward depends on the nature of the failure and the types of processes that were running when the failure occurred.

The importance of the log file is that it serves as a shorthand mechanism to replicate or remove data from a database. While mirroring database I/Os at the storing level can take a large amount of network bandwidth, possibly at high cost, transmitting log files between local and remote systems can be done relatively inexpensively. Therefore, replicating log files as shown in Figure 15-2 is a common way to protect database data from a local disaster.

After the log files are replicated from the local site to the remote site, they need to be played forward to bring the remote database up to the level of the local database as of the time the last log file was written. In essence, this is similar to taking a snapshot of the database at the time the log file was closed. The difference is that the snapshot data stays on a filing system for an extended period of time, but the database log files are regularly and

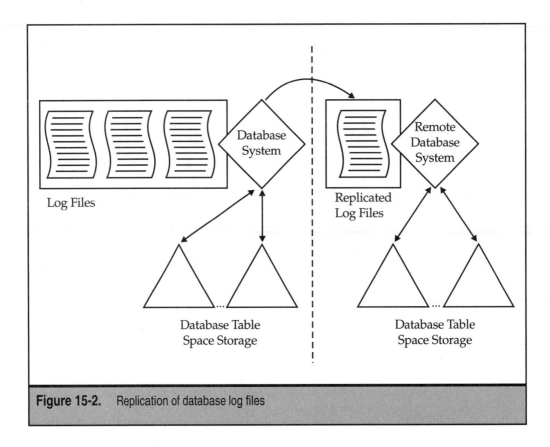

Figure 15-2.   Replication of database log files

often overwritten. The process of synching the remote database with a "log-snapshot" is shown here:

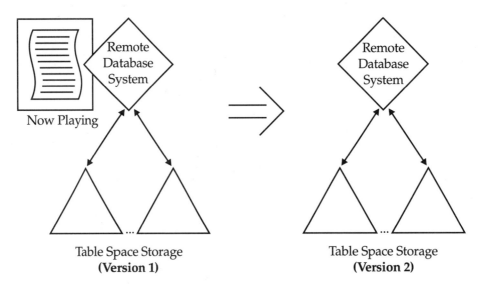

It is probably obvious, but the method of replicating log files only works if there is a computer system running the database program at the remote site that can play the logs. If the remote site only has storage subsystems, then the data will need to be mirrored. This small detail of needing a system and somebody to run it obviously adds cost and logistics problems to the log replication scheme. Therefore, it may work best if the database log files can be replicated between two different data centers where there is a staff that knows what to do.

Finishing the Job with Log File Mirroring

Through replication, which is a filing-level function, it is possible to keep a remote database in synch with the status of the last database log file. However, this does not protect the database from losing data that has been written since the last log file was replicated to a remote site.

For that reason, it makes sense to mirror the log file as it is being written from the local site to the remote site. In general, there are far fewer I/Os needed to write the log file than are needed for the database to write transactions, which means the bandwidth requirements are far less. One approach is to configure the database to write its log files to its own dedicated, local storage device and to mirror all I/O operations to this device over a wide area link, as shown here:

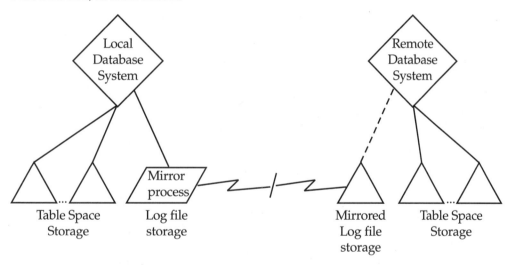

With the log files being mirrored to the remote site, a failure at the local site would result in a partially completed log file at the remote site. A database administrator can then examine the log file and determine what transactions can be rolled forward to bring the database up to date to a more recent time than the time a complete log file was played. This way, much less data would be lost following a failure of the local database system.

Now, of course, if the log file is being mirrored to the remote site, it might not be necessary to replicate the log file anymore, because there would already be a mirrored copy at the remote site. It would be advisable to retain the ability to replicate log files to provide redundancy and error correction capabilities in case there were ever any integrity problems with mirrored log files.

PACKING INTELLIGENCE INTO STORAGE DEVICES AND SUBSYSTEMS

One of the most interesting developments in network storage is the integration of intelligent processors into storage devices and subsystems. Intelligent processors have been used in storage devices and subsystems already for many years to manage their internal functions. Disk drives have evolved over time to integrate specialized processors for error recovery, logical block address translations, tagged command queuing, and RAID 5 XOR capabilities. The NASD project, discussed in Chapter 14, is primarily concerned with integrating networking functionality into disk drives.

Storage subsystems have used specialized processors for many years to provide array and subsystem management, including RAID configurations, caching, tagged command queuing, and storage channel communications. It seems apparent that storage subsystem vendors will continue to add new software to their products that make them more competitive and easier to sell. An example is a storage subsystem that integrates the storage details of a database system to achieve higher cache hit ratios for faster performance.

Deconstructing Filing Functions

With more intelligence being integrated into storage devices and subsystems, it makes sense to examine which filing functions could reside in them and how they might be used. Previously, filing was described as having two roles in the I/O path: the external representation of data and the internal structure of data in logical block storage spaces.

However, there is more to filing than I/O path functions. There are also functions for access control as well as for creating and maintaining metadata—the data that the filing system uses to describe and manage the data it holds. With these two additional functions added, a filing system has the following components:

▼ Access control

■ Data representation

■ Metadata management

▲ Data structure

Each of these will be discussed briefly in the following sections.

Access Control

The filing system's access control function is the primary security mechanism for managing user access to data in the filing system. There two basic levels of access control to consider, one that determines whether or not a data object can be accessed and another that determines how locking is managed.

File and Directory Access Control   The first access control step in the filing system involves *access permissions.* In general, access permissions are a way of matching users with the data they are allowed to access. Systems administrators establish access permissions for their users to either grant or deny access to various parts of the file system. If a user does not have permissions established for a certain file or directory, that user will not be able to open it and work on it.

File and Directory Locking   Locking was introduced in Chapter 14 in the comparison of NFS and CIFS network-attached storage appliances. One of the main issues with locking is how to manage concurrent updates to a file or directory structure when more than one user or application is working with it. Most locking implementations use a first-come, first-serve approach where the first user to access a file or directory has the ability to update data, but users that access it later are not allowed to make changes.

Data Representation

An important role for any filing function is representing the data to users and applications. In general, this is the structure that is used to identify data uniquely in the system. For instance, the data representation can include directory paths or file folders. For databases, it can indicate records in database tables that are part of particular tablespaces. Where network storage is concerned, the data representation can also include a network system identifier.

Metadata Management

Metadata is the information about the data that the filing system controls. Metadata is extremely important in maintaining records about the creation and maintenance of data as well as for facilitating searches of particular data objects stored by the filing system. Metadata is regularly updated as data is stored and retrieved to reflect changes in some of the data's descriptors. The filing system's metadata often contains access control information, but there are no requirements for access control information to reside in the same data structure as the information that describes the data.

Data Structure

A great deal has already been said in this book about the data structure component of filing. The data structure component determines and manages the logical address block locations for all data stored by the system.

Filing Functions in Network Storage

To help clarify the differences in the various filing functions, we'll now analyze some of the network storage concepts discussed previously for the way these functions are implemented.

Filing Functions in SANs

SANs were defined in Chapter 8 as the application of storing functions over a network. As such, there are no filing functions distributed over a SAN. All the filing functions are located in the host system. The filing function passes its I/O requests as logical block address operations to the underlying volume manager and/or device driver functions, where they are transferred over the network.

Filing Functions in NAS

NAS, on the other hand, was defined as the application of filing over a network. It follows, then, that most of the filing functions in a NAS environment are located in the NAS appliance. Notice, however, that the client redirector has to have some of the responsibility for representing data to the end user or application. Thus, the data representation function in NAS is distributed.

Also, in NFS NAS systems, the security mechanism between client and NAS appliance operates between systems, not on the basis of a network user login. Users are first authenticated on their local machines, but no further user authentication is performed when accessing NAS data. In that way, the access control for an NFS NAS system is done on two levels: the user access is controlled on the client, and the client system access is performed on the NAS appliance.

Filing Functions in NASD

The preceding chapter discussed the NASD research effort, which uses a separate file manager system to distribute access keys to clients wanting to access data on intelligent disk drives. In the NASD system, the data representation function is distributed between the NASD disk drive and the client, just as it is in NAS, but the access control is maintained by the file manager system. The metadata and data structure functions are located on the NASD disk drive.

Filing Functions on DAFS

Another new development in network storage, DAFS, was discussed in the preceding chapter as a way to cluster NAS appliances together for capacity scaling and reliable client/server communications. As in NAS, the data representation function is distributed between the client and the DAFS cluster. As each member of the DAFS cluster has the same file system image, the security and metadata functions are likely to be the same on each member, although it would be possible to distribute them among the members.

The data structure function is performed within the DAFS cluster, but within the cluster it is distributed among the cluster members, where each member manages the data structure for the storage subsystems it controls.

Object-Based Storage in Disk Drives

One of the new directions in network storage is called *object-based storage*, or *OBS*. OBS is a project that is related to the NASD research project and shares the design goals of making disk drives directly addressable as network attached storage. However, unlike NAS, OBS does not turn disk drives into miniature file servers, but into a new kind of a storage device that implements a filing data structure function.

OBS removes the necessity of managing the details of disk space allocation from operating, file, and database systems. There are many intriguing aspects to the concept, especially for improving transaction system I/O performance. Instead of a single database system calculating the logical block addresses for thousands of transactions per second, OBS allows databases instead to transfer transaction data with a minimal set of location information. The OBS drive does the rest by receiving the transaction data along with its location information and calculating the final logical block address.

The idea is not as far-fetched as it might seem. Disk drives already translate logical block addresses to internal block addresses within the drive. The difference for OBS is that another type of location information would be transferred to the disk drive instead of logical block addresses. This requires the development of some other type of storage protocol, not one based on logical block addresses or filenames. This is one of the main issues being addressed by the standards group developing OBS.

Potential Performance Advantages of OBS

Offloading the data structure function from one location to another doesn't do much good unless the new configuration delivers some real benefits. In the case of OBS, the idea is that many disk drives would be actively processing OBS I/O instructions, including data structure operations and the calculation of real block addresses. In theory, hundreds of OBS disk drives could be doing this as opposed to a single transaction system. Although the transaction system still needs to provide some location context, including the network location of the OBS disk drive, the effort for this is far less than that for calculating logical block addresses. This type of massive parallelism has the potential to significantly improve the overall I/O rate of large transaction systems. Figure 15-3 shows the parallel processing model for OBS-based I/O.

One of the other design goals of OBS is to create self-managing storage. OBS uses file system attributes for management purposes that allow local management of each OBS disk drive, as opposed to management through a centralized file system. This type of management, called *attribute management*, can include a wide range of functions, including error correction, space allocation, backup, mirroring/replication, and data movement. Just as a MIB (management information base) can convey management information to network devices, attribute management could be used to convey management information to storage devices and subsystems.

OBS proponents make good arguments for the technology. They claim that local management of the disk's address space is the most efficient method and that it is a waste of processing power to make the calculation twice if it is going to be done in the disk drive

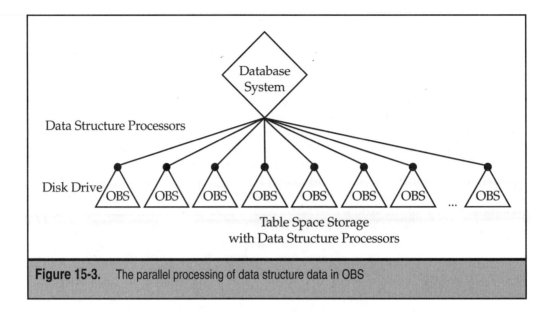

Figure 15-3.   The parallel processing of data structure data in OBS

anyway. Also, device sharing and storage sharing on an individual device become possible if the device manages its own space. While this might seem slightly strange to some readers, 100GB disk drives could be subdivided and have their storage capacity shared by several users. OBS could enable this type of sharing to take place.

Filing Functions in OBS

The distribution of filing functions in an OBS I/O system would be similar to those for a NAS appliance. Each disk drive would have its own representation, data structure, metadata management, and access control capabilities. Clients would have a redirector component of some sort that provides some element of the data representation function. Clients would also provide some amount of data structure functionality that allows them to formulate the location description that is to be decoded by the OBS disk drive.

STORAGE NETWORK FILING SYSTEM DESIGNS

The fundamental requirements for storage networking is to scale up to new capacities, provide higher levels of data availability, and provide adequate performance to match processor advances. It follows, then, as long as wiring and storing functions are both changing to adapt to storage networking, that filing should also change. In the sections that follow, we'll look at some of the new designs in storage network file systems.

Many of the concepts of object-based storage for disk drives can be applied to storage subsystems also. If disk drives can incorporate filing functions, there is no reason why storage subsystems can't. In many respects, subsystems are preferable for this purpose because they don't require the same levels of chip integration and miniaturization as disk drives.

Four Approaches to Storage Network Filing

Because there are many ways to distribute filing functionality, there can be many possible configurations and approaches to filing. This book identifies four of them:

▼   Standard NAS

■   Shared nothing clustered filing

■   Independent filing management

▲   Distributed metadata and data with direct access

The first two of these were discussed in Chapter 14. The shared nothing clustered file system is one of the potential outcomes of DAFS, although other technology besides DAFS could be used to create clusters of scalable NAS appliances.

The remaining two network storage filing approaches are discussed in the sections that follow.

Client Redirectors and Installable File Systems

For any of these filing methods to work, there needs to be some sort of client redirector function or installable file system that enables a client to access the filing service. The words "installable file system" tend to strike fear in the hearts of many. It may help to think about an installable file system as similar to the client redirector technology that has been around for decades.

The capability to use installable file systems has existed for years as a way to extend the functionality of the operating system; such file systems are accommodated by most operating systems through a set of programmatic interfaces. For the most part, the installable file system integrates with the data representation function in the I/O path. The installable file system represents its data through the system's interfaces in a way that is consistent with the system's native file system. Likewise, an installable file system provides the same types of services that the system's native file system does, but it can access data in several different ways.

The data structure function in an installable file system can be completely independent of its data representation function. In the case of storage network filing systems, the data structure function is likely to take on additional network capabilities that allow the file system to work over a network.

Figure 15-4 elaborates on this idea by showing the location of two different installable file systems in the I/O path. In this diagram, installable file system A uses the traditional path to storage hardware through a volume manager and device driver. Installable file system B is using an FTP access method that stores and retrieves data over the Internet.

Filing Systems Using an Independent Filing Manager

Chapter 10 introduced the concept of an independent connection broker function that allows multiple backup systems to share the resources of several tape drives. This idea surfaced again in Chapter 14's discussion of NASD where the NASD file manager provided the security keys to clients who would use them to access NASD disk drives.

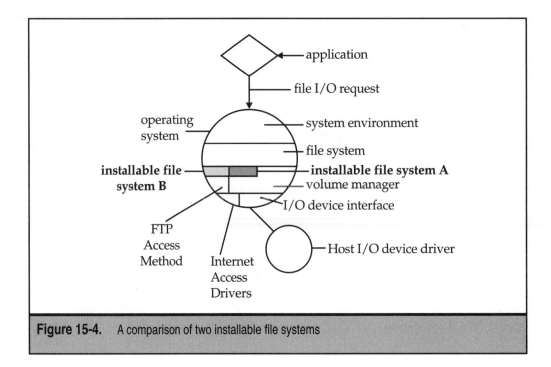

Figure 15-4. A comparison of two installable file systems

In a similar way, filing systems can be deconstructed and implemented on a large scale with an independent filing manager on an independent system or cluster. The general network configuration for this type of filing system looks like this:

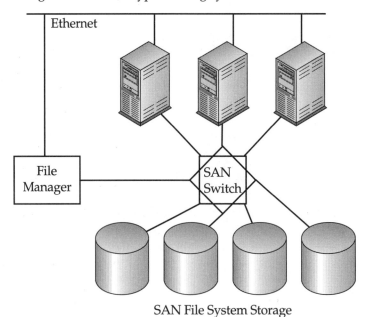

There are already several companies offering products in this category with several new development initiatives underway throughout the storage industry, and it seems apparent that the independent filing manager approach will have some momentum behind it. However, it is not at all clear whether or not these new filing systems based on this model will align themselves with standards or if they will be proprietary "archipelagos" of distributed filing.

Role of the Independent Filing Manager   The independent filing manager is a filing software function that runs on a processor or groups of processors in the network and controls the filing functions necessary to store and retrieve data over a storage network. In other words, the independent filing manager plays "big brother" and oversees all operations in the filing system.

The filing manager represents data in the filing system to the client system, which in turn represents the data to users and applications through its interface. When a user or application wants to access data in the filing system, it makes its request to the filing manager. This request is typically made over a data network link, such as Ethernet, using available TCP/IP messaging protocols. The filing manager receives the request and invokes its access control mechanism to determine if the user or application has permissions to access the data before determining whether or not the data is locked by any other users. If the client cannot access the file, the file manager sends the client some form of rejection or error message.

If the user has permissions and is not prevented from opening the file by locks, the filing manager then determines the network address and storage location of the data using its data structure function. This is an important point: the location of data is not necessarily limited to a logical block address, but contains an additional network address or name of the storage subsystem where the data is located. This network-location information is then shipped to the client system.

Client Access to Network Data   The client system receives the network location, stores it locally, and begins to access the data directly over the network using whatever storing or message protocols are implemented by the filing system. For many of the products sold as SAN file systems, the protocol used to access data stored in the network is a form of serial SCSI; however, there is no solid requirement that SCSI be used. It would be possible to use NFS, CIFS, or any other available protocol, such as a protocol being developed for OBS. Just as the wiring is independent of storing and filing implementations in storage networks, the storing protocol used is independent of the filing system that requests services from it.

The entire picture of how data is accessed through an independent filing manager is shown in Figure 15-5.

Writing Data with an Independent Filing Manager   Writes and updates to data using an independent filing manager follow a reverse-direction process where the client system communicates its need to write some amount of data to the filing manager. The filing manager invokes its data structure function, determines where the data should be placed, and sends the "write-to" location to the client.

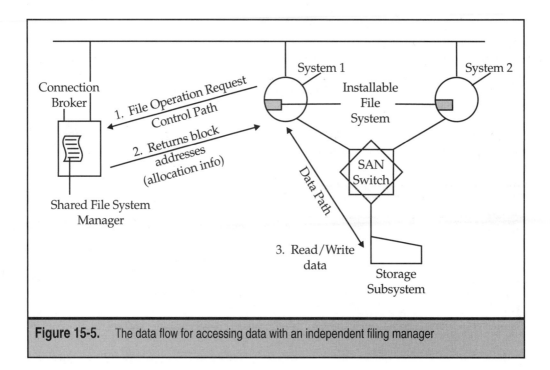

Figure 15-5.   The data flow for accessing data with an independent filing manager

There could be many variations on how writes are done. For instance, if an update to a file does not change its physical size in storage, the client could write directly to storage and inform the filing manager of any changes that are needed in the filing system.

Another matter that could be implemented in several different ways is the creation and updating of metadata. An independent filing manager system needs to have some way of identifying the owners of data and the time that data was created or updated. This requires some messaging system or protocol that communicates this information from the client to the filing manager. The metadata information could be transferred from the client to the filing manager along with its request for a "write-to" location, or it could be sent from the client after the data was actually written. In both cases, error recovery scenarios are needed that can roll back or roll forward filing metadata to be consistent with the data in the filing system.

The possible variations in writing and metadata management illustrate how difficult it may be to create industry standards for the independent filing manager approach. While the basic architecture of the two different systems might be similar, the methods used to write data and maintain metadata could be completely different and incompatible.

Benefits and Risks of an Independent Filing Manager   Independent filing manager systems can be designed to work with off-the-shelf hardware, making them fairly easy to buy equipment for and thereby reducing the cost. However, the adaptability to existing products also creates some potential security problems, which are discussed a few paragraphs later.

In general, the independent filing manager approach extracts the filing function from the host system and allows it to grow independently of all other storage network components. This means that filing can be managed independently and given resources as needed to support storage network activities.

For instance, an independent filing system could be made to support a small number of graphics production workstations where the number of files is small, but the storage capacity to hold them is large. In that case, the filing manager system could be a fairly small system because it would not be accessed excessively during the course of a normal workday.

Alternatively, an independent filing manager could be used to support a retail sales or factory automation application with an increasing number of production line monitors feeding data into the system on an ongoing basis. In this case, the amount of stored data might be small but the activity in the filing manager might be very high, requiring a more powerful system.

Compared to a single host system, with an associated filing system, the independent filing system provides a more fair method of accessing data as well as removing any particular production system from being a hindrance to data access. Just as a storage network removes the risk of having a single server become a single point of failure by making storage accessible to all systems on the network, the independence of the filing manager makes the filing function readily available on the network also. While the filing function might be broadly accessible on a network, it manages all filing functions, including reads and writes. Therefore, it is a potential single point of failure and a likely bottleneck for high-activity storage networks. That said, there are many ways to build reliability and performance scalability into this design through the use of high-speed, low-latency networks and through clustering techniques.

Security Considerations   The most obvious question mark for most independent filing systems is system security. Communications between clients and the independent filing manager travel over IP networks and can use any of the encryption and authentication technologies that exist. However, the connection between clients and storage is much more suspect. As mentioned, one of the strengths of the independent filing manager approach is that it can use unmodified off-the-shelf hardware. This means that storage subsystems are used that do not have either encryption or authentication technology implemented in them to afford them protected communications with clients. In addition, there are no facilities in off-the-shelf storage subsystems for exchanging and processing security keys with clients and no way of verifying whether I/O operations conducted by clients were authorized by the filing manager.

This is not a whole lot different from the situation in SANs today where clients access storage subsystems directly without any correlation between the file system and the storage subsystem. But storage networking filing systems are designed with the idea that they will be used in networks, whereas traditional filing systems were designed for relatively closed single-host environments. While the expectations for security might be somewhat different for storage network filing systems, it will likely take several years for security to catch up with expectations.

One potential scenario in which security is exposed in an independent filing system relates to the possibility that any client could access storage in the network without first having been authorized by the filing manager. No interlocks or keys are used to validate the I/O operation. It is possible that errors in device drivers or file redirectors could result in storage location data being inadvertently altered or retained by the system and used incorrectly or improperly. What's more, there is nothing to stop a security attack from being launched from a client system on the storage network. Again, this is not much different from the situation today on storage networks, but it is expected that storage network filing systems will widen the applicability of storage networks and incorporate more client systems, including those run by end users.

Network Filing with Distributed Metadata and Data

Another model for a storage network filing system puts pieces of the filing system in storage subsystems and distributes metadata and data throughout the network storage system. To some degree, this approach is similar to OBS as discussed previously, except that intelligent storage subsystems in a distributed metadata+data system have the physical resources available to implement more powerful processing technology and can therefore provide more filing functions than just the data structure function that OBS provides.

As is expected from network storage filing systems, the addressing model in this approach determines the storage location using both network addresses as well as a storage address. Unlike the independent filing system discussed previously where files are written to a particular storage subsystem in the network, the distributed metadata+data filing system spreads data and metadata across all the various storage nodes in the system.

A visual overview of this approach is pictured in Figure 15-6.

Characteristics of Distributed Metadata and Data Filing Systems   The distributed metadata+data system is a single, distributed system where all client systems using it have the same image of the filing system. In that respect, it is similar to the DAFS cluster discussed in the preceding chapter, where each client using the system has the view of the data stored in the system. However, unlike in a DAFS cluster where the image of the file system is replicated between cluster members, in the distributed metadata+data filing system each client reads its image from the data that is distributed in the storage network. The distributed metadata+data system enables this by using a data structure function that includes network addresses as part of its data location algorithms.

There are three fundamental architectural elements that make up a distributed metadata and data filing system. They are:

▼ Peer-to-peer communications between cluster nodes

■ Uniform distribution of metadata and data across participating nodes

▲ Subsystem-based data structure functionality

Peer-to-peer communications allow the distributed system to coordinate all activities among cooperating subsystems. While there could be a number of ways to structure the relationship between subsystems, the peer-to-peer method provides some advantages

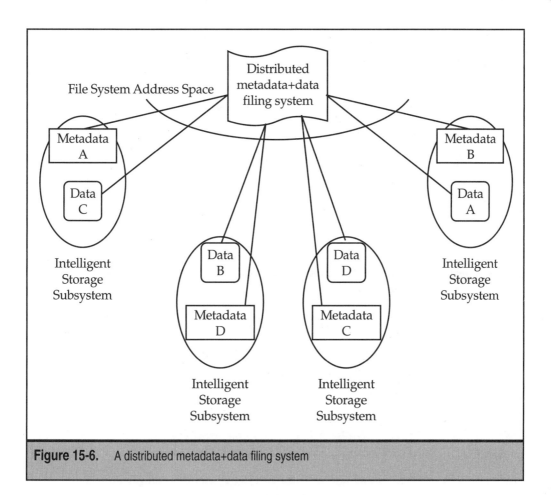

Figure 15-6. A distributed metadata+data filing system

for failover situations. The distribution of both metadata and data is done uniformly across all participating subsystems to maintain consistent performance and capacity. Finally, the subsystems in this design provide the data structure function that assigns the logical block addresses for all the data it stores. In other words, each system node is responsible for managing its own storage space, including managing locks locally. Of course, the coordination and error recovery of this kind of data distribution requires processing and network overhead to handle transmission errors as well as any failures that could occur within the subsystems, such as running out of free disk space.

Data Striping and Redundancy   A distributed metadata+data system can use RAID algorithms for spreading filing data redundantly across the storage network. This notion of object-oriented RAID is to stripe data objects across intelligent storage subsystems that perform their own data structure functions. In the discussions that follow, this type of filing system that stripes data across subsystems is called an *array-structured file system,* or

ASFS. Just as RAID disk subsystems can stripe data across multiple disks, the array-structured file system stripes files and database data across multiple intelligent storage networking subsystems.

One of the most interesting aspects of an ASFS file system is the way directory data, metadata, and file data are striped across multiple storage subsystems. For instance, directory data and metadata in the filing system are spread throughout the storage network, with redundant copies maintained on different subsystems. File data is also striped over the array of subsystems (network nodes that provide filing), independently of where the directory data and metadata have been placed. In other words, the boundaries of the filing system are defined by the number of network addresses of the participating filing subsystems.

A small file may be written as a single entity that is mirrored across two or more subsystems, and large files are split up into *file stripes,* transmitted across the network, and spread across multiple locations on multiple storage subsystems, keeping redundant copies of each file stripe.

Benefits of the Distributed Metadata and Data Filing System   One of the major advantages of a distributed metadata+data filing system is the redundancy built into the architecture to eliminate single points of failure. The implementation of redundancy in file stripes provides the ability to continue operations in case one of the distributed nodes fails.

The distributed metadata+data filing system has scalability advantages, too. Capacity can be added to the system by integrating additional filing subsystems and redistributing the data and metadata stripes across the new configuration. In the same way, the performance of the system can also be improved potentially by increasing the number of subsystems and gaining the benefits of parallelism. Distributing file data across multiple subsystems lends itself to very fast performance for reading, as several subsystems can be accessing data on many individual disk drives for a single read operation.

Another interesting advantage of this distributed system approach is the lack of a requirement for redundancy protection within a local subsystem. The filing-level redundancy in the distributed metadata+data filing system provides complete redundancy of data across the network storage space. Therefore, there are no read, modify, write penalties as there are with RAID 5. Of course, it may be desirable to use storing-level mirroring redundancy in the subsystems for added protection and read performance. Figure 15-7 gives a high-level view of how file redundancy is applied in a distributed metadata+data filing system.

Weaknesses of Using a Distributed Metadata and Data Filing System   Similarly to OBS, subsystems that work in a distributed metadata+data filing system have to have specialized technology implemented to allow them to work. Unlike the independent file manager system, off-the-shelf components might not be available to support it. This adds cost and complexity to implementing the solution. That said, it is possible to package the technology in a modular fashion. For instance, the NAS products sold by Tricord Systems use their own distributed metadata+data filing system that provides excellent, transparent scalability for NAS.

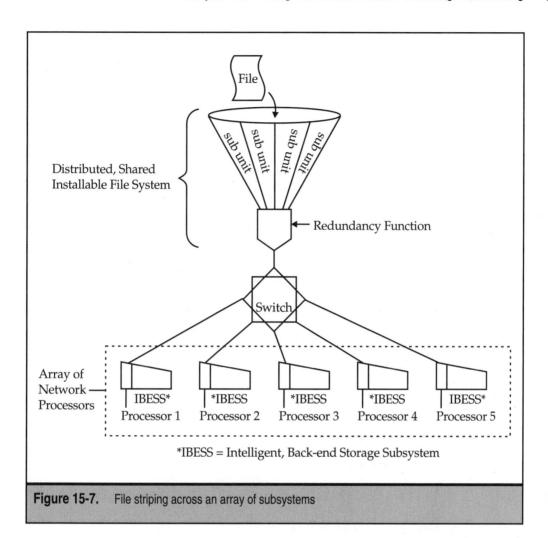

Figure 15-7.   File striping across an array of subsystems

Another difficult problem to solve with distributed filing systems, particularly when data is scattered between subsystems, is how storage management applications such as backup can work. While this type of filing system scales up for performance, the performance required of backup is extreme, as pointed out in Chapters 7 and 10. It is not clear how a large distributed metadata+data filing system could be backed up efficiently. One approach is to use an "insider" approach where one of the subsystems belonging to the filing system would be responsible for performing backups. This subsystem could be a backup-only member that does not store data but exists solely for backup purposes. Another technique that could be added would be a software snapshot, although the complexity of synchronizing snapshots across multiple networked subsystems may make for a difficult engineering project. The fact that metadata and data are distributed and accessible by many clients poses significant challenges that involve coordinating the file system operations that flush data from client cache buffers to the storage network filing system.

DATA SHARING: THE HOLY GRAIL OF STORAGE MANAGEMENT?

Traditional filing systems typically involve a single system that controls the access and structure of data stored on storage resources. In other words, traditional filing is an autocratic system with a single filing manager. This allows data structures to be maintained with a minimal amount of risk.

However, this autocratic way of managing storage is not necessarily how storage networking file systems will work. The filing systems discussed in this chapter try to make it easier for multiple client systems to participate. The capability to share data across systems and applications has the potential to provide much better data integrity as well as simplify some challenging aspects of systems management. For that reason, the idea of *data sharing* among groups of computers has been proposed and tinkered with for many years.

Benefits of Data Sharing Filing Systems

Data sharing ensures a single, current, and consistent view of data, as opposed to having several different versions stored in various places by several different systems. The errors and consequences of having multiple versions of data become greater as one moves up the food chain in the business organization. For example, a corporate accounting document that uses the wrong data could make critical mistakes in reports, resulting in ill-advised decisions and general confusion in the organization.

Many systems managers have problems maintaining multiple data versions between related systems. System-to-system data transfers often require the sending system to run an export operation, which often requires significant processing resources. Similarly, large data transfers can take a substantial amount of network bandwidth, taking a long time to run and having a negative effect on other network processes.

One application that is particularly problematic is data warehousing. Typically, a data warehouse is built from data coming from many sources. Various applications process data in the warehouse and create subsets of the data that are needed by other systems in the corporation. Each of these systems depends on having timely information delivered by the data warehouse. Depending on the success, or lack thereof, of distributing this information, several different versions of the same information may be in use by different machines throughout the company.

Data Sharing as a Solution to Version Generation Problems

Database managers working with ERP (enterprise resource planning) systems understand the value of integrating applications together across the organization. Still, the issue of getting the right versions of data to these integrated applications is a problem. So, the goal of achieving "normalized" network data through data sharing, similar to the concept of normalizing data in a database, is powerful. Normalization is a concept that is based on managing a single instance of data that can be used by all processes that need it.

Consolidating Data Management Resources Through Data Sharing

Just as storage pooling groups storage resources together and allows them to be consolidated and centrally managed, data sharing pools information together and delivers the ability to manage and protect it as a single resource. However, unlike storage sharing, where each system must manage the storage capacity allocated to it, data sharing allows data management to be accomplished by a single manager, which could significantly reduce the burden of managing data on multiple, disparate systems.

Data Sharing Implementation Issues

Filing systems for data sharing are a completely different concept from traditional filing systems. Whereas storage sharing gives each server its own virtual logical address space to work with, data sharing filing systems allow access from multiple systems to the same logical address space. Data sharing filing systems are related to clustering in that clustered systems typically need some type of data sharing scheme, but clustering is not a requirement for data sharing, as nonclustered systems can share data also.

Sharing Data on a Disk Drive

To understand the complexities of data sharing better, we'll explore a simple model where data sharing is implemented on an individual Fibre Channel disk drive that exports a logical address space through a single port.

We'll first examine the physical connections used to do this and then discuss what the logical side of the equation looks like. As commands from multiple systems are received in the drive, they are placed in a buffer or queue where they may be sorted or serviced in a FIFO fashion. Figure 15-8 shows servers A, B, C, and D connected on a Fibre Channel loop network to a Fibre Channel drive.

The systems in Figure 15-8 can be used for different applications. For instance, System A is a file server, System B is a database server, System C is an e-mail server, and System D is a Web server. As each system on this network wants to access the drive, it arbitrates to gain control of the loop, logs into the drive's L-port, and begins transferring data.

Shared Data Operations on a Single Device

Now we'll take a quick look at the anticipated operating requirements for a shared disk drive and consider how it manages access from multiple systems. Assume there is a single partition in the drive that supports all four systems. In other words, the four systems share a single logical drive. Only one partition and one addressable logical drive on the storage network are being shared by all four systems.

Figure 15-9 illustrates how the four systems could access the shared logical drive. System A is working with file A, system B is working with file B, and systems C and D are working on file C. In fact, any system could be working on any file on the disk drive at any time.

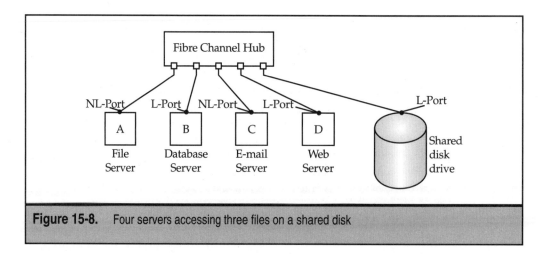

Figure 15-8. Four servers accessing three files on a shared disk

Processing Requirements of Data Sharing on a Single Device

So let's try to think about how much processing power is needed in this disk drive. To begin with, the disk drive needs to support simultaneous communications with the four systems. At any point in time, the disk drive is receiving data from one particular server. In other words, the disk drive has to be able to direct incoming frames to the proper queue for any of the servers that are communicating with it. This is an example where a dual-ported drive could allow concurrent communications with more than one system, but to simplify the model, it is not explicitly used in this example.

I/O operations for each system may take several logins. With multiple sessions taking multiple logins each, it is clear that the disk drive needs to incorporate some sort of communications management process that independently tracks the status of operations with each

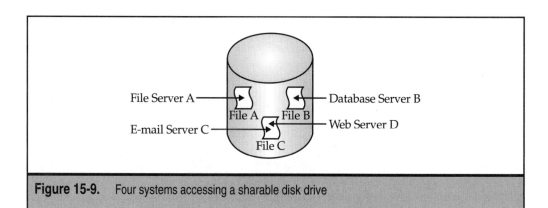

Figure 15-9. Four systems accessing a sharable disk drive

system. This means the disk drive needs to implement an intelligent error recovery mechanism that allows it to recover data or sessions independently for each distinct connection.

Once connectivity is established, it may be necessary to implement some form of security. While systems A, B, C, and D all have access to this drive, other systems may be explicitly restricted from accessing it. There is obviously a need for higher intelligence to be able to support a variety of security methods—from simple password security to complex encryption and authentication—and even recognition of more sinister security threats such as denial of service attacks.

With reliable and secure communications in place, one is free to work on the usual storage problems, such as performance. There is little doubt that caching for such a drive could be a major benefit, as it is for most drives. The value of the cache is not the question here, but rather the question is how the cache is allocated and what form of cache to use. Theoretically, each system using the drive could employ slightly different access requirements that would affect the selection of the cache. In a single disk drive, the question is how to provide a balance of resources and algorithms that benefits each of the different applications working on the drive.

There is a high probability that accesses on the disk by the four applications will not be equally distributed during short periods of time. Instead, it is highly likely that one or two systems will determine the I/O operations during a short time interval. However, over a longer period of time, say several seconds, that could change, and a different set of systems would be driving I/O operations. Trying to understand how to adapt a device cache to fit this kind of access is a challenge, and managing such a feat would probably require a fair amount of processing power. In the future, intelligent storage devices and subsystems may be differentiated by the effectiveness of their caching.

Finally, some sort of backup or data protection scheme is needed. If cold backups are performed, then all four systems need to stop accessing the drive. If hot backups are performed, it would be necessary to monitor a different copy-on-write function for each client. This is completely nontrivial. An alternative approach is to implement some sort of snapshot capability in the drive, which requires coordination among the four systems to flush their buffers at roughly the same time to allow the filing system in the disk drive to change all the necessary attributes or metadata.

Data Structure Functions in Data Sharing Filing Systems

The preceding example of data sharing in a disk drive highlights the added complexity that data sharing adds to storage networking. A data sharing device or subsystem requires much more processing power for communications, error recovery, security, and caching than typical storage used for traditional filing systems. More than just processing power, however, data sharing also requires more memory to be used as cache and may also require faster and more reliable network links for managing data stored in its own and in client systems' caches.

For that reason, data sharing may be more practical for a storage subsystem with the additional physical space and resources available. For data sharing to work to its greatest effect, all participating systems should be able to read, write, and update data in the filing system. At a minimum, this requires all participating systems to be able to run or at least initiate the data structure function. In traditional filing systems, the data structure function is implemented as a single function running in a host-based file or database system, but a data sharing system implements the data structure function in a distributed or neutral fashion.

A Unified File System View

One difficulty at the core of data sharing is satisfying the requirement for multiple users/applications working concurrently to get a single, unified view of the data that everybody can work with. This means that each participating client system has to have some way to determine where file and directory objects are stored.

A traditional filing system manages the data structure across single or multiple real or virtual storage volumes. It is possible for traditional filing systems to share data, but only if they all are designed to work together using strict rules that determine which system controls the data structure. Figure 15-10 illustrates this.

The scenario illustrated in Figure 15-10 is somewhat similar to using an independent filing manager, but where the filing functions belong to a traditional system. A stateful,

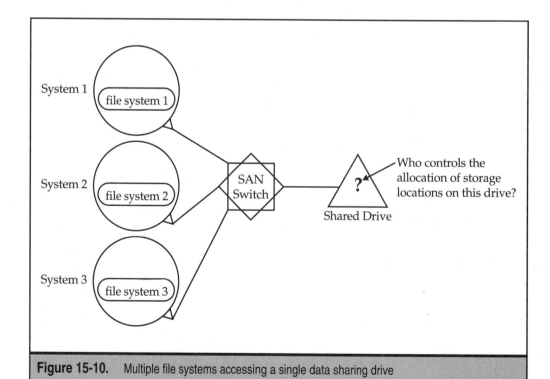

Figure 15-10. Multiple file systems accessing a single data sharing drive

consistent order needs to be maintained in order for all participating systems to be able to find and read the file system information located on the shared drive.

Locating Data Structure Information in Storage

File systems know where to find their data structure information in storage. This is normally accomplished as some number of blocks set aside for this very important purpose. In general, there are two kinds of data structure information the file system need access to: its internal reference information and its content data.

The internal reference information is used by the filing system to maintain its integrity. This data is placed in redundant locations throughout the file system for error recovery purposes to prevent disk drive failures. Content information is basically the directory structure and the sequence of location pointers that locate all the parts of a file or directory. The most important directory is the root directory. A file system can typically find everything else in the storage resource if it knows how to find the root. The diagram that follows shows a filing system locating its internal reference information on a storage device:

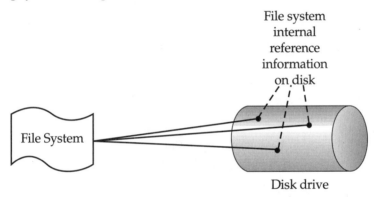

Traditional file systems were developed to work with devices connected to storage I/O buses. By nature, storage networking extends the idea of local storage to include SAN-based storage. This doesn't seem like such a big step, but it is interesting to think that the file system internal reference information can now include a network address or name that may be available to every system on the SAN. The notion that internal file system reference data is so readily accessible on the SAN could certainly have an impact on the deployment of security and protocols on the SAN.

In Fibre Channel networks, the network addressing is transparent to the file system and is handled by the device drivers and host I/O controllers that translate SCSI target-LUN addresses to Fibre Channel network names. However, this does not mean that the file system might not be able to incorporate network naming as part of its capability to locate organizational data on a real or virtual drive connected to a storage network. In other words, a network location identifier can be part of the information that a file system uses to locate its organizational data.

Distributing the Internal Reference Information

In addition to using network addresses as part of the internal reference location, file system reference data can be distributed over multiple resources. Borrowing a construct from linear algebra, the network address component creates an additional vector for the storage location. This type of network-inclusive storage addressing opens the door for filing systems to be built on top of network structures, as opposed to device structures. The diagram here shows a file system that is able to find its internal reference information scattered across multiple real or virtual drives in the SAN:

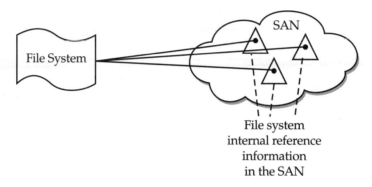

File system
internal reference
information
in the SAN

An important and subtle point to this approach is that a storage network filing system can span multiple real or virtual devices without first needing them to be aggregated together by a virtualization process in the I/O path. In other words, the capability to address storage by network location at the filing system's data structure level could potentially take precedence over the benefits of aggregating logical block addresses in volume managers.

RESOLVING LOCKS AND SEMANTIC DIFFERENCES

The topic of *locking* for NAS products was discussed in Chapter 14 with an analysis of the differences between PC CIFS-style locking and Unix NFS-style locking. In this section, we'll examine locking and client system semantic differences in data sharing systems.

Lock Management for Network Storage

Most filing systems provide some level of *locking*. Locking is a process that reserves the ability to access or update data to one user or application. The idea is to prevent another user or application from accessing or updating data while the first user or application is working with it.

The function that provides the lock mechanism is called the *lock manager*. The lock manager is responsible for managing the access to locked data as well as any actions and notifications that are needed when attempts are made to access locked data. For instance, it is possible that a lock manager can use advisory locks, warning the users or applications that the data they have accessed is locked. Without the ability to enforce the lock, the data can be subsequently updated. In that case, the lock manager may be able to notify other clients who have opened the file that it has been updated, advising them to reload the data.

The lock manager for a database system could provide locking at the following levels:

▼ **Table level** Only one application is allowed to update at a time.

■ **Record level** Records are locked during updates; multiple systems can access other records.

▲ **Field level** Individual fields are locked, allowing access to other parts of the record and all other records.

Similarly, the lock manager for a file system could provide locking for:

▼ **Directory level** Only one application can update files within the directory.

■ **File level** One application is allowed to update.

▲ **Byte ranges** within files

Transparency of the Lock Manager

Locking technology has been successfully used for many years and by many users. However, the matter of locking shared data in a SAN is likely to be a different experience for end users, adding several new wrinkles. In the discussion that follows, it is assumed that locking is managed at the subfile level and that directory-level or file-level locking is not under the microscope.

Usually when new technology, such as a data sharing filing system, is introduced, it is important that new functions be able to be used *transparently*. In other words, the new features should not change the way users work. Unfortunately, transparency for data sharing may not be possible due to the nature of resolving conflicts for multiple clients.

A lock manager for a data sharing environment could build a lock resolution hierarchy based on several items, such as user profiles, prioritization or policies, and order of access to data, as in a first-come, first-lock manner. The determination of how locks are assigned to clients is not a trivial matter. Users are not necessarily accustomed to working with files and finding out that the paragraph or spreadsheet cells they are working with cannot be modified.

Nor are they accustomed to receiving a notice telling them that the data they are working with has been changed and they need to reload it. The whole notion of notifying users about locks and freeing of locks is an interesting puzzle. If users try to write data and are told that it is temporarily locked, should the lock manager tell them when the lock is cleared? If so, how does it identify which specific lock has cleared? What if a user wants to override a lock of a subordinate colleague? Should there be a method for doing so? If so, how does an organization keep this from becoming abused or hacked and a threat to data availability? There are bound to be many interesting requirements that spring up as the technology is adopted.

Semantic Integration

Another interesting challenge in data sharing is *semantic integration,* which deals with the differences between file system operations in different filing and operating systems. For instance, various network operating systems differ in how files are named, opened, locked, deleted, updated, and so on. If a user on a Unix system creates a filename that is illegal on a Macintosh system, how is that filename represented to the Macintosh user?

A file operation may also be supported on one client system, but not another. Semantic integration within the data sharing filing system attempts to resolve these differences by providing alternative functions or user guidance of some sort. It is certainly one of the important areas for the development of data sharing filing systems and will likely differentiate them in the market.

FILE-LEVEL VIRTUALIZATION

The final section of this chapter looks at virtualization technologies that can be implemented at the filing level to provide storage management benefits.

The Grandfather of File-Level Virtualization: HSM

File-level virtualization has existed for many years as *hierarchical storage management,* or simply *HSM.* The idea of HSM is fairly simple: remove data that is not being used any longer, and make room for new data that is being created. The old data is said to be migrated to "near-line" storage for safekeeping and fairly fast retrieval. Near-line storage is storage that is not part of a file system's storage but can be accessed relatively quickly. The implication is that near-line storage involves some type of removable storage media.

HSM typically uses tape or magneto-optical recording media as the near-line storage media that can be quickly accessed through the use of libraries and autochangers. In general, access to data on optical disks is much faster than it is on tape, and in fact this has been one of the few applications where magneto-optical storage has succeeded as general-purpose storage. Most other uses of magneto-optical technology have been in support of specific imaging applications.

The Virtualization Entity: the Stub File

The key to HSM and any other file-level virtualization process is something called a *stub file.* A stub file takes the place of the original, migrated file within the filing system. When a file is migrated, it is copied to another storage device or media, deleted from its original location, and replaced by a stub file that has the same name and attributes, although it is much smaller. This allows the storage space that was being used by the original file to be returned to the filing system's free block list and reused by the system. The goal of most

HSM systems is to continue representing migrated data as if it still resided in the file system, while significantly reducing its capacity needs.

Recalling Migrated Data in an HSM System

A special daemon process or watchdog program runs continually in the background, intercepting every file access request that is passed to the filing system by the system's kernel. If an attempt is made to access a stub file, the HSM system steps in and performs a *recall* operation that copies the migrated file back from near-line storage, instead of reading the file from the system's normal access process and data structure.

When the file is recalled, the HSM system typically writes it back into its original location in storage. The process that does this is more or less the reverse of the migration process: the migrated file on near-line storage is read, the stub file is deleted, and the original file is written along with its original attributes and metadata.

Automating HSM

An important aspect of an HSM system is its capability to run automatically without user or administrator intervention. In other words, its operations need to be transparent. The transparency of an HSM system results from the automation that supports it. The HSM system will be viewed as successful if the level of automation allows the system to work without user or administrator intervention. The recall process is automated by nature, but the migration process needs to be stimulated somehow to start its operations.

One of the primary elements of automating HSM is determining the control thresholds that signal the start and end of the automated migration processes. One threshold is called the *high-water mark.* When the used capacity of the filing system exceeds this threshold, the migration process begins. The other common threshold is called the *low-water mark.* After the migration process has removed enough data to reach the low-water mark, migration stops. In other words, the high-water mark is used to signal the start of migration operations, and the low-water mark is used to signal the end of migration operations.

Wringing out HSM

HSM provides storage scalability by shifting the bulk storage capacity used by dormant files to some other kind of storage. This sounds pretty good, and in fact, it works pretty well, but it is not clear that the benefits outweigh the risks.

One of the risks involves the difficulty in backing up a system running HSM. A backup process that accesses stub files and recalls all of them is a virtual disaster. Therefore, it is important to use a backup product that integrates with the HSM system to prevent this from happening. It is a well-known issue for the developers of HSM technology, and as a result, they usually know about solutions that prevent this from happening.

The larger problem with HSM is what happens if stub files become corrupted or are deleted; in that case, the automatic recall of data cannot occur and it may be necessary to locate the data on removable media to restore it. Depending on the amount of media used to store migrated data, this could take days. A more serious problem is what happens if the removable media containing the data are lost or destroyed? The answer is, the data is probably lost and cannot be recovered.

OnLine File-Level Virtualization

HSM in the form described has been used for decades with limited success. While nearly everybody agrees that its benefits for capacity are valuable, the additional management effort of managing removable media and the risk of not being able to recall data makes HSM less desirable.

Storage networking brings a new twist to the old HSM model by allowing online storage to be used in place of removable media. There is no particular requirement for automated tape and optical libraries in HSM systems. There is a requirement, however, to make the process easier and more transparent. It follows, then, that NAS storage on an Ethernet network or a virtual storage volume on a SAN could also be used to copy migrated data from a system.

Online storage has significant performance and thus, usability advantages over removable media. The migration and recall of data to a storage network resource happens far faster than with a tape or optical platter.

Dynamic Storage Optimization

One of the potential uses for online file virtualization is to accelerate system performance. The idea is fairly simple: instead of looking for dormant files to migrate, a *dynamic storage optimization* process can move files into high-speed, low-latency storage subsystems to increase I/O performance. For instance, if an administrator knows that certain files will be used for an upcoming application run, the administrator could place those files in a high-speed device such as an SSD to accelerate the I/O rates for the data.

The concept of dynamic storage optimization is shown in Figure 15-11.

It is possible that this concept could be applied to a regular application processing schedule so that certain key application files would be moved into high-performance storage prior to the beginning of their run. When the application has finished processing, the files would be copied back into their permanent storage location for safe keeping.

This idea proposes a different type of storage concept, in which the files and applications that are currently running are placed in a high-performance storage subsystem. In essence, this could be done today with solid-state disk technology, but the software to enable it has not been developed yet.

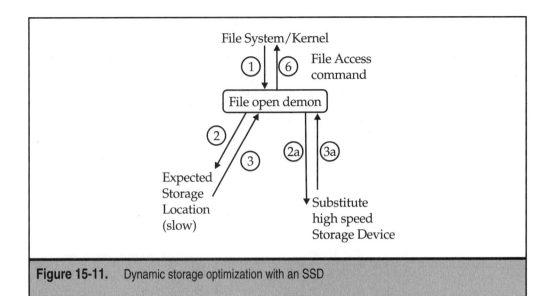

Figure 15-11.   Dynamic storage optimization with an SSD

SUMMARY

This chapter looked at filing technologies in storage networks. A variety of technologies were analyzed, including journaled file systems, snapshots, dynamic file system expansion, database replication, and direct file I/O for database systems. The use of these technologies is making it significantly easier to create larger and more scalable filing systems that better meet the needs of storage networks.

Then several technologies were discussed that use embedded processors to distribute filing technologies into the devices and subsystems that store the data. Object-based storage holds the potential to accelerate database performance by moving the data structure function into many disk drives working in parallel. Similar, expanded concepts for distributed filing systems place more of the filing components in storage subsystems or third-party systems and provide the means to scale up and build reliability through processor integration.

The final part of the chapter was a brief look at HSM and file-level virtualization. The idea of HSM is old, but the concept has the potential of being reinvented as the capability to dynamically assign data to faster storage subsystems. Whether this is accomplished remains to be seen.

Readers interested in filing technology may find it difficult to find much material to read. The cursory introduction to these topics in this book is intended to help the reader get started down the path of understanding this complex area. Hopefully, as the applications of storage networks become accepted in the market, the topics of this chapter will become more available as products and accessible through other books, white papers, product descriptions, and such.

EXERCISES

1. Assume you have a local database system that rotates writing through three log files. Write an algorithm for replicating these three log files to a remote database over a wide area network at T1 speeds (56 Kbps). Include how the log files will be applied to the remote database system.

2. Draw the network diagram for Exercise 1.

3. Write an algorithm for dynamic storage optimization that places nightly batch files and applications in an SSD to improve performance. Include how data is returned to its permanent storage location and how the SSD can be used for other applications according to a schedule.

CHAPTER 16

Storing and Retrieving Data on Public Networks

The integration of the Internet with storage has been taking place for many years but has accelerated recently along with the rapid emergence of the World Wide Web. This chapter looks at some of the storage/Internet integration efforts underway in the market, beginning with an analysis of storage technologies that can support the operation of Web sites. Then the chapter moves toward an exploration of storage service providers, or SSPs, that have the potential to form a whole new segment of the storage industry.

The last part of the chapter looks at the technologies and services that can be used by individuals such as FTP (File Transfer Protocol). Other technologies, such as WebDAV, are relatively new and have not been used much yet but hold a great deal of potential for future developments

INTERNET INFRASTRUCTURE STORAGE

While there are several interesting possibilities for storage applications on the Internet, the capability of storage and I/O technologies to keep pace with the changes of Internet computing is an essential ingredient for many IT organizations. This section examines the deployment of storage and I/O technology for server-side and client-side environments.

Scaling to Server-Side Requirements

Most Web servers do not have enormous amounts of data stored on them. For instance, a Web server with 50GB of online disk capacity is considered to be a fairly good-sized Web server. Of course, there are always exceptions to the norm, and there are large Web servers with terabytes of data. There is also an important difference between a Web server and a Web site. It's fairly normal for a Web site with huge amounts of data to be built from many smaller servers. Still, the overwhelming majority of Web sites have less data on them than internal network servers.

What Web sites may lack in data volumes they more than make up for in traffic. Busy Web sites can have millions of file accesses, or *server hits*, per day. High-traffic sites can easily become I/O bound as the number of requests exceeds the capability of the I/O infrastructure to supply them.

I/O Loading in Web Servers

Internet companies with high-traffic sites are not eager to discuss performance problems in public, but I/O operations have certainly been recognized as a serious system bottleneck on many occasions. I/O performance is particularly difficult for sites that attempt to provide customized information to thousands of users simultaneously. For instance, the customized profile information and the corresponding data a user sees on his or her favorite Web site has to be assembled from disk storage before it is transmitted across the Internet. Sites with millions of users sometimes experience heavy I/O loads in trying to satisfy the customized information demands of their users.

Even more difficult is the task of providing online personal information that users will access on demand from any location, such as appointment information, phone numbers, and Web-based e-mail. These information items have to be stored and accessed for each user of the system. As the number of users can be in the millions for such free services, the potential for I/O congestion is very real.

Search Engines and Storage

Internet search engines work by reading information from Internet sites and building a large text-indexed database that represents the content. The many different types of search technologies are beyond the scope of this book, but the point is that an enormous amount of information is collected and made available. After the database index has been generated, it is typically copied into a disk cache to provide the fastest performance. Heavily used search engines such as Yahoo!, Google, Excite, Alta Vista, and Lycos would be unusable if the performance of their engines was gated by disk I/Os of the search engine index. The cache used for storing the index is normally host-resident cache, but it could also be subsystem-resident cache.

Unfortunately, the size of these index files can exceed the maximum installable memory of Web servers by many gigabytes. For instance, a server with a 12GB memory limitation cannot store a 120GB search index. In these cases, the index is spread over many systems, and inquiries are distributed to the appropriate system. A complete copy of the database file and table structure may be stored on devices connected to each index server (see Figure 16-1).

This kind of indexing implementation works, but it has some significant cost drawbacks. First, the amount of money spent on multiple index server systems is high, especially if one considers the need to fill them with the maximum amount of memory possible. In addition, the database file that the index references has to be copied onto multiple storage subsystems. As this number of subsystems increases, the amount of time to do the copying gets larger and larger, the likelihood that errors will occur also grows, and the difficulty synchronizing index updates across multiple servers becomes a real headache. Finally, the requirement to duplicate all the equipment for fault tolerance doubles the cost of this implementation.

Implementing Volume Management and SSDs for Search Index I/O   A storage-centric solution, as opposed to a server-centric solution, could be used to reduce the cost and make the system more manageable. For starters, the system cache memory in each index server that is used to store the index segment could be replaced by a larger block of memory in a fast solid state disk (SSD) device. The performance characteristics for SSDs supporting this application are likely to be aggressive—in the range of microseconds, as opposed to the millisecond-range performance delivered by disk subsystems. Considering that host system memory is accessed in the nanosecond range, anything to make SSDs perform faster would be welcome. For instance, an InfiniBand interface using VI or some other fast protocol might be able to increase SSD response time into the submicrosecond range.

This assumes that there are SSDs large enough to hold the index file, which is not necessarily a valid assumption. Therefore, it may be necessary to use volume management software to concatenate multiple SSDs and create a single large virtual SSD. This virtual SSD

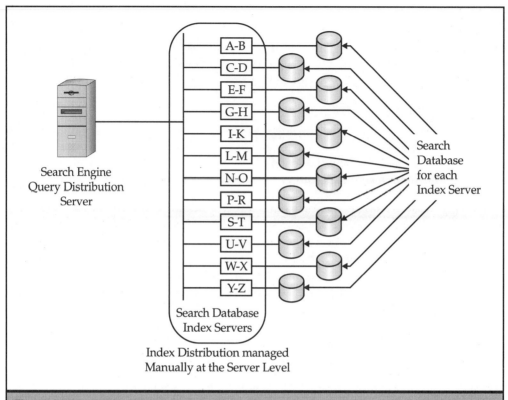

Figure 16-1. Indexes distributed manually across server memory caches

could hold the entire search index file and provide excellent performance. Figure 16-2 illustrates this volume manager/SSD approach and shows the I/O path involved when connecting five such SCSI SSDs of 24GB each to create a single virtual 120GB index volume.

This type of storage-centric approach eliminates the need for multiple index servers. As a by-product, it also eliminates the need to have a copy of the database stored on separate disks or subsystems for each index server. Not only that, but as the size requirements increase, additional SSDs can be incorporated by the volume manager software.

Using an Array-Structured Network File System for Scaling Search Engine I/O This still leaves a situation in which a single index server is both a potential bottleneck and a single source of failure. An alternative approach, more hypothetical than real, is to use an array-structured network file system, as discussed in Chapter 15, to store the index file across multiple SSDs. This way, multiple index servers could access the same index file simultaneously over the storage network. The SSD subsystems would probably need to include the appropriate distributed storage and network processors to provide the functionality and the performance required.

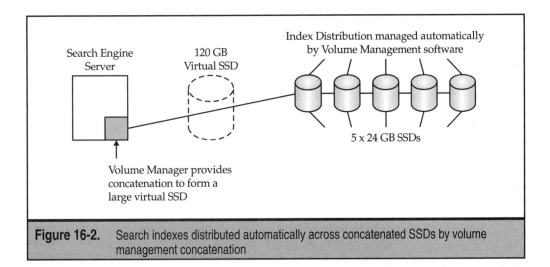

Figure 16-2. Search indexes distributed automatically across concatenated SSDs by volume management concatenation

The site's database files could be stored in a similar fashion on distributed disk subsystems. The end result would be a large, scalable network I/O system that easily adapts to increased user loads and ever-increasing search databases and indexes. Figure 16-3 shows a Web site storage network in which an installable file system resides in search engines that have access to an object-striped file in an array of SSDs. The database file that the index file relates to is also striped in this example.

General Requirements for Web Server I/O

Search engines are an interesting, but special, case of Web servers. There are many more transaction and HTTP servers on the Internet than there are search engine servers. This section discusses a variety of network storage technologies and approaches that could be employed to provide higher-performance, scalable, and more reliable Internet storage.

Performance requirements vary a great deal, depending on the type of traffic and the type of data. Most Web servers do not have the I/O performance requirements that search engines do. For example, streaming audio servers do not need to provide responses immediately, but once they start streaming data, they need to be able to maintain a sustained rate.

The primary requirements for Web site storage are to provide the following:

▼ Flexibility

■ Scalability

▲ Availability

Stable Storage Amid Rapid Server Changes

Web sites can grow and change quickly. While Web site architectures do not change daily, they can change a couple of times a year. Managing a Web site is often a wild ride for network and storage administrators. The requirement to add or upgrade servers and

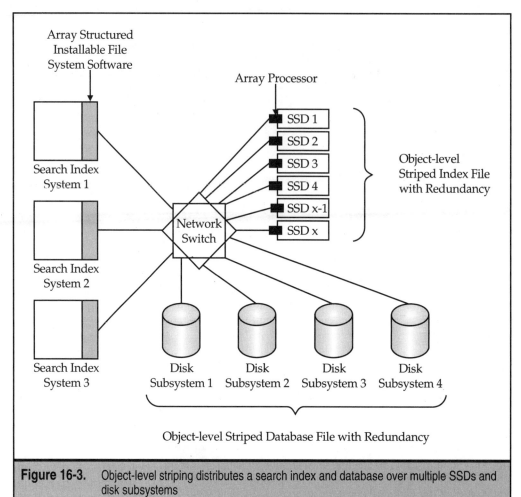

Figure 16-3. Object-level striping distributes a search index and database over multiple SSDs and disk subsystems

reorganize applications across those servers is fundamental to managing large Web sites. The trick is to make changes without any resulting downtime.

The storage infrastructure for these sites should support server changes while minimizing configuration changes to storage. In other words, the storage network should isolate the configuration of storage from the configuration of servers.

Mirroring and RAID for Data Availability in Web Sites

Web sites are typically 24 × 7 operations. There aren't any good times to have a Web site respond with *404 file not found* errors due to storage failures. The storage infrastructure for a Web site should be able to provide high data availability. Disk mirroring or parity RAID should be used to provide availability of data in case of disk failures. Some points to keep in mind include the following:

▼ RAID 3 provides almost no benefit, as the Internet connection between the Web site and the user cannot keep pace with RAID 3's streaming data delivery.

■ RAID subsystems that provide independent access to member disks, such as RAID 5, provide the best sustained transfer rates for high volume Web servers. RAID 0+1 is also very effective.

■ RAID 5 write penalties are typically minimal due to the very high read/write ratios in typical Web sites.

■ Transaction processing servers with higher write percentages can benefit from RAID 1 or RAID 0+1 to eliminate the RAID 5 write penalty.

▲ Having larger numbers of small disks in an array increases the number of disk arms and can increase system throughput in high-volume Web servers.

NAS for Web Sites   Network attached storage provides a simple and flexible mechanism to access storage resources. The general idea is to implement a site file server, several servers, or a clustered file server that provides file I/O for all other systems in the site. As production Web servers are changed, the applications running on them can use a consistent and common file access mechanism. Managing systems in the site is made easier by not having to worry about the storage resources for each individual server. Instead, site servers can be configured for minimal storage resources to support system booting and operating system functions, while the storage resources for the site can be managed through a single NAS system.

Figure 16-4 shows a before/after picture of a Web site. The before picture shows a three-system Web site, all systems accessing their files from a NAS system. The after

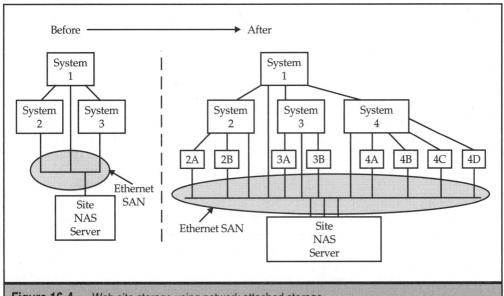

Figure 16-4.   Web site storage using network attached storage

picture shows the same site with 12 servers, each of them accessing the same NAS server. The NAS server has grown both in storage capacity and in network capacity through the addition of two additional network connections.

One of the advantages of using NAS for Web site storage is the fact that NAS wiring and the Web site wiring are the same. In essence, this makes it easier to purchase, install, and manage the storage network that supports the Web site. This does not mean that the NAS traffic has to flow over the same physical network as the Web server traffic; instead, the NAS storage network (the old SAN made of NAS switcheroo) could be an independent Ethernet network.

One of the potential problems of using NAS for Web sites is the potential problems inherent in using NAS for database storage. The challenge of using a stateless I/O mechanism, as NAS does, with a stateful application I/O process, such as databases have, may be capable of being solved by NAS vendors. Several variables come into play for such a configuration, including the size of the database, the activity level of the database, and the recovery accuracy needed should the database fail.

SANs for Web Sites SANs provide separation of storage resources from Web site systems. Site systems can be easily replaced and upgraded without having to unplug or move storage resources. Notice, however, that Web applications cannot be redeployed across Web systems without copying data from one server disk subsystem to another. If an application is moved from one server to another, it is likely that zone assignments, LUN masks, or port configurations will need to be changed to allow the application to continue to access its data. In any event, the changes required can be done logically, and do not involve moving physical connections or equipment.

SAN storage pools have the potential to save Web site managers a great deal of worry and time. Storage pools that are established on application boundaries provide a centralized approach to managing the storage resources for a Web site. As new needs and applications are discovered and implemented, storage capacity can be "carved out" of installed, but unallocated, storage. Figures 16-5 and 16-6 show the before and after views of a pool of virtual drives assigned by application, as opposed to server boundaries. The storage pool in this case is implemented across three similar dual-port/dual-controller storage subsystems.

Looking at Figures 16-5 and 16-6, the *before* picture shows three servers with five applications spread across three pooled storage subsystems. Each subsystem has a significant amount of unallocated storage capacity representing either empty disk drives or empty drive bays. Note that while storage capacity was allocated by application, the port assignments on subsystem ports are assigned by server.

The *after* picture shows each application being moved to its own dedicated server, and a new application, streaming audio, implemented on a sixth server. The e-mail storage has been expanded to use the remaining unallocated space on subsystem 1, subsystem 2 did not change, and subsystem 3 added streaming audio data and still has some remaining unallocated capacity. Each subsystem supports a connection to two site servers.

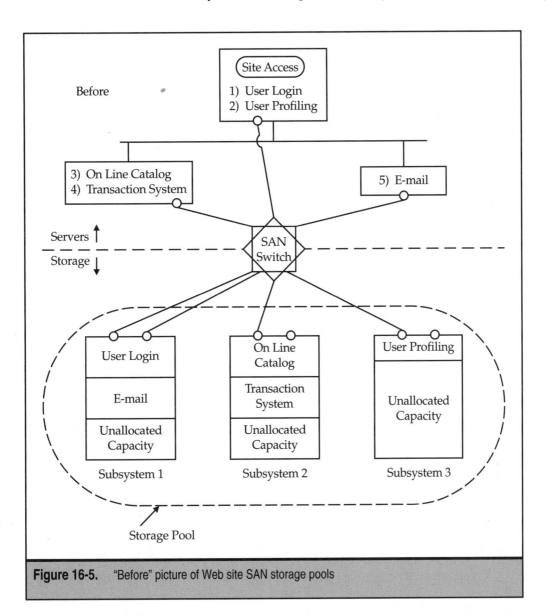

Figure 16-5.   "Before" picture of Web site SAN storage pools

Differences Between SAN and NAS Web Site Implementations   While both SAN and NAS technology can be used to provide storage services for Web sites, there are some significant differences to consider:

NAS does not support all applications equally well. Some applications require block I/O and do not work with file I/O provided by a NAS server. In this case, either bus-attached SCSI or SAN technology is needed. In contrast, SANs support all applications.

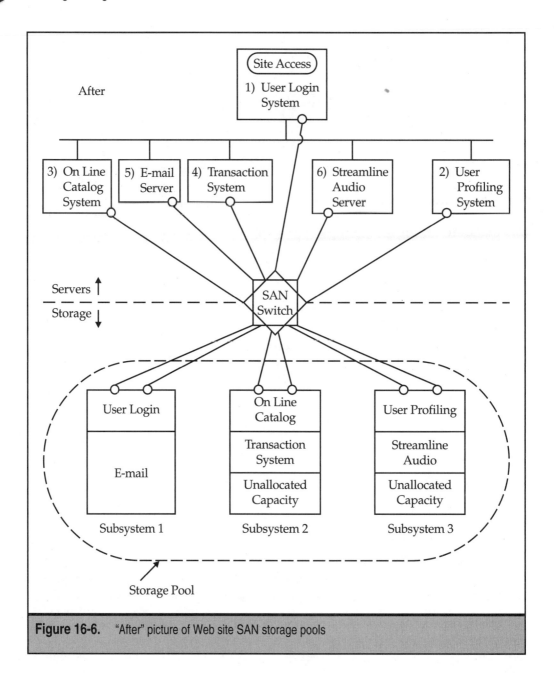

After

Figure 16-6. "After" picture of Web site SAN storage pools

SANs require storage administration for each server. Each server in a SAN requires storage to be configured and installed. In addition, each server requires some amount of storage management, such as backup. By contrast, a NAS solution centralizes all storage management on a single file server.

NAS and SAN solutions can be single points of failure. A single NAS server that fails or is powered off for maintenance or upgrades can shut down an entire Web site. The same thing could happen if a single multiport disk subsystem that provides all storage services for the Web site fails.

Capacity maximums are lower in NAS products. All products have limited capacity. In the case of a NAS product, the physical configuration limitations determine the capacity of a single integrated file system. Typically, two NAS products cannot be combined as a single named or addressable entity under a single file system. SAN disk subsystems also have capacity limitations, but they can be combined by storage management applications to create much larger virtual devices managed by a single file system.

SANs can accommodate specialized technologies more easily. SANs can utilize virtually any kind of device. NAS products, on the other hand, typically qualify each device used as part of their solutions. This effectively restricts certain devices from being used with NAS implementations.

Read-ahead caching in NAS products is more effective. Because NAS products have their own integrated file system, read-ahead caching is 100 percent accurate. By contrast, block I/O caching in SANs should only be expected to be far less accurate. For longer data files such as graphics and streaming audio/video, this can be a big advantage for NAS storage. However, the maximum amount of cache available in SAN storage subsystems can be larger than the maximum amount of cache in NAS products. This is an implementation issue that depends on the cache memory capacity provided by manufacturers.

Zambeel's Approach for Super-Scalable Web Site Storage   Today's SAN and NAS products are the applications of traditional storing and filing on networks. However, they hardly define the total realm of possibilities for storage network technology.

One of the areas that is likely to see development in the future is the file system. In this book, filing has been described as having the dual functions of representing data externally as well as managing the data structures on disk. Object-based storage, discussed in the previous chapter, is an architecture that disintegrates these file system functions and runs them as a distributed process.

In a similar vein, new filing technologies could look into the internal mechanisms of file systems further and distribute their functions across high-speed networks to multiple systems. An example of this approach is being developed by a new company named Zambeel. The Zambeel system is targeted at very large storage requirements with a modular file system design that allows several file system components to scale independently. This design has the advantage of delivering the most efficient mix of intelligent storage equipment to match the varied data characteristics of any particular site.

INDUSTRIAL STRENGTH INTERNET STORAGE SERVICES

One of the more interesting developments in Internet computing recently has been the emergence of SSPs, or storage service providers. SSPs provide Internet storage services and resources targeted at data center operations. The idea of an SSP is one of the most radical concepts to come along in storage for a long time. While network storage separates storage from systems, storage service providers separate the management of storage from data center operators. In general, this involves removing the storage from the data center and placing it at the SSP location, but it can also involve managing storage within the corporate data center.

Internet Data Center Storage Services

SSPs have been able to gain traction with Internet companies and corporations with significant Web site deployments who need help managing their Web site storage. The fit appears to be pretty good; Web site operators have plenty of technical and business challenges to worry about without worrying about their storage requirements, and SSPs have the skills and capabilities to do a much better job at storage management than their customers can.

The primary issue for Web site operators is being caught with an unexpected storage capacity crunch that threatens the availability or integrity of data on their site. There seems to be little argument that Web site downtime is viewed as a severe problem. Hence, SSPs can alleviate problems with the day-to-day management of storage and provide a level of "storage insurance" to proactively prevent storage crises from occurring. Even if the SSP gets caught by surprise by unexpected site dynamics, it is in a much better position to respond to storage problems than the average IT organization.

Colocation Internet Data Centers

Internet data center colocation facilities are specialized environments run and managed by companies with data center operations and expertise. In essence, they provide facilities rental and management on behalf of their Web site subscribers. Internet data centers vary considerably in the types of facilities and services they offer, but in general their primary value is Internet connectivity management, security, safety, and flexibility. Customers can focus on their Web site applications and leave the details of operating the networking and processing equipment to specialists.

The Internet data center can function as an SSP or can work with one or more SSPs and lease them space within its buildings to set up their storage operations. The storage site can contain any mix of storing and filing products connected through a wiring infrastructure that runs through the data center.

SSP Functions

An SSP can provide several storage applications and services to its subscribers, including:

▼   Primary disk storage

■   Network attached filing

■   Capacity planning/sizing

■   Volume management

■   File system management

■   Backup and recovery, including off-site storage

▲   Remote mirroring/vaulting

An SSP can offer these capabilities in a variety of packages or as à la carte items to their subscribers. The requirements depend a great deal on the dynamics of each individual Web site. For instance, a Web site running transaction services will likely require different types of storage than a site with a large number of servers in a server farm that stores a lot of personalized data such as e-mail and calendars for subscribers. Web site owners might seek help from SSPs to help make decisions about the type and amount of storage required for their various applications.

Some of the services an SSP can provide may require access to its customer's server equipment. For instance, an SSP that manages volume manager software on a Web server certainly needs access to the server to perform this work. The same goes for file system services on Web site servers.

An example of how this might work is a volume expansion for a Web server that is approaching the capacity limitations of its current disk volume. Assuming in this case that the storage network involved is a SAN, new larger-capacity storage (real or virtual) could be connected to the SAN and configured as a mirror to the existing volume through volume management software. After the new mirror volume is fully synchronized with the original volume, the original volume can be taken offline, again through a volume manager operation. At this point, the new usable storage capacity will be the same as the original because it was populated by a storing-level mirroring function. In other words, the file system data structure needs to be adjusted (expanded) to take advantage of the additional capacity in the new volume. So, the last step for the SSP would be to run a dynamic file system expansion operation on the file system.

Obviously, this process requires a file system that supports dynamic file system expansion. It also requires that the SSP has access to the server to perform the volume manager and file system operations. It is also not something an inexperienced Web site manager would want to do without professional assistance and is probably best left entirely to experienced storage professionals.

Segregation of Subscriber Data   In order to prevent unauthorized or incorrect access to their subscriber's data, an SSP needs to implement segregation technologies such as SAN zoning and storage subsystem port zoning (LUN masking). NAS servers can provide segregation through access rights in the NAS file system, just as they do for end users within an organization. As an alternative, the SSP can provide separate NAS appliances for each of its subscribers. However, the scalability of these appliances needs to be carefully thought through before using this approach.

Remote Data Center Storage Services

A logical extension for SSPs is to provide their services outside the locality of the Internet data center to include data centers that can be connected over public or private networks to remote SSP storage centers. Data center managers' rational for using such services is basically the same as for Web site owners: they lack the skills to keep up with the demands of storage management.

On the surface, this type of service runs contrary to the philosophy of enterprise storage, which claims that data is the most important IT resource and ought to be centralized on a safe and secure storage platform, as opposed to being held captive to particular servers. But the SSP's role is not necessarily intended to move data out of the data center but instead to augment a strong centralized storage policy through enhanced management and recovery capabilities. SSPs can potentially provide a great deal of value through storage pooling, remote mirroring, snapshots, data replication, serverless backup vaulting, and historical archiving of data for their subscribers.

Filing Issues for Remote Storage Services   If the client connects to the SSP through a SAN, the ability to manage data at the SSP could be severely limited. One of the most likely problem areas is backup of data at the SSP site. The file system's metadata and data structure information is processed in the server system at the subscriber's own data center. As a filing application that can back up and restore individual data objects, the backup system needs access to this file system information. Without access to the file system, the only backup that can be done is a block-based full image copy. Backup is not the only storage application affected. Any other filing application, including historical archiving and versioning, also depends on access to file system information.

The technology certainly exists for the SSP's storage management products to communicate with the various file systems at the subscriber's data centers. Essentially, the problem is a geographic expansion of a data mover as described in Chapter 10. Although the technology may be available to make it all work, data center operators might not want to grant access to their file system information through a remote network, for very good security reasons.

With the assumption that subscribers want data to be stored locally and at the remote SSP site, there are two potential avenues to take. The first is to use filing-level replication as opposed to storing-level mirroring. This will not yield the type of instantaneous data protection of mirroring, but it certainly does allow the SSP to provide file-oriented services. The second approach is more theoretical in nature, as it involves using object-based storage that transfers filing information along with data from the subscriber's data center to the SSP. In both approaches, the SSP has its own filing implementation that allows it to manage subscriber data as files and data objects.

PERSONAL STORAGE SERVICES AND TECHNOLOGIES

Individuals have been storing and sharing data on the Internet for decades already and will continue to do so at even greater levels in the future. Some of the contributing factors driving Internet storage are:

▼ Communities of users exchanging photos, music, and other files electronically

■ Ease of access to Internet applications with storage services

▲ Increasing bandwidth for storage transfers

A great deal of technology being developed allows people to access the Internet from almost any location using small handheld appliances such as cellular phones and palm computers. While these devices offer ultimate portability, they do not have the capability to store large amounts of data or share that data with others. It is highly likely that users of these products will use the resources of the Internet to store and retrieve data. The partial universe of systems and devices needing Internet storage are shown in the following drawing:

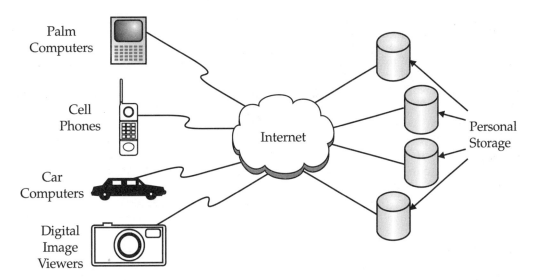

People can access the Internet from computers at work, at home; in their cars; at friends' and relatives' houses; at airports, hotels, printing centers, and Internet cafes—almost any computer anywhere can have public access to the Internet. With so many places to access data, it follows that one of the best places to store data is an Internet site. In fact, it seems almost obvious that Internet storage will be used as the central repository for mobile electronic workers, and as the optimal storage facility for synchronizing data.

Data synchronization is certainly not a new application, as many have used it to manage different versions of files on laptops and desktop machines. With an Internet-wired world, the increasing number of machines/devices a person uses makes it even more important to synchronize and manage multiple generations of data files. Internet services that provide these functions already exist and will likely become more prevalent in the future. The following diagram shows some of the multiple access points individuals will use to access data on the Internet:

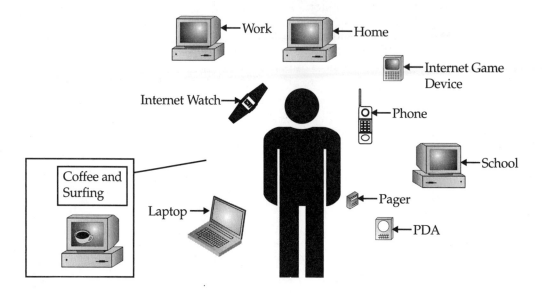

New collaborative applications designed to facilitate virtual workgroups have been developed that use centralized Internet storage. The following illustration shows a small team of workers in separate locations sharing data over the Internet:

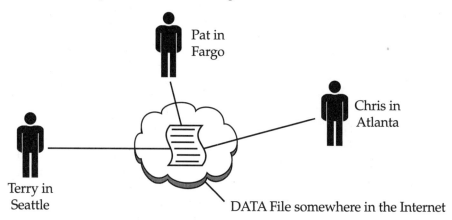

Internet Storage Methods

For many, the World Wide Web is synonymous with the Internet. However, for the purpose of using the Internet for storage, it is a good idea to maintain a clear distinction between the Internet and the World Wide Web. The World Wide Web allows people to access all kinds of information from almost any place in the world; however, Web users have not been using it much to access the information most important to them—their own.

Instead, people have been storing and retrieving data on the Internet using FTP (File Transfer Protocol) for years before Web browsers existed. FTP was developed as a command line interface that can be run on systems—including PC DOS systems—lacking sophisticated graphics capabilities. It is an extremely flexible and mature utility that works very well for both storing and retrieving data.

Another Internet facility called *Gopher,* named after the mascot of the University of Minnesota—the "golden gopher"—was also used to store and retrieve data on the Internet prior to the advent of the World Wide Web. Gopher provided a graphical representation of directory structures on Internet servers and allowed users to navigate their directory trees and select files for downloading. Considering that these directory representations were actually directory files, one can see how Gopher anticipated the linking capability within documents that served as the impetus for HTTP. Today, Gopher functionality is integrated into Web browsers, although its use is relatively rare.

Finally, data can be stored and retrieved using the HTTP (Hypertext Transfer Protocol) used by Web browsers to access Web files from embedded links. The capability to store files is included in HTTP, but its use as a storage mechanism in lieu of FTP has been somewhat slow to be adopted.

Figure 16-7 shows the three methods of storage described in the preceding sections. On the left is the pre-Web FTP method used to upload and download files. The center is occupied by FTP and Gopher. The right side adds HTTP to create the World Wide Web, in addition to providing FTP and Gopher capabilities.

Storing and Retrieving Data with FTP

Referring to Figure 16-7, the common facility across all three application environments is FTP. Considering its place in history, it is also the most popular mechanism for storing files on the Internet.

FTP is a client/server architecture. FTP client software runs on almost any system accessing the Internet. FTP server software can run on servers supporting other processes, such as HTTP Web services and e-mail services. FTP communications start when the FTP client establishes a control session with the FTP server that can be used to initiate multiple file transfers to or from the FTP server.

What You Need to Store Your Data on the Internet   To access an FTP site, you need the following:

▼   The server name of an active FTP server

■   A valid password, if it is a secure FTP site

▲   FTP client software or an FTP-capable application

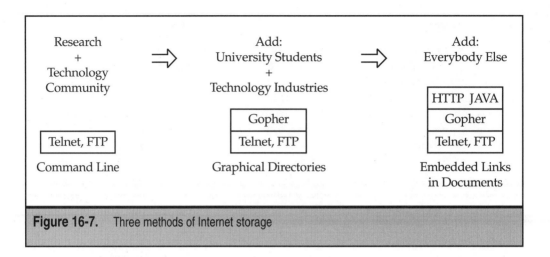

Figure 16-7.   Three methods of Internet storage

There are both *secure* FTP sites and *anonymous* FTP sites. Secure FTP sites require a password to access them. Anonymous FTP sites allow anybody to download files from them but typically do not allow any file uploads. Anonymous FTP sites implement a trivial password scheme that usually allows a client to supply their own e-mail address as a password.

Readers interested in establishing or experimenting with personal storage capabilities on the Internet can contact their ISP and request an account for a personal Web site. The ISP should be able to state whether there are any charges, and will create an FTP user account on an FTP server. After receiving the Web site account information complete with server name and password, you should be able to read and write data from the FTP site.

FTP Application Availability   Most operating systems sold today come equipped with a text-based FTP program for those users familiar with FTP's command line interface. However, it is rarely necessary to perform FTP operations from a command line. There are many excellent FTP software packages to choose from, and most are available over the Internet through software download sites. For example, **www.tucows.com** has many FTP programs available for Windows systems.

However, it is not necessary to have an FTP program to be able to store and retrieve data from an FTP site on the Internet. Applications such as Microsoft Office applications provide access to files stored on FTP sites. For example, Microsoft PowerPoint presentations can be uploaded to a private FTP site from within the application and accessed later from a remote site. This makes it possible to retrieve files while traveling that may have been left behind at home or at the office. It is possible to sit down at virtually any Internet coffeehouse or Kinko's Copy Center that has Windows systems and Internet access and access your files. Notice that this does not require a browser. This access is provided completely through a user application; the system does not even need to have a browser installed to work.

Web-Based Storage

Just as browserless FTP transfers are based on a client/server model, file transfers over HTTP are also based on a client/server process. Therefore, any new function has to be implemented in both client and server components. This codevelopment can take years, especially in highly competitive areas where many technologies and capabilities are involved. New functions sometimes do not become useful until a clearly defined standard is formed to provide interoperability between different vendors' products.

RFC 1867

Internet technology has obviously undergone significant development over the last several years. One successful development has been the creation and adoption of RFC 1867 into the HTML specification, which specifies the use of HTML *forms* for uploading files from clients to Web servers using HTTP (Hypertext Transfer Protocol) as the transfer protocol. Whereas FTP was developed years before browsers or the World Wide Web existed, RFC 1867 is browser-based technology designed to provide functionality for Web applications or services. RFC 1867 was originally proposed in 1995 by two Xerox researchers, Larry Masinter and Ernesto Nebel, and since its introduction has been implemented broadly in browser and Web server software.

The significant aspect of RFC 1867–based storage is that the facility is provided as an HTML Web page, as opposed to being a separate client-side application. The file transfer begins by presenting the user with a form to fill out in his or her browser. The filled form contains the name and location of the file(s) they want to transfer. The actual transfer is accomplished by *posting* the form to a Web server with the file identified as a field in the form. In other words, the file information is carried inside the form data. A corresponding function running on the Web server receives the form, identifies the file(s), and stores it according to the design and implementation of the application or service. Figure 16-8 shows the process of uploading a file to an Internet storage location using RFC 1867.

Web-Based Distributed Authoring and Versioning, or WebDAV

One of the problems with any storage resource is managing the data in it after it gets put there. Unfortunately, the tools for managing Internet-resident data are not very useful today, compared to the tools available for managing data in LANs and SANs. Indeed, it appears that the Internet is not used as widely as it could be for storing data. One problem discussed previously is the confusion and lack of knowledge among users as to how data gets deposited in the Internet in the first place. But beyond that, there is great uncertainty about how to move it, copy it, edit it, or delete it after it is initially put on the Web.

Managing Data with WebDAV   In response to the lack of manageability of Internet/Intranet data on Web servers, a group of industry volunteers led by Jim Whitehead, a Ph.D. candidate at the University of California, Irvine, developed new protocol extensions to HTTP 1.1 called WebDAV, for Web Distributed Authoring and Versioning.

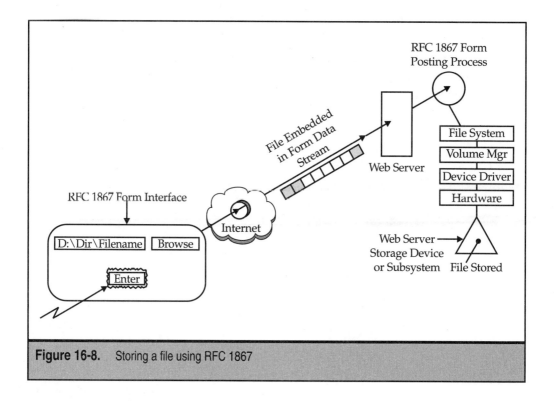

Figure 16-8.   Storing a file using RFC 1867

According to the charter of the WebDAV working group, WebDAV is intended to "define the HTTP extensions necessary to enable distributed Web authoring tools to be broadly interoperable, while supporting user needs." From a network storage perspective, this says that WebDAV will deliver the ability to write and read sharable data over the Internet. WebDAV contains the underpinnings to create shared, concurrent access to distributed Internet file systems.

As a protocol, WebDAV can be used to carry embedded management information about data stored at an Internet storage repository. This information, expressed as XML (Extensible Markup Language) data, can interact with a wide variety of functions in storage servers, including policy-based management agents for data and storage management applications. In addition, WebDAV is designed to support distributed and dispersed workgroups that cross regional and organizational boundaries. The ability to create distributed software development environments is a direct target of the technology.

WebDAV is defined in RFC 2518, which can be viewed at Carnegie Mellon University's Web site at **http://andrew2.andrew.cmu.edu/rfc/rfc2518.html**, as well as other locations. An active Internet Engineering Task Force (IETF) is working on the technology with volunteers from IBM, Microsoft, Xerox, and Novell, among others. Their work can be reviewed at **http://www.webdav.org**. This Web site has a list of client and server applications that have implemented the WebDAV specification.

Embedded Control in WebDAV   XML is used by WebDAV to convey *properties* associated with Internet data, such as the creation and transmission of descriptive metadata. WebDAV properties can be manipulated by the WebDAV protocol. An associated protocol called the DAV Searching and Locating protocol (DASL), can search for WebDAV data by its XML properties. WebDAV also provides the ability to remotely establish and change access control information for data stored on Internet servers. This could obviously pose a security challenge, but it also opens the possibility for distributed project administration.

The Future of WebDAV   Today, WebDAV is an unproven technology with limited implementations. The scope of the work defined in WebDAV appears to be fairly large and could result in significant changes to Web storage, applications, and security. In other words, WebDAV contains some big ideas that could take several years to develop. Therefore, it is somewhat difficult to predict how quickly the technology will become adopted.

Personal Internet Backup Software and Services

One of the earliest Internet-based storage applications to arise since the emergence of the World Wide Web is system backup and recovery. It makes a certain amount of sense to vault data to an Internet site, considering the chances are pretty good that the Web site will not be destroyed by the same disaster that strikes a system in the office or at home.

For the most part, Internet online backup has been implemented as client/server, browserless technology using FTP as a transfer protocol. Unlike tape backup applications in which tape format compatibility is an ongoing concern, it is unlikely that the data written to a particular online service would be moved to another online service. Therefore, very little attention is paid to the storage format used on such sites.

Although the technologies are similar, the application challenges posed by Web backup are almost the opposite of the problems posed by Internet data sharing. In general, backup data should be private and not accessible by others, unless they are chartered to retrieve it. This can include a single user who may have copies of data files on both a desktop system and a laptop computer.

Characteristics of Internet Backup

Several services are available for online backup, providing a variety of functions, including such things as the ability to make CDs of backup data and ship them to subscribers and mix online backup with actual tape backup. The scheduling capabilities and user interfaces of the various products vary significantly. In general, there is a graphical user interface that provides point-and-click selection and exclusion of specified files and directories, and a scheduler that allows unattended backup operations to commence in the middle of the night.

While all the online backup products have differentiating features, there are a few basic similarities among the various Internet backup products:

▼   Electronic distribution of client software

■   Free trial offers and capacity-based pricing

- Local encryption at the client side
- Ability to move many files in a single operation
- Performance limited by Internet line speed
- ▲ Partial file backup technology

Internet backup applications are mostly sold and distributed over the Internet. Product updates can be managed with complete transparency to the end user. In fact, sometimes the installation of the product is not completed until the Web site is accessed for the first time. For the most part, Internet backup is not a free service, whereas file transfer and storage as discussed previously often are. However, most products offer a 30-day trial period. This should be plenty of time to adequately determine if the product will work for most environments.

Subscribers are asked to provide an encryption key, or sometimes an encryption phrase, that is used to encrypt files before they are uploaded. It is up to subscribers to remember their user ID and encryption key to be able to restore or download files. This poses some interesting problems for disaster recovery. For example, a fire that destroys a small office is likely to destroy any written records containing account numbers and encryption keys. In that case, the software can be downloaded again and reinstalled; the subscriber must then contact the technical support department of the backup service, which will give them their vital access info. It's not clear how such a "phone trust" system can be secure, but the practice is widespread among backup services. The process is illustrated here:

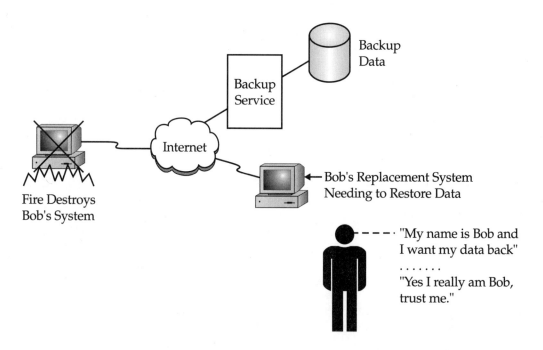

One of the advantages of Internet backup is the ability to transfer large numbers of files in a single user operation. When one has a large number of files to upload or download, backup provides the most service for the least amount of administration overhead. Unfortunately, the performance of Internet backup can leave a lot to be desired. A 56 Kb/s modem cannot come close to the speeds of backing up to a locally attached tape of removable media device. DSL and cable modem speeds at approximately 150 Kb/s are roughly equivalent to backing up to a floppy disk drive.

Compression technology can be used to increase the performance of Internet backup file transfers. In general, this can have the effect of doubling backup performance, but it depends on the data being transferred. It is interesting to see how certain files such as PDF documents are mostly uncompressible, while other types of files, such as HTML files, are highly compressible. So, compressing files during backup can be useful, but it may not provide the anticipated results.

For that reason, Internet backup services have implemented the ability to transfer partial files, instead of entire files. This means that the client software has to have the ability to recognize which parts of a file have changed, and only send those parts to the Web site for storage. It also means the server software has to be able to integrate the partial file uploads with the existing file versions they now have. While this is not impossible, it is not necessarily trivial either. Besides capturing the changed data in the client system, it is also necessary to establish a consistent method for subdividing files and identifying any changed sections. Partial file transfers and storage are depicted in the following diagram:

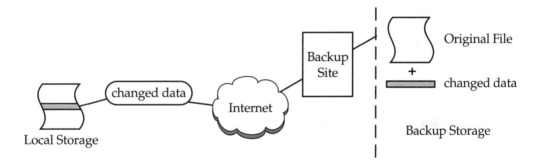

The two technologies used to provide partial file backup are called *delta block* and *binary patch*. Delta block technology employs a method of parsing files into small block ranges. A checksum is calculated for each block range. When backup starts, new checksums are generated for each block range and compared with previous checksum values. If there are differences, the updated block ranges are transferred.

Binary patch has a similar way of identifying changed data in a file, but instead of transferring the data in block sections, it uses a technique similar to those used for application software for installing "patches." It appears that both techniques work well to improve backup performance. Delta block technology may have some advantages in the ability to re-create multiple historical versions of a file, but this ability is not highly touted in the existing Internet backup products.

Servers used for the "back end," or Web side, of these backup sites have specialized application software that provides the security and file management for backup data. In addition, the equipment used at these sites also differs considerably. Some use site mirroring across geographic boundaries, and others use regular tape backups and then store their backup tapes off-site.

SUMMARY

Both NAS and SAN products have strong features to help IT organizations build high-availability 24 × 7 Web sites. The pace of change of the Internet is application driven, not server or storage driven. Therefore, server and storage infrastructure strategies that are modular and organized along application boundaries are most likely to provide the growth potential needed to maintain a thriving and healthy Web site.

This chapter also looked at the types of services and technologies being offered to business and individual customers over the Internet. This is a fast-changing environment that will no doubt see a great deal of creativity and innovation in coming years. The ability to store, access, share, and exchange data over the Internet using a number of methods will provide new ways of working in the near future. One of the more interesting aspects of this is the arrival of SSPs, which could become a whole new part of the storage industry.

EXERCISES

1. Design the storage for a Web site server farm with 50 servers and 10 terabytes of storage. Assume that most of this access is for stored files as opposed to database transactions.

2. You have the job of developing the backup strategy for an SSP. Assume your customers want the ability to recover individual files within 12 hours after notifying you. Use any combination of filing and storing products. What kind of access will you need to your customer's systems?

CHAPTER 17

Managing Storage Networks

In order for storage networks to live up to their potential, they need to have management tools that enable stable operations and quick responses to problems when they occur. A great deal of this book was spent discussing some of the different management tools available, but none of the previous discussions considered the type of comprehensive and large-scale network management systems that IT organizations use to manage their local and wide area IP networks. This chapter analyses the general state of storage networking management systems and looks at some of the ways it is likely to evolve to meet the manageability requirements of IT managers.

One of the major difficulties of managing storage networks at a high level is the inability to integrate the management of wiring, storing, and filing functions. It is not so much a failure of management systems to integrate the management of all three functions, but the nature and independence of storing and filing that makes it difficult. Perhaps someday, all three storage network functions will be able to be more closely integrated, but for now, one should not expect a single management system to cover all of them.

MANAGEMENT DESIGNS

Before discussing how storage networking management tools work, we'll spend a short period of time reviewing the management functions desired from each of them. In general, a management tool should provide the ability to:

▼ Monitor status of components periodically and on demand

■ View historical data and provide trend analysis

■ Filter out insignificant data

■ Establish parametric priorities

■ Notify on excessive or failure conditions

■ Adjust configuration

▲ Enforce security

The first requirement of most management systems is to monitor the status of the entities its manages. Most of the time, status checking is done on a periodic basis, but it is also common for administrators to want to retrieve status data instantly when they feel something might be working incorrectly. As this data is created, it is usually considered worthwhile to maintain it in historical records for some period of time. It follows that the management system needs to have a data structure for storing and retrieving status data. In addition, the management system needs to provide a human interface for controlling operations and providing analysis of stored data.

Catastrophes, Pathologies, and Bugs

There are many ways to characterize network problems. One simple way is to generalize among:

▼ Catastrophic failures

■ Bugs

▲ Pathological problems

Catastrophic Failures

A *catastrophic failure* is one that occurs suddenly without warning and causes an immediate failure in the network. Catastrophic failures can be small in scale and relatively easy to overcome, such as when a backup tape breaks and backup fails. They can also be large and extremely difficult to overcome, such as when industrial equipment like a backhoe or welder destroys fiber optic network cables.

Catastrophic failures are usually obvious and can often be detected without sophisticated management equipment. When a system, storage subsystem, or network link fails, there are usually people or other systems that are immediately affected by it. That does not mean that it is immediately obvious where the problem is. It is not always instantaneously clear that a communication failure is a network failure or a failure in the host system or in the storage subsystem.

The best way to protect against catastrophic failures is to use redundancy techniques that allow secondary networks or equipment to step in and take over when a failure occurs. Disk mirroring is an example of how a controller or software can provide continuous operations when a disk drive failure occurs. Clustering technology, as discussed in Chapter 13, provides the highest level of redundant protection at the highest cost.

But redundancy does not provide a solution to fix the problem; it only provides continuous operations for certain types of failures. In other words, redundancy only buys the administrator time. Whether or not redundancy is being used, it is usually desirable to accurately identify the source of the problem as quickly as possible. That is where network management equipment can be most useful. A network management system that identifies failed network components can save a great deal of time.

Bugs

Bugs are usually software or logical problems that cause failures or improper system responses to unanticipated conditions or data. Bugs in storage I/O systems are not unheard of, but thankfully they are relatively rare.

One way to keep bugs to a minimum is to limit the complexity of a system, thereby limiting exposure to unanticipated conditions. This is one of the areas of concern for storage networking. The question is, as storage networks grow and add functionality, is there also an increasing likelihood of discovering bugs? There is no good answer to this question, except that it is always prudent to make changes slowly when possible and to try to test combinations of technology thoroughly before deploying it. There is no question that some storage networking vendors place a larger emphasis on testing than others. Nobody wants to be a guinea pig for a storage network implementation that is unproven and untested.

One of the biggest problems for solving bug problems is reproducing them. Once a bug can be reproduced, then it is usually necessary to collect data that engineers can examine to determine the source of the problem. Depending on the type of problem, a storage network management system could help collect data for this purpose.

Pathological Problems

A *pathological problem* is one where a hardware or software component starts failing intermittently with greater frequency over time. Often pathological problems turn into complete, catastrophic failures at some point in the future.

Pathological problems can be very frustrating to identify because they are not always reproducible. Similar to visiting the doctor to discuss a disappearing symptom that has hidden itself again, pathological storage network problems do not necessarily lend themselves to analysis and troubleshooting. One of the ways to troubleshoot these types of problems is to use statistical methods that monitor trends and activities over time. The idea is simple: track all activities or sample some number of activities at certain time intervals and look for how often problems occur.

But monitoring trends and statistics for storage networks can be challenging. In essence, this is a bit like looking for needles in haystacks. For starters, one usually needs some idea of what it is one is looking for and hope that somebody has built a management tool to monitor the problem. Then the data has to be collected somewhere and made available for analysis. The collection of statistical data for storage I/O is far from trivial and can generate an enormous amount of data very quickly. Storage network transmission speeds are often very fast, and system performance can be sensitive to transmission latency. If the management process introduces delays in I/O operations, it is probably more of a hindrance than it is an assistant.

Physical components such as network equipment and storage devices are relatively easy to monitor, but if one is trying to manage filing systems by collecting statistical data (more metadata actually), the issue of creating this management data can becomes an enormous problem. With millions of individual items in a filing system, the data structures for this management information have to be scalable. For instance, it is conceivable that an administrator might want to have a trend analysis of the activity levels in a filing system, charting the access characteristics of certain data objects over time, including which process was being used and how long the object was being actively updated or read. While this seems simple enough conceptually, it would be very difficult to implement a general-purpose tool that allowed a variety of historical reports to be generated.

The filing systems themselves often have this information available for its current state, but usually not with much historical content.

It is usually important for the management system to filter certain information from being recorded or presented to the administrator. There is only so much detail that a typical systems administrator can respond to as part of his or her daily routine. Therefore, management systems normally implement thresholds and/or severity levels that determine when a potential problem needs attention.

Thresholds   *Thresholds* are numerical boundaries that help administrators determine when a serious problem may be occurring. The concept of thresholds is based on the fact that minor errors in storage networks are always occurring and that one should expect a storage network to work well with some low-level statistical error levels. For example, a switch may drop a certain percentage of all the frames or cells it forwards. Some of these may be due to congestion, and some may be due to receiving "bad" frames that do not pass integrity (parity) tests.

When the error rate for a certain event passes its threshold, it indicates that a more serious problem may be brewing somewhere in the network. Typically, a storage network management system will create some sort of alert or warning message about the error. It is then up to the administrator to determine whether or not this message indicates an actual problem or if there is some other reason for it. For example, the threshold may have been set too low or there may have been some other circumstances contributing to the threshold being exceeded.

Severity Levels   One way to determine if a failure requires attention is by its *severity level*. Whereas thresholds are quantitative in nature, severity levels are qualitative. Severity levels are typically associated with some numerical weighing factor, such as "on a scale from 1 to 10, is this sort of bad or is this a lose-your-job kind of problem?"

Problems, errors, and failure messages that have severity levels are typically generated by systems and indicate what the impact of the error could be. For the purposes of the discussion here, we'll talk about three severity levels: notices, warnings, and "it's too late already." Notice that severity level messages should not be ignored, but they don't always need an urgent response. They tend to be oriented to providing information to the administrator about a potential problem at some point in the future. Notices typically do not indicate something is failing; in fact, they often indicate something is working. Messages with "warning" severity usually indicate that something is not working correctly and that the system cannot do what you are trying to do with it. Warnings about storage I/O should be treated as a high priority because they may indicate that the storage I/O network is not working the way you expect. "It's too late already" severity indicates that something has already gone wrong and that corrective measures need to be taken. It is possible that data may already have been lost as the result of one of these messages. System operations should stop and the problem understood, resolved, or circumvented before continuing.

SNMP Enterprise Network Management

SNMP (the Simple Network Management Protocol) has evolved into a dominant industry standard for managing networks. It is a technology that is applicable to networks of all sizes, from small networks to large corporate networks. While SNMP can be used to change the behavior of equipment in the network, SNMP is mostly used to monitor the status of the network and to quickly identify where problems may be occurring. SNMP is the prevailing management technology used to manage the wiring component of storage networks.

SNMP management systems are designed around four architectural elements. These are:

▼ The management station

■ Management agents

■ Management information bases (MIBs)

▲ The SNMP protocol

Management Station

Traditionally, there is a single *management station* that collects all the information about the network, analyzes it in relation to threshold levels, and presents the status to network administrators. The management station in an SNMP management system is the primary administrative console for all sizes of network management systems, including enterprise network management products. In general, the information collected in the management station is available for viewing by administrators working on other stations in the network.

Nothing special is required to make most other SNMP management components, such as agents and MIBs, work with most SNMP management stations. However, most SNMP management systems incorporate extended graphics capabilities and programming interfaces that allow additional capabilities beyond those prescribed by the SNMP standard. For instance, some SNMP management systems provide the capabilities to visually represent the location and functions of the managed entity in a more intuitive fashion.

Management Agents

The information collected, analyzed, and presented by the management station is supplied by the various *management agents* in the network. Management agents are similar to backup agents in that they are designed to run across a variety of platforms and equipment. They integrate with programmatic interfaces in the managed entities in the network to collect the data that is stored in the MIB (discussed in the text that follows). They are different from backup agents in that they can work with multiple management stations.

For instance, network management agents are typically designed for all types of networking equipment, including switches, routers, bridges, and hubs, as well as for a variety of platforms. Where storage products are concerned, various vendors have developed SNMP agents for monitoring storage subsystems. Agents can be designed for almost any type of network hardware or system function, although management by SNMP agents is not always as precise as desired.

SNMP MIBs

The *MIB,* or *management information base,* is the numerical representation of the status and performance variables that are monitored or managed by SNMP agents and the management station. For instance, a variable could be assigned to monitor the peak transfer load per second for each port in a switch. The language used to create MIBs, called ASN.1, was adopted for its capability to represent basic networking information. In general, MIBs can be used to represent quantitative data, but they do not work as well for representing larger types of systems, such as storage. For example, a MIB could be developed to collect data for file access characteristics in a large file system. However, such a MIB would be extremely large and difficult to manage. There are better data structures, such as databases, for this type of analysis.

The SNMP Protocol

The *SNMP protocol* (my apologies for the acronym redundancy) is an application-layer protocol that runs on top of TCP or UDP, similarly to the NFS or CIFS protocols used by NAS appliances. There is nothing inherently special about how SNMP works within the network, as it uses the same IP-based facilities as other network applications. Nearly all vendors making networking gear use SNMP as the primary network management interface in their products.

SNMP Data Exchanges

The SNMP management station exchanges data with agents running in managed entities. There are three fundamental SNMP operations: gets, sets, and traps. *Gets* are operations where the management station retrieves data from the agent in the managed entity. *Sets* are the inverse operation, where the management station sends data to the agent, which places it in the MIB. A management program in the managed entity reads the data and interprets it to change its configuration or operating processes. *Traps* are the process whereby an agent notifies the management station of an exception condition that exceeds a threshold and may need attention from an administrator.

SNMP in Storage Networks

As the default network management technology in use today, SNMP is also the most common approach taken to manage storage networks. This is true for Fibre Channel SANs as well as for Ethernet/TCP/IP SANs and in storage networks built around NAS appliances.

SNMP for Managing NAS Environments

NAS storage typically runs in Ethernet/TCP/IP networks that are managed by SNMP management systems. As usually nothing is required to make Ethernet networks support NAS appliances, there is nothing unique about the way SNMP works in networks with NAS. NAS products can incorporate MIBs and agents so that they can be managed by SNMP systems to collect such information as I/O activity levels and capacity statistics.

That said, it should be understood that there can be significant differences in the variety of SNMP management support among NAS products. In fact, this is one of the most important ways that NAS vendors differentiate their products. Prospective customers are encouraged to make sure they understand what capabilities are available on products they are considering and what the system and network requirements are to be able to use those management capabilities.

Out-of-Band Management in Fibre Channel SANs

In Fibre Channel networks, SNMP is commonly implemented as *out-of-band* management, where the flow of management information follows a completely different path than the storage I/O traffic. The primary reason for this is that most Fibre Channel equipment vendors have chosen not to implement multiprotocol capabilities in their Fibre Channel ports. In other words, they do not support SNMP as an upper-layer protocol in Fibre Channel. Instead, TCP/IP is supported over completely independent 10/100 Mb/s Ethernet connections.

The primary reason separate network interfaces were implemented for out-of-band network management in Fibre Channel was to enable network management in the first place. There were no IP tunneling products, as discussed in Chapter 12, when Fibre Channel solutions began shipping. Without a way to get SNMP data into and out of the Fibre Channel SAN island, manufacturers had no choice except to implement out-of-band management.

While out-of-band management refers to the use of non–storage network links to manage the network, there are some additional aspects of storage networks that contribute to the use of out-of-band management. SCSI-3, based on parallel SCSI, incorporates the same basic operating environment as SCSI buses in SANs. Parallel SCSI was highly optimized for performance and reliability, as opposed to TCP/IP networks, which were optimized for flexibility and ease of connectivity. Because parallel SCSI was so reliable and because it was integrated with server platforms, management of parallel SCSI was never seen as a requirement. In fact, injecting management into SCSI buses would likely result in slower and less reliable I/O operations. Not only that, but parallel SCSI buses were stable, simple configurations without any intermediate wiring devices involved. Therefore, in parallel SCSI there are no switch or hub performance variables to monitor, which is arguably the primary function of network management.

The situation with Fibre Channel SANs is obviously different, as there are switches, bridges, routers, hubs, and other network equipment to monitor. For the foreseeable future, it appears that Ethernet/IP management ports will be required for all Fibre Channel products, although some manufacturers may attempt to provide support for SNMP through Fibre Channel ports using another upper-layer protocol option such as IP or VI.

In-Band Management for Ethernet/TCP/IP SANs

Ethernet/TCP/IP SANs will undoubtedly use *in-band* SNMP management. It may be preferable to shunt network management traffic through separate management ports and paths to prevent any interference of storage I/O from network management traffic.

This allows the storage I/O function to run unencumbered by management processes. However, the bandwidth consumed by network management frames is insignificant compared to the bandwidth consumed by storage I/O. In addition, the processing power needed for network management is roughly the same whether or not different storage and management circuitry is used.

Strengths and Weaknesses of SNMP Management for Storage Networks

The biggest advantage of using SNMP for storage networks is the fact that SNMP management is pervasive and available. There is a large talent base that knows how to make it work and integrate it into a wide variety of management implementations. In essence, SNMP support is a fundamental market requirement for storage networking. At a minimum, it is essential that problems with storage networks be recognized fairly quickly to allow administrators to respond to the situation.

Beyond that, SNMP is not a great way to manage much of what is *storing* or *filing* in storage networks. To begin with, MIBs were never designed for storage or filing resources and are not likely to provide the kind of control to really help administrators manage storage effectively. In addition, SNMP is relatively slow and is not capable of providing any real-time management of storage devices where the response time to failures must be much faster. While SNMP can be used to report failures, it should not be thought of as a technology that is capable of automating pathing functions in real time to provide an automated fault-tolerant storage network. In short, SNMP works well enough for administration alerts, but do not expect it to provide much more than that.

The limitations of SNMP for pathing imply another subtle weakness of using SNMP for storage management. A great deal was discussed in this book already regarding the value and importance of virtualizing storage through multiple logical block address transformations. There is no question that it would be valuable to be able to manage the network connections to these aggregated logical block address spaces together. Unfortunately, with SNMP, there is no way to do this easily.

In general, storing functions are not developed to be tightly integrated with wiring functions—they simply assume the wiring is working and then do their best to manage data transfers with the wiring that is available. There is typically no provision for the storing function and the wiring function to communicate about each other's workloads and status. Therefore, there is no opportunity to provide management "hints" one way or the other that would be integrated.

Web-Based Management

Another common way to manage storage network products is via a Web browser. This method uses the same HTTP (Hypertext Transfer Protocol) that is used to access Internet Web sites. In general, Web-based management requires that each managed entity act as a Web server for the browser-administrator stations that access it. One of the advantages of Web-based management is that a manufacturer can create almost any kind of management capabilities desired. In addition, a Web-based management utility allows the product to be accessed from virtually any local system.

The strength of Web-based management is also its greatest weakness. While each manufacturer can develop completely customized Web-based management for its products, doing this makes it virtually impossible to consolidate all the data for the various SAN products into a single comprehensive view of the network. Different products from the same manufacturer may be able to be managed as a unified set, but products from different vendors will be managed separately. This, of course, makes it more difficult to grasp the complete network status.

Management of Storage Tunneling

Storage tunneling, as discussed in Chapter 12, presents a few additional challenges for network administrators. While the same SNMP management system can be used to manage both Fibre Channel and Ethernet/TCP/IP networking equipment, it may be somewhat difficult to correlate the activities and information on the Fibre Channel side with those on the Ethernet/TCP/IP side. It is much easier to track the storage traffic if the tunnel is made from a dedicated Ethernet/TCP/IP network.

Storing Management

The management of storing functions was discussed already at great length in Chapters 4, 5, and 6. Historically, there have been many different ways to implement storing functions. They are often included as operating system utilities and sometimes sold as device drivers that accompany host bus adapters. One of the most powerful storing management products is the volume manager. Volume managers provide the ability to combine disk drives and subsystems together in a wide variety of ways and can work with file systems as a matched pair.

Host I/O Monitoring Software

Another storing-level product to help manage storage networks is host I/O monitoring software. In a nutshell, an I/O monitor records data about all the I/O operations in a system, across all storage channels. The output from this type of product can provide important information used to troubleshoot I/O problems.

I/O monitoring software can generate a tremendous volume of data in a relatively short period of time. Scanning through the output is not for the faint of heart and usually requires experience or special training to correctly interpret the data. In general, the analysis of the monitor's output is most helpful when trying to identify performance problems with a transaction processing system, including identifying hot-spot bottlenecks.

Readers interested in finding out more about I/O monitoring software and I/O analysis in general may want to visit the Web site for the Evaluator Group at **www.evaluatorgroup.com**.

Storage Resource Management

A relatively new concept in storage network management that appears to be taking hold is called *storage resource management* or *SRM*. In short, SRM provides a dynamic view of storage capacity and utilization in storage networks. As such, SRM allows administrators to view the status of their storage plant from a centralized management console. While this is a fairly simple concept, it is incredibly powerful in the way it saves time administering large storage networks.

Managing large amounts of storage has been discussed previously as one of the reasons for implementing storage networks. SRM is a management concept that realizes the benefits of storage networks. Using an SRM system, a single administrator can monitor the status of many storage subsystems in a matter of minutes.

The basic idea of SRM is to collect data for a number of different storage I/O functions and to consolidate this data in a centralized location. In addition, SRM monitors threshold levels to determine potential problems and alert administrators.

SRM systems can be implemented in different ways, but in general they require both storing- and filing-level interfaces to capture the complete breadth of management information desired. SRM systems follow the model of network management where agent technology is used, running on various platforms and storage equipment that can collect data, report status, and respond to instructions from the SRM console.

In order to know such things as the amounts of free space in any storage volume, the SRM system must be able to work with the file system because only the file system knows what blocks in the data structure are available at any time. Also, to collect information about I/O rates, SRM systems must be able to work at the storing level because filing functions do not typically know much about storing processes.

Configuring SRM

While SRM sounds wonderful, and it can be, there is a fair amount of work to be done setting up a system initially. SRM systems typically have default configurations that establish thresholds to monitor capacity. Like most management systems, the default values will probably need to be adjusted to fit the environment they are running in.

This means that administrators need to spend time learning how the SRM system works to manipulate its functions. More importantly, administrators should try to understand the data access patterns of their applications, as they will likely differ from application to application.

Limitations of SRM

SRM systems do not necessarily imply that they will respond to situations. Typically, other administrative actions must be taken to alleviate the problems the SRM system discovers.

Depending on the technology in use, the response to an SRM system warning could be a relatively simple process or a difficult process. Whatever the administrative response is, it is probably better to start working on the problem early than it is to deal with it as an emergency later.

SCSI Enclosure Services

A standard specification known as *SCSI Enclosure Services (SES)* has been created that identifies the various components of disk subsystems and their metrics for reporting their operating statistics. SES is a fairly broad and large specification, so there are bound to be differences in its interpretation, but it should prove to be very useful as it becomes more widely implemented in products and storage management systems.

SES can be used to provide status information, warnings, and alarms for various aspects of a storage subsystem, including power, cooling, configuration, and physical security. For instance, a large-disk subsystem may have the capability to monitor and report on environmental changes, such as temperature and humidity inside the subsystem. SES can also provide warnings and alarms for unauthorized attempts to remove storage devices from a locked storage subsystem.

Virtualization as a SAN Management Tool

Storage virtualization is one of the hottest topics in storage networks today. Chapter 10 already discussed this topic in a fair amount of detail as *storage pooling* and as the translation of logical block addresses in the I/O path by volume management software, host adapters, subsystem controllers, and storage domain controllers. However, to be fair to the concept of storage virtualization, as it is being discussed in the industry, a closer look at the nuances of the technology is needed. In general, storage pooling is a storing application that runs as a process in a large storage subsystem that may also control downstream external storage components. Storage virtualization, in contrast, is being discussed as an external storing application that is located in front of one or more storage subsystems/devices in the I/O path.

Storage virtualization provides the ability to create and manage virtual storage devices and LUNs. Using virtualization, the blocks that are aggregated through block translation can be made available as unique and separate storage entities that can take advantage of other storage networking services and technologies such as zoning and caching.

To make things easier to understand, in the paragraphs that follow, we'll refer to a *virtualization machine* that provides the block translation and presents block addresses as devices or LUNs to other systems and subsystems in the SAN. A virtualization machine could be built out of off-the-shelf computing equipment or as a completely specialized package.

For example, a virtualization machine could aggregate the storage of assorted storage subsystems and present these address ranges to the rest of SAN as virtual devices in the SAN. The virtualization machine could provide a variety of storing functions including mirroring, RAID, caching, and remote replication. Working with disk subsystems that have RAID capabilities already, the virtualization machine provides a higher level of virtualization, resulting in multilevel RAID, sometimes referred to as *plaid*. It's not clear that this is all that useful, except possibly for I/O systems such as transaction processing systems where it is valuable to spread out hot spots over as many disk arms as possible.

Caching and Virtualization

Memory in the virtualization machine could be used for caching all these devices or a subset of these devices. In fact, a virtualization machine could be used to build a large amount of inexpensive caching in the SAN and direct it at specific disk targets, or even address ranges where hot spots have been identified. As an extreme example, consider a high-capacity disk drive with a single disk arm. It is theoretically possible for several virtualization machines to export certain extents on the disk drive and to provide a relatively large amount of caching for each one. In a similar vein, the storage capacity of several SSDs could be aggregated and used to mirror the address ranges where hot spots occur. Obviously, the characteristics of the cache, as discussed in Chapter 5, need to be carefully thought out and well understood to ensure data is written back to nonvolatile storage.

Open Systems Market Dynamics of Virtualization

The volume management techniques used in storage virtualization are certainly nothing new, as they have been provided by disk subsystem and volume management vendors for many years. These products have created and managed disk extents for many years. When it comes to disk subsystems, their virtualization and management capabilities have been valued at a premium by the market. When one separates the disk drives from the subsystems, it is obvious that most of the value is associated with the virtualization and management—and not the disk drives.

Storage virtualization products have the potential to take the virtualization and management capabilities of disk subsystems and apply open systems market dynamics. By using inexpensive and capable PC commodity hardware and memory, it is theoretically possible to create high-capability and fairly reliable virtualization machines that are far less expensive than corresponding proprietary disk subsystem implementations.

Potential Shortcomings of Virtualization

As mentioned previously in this chapter, as the complexity of systems increases, these systems are more likely to encounter unanticipated conditions and bugs. Bugs in storage I/O could cause catastrophic failures. There is no question that virtualization adds complexity.

One of the differences between virtualization machines and disk subsystems/volume managers is that disk subsystems and volume managers were designed to operate on physical disks, not just on logical block address spaces. Often these products write configurations on each of the disks they manage. This does not seem like such a big deal, but it can come in handy when troubleshooting. As entities that work primarily on logical block address spaces, it is not clear where virtualization would write similar disk-level information that could be located and recovered after a failure.

What is more important perhaps, is that one needs to be mindful of the mechanical disk processes that provide the actual storage function. They are very real mechanical limitations in the number of disk arms and the rotational speed of the drives. Using an open-systems approach to storage virtualization it is potentially possible to lose track of how many different filing systems may be accessing the same physical disk. The problem is that once an administrator discovers this type of problem it could be difficult, time consuming, and expensive to provide a remedy.

In general, there are many potential benefits of storage virtualization, but caution needs to be taken to ensure that storage configurations can be put back together following a disaster scenario. The metadata the virtualization machine needs to aggregate resources needs to be safely kept somewhere and all storage management processes such as backup, mirroring, and replication need to be considered.

SUMMARY

This chapter presented a brief overview of the management systems for managing storage networks. While most of the book already discussed various details of storage management, this chapter looked at some of the issues of managing storage networks from an enterprise management perspective. Unfortunately there do not appear to be products that integrate the management of all three storage network components—wiring, storing, and filing—together in a single system.

Three fundamental management systems were discussed. The first was SNMP, which is the established standard for managing Ethernet/TCP/IP networks. Next, SRM, or storage resource management, was discussed as a way to monitor and manage storage devices and subsystems as well as some of the filing components that reside in them. Finally, the topic of virtualization was discussed again, with more of an emphasis on its being implemented as SAN products, as opposed to simply being a way to provide logical block translation.

EXERCISES

1. Develop an SNMP management system for a storage virtualization system using an external storage domain controller that stripes data across four downstream RAID subsystems.

2. Using the SNMP management system developed in Exercise #1, where do you plan to put the SNMP agents? What information will they provide to the management console? What information do you think they might not be able to provide?

INDEX

D

▼ E

▼ F

G

 H

I

J

K

L

M

▼ N

O

S

X

Z

INTERNATIONAL CONTACT INFORMATION

AUSTRALIA
McGraw-Hill Book Company Australia Pty. Ltd.
TEL +61-2-9417-9899
FAX +61-2-9417-5687
http://www.mcgraw-hill.com.au
books-it_sydney@mcgraw-hill.com

CANADA
McGraw-Hill Ryerson Ltd.
TEL +905-430-5000
FAX +905-430-5020
http://www.mcgrawhill.ca

**GREECE, MIDDLE EAST,
NORTHERN AFRICA**
McGraw-Hill Hellas
TEL +30-1-656-0990-3-4
FAX +30-1-654-5525

MEXICO (Also serving Latin America)
McGraw-Hill Interamericana Editores S.A. de C.V.
TEL +525-117-1583
FAX +525-117-1589
http://www.mcgraw-hill.com.mx
fernando_castellanos@mcgraw-hill.com

SINGAPORE (Serving Asia)
McGraw-Hill Book Company
TEL +65-863-1580
FAX +65-862-3354
http://www.mcgraw-hill.com.sg
mghasia@mcgraw-hill.com

SOUTH AFRICA
McGraw-Hill South Africa
TEL +27-11-622-7512
FAX +27-11-622-9045
robyn_swanepoel@mcgraw-hill.com

**UNITED KINGDOM & EUROPE
(Excluding Southern Europe)**
McGraw-Hill Education Europe
TEL +44-1-628-502500
FAX +44-1-628-770224
http://www.mcgraw-hill.co.uk
computing_neurope@mcgraw-hill.com

ALL OTHER INQUIRIES Contact:
Osborne/McGraw-Hill
TEL +1-510-549-6600
FAX +1-510-883-7600
http://www.osborne.com
omg_international@mcgraw-hill.com